Punish Treason, Reward Loyalty

CONSTITUTIONAL THINKING

Sanford Levinson
Jeffrey K. Tulis
Emily Zackin
Mariah Zeisberg
Editors

Punish Treason, Reward Loyalty

The Forgotten Goals of Constitutional Reform after the Civil War

THE FORGOTTEN FOURTEENTH AMENDMENT, VOLUME I

Mark A. Graber

UNIVERSITY PRESS OF KANSAS

Published by the University Press of Kansas (Lawrence, Kansas 66045), which was
organized by the Kansas Board of Regents and is operated and funded by Emporia State
University, Fort Hays State University, Kansas State University, Pittsburg State University,
the University of Kansas, and Wichita State University.

Library of Congress Cataloging-in-Publication Data

Names: Graber, Mark A., author.
Title: Punish treason, reward loyalty : The forgotten goals of constitutional
    reform after the Civil War / Mark A. Graber.
Description: Lawrence : University Press of Kansas, 2023. | Series:
    Constitutional thinking | The forgotten Fourteenth Amendment |
    Includes index.
Identifiers: LCCN 2022049639 (print) | LCCN 2022049640 (ebook)
    ISBN 9780700635030 (cloth)
    ISBN 9780700635047 (ebook)
Subjects: LCSH: United States. Constitution. 14th Amendment. | Privileges
    and immunities—United States. | Civil rights—United States. | Due
    process of law—United States.
Classification: LCC KF4558 14th .G69 2023 (print) | LCC KF4558 14th (ebook) |
    DDC 342.08/5—dc23/eng/20230504
LC record available at https://lccn.loc.gov/2022049639.
LC ebook record available at https://lccn.loc.gov/2022049640.

British Library Cataloguing-in-Publication Data is available.

Printed in the United States of America

10 9 8 7 6 5 4 3 2 1

The paper used in this publication is acid free and meets the minimum requirements of
the American National Standard for Permanence of Paper for Printed Library Materials
Z39.48–1992.

For the Friday afternoon group: Jack, Sandy, Stephen, and Jonathan

CONTENTS

AMENDMENT XIV (1868)

Section 1.
All persons born or naturalized in the United States, and subject to the jurisdiction thereof, are citizens of the United States and of the state wherein they reside. No state shall make or enforce any law which shall abridge the privileges or immunities of citizens of the United States; nor shall any state deprive any person of life, liberty, or property, without due process of law; nor deny to any person within its jurisdiction the equal protection of the laws.

Section 2.
Representatives shall be apportioned among the several states according to their respective numbers, counting the whole number of persons in each state, excluding Indians not taxed. But when the right to vote at any election for the choice of electors for President and Vice President of the United States, Representatives in Congress, the executive and judicial officers of a state, or the members of the legislature thereof, is denied to any of the male inhabitants of such state, being twenty-one years of age, and citizens of the United States, or in any way abridged, except for participation in rebellion, or other crime, the basis of representation therein shall be reduced in the proportion which the number of such male citizens shall bear to the whole number of male citizens twenty-one years of age in such state.

Section 3.
No person shall be a Senator or Representative in Congress, or elector of President and Vice President, or hold any office, civil or military, under the United States, or under any state, who, having previously taken an oath, as a member of Congress, or as an officer of the United States, or as a member of any state legislature, or as an executive or judicial officer of any state, to support the Constitution of the United States, shall have engaged in insurrection or rebellion against the same, or given aid or comfort to the enemies thereof. But Congress may by a vote of two-thirds of each House, remove such disability.

Section 4.
The validity of the public debt of the United States, authorized by law, including debts incurred for payment of pensions and bounties for services in

suppressing insurrection or rebellion, shall not be questioned. But neither the United States nor any state shall assume or pay any debt or obligation incurred in aid of insurrection or rebellion against the United States, or any claim for the loss or emancipation of any slave; but all such debts, obligations and claims shall be held illegal and void.

Section 5.

The Congress shall have power to enforce, by appropriate legislation, the provisions of this article.

Source: www.law.cornell.edu/constitution/amendmentxiv.

It is a special pleasure to write the foreword to Mark Graber's new book, published as part of the University Press of Kansas's Constitutional Thinking series coedited by Sanford Levinson, Jeffrey K. Tulis, Emily Zackin, and Mariah Zeisberg. It has been a long time in the writing, and we are all convinced that the wait was worth it. It is the first volume of a projected multivolume magnum opus by one of the leading scholars in the field of American constitutional development. Even more important, it promises to transform the way that the scholarly community—and perhaps even the public at large—think of the Reconstruction Amendments added to the United States Constitution in the aftermath of the internecine conflagration that formally began in 1861.

As Graber has demonstrated in earlier work, the potential for—and perhaps inevitability of—the Civil War was baked in to the Constitution of 1787. The structure of congressional politics guaranteed the priority of state and regional loyalties over an enduring Union, and many overt compromises were made with slaveholders. When "compromise" is viewed as "selling out," it is no surprise that what we today call "polarization" becomes rife. Divided houses perhaps can remain standing for a long time—if, that is, the inhabitants really wish to remain together. But even ostensibly well-constructed houses can prove unavailing if the inhabitants increasingly mistrust and even loathe one another and wish desperately for a divorce based on "incompatibility" (let alone domestic violence). Such was the reality of American politics in the 1850s.

As Lincoln proclaimed in his Second Inaugural Address, "the war came" in 1861. Among its consequences, in addition to at least 750,000 slain soldiers, were the Thirteenth, Fourteenth, and Fifteenth Amendments. Graber has valuable things to say about all of this, but what makes his book a paradigm-shifter is surely his treatment of the Fourteenth Amendment. If one asks even the best-educated academics what the Fourteenth Amendment is about, they will almost surely focus exclusively on Section 1, with its language about the "privileges or immunities" attending citizenship in the United States and the guarantees of due process and equal protection that help construct the legal order. More sophisticated lawyers might mention Section 5, which seemingly grants Congress an important role in the implementation of its guarantees—although every lawyer today knows that the Supreme Court claims ultimate responsibility for the enforcement of

Section 1. In-depth courses on the Fourteenth Amendment are devoted to the study of Supreme Court decisions, and the Fourteenth Amendment is at the heart of the modern judiciary's self-proclaimed prerogative as an institution that protects individual and group rights.

Graber's central contribution is to remind us that the Fourteenth Amendment actually contains *five* sections and that the least-taught and rarely litigated—Sections 2, 3, and 4—are in fact crucial to understanding the visions of political futures contained within the overall structure of the amendment. Because these obscure sections are rarely or never litigated, the "Supreme Court's Fourteenth Amendment" does indeed consist of only Sections 1 and 5. The middle three sections have simply receded from public consciousness. Even legal historians seem satisfied to focus exclusively on Section 1.

In this book Graber demonstrates beyond any shadow of a doubt that, at the time the Fourteenth Amendment was passed, the other sections were viewed by Congress to be at least of equal—and quite possibly greater—importance to what Eric Foner has called the "second founding." Such a refounding would require far more than simply plugging new language into the Constitution. Almost all of the Radical Republicans—the party faction most committed to the idea that the United States *needed* a second founding if it was to genuinely provide the "new birth of freedom" promised in the Gettysburg Address—agreed with James Madison's caution about placing mere "parchment barriers" in the Constitution without an adequate guarantee that they would in fact be enforced against vigorous opposition. Given the jurisprudence of the United States Supreme Court leading up to the Civil War, why would one expect the Court to offer capacious, or even radical, interpretations of what Justice Robert Jackson once referred to as the "majestic generalities" contained in Section 1? Even if, as some historians emphasize, there was throughout the earlier period a tradition of "antislavery constitutionalism," to be "antislavery" did not guarantee that one was sympathetic to full inclusion of formerly enslaved persons within the American polity. After all, Lincoln himself was a devotee of colonization—emigration of Black persons from the United States to Africa, Haiti, or, as Lincoln suggested, Panama—well into his presidency.

Whether or not the founders included the magic words "property in man" in the Constitution to formally recognize slaveholders' interest in human chattel was essentially irrelevant for federal judges charged with interpreting the Constitution. (In fact the original 1787 text did *not* include such language, an omission that Madison was proud to take responsibility for and that the modern historian Sean Wilentz has made central to his own argument about American constitutionalism.) As the law professor Kermit

Roosevelt has emphasized, sincere opposition to slavery was subordinated to what were thought to be the twin imperatives of, first, creating the Union in 1787 and then of maintaining it thereafter. The Supreme Court's acknowledgment of these imperatives arrived with its enforcement of the Fugitive Slave Laws of 1793 and then the even more draconian slave law passed as part of the Compromise of 1850. Ostensibly "free" states had to return enslaved persons who had escaped from any state endorsing slavery. But equally important was the original "three-fifths" compromise that awarded slave states greater voting power in the House of Representatives and the Electoral College by counting slaves as three-fifths of a person—not to mention the guarantee of the international slave trade until 1808 (when, in fact, it was prohibited by Congress). These policies were not dependent whatsoever on the publication of favorable judicial opinions; they simply reflected the reality of American constitutional politics and the political commitment to maintaining the Union alongside slaveholders.

Lincoln agreed that the Union came first. He might have hated slavery, but he hated the idea of disunion even more, and he was more than willing to defend a series of compromises on slavery. His 1856 speech in Peoria that established his reentry into politics eloquently denounced slavery and the passage of the Kansas–Nebraska Act, but it also endorsed the Missouri Compromise of 1820 and the Compromise of 1850, both brokered by his political hero, Henry Clay. Even in his First Inaugural Address, he emphasized that his presidency would pose no threat at all to slavery in the states where it already existed. He drew his own line at extending slavery into the territories. But during the Civil War he wrote a famous letter to Horace Greeley in which he indicated that most important goal to him was preserving the Union. If abolishing slavery would do that, so be it (as he decided was the case in 1863); but if the South could be enticed back into Union with the preservation of slavery, then that, too, might well be acceptable, so long as they accepted that there would be no expansion of slavery into the territories.

Lincoln was assassinated before he had to commit himself to a specific policy of "reconstruction," a truly double-edged word. Did "reconstruction" mean rebuilding the exact house destroyed in the hurricane of war, perhaps with a few tweaks to account for changed circumstances yet standing resurrected as a testament to the resilience of a nation that wanted to return to the Constitution of 1787? Or did "reconstruction" mean starting from a new foundation and adopting a very different architecture than the one whose failures caused the catastrophic devastation of 1861–1865? What did Lincoln really mean by declaring his commitment to a policy of "malice toward none, and charity for all," in a world where the Civil War was the result of the malice toward and lack of charity for enslaved Black people? Would the crucible of battle be followed by a transformation of the hearts and minds of the losers? Or would the battleground shift toward KKK insurgency and litigation adjudicated before judges likely to be unsympathetic with more radical understandings of "reconstruction"?

Lincoln, like his successor, Andrew Johnson, was arguably committed to what has come to be called "presidential Reconstruction"—that is, placing ultimate authority over the defeated leaders of the Confederate States of America in the hands of the chief executive. He had vetoed the Wade–Davis Bill in 1864 that established more onerous terms for reentry of the secessionist states—assuming, of course, that in some sense they had indeed left—than those he had suggested were acceptable for Arkansas and Louisiana. Meanwhile, Radicals like Charles Sumner and Thaddeus Stevens were strongly committed to Black suffrage (the subject of the Fifteenth Amendment in 1870), but many other white Radicals were more conservative than Sumner and Stevens; Lincoln's position was not clear. It is important to remember that historian Michael Les Benedict some decades ago established that those we might tend to lump together as "radicals" were quite divided among themselves. In the language of modern political science, Radical Republicans were a "they" and not an "it." John Bingham, a chief figure behind Section 1 of the Fourteenth Amendment, was described by Benedict as decidedly conservative within the Republican Party. Lincoln's famed cabinet—his "team of rivals"—had only one true radical: Secretary of the Treasury Salmon P. Chase. Yet he was no radical within the terms of antislavery politics outside of Congress, and even he, a former Democrat, was sufficiently consumed by his (unfulfilled) ambition to be elected president that his views on Reconstruction became considerably more conservative over time. We simply do not know how Lincoln would have navigated the difficult political challenges that Mark Graber elucidates in this volume. One can be sure that Lincoln would have supported *some* version of Reconstruction, of course. That being said, the devil would be in the details.

The only thing one can say with confidence is that Lincoln would have been far more skillful politically in managing conflicts within the Republican Party coalition than his successor. Andrew Johnson opposed the *entire array* of Republican Reconstruction proposals and subverted those that were adopted. Despite the efforts of congressional Republicans, Johnson's vision ultimately supplanted theirs. It became the dominant policy regime for more than a century afterward. Our own amnesia about the Fourteenth Amendment is a testament to Johnson's victory, which has obscured the central political issues debated within the Thirty-Ninth Congress as it approached the task of constitutional reform. It has been hard for us to remember the *existence* of Sections 2 through 5, let alone imagine *why* they are in the Constitution. That is the central question of this volume.

Graber's work shows that central to the congressional discourse on the Fourteenth Amendment was the effort to *prevent rebel rule*. The Republican strategy for doing so was about constitutional politics, not constitutional law: their speeches in the *Congressional Globe* provide evidence of a strategy not focused primarily on protecting Black civil rights in court but rather on empowering those people—white and Black—who remained loyal to the Union. Graber argues that the vague phrases in Section 1 held little to no original meaning for the legislature because the Thirty-Ninth Congress's concern was primarily about, in Walter Murphy's formulation, "who" and not "what."[1] But on this matter Graber steps out of Murphy's paradigm when he identifies *partisan* supremacy—not only legislative supremacy—as a fully cogent and working constitutional ideology necessary to understanding the American constitutional order. Partisan supremacy as an ideology of constitutional understanding is barely, if at all, on the register of political scientists, lawyers, and historians in constitutional studies. After Graber's volume, we believe it deserves to be elaborated and interrogated in all of these fields.

In a rebuke to modern inheritors of the Republican project, Graber shows that, in these debates, *Black political identity functioned generally as a proxy for loyalty to the Union* rather than being centered within a conversation on human dignity. Even more striking, when the Thirty-Ninth Congress faced a choice between empowering loyal whites and empowering loyal Blacks, as when considering Colorado statehood, Nebraska statehood, and restoring Tennessee to the Union, they abandoned loyal Blacks and chose to empower loyal whites. Graber thus provides ample evidence for the relevance of Derek Bell's interest-convergence thesis—the idea that Black civil rights are advanced when those rights converge with the interests of whites.

Thus we get Sections 2 and 3, which were designed to turn a Pyrrhic victory into an actual victory. Not only would Southern denial of suffrage to African American males lead, at least in theory, to diminished representation of the South in Congress; official institutions would be culled of those deemed "traitors" or "rebels" against the United States. Moreover, Section 4 recognized that former slaveholders might find a sympathetic audience should they claim that confiscation of their "property" required "just compensation" as required by the Fifth Amendment. Abraham Lincoln, after all, had supported "compensated emancipation" well into his presidency, and there was nothing frivolous about arguments that the national government might owe compensation to slaveholders, especially to those who had not provided active aid to the Confederacy. Section 4 took such arguments completely off the table.

Republicans were pluralistic, of course, and discourse in the *Congressional Globe* cannot lend proof to any actor's motivations. But what is clear after this volume is that the discursive field from which the Fourteenth Amendment emerged was emphatic on the value of creating a constitutional politics that *empowered loyalists*. Though the South did not secede again, and Unionist-elected representatives maintained control of national institutions for another century, the South did not turn out to be a lasting source of support for the Republican Party. Republicans had hoped that they could rewrite the Constitution to establish a genuine hegemony in Southern states for their own party. When that turned out to be a failed hope, they shifted their sights to the Midwest (via so-called state-packing), and most (but not all) Republicans simply averted their gaze and acquiesced to Jim Crow. While this pivot speaks to the capacity of parties to achieve their goals in politics, Graber's finding also reminds us of the horrific collective failures that are already built into legislative representation within the Constitution.

Mark Graber's genuine magnum opus, based on total immersion in the congressional debates of the time, promises to transform the way that all of us imagine the Reconstruction Amendments from a modern perspective. At the very least, he enables us to realize that the separation of law from politics is much too facile; that law, especially formal constitutional amendments, emerges out of politics and, especially with regard to Sections 2 through 4 of the Fourteenth Amendment, instantiates a different vision of politics than the misleading, judiciary-centered vision taught to students. Actual constitutions are not written by disinterested parties operating behind what John Rawls famously called the "veil of ignorance." Instead, those drafting constitutions are well aware of the implications of any given decision, especially those involving the basic structures of the polity. Constitutions—not to mention laws passed by the procedures established by a given constitution—are made (and interpreted) by members of winning political coalitions who wish to maintain themselves in power, sometimes because they genuinely perceive their political opponents as threats to fundamental values such as racial justice, and sometimes simply because they are committed to the ongoing wins of their own coalition. The Fourteenth and Fifteenth Amendments are tributes to this reality. No one who absorbs the lessons that Mark Graber teaches in these pages will ever be able to think of constitution formation in general, or the particularity of the Reconstruction Amendments, in the same way as before. We are proud to introduce this book as constitutional thinking of the very highest caliber.

Sanford Levinson
Jeffrey K. Tulis
Emily Zackin
Mariah Zeisberg
Coeditors, Constitutional Thinking Series

ACKNOWLEDGMENTS

I have been extraordinarily fortunate in the people who have carried, guided, and accompanied me down my life path that has led to this volume. I was first carried by two exceptionally loving and giving parents, Anita Wine Graber and Julius Wolf Graber. Through example and encouragement, they fostered commitments to *tikkun olam*, to the acquisition of useful knowledge, and to the exploration of what at first glance may not seem to be useful knowledge. When I was old to enough to walk holding their hands, they were carrying Peter and Eric. Both are extraordinarily decent people who are living extraordinary lives. They have influenced my path and this volume more than they will know.

My tour guides at Jacob Gunther Elementary School, Jerusalem Avenue Junior High School, and Wellington C. Mepham High School fostered a love of reading, a fascination with history, and an often obnoxious iconoclasticism while putting up with my obsessions with chess, the clarinet, and basketball. Special thanks to Mrs. Dowd, Mr. Ambroso, Mr. Cohen, and Mr. Rapport. Each modeled why the teaching professon is so vital.

At Dartmouth College, I found both guides and companions. Two professors stand out in a group of outstanding educators. Professor Willis Doney — my thesis adviser, an internationally known Descartes scholar, and my first academic mentor — helped me in understanding academic rigor. George Young taught me Russian history and, more important, the pedagogical importance of communicating enthusiasm to students. My brothers and sisters at the Phi Tau fraternity provided much-needed bridge games, square dancing, conversations about the meaning of life, and chatter about more tangible matters. Several of them, most notably Jeff Weeks, James Lyons, and Betsy Lyons, have remained lifelong friends.

Rogers Smith, my dissertation adviser in the Yale University's Department of Political Science, guided my transition from student to professor/ scholar. Rogers plays a founding role in the study of American political development as a scholar and as a mentor to many of the most prominent practitioners over the past forty years. I am honored to be his first PhD student, even, as I suspect, the product he has turned out has improved considerably over the years. Rogers was generous with his time, acute with his commentary, and consistently encouraging, particularly at times when encouragement was desperately needed. Douglas Rae, Stephen Skowonick, and David Mayhew also provided valuable guidance to a graduate student who had more than his fair share of stumbles along the scholarly road.

At the beginning of my professional career, I was lucky enough to be guided by Jim Fishkin, who was the chair of the search committee that hired me at the University of Texas and then for his sins became chair of the department. At least 10 percent of my weight was gained at dessert parties at his home. Scot Powe, Walter Dean Burnham, and Sandy Levinson were also vital guides during my scholarly wanderings. Each is a terrific scholar and even better person, though I regret Dean must now be referred to in the past tense. I owe much of my understanding of the interaction between law and politics to Scot and Dean. Sandy inspired my slow move to constitutional politics from constitutional law. He deserves special mention for promoting my work, even if I cannot convince him that now is not the moment for a constitutional convention. Readers should look at the LevinsonFest blogs on Balkanization to learn or, more likely, be reminded of the remarkable depth and breath of this remarkable scholar.

Different companions joined me when I moved to the Political Science Department at the University of Maryland, College Park and then the University of Maryland Carey School of Law. Deans Karen Rothenburg, Phoebe Haddon, Donald Tobin, and Renée Hutchins provided material and immaterial support for my writing, as did Jon Wilkenfeld, the longtime chair of Government at College Park. Richard Boldt, Doug Colbert, Peter Danchin, Deborah Eisenberg, Steve Elkin, Don Gifford, Leslie Henry, Michael Pappas, Jana Singer, Karol Soltan, Maxwell Stearns, Michael Van Alstine, Gordon Young, and many others deserve special credit for listening to essentially the same project over and over again while consistently offering fresh insight.

I benefited from the academic companionship of numerous scholarly friends who were dedicated to collapsing what I have called the "New Deal constitutional universe." Foremost among my companions are Paul Frymer, Howard Gillman, Leslie Goldstein, Ran Hirschl, Ken Kersch, Julie Novkov, Amnon Reichman, Kim Lane Scheppele, Howard Schweber, Alexander Tsesis, Keith Whittington, and Emily Zackin. As I have written in other dedications, I rarely if ever know where my ideas begin and theirs end. Antonia Baraggia, Gabor Halmai, Heinz Klug, Richard Albert, Yaniv Roznai, and Rivka Weill have become new companions as I try to branch out as an amateur comparative constitutionalist. I have also been inspired by the work of scholarly friends who regularly indulge me by participating in the annual Maryland Schmooze. Mark Tushnet, the founder of the Schmooze, deserves special mention as both a mentor and scholarly inspiration. Other frequent Schmoozers who have been academic companions include Hank Chambers, James Fleming, Linda McClain, Robert Tsai, and Rebecca Zietlow. David Schwartz, who graciously invites me to the Wisconsin Schmooze, has also helped me think through ideas and, more important, exposed me to the ideas of others. Steven Lichtmann, the organizer of the New England Political Science Association, has happily introduced me to a generation of younger scholars who are making their paths in the scholarly world.

Punish Treason, Reward Loyalty has followed a similarly winding path to publication. The road began with a great many out-of-town tryouts. I am grateful for the comments I received when presenting versions or parts of this book at Hofstra Law School, New York University School of Law, the City University of New York, Staten Island, the Loyola University Chicago School of Law/George Washington University Law School annual Constitutional Law Colloquium, the Midwest Political Science Association, the Interdisciplinary Center in Tel Aviv, the University of Wisconsin School of Law, Texas State University, Chicago-Kent College of Law, Duke University School of Law, South Texas University, the University of Texas School of Law, Washington and Lee University School of Law, Cornell Law School, Yale Law School, University of Georgia School of Law, the American Association of Law Schools, Princeton University, the University of Virginia School of Law, the American Political Science Association, and the New England Political Science Association. Richard Albert was his usual extraordinary self when organizing an online symposium at the University of Texas on the manuscript. Rebecca Zietlow provided superb commentary. Ran Hirschl, Emily Zackin, Mariah Zeisberg, and many others provided probing questions. I hope that the first two chapters of *Punish Treason, Reward Loyalty* reflect their concerns.

As a friend and editor, David Congdon has proved a worthy successor to Fred Woodward, Michael Briggs, and Charles Myers. Together they have produced a marvelous list in American constitutional development and demonstrated quiet patience with the length of time needed to produce this manuscript. Greg Downs and David Bateman did a sterling job as readers, identifying strengths but also pushing me aggressively to make the work better. No doubt I should have listened to them more, but their advice was most welcomed. Sandy Levinson, Jeff Tulis, Emily Zackin, and Mariah Zeisberg kindly included this work in their Constitutional Thinking series. Special thanks are due to the outstanding production and publicity teams at the University Press of Kansas. Kelly Chrisman Jacques, the managing director of the press, assembled a terrific group that including Jon Howard, who thoroughly copyedited this work; Karl Janssen, who is responsible for the cover design; Alec Loganbill, the production assistant and second set of eyes at all stages of the proofing; Derek Helms, the marketing and publicity director; and Suzanne Galle, the assistant marketing manager. Sergey Lobachev did a wonderful job with the index.

Jack Balkin, Sandy Levinson, Jonathan Gienapp, and Stephen Griffin have been my most frequent academic traveling companions in recent years. Jack organized a wonderful salon in which we gossip about Yale Law School, discuss the state of American constitutional politics, and comment on various manuscripts with such guests as Reva Siegel, Pamela Karlan, and Andy Koppelman. Jack, Sandy, Jonathan, and Stephen have enriched my understanding of American constitutionalism in ways they defy description. They are probably as responsible for the ideas that follow as I am. The dedication is an inadequate payment of my intellectual debt to them.

No dedication adequately expresses the debt I owe to Julia Bess Frank, who has been my daily companion down life's path for the past forty years. A special scholar, doctor, spouse, and parent, as well as a theater and cycling buddy, Julia brightens every day I have and every word I write. Together we carried Naomi, Abigail, and Rebecca down their life paths. We served as tour guides and are now their companions. My hope is that when each writes an acknowledgement of some sort thirty years from now, they will feel their lives as blessed as my life has been.

An aspiring actor finally lands a role in a major Shakespearean company, playing the part of Osric in *Hamlet*. He is thrilled to have a few lines, umpire the final duel, and portray a character who, unlike many others, survives. After the first week of the play's run goes well, our excitable thespian decides a celebratory trip to the local tavern is in order. There he meets a young woman. They get to talking. "What do you do?" his companion asks. Our hero replies, "I'm an actor." "Are you in a show?" she continues. "Yes," he proudly answers, "I am in *Hamlet*." She responds, "I am not a theater person. What is *Hamlet* about?" "Well," he says, "there is this guy called Osric. . . ."[1]

Of Osric and Contemporary Constitutionalism

Commentary on the Fourteenth Amendment retells this Osric story. The Fourteenth Amendment in contemporary constitutional politics is a star vehicle. Section 1, which includes the Citizenship, Privileges and Immunities, Due Process, and Equal Protection Clauses, is the performer.[2] Section 5, which vests Congress with the power to implement the entire Fourteenth Amendment, has a bit part, but only with respect to Section 5's relationship with Section 1. Sections 2, 3, and 4 are often offstage entirely.[3] The Fourteenth Amendment as drafted by the Republican members of the Thirty-Ninth United States Congress was an ensemble production.[4] Sections 2, 3, and 4 had major roles, with Section 2 gaining star billing. Section 1, if not Osric, was no more than Polonius, Horatio, Ophelia, or Laertes—and certainly not Hamlet, Gertrude, or Claudius. Section 5 supported every provision in the previous sections.

The Faux Star Story

The Fourteenth Amendment as *Osric: The Musical* was originally produced by the Supreme Court in the *Slaughter-House Cases*. The first big number in that production sings out:

> [The Black Codes][5] . . . forced upon the statesmen who had conducted the Federal government in safety through the crisis of the rebellion, and who supposed that by the thirteenth article of amendment they

had secured the result of their labors, the conviction that something more was necessary in the way of constitutional protection to the unfortunate race who had suffered so much.[6]

Subsequent revivals faithfully reproduce the three central plot devices that structure *Slaughter-House*'s presentation of the post–Civil War amendments. The Black Codes that former Confederate states passed in the immediate wake of the Civil War demonstrated the need for new constitutional rights guarantees.[7] As one federal judge noted, "distinguished historians from various viewpoints all agree that one of the primary reasons for the fourteenth amendment was the existence of 'Black Codes.'"[8] The primary purpose of the Fourteenth Amendment was to protect persons of color.[9] Nikolas Bowie and Daphna Renan claim that "Congress . . . proposed the Fourteenth Amendment to place its power to pass . . . civil-rights legislation on firm constitutional footing."[10] Section 1, which provides those new rights protections for persons of color, is "the heart of the Fourteenth Amendment."[11] "What has made the amendment famous," Steven Calabresi and Lena Barsky declare, "is its second sentence in Section 1."[12]

Section 1 gets star billing in the revivals of the Fourteenth Amendment that take place in courtrooms, legislative chambers, and law reviews across the United States in large part because that text is central to contemporary disputes in constitutional law that arise over the meaning of what Sandy Levinson calls the "Constitution of Conversation."[13] Levinson's "Constitution of Conversation" consists of the commonly litigated provisions in the text whose official interpretation is crucial to the most important controversies in constitutional law during our time. To paraphrase Alexis de Tocqueville, "scarcely any [constitutional law] question arises in the [contemporary] United States that is not resolved, sooner or later, into a [Fourteenth Amendment] question."[14] The constitutional status of affirmative action depends on the proper interpretation of the Equal Protection Clause.[15] The constitutional status of state gun control legislation depends on the proper interpretation of the Due Process Clause[16] and, perhaps, the Privileges and Immunities Clause.[17] The constitutional status of same-sex marriage depends on the proper interpretation of both the Equal Protection and Due Process Clauses.[18] When the Supreme Court considers whether the federal government has violated the rights enumerated in the first eight amendments to the Constitution, the justices rely heavily on precedents that interpret those rights as incorporated by the Due Process Clause of the Fourteenth Amendment.[19] The Supreme Court's decision declaring unconstitutional under the First Amendment congressional legislation prohibiting protestors from burning the flag of the United States[20] made multiple references to a past decision declaring unconstitutional under the Fourteenth Amendment state legislation prohibiting protestors from defacing the flag.[21] The four blockbuster decisions that ended the Supreme Court's 2021–2022 term all directly turned on the proper interpretation of the Due Process Clause of the Fourteenth Amendment[22] or concerned provisions in the Bill of Rights that the justices had previously determined were incorporated against the states by the Due Process Clause of the Fourteenth Amendment.[23]

Sections 2, 3, and 4 of the Fourteenth Amendment are relegated to the "Constitution of Memory"—those constitutional provisions that once played or were intended to play vital roles in American constitutionalism but do not play any role in current constitutional politics.[24] Congress has never exercised Section 2 powers.[25] The persons banned from holding office under Section 3 have been dead for over a century, although the response to Donald Trump's insurrection on January 6, 2021, inspired a brief revival.[26] Section 4's claim that the national debt not be repudiated enjoyed a short revival during present-day debates over raising the debt ceiling[27] but has otherwise been an historical obscurity. The Union soldiers and their families who might be owed pensions under Section 4 are long dead, as are persons who might have any claims to compensation for former slaves or Confederate war bonds.

Contemporary demands for constitutional performances that emphasize restrictions on government power buttress Section 1's star status. Conventional wisdom insists that constitutionalism is "by definition limited government" committed to constraining powerholders.[28] Twentieth and twenty-first century liberal constitutionalism emphasizes rights provisions as the most important, often exclusive means for constraining government power.[29] Giovanni Sartori declares, "[a] frame of government [must] provide for a bill of rights and the institutional devices that would secure its observance."[30] The Citizenship, Privileges and Immunities, Due Process, and Equal Protection Clauses of the Fourteenth Amendment are centerpieces to what Lorraine Weinrib describes as "the postwar constitutional paradigm," a vision of politics that sees constitutions as "rights-protecting instruments" designed to "build[] the primacy of equal citizenship and inherent human dignity into the basic structure of liberal democracy."[31] If the point of the constitutional show is to protect fundamental rights, then the spotlight never leaves the fundamental rights provisions. Those provisions in the Constitution of the United States are found in Section 1 of the Fourteenth Amendment.

Sections 2 and 3 of the Fourteenth Amendment seem orthogonal to the liberal constitutional project. Neither section announces rights. Both make rules for staffing the quasi-majoritarian institutions liberal constitutional theory assumes cannot be trusted to protect rights. Neither Section 2 nor Section 3 seems relevant to liberal schemes for enforcing rights through judicial review, or what Ronald Dworkin called "the forum of principle."[32] The constitutional rules for allocating representation and setting qualifications for officeholding do not directly affect the "[a]djudication of rights claims" that "serves to protect . . . constitutional principles against inimical legislation and state action" that Weinrib maintains is central to the postwar constitutional paradigm,[33] although Section 3 forbids some former Confederates and participants in future insurrections from sitting on federal and state benches. Both Section 2 and Section 3 lack textual connection with the rights enumerated in Section 1 that are at the core of the liberal constitutional project other than their being part of an apparent omnibus constitutional amendment. Commentary that focuses on rights guarantees rarely if ever makes any historical connection between the rights and structural provisions of the Fourteenth Amendment.

The spotlight shone on Section 1 casts the Fourteenth Amendment as an "omnibus" whose provisions have little in common other than being in the same measure.[34] The same congressional logrolls that explain why a single bill may increase pay for Marines serving overseas and provide for roads to be improved in Nebraska apparently explain why the Fourteenth Amendment includes an equal protection clause, a clause banning certain Confederates from holding certain offices, and provisions on the national debt. Omnibus bills often appease small constituencies whose votes are needed to pass important legislation of general interest. The contemporary Fourteenth Amendment from this perspective seems analogous to contemporary spending bills where the analogies to Section 1 are the provisions detailing the military budget, and the analogies to Sections 2, 3, and 4 are the riders added that, say, provide federal funds to improve a library in Sioux City, Iowa, declare July 27 "National Bird-Watching Day," and congratulate the US Checkers Team for their fifth-place finish at the world championships.[35]

The Project

The Forgotten Fourteenth Amendment: Punish Treason, Reward Loyalty begins a multivolume project that restores to contemporary memory the

Fourteenth Amendment drafted by those Republican and Unionist members of the Thirty-Ninth Congress who supported congressional Reconstruction. This volume details how the Republican framers regarded constitutional reform as central to their effort to prevent "rebel rule" by empowering and protecting the persons, white and Black, who remained loyal to the Union during the Civil War. Volume 2 will explore how members of the Thirty-Ninth Congress thought the Constitution of the United States constrained, created, configured, and constituted politics immediately after the ratification of the constitutional ban on slavery. Volume 3 will discuss the debates in Congress over proposed constitutional reforms, from the stand-alone debt, apportionment, and civil rights amendments to the final omnibus. Volume 4[36] will document and explain the swift rise of Section 1 in the 1870s.

This volume and the volumes to come examine the Fourteenth Amendment in light of the problems that seemed pressing to those Republican and Unionist members of the Thirty-Ninth Congress who favored congressional Reconstruction, the conceptual apparatus they brought to bear on those problems, and the choices they believed were politically feasible promise to advance knowledge about Reconstruction, the Fourteenth Amendment, and constitutionalism. With respect to Reconstruction and the Fourteenth Amendment, these volumes will:

- Highlight the importance of Sections 2, 3, and 4 to the representatives in the Thirty-Ninth Congress who drafted the Fourteenth Amendment and (Representative John A. Bingham of Ohio aside) their relative indifference to Section 1;
- bring to light all the debates that took place in the first session of the Thirty-Ninth Congress (December 4, 1865–July 28, 1866; see pages 260–265 for a complete calendar) over constitutional reform and related subjects, most notably the debates over presidential and congressional Reconstruction;
- place at the center of Reconstruction and constitutional reform the Republican concern with preventing rebel rule by empowering and protecting the loyal;
- emphasize how the persons responsible for the Fourteenth Amendment were more concerned with configuring and constituting constitutional politics than with constraining and creating constitutional politics; and
- underscore the importance of legislative primacy and partisan supremacy to Republican constitutional thinking about constitutional

authority immediately after the Civil War and the impact those commitments had on the Fourteenth Amendment.

With respect to constitutionalism, these volumes will:

- Shift the focus of constitutional thinking from constitutional law to constitutional politics, from questions about what constitutional provisions mean to questions about how constitutions work;
- introduce legislative primary and partisan supremacy as means for allocating constitutional authority;
- maintain that constitutions are better conceptualized as mechanisms for empowering than for limiting government; and
- elaborate problems with originalism as a means for interpreting constitutional provisions designed to construct and constitute constitutional politics rather than to constrain and create constitutional politics.

The Fourteenth Amendment that proponents of congressional Reconstruction framed was designed to prevent "rebel rule" in the nation and in the former Confederate states. The main impetus for the Fourteenth Amendment was the Thirteenth Amendment, which, by counting disenfranchised former slaves as full persons, threatened to restore to local and national power a revived coalition of former slaveholders, white supremacists, and Northern Democrats. The Republicans responsible for the Fourteenth Amendment thought preventing rebel rule required new anti-secession, financial, political, and civil rights guarantees that would empower and protect loyal freedmen, loyal Southern Unionists, loyal soldiers and their families, and loyal Northern creditors. Rights provisions were important to this enterprise, but they were rarely given place of pride in the numerous arias that individual Republicans sang on the floor of Congress. When drafting and debating the really big, show-stopping provisions, Republican recitations considered at great length the political guarantees and securities that became embodied in Sections 2 and 3 of the Fourteenth Amendment, but most framers paid little attention to the rights guarantees that became embodied in Section 1. More Republicans when making speeches on congressional Reconstruction called for constitutional amendments providing financial guarantees for loyal creditors than championed constitutional guarantees providing civil rights guarantees for persons of color.

The heart of the Fourteenth Amendment was a series of constitutional reforms aimed at protecting and empowering those persons, white and Black, who remained loyal to the United States during the Civil War.

Representative Thaddeus Stevens of Pennsylvania and his political allies feared that, unless the basis of representation was adjusted (Section 2) and former rebels politically enfeebled (Section 3), the Thirteenth Amendment and other existing constitutional protections for loyal citizens would be disobeyed, invalidated, neglected, denied, circumscribed, circumvented, or captured. Stevens reminded Congress repeatedly that the post–Civil War Constitution would be a parchment barrier in the hands of a revived Jacksonian coalition of Southern Democrats and their Northern Doughface allies. Southern Blacks would be practically re-enslaved, Southern Unionists persecuted, and Northern creditors stiffed under rebel rule—no matter what rights guarantees might be found in the constitutional text. Regarding the central problem of Reconstruction as one of constitutional politics rather than one of constitutional law, the Republicans and allied Unionists responsible for the Fourteenth Amendment concentrated on elaborating better constitutional foundations for continued rule by the majority party of the people who remained loyal to the government during the Civil War and ratified the Thirteenth Amendment. Republicans cheerfully endorsed the more substantive rights provisions in Section 1 and Section 4. Nevertheless, the Republican leadership in the House and Senate understood that the rights, restrictions, and powers enumerated in Sections 1, 4, and 5 of the Fourteenth Amendment, as well as those rights and powers enumerated in Sections 1 and 2 of the Thirteenth Amendment, would be interpreted and implemented in good faith only if Sections 2 and 3 successfully configured American constitutional politics to prevent rebel rule and empower the loyal.

The rights of African Americans played a different, more complicated, and more ambiguous role in Republican thinking about constitutional reform than in the accounts offered by the *Slaughter-House* majority or by contemporary revivals. Former slaves have a prominent role in historically faithful productions of "The Greatest Hits of the Thirty-Ninth Congress, First Session." During the first six months of 1866, Congress passed the Second Freedmen's Bureau Bill,[37] which was vetoed by President Andrew Johnson,[38] passed the Civil Rights Act of 1866,[39] overturned President Johnson's veto of that measure,[40] and then passed a modified version of the Second Freedmen's Bureau Bill[41] over another Johnson veto.[42] The House of Representatives voted to enfranchise persons of color in Washington, D.C.[43] Nevertheless, Section 1 did not play a major role in scenes devoted to Republican efforts from December 1865 to July 1866 to secure racial equality in the United States. The leading proponents of Black rights in the Thirty-Ninth Congress, most notably Senator Charles Sumner of Massachusetts, maintained that former slaves were adequately protected by the Constitution in effect on January 1, 1866. Bingham aside, Republican proponents of congressional Reconstruction maintained that the Thirteenth Amendment already gave the national government the power necessary to protect all the rights of former slaves that Black Codes in the South denied and Republican majorities wanted to protect. The question that divided Republicans during the first session of the Thirty-Ninth Congress was whether persons of color should be empowered as well as protected. Many Republicans insisted that rebel rule could be prevented only if persons of color were directly enfranchised by constitutional amendment, directly enfranchised by federal statute passed under the Thirteenth Amendment or the Guarantee Clause, or indirectly enfranchised by apportionment reforms that would compel former Confederate states to grant former slaves the ballot in order to have adequate representation in the national government. Others insisted that Congress need not directly or indirectly attempt to enfranchise persons of color and that rebel rule could be prevented if loyal whites were empowered. This view predominated during the first months of 1866.[44] When Republican majorities in the first session had a choice between empowering loyal whites and empowering loyal Blacks, as when considering Colorado statehood, Nebraska statehood, and restoring Tennessee, they chose to empower loyal whites.

Some Conceptual Tools

This and the subsequent volumes employ some concepts or conceptual tools that are almost never used in studies of the Fourteenth Amendment and are too rarely used in constitutional studies more generally. The focus is on how the persons responsible for the Fourteenth Amendment thought their constitutional reforms would work rather than on what they thought their newly framed constitutional provisions meant.[45] The volumes in The Forgotten Fourteenth Amendment series document the Republican emphasis on configuring and constituting politics. John Bingham was the only member of the Thirty-Ninth Congress who shared more contemporary obsessions with provisions that constrain and create politics. What Stevens and his political allies were doing when they framed the Fourteenth Amendment can be explained only in light of their background commitments to partisan supremacy and legislative primacy as the appropriate allocation of authority over the interpretation and implementation of constitutional provisions. Future volumes will detail at some length these Republican concerns with configuring politics, constituting politics, partisan supremacy, and legislative primary, but a brief introduction seems useful in this preface.

Conventional constitutional histories, particularly those undertaken in the legal academy, assume that constitutions work primarily by constraining politics. Constitutions are mechanisms for limiting government. The point of constitutional *reform* is to provide new, fixed legal restrictions on government. The point of constitutional *history* is to determine the original meaning of those legal restrictions. Whether those original meanings should bind future generations is a subject for constitutional theorists, not constitutional historians.

Conventional constitutional histories also recognize that constitutions work by creating politics. Constitutions are mechanisms for empowering as well as limiting government. Max Edling captures this dimension of American constitutionalism in his 2003 book *A Revolution in Favor of Power*. The point of constitutional reform in the United States during the late eighteenth century, Edling and others observe, was to provide the national government with new, fixed legal powers.[46] The point of constitutional history is to determine the original meaning of those legal powers. Whether those original meanings should bind future generations is likewise a subject for constitutional theorists, not constitutional historians.

The Republicans who framed the Fourteenth Amendment thought constitutions work by configuring politics. They regarded constitutions as mechanisms that privilege coalitions with particular interests and values. By structuring government in ways that empower some political movements at the expense of others, constitutions guarantee to the extent feasible that the privileged coalitions will control the future interpretation and implementation of constitutional limitations and powers that are often phrased in grand, abstract terms. John Bingham aside, Republican members of the Thirty-Ninth Congress believed the Thirteenth Amendment's Constitution, the Constitution after the ban on slavery was ratified, adequately constrained and created politics. The newly ratified Thirteenth Amendment and such long-standing constitutional provisions as the Guarantee Clause provided Congress with more than sufficient powers to protect the rights of former slaves and white Southerners who remained loyal to the Union during the Civil War. What Republicans dreaded was that future Congresses would not exercise those powers unless politics was restructured. The point of constitutional reform was to configure politics in such a way that would enable the people who remained loyal to the Union to control how the Thirteenth Amendment was interpreted and implemented in the foreseeable future. The point of constitutional history is to determine *who* Republicans wanted to interpret and implement the Thirteenth Amendment and to detail the processes Republicans sought to put in place for empowering the sympathetic to interpreting and implementing it. The point of constitutional theory is to adjudicate those debates among persons committed to the free labor and racial equality that the Thirty-Ninth Congress left to be resolved by Republicans in the future.

The Republicans who framed the Fourteenth Amendment also thought that constitutions work by constituting politics. They regarded constitutions as mechanisms that help fashion a citizenry with particular interests and values. The persons responsible for the post–Civil War amendments believed a properly configured politics would change racial attitudes in the South. Many white Southerners would become more racially tolerant if a restructured constitutional politics freed them from the thralls of the slaveholding class responsible for secession. Less-affluent whites would gradually lose their racial prejudices when practically compelled to form biracial coalitions with Black voters. The point of constitutional reform was to bring about the conditions necessary to shape a citizenry more committed to racial equality. The point of constitutional history is to explain the constitutional sociology that Republicans believed would generate popular majorities in the United States who recognized persons of color as equal citizens in the United States. Constitutional theory is pointless unless the Constitution continued to fashion a citizenry committed to some version of Republican understandings of free labor and racial equality. The Fourteenth Amendment would not work, Stevens and his political allies knew, should most Americans revert to antebellum attitudes toward slavery and white supremacy.

Republicans committed to constitutional reforms that configured and constituted politics emphasized parties as the institutions primarily responsible for interpreting and implementing new constitutional provisions. Commitments to judicial supremacy make sense only when the point of constitutional reform is to provide new fixed legal constraints and new fixed legal powers. Chief Justice John Marshall pointed out in *Marbury v. Madison* that "it is the province and duty of the judiciary to say what the law is."[47] The Republican framers of the Fourteenth Amendment understood that popular constitutionalism is more appropriate when reformers are trying to configure politics in ways that make certain outcomes more likely and constitute politics in ways that fashion more citizens sympathetic to their general vision. Stevens and his political allies spoke frequently about the need to maintain Republican Party strength and unity, but they hardly ever mentioned the federal judiciary when constitutional reform was on the table. Political parties and popular movements, they recognized, are the primary vehicles in the United States for organizing politics and altering the values underlying political action. Courts have little to do with the processes that privilege legislation promoting racial equality and increase support for such policies.

Partisan supremacy and legislative primacy are two elements of the popular constitutionalism underlying the Fourteenth Amendment. Partisan supremacy, as articulated by Martin Van Buren and Thaddeus Stevens, regards dominant political parties as vested with the authority to settle constitutional disputes.[48] Abraham Lincoln's attack on judicial supremacy is the most famous articulation of partisan supremacy in American history. Lincoln claimed he was entitled to reject the Supreme Court's decision in *Dred Scott v. Sandford*[49] as the established law of the land because he was the leader of a victorious political party and not, as departmentalist logic suggests, because he was president of the United States.[50] Legislative primacy regards Congress as the institution primarily responsible for interpreting and implementing the post–Civil War amendments. Courts assess the constitutionality of federal legislation but are not expected to implement independently the post–Civil War Amendments in the absence of clear violations.[51] The debate over school segregation when the Civil Rights Act of 1875 was framed illustrates legislative primary. Many Republicans maintained Congress had the power under the Thirteenth and Fourteenth Amendments to ban segregated schools. No one maintained that courts could ban segregated schools in the absence of federal legislation.[52]

Understanding the Fourteenth Amendment in terms of Republican commitments to configuring politics, constituting politics, partisan supremacy, and legislative primacy plays havoc with traditional searches for original meanings. The quest for original meaning makes sense when framers are constraining or creating politics or otherwise intend constitutional provisions to have fixed legal meanings.[53] We can ask of such provisions: What did people think they meant when they were ratified? Republicans had no intention to constrain or create politics when they framed Section 1 of the Fourteenth Amendment. The vague phrases were just that—vague phrases. Thaddeus Stevens and his political allies were concerned with who would interpret and implement those phrases in the foreseeable future, not with fixing their meaning in the present. Provisions designed to be liquated by a particular kind of constitutional politics over time do not have the fixed legal meanings required by the most popular forms of constitutional originalism in the twenty-first century. Sections 2 and 3, which were designed to have fixed legal meanings, are the heart of the Fourteenth Amendment, not Section 1, whose meaning was subject to the workings of Sections 2 and 3.

Hidden in Plain Sight

The forgotten Fourteenth Amendment has been hidden in plain sight for more than a century. *Punish Treason, Reward Loyalty* and succeeding volumes rely extensively on the same *Congressional Globe* that scholars routinely use as the primary source when writing about the post–Civil War amendments. Readers will find no letters from an obscure congressperson found recently in an old attic or columns from an unknown pundit published by a newspaper that went out of business in 1867. This is not a book claiming that one speech or one paragraph in a speech made by a congressional backbencher on May 1, 1866, provides the key that unlocks the meaning of the Fourteenth Amendment. The following pages offer no esoteric readings[54] that treat Charles Sumner as directing his rhetoric primarily at a future elite (me) capable of discerning hidden meanings in the oratory. Republicans publicly, plainly, and repeatedly stated that the Fourteenth Amendment was needed to change the structure of constitutional politics, not the edicts of constitutional law. The argument, pursued to the point of severe overkill, is that almost every proponent of the Fourteenth Amendment who spoke at any length (other than John Bingham) declared openly that the core of that constitutional reform was some combination of Sections 2, 3, and 4. As Sandy Levinson has pointed out to me, the Republican framers were not Rawlsian figures sitting behind a veil of ignorance wondering what kind of constitution they might want if, when the veil was lifted, they turned out to be Democrats. Stevens and his political allies believed that only Republicans could be trusted to vindicate the slaughter of the Civil War—to guarantee that the victims did not "die in vain." The Reconstruction Amendments were openly designed to guarantee the continued supremacy of Republican public officials.

Scholars have overlooked the animating spirit of the Fourteenth Amendment even though Republican members of the Thirty-Ninth Congress were engaged in conventional constitutional politics. The main theses of this and succeeding volumes would inspire little more than yawns were the subject another major constitutional reform in the United States or, better yet, another country.[55] A central point of constitutional reform was to entrench the party of the constitutional reformers. Not exactly a "Stop the [University] Presses" scholarly headline. The constitutional reform was spearheaded by long-standing legislative leaders (i.e., Stevens) rather than by a member of the national legislature (i.e., Bingham) who is rarely mentioned in any history of times not devoted to that specific constitutional reform. Not exactly shocking.

Seventeen eighty-seven might have provided the model for understanding 1866. Both Republican and Federalist founders sought to reconfigure constitutional politics in order to privilege their constitutional visions. That fundamental rights are best protected by the structure of politics rather than by parchment barriers[56] is a staple of the literature on the Constitution drafted in Philadelphia. Consider only scholarship devoted to *Federalist No. 10*, the essay claiming that a large republic is the better guarantor of religious freedom than free exercise or establishment clauses.[57] Any investigation that began with the premise that the Republican framers of 1866 were just as concerned as the Federalist framers of 1787 with privileging the power of some worthies[58] at the expense of other potential powerholders would find that thesis confirmed repeatedly in the *Congressional Globe*.

The forgotten Fourteenth Amendment stares Americans in the face. The Republican leadership was not shy about speaking—and speaking about their partisan ambitions. From December 1865 to May 1866, hardly a week went by without multiple long speeches by various Republicans in Congress discussing the need for constitutional reforms that would ensure that former rebels did not control the national government and that loyal persons of all races would get their due rewards. Numerous congresspersons, many of them prominent, gave more speeches and longer speeches emphasizing the importance of political protections for existing fundamental rights than John Bingham gave emphasizing the need for new fundamental rights guarantees. If there are any esoteric meanings in the Thirty-Ninth Congress, they concern the fundamental rights provisions in Section 1 whose "euphony and indefiniteness of meaning were a charm,"[59] not Sections 2, 3, and 4, provisions the congressional leadership word-smithed to ensure maximum clarity.

This apparently remarkable failure to see the obvious has strong roots in Reconstruction history. A consensus developed by the end of Reconstruction that the primary purpose of the Fourteenth Amendment was to provide newly freed slaves with certain fundamental rights that were being violated by the Black Codes. Section 1 was center stage when the Supreme Court decided the *Slaughter-House Cases*[60] in 1872, a mere four years after the Fourteenth Amendment was ratified. Section 1 was center stage when Congress debated the Civil Rights Acts of 1871[61] and 1875.[62] The Amnesty Act of 1872 aside,[63] one would need the detection skills of a Hercule Poirot or the most sophisticated CSI crime lab to discern traces of Section 2, Section 3, or Section 4 in any prominent congressional debate that took place after the Amnesty Act of 1872. Why Republicans in the early 1870s might misrepresent their ambitions in the mid-1860s is a mystery no one has yet identified, much less explained.[64]

The siloed construction of the American academy after World War II further explains the uncritical acceptance of Republican claims in the 1870s that constitutional reform in 1865–1866 was directed only at adding new fundamental rights to the Constitution. The forgotten Fourteenth Amendment exists in the cracks between law, history, and political science. Each discipline is structured by disciplinary blinders that render largely invisible the Republican effort in the Thirty-Ninth Congress to reconfigure constitutional politics. Law professors wear disciplinary blinders that enable them to see only the few passages in the *Congressional Globe* that bear on the proper interpretation of the provisions in Section 1 relevant to such contemporary problems as racial equality and abortion. Historians and political scientists have largely yielded constitutional history to the legal academy. Those historians and political scientists interested in constitutional history often wear disciplinary blinders that enable them to see only those passages in the *Congressional Globe* that highlight the struggle for and ideals about racial equality. Those who see Sections 2, 3, and 4 do not see clearly. The result is a voluminous literature on Section 1 written by lawyers largely, and an extensive literature on racial equality during Reconstruction written by historians and a few political scientists, but only scant attention paid to the role Sections 2, 3, and 4 were expected to play in reconfiguring constitutional politics in congressional Reconstruction.

The Legal Blinders

The practice of constitutional interpretation constructs the blinders persons trained in law wear when they study the drafting of the Fourteenth Amendment. Lawyers look to history only when the meaning of constitutional provisions is unclear. The Citizenship, Privileges and Immunities, Due Process, and Equal Protection Clauses of Section 1 are open-ended. The meaning of Sections 2, 3, and 4 is more, though not perfectly, straightforward. Lawyers turn to history only when resolving those contemporary problems that are likely to be litigated before the Supreme Court of the United States. Every major rights question that has arisen for the past seventy years turns in part on the interpretation of Section 1. Rarely have contemporary constitutional disputes turned on the proper interpretation of Sections 2, 3, and 4.

Constitutional history in the legal academy is largely a species of constitutional interpretation.[65] The point of historical inquiry is to determine how constitutional provisions should be interpreted in the present. Cass Sunstein maintains that lawyers explore the past to find "elements in history that can be brought fruitfully to bear on current problems."[66] Lawyers as advocates are interested in the Thirty-Ninth Congress because they want to make arguments about how the Fourteenth Amendment was understood when that text was drafted and ratified.[67] Randall Kennedy articulates this presentist perspective when he observes that "[n]othing more securely links Reconstruction to the present than the constitutional and statutory law enacted then that remains on the books, powerfully affecting the texture of our current political life." "One thing that cements this linkage," he continues, "is the popular, albeit contested, belief that 'original intent' should play an important, if not decisive, role in determining how statutes and constitutional provisions are applied in resolving contemporary controversies."[68] Originalists claim that constitutional provisions mean what they meant when they were ratified.[69] Interpretive pluralists think that what constitutions meant when they were ratified is relevant to contemporary meaning.[70] Jurists who take either approach when researching the Thirty-Ninth Congress tend to ask only one question: What did the Republican framers mean by the language they used in the Fourteenth Amendment?[71]

Lawyers as advocates have little interest in how constitutional provisions were intended to work, particularly when function is independent from meaning. Who the framers expected to occupy government offices and the policy implications of equal state representation in the Senate are issues for historians and political scientists, not for lawyers interesting in the meaning of constitutional language. Debates over whether the Republican commitment to federalism doomed Reconstruction are for history journals and university presses, not for law reviews. Changes in the composition of the Supreme Court may be relevant to constitutional interpreters who engage in doctrinal analysis, not changes in the structure of political parties and electoral competition.

Far more historical investigation seems necessary to determine the meaning of the provisions in Section 1 than to determine the meaning of Sections 2, 3, and 4. The text of the Equal Protection Clause provides little assistance to constitutional decision makers, given that all laws regulate some subjects but not others.[72] History promises guidance for persons trying to determine which of the nearly infinite conceptions of equality[73] is or ought to be the official law of the land. History explains far better than constitutional text, for example, why race discriminations are more likely to offend the Fourteen Amendment than discriminations between different groups of butchers.[74]

The text of Sections 2, 3, and 4 provide far more guidance to constitutional decision makers even though interpretive problems exist. Few interpreters need to review the *Congressional Globe* when determining the meaning of "male" in Section 2 or "pensions and bounties" in Section 4.

The legal preoccupation with the "Constitution of Conversation"—those constitutional provisions that are routinely litigated in contemporary constitutional politics[75]—places Section 1 at the center of constitutional inquiry. Scarcely any constitutional rights issue arises in the contemporary United States that does not concern the proper interpretation of the Due Process or Equal Protection Clauses of the Fourteenth Amendment. Justice Clarence Thomas would have the Privileges and Immunities Clause do much of the work that the Due Process Clause does today.[76] Bitter controversies rage over birthright citizenship, which turn on the proper interpretation of the Citizenship Clause.[77] Law professors engage in these debates by publishing influential articles and books exploring whether some provision in Section 1 incorporates the Bill of Rights,[78] mandates desegregated schools,[79] or supports the right to bear arms.[80] No relevant historical stone is left unturned when the Supreme Court is reconsidering the constitutional status of reproduction choice[81] or the use of race in university admissions.[82]

Sections 2, 3, and 4 belong to the "Constitution of Settlement"[83] or the "Constitution of Memory"[84] that warrant no sustained legal attention. The Constitution of Settlement consists of those provisions, such as the requirement of state equality in the Senate, whose meaning is clear and uncontroversial. That Constitution receives no sustained legal attention because broad agreement exists on how to interpret those specific provisions. Debate exists over their wisdom[85] but not about their semantic meaning. The Constitution of Memory consists of those provisions, such as the Third Amendment, that once played or were intended to play vital roles in American constitutionalism but do not play any role in our current constitutional politics. No contemporary constitutional debate turns on the best interpretation of such anachronistic provisions as the congressional power to issue letters of marque and reprisal.[86] The forgotten Fourteenth Amendment suffers from this double curse. The texts are straightforward. The rules in Section 2 for apportioning representatives among the states are a model of clarity, at least when compared to the rights provisions in Section 1. No issue in Sections 2, 3, and 4 has occupied a significant place on the constitutional agenda for nearly a hundred and fifty years. Debates about the debt ceiling occasionally flare up, as have modern concerns with who is eligible for federal office under Section 3. Still, the rare law review article on those matters[87] has yet to capture the attention of the legal academy or any broader legal audience.

The search for legal meaning extends to Section 5, which empowers Congress to implement the Fourteenth Amendment. Prominent law professors recognize that the persons responsible for the post–Civil War amendments believed Congress was the institution primarily responsible for implementing the substantive provisions of the text.[88] Many legal scholars think Supreme Court decisions such as *Boerne v. Flores*[89] and *United States v. Morrison*[90] too narrowly interpret Section 5.[91] Some law professors call for Section 5 to be interpreted consistently with principles of popular constitutionalism.[92] Wearing disciplinary blinders nevertheless inhibits legal scholars from asking what Republican framers did to ensure that Congress would faithfully implement the Fourteenth Amendment once Southern representatives were seated in the House of Representatives and Senate. Legal commentaries on congressional power to implement the Fourteenth Amendment are commentaries on federal power to implement Section 1 of the Fourteenth Amendment. One would never know from the legal literature that Section 5 empowers Congress to implement Sections 2, 3, and 4. Related disciplinary blinders explain why commentaries on congressional power to implement the Fourteenth Amendment do not wonder whether the framers, if the Fourteenth Amendment was designed to empower Congress rather than courts, might have understood the Fourteenth Amendment in light of those interpretive modalities more common to elective political institutions than those routinely employed by a life-tenured court.[93] Legal commentaries on congressional power to implement the Fourteenth Amendment assume the Republican framers regarded the modalities appropriate for constitutional texts directed at courts as appropriate for constitutional texts directed at the national legislature.[94]

This disciplinary emphasis on the proper interpretation of those constitutional provisions bearing on constitutional problems of the twenty-first century explains why contemporary law professors interested in constitutional history scour the *Congressional Globe* for the few quotations on Section 1 relevant to the concerns of their day while ignoring the hundreds of pages devoted to the Republican concerns during Reconstruction with rebel rule and the structure of constitutional politics that inspired the Fourteenth Amendment. Republicans during the Thirty-Ninth Congress said little about what they meant by the phrase "privileges and immunities." Bingham was the only member of Congress who spoke more than once on that subject; his comments and few others are all the *Congressional Globe* yields for scholars looking to congressional speeches in 1866 for answers to questions about whether Section 1 was intended to incorporate the Bill of Rights, protect the right to bear arms, or support some other item on modern constitutional agendas. Twenty-first century eyes searching for rare nuggets about the original meaning of "equal protection" glaze over the numerous Republican speeches insisting that former Confederate states repudiate war debts that dotted the constitutional landscape when the Fourteenth Amendment was drafted. The clear text of Section 4 effectively blinds legal scholars to the Republican emphasis on constitutionalizing financial guarantees for Union creditors and Southern Unionists, as well as their commitment to ensuring no slaveholder was compensated for the loss of human chattel. No pressing contemporary constitutional issue renders visible the substantial evidence on the original understanding of "neither the United States nor any State shall assume or pay any debt or obligation incurred in aid of insurrection or rebellion against the United States." Claims about past priorities follow from concerns with modern priorities. If legal training provides disciplinary blinders that enable law professors to see only Republican discussions relevant to Section 1, then persons with legal training who study the Thirty-Ninth Congress are likely to conclude that Section 1 is the core of the Fourteenth Amendment.

The History/Political Science Blinders

Historians and political scientists do not wear these legal blinders. A robust literature exists in history and political science discussing how the Constitution of 1787 was intended to work rather than outlining what various provisions were thought to mean. From Charles Beard to the present day, a staple of historical work has been concerned with who the Federalist framers intended to empower.[95] The title aside, Jack Rakove's acclaimed *Original Meanings* emphasizes how the framers thought various governing institutions would function and function in tandem.[96] Michael Klarman details how the persons responsible for the Constitution relied on "huge districts for congressional representatives[] and indirect elections and lengthy terms in office for both senators and presidents" to enable "the federal government to be insulated from . . . populist politics."[97] A robust literature is developing in comparative constitutionalism detailing the practices of constitutional politics across the globe.[98] Ran Hirschl's influential "hegemonic preservation" thesis maintains "when their policy preferences have been, or are likely to be, increasingly challenged in majoritarian decision-making arenas, elites that possess disproportionate access to, and influence over, the legal arena may initiate a constitutional entrenchment of rights and judicial review in order to transfer power to supreme courts."[99] Adam Chilton and

Mila Versteeg examine the political conditions under which enumerated rights in national constitutions influence public policy.[100]

Prominent historians and political scientists discuss many themes in The Forgotten Fourteenth Amendment series. Gregory Downs, Lisset Marie Pino, and John Fabian Witt highlight the relation between military rule in the South and constitutional reform.[101] Michael Les Benedict and Earl Maltz highlight the importance of the congressional debate over the apportionment resolution, a stand-alone version of what became Section 2.[102] Benedict's magisterial *A Compromise of Principle* emphasized the differences among particular Republicans and differences in Republicans as a whole over time over whether to achieve African American suffrage directly, indirectly, or at all. Richard Vallely notes the emphasis the Republican framers placed on the apportionment provisions in Section 2.[103] Forrest Nabors emphasizes the Republican commitment to breaking up the slaveholding oligarchy of the South.[104] Mark Wahlgren Summers stresses Northern fears that Southerners might renew their attempt at secession under more favorable conditions.[105] Harold Melvin Hyman and William Blair detail the importance Republicans placed on rule by the loyal.[106] Garrett Epps discusses the problem of loyalty and revised slavery in the postbellum South.[107] Laura Edwards emphasizes how fundamental rights were to be "secured . . . through federal power."[108] Eric Foner, the dean of Reconstruction historians, recently acknowledged the significance of the "other" provisions in the Fourteenth Amendment. The first paragraph of Foner's classic book *The Second Founding* states: "The Fourteenth [Amendment] constitutionalized birthright citizenship and equality before the law and sought to settle key issues arising from the war, such as the future political roles of Confederate leaders and the fate of the Confederate debt."[109] Charles Fairman's very brief discussion of the Fourteenth Amendment in his contribution to the *Holmes Devise* histories of the Supreme Court points out: "Section 1 . . . was at the moment regarded as less controversial and of less consequence than the next two sections, now virtually forgotten."[110] Combine these insights, lengthen the discussion considerably, and you have *The Forgotten Fourteenth Amendment* books.

Historians and political scientists have yet to combine or fully develop these insights. The individual rights set out in Section 1 remain the core of the Fourteenth Amendment in both the humanities and social sciences. Book titles such as *Until Justice Be Done* and *The Fourteenth Amendment and the Fight for Equal Rights in Post–Civil War America* capture the focus on rights provisions across disciplines. Kate Masur's brilliant discussion of

antebellum fights for African American equality in Northern states epito-
mizes the hold of conventional wisdom about constitutional reform in the
1860s on even the best contemporary historians. Masur does a marvelous
job uncovering the role of Northern Black Codes in the prehistory of Section 1, but those findings merely cement the centrality of Section 1 to the
Fourteenth Amendment. She writes:

> Protections for civil rights remained a priority. Just as Republicans
> across the ideological spectrum had supported the Civil Rights Act,
> so too did they support a constitutional amendment that would make
> federal protection for basic civil rights more secure. Many Republi-
> cans understood the need for an amendment not only because of the
> southern states' black codes or because of uncertainty about the con-
> stitutionality of the Civil Rights Act, but also because for decades they
> had been fighting against racially discriminatory laws in the states and
> trying, mostly unsuccessfully, to get Congress or the federal courts to
> support their efforts.[111]

A prominent legal historian claims John Bingham is the "father of the Fourteenth Amendment"[112] even though Bingham had little influence or interest
in Sections 2, 3, and 4. Historians writing about Republican divisions over
Black suffrage treat that dispute as being over the future law of racial equality rather than between champions of different visions of the constitutional
politics necessary to implement the Thirteenth Amendment's promise of individual freedom.[113] By placing individual rights and legal guarantees at the
heart of the Fourteenth Amendment, historians and political scientists are
no better positioned than academic lawyers to see the Republican framers'
effort to change the structure of constitutional politics even though this was
the thrust of almost every major speech given by the Republican leadership
in Congress.

Sheer numbers explain some disciplinary blindness. Basic features of
constitutional history remain undiscovered because few historians or political scientists are looking.[114] More law professors probably present papers
on constitutional history in any given week at a local legal theory workshop
than political scientists and historians present at major national conferences.
The number of papers on constitutional history at the annual meetings of
the American Historical Association and the Organization of American
History is stunning low. The 2022 annual meeting of the American Historical Association had only one panel on constitutional history. Had the
percentage of professional historians interested in constitutional framing
remained constant for the last seventy years, a fair probability exists that

some historians would have recognized that the Republican framers were as wary as the Federalist framers were of parchment barriers and would have developed full-scale projects elaborating that theme.

The academic division of labor creates other disciplinary blinders. Law professors tend to write about constitutional amendments or federal statues such as the Civil Rights Act of 1866. Historians and political scientists write more often about Reconstruction as a whole or specific aspects of Reconstruction. Michael Les Benedict observes that "[a]cademic historians . . . see the framing and ratification of the Thirteenth, Fourteenth, and Fifteenth Amendments as part of a longer, broader, and essentially political process in which Americans have developed fundamental principles of governance."[115] Some tendency may exist for historians and political scientists to regard law professors as adequately covering the framing and ratification of the Fourteenth Amendment. Rather than review the assumed already thoroughly digested records of the Thirty-Ninth Congress, the better strategy has been to plumb other sources relevant to political and constitutional developments during Reconstruction but not directly relevant to the framing and ratification of the Fourteenth Amendment. The Fourteenth Amendment is only a short subchapter in Eric Foner's magisterial *Reconstruction*. The text occupies even less space in other important studies of American constitutional politics after the Civil War.[116] Vallely's discussion of Section 2 occupies a page in his analysis of Black voting rights during the first and second Reconstructions.[117]

Many scholars in PhD programs whose writings touch the Fourteenth Amendment study the history of civil rights rather than constitutional history per se. They ask why persons of color failed to become legal equals during Reconstruction. Historical research concerned with the implementation of laws protecting persons of color is as likely as legal research concerned with the meaning of those laws to focus almost exclusively on the rights enumerated in Section 1. The other provisions of the Fourteenth Amendment are for historians with other disciplinary concerns. Historians of financial markets study the status of public credit.[118] Section 3 is for historians interested in loyalty oaths, amnesty, and the fate of white Southerners, not for historians interested in civil rights and the Southerners of color.[119]

The revisionist conclusion that Reconstruction was a failure[120] is partly a product of this set of disciplinary blinders. Judged by the goals Republicans repeatedly announced in 1866 rather than modern ambitions, constitutional reform in the postwar period was largely (if incompletely) successful. Southerners made no attempt to secede after 1865, representatives from the Union states controlled the national government for the next hundred years, and all the provisions in Section 4 were scrupulously honored.[121] Students of financial markets, whose gaze rests upon Republican speeches during the debates over the Fourteenth Amendment expressing concern for the public credit, might be as inclined to regard Reconstruction as an unambiguous triumph. Students of racial equality, whose gaze rests upon (the fewer) Republican speeches during the debates over the Fourteenth Amendment expressing concern with the constitutional rights of former slaves, are inclined to view constitutional reform during that period as being defeated.

Law professors influence the questions that historians and political scientists ask when exploring constitutional questions, even when the legal academy exerts less influence over the answers. A small cottage industry exists questioning, on historical grounds, the legal search for the original meaning of constitutional provisions. Historians point out that no consensus exists on particular meanings, that framing and ratification processes are not designed to reach consensus on original meanings, and that the Constitution is not the kind of text that would have an original public meaning.[122] Still, this "law literature" fixates the few historians and political scientists studying the Constitution on meaning. Historians and political scientists ask whether constitutional provisions have original meanings rather than what those original meanings are. By making original meaning the focus of the enterprise, the legal academy keeps scholars in the humanities and social sciences focused on the same texts that law professors invoke when making claims about what the Republican framers meant by such phrases as "due process," "privileges and immunities," and "equal protection." The main difference among different scholarly disciplines is that many lawyers think these texts speak clearly to the present, while the vast majority of historians and political scientists think those texts are ambiguous and rooted in assumptions long abandoned.

Recent scholarship on the impact of abolitionist thought, Black abolitionist thought in particular, on Reconstruction exhibits both the considerable virtues and partial blinders of historical thinking about constitutional reform after the Civil War. Mazur,[123] Martha Jones, and Simon Gilhooley have done a magnificent job documenting how African American constitutional politics before the Civil War influenced the rights Republicans sought to protect after the Civil War. They are correct to note that the focus of most African Americans and the most radical abolitionists was on the rights persons of color should enjoy under the postbellum constitution. They are correct to note Black pre–Civil War agitation shaped the Civil Rights Act of 1866 and the Second Freedmen's Bureau Bill. Their focus on African American demands for rights, however, risks shifting the spotlight too far from the antislavery concern with structure. Unlike African Americans and radical white abolitionists, most proponents of congressional Reconstruction were fixated on the slave power rather than on slavery per se. The origins of the Fourteenth Amendment lay in antebellum (white) antislavery complaints that constitutional politics tilted too far southward rather than the Black and abolitionist fight against human bondage. Abolitionists such as Frederick Douglass and Charles Sumner were more noble than antislavery advocates such as William Pitt Fessenden; but Thaddeus Stevens aside, Republicans more sensitive to the impact of slavery on free white labor had a far greater impact on the Fourteenth Amendment than Republicans more sensitive to the impact of slavery on involuntary Black labor. The contemporary focus on Black abolitionist influence on Section 1 reflects the priorities of persons of color and radical abolitionists outside of Congress, as well as contemporary concerns with racial equality, rather than the priorities of the persons in Congress actually responsible for drafting the Fourteenth Amendment.

Marbury v. Madison[124] fashions separate disciplinary blindness. Conventional wisdom maintains that John Marshall's decision establishing judicial review was a crucial step in the process that legalized the Constitution. Americans replaced a regime in which what the Constitution meant was partly determined by a constitutional politics structured to privilege certain interests or combination of interests with a regime in which what the Constitution meant was determined entirely by the federal judiciary interpreting constitutional law.[125] Both strains of thinking about constitutional authority were vibrant in the late eighteenth century. *Federalist No. 31* articulates a more popular constitutionalism. Hamilton wrote that "all observations founded upon the danger of usurpation ought to be referred to the composition and structure of government, not to the nature or extent of its powers."[126] *Federalist No. 78* articulates a more legal constitutionalism. Constitutional "limitations," Hamilton asserted, "can be preserved in practice no other than through the medium of courts of justice, whose duty it must be to declare all acts contrary to the manifest tenor of the Constitution void."[127] *Marbury* signaled the triumph of legal constitutionalism. Writing more than a hundred and fifty years later, all nine Supreme Court justices in *Cooper v. Aaron* concurred: "*Marbury v. Madison* . . . declared the basic principle that the federal judiciary is supreme in the exposition of the law of the Constitution[] and that principle has ever since been respected by this Court and the Country as a permanent and indispensable feature of our constitutional system."[128] The law of the Constitution, this broadly accepted account of judicial supremacy contends, has changed considerably, but no one should bother looking to Reconstruction or any other moment in American history for a significant effort to reconfigure the constitutional politics that determines the official law of the land. The Constitution of the United States since *Marbury* works when the Supreme Court protects constitutional rights and maintains the constitutional limits on government powers, and when other governing officials adhere to the constitutional law declared by that esteemed tribunal. That has been the structure of constitutional politics in the United States for more than two hundred years and was the structure of constitutional politics that provided the background for the post–Civil War amendments. Or so goes conventional wisdom.

Marbury revisionism peters out by the Civil War. Contrary to *Cooper*, historians and political scientists have documented the vibrant tradition of popular constitutionalism that existed during the first years of the American Republic. Sylvia Snowiss notes resistance to treating the constitutional as a purely legal text during the early national period.[129] Saul Cornell and Gerry Leonard point out that Van Buren Democrats in Jacksonian America believed that mass political parties were the best vehicle for making the Constitution work.[130] Larry Kramer details strong commitments to popular constitutionalism throughout antebellum America.[131] Lincoln's First Inaugural in these contemporary histories is the last gasp of serious American efforts to locate constitutional authority outside the courts.[132] Then the guns fire on Fort Sumner, and popular constitutionalism in American scholarship falls silent. Kramer spends almost a hundred and fifty pages documenting challenges to judicial supremacy from the framing to Lincoln assuming office. A page or so later, readers are in the 1890s, with no mention of any instance of popular constitutionalism in the previous thirty years.[133]

Partly blinded by *Marbury*, scholars disregard clues left by Republican framers that their goal was to reconfigure constitutional politics rather than provide new sources of constitutional law for judges to interpret and implement. Section 5 provides one such hint: all the provisions of the Fourteenth Amendment are to be enforced by Congress. Courts are nowhere mentioned. Republican attacks on the federal judiciary during the Civil War and Reconstruction[134] offer another sign that judicial supremacy was not the unquestioned practice of constitutional authority when the Thirty-Ninth Congress was in session. These tea leaves have not been read, or sometimes they have been misread. Historians and political scientists do not link the enforcement clauses of the post–Civil War amendments to the movements for popular constitutionalism before the Civil War. Section Five receives almost no attention in constitutional histories of the 1860s that are not dedicated to deciphering the meaning or original meaning of the Fourteenth

Amendment. William Lasser and Stanley Kutler regard Republican attacks on judicial power during the 1860s as instances of naked partisanship with no connection to the Fourteenth Amendment. Jurisdiction stripping and related measures, in their view, were directed at a court temporarily controlled by political rivals rather than rooted in a fundamentally different understanding of constitutional authority that might make visible what Republicans were doing when they debated and drafted Sections 2, 3, and 4. Unable to keep his eyes wandering too far from *Marbury*, Kutler states that "most Republicans [at the time] recognized that southern domination of the judiciary, and not the Court's functional capacities, had to be changed."[135] "John Marshall had for decades shown that the federal judiciary was the natural ally of federal power," Lasser agrees, "and the Republicans had not forgotten that lesson."[136]

The Dunning School (named after William A. Dunning [1857–1922], a scholar of the Civil War and Reconstruction) fashioned a different set of disciplinary blinders, even as contemporary scholars properly scorn that school's racist interpretation of Reconstruction. The Dunning School traditionalists who flourished in the first half of the twentieth century condemned the Republican framers for promoting racial equality at the expense of traditional states' rights.[137] The generation of historians who came of age during the civil rights movement celebrated the Republican framers for promoting racial equality at the expense of traditional states' rights.[138] Contemporary revisionists complain that the Republican framers when promoting racial equality did not sufficiently weaken traditional states' rights.[139] The revisionist and contemporary historians who aggressively reject the Dunning School's normative commitment to white supremacy nevertheless appear to accept uncritically the Dunning School's understanding that the point of constitutional reform was to constitutionalize the rights former slaves needed to become legal equals in the United States. The debate between different generations of historians is over the motivation, merits, and success of Republican efforts during Reconstruction to promote racial equality at the expense of traditional states' rights.[140]

Revisionists committed to scrubbing Reconstruction history of Dunning School racism pay no more attention than members of the Dunning school to the provisions of the Fourteenth Amendment that do not seem directed at securing racial equality or limiting state prerogatives. Neither Dunning School traditionalists nor contemporary historians who write about the Fourteenth Amendment discuss at any length the plight of white Unionists or the fears of Northern creditors, even though both concerns were repeatedly expressed by members of the Thirty-Ninth Congress. Dunning School traditionalists and contemporary revisionists pay substantial attention to proposals to enfranchise persons of color, but, Benedict aside, neither take seriously alternative means for entrenching Republican rule that the Republican founders debated extensively. Section 2 was a defeat for proponents of racial equality rather than the constitutional reform Republicans thought would entrench rule by the loyal people of the United States.[141]

The main historical divide between Dunning School traditionalists and contemporary revisionists is their treatment of the Republican framers' commitment to federalism.[142] Dunning School traditionists, echoing post–Civil War Democratic complaints, charged Republicans with abandoning constitutional federalism. Dunning regarded the Civil Rights Act of 1866 as "out of all relation to our constitutional system."[143] Contemporary revisionists see the Republican framers as too committed to constitutional federalism. Benedict insists that "Americans were as concerned with preserving the Constitution as they were with changing it to protect liberty and equal rights."[144] The revisionist literature that developed in the wake of the Great Society maintained that constitutional reformers during Reconstruction were institutionally conservative, even as they altered the rights inherited institutions were designed to protect. Forrest Nabors observes:

> The American founders already devised a system of government informed by the same principles that later informed the framing of the [Fourteenth] [A]mendment. However, the Fourteenth Amendment for the first time specified the conditions that needed to be met in order to satisfy the definition of *republican* in the guarantee clause and was intended to be a revolution in federal *enforcement* of republicanism and republican citizenship in the states. There never need be nor should there have been any conflict between the Fourteenth Amendment, properly applied, and federalism. All states could continue to be self-governing, exercising any powers not explicitly delegated to the national government, and free from national government interference, *as long as they continued to be genuinely republican in form.*[145]

Reconstruction failed, much conventional wisdom insists, precisely because the Republican framers focused solely on rights without adjusting the constitutional politics necessary to make governing institutions more conducive to implementing those new rights.[146]

Contemporary understandings of the Fourteenth Amendment are structured by this combination of institutional conservatism and rights progressivism that dates from the reaction to Dunning School history. When challenging Dunning School claims that Republicans were committed to

subverting American federalism, modern revisionists regard the rights provisions of Section 1 to be the core of the Fourteenth Amendment. Nothing in the Fourteenth Amendment reconfigures the national constitutional
politics that influence how and how aggressively the federal government
enforces the Thirteenth Amendment and the rights provisions in Section 1.
This single-minded focus on rights renders Sections 2, 3, and 4 invisible,
and obscures Republican emphasis on how the post–Civil War Constitution
would work, as opposed to Republican beliefs about the rights Republicans
thought the post–Civil War Constitution would protect.

Interdisciplinary Visions (and Blinders)

Punish Treason, Reward Loyalty begins a project on the borders of law, history, and political science. The volumes in the *Forgotten Fourteenth Amendment* series explore how the Republican framers sought to reconfigure
constitutional politics through constitutional reforms designed to ensure,
to the extent humanly feasible, that the party of the persons who remained
loyal to the Union during the Civil War controlled the national government,
controlled state governments in the former Confederacy, and controlled the
official meaning of the Thirteenth Amendment. The *law* is the Fourteenth
Amendment, whose original and contemporary meanings are the subjects of
extensive contestation in the legal academy. The *history* is that of the Thirty-
Ninth Congress responsible for drafting the Fourteenth Amendment. The
political science is the focus on how members of the Thirty-Ninth Congress
thought the Fourteenth Amendment would work rather than the traditional
legal emphasis on what the Republican framers thought the provisions of
the Fourteenth Amendment meant.

Interdisciplinary scholars see differently, not more. Scholars who spend
time examining law, history, and politics do not master doctrine as well as
law professors devoted solely to their craft; do not master the distinctive
voices of the past as well as historians devoted solely to their discipline; and
do not master the forces that structure politics as well as political scientists
devoted solely to that field of expertise. Law professors offer far more re-
fined doctrinal analysis than can be found in these volumes. A historian
would spend considerably more time in the archives rather than rely on
the *Congressional Globe* as the near-exclusive source for Republican understandings of the Fourteenth Amendment. A political scientist would have
made greater use of the sophisticated political models developed by scholars
of American political development such as Karen Orren and Stephen Skowronek.[147] Martin Shapiro observes that a person who studies the politics of

forestry is likely to be considered a great forester by political scientists and a great political scientist by foresters.[148] This study in that spirit may be considered good political science and law by historians, good history and political science by lawyers, and good law and history by political scientists.

The best excuse for this exercise is that the problems of the world do not sort themselves by disciplinary boundaries. The failure of scholars wearing disciplinary blinders to even see Sections 2, 3, and 4 highlight how interdisciplinary approaches are necessary for identifying certain problems in the world and for providing the tools for answering them. The borders between law, history, and political science resemble the borders between suburban towns, which often are as lively and populated as the town center, rather than the borders between towns in the rural West, which consist of empty spaces and are populated by two species known only to environmentalists. A political world in which Levittown, East Meadow, and North Bellmore, New York, are governed separately will better identify and respond to the problems at the heart of each town than the problems that afflict those who live and work at the porous borders. An academic world in which persons interested in law, history, and political science are separated into different disciplines and housed in different buildings is similarly likely to focus on the problems at the core of each discipline and slight the problems that exist on the peripheries. The way in which constitutional reformers in the United States in 1866, previous constitutional reformers in the United States, and constitutional reformers across the globe have sought to reconfigure constitutional politics in order to privilege particular constitutional visions presents one such problem at the intersection of law, history, and political science that has been slighted by the structure of the academy. Academic life needs to be less siloed so that these and related issues are more visible and better subject to scholarly inquiry.

The debates in 1787 and in 1866 highlight the priority that the Federalist and the Republican framers gave to questions about how constitutions work as opposed to questions about what constitutions mean. Neither Federalist nor Republican framers haggled over words. During the initial drafting in 1787, the many stylistic changes that the Committee on Detail made that contemporary Americans think dramatically changed the Constitution were largely uncommented upon during the Philadelphia convention.[149] Many Republican members of the Thirty-Ninth Congress thought that John Bingham had a taste for abstract phrases whose meaning was obscure,[150] but that lack of clarity did not inspire substantial debate over Section One of the Fourteenth Amendment. The Federalist and Republican framers were concerned with who would control future understandings of such vague phrases as the "general welfare" and "equal protection of the laws." Effective and just constitutional government depended on a sound constitutional politics, not elegant wordsmithery of rights and powers provisions.

Chief Justice John Marshall pointed to an important difference between inherited and contemporary understandings of constitutionalism when in *McCulloch v. Maryland* he declared: "A constitution, to contain an accurate detail of all the subdivisions of which its great powers will admit, and of all the means by which they may be carried into execution, would partake of the prolixity of a legal code." He continued: "Its nature, therefore, requires only that its great outlines should be marked, its important objects designated, and the minor ingredients which compose those objects be deduced from the nature of the objects themselves."[151] The United States Constitution was sparse because Marshall and members of his generation thought the persons responsible for constitutions sought to construct political systems that privileged getting the "right" persons in place for deducing the "minor ingredients,"[152] whether those persons be propertied cosmopolitans or antislavery Republicans. Contemporary constitutions are much longer.[153] Contemporary framers spell out the minor ingredients because constitutional law in modern constitutionalism does far more work than constitutional politics.[154]

The Republican framers stood with Marshall in their emphasis on constitutional politics rather than constitutional law. The persons who drafted the Fourteenth Amendment sought to ensure that the right people would be in power to discern the minor ingredients rather than bind future Americans to a detailed legal code. We can understand what Stevens and his political allies were doing in 1866 only when we combine the conceptual tools of law, history, and political science in ways that enable us to see all their words, understand the full scope of their aspirations, and comprehend their attempt to reconfigure constitutional politics as the best means for realizing their aspirations. Once we see the original concern with constitutional politics more clearly, we might even be positioned to observe how, as Stevens and his Republican allies would perceive, a contemporary political system obsessed with constitutional law nevertheless rests on a foundation of constitutional politics. American incapacity to achieve full racial equality and other contemporary constitutional predicaments may stem from mismatches between political institutions and political commitments in the United States, rather than from particular failings in American constitutional law or the judges handing down that constitutional law.[155]

Introduction
Three Republican Soloists and the Republican Chorus

Three performances by Republican members of the Thirty-Ninth Congress capture the specific themes of *Punish Treason, Reward Loyalty*. Representative Thaddeus Stevens of Pennsylvania belted the opening number on Reconstruction just after the Thirty-Ninth Congress opened. Representative Jehu Baker of Illinois sang at length at the end of January about the status of former Confederate states in the Union. Representative John A. Bingham of Ohio delivered a finale in July on the restoration of Tennessee. Stevens led the Republican chorus in the House of Representatives, although members frequently did not sing in his key. Baker was a typical member of the Republican chorus, many of whom performed very similar solos during the Saturday open microphone session at the House of Representatives. Bingham sometimes carried the same tune, but at crucial junctures he hummed an entirely different melody from that of his fellow choristers.

The Stevens, Baker, and Bingham recitals have gone unheard by Fourteenth Amendment scholarship. No major text on the Fourteenth Amendment or Reconstruction discusses those specific performances. The best explanation for their absence may be the label in the *Congressional Globe*. The ostensible subject of the Baker and Stevens solos, according to the *Congressional Globe*, is "Reconstruction."[1] Bingham's solo falls under the label "Admission of Tennessee."[2] Fourteenth Amendment scholarship, whether concerned with the history of the text or the original meaning of the text, is remarkably limited to performances given under the label "Constitutional Amendment" and the like in the *Congressional Globe*. This selection bias explains why Republican presentations on the continued exclusion of Southern representatives from Congress, President Johnson's December Message to Congress on Reconstruction, various proposals to restore Southern representation, other Reconstruction measures, and other subjects of legislation, most notably the post office bill, where debates over Reconstruction broke out, do not play a role even as substantial as Osric's in the Fourteenth Amendment story. Every Saturday from January to June 1866, the House of Representatives allowed individual members to sing out on the issues of the day, which almost always resulted in multiple solos on Reconstruction and the constitutional reforms necessary before former Confederate states could be represented in Congress again. These performances appear nowhere in the literature on the Fourteenth Amendment.[3] Unlike Rosencrantz and Guildenstern, the exclusion resolution and related matters are not even celebrated in a separate production. Despite the important federalism and separation of powers issues raised by the status of the former Confederate states, no major contemporary work on Reconstruction is devoted to these debates.[4]

This is a serious mistake. The first major theme of *Punish Treason, Reward Loyalty* is that no aspect of the Fourteenth Amendment can be understood in the absence of an engagement with the debate over the status of the former Confederate states. During the debates over Reconstruction and related matters, members of the Thirty-Ninth Congress routinely discussed constitutional reform. Republicans, Democrats, and Unionists considered whether constitutional reform was necessary, the threats that proponents of constitutional reform believed warranted amendment, and how various amendments would respond to those threats. Many speeches contained analyses of what proposed texts meant, the stuff that is at the heart of contemporary Fourteenth Amendment scholarship. By limiting themselves to speeches given only when the text was explicitly under consideration, scholars have missed most of the speeches on constitutional reform delivered during the Thirty-Ninth Congress.

Stevens, Baker, and Bingham all played variations of the same theme: the need for constitutional reforms that prevented rebel rule by empowering and protected the loyal. They differed primarily on points of emphasis. Stevens obsessed over constitutional reforms that empowered the loyal and prevented rebel rule, even as he supported constitutional reforms that protected the loyal. Baker insisted on a package of anti-secession, financial, political, and civil rights guarantees that empowered and protected the loyal against the looming specter of rebel rule. Bingham maintained that constitutional reforms that protected the loyal were the best means for warding off rebel rule, even as he supported constitutional reforms that empowered the loyal. Stevens was far more typical of Republicans in thinking that constitutional protections for the loyal would work only if constitutional reforms empowered the loyal. Bingham was the only Republican who intimated that constitutional protections for the loyal might work even in the absence of any constitutional reforms that empowered loyal citizens. Bingham was far more typical than Stevens when the Ohio Republican confidently proclaimed that empowering loyal whites might adequately protect loyal Blacks.

The demand made in numerous petitions that Congress should "punish treason and reward loyalty"[5] captures the two related concerns that animated Stevens, Baker, Bingham, and the members of Congress responsible for the Fourteenth Amendment. The second theme of *Punish Treason, Reward Loyalty* is that the Fourteenth Amendment was the outcome of a debate among proponents of congressional Reconstruction over the package of reforms that would best discipline traitors and benefit the faithful. Rebel rule had to be prevented. The persons responsible for secession had to be politically neutered, if not subject to penal and economic sanctions. Loyal Americans had to be protected and empowered. Politics had to be reconstructed so that loyal majorities would control forever the former Confederate states and the national government. Bingham aside, no one thought that new *constitutional* civil rights guarantees were central to the processes by which rebel rule could be prevented and loyal Blacks and whites empowered and protected.

The Arias

STEVENS

Stevens's first speech on Reconstruction called for constitutional reforms that "secure[d] perpetual ascendancy to the party of the Union . . . so as to render our republican Government firm and stable forever."[6] Constitutional reform was necessary because, under the Constitution of December 1865, former Confederate states might obtain thirty-seven members of the House of Representatives and thirty-seven votes in the Electoral College for disenfranchised persons of color. This "slavocracy bonus" would enable the antebellum Jacksonian coalition of slaveholders and doughfaces to regain control of the national government. The result would be "[t]he oppression of the freedmen, the reamendment of their state constitutions, and the reestablishment of slavery."[7] Apportionment reform would alleviate this threat by placing the South in a dilemma: former Confederate states would either have to enfranchise persons of color, which would "continue the Republican ascendancy,"[8] or have their representation reduced by almost 40 percent, which would "render them powerless for evil."[9]

Stevens was typical in maintaining that the main impetus for constitutional reform was the threat of rebel rule magnified by the potential impact of the Thirteenth Amendment on representation in the national government.[10] Proponents of congressional Reconstruction repeatedly maintained that the South intended to rise again. Many Republicans echoed Stevens's warning that the constitutional ban on slavery, which made all persons of color in the former Confederacy full persons for apportioning members of Congress and the Electoral College, threatened to return control of the national government to the slave power that had dominated antebellum politics. Constitutional amendments and statutory reforms adopted to ensure that the Union reaped the fruits of victory in the Civil War would become weak parchment barriers should Democrats again dominate national affairs. The Thirteenth Amendment would be either repealed, ignored, or circumvented.

Stevens was as typical in his concern with constitutional politics. Most Republicans believed Congress already had the power under the Thirteenth Amendment, the Guarantee Clause, and other constitutional provisions to pass the rights legislation they believed necessary to protect persons of color and loyal Unionists in the former Confederate states. Disputes existed over the necessary reforms, in particular over whether Congress should grant persons of color the right to vote and give former slaves homesteads. Nevertheless, no proposal failed during the first session of the Thirty-Ninth Congress because crucial Republicans thought the measure desirable public policy that, alas, the national government had no constitutional power to enact. Voting rights failed because congressional majorities before July 28 were not willing to enfranchise persons of color immediately. Stevens and his political allies were more concerned with the constitutional rules that determined who made and maintained civil rights legislation than with the existing constitutional powers to make and maintain civil rights legislation. The pressing issue before proponents of congressional Reconstruction was how to reform constitutional politics so that Republicans and their Unionist allies would continue to have the power to make and maintain whatever Reconstruction policies they felt necessary. Constitutional politics had to be reconfigured, Republicans agreed, so that Republicans would maintain the control over the national government necessary to ensure that the Thirteenth Amendment and other provisions would be used as intended by their framers to eradicate slavery, the slave system, and the slave power.

Stevens was also typical in identifying the Republican Party with the people who had remained loyal to the Union during the Civil War. Proponents of congressional Reconstruction inherited from Jacksonians the view that party competition in the United States was between the party of the popular majority that was committed to maintaining the Constitution and the party of unrepresentative elites committed to perverting the Constitution through minority rule.[11] The Republican Party, Republicans insisted throughout the first session, was the party of the popular majority that was faithful to the Constitution. Democrats were the party of rebels and Copperheads bent on constitutional subversion. Americans would enjoy the fruits of the victory in the Civil War only if, as Stevens and his fellow partisans maintained, the Republican Party retained control of the national government. Constitutional reforms aimed at "secur[ing] perpetual ascendancy to the party of the Union" were the best means of politically entrenching what Republicans believed were constitutional commitments to free labor and racial equality.

Stevens differed from fellow Republicans in his single-minded emphasis on constitutional reforms that provided sound political foundations for Reconstruction. While he supported financial and civil rights guarantees, both his first speech on Reconstruction and his later speeches in the Thirty-Ninth Congress focused almost entirely on the political guarantees he believed necessary to ensure loyal Republican control of the federal government and the governments in former Confederate states. Stevens's opening speech on Reconstruction emphasized apportionment reform. Later speeches concentrated on disenfranchising former Confederates and enfranchising persons of color, at least in the South. Most Republicans shared Stevens's focus on constitutional politics, but they paid far more attention than he did to the anti-secession, financial, and civil rights guarantees they believed were necessary to prevent rebel rule.

Stevens also differed from most fellow Republicans when he emphasized empowering and protecting persons of color. His opening speech on Reconstruction worried about "[t]he oppression of the freedmen, the re-amendment of their state constitutions, and the reestablishment of slavery." His Fourteenth Amendment was designed explicitly to secure the political foundations necessary to implement the Thirteenth Amendment. Nowhere did Stevens emphasize the threat that rebel rule presented to loyal white people. A few Republicans, most notably Sumner, were as focused on securing racial equality. Far more proponents of congressional Reconstruction spoke at length about empowering and protecting loyal whites in addition to former slaves. Constitutional reform in their more common view extended far beyond fashioning a constitutional politics conducive to free labor and racial equality.

BAKER

Baker in a speech that occupied slightly less than six pages of the *Congressional Globe* used "rebel" or "rebels" forty-forty times[12] and "loyal" thirty-one times.[13] He spoke of "rebel States," the "rebel debt," "rebel communities," the "rebel mob," the "rebel population," and of persons who were "rebels." While Baker sometimes used "rebel" as a noun or adjective when describing events that took place during the Civil War, many uses proclaimed that rebels and rebel rule remained a viable threat to republican (lowercase *r*) government in the United States despite the surrender of the Confederate/rebel army. "We want a constitutional barrier," Baker demanded, "against this impending irruption of rebel celebrities into the chief seats of the Republic, which they have been unable to subvert by stealth, fraud, and perjury, or to overthrow by armed forces in the field."[14] "Loyal people"—a phrase Baker used twelve times—were responsible for erecting the constitutional barriers. "The loyal people of this nation, through their Representatives in Congress," he declared, "should be the judge of what great and just guarantees will make them secure in the future before readmitting to full power in the system those States which have . . . filled the grave-yards of the North and the battle-fields of the South with the moldering bodies of the patriotic children of the Republic."[15] Constitutional reform was designed to prevent rebel rule by empowering and protecting the loyal. "[A]n amendment apportioning representation in Congress . . . according to the number of people who are represented in each State respectively," Baker thought, would "protect[] the loyal people of the nation from the crying injustice and palpable danger of restoring the late rebel communities."[16]

Baker's speech on January 27, 1866, proposed the numerous constitutional and statutory reforms he thought would ensure that the Confederacy did not rise again. The package included anti-secession, financial, political, and civil rights guarantees, all of which Baker defended at some length. The first set of "great and just guarantees" was a series of constitutional amendments:

> First, an amendment placed in the fundamental law of the whole land, putting it above all question and all cavil, that no State has a right to secede from the Union at her sovereign will and pleasure. Secondly, an amendment . . . giving the people of the Union and the people of every State perfect repose, perfect security against the possibility of ever being burdened with the payment of the enormous rebel debt which was contracted in the satanic effort to lay the Republic in ruins. Thirdly, making representation, and consequent power in this Government, bear an exact proportion to the measure of political justice practiced by each State in the Union. . . . Fourthly, an amendment forever excluding all rebels from the high offices, civil and military, under this

Government—thereby giving bloodless satisfaction to justice, and a deadly blow to the aristocracy out of which the rebellion sprung.[17]

The second set of "great and just guarantees" was a series of civil rights statutes combating racial discrimination. These measures, Baker declared, were "needful and proper to make real the civil liberty which has been pledged to the colored people of the South."[18]

Baker was a typical Republican proponent of congressional Reconstruction. He played no leadership role in Congress, and his speeches were not influential. No Republican member of the Thirty-Ninth Congress quoted the words Baker spoke on January 27. No contemporary historian even mentions any contribution Baker made to the Fourteenth Amendment. Baker was typical in that if one could somehow average the speeches that proponents of congressional Reconstruction gave during the first session on constitutional reform, the result would resemble the speech Baker gave on January 27.

Baker was typical in his unrestrained use of "rebel" and "loyal." Few Republicans spoke for more than five minutes on Reconstruction without using either "rebel" or "loyal" as an adjective or noun. Rebel rule was the problem. Empowering and protecting the loyal was the solution. Proponents of congressional Reconstruction, when making speeches on that issue and constitutional reform, spoke frequently of rebels who remained a political force in 1866 to emphasize broad concerns with Southern constitutional politics that often included, but always extended beyond, race relations in the former Confederacy. Members of what was becoming the Party of Lincoln emphasized how the threat rebel rule presented to national unity, national finance, Southern Unionists, republican government, and former slaves required fundamental alterations in the structure of Southern and national constitutional politics. These fundamental alterations empowered and protected the faithful. Each of Baker's proposed constitutional reforms either punished treason or rewarded loyalty.

Baker was as typical in thinking that an aristocratic slaveholding elite bore the blame for secession and the Civil War. Republicans during the 1850s depicted the South as dominated by oligarchs who, through economic and social power, maintained their "peculiar institution" by perverting public opinion. Secession and Civil War were less the consequence of a popular uprising against the national government than a manifestation of this powerful minority's disdain for democracy. Poor Southern farm boys went to their slaughter at Gettysburg and elsewhere because, having lived in a closed society structured by proslavery and racist propaganda, they knew no better. If constitutional reform could neuter the antebellum slaveholding elite, Baker and his political associates were convinced, then poorer whites in the South would soon discard their antebellum racial prejudices. The new constitutional politics Republicans were fashioning would fashion commitments to free labor and racial equality throughout the nation.

Baker offered a typical Republican reform package for reconstructing the South. Republican member after Republican member of the Thirty-Ninth Congress echoed Baker's understanding of the "great and just guarantees" necessary before representatives of the former Confederate states could be seated in Congress. Most reform packages included financial, political, and civil rights guarantees. More than a few included anti-secession guarantees. The Republican majority united on the need for adjusting the constitutional basis of representation and stabilizing national finances by some combination of constitutional guarantees for payment of the Union debt, constitutional prohibitions on compensation for freed slaves, constitutional bans on states paying Confederate creditors, and a constitutional amendment repealing the ban on export taxes in Article I, Section V, Paragraph 5 of the Constitution. A powerful Republican consensus supported further legal protections for former slaves, but no consensus existed on the legal form such protection should take. Some Republicans called for constitutional provisions protecting the rights of persons of color. Others, like Baker, insisted that the Thirteenth Amendment and Guarantee Clause of Article IV provided a sufficient basis for the necessary legislation that should be passed before Southern representatives took their seats. Still others took an in-between position, claiming a constitutional amendment would be necessary only if civil rights legislation ran into constitutional difficulties.

Baker was not atypical in his failure to discuss the Black Codes when considering the challenges of reconstructing former Confederate states. Many Republican speeches on Reconstruction condemned those states for passing laws reducing former bondsmen to near slavery. Others placed greater weight on other manifestations of rebel rule. Stevens and a few Radical Republicans aside, those Republicans who condemned the Black Codes condemned just as vigorously the Southern persecution of white Unionists and calls for payment of the Confederate debt. Government had an obligation to protect loyal freedmen, Baker and other Republicans agreed, but government had the same obligation to protect loyal white Unionists, loyal Northerners who moved south, loyal Union soldiers, the loyal widows and children of Union soldiers who died in battle, and loyal creditors who purchased Union bonds.

BINGHAM

Bingham's speech on the restoration of Tennessee—with an important twist—offered a popular understanding of how to prevent rebel rule by empowering and protecting the loyal. The issue on the floor was whether Tennessee had a state constitution that was "republican in form," even though state law restricted the ballot to white men. Bingham when leading the fight for restoration insisted that Tennessee met republican standards. In his view, republican government authorized rule by the loyal majority. Tennessee had empowered the loyal by disenfranchising rebels. Denying Confederate supporters the ballot presented no republican problem, Bingham pointed out, because "traitors forfeited their political rights, privileges, and powers under the governments, both State and national."[19] If the loyal white majority wished to disenfranchise the loyal Black minority, that was also of no republican concern. Loyal majorities were entitled to distribute the suffrage as loyal majorities thought best. "[T]he right of the law-abiding majority of the people to govern," Bingham reminded the House of Representatives, was "the very principle out of which the Constitution and the Union have been maintained through these five years of war."[20]

Bingham assured Radical Republicans that they need not worry about the white majority oppressing the Black minority or white Unionists. The proposed Fourteenth Amendment would solve this problem by giving the national government the power to protect "the rights of loyal colored men or of any men."[21] Loyal people were protected, even when not empowered, because the Constitution of the United States guaranteed that protection. The Fourteenth Amendment would vest Congress with "the power . . . to throw the shield of the law of the land over these unfortunate human beings, lately slaves, now emancipated citizens, who with their ancestors have through many generations and many centuries been the victims of cruelty, outrage, oppression, and wrong."[22]

Bingham's speech on the restoration of Tennessee read from the script that Stevens developed and Baker followed right down to the nineteen references to "rebel" or "rebels" and the thirty-three references to "loyal" in an interrupted speech that occupies less than three pages in the *Congressional Globe*. Tennessee could be restored because rebel rule had been prevented by state constitutional provisions empowering and protecting the loyal. Tennessee had disempowered all Confederate supporters. Bingham observed that the state "constitution declared that rebels shall not exercise any of the political power of the State or vote at elections."[23] This left the state government in the hands of the persons who had supported the Union during the Civil War. The Ohio Republican asserted that "a majority of the loyal freemen, citizens of the United States, shall be permitted to control the destiny and political power of that State."[24] "[T]he loyal men of Tennessee," he proclaimed confidently, "shall be represented by loyal men." That the loyal white people of Tennessee chose to disenfranchise the loyal Black people of Tennessee hardly distinguished that state from any other state in the Union. "If the majority of the people of Ohio have the right to control the political power of the State," Bingham observed, "the majority of the loyal people of Tennessee have the same right."[25]

Bingham was typical is his references to "the rights of loyal colored men" and "loyal black men."[26] While proponents of congressional Reconstruction maintained that former slaves should enjoy certain fundamental rights, they asserted repeatedly that the Thirty-Ninth Congress should protect those rights at that time because persons of color had been faithful to the Union during the Civil War. African American loyalty and military service played especially vital roles when Radical Republicans called for bans on race discrimination in voting laws. Persons of color should be granted voting rights, some party members maintained, because persons of color could be trusted to cast loyal ballots. Even Bingham, noting that Black disenfranchisement was not baked into the Tennessee state constitution, declared: "It cannot be said of loyal Tennessee . . . that a citizen who has battled for the Republic through four years of war, who is covered with wounds received in its defense, is declared by the constitution forever disqualified to vote."[27]

Bingham was as typical in preferring loyal whites to loyal persons of color in circumstances where the interests and rights of loyal whites clashed with the interests and rights of loyal persons of color. Empowering the loyal, Bingham and most Republicans agreed, did not entail empowering persons of color in jurisdictions where they believed a substantial number of loyal whites resided. If enough loyal whites existed to form a government without the assistance of loyal Blacks, most Republicans during the first session of the Thirty-Ninth Congress[28] favored allowing loyal whites to retain the exclusive right to vote and hold office. Bingham was successful in gaining congressional support for the right of the loyal white citizens of Tennessee to disenfranchise the loyal Black citizens of that state. Bingham and many Republican members of the Thirty-Ninth Congress supported Colorado and Nebraska statehood even though both jurisdictions disenfranchised persons of color and had a history of race discrimination. The Republican majority, while drafting the Fourteenth Amendment, favored empowering persons of color only when doing so was necessary to prevent rebel rule.

Bingham was nevertheless singing an entirely different melody when he asked loyal persons of color to have faith that they would be protected by the civil rights guarantees embodied in the Fourteenth Amendment—even in jurisdictions where only loyal whites were empowered. While the Ohio Republican supported financial and political guarantees, his speech on the restoration of Tennessee, and his other speeches on national constitutional reforms, focused almost exclusively on civil rights guarantees. No other Republican emphasized rights guarantees to the same degree. Such proponents of congressional Reconstruction as Baker discussed civil rights guarantees; unlike Bingham, however, they emphasized that civil rights guarantees would work because constitutional reforms altering the structure of constitutional politics would ensure that the national government was committed to making those civil rights guarantees work. Bingham sang without Republican choral support when during the speech on the restoration of Tennessee he predicted that the civil rights guarantees in the proposed Fourteenth Amendment would protect persons of color without making any mention of why, once rebel rule had been prevented through the empowerment of loyal whites, popular majorities in Congress would remain interested in protecting persons of color.

Things to Come

The following pages describe the Republican Party's effort during the first session of the Thirty-Ninth Congress to prevent rebel rule by protecting and empowering those Americans, white and Black, who were loyal to the Union during the Civil War. The focus is almost entirely on the first session, which was gaveled in on December 4, 1865, and ended on July 28, 1866.[29] That session began by excluding representatives of the former Confederate states from the national legislature and ended with the swearing-in of representatives from Tennessee after that state ratified the Fourteenth Amendment framed by members of the Thirty-Ninth Congress. *Punish Traitors, Reward Loyalty* makes no more effort than did representatives or senators in 1866 to distinguish speeches on Reconstruction from speeches devoted specifically to the Fourteenth Amendment. Republicans, Democrats, and Unionists regarded those topics as identical. Both concerned the guarantees for future loyalty and against future secession that the national government could properly demand before allowing former Confederate states to be represented in Congress and to enjoy the other prerogatives enjoyed by states of the Union.

Chapter 1 details the debates over presidential and congressional Reconstruction that structured debates over the Fourteenth Amendment.

President Andrew Johnson and his political allies in Congress believed that the president was responsible for settling the status of former Confederate states in the Union. The president as commander in chief determined when the Civil War was over and what guarantees the Union could insist on as terms of surrender before former states could have their antebellum prerogatives restored. Proponents of congressional Reconstruction maintained that the national legislature settled the status of former Confederate states in the Union. Congress, as the repository of the war power conferred by the terms of the Constitution, determined when the Civil War was over and what guarantees the Union could insist on as terms of surrender before former states could have their antebellum prerogatives restored. President Johnson and his allies maintained that former Confederate states had never left the Union. If state leaders recanted secession, slavery, and the Confederate war debt, then their state should again be represented in Congress. Most Republicans maintained that former Confederate states were out of "practical relations" with the Union. Many insisted that secession ordinances had caused states to revert to territories. Proponents of congressional Reconstruction demanded far more significant guarantees than did proponents of presidential Reconstruction of future loyalty and against future secession.

Chapter 2 explores the problem of rebel rule that animated Republican demands for guarantees of future loyalty and against future secession that the Thirty-Ninth Congress transformed into the Fourteenth Amendment. During the months after Confederate military forces surrendered, journalists, army officers stationed in the South, memorialists, and African American petitioners warned members of Congress that a revived coalition of former slaveholders, white supremacists, and Northern Democrats were attempting to win in electoral politics what they had lost during the Civil War. Democrats dismissed as "fake news" reports that persons of color and white Unionists were being persecuted in the former Confederacy.[30] Stevens and his political allies were far more alarmed by events in the South and by an unforeseen political consequence of emancipation. When discussing constitutional reform, the members of the congressional majority emphasized how the Thirteenth Amendment, by repealing the Three-Fifths Clause, added significantly to Southern power in the House of Representatives and the Electoral College. Prominent champions of free labor and racial equality feared that the newly ratified constitutional ban on slavery, by permitting former Confederate states to count disenfranchised persons of color as full persons for purposes of allocating representatives in Congress and members of the Elected College, offered former slaveholders the opportunity in the near future to resume minority control of the national government. Once in power, proponents of congressional Reconstruction dreaded, the powerful Southerners who had always dominated the Democratic Party would repeal laws that Republicans had passed under the Thirteenth Amendment; restore to a fair degree antebellum labor relations in the South; pay off Southern war creditors while refusing to honor Civil War obligations to Union widows and Union creditors; and, when challenged, interpret in bad faith constitutional provisions designed to protect those whites and Blacks who had been loyal during the Civil War. Constitutional reform, Republicans repeatedly asserted, had to be directed at any constitutional provisions and practices that might enable traitors to rule the South and national government in the very near future.

Chapter 3 discusses empowering and protecting the loyal as the Republican solution to potential rebel rule. A bipartisan consensus existed in the Thirty-Ninth Congress that only loyal people should govern. Bitter partisan disputes existed over who was faithful to the Union in 1863 and in 1866. President Johnson and his political allies maintained that most Southerners (aside from the Confederate leadership) could be trusted. Democrats were as loyal, if not more loyal, than Republicans. Southern Blacks had and would continue to ally with the planting elite in the South rather than with the loyal Unionists in the North. Proponents of congressional Reconstruction promoted a very different set of loyal persons. Republicans insisted that Republicans were the party of the persons who remained loyal to the Union, that most white Southerners could not be trusted with political power as long as they remained dupes of the slaveholding elite, and that persons of color were the only significant loyal class in the South. Proponents of racial equality insisted that Black citizens deserved protection and empowerment, at least as much as a reward for being loyal during the Civil War as because they were being deprived of fundamental rights. Black suffrage was defended almost exclusively as justified by Black loyalty.

Chapter 4 lays out the anti-secession, financial, political, and civil rights guarantees that various proponents of congressional Reconstruction proposed as the means for preventing rebel rule in the former Confederate states and in the nation by empowering and protecting loyal persons. The multifaceted constitutional reform packages different Republicans championed when making speeches on Reconstruction and other matters demonstrate that an omnibus of some sort was always in the cards. The main questions before the Joint Committee of Fifteen on Reconstruction and the Thirty-Ninth Congress were the precise content of specific constitutional reforms and whether those constitutional reforms should be bundled together or voted on as separate amendments. Most Republicans made political guarantees their highest priority. Rebel rule in the South and nation could be forestalled, in their view, only if Americans adjusted the basis of apportionment, enfranchised persons of color, barred Confederate leaders from holding public office, disenfranchised all Confederates for a period of time, or adopted some combination of these means for modifying constitutional politics in the United States. Almost all reform packages included financial guarantees—most notably a constitutional amendment forbidding repayment of Confederate debt. Constitutional bans on secession were popular during the winter but largely disappeared after March 1866. Constitutional provisions banning Black Codes and related state laws did not receive the same level of support as political and financial guarantees. Most Republicans called for bans on race discrimination in civil rights, but many maintained that legislation under the Thirteenth Amendment, rather than new constitutional provisions, was the best means for protecting persons of color. Enthusiasm for a constitutional amendment banning race discrimination in civil rights dropped considerably after Congress passed the Civil Rights Act of 1866 in March.

Chapter 5 details how, in the case of Colorado statehood and related matters, most Republicans during the first session of the Thirty-Ninth Congress preferred empowering loyal whites to protecting the rights of African Americans. Colorado had been loyal to the Union during the Civil War but presented a state constitution that prohibited persons of color from voting. Over Sumner's strenuous objections, Republican majorities in the House and Senate voted in favor of statehood. Colorado would be a fully Republican state, in their view, which was more vital for preventing rebel rule than Colorado being something less than a republican state. This tension between empowering loyal whites and protecting persons of color frequently resurfaced in Congress throughout July 1866, with the same outcome. The congressional majority that framed the Fourteenth Amendment during debates over restoring Tennessee, granting statehood to Nebraska, and seating Senator David Patterson of Tennessee voted to empower white persons who had been loyal to the United States during the Civil War, even when those loyal whites demonstrated no commitment to empowering or protecting those persons of color who had been at least as, if not substantially more, faithful to the Union cause.

Coda

Constitutional civil rights guarantees for former slaves were no more central to Reconstruction and constitutional reform in 1866 than Osric is to

Hamlet. Bingham aside, proponents of congressional Reconstruction after the Thirteenth Amendment was ratified were more concerned with the existing structure of constitutional politics than with the existing constitutional powers of the national government or existing constitutional rights. Constitutional reform was designed to prevent rebel rule. Black Codes were one manifestation of rebel rule, but so were the persecution of white Unionists in the South, the possible repudiation of the national debt, and the threatened repayment of the Confederate debt. Republicans sought to prevent rebel rule by empowering all persons, Black and white, who remained loyal to the Union during the Civil War. The New York financiers who loaned money to the Union cause and the Ohio widows whose husbands died fighting the rebels were as much on the minds of the persons responsible for Reconstruction and the Fourteenth Amendment as were the South Carolina bondsmen made free by the Emancipation Proclamation and Thirteenth Amendment.

The aspiring thespian whose story begins this volume may nevertheless have much in common with the Republicans and allied Unionists who drafted the Fourteenth Amendment. In one telling of the stories, all these characters are egoists who see the world only from their selfish perspectives. Our young thespian thinks that Shakespeare's *Hamlet* is about his Osric character. Proponents of congressional Reconstruction were far more interested in empowering and protecting themselves and white people like themselves than in empowering and protecting persons of color. In a different telling, all these characters are naïve enthusiasts. Our young thespian has thrown himself into the role of Osric. Members of the majority in the Thirty-Ninth Congress believed sincerely that history was on the side of free labor and racial equality. Those causes made extraordinary gains during the last two years of the Civil War and the first year of Reconstruction, as stories of Blacks' military valor weakened racial prejudice in the North.[31] Persons who witnessed these events firsthand—from the Emancipation Proclamation to the submission of the Fourteenth Amendment to states for ratification—might have convinced themselves that permanently dethroning the slaveholding elite both nationally and in the former Confederate states was the last step necessary to bring about a new era of race relations in the United States and the American South. The extent to which either, both, or still other accounts best describe the persons responsible for the Fourteenth Amendment awaits the many pages—and perhaps several volumes—to come.

The Exclusion Debate

Representative Thaddeus Stevens of Pennsylvania and his political allies most frequently announced their proposals for constitutional and statutory reforms when justifying their decision not to seat representatives from the former Confederate states. Senator Charles Sumner of Massachusetts, minutes after Reverend Edgar Gray delivered the prayer opening the first session of the Thirty-Ninth Congress, introduced a resolution declaring "it is the first duty of Congress to take care that no State declared to be in rebellion shall be allowed to resume its relations to the Union until after the satisfactory performance of five several conditions."[1] Republicans offered variations on Sumner's themes and conditions when commenting on President Andrew Johnson's first annual message, which urged the Thirty-Ninth Congress to seat representatives from the former Confederate states;[2] when defending the ongoing congressional decision to exclude from the House and Senate representatives from former Confederate states;[3] when discussing the bill for restoring Southern states that accompanied the Joint Committee on Reconstruction's Fourteenth Amendment;[4] when debating new federal civil rights statutes; and when considering proposed constitutional amendments. As remains the case, germaneness was not a bar to discussing what a representative believed was the most pressing issue of the day. Debates over the status of former Confederate states in the Union and the constitutional reforms necessary for Reconstruction broke out when Congress consider numerous other matters, most notably the staffing of the post office.[5]

The status of former Confederate states occupied the first session from beginning to end. The debate began on the first day of the legislative session when, by arrangement with Stevens, Edward McPherson, the Clerk of the House, refused to announce the names of persons elected from the former Confederate states during the first roll call.[6] Republican majorities during the following months rebuffed President Johnson's repeated pleas to restore swiftly the right of former Confederate states to be represented in Congress.[7] On February 20, 1866, responding to such a call in the presidential message vetoing the Second Freedmen's Bureau Bill,[8] the House passed a resolution, recommended by the Joint Committee, declaring:

> That in order to close agitation upon a question which seems likely to disturb the section of the Government, as well as to quiet the uncertainty which is agitating the minds of the people of the eleven States which have been declared to be in insurrection, no Senator or Representation shall be admitted into either branch of Congress from any of said States until Congress shall have declared such State entitled to such representation.[9]

The Senate passed the exclusion resolution several weeks later.[10] Stevens in the hours before the Congress adjourned proposed another Reconstruction bill, setting out new conditions for former Confederate states to be represented in Congress.[11]

Reconstruction and the Fourteenth Amendment

The congressional debates in the first session over the status of former Confederate states are so entwined with the debates over various proposed fourteenth amendments as to be incapable of being disentangled by anyone other than a contemporary constitutional lawyer. Proponents of congressional Reconstruction, when considering the status of the former Confederate states, described the circumstances that they believed necessitated constitutional and statutory reforms. They delineated the constitutional and statutory reforms they believed necessary. Various proposed fourteenth amendments were the outcome of these deliberations. Prominent Republicans acknowledged the intimate connections between exclusion and constitutional reform. Senator William Pitt Fessenden of Maine during the debate over the exclusion resolution observed that "the constitutional amendment [the apportionment resolution] which is before this House . . . is intimately involved with the very question now under consideration."[12] He explained:

> If we think that constitutional amendments are necessary arising from the condition in which we have been, it is our duty to propose them. If we think that additional laws are necessary, it is our duty to pass those laws. If we think it is proper to impose conditions, not conditions that would degrade or disgrace any State, for when they come back they

must come on terms of equality—but if we think it is necessary to impose some conditions even upon these States on their return, it is our duty to do that before we admit their members to seats on this floor or the floor of the other House.[13]

The debates over Reconstruction and the Fourteenth Amendment frequently bled into each other. Members of Congress when officially debating various versions of the Fourteenth Amendment discussed the status of states in the Union and congressional responsibility for Reconstruction. During the debates over the exclusion resolution, President Johnson's annual message, the restoration bill, and other related measures, members of Congress offered their opinions on various proposed Fourteenth Amendments.[14] No better illustration exists of the capacity of the legal mind to "think about a thing inextricably attached to something else without thinking of the thing which it is attached to"[15] than the hiving off of the debates on the status of former Confederate states from the debates on constitutional reform in the recent legal literature on the Fourteenth Amendment.[16]

The Joint Committee on Reconstruction embodied the entangled controversies over constitutional reform and the status of former Confederate states during the first session. After electing leadership and agreeing on procedural rules, the House of Representatives without debate approved a resolution that Stevens proposed establishing the Joint Committee on Reconstruction, which would be charged with responsibility for determining what legislation and constitutional amendments were necessary before excluded representatives could be seated in Congress. That proposed resolution declared:

[A] joint committee of fifteen members shall be appointed, nine of whom shall be members of the House and six members of the Senate, who shall inquire into the condition of the States which formed the so-called confederate States of America, and report whether they or any of them are entitled to be represented in either House of Congress, with leave to report at any time by bill or otherwise: and until such report shall have been made and finally acted upon by Congress, no member shall be received into either House from any of the said so-called confederate States."[17]

Senate Republicans on December 12, after defeating a motion requiring equal Senate representation on the committee and another motion asserting Senate power not to be bound by any committee recommendation, approved the resolution establishing the Joint Committee, but members struck out the provision excluding Southern representation until the Joint Committee reported back to Congress.[18] The House approved that revision the next day.[19] Fessenden was appointed to chair the committee. The Speaker of the House, Representative Schuyler Colfax of Indiana, appointed Representatives Stevens, John A. Bingham of Ohio, George S. Boutwell of Massachusetts, Henry T. Blow of Missouri, Roscoe Conkling of New York, Justin Morrill of Vermont, Elihu Washburne of Illinois, Henry Grider of Kentucky, and Andrew J. Rogers of New Jersey to the Joint Committee.[20] The Senate selected Senators Fessenden, Jacob Howard of Michigan, Ira Harris of New York, James W. Grimes of Iowa, George H. Williams of Oregon, and Reverdy Johnson of Maryland.[21] Grider, Rogers, and R. Johnson were Democrats. The other members of the Joint Committee were Republicans. No Unionists served.

The committee's final report explicitly connected Reconstruction and the Fourteenth Amendment by simultaneously sending to Congress a proposed Fourteenth Amendment and proposed legislation restoring to full rights in the Union any former Confederate state that ratified the amendment.[22] The report began by declaring that members were tasked with determining whether the former Confederate states "were entitled to representation in Congress."[23] The Fourteenth Amendment set out the terms on which a final peace could be made and the former Confederate states permitted to enjoy their ancient prerogatives in the Union.[24] The minority report was devoted almost entirely to the status of the former Confederate states in the Union, making only brief reference to some provisions in the proposed amendment and no reference at all to either the proposed Section 1 or to any other matter concerning race relations in the United States.[25]

The Fourteenth Amendment remained entangled with the status of former Confederate states, even after Congress sent the text to the states for ratification. Members of Congress when debating the Joint Committee's proposed Reconstruction Act considered whether states should be admitted upon their ratification of the Fourteenth Amendment or only if the Fourteenth Amendment was ratified; the consequences for former Confederate states should Union states not ratify the Fourteenth Amendment; whether Tennessee and Arkansas, which were further reconstructed than other former Confederate states, upon their ratification should be allowed representation in Congress even if less reconstructed states had to wait for national ratification; and whether Congress should condition restoration of former Confederate states on further constitutional reform, most notably former Confederate states adopting state constitutional provisions enfranchising persons of color.[26] The precise label attached to the debate by the *Congressional Globe* mattered little. Senators and Representatives continued to mix commentary on the justifications and content of the Fourteenth Amendment with commentary on the status of states in the Union regardless of the nominal subject under debate.[27] The Fourteenth Amendment remained fair game when the matter officially being considered was the exclusion of former Confederate states, just as the exclusion of former Confederate states was always fair game when the matter officially being considered was the Fourteenth Amendment. The Fourteenth Amendment, Lisset Marie Pino and John Fabian Witt observe, replaced military rule in the South and, in their opinion, was a premature if not inferior substitution.[28]

Congressional votes confirm the tight connection between the status of former Confederate states and the omnibus Fourteenth Amendment. The coalition that supported excluding from Congress representatives from "rebel states" (see tables A.1 and A.2 in the appendix), was almost identical to the coalition that eventually passed the omnibus Fourteenth Amendment. No Democrat in the Thirty-Ninth Congress voted for either the exclusion resolution or the omnibus Fourteenth Amendment. Three very conservative Republicans in the Senate, James R. Doolittle of Wisconsin, James Dixon of Connecticut, and Edgar Cowan of Pennsylvania, did not vote for either. Except for Representatives Robert S. Hale of New York, Henry J. Raymond of New York, William A. Newell of New Jersey, and Senators William M. Stewart of Nevada, James H. Lane of Kansas. and Edwin D. Morgan of New York, every Republican who voted for the omnibus Fourteenth Amendment had previously voted for the exclusion amendment.[29]

Members of the Thirty-Ninth Congress when debating President Johnson's proposed Reconstruction policy, the exclusion resolution, the admission of Tennessee, various restoration bills, civil rights legislation, proposed constitutional amendments, and other related (and sometimes unrelated) matters considered the impact that secession ordinances had on the status of states in the Union, whether the Civil War had ended, the conditions under which former Confederate states would be entitled to resume their previous status in the Union, and who was constitutionally authorized to make these judgments. President Johnson, congressional Democrats, many Unionists, and a handful of very conservative Republicans supported presidential Reconstruction. They insisted that secession ordinances had no legal consequences. The president, as commander in chief, was responsible for determining when the Civil War was over and the terms of Confederate surrender. Once the president declared former Confederate states were again loyal to the Union, they were entitled to immediate representation in Congress without any further congressionally imposed conditions, although each branch of Congress retained the power to refrain from seating disloyal representatives in that institution. The overwhelming majority of Republicans and many Unionists in both the House and the Senate insisted on congressional Reconstruction. They maintained that secession ordinances deprived former Confederate states of their ancient prerogatives in the Union. Congress, as the lawmaking power of the country, was responsible for determining when the Civil War was over and what guarantees or securities were necessary before former Confederate states were entitled to resume their antebellum status in the Union. The president could begin Reconstruction in the absence of a congressional policy, but a federal statute was necessary for former Confederate states to again be represented in Congress.

Presidential Reconstruction

President Johnson, every Democrat in Congress, many Unionists, and a very few conservative Republicans fought a largely unsuccessful rearguard action throughout the Thirty-Ninth Congress against the majority decision to exclude from the House and Senate all representatives from the former Confederate states, with the exception of representatives from Tennessee, who were admitted only after the Fourteenth Amendment passed both legislative chambers and was sent to the states for ratification. Their opposition relied on federalism and separation of powers principles. Proponents of presidential Reconstruction insisted that the rebellious activities from 1860 to 1865 done by however many individuals constituted treason but did not and could not change the status of any state in the Union. The president, they claimed, was the government official responsible for defeating the rebels who had illegally commandeered the machinery of government in eleven states, had the authority to establish the terms on which the insurrection would be considered over, and was constitutionally empowered to determine whether those conditions had been met.

The Joint Committee's minority report was devoted to demonstrating that former Confederate states were entitled to representation in the Thirty-Ninth Congress. The three Democrats on that committee, R. Johnson, Rogers, and Grider, insisted on the principle "once a state, always a state." Their report (titled "Views of the Minority") declared that "[a] State once in the Union must abide in it forever. She can never withdraw from or be expelled from it."[30] Secession was a nullity that had no legal impact on the status of states within the Union. The minority report further maintained that "such States during the entire rebellion were as completely component States of the United States as they were before the rebellion, and were bound by all the obligations which the Constitution imposes and entitled to all its privileges."[31] The three committee Democrats thought the contrary view implied that states could, albeit illegally, get out of the Union. The dissenting committee members pointed out,

> [t]o concede that, by the illegal conduct of her own citizens, she can be withdrawn from the Union, is virtually to concede the rights of secession. For what different does it make as regards the result whether a State can rightfully secede[] (a doctrine, by-the-by, heretofore maintained by statesmen north as well as south[]) or whether by the illegal conduct of her citizens she ceases to be a State of the Union?[32]

Once a state ceased rebelling that state was entitled to resume an equal status in the Union. "[T]he moment the rebellion was suppressed," the minority insisted, "the ancient laws resumed their accustomed sway, subject only to the new reorganization by the appointment of the proper officer to give them operation and effect."[33]

The president, as commander in chief, was the person responsible for determining when the rebellion had been suppressed and for appointing the officers who would supervise the reconstruction of former Confederate states. The Democrats on the Joint Committee stated: "This organization and appointment of the public functionaries, which was under the superintendence and direction of the President, the commander-in-chief of the army and navy of the country, and who, as such, had previously governed the State, from imperative necessity, by the force of martial law."[34] Congress had no say in the process by which states might draw up new constitutions. "The minority declared that "[t]he power to establish or modify a State government belongs exclusively to the people of the States" and that "their decision is obligatory upon everybody[] and independent of all congressional control if such government be republican."[35] Congress could constitutionally determine only whether elected representatives met constitutional requirements, a decision that was vested in each house of Congress, not Congress as a whole.[36] Any representative "able and willing" to take the oath of office mandated by Article VI had the right to be seated in Congress.[37]

Members of Congress who favoring seating Southern delegations anticipated and elaborated the claim in the minority report that secession ordinances had no legal effect.[38] Opponents of the exclusion resolution began from the near-unanimous consensus in the Thirty-Ninth Congress that no state had a right to secede from the Union. Rogers spoke for all Democrats other than Representative Benjamin G. Harris of Maryland[39] when he declared "the foundation stone which lies at the base of our whole structure of government[] denies the right of any State to withdraw from the compact into which it entered when it, with other States, formed the American Union."[40] If states could not lawfully secede, proponents of presidential Reconstruction reasoned, then secession ordinances could not impair constitutional rights and duties. Representative Aaron Harding of Kentucky summed up the Democratic position with a simple syllogism: "[I]f . . . the Constitution is the supreme law of the land, every ordinance of secession in the South being opposed to the Constitution and seeking its overthrow of necessity must have been absolutely null and void," he declared, "and being void must be regarded as wholly inoperative[] and therefore could not work any change in the constitutional relations of the States to the Federal Government."[41] Proponents of presidential Reconstruction competed throughout the first session of the Thirty-Ninth Congress to determine who could make this point most persuasively and, if not most persuasively, most frequently. Representative William E. Finck of Ohio pointed out that "[t]he ordinances of secession were invalid and unconstitutional." As a result, the former Confederate states "had never been out of the Union, but have always continued to be, and are to-day, States within the Union."[42] Alabama was as much a state in the Union in 1866 or in 1863, opponents of the exclusion resolution agreed, as Alabama was in 1860 or in 1840. "[T]hat they are still States in this Union is the most sacred truth and the dearest truth to every American heart," Doolittle contended.[43]

A few Democrats pointed out paths not taken to secession. Secession might have occurred by mutual agreement. R. Johnson insisted that "they are States in the Union, and . . . they never could have been placed out of the Union without the consent of their sister States."[44] Military triumph would have been a second possible path to lawful secession. Representative Francis C. Le Blond of Ohio stated that "a State once in the Union is always in except by a successful revolution."[45]

Proponents of what might be labeled "contingent secession" were nevertheless a minority of the congressional minority. Most proponents of presidential Reconstruction insisted that leaving the Union was a constitutional impossibility. Representative Daniel W. Voorhees of Indiana asserted "no State, or any number of States confederated together, can in any manner sunder their connection with the Federal Union."[46] Representative Charles Sitgreaves of New Jersey contended "no State could or should put itself out of the Union, either by peaceable secession or force of arms."[47]

Proponents of presidential Reconstruction frequently asserted that denying former Confederate states representation in Congress was inconsistent with the basic principles underlying the Civil War. Doolittle stated: "The ground we occupied was this: that no State nor the people of any State had power to withdraw from the Union."[48] Representative Green C. Smith of Kentucky insisted "the entire action of Congress [and] all the speeches made by Union men" during the Civil War "were made distinctly and emphatically maintaining the ground that those eleven States were not out and could not get out of the Union."[49] President Johnson's political supporters maintained that the Union fought to maintain the federalism status quo, not to undermine the existing relationships between the federal government and the states. Senator Willard Saulsbury, Sr., of Delaware pointed out that "[t]hroughout the whole contest the battle-cry was 'the preservation of the Union' and 'the union of the States.'"[50]

Democrats and other opponents of exclusion acknowledged that the rights of former Confederate states were suspended during the Civil War;[51] but that conflict was now over. President Johnson informed Congress on December 4, 1865, that Abraham Lincoln had "brought the civil war substantially to a close" and that Southern "[r]esistance to the General Government appeared to have exhausted itself."[52] Two weeks later he declared "the rebellion waged by a portion of the people against the properly constituted authority of the Government of the United States has been suppressed."[53] Proponents of presidential Reconstruction in Congress agreed with the president's proclamation. "[T]he war has ceased," Senator Garrett Davis of Kentucky contended. "There is not," he continued, "and has not been for months, any rebellion, or insurrection, or resistance, or a single armed soldier or citizen in those States, or any one of them, against the United States or their authority."[54] Senator James Guthrie of Kentucky bluntly declared "the rebellion has been suppressed."[55]

Proponents of presidential Reconstruction maintained that the restoration of peace had important political and constitutional consequences. The Confederacy, which never had legal existence, no longer had extralegal or illegal existence. Senator James Nesmith of Oregon stated: "All these hostile organizations are defunct. They are dead, and will know no resurrection."[56] Wartime measures no longer had constitutional sanction. G. Davis called for restoring habeas corpus because "there are now no cases of invasion or rebellion . . . anywhere in the United States."[57] Loyalty reigned supreme. President Johnson observed that "[t]he people throughout the entire South evince a laudable desire to renew their allegiance to the Government."[58] Loyal Southerners were eagerly seeking to join their loyal fellow citizens in the joint project of governing. Smith stated "these men come here through the actions of loyal Governors and loyal Legislatures . . . and they come here by the vote of thousands and thousands of loyal voters electing them to seats in this Hall."[59]

The suspended status of former Confederate states ceased the moment the rebel insurgence ended. Representative Anthony Thornton of Illinois, quoting General William Sherman, insisted that "[w]henever the people of Georgia quit rebelling against their Government, then the State of Georgia will have resumed her functions in the Union."[60] "Upon revocation of the proclamation, and a cessation of the state of things which prompted these arbitrary measures," Thornton continued, "the Constitution and laws woke from their lethargy[] and again became our shield and safeguard."[61] States no longer in rebellion had their antebellum status fully restored. The former Confederate states, Representative Charles A. Eldredge of Wisconsin demanded, "should resume their appropriate and constitutional positions in the Union without delay."[62] Saulsbury proposed a resolution declaring, "[a]nd whereas the said civil war has ceased, Therefore, *Resolved*, That the Senate . . . will preserve the Union with all the dignity, equality, and rights of the several States, the said southern States included, unimpaired."[63] "All" meant each and every right states had enjoyed before the Civil War. States that had never legally been out of the Union were entitled to the same rights as states that never claimed to be legally out of the Union. R. Johnson, one of the leading constitutional lawyers of the Civil War and the Reconstruction Era, stated that, with "[t]he insurrection terminated, the authority of the Government thereby reinstated, *io instante* they were invested with all the rights belonging to them originally; I mean as States."[64] Aa. Harding asserted "[w]hen the rebellion in the South was subdued, and the insurgents yielded obedience to the Constitution and laws, then the States were in law restored to all their constitutional rights in the Union."[65]

Statehood came with numerous and vital privileges. Representation in Congress was the most important right former Confederate states were entitled to exercise after rebels were swept from state governments. "[I]f these States are in the Union, if they have never been out of it," Finck stated, "they are in the Union as equal States, with all the rights and privileges which belong to States in this Union, and are entitled to be represented on this floor by the same authority as the States of Pennsylvania and Ohio."[66] That right might have been suspended during the Civil War, but no state prerogatives were permanently lost. Representative Samuel J. Randall of Pennsylvania maintained that "the right of representation as belong to the loyal people of the South has never ceased."[67] Local power to control state government was another right that automatically resumed after rebellion ended. "[W]hen armed resistance to Federal Authority ceased in the southern States, and the Federal authority was acknowledged," Saulsbury insisted, "those States never having been out of the Union, . . . their ordinances of secession being absolute nullities, the people of those States had a right to . . . put into operation the machinery of government, without the intervention of the President or Congress or anybody else."[68] Former Confederate states were entitled to decide whether to ratify the Thirteenth Amendment and other new constitutional provisions. President Johnson informed Congress "[t]he next step which I have taken to restore the constitutional relations of the States has been an invitation for them to participate in the high office of amending the Constitution."[69] Proponents of presidential Reconstruction pointed to the participation of former Confederate states in the amendment process as demonstrating they were part of the Union. Grider proposed a resolution declaring "it is illogical and unconstitutional to hold that States are in the Union to vote for constitutional amendments and yet not entitled to representation in Congress."[70]

Continued exclusion was inconsistent with constitutional principle, violated constitutional law, and created a serious constitutional conundrum. If the people of the South were being taxed by the federal government, then fundamental constitutional commitments entailed that they be represented in the federal government. Smith observed "there cannot possibly be a republican form of government unless representation accompanies taxation."[71] Exclusion violated Article I and Article V, which require state equality in the Senate. "[I]f they be States," Saulsbury maintained, "they shall each be entitled to two Senators on this floor."[72] Numbers did not matter. Representation was constitutionally required no matter how few persons were authorized to vote and hold office. Just as low-population New England states had the same right to representation as heavily populated New York, so states with few loyal voters had the same right to representation as states with many loyal voters. "[I]f it be true that in such a case one tenth alone must be allowed to vote," Smith stated, "that one tenth should be regarded as the State."[73] The consensus that Andrew Johnson was the constitutional president of the United States, opponents of exclusion maintained, rested on Tennessee being as much a state in the Union as Illinois. Representative James Brooks of New York observed that, "if Tennessee is not in the Union, and has not been in the Union, and is not a loyal State, and the people of Tennessee are aliens and foreigners to this Union, by what right does the President of the United States usurp his place in the White House."[74]

The president was responsible for determining when a state was sufficiently reconstructed to merit representation in Congress. G. Davis maintained that "the power to determine when any portion of the country is in a state of insurrection belongs to the President exclusively."[75] Guthrie asserted that the Article II power to "take care that the laws be faithfully executed" authorized the president "to put down a rebel government and put a government that is friendly to the United States."[76] These presidential powers included the power to demand guarantees of future loyalty and good behavior. Raymond derived the right to demand guarantees from the first sentence of Article II, Section 2. Any conditions on changing the suspended status of former Confederate states, he declared, were "terms of surrender." As such, Raymond concluded, "it belongs . . . to the President as Commander-in-Chief of the Army and Navy of the United States to make them, and to fix the limit as to what they shall embrace."[77]

Opponents of exclusion heartily endorsed the conditions for restoration demanded by President Johnson. Abolition was the priority of presidential Reconstruction. The president's first annual message to Congress declared "the evidence of sincerity in the future maintenance of the Union shall be put beyond doubt by the ratification of the proposed amendment to the Constitution, which provides for the abolition of slavery forever within the limits of our country."[78] President Johnson just as forcefully insisted that former Confederate states repudiate secession and all state debts contracted to fight the war.[79] With his encouragement, the eleven states that had attempted to secede ratified new state constitutions that abolished slavery, rescinded and declared void all secession ordinances, and foreswore repayment of the Confederate debt.[80] Almost all Democrats, many Unionists, and a few Republicans thought this was enough. Smith urged Congress to seat the Tennessee delegation because that state "has repudiated the rebel debt; she has passed the constitutional amendment; she has rendered null and void all the ordinances of secession; and she has sent here to represent her men who have been in the war on the side of the Government from 1862 to its close."[81]

Several proponents of presidential Reconstruction paid lip service to the rights of emancipated slaves. Representative Thomas M. Stillwell of Indiana added a measure of racial justice to the conditions for restoration. He offered a resolution calling for the seating of representatives from former Confederate states that "have submitted to the laws of the United States, adopted a republican form of government, repealed the ordinance of secession, passed the constitutional amendment forever prohibiting slavery, repudiated the rebel war debt, and passed laws protecting the freedmen in his liberty."[82] Cowan claimed, "Everybody admits that the negro ought to have his natural rights secured to him." These natural rights included "the right to life, liberty, and the pursuit of happiness, the protection of property, limbs, and reputation, . . . the right to sue and be sued, and to testify in courts of justice."[83] The few opponents of exclusion who spoke of racial justice as a condition for representation, however, typically assumed that condition had been or was being met. President Johnson was particularly confident that former Confederate states were committed to granting persons of color practical freedom. "[I]n nearly all of them," he informed Congress, "measures have been adopted or are now pending, to confer freedmen rights and privileges which are essential to their comfort, protection, and security."[84] Stewart thought further exclusion unnecessary because the national government was already empowered to protect persons of color in former Confederate states. "What sterner guarantee of the effectual abolition of slavery and the restoration to civil rights of the freedmen can be given," he asserted, "than the pledge recorded in the supreme law of the land proclaiming their liberty, and authorizing Congress to provide for its maintenance."[85]

Once the president declared a state loyal, that state had a right to be represented in Congress without further conditions. R. Johnson insisted, "[W]hat have you in such as case as this have the right to demand? Submission to the authority of the Government, and that you have got."[86] Voorhees agreed that "[p]eace and obedience to law are the only guarantees for the future which any Government can justly require of its citizens."[87] This condition had been met both by presidential decree[88] and Democratic observation. Voorhees proclaimed "peace and obedience reign" in the former Confederate States.[89] Nesmith spoke of "their sincere, generous, and earnest proffer of allegiance and devotion to" the federal government.[90] No federal official or institution could require more of a state whose loyalty had been secured. Representative Lovell H. Rousseau of Kentucky asked, "[W]hat do we want with guarantees from the insurrectionary States? What right has the nation to ask guarantees from a portion of the people?"[91] States could not be required to ratify further federal constitutional amendments. "[I]f they are States," Representative George R. Latham stated, "Congress has no more right to compel them to adopt any measure than it has to adopt it for them and transfer it to their code."[92] The federal government had no more power to demand changes in the state constitutions of loyal states. Nesmith "den[ied] all power in Congress, or the President or in both combined, to make a State constitution, or to dictate any provision which shall be contained in it."[93]

The Democrats, Unionists, and very conservative Republicans who supported presidential Reconstruction acknowledged that each chamber of Congress, when exercising the constitutional power under Article I to determine whether state elections and state election winners met constitutional conditions, was authorized to determine whether particular representatives were sufficiently loyal to be seated. President Johnson's first annual message admitted "it is for you, fellow-citizens of the Senate, and for you, fellow-citizens of the House of Representatives, to judge, each for yourselves, of the elections, returns, and qualifications of your own members."[94] The president's political supporters rejected claims that members of the House and Senate could jointly bind themselves in advance to adopting common criteria for seating representatives from the rebel states. Doolittle stated, "on the subject of representation in this body, it is not within our constitutional power to delegate our power to any other body, or to any committee which we ourselves do not control."[95] "The Constitution makes each House, separately, the exclusive judge," J. Dixon asserted.[96] Exclusion was justified only when a representative lacked the appropriate credentials. Representative Charles Goodyear of New York insisted that "the simple constitutional prerogative" of the House was "to judge of the qualifications of its members without regard to the constituent state."[97]

Those Republicans and Unionists who opposed exclusion leaned heavily on the test oath, which required members of Congress to swear to past, as well as to present and future, loyalty.[98] If loyal voters from former Confederate states sent to Congress representatives who had been loyal to the Union during the Civil War, they insisted, those representatives were entitled to seats in the House and Senate. J. Dixon required only "loyal men who can take the required oaths, provided they come from States which present themselves in an attitude of harmony and loyalty."[99] Representative Charles E. Phelps of Maryland maintained: "You have a test oath searching and stringent enough to satisfy the most exacting. Under it no traitor can enter Congress or hold a Federal office."[100] A few Democrats accepted the test oath as a barrier to and basis of representation. S. Randall pointed out: "We have all taken it, and at present no new members can be admitted without taking it."[101]

Most Democrats were less demanding, requiring only that representatives from former Confederate states foreswear future secession. "They proffer the only test you have a right to require," Thornton asserted, "obedience to the Constitution and laws of the land."[102] Past transgressions should be forgiven when future loyalty was sincerely promised. Guthrie would modify the test oath "so that those who have repented of their disloyalty may not be excluded."[103] Other Democrats declared the test oath unconstitutional. Finck insisted that, "if Congress had authority to prescribe the test oath of 1862, it has the power to add other and different qualifications for Senators and Representatives than those provided in the Constitution, and thus change the organic law by legislative enactment."[104] Article VI, Paragraph 3, which declares "Senators and Representatives . . . shall be bound by Oath or Affirmation[] to support his Constitution" set out the only pledge that President Johnson's political allies believed Congress could require of members. If "they send their Representatives to the other House and their Senators here, and those Representatives and Senators are willing to take the oath to support the Constitution of the United States, and no other oath," Saulsbury stated, "I respond affirmatively that those States have a right to be represented by the men so chosen."[105] Representative Burwell C. Ritter of Kentucky declared "when a State is in a condition to exercise the functions of a State that Congress has no right or authority to require anything more than to judge the legality of the election and qualification of its members, and to require that they shall take the oath prescribed by the Constitution."[106]

Those members of Congress who opposed the exclusion resolution and the Fourteenth Amendment were united in opposition to granting persons of color the right to vote by statute or constitutional amendment. President Andrew Johnson insisted that neither he nor Congress had power to condition restoration of the Southern states on universal suffrage. After noting "the uniform usage for each States to enlarge the body of its electors, according to its own judgment," the *Tennessee Unionist* declared that "a concession of the elective franchise, by act of the President of the United States . . . would have created a new class of voters, and would have been an assumption of power by the President which nothing in the Constitution or laws of the United States would have warranted."[107] Thornton offered a resolution declaring "any extension of the elective franchise to persons in the States, either by act of the President or Congress, would be an assumption of power that nothing in the Constitution would warrant."[108]

Democrats opposed Black suffrage by any means, whether those means be presidential proclamation, congressional statute, or constitutional amendment. Finck asked:

Are the principles of the old Constitution to be abandoned, and the whole character of our system of government changed, in order that the white men of eleven States may be disfranchised, and the negro clothed with political rights? Is it possible, sir, that within the limits of our Republic white men will combine to degrade their own race and kindred in order to confer political power into the hands of black men?[109]

Most officials opposed to Black suffrage did so as white supremacists.[110] A few based their opposition entirely on federalism principles. President Johnson, although a white supremacist, adopted a softer tone than most Democrats when he asserted "the freedmen, if they show patience and manly virtues, will sooner obtain a participation in the elective franchise through the States than through the General Government."[111]

Congressional Reconstruction

Stevens and his political allies disputed the Democratic/conservative position on the status of former Confederate states, the state of the Civil War, presidential power during Reconstruction, and the conditions under which former Confederate states could be represented in Congress. Secession had legal and constitutional consequences, although not those intended by Confederate rebels. Congress determined by law when the Civil War ended, the conditions of peace, and whether former Confederate states met those conditions. Representative John D. Baldwin of Massachusetts expressed the dominant Republican consensus on the federalism and separation of powers issues raised by the status of former Confederate states when he declared that

> every insurgent State became utterly disorganized. . . . This necessarily withdrew those State from practical relations with the Government, and it suspended their representation in Congress, for such representation implies an organized State, with a government duly recognized by Congress as valid and republican. . . . Before they can return to the condition from which they fell they must be loyally reorganized with the forms of government duly recognized by Congress as satisfactory; and all this with due regard to the fact that the nation has in those States not only the rights of sovereignty, but also, superadded to these, the belligerent rights of conquest.[112]

Representative William Windom of Minnesota itemized the Republican position on congressional Reconstruction:

1. That the secession of a State and the rebellion of its people "deprives it of all civil government" and abrogates all its rights and privileges in the Union, but does not in any way affect its obligations to the Union.
2. That such State can be restored only by the act of the loyal people, expressed through their representatives in Congress, and until such

restoration takes place its people have no right to demand representation.

3. That it is the duty of Congress to first ascertain whether or not the
people of the South are in a condition to participate, safely, in admin-
istrating the Government. If they are, to restore them at once. If they
are not, to provide, as conditions-precedent to their admission, such
irreversible guarantees as will insure the safety of the Republic and
prevent future rebellions.[113]

These "irreversible guarantees" evolved into the Fourteenth Amendment.

The *Report of the Joint Committee on Reconstruction*, penned by Fessenden and signed by every Republican on the committee, elaborated at
length the case for excluding Southern representatives from Congress. Secession obliterated all legitimate government in the former Confederate
states. The committee majority determined that, when rebels passed secession ordinances, they "destroyed their State constitutions in respect to the
vital principle which connected their respective States with the Union and
secured their federal relations; and nothing of those constitutions was left of
which the United States was bound to take notice."[114] Lacking a legitimate
state constitution, residents of former Confederate states no longer had the
means of self-government. They were members of "disorganized communities, without civil government, and without constitutions or other forms
by virtue of which political relations could legally exist between them."[115]
Secession obliterated state rights without altering the duties of the people
in the seceding states to their fellow citizens in the Union. The committee
report stated "while they can destroy their State governments, and place
themselves beyond the pale of the Union, so far as the exercise of State
privileges is concerned, they cannot escape the obligations imposed upon
them by the Constitution and the laws, nor impair the exercise of national
authority."[116] Congress could tax rebels and emancipate their slaves because
secession did not affect federal constitutional or statutory law. Lacking
legitimate state governments, but still bound to the federal government,
Southern people were "reduced to the condition of enemies conquered by
war."[117]

The federal government was responsible for reconstructing former Confederate states so that they could again be represented in Congress. The
notion that popular majorities in rebellious states could decide unilaterally
at any point to resume their status as states in the Union was nonsense. The
Republicans on the Joint Committee wrote:

It is more than idle, it is a mockery to contend that a people who have thrown off their allegiance, destroyed the local government which bound their States to the Union as members thereof, defied its authority, refused to execute its laws, and abrogated every provision which gave them political rights within the Union, still retain through all, the perfect and entire right to resume, at their own will and pleasure, all their privileges within the Union, and especially to participate in its government, and to control the conduct of its affairs.[118]

Congress was the federal institution vested by the Guarantee Clause and other constitutional provisions with the authority to determine by legislation when former Confederate states could be restored to their antebellum status. The national legislature had "the authority to fix the political relations of the States to the Union" in light of the "duty . . . to guarantee to each State a republican form of government, and to protect each and all of them against foreign or domestic violation, and against each other."[119] The House and Senate when reconstructing former Confederate states required various guarantees or securities. The committee report spoke of "[t]he necessity of providing adequate safeguards for the future, before restoring the insurrectionary States to a participation in the direction of public affairs."[120] After elaborating at great length the case for congressional Reconstruction, the report very briefly and without explanation set out the guarantees and securities contained in the proposed Fourteenth Amendment.[121]

Most Republicans agreed with Democrats that secession was legally impossible[122] but insisted that secession had substantial legal consequences. Secession, the House by a 102–36 vote resolved, "deprived the people of the States in which it was organized of all civil government."[123] "[A] people who were habitually disobedient to their own laws," Representative Samuel Shellabarger of Ohio claimed, "is blotted out."[124] Proponents of congressional Reconstruction insisted that the secession ordinances "forfeited" the rights of the seceding states to representation in Congress.[125] Stevens on December 18, 1865, declared "the late rebel States have lost their constitutional relations to the Union[] and are incapable of representation in Congress, except by permission of the Government."[126] A far more conservative Republican, Representative Columbus Delano of Ohio, endorsed the Republican leadership's efforts to prevent representatives from those states that attempted secession from being seated in the House or Senate. He maintained that the "proper relations" of the former Confederate states had "been so interrupted and changed as to deprive them of the absolute right to demand the admissions of members to this floor without conditions and proper qualifications for membership."[127]

Secession deprived the former Confederate states of every right as states in the Union, not just the right to be represented in Congress. A state by "rebellion," Windom insisted, "abrogates all its rights and privileges in the Union."[128] States that were out of the Union did not count toward determining whether the Thirteenth Amendment was constitutionally ratified. Sumner pointed to the constitutional requirement that amendments be submitted to "the Legislatures of the several States." Only Union states, he continued, could ratify the proposed constitutional ban on slavery because the former Confederate states, "by reason of rebellion, were without Legislatures."[129] Stevens sought to "establish a principle that none of the rebel States shall be counted in any of the amendments of the Constitution until they are duly admitted into the family of States by the law-making power of their conqueror."[130] Excluding former Confederate states from the constitutional reform enterprise was crucial to the success of that endeavor. Stevens asked fellow Republicans "whether they believe [any proposed constitutional amendment] could be adopted if the eleven confederate States are to be counted as States in making the requisite three fourths."[131] Representative Ebenezer Dumont of Indiana elaborated on the case for not permitting states that passed secession ordinances to participate in the amendment process when declaring:

> How wrong it is not to admit South Carolina at once in order that the constitutional amendments now pending may be defeated! If admitted she would aid in their defeat in two ways. First, she would vote against them; and second, she must be counted as one of the States, and the amendment must be ratified by three fourths of the States, counting her in as one.[132]

Republicans reached no consensus on the precise mechanisms by which secession deprived jurisdictions of their rights as states in the Union. Proponents of congressional Reconstruction claimed that the former Confederate states had reverted to territories[133] or otherwise "ceased to be States,"[134] were "entitled to no other appellation than that of conquered country,"[135] were "disorganized,"[136] "disconnected,"[137] or dead states,[138] perhaps from committing "suicide."[139] Former confederate states had "vacated their rights . . . as State organizations,"[140] had their "rights and powers . . . impaired,"[141] were experiencing a "lapse" of government,[142] were "suspended,"[143] "paralyzed,"[144] had all legitimate government "destroyed,"[145] or had been "usurped."[146] Such states no longer had any government[147] or

lacked a republican form of government that was constitutionally authorized to send representatives to the national legislature.[148] Senator James W.
Nye maintained that former Confederate states were guilty of "treason" and
could "be politically punished" by having the "State government . . . taken
away."[149] Many Republicans quoted or paraphrased Abraham Lincoln's
claim that the former Confederate states were out of "practical relations
with the Union."[150]

Republicans displayed the same ecumenical spirit when considering
whether the former Confederate states remained states. Some Republicans
insisted secession destroyed statehood. "I do not admit that these eleven
once States are for present purposes of Government to be recognized as
States," Boutwell asserted.[151] Representative Sidney Clarke of Kansas stated
"the rebellious States are out of the Union so far as any right exists on the
part of said States to claim anything from the Federal Government."[152] Others insisted that secession deprived a state of rights and privileges but not
statehood. Senator Henry Wilson of Massachusetts argued: "These States
are members of the Union, but their practical relations with the Government
are not yet completely established."[153] Representative Henry L. Dawes of
Massachusetts maintained: "They have always been States, but States disorganized, and therefore unable to elect Representatives."[154]

Proponents of congressional Reconstruction made little effort to resolve
these academic differences over the status of former Confederate states.
Most Republicans acknowledged that maintaining the party consensus that
such states as South Carolina and that state's partners in crime had no right
to be represented in Congress was far more important that developing a
party consensus on the theory that best justified the exclusion resolution.
Bingham declared: "I care not whether the President says that their functions are suspended or whether he says that they have ceased to be States for
municipal purposes, it is one and the same thing in law."[155] Senator Timothy
O. Howe of Wisconsin agreed. "Nor do I think it worthwhile for the great
Union party to divide," he stated, "upon the question whether the Constitution requires us to say that the functions of a State in a given emergency
are 'suspended' or 'destroyed.'"[156] Republicans were indifferent as to how
party members conceptualized former Confederate states. Representative
Martin Welker of Ohio refrained from discussing "whether they shall be
regarded as mere Territories[] or as States with 'suspended vitality.'"[157] David Burdick petitioned Congress "to spend no more time in discussing the
theory whether rebellious States are in or out of the Union" and to "immediately use our power to protect the loyal from oppression."[158]

Former Confederate states had no more capacity to declare unilaterally the Civil War was over than to undo unilaterally the legal consequences of secession. The Civil War ended only when a Congress controlled by Republicans declared that the Civil War had ended. "Congress . . . alone," Senator Jacob Howard of Michigan stated, as "the war-making and war-conducting power . . . can recognize or reestablish the state of peace after a state of war has intervened."[159] Presidential power to declare and end martial law was not a power to determine when a rebellion was over. "The President might exercise a temporary military power," Sumner declared, "but Congress must lay the foundations of permanent peace."[160]

Proponents of congressional Reconstruction thought the secession crisis remained in full bloom. Professor Gregory Downs observes: "Congressional Republicans . . . united around the idea that the country remained in a 'time or war.'"[161] Dawes spoke for his partisan peers when insisting that the former Confederate states "are still in rebellion, or not yet sufficiently out of it."[162]

If, as everyone agreed, rebel states could send not representatives to Congress during the Civil War,[163] then those states could not be represented in Congress until the Civil War was officially over. Former Confederate states were entitled to representation only "[w]hen the war of rebellion is closed and peace is proclaimed," Representative Benjamin F. Loan of Missouri declared when explaining his vote for the exclusion resolution.[164] No such cease-fire had been declared. Republicans, Senator Lyman Trumbull of Illinois stated, had not yet "seen . . . the angel of peace."[165]

Congress determined when rebellious states could be represented in the national union.[166] "[I]f you test this proposition by the simplest principles of constitutional law," Senator John Sherman of Ohio stated, "there can appear no doubt that Congress has sole and exclusive power over this subject."[167] Senator Benjamin F. Wade of Ohio bluntly proclaimed that "it is for Congress and nobody else to settle."[168] This congressional power included the power to set conditions for restoration and the power to determine whether these conditions had been met. Trumbull insisted that "it is proper, and the only proper way, for Congress by joint action to determine whether after a State government has been overthrown in any of the States the new organization which has been set up is entitled to representation or not."[169] Congress, Sumner agreed, assessed "when that state of things existed which would entitle the rebel States to perform their functions as integral parts of the Union."[170]

The Guarantee Clause of Article IV provided the main foundation for congressional power. Colfax, upon being chosen Speaker of the House, informed his peers, "[r]epresenting, in its two branches, the States and the people, [Congress's] first and highest obligation is to guaranty to every State a republican form of government."[171] Official edicts emphasized the Guarantee Clause as the basis of congressional Reconstruction. The House of Representatives on February 19, 1866, by a 104–35 vote approved a resolution offered by Representative John W. Longyear of Michigan declaring, "whenever the people of any State are thus 'deprived of all civil government,' it becomes the duty of Congress . . . to enable them to organize a State government, and in the language of the constitution to guaranty to such State a republican form of government."[172] Sumner elaborated on the Guarantee Clause in his numerous and lengthy Senate speeches. He insisted that "it has become the duty of Congress . . . to provide governments, republican in form, for such States"[173] and that "Congress must . . . determine what is a republican form of government."[174] Republican backbenchers shared this enthusiasm for Article IV, Section 4. "It is just as much our duty," Representative Sidney Perham of Maine declared, "to see that the government of a State continues republican in form as to require it as a condition of admission."[175]

Republicans were as ecumenical on the source of congressional power as they were on the status of former Confederate states. Sumner thought the war power supplemented the Guarantee Clause as authorization for congressional control of rebel states. Giving a eulogy for Senator Jacob Collamer of Vermont, he quoted Collamer's insistence that "when reestablishing the conditions of peace with that people, Congress, representing the United States, has power in ending this war as any other war to get some security for the future."[176] Stevens thought the congressional power to admit new states provided the source of legislative power. "They must come in as new States or remain as conquered provinces," he informed Congress. "Congress—the Senate and House of Representatives, with the concurrence of the President—is the only power that can act in the matter."[177] A later speech pointed to international law. "[T]he law of nations, which is a part of the Constitution," Stevens stated on May 1, 1866, "enables us to govern conquered provinces."[178] Representative Halbert E. Paine of Wisconsin thought the Territorial Clause was relevant. "If in the judgment of Congress it shall be necessary to organize and govern the late rebel States as Territories, upon Congress will devolve the duty of providing for their organization and government."[179] Representative Rufus P. Spalding of Ohio won the overkill award by claiming congressional Reconstruction was an exercise of the power to "'admit new States,' the guarantee clause, the necessary and proper clause, the territorial clause,[180] the power to govern the District of Columbia, and the power 'to make rules concerning captures on land and water.'"[181]

Congressional Reconstruction was not grounded in Article I, Section 5, which declares: "Each House shall be the Judge of the Elections, Returns and Qualifications of its own Members." Republicans who favored exclusion thought President Johnson and his supporters were mistaken when those proponents of presidential Reconstruction limited congressional power over seating representatives to implementing this provision. Properly interpreted, almost all Republicans agreed, Article I, Section 5 concerned only the qualifications of persons to be representatives, not the right of a state to be represented. Article I, Section 5 did not touch on the status of states in the Union, which was central question of Reconstruction and the exclusion resolution. Whether North Carolina in 1865, Texas in 1845, or Finland in 1965 had a right to have representatives in either branch of the national legislature was for the entire Congress to resolve under some combination of the national powers to guarantee republican governments, admit new states, declare war, and govern territories. "It is for Congress to determine," Trumbull stated, "whether there is a State that has a right to send Senators here."[182] Whether a person claiming election had a right to be seated in either the House or the Senate, the subject of Article I, Section 5, raised different considerations and was settled by a different process than whether a state had a right to be represented. The House of Representatives and Senate, acting separately under Article I, Section 5, Trumbull claimed, determined "whether there is a constituency having a right to elect, whether they have sent persons qualified, and whether they have elected them properly."[183] The House decided whether a person claiming to have been elected by a congressional district in Florida was elected by loyal voters, was over twenty-five years old, and had actually won the congressional race. Congress as a whole—the House of Representatives and the Senate—determined whether Florida was a state that could send representations to the House.

Political, as well as constitutional, logic placed primary authority for the former Confederate states in the lawmaking branch of government. Presidential Reconstruction was inappropriate institutionally because the president was not a lawmaker. "It is the province of the President to execute the national will," Howe stated, "not to expound it."[184] Congress was better structured to give members both the knowledge and independence necessary to determine the conditions of reconstruction. Howe declared:

> To Congress it ought to be delegated, because its members coming more directly from the people, and from many different localities, are supposed to be better informed as to what is the popular will than any individual can be. To Congress it ought to be delegated, because

its members have no personal interest in the decision of the question. The people of those revolting districts will have no more and no less influence upon the reelection of the members of these Houses whether the functions of States are restored to them or not.[185]

If treason was the problem, then reconstruction by the branch of government that embodied the faithful was the solution. Nye asserted: "Congress represents the loyalty of the nation, South as well as North."[186]

Representative Ebon C. Ingersoll of Illinois maintained that secession had consequences for former Confederates as well as for former Confederate states, consequences that provided supplemental grounds for congressional Reconstruction. In his view, "the people of the southern States did, by treason and rebellion, become alien enemies to the Government."[187] As noncitizens, traitors had no political rights. "The right to vote was forfeited by the crime of treason," Ingersoll claimed, "and that crime has not been expiated."[188] Congressional action was as necessary for restoring full citizenship as for restoring full statehood. Ingersoll pointed out that "[t]he President cannot change an alien into a citizen. . . . Congress alone is vested with that power."[189] This congressional responsibility for restoring citizenship obligated the national legislature to govern former Confederate states until citizenship was restored. Ingersoll concluded that, "if within any certain State all its inhabitants become alien enemies, the Congress of the United States is alone vested with the power to establish a government for them, to make laws for them, to control them so long as they shall remain alien enemies."[190]

Congress required "adequate security"[191] or "guarantees"[192] before restoring former Confederate states and repatriating former Confederate citizens. H. Wilson "demand[ed] the amplest of guarantees for the future."[193] Numerous petitions and remonstrances railed "against the admission of southern States until proper guarantees are secured"[194] or asked Congress not to allow former Confederate states to be represented in Congress "until adequate security has been obtained against its renewing the attempt to secede."[195] Sumner offered a petition from citizens of Massachusetts calling for "security for the future" and "irreversible guarantees."[196]

Returning local control to residents of former Confederate states would be catastrophic, almost all Republicans believed, until a strong reform package was adopted. Representative Fernando Cortez Beaman of Michigan maintained that "admit[ting] without delay these traitors direct from the battlefield" would enable them to "attempt to accomplish by political skill and dark intrigue what they failed to do by the sword."[197] Members of the majority party warned that the Civil War would have been in vain should

Reconstruction be prematurely abandoned. "It is our duty, as statesmen, by wise and considerate measures," Representative Reader W. Clarke of Ohio stated, "to secure the country the fruits of victory achieved by our arms."[198] Given the opportunity, representatives from the slave states to Congress would join with Democrats to defeat any subsequent constitutional proposal and probably any subsequent statutory proposal that protected Southern Unionists, persons of color, Northern creditors, persons entitled to Civil War pensions, and others who had remained loyal during the Civil War. Representative John M. Broomall of Pennsylvania asked: "[C]an we safely entrust to these governments the rights and interests of the Union men of the South?"[199]

A consensus quickly formed that these guarantees and securities should at least be partly embodied in amendments to the Constitution of the United States. A few Republicans proponents of congressional Reconstruction during the first days of the Thirty-Ninth Congress called for state constitutional reform while demanding far more extensive and secure conditions than President Johnson and his supporters did when championing state constitutional reform. Sumner on December 4, 1865, insisted that popular majorities in the seceding states had to make five promises to the Union for their state to be restored to full status in the Union.[200] Representative John A. Kasson of Iowa called for "a fundamental compact between each of [the seceded] States, and the United States, irrepealable without mutual consent."[201] Within days, federal constitutional and statutory reform took over center stage. Stevens began the congressional debate on Reconstruction by calling for a package of constitutional amendments and federal statutes to be passed before representatives from former Confederate states were seated.[202] Beaman asserted, "We should . . . obtain, by constitutional amendment or otherwise, some guarantee for future good conduct before consenting to place such men in power."[203] A fourteenth amendment, and perhaps fifteenth, sixteenth, and seventeen amendments, together represented a necessary condition for former Confederate states to be granted their previous rights in the Union.

Structure, Race, and Rebels

The debate over the status of former Confederate states was no more a controversy entirely about presidential power than the debate about secession was a controversy entirely about states' rights. South Carolina in 1860 may have proclaimed undying devotion to states' rights, but secession was about slavery.[204] Southerners were enthusiasts for federal power when federal power promoted human bondage.[205] Many Northerners discovered the virtues of nullification when federal officers sought to implement federal fugitive slave laws.[206] Sincere commitments to certain structural principles were in short supply during and immediately after the Civil War. Democrats who vigorously championed presidential Reconstruction were hardly enthusiasts for presidential power during the Civil War.[207] Many Republicans who would eventually seek to impeach President Johnson for abuses of executive authority from 1860 to 1865 felt differently when Lincoln was exercising presidential power. Most approved the Emancipation Proclamation while objecting to Lincoln's more lenient proposals for Reconstruction.[208] Party members divided over whether the president could suspend habeas corpus unilaterally.[209] Had Stevens assumed the presidency after Lincoln's assassination and implemented his preferred Reconstruction program by executive decree, the congressional debate over the separation of powers issues raised by the exclusion resolution would likely have had a very different partisan structure.

Events immediately before and during the Civil War also cast doubt on whether different commitments to racial equality fully explain political divisions over Reconstruction policies. Eric Foner famously notes that more Northerners opposed the slave power than slavery.[210] Republicans gained adherents because they convinced voters in free states that human bondage threatened the interests of Northern whites and violated the rights of enslaved persons of color. "We want [the territories] for the homes of free white people," Abraham Lincoln notoriously asserted.[211] The heroics of Black soldiers on the battlefield generated a surge in support for racial equality in Union states.[212] Still, as will be detailed in coming chapters, while Republicans during the Thirty-Ninth Congress expressed similar commitments to the rights of loyal Blacks that they had once expressed to the rights of Black slaves, concerns for Black freedmen were as entwined with concerns for white persons as had been concerns for Black slaves.

Differences over the location of constitutional reforms may best capture the most fundamental divide between proponents of presidential Reconstruction and congressional Reconstruction. To a fair degree, proponents of presidential Reconstruction and congressional Reconstruction demanded similar substantive guarantees from former Confederate states. Former Confederate states were expected to repudiate secession, abolish slavery, foreswear repayment of the Confederate debt, and elect loyal state and federal officials. President Johnson and some of his political allies even acknowledged that persons of color should enjoy certain fundamental rights. Proponents of presidential Reconstruction, however, trusted defeated secessionists to adopt and maintain these commitments. They argued that, after ratification of the Thirteenth Amendment, all that was needed was state constitutional and statutory reform. President Johnson and his political allies looked southward and saw prodigal sons who had repented of their error and were eager to resume playing the constitutional game by the constitutional rules. Proponents of congressional Reconstruction had no faith in defeated secessionists. They insisted on federal constitutional and statutory reform. Stevens and his political allies looked southward and saw rebels making insincere commitments in order to regain the control over state and national governments necessary to resume their nefarious schemes against loyal Blacks, loyal Southerners, loyal creditors, and the loyal people of the North who had joined the Republican Party's crusade to save the Union.

The Problem of Rebel Rule

The debates over presidential and congressional Reconstruction that took place in the wake of the Civil War were part of a broader sectional struggle over control of the South and control of the Union. Former slaveholders, inverting Clausewitz, treated constitutional politics as war by other means. Representative Benjamin F. Loan of Missouri insisted:

> Defeated but not conquered, subdued but not subjugated, their determination to destroy this Government and to erect another on its ruins, the chief corner-stone of which is to be African slavery, remains as fixed and steadfast as it was when they embarked in rebellion in 1860–61. The decision of war to which they first appealed having been given against them, they seek to transfer the contest to the Halls of the grand council of the nation, into which their chosen agents are now demanding admission, and where it is hoped, if they can once enter, they can by diplomacy and fraud achieve that success which they failed to secure by force.[1]

Representative Samuel W. Moulton of Illinois pointed out that while "rebels admit that they have been conquered in the field, . . . they insist that they can obtain by diplomacy, craft, and fraud all that they desire."[2] The Republican and Unionist members of the Thirty-Ninth Congress who supported the exclusion resolution and the Fourteenth Amendment shared this fear that the Union was in danger of winning the war but losing the peace. Representative John R. Kelso from Missouri warned: "If the rebels are allowed to vote, their ballots will be cast for our destruction, as their bullets have heretofore been, and it may be with more fatal effect."[3] "[T]he rebels are seeking to gain by the ballot," a Unionist Arkansas paper agreed, "what they could not gain by the bullet."[4]

Proponents of congressional Reconstruction had good reason to believe that postwar constitutional politics might transform the Thirteenth Amendment into a parchment barrier in much the same way that antebellum constitutional politics, as manifested most notably by *Dred Scott v. Sandford*[5] and the Kansas–Nebraska Act,[6] had perverted what they perceived were the antislavery commitments of the original Constitution.[7] Republicans regularly heard reports from the South detailing how former slaveowners planned to dominate the country by renewing their previous alliances with Northern Democrats. This alliance, if successfully consummated, would enable former Confederates to circumvent the Thirteenth Amendment and otherwise prevent Union states from enjoying the material and ideological fruits of their battlefield victory. Republicans learned to their horror that they had inadvertently empowered this conspiracy when ratifying the constitutional ban on slavery. The Thirteenth Amendment, by repealing for all practical purposes the Three-Fifths Clause of the Constitution, threatened to undermine the constitutional politics necessary to make the amendment a living reality. If the basis of apportionment was not changed, then former (and future) slaveholders would increase their seats in the House of Representatives and votes in the Electoral College, because disenfranchised persons of color would count as full persons when the federal government allocated representation in these institutions. These extra votes might easily provide the margins rebels need to control the national government and regain in peace what had been lost in war.

The status of free slaves was only one of the numerous problems Republicans perceived when they looked southward. The proponents of congressional Reconstruction who were responsible for the Fourteenth Amendment expressed at least six concerns with the future direction of constitutional politics in the United States.

- Southerners remained as hostile to Union and as committed to the principles underlying secession in 1866 as they had been in 1860–1861.
- A largely unreconstructed Southern electorate was staffing state and federal offices with the same persons who led the fight for secession in Southern legislative chambers and on blood-soaked Southern battlefields.
- Unreconstructed Southerners in control of state governments were engaging in or turning a blind eye to a merciless campaign against white Unionists.
- Unreconstructed Southerners in control of state governments were

adopting public policies or turning a blind eye to private devices for practically re-enslaving persons of color.

- Unreconstructed Southerners, aided by the repeal of the Three-Fifths Clause, were seeking to control the national government through an alliance with unrepentant Democrats. Such control would solidify unreconstructed Southern rule at home and secure national policies or national toleration of state policies that compensated former slaveholders, repudiated the Union war debt, abandoned obligations to Union soldiers and their survivors, assumed or paid the Confederate war debt, and honored obligations to Confederate soldiers and their survivors.

If unreconstructed Southerners could not achieve their goals politically, they might repeat their secessionist experiment under more fortuitous circumstances or involve the United States in a foreign war.

The fears that animated congressional Reconstruction were united by the dread of rebel rule. Republicans insisted that former rebels would dominate an unreconstructed South. Disloyal former Confederates in state governments would persecute loyal white Unionists and devise a forced labor system for controlling loyal persons of color. Disloyal Confederates in the national government, uniting with disloyal Copperhead Democrats, would ruin the national credit by funneling money to former slaveholders rather than paying the national debt. History threatened to repeat the constitutional politics of the previous decade, without the happy ending. Either the slave power would regain control of the national government, or Southern states would again secede—this time successfully.

The broad concerns with rebel rule expressed by proponents of congressional Reconstruction outside and inside Congress belie the common claim that the Fourteenth Amendment or Section 1 of the amendment was "in large part a reaction to the[] . . . Black Codes."[8] The Black Codes played an important role in Republican thinking about Reconstruction and the problems of rule by disloyal rebels. Numerous Republicans mentioned those laws as demonstrating that Southern elites were not reconciled to the outcome of the Civil War. Nevertheless, Northerners no more viewed the problem of rebel rule entirely through the prism of racial equality than they had viewed the antebellum slave power entirely through the prism of Black rights.[9] While some Republicans' speeches on Reconstruction policy emphasized the plight of Southern Blacks, others stressed the fate of loyal Southern whites. Most proponents pointed to numerous baneful consequences should former Confederates regain state and national power. Members of the majority party in the Thirty-Ninth Congress had as great a tendency to express concern that rebel rule would imperil Northern finance as brutalize Southern Blacks. Treating Black Codes as the primary target of the Fourteenth Amendment is analogous to treating a circus as primarily about clowns, a treatment that ignores both the other performers and performances and, as important, how a circus is constructed by the ways in which the clowns interact with the other performers and performances.

What's in a Word: "Rebel"

The use of "rebel/rebels" as an adjective and as a noun highlights the commonalities and divisions that structured debate over Reconstruction and the Fourteenth Amendment in the Thirty-Ninth Congress. The frequency with which almost all members used "rebel" as a noun and adjective captures the consensus in Congress that secession was wrong and that the former Confederate/rebel states had no right to leave the Union. President Andrew Johnson and his political allies typically spoke of "rebels" only when referring to past events. Those Republicans and Unionists who supported congressional Reconstruction and the Fourteenth Amendment were far more likely to refer to "rebels" than the proponents of presidential Reconstruction and, more important, far more inclined to speak of present "rebels" than their partisan rivals. Representative Thaddeus Stevens of Pennsylvania and his political allies spoke of "rebels" as an omnipresence in the constitutional politics of the here-and-now. The linguistic divide in the Thirty-Ninth Congress was whether most white residents in the former Confederate states were or merely had been "rebels."

Tables A.3, A.4, A.5, and A.6 detail how, with important exceptions, Republicans, Unionists, and Democrats, proponents and opponents of the Fourteenth Amendment, and proponents and opponents of congressional Reconstruction all used "rebel" as a noun or adjective at some point. Almost all representatives and senators who spoke for an hour or more on a subject related to Reconstruction made a reference to "rebel/s." Many did not need a germaneness excuse. The few representatives and senators who did not use "rebel" in a speech rarely if ever spoke during the first session of the Thirty-Ninth Congress.

The common use of "rebel" reflected the broad antipathy to secession in the Thirty-Ninth Congress. The members repeatedly referred to South Carolina and allied jurisdictions as "rebel states." Senator James W. Grimes of Iowa, a Republican, was one of many senators who routinely spoke of "the condition of the rebel States."[10] Senator Thomas A. Hendricks of Indiana, a Democrat, referred to "all questions in relation to the rebel States."[11] Democrats and Republicans agreed that Robert E. Lee commanded a "rebel army."[12] Representative Andrew J. Rogers of New Jersey, a Democrat, detailed how New Jersey volunteers "saved the capital of the neighboring State of Pennsylvania from capture by rebel forces."[13] Representative Elihu B. Washburne of Illinois, a Republican, described how during the Battle of the Wilderness "in the lines of the rebel center" there was a "prolonged and terrific rebel shout and hiss."[14] This consensus that the South had rebelled generated an important policy consequence. Broad agreement existed that Confederate loans were a "rebel debt" and that this "rebel debt" should not be paid. Rogers "understood it to be one of the principal axioms of the parties on both sides of the House to discountenance . . . any assumption for the payment of the rebel debt, either of any of the rebel States, or of the so-called confederate government."[15]

Proponents of presidential Reconstruction differed in the frequency with which they used "rebel" as a noun or adjective. President Johnson's Republican allies and Unionists from Kentucky, most notably Senator Garrett Davis and Representative Green C. Smith, employed "rebel" as frequently as proponents of congressional Reconstruction. The Senate Democrats who spoke most frequently against the exclusion resolution, Senators Reverdy Johnson of Maryland, Willard Saulsbury, Sr., of Delaware, and Hendricks hardly ever used "rebel" as a noun or adjective, even when making long speeches against Republican policy. The House Democrats who spoke most frequently in debates on Reconstruction, Rogers and Representative William E. Finck of Ohio, used "rebel" more frequently than did Senate Democrats, though far less frequently compared to Republican opponents of the exclusion resolution and to Unionists from Kentucky.

Proponents of presidential Reconstruction usually limited their use of "rebel" to describe the past. Kentuckians sometimes spoke of present "rebels" in their state when comparing them to the more numerous loyalists. Smith complained about policies that "incarcerate good Union men and allow rebels to go free."[16] President Johnson's allies who represented states or districts other than or outside of Kentucky more often restricted their use of "rebel" to describe persons or events that took place during the secession crisis or the Civil War. Senator James R. Doolittle of Wisconsin used "rebel" with some frequency when discussing the recent past, but he almost never used "rebel" to describe present persons, groups, or actions. The "rebel Governor of Tennessee" held office during the Civil War while an "open rebel" campaigned for a state judgeship,[17] but the senators-elect from Tennessee did not represent a "rebel constituency" or a "rebel state." Opponents of the exclusion resolution used "rebel" with some frequency when rejecting claims that persons or groups were presently disloyal to the United States or when criticizing Republican uses of "rebel." Senator James Guthrie of Kentucky did "not pretend to deny" that "there have been rebels and disloyal persons in the State of Kentucky," but he insisted that the state was "not in the hands of rebels."[18] Democrats chaffed when Republicans called them disloyal. Representative Samuel Randall of Pennsylvania, when urging that the loyal people of former Confederate states be represented in Congress, declared: "I am no defender either of rebels or of the rebellion."[19]

Republican proponents of the exclusionary resolution repeatedly referred to "rebels,"[20] "rebel States,"[21] the "rebel debt,"[22] and "rebel voters."[23] Representative George W. Julian of Indiana spoke of "rebel representation" and the "rebel class."[24] Representative John F. Benjamin of Missouri referred to the "rebel element."[25] Senator John B. Henderson of Missouri decried "rebel influence" and "rebel tyranny."[26] After pointing out that "the Governor of Alabama was appointing two rebel Senators judges of the supreme court," Senator Richard Yates of Illinois maintained: "We know that the only passport to southern office, to the Legislature and to Congress, is fidelity in the rebel army and in the rebel cause."[27] Senator Henry Wilson of Massachusetts compared the Republican "struggle to put rebels under the laws of the country" with the Democratic "struggle to enable rebels to frame the laws of the country."[28] Senator Henry S. Lane of Indiana "tremble[d] in view of the evil consequences which would result, from the admission of rebel members, to your national debt, to the national credit, the plighted faith of the nation to your invalid soldiers, the plighted faith of the nation to your living and dead heroes."[29] Many Republicans gave speeches that used "rebel" more than twenty-five times.[30] Moulton and Loan battled for the record by using "rebel" as a noun or adjective sixty-five and sixty times, respectively, in what appear to have been less than two-hour speeches.[31] Republican speakers repeated "rebel" in rapid succession when emphasizing the threat of rebel rule. Representative Reader W. Clarke of Ohio captured many Republican uses of "rebel" when he stated:

> If we propose to sponge out the rebel debt, we are told it would violate the Constitution. If we propose to disfranchise leading rebels who have been conspicuous in treason, we are told it would be unconstitutional. If we propose equalizing representation in Congress so that a South Carolina rebel shall at most, not possess more political power than

a loyal Ohioan, we are told it would be unconstitutional. If we propose to amend the Constitution, without first inviting the whole rebel delegation to seats in this body, it is denounced as unconstitutional.[32]

The above quotations demonstrate the Republicans' propensity for using "rebel" as a noun or adjective to describe persons or events in the present or future. The "rebel representation," "rebel class," "rebel representation," "rebel Senators," "rebel army," "rebel cause," "rebel members," "rebel debt," "leading rebels," "a South Carolina rebel," and "the whole rebel delegation" either existed in 1866 or might exist shortly thereafter. Representative Samuel Shellabarger of Ohio captured the frequent and present use of "rebel" when pointing to the dire consequences of a national government and state governments staffed by traitors. He asked:

[H]ow long may this nation survive with a Senate elected by rebel Legislatures; or with treaties made by Senators chosen by rebel States; or with a President selected by electors chosen by the Legislature of South Carolina; or with a President elected in a House of Representatives where each rebel State casts one vote; or with a House of Representatives elected by electors whom a rebel legislature would authorize to vote; or with officers over United States forces appointed by rebel governors; or with such constitutional amendments as would be ratified by rebel legislatures; or with a traitor for President whom you could only remove by the impeachment of a Senate elected by rebel legislatures; or with such foreign ministers and other officers of the United States as such a Senate would confirm; or with a prohibition upon your closing the ports of the eleven rebel States to a commerce supplying them with all the supplies of war, unless you also closed all the ports of the other States?[33]

The South was rebels all the way down, and those rebels remained a threat to constitutional government in the United States.

The difference between Republicans' and Democrats' uses of "rebel" captures the fundamental problem of Reconstruction that the Fourteenth Amendment was designed to resolve. If Republicans were correct that rebels in 1866 still existed in substantial numbers, then how could loyal Americans prevent a repeat of the secession experiment that had taken place in 1860? More to the point: If rebels in 1866 still existed in substantial numbers, how could Republicans prevent the renaissance of the slave power that they believed had governed the United States before 1860?

The Postwar South

Members of the Thirty-Ninth Congress were deluged by on-the-ground bulletins from free-state journalists, Southern correspondents, Unionist memorialists, and African American petitioners detailing how the slave power intended to win the peace what was lost in the war. Northern reporters who toured the South described how "the Slave South, though vanquished, was unbowed, and . . . its people intended to re[-]create its prewar system as closely as they could[] and then return to dominate the Union."³⁴ Many senators and representatives corresponded with Southern elites, who confirmed and elaborated on the evidence journalists provided of ongoing disloyalty in the former Confederate states. The provisional governor H. G. Brownlow of Tennessee informed Representative Jehu Baker of Illinois: "I believe the whole South is full of rebellion, and that the rebels are seeking to accomplish by legislation and through Congress what they failed to do upon the field of carnage—destroy the Government."³⁵ A. Warren Kelsey informed Senator Charles Sumner of Massachusetts: "They have simply changed their base from the battle-field to the ballot box, believing, as they very frankly admit, that greater triumphs await them there than they could ever hope for in the field."³⁶ Southern Unionists issued memorials depicting a South that had been defeated only in martial combat. A memorial from Tennessee Unionists stated:

> The designs of the great secession majority of Tennessee may have changed by the events of the war, and so may have been their opinions of their own strength, and of the strength of the Government, but unless your memorialists greatly misunderstand them, their sentiments, sympathies, and passions remain unchanged. They welcome peace because they are disabled from making war; they submit because they can no long resist; they accept results they cannot reject, and profess loyalty because they have a halter around their necks. They recognize the abolition of slavery because they see it before them as a fact; but they say it was accomplished by gross violations of the Constitution— that the negro is free only in fact, but not in law, or of right.³⁷

African American petitioners described the brutality of white Southerners who refused to admit either defeat or the birth of a new, more egalitarian racial order. The delegates at the Colored People's Convention of the State of South Carolina issued a "Declaration of Rights and Wrongs":

> We have been deprived of the free exercise of political rights, of natural, civil, and political liberty.

The avenues of wealth and education have been closed to us.

The strong wall of prejudice, on the part of the dominant race, has obstructed our pursuit of happiness.

We have been subjected to cruel proscription, and our bodies have been outraged with impunity.

We have been, and still are, deprived of the free choice of those who should govern us, and subjected unjustly to taxation without representation, and have bled and sweat for the elevation of those who have degraded us, and still continue to oppress us.[38]

The Civil War transformed enslaved people into oppressed people, but to journalists, memorialists, correspondents, and petitioners the war otherwise appeared to have had little impact on Southern race relations and political culture.

THE PAST AND PRESENT AS PROLOGUE

Journalists, correspondents, memorialists, and petitioners informed national officials that former rebels expected that their near future would resemble their disloyal past. Carl Schurz, who was sent to the South on a fact-finding mission by President Johnson, stated that "one reason why the southern people are so slow in accommodating themselves to the new order of things is[] that they confidently expect soon to be permitted to regulate matters according to their own notions."[39] "[T]he men who tried hardest to break up the Government," a South Carolinian wrote, wished to "recommence the agitation with their tongues, and by their arguments and votes."[40] Those Unionists who celebrated apparent victory on the battlefield were dangerously unaware that the war had at most paused and certainly had not ended. A correspondent observed:

[T]he spirit of rebellion is not dead, and will never die while Democratic leaders in the South are relieved of their treachery and turned loose to stir up sedition and to incite rebellion. The men make loud professions of loyalty, and their press reverberates the echo from hill and valley, but you have only to read their fanfaronades on loyalty to satisfy yourselves of the bitter hatred that fills their breasts against the Union, and the burning hate with which they will proceed to pour out the vials of their wrath upon all Union men, when once they can secure seats in Congress and get possession of the reins of State government. In their hearts they cling as ardently to State sovereignty as ever, and once give them the power . . . they will tax the loyal people to the full value of the slave property destroyed by the war.[41]

Former Confederates might take several paths to final victory. Restoration might be done peaceably. The journalist Sidney Andrews noted a resolution at the South Carolina constitutional convention declaring that, "under the present extraordinary circumstances, it is both wise and politic to accept the condition in which we are placed; to endure patiently the evils which we cannot avert or correct; and to await calmly the time and opportunity to effect our deliverance from unconstitutional evils." History might repeat with a second attempt at secession and a second civil war. Southerners, the journalist John Trowbridge thought, were committed to "reviv[ing] the cause of the Confederacy whenever there should occur a favorable opportunity."[42] Both peaceful and military options remained on the former Confederates' table. Kelsey observed that "if the northern people are content to be ruled over by the southerners they will continue in the Union; if not, the first chance they get they will rise again."[43]

Surrender had not altered the fundamental values of Southern elites. Nullification, secession, and state sovereignty remained their core commitments. "The State rights heresy" was almost as dominant in the first round of Southern constitutional conventions held in 1865, correspondents found, "as in that of 1861."[44] Andrews informed Northern readers that "[t]he supremacy of the Constitution of the United States is formally acknowledged, but the common conversation of all classes asserts the supremacy of the State." He pointed to "an open enunciation of the supremacy of the State over the general government."[45] Kelsey insisted that "so far as secession is concerned, that is, the doctrine of State rights, it is more deeply rooted than ever among them"[46] Home rule remained the first tenet in the Southern catechism. The journalist Whitelaw Reid reported the blunt sentiment that "Louisiana must be governed by Louisianians."[47]

Home rule was tied to racial subordination. "[N]inety-nine in every hundred of the men, women, and children." Kelsey wrote, "believe sincerely . . . that the South of right possesses and always possessed the right of secession" and "that negro slavery was and is right."[48] A Union military officer stationed in the South observed that "[t]heir preference for the 'divine institution,' and their intellectual belief in the right of a State to secede, are as much articles of faith in their creed at the present moment as they were on the day when the ordinance of secession was unanimously adopted." He concluded: "Their political principles, as well as their views on the slavery question, are the same as before the war."[49]

Southerners committed to states' rights were as unrepentant and as sectionalist as ever. "Treason," Schurz reported, "does, under existing conditions, not appear odious in the south."[50] Virginia unionists asserted: "They assume that they have done no wrong but acted nobly and honorably in rebelling against the Government of the United States."[51] Loyalty was a very scarce commodity in former Confederate states. A correspondent from Virginia wrote that "[t]he feeling of disloyalty is as strong here now as it was during the war."[52] The journalist John Richard Denning stated that "[t]he vast majority of the people were as disloyal . . . as we may suppose them to have been in 1862."[53] Military defeat aggravated disloyal sentiments among former Confederates. Brownlow informed Representative Schuyler Colfax of Indiana, the Speaker of the House, that "[t]hose who suppose the South is 'reconstructed,' and that her people cheerfully accept the results of the war are fearfully deceived. The whole South is full of the spirit of rebellion and the people are growing more bitter and insolent every day."[54]

Correspondents found little evidence of nationalism during their Southern tours. Schurz noted "an entire absence of that national spirit which forms the basis of true loyalty and patriotism."[55] "[T]here is, as yet, among the southern people," he wrote,

> an utter absence of national feeling. I made it a business, while in the south, to watch the symptoms of "returning loyalty" as they appeared not only in private conversation, but in the public press and in the speeches delivered and the resolutions passed at Union meetings. Hardly ever was there an expression of hearty attachment to the great republic, or an appeal to the impulses of patriotism; but whenever submission to the national authority was declared and advocated, it was almost uniformly placed upon two principal grounds: That, under present circumstances, the southern people could "do no better"; and then that submission was the only means by which they could rid themselves of the federal soldiers and obtain once more control of their own affairs.[56]

Defeated Southerners routinely expressed deep antipathy to the national government, the North, Northerners, and persons of color identified with the Northern war effort. Denning described "the general feeling of hostility to the Government."[57] Sumner quoted a correspondent who declared that "the spirit of the people [is] more hostile to the Government than at the breaking out of the war."[58] Southern hatred of the North was intensifying. A correspondent informed Schurz: "The political and commercial combinations against the north are gaining in strength and confidence every day. Political, sectional, and local questions, that I had hoped were buried with the dead of the past four years, are revived."[59] This hostility extended to Northerners and persons of color who had allied with Northerners. The fictional scenes in *Gone with the Wind* where Melanie Hamilton expresses contempt for all things Northern were regularly reenacted in the actual postbellum South. An officer of the Freedmen's Bureau informed Congress: "Nearly all the females and young men . . . are open and defiant in their expressions of hate for Yankees and negroes."[60] He declared: "There is not one spark of love for the Union in all that I have seen or can judge: but bitter, unrelenting hate, full of the spirit of hell and death to the black man and his white benefactor."[61] All segments of the Southern community united in their loathing for the free states and free-state citizens. A Texas correspondent reported "The minister of the Gospel, of all denominations, the instructors of the youth of the country, the women, and all the young men, all hate the North with a degree of intensity that cannot be exaggerated."[62]

The political commitments of Southern elites had not changed in large part because Southern elites had not changed. Southern politics in 1865 and early 1866 anticipated a popular contemporary rock lyric: "Meet the new boss; same as the old boss." Alabama Unionists observed that "nearly all the offices of the State government are in the hands of those who are hostile to the national Government. Some of the former officers of the confederacy have either been reappointed or reelected by rebel votes."[63] Schurz reported on "the rapid return to power and influence of so many of those who recently were engaged in a bitter war against the Union."[64] Virginia Unionists confirmed Schurz's report. Their memorial to Congress claimed that "the same traitors who had set a price upon the heads of many of us because we were Union men . . . possessed themselves of the political control of affairs within that portion of the lately conquered territory known as Virginia."[65] Service to the Confederate cause was an electoral badge of honor. "No man has a better claim to their sympathy," one of Sumner's correspondents pointed out, "and none stand a better chance of election, than those who were the last to give up."[66] Andrews did not "hear of the success of a single candidate who opposed the war or was even lukewarm in its support, while as between war men the result is generally in favor of the most radical."[67] The transition from Southern rebel to Southern official was often nearly immediate. Reid found that "the men who were taking the offices were the men who had just been relieved of duty under their Rebel commissions."[68] Such persons were committed to "the necessity for giving it up just so much of their old policy as that defeat compelled them to give up — not a whit more."[69]

Electoral practices buttressed the power of long-standing Southern and rebel elites. Former rebels gained power after the war by making the same sectional appeals that had been successful before the war. Sectional rhetoric, if anything, was rising. A South Carolina correspondent reported to Sumner that "[m]ore inflammatory speeches were not made in 1860 than have been delivered during the late canvass."[70] Electoral rules remained subject to manipulation so as to maintain the sectional status quo. Northerners moving to the South had no guarantee that they could cast ballots. Virginia Unionists noted proposals to "disfranchise loyal men by requiring a residence in Virginia of five years[] as a qualification for voting."[71]

Former rebels in power vigorously suppressed what they perceived as Northern heresies. Political dissent, particularly on racial issues, was no more tolerated in the postwar South than in the antebellum South.[72] A Virginian informed Sumner that "it is not safe to speak one's sentiments . . . ; liberty of speech does not exist."[73] A Texas correspondent agreed that "any man of racial views who comes down here to plant cotton will be in constant danger, night and day, unless he holds his tongue."[74] The main difference between the South of 1860 and the South of 1866 was that suppression immediately after the Civil War occurred exclusively through private violence rather than, as had been the case in the antebellum South, partly through public sanction. After noting "[i]t cannot be said that freedom of speech has been fully secured in either of the three States which I have visited," Andrews observed that "any man holding and openly advocating even moderately radical sentiments on the negro question, stands an excellent chance, in many countries of Georgia and South Carolina, of being found dead some morning,—shot from behind, as is the custom of the country."[75] "When [Denning] asked if there is any town in the State where they thought a man might, with safety to his life, publicly advocate, or be generally known to advocate, the propriety of allowing intelligent, educated Negroes to vote, the reply was uniformly in the negative."[76] Former rebels in office and in jury boxes turned a blind eye to the private suppression of speech. A Texas correspondent stated: "If any man from the North comes down here expecting to hold and maintain 'radical' or 'abolition' sentiments, let him expect to be shot down from behind the first time he leaves his house, and know that his murderer, if ever brought to justice, will be acquitted by the jury."[77]

This private violence extended to any person who former Confederates identified with the new post–Civil War order. General George Henry Thomas noted that "two companies of the militia had sworn that in their counties no negro who did not work for his old master, and no Yankee could live; that they would 'drive out the thieving Yankees and shoot'" all African Americans.[78] The New York *Herald* noted that in Georgia "[t]he shooting or stringing up of some obstreperous" former enslaved person "is so common an occurrence as to excite little remark" and that the same perpetrators "make it uncomfortably warm for any new settler with demoralizing innovations of wages for" free persons of color.[79] Freed slaves were routinely victims of organized violence. An officer of the Freedmen's Bureau observed: "You have never conceived of the abuse, the cruelty, the premeditated butchery now practiced upon the colored race in this region and the bordering counties of Texas. Not a day or a night passes but what many victims are murdered by the white confederate citizens." That letter to H. Wilson concluded that a "leading man in this place told me a few days ago that they should not rest till paid for their freed slaves; if they could not get this they would exterminate them."[80]

Former rebels victimized their former slaves with impunity. The Southern *Loyalist* summed up the general attitude of unrepentant Confederates: "If you . . . think I am going to give" former slaves "any rights that you had not under the old State laws, you are damnably mistaken."[81] A petition from freed slaves in Mobile, Alabama, set out a long list of grievances detailing how a combination of public actions, public inactions, and private mayhem threated the existence of Southern free persons of color in the wake of the Civil War:

> [T]hey say that in the city where they were assembled in convention several of their churches had been already burned to the ground by the torch of the incendiary, and threats are frequently made to continue the destruction of their property; the means of education for their children are secured to them only by the strong arm of the United States Government against the marked opposition of their white fellow-citizens, while throughout the whole State the right to participate in the franchises of freemen is denied as insulting to white men, and a respectful appeal addressed by some of their people to the late State convention was scornfully laid upon the table, some of the members even refusing to hear its reading. They also state that many of their people daily suffer almost every form of outrage and violence at the hands of whites; that in many parts of the State their people cannot safely leave the vicinity of their homes; they are knocked down and beaten by their white fellow-citizens without having offered any injury or insult as a cause; they are arrested and imprisoned upon false accusations, their money is extorted for their release, or they are condemned to imprisonment at hard labor; that many of their people are now in a condition of practical slavery, being compelled to serve their former owners without pay and to call them "master."[82]

Correspondents played numerous variations on these themes. They declared that "the negroes have been cruelly treated, not only by the civilians, but also by the civil authorities here"; observed "a most cruel, remorseless and vindictive spirit toward the colored people"; detailed how "they are exposed to unutterable hardship and cruelty"; reported on "the outrages that are being perpetrated upon unoffending colored people by the State militia"; wrote about "cruel grievances that are unredressed"; emphasized the "numberless atrocities that have been perpetrated against the freedmen"; and pointed out that "the poor colored people are in a constant state of alarm."[83]

Governing officials adopted and implemented laws in ways designed to undermine the constitutional ban on slavery announced by the Thirteenth Amendment. Virginia Unionists complained of practices

> intended to degrade and humiliate the colored population, to deprive them of the benefits of their freedom, and to subject them to the power of the whites by means of unjust and intolerably oppressive vagrant laws, and others, passed to satisfy the positive requirements of the national Government, ostensibly allow colored persons the right to testify in cases to which such persons are parties, but give even justices of the peace the power to decide, arbitrarily and peremptorily, upon the credibility of such testimony, and to exclude it from the jury, without appeal from such decisions.[84]

Former Confederates employed both criminal law and civil law to practically re-enslave persons of color. African American defendants accused of crime faced a nearly irrebuttable presumption of their guilt. A. J. Fletcher, the provisional secretary of state in Tennessee, informed Congress: "If a negro is put upon his trial in many localities it amounts to a conviction and the maximum penalty allowed by law."[85] Southern civil law was just as hostile to racial equality. Sumner's correspondents pointed out: "It is a simple truth that black men are not allowed to use their own property to the best advantage, or in any way to make use of their capacities as would be likely to elevate them in social position."[86] Many white planters refused without legal sanction to pay former slaves their earned wages.[87]

Official practices that oppressed people of color supplemented private violence that former rebels in office made little effort to prevent or punish. A Georgia correspondent asserted: "The hatred toward the negro as a freeman is intense among the low and brutal, who are the vast majority.

Murders, shootings, whippings, robbing, and brutal treatment of every kind are daily inflicted upon them, and I am sorry to say in most cases they can get no redress."[88] Another correspondent wrote that "the black man does not receive the faintest shadow of justice. . . . It is a simple truth that most flagrant crimes against the blacks are not noticed at all."[89]

White Republicans in the former Confederacy did not fare much better than their neighbors of color. Schurz observed that Southern "animosity against 'Yankee interlopers' is only second to their hostile feeling against the negro."[90] The "existence" of those "who during the war had been to a certain extent identified with the national cause," he pointed out, "was of a rather precarious nature."[91] A correspondent wrote that "the desire to persecute and break down all true loyal men is exhibited on every hand with even more sly ferocity than while the war of sections raged."[92] Correspondents from Tennessee reported especially severe hatred of the loyal minority. A Colonel Stokes informed Representative Hiram Price of Iowa that "there is now a feeling as bitter toward the Union men of the South as there ever was in 1860 or 1861."[93] Law and order had broken down with respect to those white citizens who had been faithful to the Union during the Civil War. A Unionist committee in Tennessee complained how "[q]uiet and peaceful citizens are met on our most public highways and robbed of their money and property, often cruelly beaten and abused, and in many cases murdered outright."[94] Conditions were as bad in Georgia. A correspondent reported: "All this neighborhood is infested with mounted hands of desperadoes, who are ex-rebel soldiers, and who are murdering Union men and negroes by the scores. . . . [T]he very streets of Augusta are unsafe for northern men after dark."[95]

Loyal whites in the South were far less likely to be murdered, butchered, or physically abused than former slaves, but they suffered frequent deprivations that were not legally remedied. Southern Unionists informed Congress that the "power and influence" of loyal judges "cannot prevent rebel juries from practicing the grossest injustice toward loyal men, while it is almost impossible to bring rebel offenders to justice."[96] Soldiers stationed in the South often suffered the same legal wrongs as loyal Unionists. A petition from Unionist citizens residing in northern Alabama stated: "[T]he loyal people, and particularly those who have in any way aided the cause of the national Government during the war, are entirely at the mercy of their enemies, the rebels; and they cannot obtain an impartial judgment in any court of justice. In many cases Union soldiers have been and are yet imprisoned without the shadow of a legal cause and their property taken from them."[97]

THE FUTURE

Journalists, correspondents, petitioners, and memorialists warned that conditions would worsen considerably should Reconstruction be prematurely abandoned. Loyal governments would be immediately destroyed. Persons of color would be reduced to practical slavery. White Unionists and Republicans would be hunted down and banished. Northern finance would collapse when Southern representatives in Congress, allied with their former Democratic allies, obtained payment of the Confederate war debt, compensation for emancipated slaves, and repudiation, at least in part, of the Northern war debt. Civil war might be renewed. "I have conversed with men of all classes here," one correspondent reported, "and they say openly that they were not conquered but only laid down their arms because it was expedient to do so; and they intended to resume hostilities the moment they see a chance of doing so with advantage."[98]

Immediate restoration promised rebel rule. "[I]f the military forces were all withdrawn from Tennessee," Brownlow predicted, "the Legislature at once would be dispersed by a rebel mob."[99] Rebels restored to their customary positions in Southern politics would immediately act on long-standing commitments to slavery and secession. Fletcher warned members of Congress that the proponents of "a just but lost cause" in Tennessee "will form a compact party in the State, held together by hatred for those whom they have branded as Tories for deserting the South in her extremity, by a determination to keep the negro in a condition as near to slavery as possible, and probably by a desire to keep the South united with a view to ulterior designs."[100]

Southern Republicans and white Unionists warned members of Congress about the devastating consequences to persons of color should Northern troops be removed from the South and antebellum elites returned to power. Senators and representatives learned from correspondents and memorialists about Southern intentions to restore human bondage and the antebellum racial status quo. "The whole thing may be summed up in one word: *the South is determined to have slavery—the thing, if not the name*," one of Sumner's correspondents from Alabama stated. That letter continued: "And if all restraint is removed, it is as certain as fate that their condition will be far worse than it ever was before. It will be the old system with all its mitigations rescinded and all its horrors intensified."[101] Former slaveholders would employ Southern contract law and criminal law to retain the antebellum labor system. A Virginia correspondent informed Congress:

[I]f they were left without these courts the whites would keep them forever in bondage by keeping them in debt, and I am afraid that the legislation of the States will be to the effect of establishing here the Mexican system of Peonage by using some very extraordinary terms to coerce "hatched-up" accounts against the blacks.[102]

Persons of color would find no legal respite in any other law of the community. The Union State Central Committee of Tennessee observed that redemption would mean that, "[a]s far as possible, restrictions will be thrown around the negro, and his elevation in the scale of being discountenanced, if not actually prohibited; he will be excluded from the courts, from common schools, and probably from all means of education, from business and privileged occupations, and perhaps from the acquisition of property."[103] The foundations for white supremacy would strengthen as Southern elites moved from local statehouses to Congress. Former slaveholders in control of the national government, Trowbridge informed readers, would "obtain the exclusive control of the freedmen and to make such laws for them as shall embody the prejudices of the late slave-holding society."[104]

The Thirteenth Amendment would be a parchment barrier in this unreconstructed South. Southern governments if restored prematurely, Northern journalists and Southern correspondents reported, would immediately develop a labor system designed to maintain white supremacy. Schurz noted a Southern "desire to preserve slavery in its original form as much and as long as possible . . . or to introduce into the new system that element of physical compulsion which would make the negro work."[105] A correspondent informed Schurz that former slaveholders "hope to obtain control of the State, and then to pass laws with reference to the colored people which shall virtually re-establish slavery."[106] This revised system of labor, Schurz declared, would be "intermediate between slavery as it formerly existed in the South, and free labor as it exists in the North, but more nearly related to the former than the latter."[107] Black life would be little different than before the Civil War. A Northern army officer on Southern duty observed, "a lingering hope yet remains with many, that although African slavery is abolished, the States may yet legislate as to place the negro in a state of actual peonage and submission to the will of the employer."[108] Another army officer asserted that, "should the care and protection of the nation be taken away from the freedmen, those people will have their way, and will practically re-establish slavery, more grinding and despotic than of old."[109]

Southerners openly acknowledged their desire to return to the antebellum status quo. A former Confederate officer told Andrews that "some system of peonage or apprenticeship will be established as soon as the State gets full control of her affairs."[110] Few hid their disdain for the letter and spirit of the Thirteenth Amendment or their commitment to developing "constitutional workarounds"[111] the instant former rebels again controlled Southern destiny. "If the Freedmen's Bureau is withdrawn," a former slaveholder informed Trowbridge, "things will work back again into their old grooves." Every former slave is "going to be made a serf, sure as you live."[112]

White Unionists in this restored regime would be terrorized. Southern Republicans spoke of a "deep-seated hatred, amounting in many cases to a spirit of revenge toward the white Unionists of the State."[113] Journalists, correspondents, petitioners, and memorialists agreed that the life expectancy for white Republicans who remained in the South after restoration would be short. Andrews reported that "[t]here are many counties . . . in which Northern labor and capital would not be safe but for the presence of the military."[114] "[S]hould the army be withdrawn," a correspondent informed Schurz, "freedom-loving men would find a southern residence unsafe."[115] A memorial from Virginia Unionists noted: "The moment the military power is withdrawn from among us, and the loyal men of Virginia are left to the protection of the so-called 'State government,' their only safety with be in immediate flight."[116]

Conditions in Tennessee, the former Confederate state with the largest white Unionist population, would be particularly dire should Congress abandon Reconstruction. Brownlow informed the national legislature that "many of the rebels now speak openly and say Union men and Yankees shall not live in the country"[117] and predicted how "Union men will be driven from the State, forced to sacrifice what they have and seek homes elsewhere."[118] Unionists allied with persons of color would be subject to gross abuses. "Assuming the restraints of the General Government are all to be removed from Tennessee," Brownlow wrote, "[i]n two cases out of every three the school-houses" used to educate persons of color "would be burned and the teachers rode upon a rail."[119] State courts would have no more regard for the rights of white Unionists than they would for former slaves. Fletcher anticipated that "[a] rebel judiciary will be elected and much that has been done by the present loyal State government will be declared void. Violence to Union men during the war will go unpunished, the government of the confederacy set up as a de facto government, and its laws of conscription, confiscation, impressment, &c., held valid for the time."[120]

Restored Southern elites threatened Northern financial interests as well as the bodies of former slaves and white unionists. Journalists, correspondents, petitioners, and memorialists predicted that former slaveholders, upon being permitted to take congressional seats, would repudiate the debt the United States incurred when fighting the Civil War or support exempting Southerners from paying the taxes needed to service that debt. Former Confederates would insist the national government assume the debts former Confederate states incurred during the Civil War or permit those states to repay their debts. Rebels in power would demand Southerners be compensated for emancipated slaves but abandon promised benefits for Northern soldiers and their survivors. Trowbridge detailed how Southern financial designs extended far beyond the South. Defeated Confederates, he warned, wished "to govern not only their own states but to regain their forfeited leadership in the affairs of the nation; to effect the repudiation of the national debt or to get the Confederate debt and the Rebel state debts assumed by the whole country; to secure payment for their slaves, and for all injuries and losses occasioned by the war."[121] Several correspondents outlined bold Southern plans for enriching the slaveholding elite and crippling the Northern economy. "The programme of the southern States, should they be fortunate enough to get into Congress," one correspondent declared, would be as follows:

First. They are to repudiate the national debt *in toto*.

Second. They are to pay all the southern slaveowners for all their negroes emancipated by the President's proclamation.

Third. They are to stop all pensions now given to Union soldiers, their widows and orphans, unless a like pension is given to the confederate soldiers, their widows and orphans.

Fourth. No officer or any leading rebel shall be punished for his treason against the Government.[122]

The financial threat was a constant refrain in bulletins from the South, even as the financial details varied. "[I]t is very probable that one or two or all of three things will be attempted within three years after the southern members of Congress are admitted to seats," a correspondent stated, including "the repudiation of the national debt, the assumption of the confederate debt, or the payment of several hundred million dollars to the South for property destroyed and slaves emancipated."[123] Southern promises to the contrary in early 1866 had no more present value that confederate bonds in early 1866. Andrews reported one speech in the Georgia state convention asserting: "Let us repudiate only at the express command of military power; and then, when we are again in the enjoyment of our rights in the Federal Union, and are once more a free and independent sovereignty, let us call another Convention and assume the whole debt."[124]

Former rebels anticipated restoring the political control over local and national politics necessary to achieve their racial and financial ambitions. Southerners, Kelsey reported, were "sanguine . . . that they can easily resume the reins of office."[125] Patience and prudence, former Confederate leaders assured their followers, would provide more successful than bullets and shot. Former slaveholders seeking power declared, "I believe that when our votes are admitted into that Congress, if we are tolerably wise, governed by a moderate share of common sense, we will have our own way."[126] Divided Northerners would yield power to a united South. "They argue that at least ninety-five in every two hundred votes at the North are sure to be thrown in their favor," Kelsey informed Congress, "and they can now rule the Union by giving up, which is cheaper than to persist in their idea of a separate government."[127] White Southern Unionists believed this confidence well placed. A white Republican from Alabama wrote about his fears that "the most corrupt men in the South will again get to power[] and sway the destinies of this section of the country."[128]

This faith in the revival of Southern control over national politics was rooted in the probability that the antebellum alliance between Southern planters and Northern doughfaces/Copperheads could be restored almost immediately after restoration. Reid informed his Northern readers that defeated secessionists intended "to combine with the Northern Democracy and such weak Republicans as Executive influence could control, repeal the test oath, thus admit all other Southern applicants, and turn over the Government to a party which, at the North, had opposed the war for the Union, and at the South had sustained the war against it."[129] Correspondents confirmed that former Confederates were confident Northern Jacksonians would grease their path to power. A Louisianan informed Congress that political leaders in that state believed that "the only true policy for the southern people to adopt is to support the Democratic party in opposition to the Republican party of the North."[130]

Former rebels made no secret of their political ambitions and the political tactics necessary to achieve those ambitions. Prominent Southerners when interviewed claimed that "[w]e'll unite with the opposition up North, and between us we'll make a majority. Then we'll show you who's going to govern this country."[131] "We must strike hands with the Democratic party of the North[] and manage them as we always have," another boasted.[132] Former Confederates running for public office openly declared their intention to restore the antebellum balance of sectional power. Andrews heard candidates call for "the speedy overthrow of the party now in power" and urge former slaveholders to "be quiet till we are strong enough, through the aid of the Democratic party of the North, to get a constitutional government."[133] Judge David Campbell Humphreys of Alabama, in a widely reported campaign speech, declared: "Gentleman, our safest place is in the Union. Grant it the idea of chattel slavery is dead, if you please; our Democratic allies will give us back the race in the condition of forced laborers, and it does not matter in which state we have them, if we have them under our control."[134]

Slaveholders and their potential Northern Democratic coalition partners celebrated the way an unanticipated consequence of the Thirteenth Amendment threatened to fashion a constitutional politics that privileged a revived slave power's efforts to nullify in practice, if not as a matter of fundamental law, the constitutional ban on slavery, brutalize white Republicans, and take control of national finances. The Thirteenth Amendment repealed the Three-Fifths Clause of Article I, Section 2. The good news for Republicans was that they had long detested how that provision augmented the slave power. The good news for the slave power was that repeal without Reconstruction promised to augment the slaveocracy bonus (the extra votes for persons of color who did not vote) that served as the foundation for Southern power in the antebellum Union.

Antebellum Northerners railed against the Three-Fifths Clause as the primary means by which the undemocratic slave power ruled the country. That provision, Salmon Chase and Charles Cleveland complained, "has virtually established in the country an aristocracy of slaveholders."[135] Three-fifths mattered and mattered often. The additional votes that slave states gained because slaves were counted as three-fifths of a person when allocating seats in the House of Representatives and members of the Electoral College provided the margin of difference in the presidential election of 1800, the congressional vote on the Kansas–Nebraska Act, and other matters on which antebellum Americans were divided by section.[136] Antislavery advocates before the Civil War unsuccessfully sought to reduce Southern influence on constitutional politics by proposing constitutional amendments that would prohibit enslaved persons from being counted at all or from being counted in new states when seats in the House of Representatives and members of the Electoral College were allocated to those jurisdictions.[137]

The Thirteenth Amendment's edict freeing persons of color—instead of reducing the power of former slave states, as antislavery advocates had previously demanded—promised to increase white Southern influence on national policy. Disenfranchised former slaves became full persons for representational purposes. This result, without further constitutional change, magnified the power of former Confederates in the Union far beyond antebellum levels. Robert Dale Owen informed President Johnson:

By the constitution the representative population is to consist of all
free persons and three-fifths of all other persons. If, by next winter,
slavery shall have disappeared, there will be no "other persons" in
the South. Her actual population will then coincide with her representative population. She will have gained, as to Federal representation, 1,600,000 persons. She will be entitled, not as now to eighty-four
members, but to ninety-four; and her votes for President will be in
proportion; . . . if color be deemed cause of exclusion, then all the political power which is withheld from the emancipated slave is gained
by the Southern white if freed slaves were denied the ballot, [and] each
Southern white voter would exercise three times the political power
of a Northern voter.[138]

This boost to white Southern political power through an augmented slaveocracy bonus, former slaveholders dreamed, might be sufficient to enable
the former slave states to regain control over the national government. The
Richmond Examiner summarized these Southern hopes when asserting that
"[u]niversal assent appears to be given to the proposition that if the States
lately rebellious be restored to rights of representation according to the federal basis, or to the basis of numbers enlarged by the enumeration of all the
blacks in the next census, the political power of the country will pass into
the hands of the South, aided it will be, by Northern alliances."[139]

The free-state journalists who travelled southward after the Civil War,
and Southerners who corresponded with Republican senators, were not
sure these rebel plans would succeed, but they were confident that strenuous efforts would be made to restore the antebellum constitutional status
quo respecting slavery and national finance. Every Southern political effort
was directed toward reviving the Old South and the constitutional politics
of the Old South. Kelsey noted how the traditional Southern leadership
promised to "strain every nerve to regain the political power and ascendancy they held under President James Buchanan."[140] "What harm they can
do the Union by political action, I do not know," Denning admitted, "but
whatever harm they can do will, I think, be done."[141]

"Fake News": Presidential Reconstruction Looks Southward

Democrats, Unionists, and the very conservative Republicans who supported presidential Reconstruction ignored or sneered at these reports of
Southern outrages and Confederate ambitions. President Johnson and his
political allies insisted that the North had won the battle for Southern minds

as well as for Southern bodies. Former Confederates could be trusted with political power. Former slaves were secure in their freedom. The main threat to national unity was the willingness of Radicals to embellish Southern incidents for political gain.

President Johnson reported to Congress that the angel of peace had appeared in the land of cotton. "Resistance to the General Government appear[s] to have exhausted itself," he insisted.[142] This acquiescence was grounded in renewed allegiance rather than military defeat. President Abraham Lincoln's successor claimed that former Confederates "are yielding obedience to the laws and government of the United States with more willingness and greater promptitude than under the circumstances could reasonably have been expected."[143] He expressed "[a]n abiding faith" that Southern "actions will conform to their professions" and that "their loyalty will be unreservedly given to the Government."[144] This loyalty was manifested by the ratification of the Thirteenth Amendment and the actual or imminent passage of laws protecting persons of color. President Johnson was confident that former slaveholders would freely "confer upon freedmen rights and privileges which are essential to their comfort, protection, and security."[145] Life in the South was not yet idyllic, but sporadic disruptions were a natural result of "the demoralizing effects of war" and the "great and sudden change in the relations between the two races."[146] The disturbances that took place were "local in character, not frequent in occurrence, and are rapidly disappearing as the authority of the civil law is extended and sustained."[147] The former slave, the Tennessee Unionist confidently predicted, "will receive the protection to which he is justly entitled."[148]

General Ulysses S. Grant supported President Johnson's opinions on Southern minds and bodies. Grant, after touring the postwar South at the President's behest, insisted that former Confederates understood that questions about "slavery and State rights, or the right of a State to secede from the Union," were "were settled forever by the highest tribunal, arms, that a man can resort to."[149] With military defeat came remarkable conversion. Grant's report to President Johnson maintained that leading Southerners "not only accepted the decision arrived at as final, but that now, when the smoke of battle had cleared away and time has been given for reflection, this decision has been a fortunate one for the whole country."[150] Remaining problems in the South were temporary and the consequence of the rapid transformations taking place in the region. Grant observed: "It cannot be expected that the opinions held by men at the South for years can be changed in a day."[151] Black and white adjustment required only time, not constitutional and statutory reform. Former slaves had significant misapprehensions about freedom. "In some instances," Grant reported, "the freedmen's mind does not seem to be disabused of the idea that a freedman has the right to live without cure or provision for the future."[152] Other freedmen were falsely convinced "that the lands of their former owners will, at least in part, be divided among them."[153] Once former slaves understood what was entailed by freedom and the boons they would not be granted, life in the former Confederate states would settle down to a new and improved postbellum normal.

The Democrats on the Joint Committee on Reconstruction in their minority report quoted Grant's observations when endorsing his Panglossian vision of the postwar South.[154] *Grant v. Lee* settled what proponents of presidential Reconstruction believed were the central issues of the Civil War. The minority report asserted: "Secession, as a practical doctrine ever hereafter to be resorted to, is almost utterly abandoned. It was submitted to and failed before the ordeal of battle."[155] No one need worry about the allegiance of former Confederate representatives. The committee Democrats declared that "representatives from the southern States would be perfectly loyal."[156] Loyal unionists had no reason to fear a re-empowered South financially. Many former Confederates would support wholeheartedly such measures as "the repudiation of the rebel debt," "the denial of all obligation to pay for manumitted slaves," and "the inviolability of our own debt."[157] The minority report was silent on race relations in the new South. The Democrats on the Joint Committee did not discuss slavery or any racial matter that had recently occupied, was occupying, or might in the near future occupy either Congress or the former Confederate states.

Members of Congress who supported President Johnson's Reconstruction policies echoed these claims that the Southern leopard had changed its spots. R. Johnson stated "they have seen the error of their ways" and "were as anxious to return as in their insanity they were anxious to leave us."[158] Finck agreed that "[t]he people of these states have wisely and really abandoned all further resistance, and have . . . determined to yield a cheerful obedience to the Constitution and laws of the United States and to discharge their duties and obligations as loyal citizens."[159] Support for slavery and state rights had evaporated. Senator Edgar Cowan of Pennsylvania asked: "Have we not heard from almost all the public men of the South that that question was put to the arbitrament of the sword, that they have lost, and that they submit[?]"[160] This transformation of Southern opinion included a new appreciation for Black freedom. "Everybody admits," Cowan stated, "that they negro ought to have his natural rights secured to him."[161] He informed the Senate that "the people of the southern States themselves . . . are in favor of opening the courts to all these classes of people."[162]

Democrats, to employ an anachronistic phrase, described reports of Southern defiance and barbarism as "fake news." G. Davis had "very little faith in the various letters of information" describing outrages in the former Confederate states and "no confidence whatever . . . in the testimony which the men in employment of the Freedmen's Bureau give."[163] Cowan quoted President Johnson and Grant at length when maintaining that reports of Southern disturbances concerned "exceptional cases."[164] Journalistic accounts were exaggerated, unreliable, and unrepresentative of Southern opinion or behavior.[165] After noting that complaints often took the form of "*ex parte* statements made by anonymous letter-writers,"[166] Cowan declared:

> One man out of ten thousand is brutal to a negro, and that is paraded here as a type of the whole people of the South, whereas nothing is said of the other nine thousand nine hundred and ninety-nine men who treat the negro well. One man expresses a great deal of dissatisfaction at the present state of affairs, and that is paraded here, while nothing is said of the other ten thousand men who are contented to accept it and make the most of it.[167]

G. Davis made a similar point when conceding "[t]here may have been a melee, a military conflict there, and there may have been some raids in which there was a collision between whites and blacks, where outrages were perpetuated," but the notion that persons of color had "no redress for such wrongs" was "as basely false as it is possible for anything to be."[168] Senator William Stewart of Nevada insisted that Republican claims about Southern outrages were self-defeating. In his view, "if . . . the evidence . . . established that the great mass of the people of the South are capable of the atrocities imputed to them by the anonymous witnesses paraded before this Senate, then a union of these States is impossible."[169]

"Rebels Rule": Congressional Reconstruction Looks Southward

Proponents of congressional Reconstruction endorsed wholeheartedly the pessimistic account of unreconstructed Southern politics proffered by free-state journalists, Southern correspondents, Unionist memorialists, and African American petitioners.[170] Stevens and his political allies repeatedly painted a dire portrait of what was happening in the former Confederacy and what would happen in and to the nation if Southern politics was not reconstructed. The Black Codes played prominent roles in many congressional speeches, but so did the fate of white Unionists, the Confederate debt, and the national debt. All were manifestations of rebel rule—what proponents believed to be the central problem facing the Thirty-Ninth Congress. Continued rebel rule in the unreconstructed South threatened to undermine the Thirteenth Amendment, destroy the beginnings of a Southern Republican Party, and ruin Northern finances. Freed persons of color, white Unionists, and Northern financial interests would not enjoy constitutional or legal protection in practice so long as Southern politics remained dominated by former Confederate elites.

Republicans in Congress slightly reworked the basic themes played by journalists, correspondents, memorialists, and petitioners, particularly after passing the Civil Rights Act of 1866. Journalists and petitioners tended to emphasize racial injustice in the former Confederate states. Many proponents of congressional Reconstruction in the Senate and House of Representatives spoke passionately against the Black Codes, but most spoke far more often and at least as passionately about the plight of white Republicans in the South and the fate of Northern financial interests. Journalists noted electoral inequalities only in passing. Stevens and his political allies were far more focused on the consequences of enhanced Southern representation in the Congress and Electoral College provided by the Thirteenth Amendment.

THE JOINT COMMITTEE AND REBEL RULE

The Report of the Joint Committee on Reconstruction, issued to explain the committee's proposed Fourteenth Amendment, was devoted to documenting and combating the threat of rebel rule. Senator William Pitt Fessenden of Maine and the other Republicans on the Joint Committee described a South in which traitors ruled. Presidential reconstruction had failed. "Allowed and encouraged by the Executive to organize State governments," the *Report* asserted, "they at once place in power leading rebels, unrepentant and unpardoned, excluding with contempt those who had manifested an attachment to the Union, and preferring, in many instances, those who had rendered themselves the most obnoxious."[171] Treason was a mark of honor. The Republicans on the Joint Committee observed that, "[i]n the face of the law requiring an oath which would necessarily exclude all such men from federal offices, they elect, with very few exceptions, as senators and representatives in Congress, men who had actively participated in the rebellion, insultingly denouncing the law as unconstitutional."[172] Remorse, contrition, and devotion to Union were scarce commodities. Fessenden, the primary author of the *Report*, maintained, "[p]rofessing no repentance, glorying apparently in the crime they had committed, avowing still . . . an adherence to the pernicious doctrine of secession, and declaring that they yielded only to necessity, they insist, with unanimous voice, upon their rights as States, and proclaim that they will submit to no conditions whatever as preliminary to their resumption of power under that Constitution which they still claim the right to repudiate."[173]

The postwar South was the antebellum South with a lower percentage of young men of military age in the general population. Attitudes in the land of cotton were unchanged. The *Report* claimed that "[t]he evidence of an intense hostility to the federal Union, and an equally intense love of the late confederacy, nurtured by the war, is decisive."[174] The same principles that animated Southern politics in 1860 animated Southern politics in 1866. The Joint Committee spoke of "a generally prevailing opinion which defends the legal right of secession, and upholds the doctrine that the first allegiance of the people is due the States, and not to the United States."[175] The same people who controlled Southern politics in 1860 controlled Southern politics in 1866. *The Report* asserted that "the elections which were held for State officers and members of Congress had resulted, almost universally, in the defeat of candidates who had been true to the Union, and in the election of notorious and unpardoned rebels, men who could not take the prescribed oath of office, and who made no secret of their hostility to the government and the people of the United States."[176] Public opinion remained controlled by rabid secessionists. Republicans on the Joint Committee pointed out how "the southern press . . . abounds with weekly and daily abuse of the institutions and people of the loyal States, defends the men who led, and the principles which incited, the rebellion, denounces and reviles southern men who adhered to the Union; and strives, constantly and unscrupulously, by every means in its power, to keep alive the fire of hate and discord between the sections."[177]

Loyalty to the Union and to the amended constitution were at a premium in the former Confederate states. The Confederacy had surrendered only because they were outgunned, not because they realized secession was treason. The *Report* stated "they only yielded when, after a long, bloody, and wasting war, they were compelled by utter exhaustion to lay down their arms; and this they did, not willingly, but declaring that they yielded because they could no longer resist, affording no evidence whatever of repentance for their crime, and expressing no regret, except that they had no longer the power to continue the desperate struggle."[178] No Republican on the Joint Committee took seriously rebel commitments to state constitutional reform. Southern support for antislavery state constitutional amendments and for repealing secession ordinances were "nothing more than an unwilling admission of an unwelcomed truth."[179] Should the former Confederate states remain un-reconstructed, secession might be repeated and the fruits of the Northern victory in the Civil War undone. "Treason," the *Report* stated, "defeated in the field, has only to take possession of Congress and the cabinet."[180]

Pervasive disloyalty in the postwar South threatened three classes of loyal persons. The first group included former slaves. The *Report* detailed how the "feeling in many portions of the country towards emancipated slaves . . . is one of vindictive and malicious hatred" and a "deep-seated prejudice against color" that "leads to acts of cruelty, oppression, and murder, which the lo-cal authorities are at no pains to prevent or punish."[181] Fessenden and his colleagues observed, "[t]here is no general disposition to place the colored race . . . upon terms even of civil equality."[182] The second group included white Unionists. Former Confederates did not discriminate on race when oppressing loyalists. The Republicans on the Joint Committee pointed out that "[t]he general feeling and disposition among all classes are yet totally averse to the toleration of any class of people friendly to the Union, be they white or black."[183] "Southern men who adhered to the Union," the *Report* declared, "are bitterly hated and relentlessly persecuted."[184] White Republi-cans who moved to the South suffered the same fate. Fessenden and friends stated that "[o]fficers of the Union army on duty and northern men who go south to engage in business[] are generally detested and proscribed."[185] The third group of threatened loyal citizens included Northern creditors. Members of the Joint Committee stated, "the people of the rebellious States would, if they should see a prospect for success, repudiate the national debt."[186] Financial ruin was likely because former Confederates would pay federal taxes "only under a great compulsion and with great reluctance," even while imposing substantial exactions on loyal citizens so that "com-pensation . . . be made for slaves emancipated and property destroyed dur-ing the war."[187]

If constitutional reform was directed primarily at expanding the rights of former slaves and repealing Southern laws discriminating against per-sons of color, then the Republican members of the Joint Committee did a magnificent job keeping this ambition secret. The Black Codes played no special role in the committee's report. Southern threats to freedmen received no greater billing than Southern threats to white Unionists, national credi-tors, or other persons who remained loyal during the Civil War. Fessenden's summary of the issues facing the national government and motivating the committee's draft of the Fourteenth Amendment did not mention racial in-justice at all:

The question before Congress is, then, whether conquered enemies have the right, and shall be permitted at their own pleasure and on their own terms to participate in making laws for their conquerors; whether conquered rebels may change their theater of operations from the battle-field, where they were defeated and overthrown, to the halls of Congress, and, through their representatives, seize upon the government which they fought to destroy; whether the national treasury, the army of the nation, its navy, its forts and arsenals, its whole civil administration, its credit, its pensioners, the widows and orphans of those who perished in the war, the public honor, peace and safety, shall all be turned over to the keeping of its recent enemies without delay, and without imposing such conditions as, in the opinion of Congress, the security of the country and its institutions may demand.[188]

This was a call to prevent rebel rule and protect potential white victims of a renewed Jacksonian alliance, not a manifesto for racial equality.

THE PAST AND PRESENT AS PROLOGUE

Republican members of Congress endorsed the central conclusion of free-state journalists and the Joint Committee when agreeing that the Southern leopard had not changed its spots. Senator Timothy O. Howe of Wisconsin bluntly stated "these men have not surrendered their cause . . . , [and] the sentiments and purposes of that people are unchanged."[189] Senator Benjamin F. Wade of Ohio observed that "their fell purpose and intent had not been relinquished one jot or tittle yet."[190] Little difference existed between Southern ambitions before and after Appomattox. Representative William Lawrence of Ohio detected in the first round of state constitutional conventions "[t]he purpose to maintain the State-rights heresy of judging of the extent of and resisting the national authority."[191] "The determination of the intelligent, influential classes at the South," Representative Henry W. Van Aernam of New York pointed out, "is manifestly to keep just as much as possible of slavery, aristocracy, State sovereignty, and disloyalty to make our victory as barren of results as they can; and defeated by arms, still to conquer by political action and party intrigue."[192] Unrepentant and unreconstructed, the former Confederate states, when the Thirty-Ninth Congress met, lacked any capacity for renewed statehood. "[T]he condition" of former Confederate states, Baker asserted, "is . . . totally incompatible with any valid claim to present resumption of representation in this Government."[193]

Military defeat had tempered Southerners' willingness to engaged in military combat, but not their commitment to the principles that inspired secession. R. Clarke asserted that "[t]he war did not squelch out rebellion; it simply disarmed it. It did not burn out treason; it lowered its front and taught it to be silent, and that silence is the peace we have—nothing more."[194] "They are not satisfied with the results of the rebellion," he elsewhere stated, "and they seem resolved upon another effort to reclaim their lost fortunes; and they are beginning in this way to educate their followers up to the spirit of their purpose."[195] Defeat in combat changed the fronts on which Southerners did battle but not the cause Southerners were fighting for. "That which they failed to accomplish by force or arms," H. Lane maintained, "they seek to accomplish by the ballot."[196] Senator George Williams of Oregon pointed out:

> True, we have conquered these people in battle, but what of that? No man was ever converted from an enemy into a friend by the summary logic of shot and shell. . . . The demonic spirit that animated this rebellion, the same that mutilated and starved and butchered our martyred heroes, that inoculated the veins and rotted off the strong arm of the northern warrior with the deadly venom of the lazar-house, that baled the yellow fever as merchandise for this capital, and that ended by assassinating our President, still lives, unrepentant, unsubdued, ferocious, and devilish as ever. The battle still rages, as it did in these Halls long before the outbreak of rebellion, but under a new phase. . . . If arms have failed, there are other weapons, rejected by the South in its blind and unreasoning arrogance, which have proved in other times more potent in its hands than the puny sword that has just been shattered like a potsherd in its collision with the iron muscle of the sinewy laboring man of the free States.[197]

A war of arms was being converted into a war of words and political strategy. "[T]he only difference between the men who twelve months ago were defying the constituted authorities," Representative John L. Thomas, Jr., of Maryland opined, "is, that then they had arms in their hands and armies in the field, now they have neither, but the disposition to have both; ay sir, they have the determination to seize hold of the political power, and to use it if possible to punish those who have made them submit to the laws."[198] Representative William Windom of Minnesota observed that "the conflict of principles still rages with increased vigor."[199]

Southern elites felt remorse for losing battles, not for committing treason. G. Williams observed: "They confess that they are subdued, but only, as they tell us, by the power of numbers—the mere brute superiority of the North. They do not profess contrition for their great crime. They do not even admit that they have sinned."[200] "Their lips acknowledge their allegiance to your Government," Senator Daniel Clark of New Hampshire agreed, "and they will keep it, because they have not strength to break it; but the heart is not warmed by any genuine loyalty."[201] No Southern apology was forthcoming for the immense destruction of Union life and Union property caused by secession. Representative Fernando C. Beaman of Michigan asked: "Have the people any evidence of repentance for such flagitious crimes?" "If so," he continued, "what is it? Does it appear in the daily conversation, in the public speeches, in the halls of legislation, or in the press of the South, the burden of all which is 'a just but lost cause?'"[202]

Southerners who displayed no remorse for treason demonstrated no fidelity to the Union. Representative Henry C. Deming of Connecticut maintained "[t]here is no loyalty there which would support what I regard . . . as indispensable to the present and future safety of this imperiled nation."[203] Those former Confederates who were not openly hostile to the Union were hypocrites. Howe described Southern politics as divided between a faction "endeavoring to awe the Government with professions of defiance" and a faction "endeavoring to cheat it with professions of friendship."[204] The concessions that Southern charlatans made were insincere and temporary. Deming stated "the evidence is complete and overwhelming that southern loyalty consists in submission to necessity, and that their implacable animosity to the Federal Government, and to those great measures which have been inaugurated for liberating and enfranchising the slave, is merely biding the time when, by the return to those Halls of its full complement of Senators and Representatives, the misfortunates of the field may be redeemed in the forum."[205] Superior arms and armies made no converts. Representative Sidney T. Holmes of New York pointed out that Southern commitments to state constitutional amendments banning slavery were "forced upon them by Federal bayonets."[206]

The Civil War had no impact on public opinion in the former Confederate states. Howe maintained that "the sentiments and purpose of that people are unchanged"[207] and "a large and controlling portion of them are still really hostile to the United States."[208] Representative Hamilton Ward, Sr., of New York observed that "[t]he same ministers that preached treason, the same presses that proclaimed it, now lead the people and control their opinions."[209] If anything, anti-Union sentiment was growing. Representative Ralph Hill of Indiana maintained that "[t]he practical workings of the course pursued since the surrender of the armies of the rebellion . . . unfortunately has been but to encourage and develop hostility to the Government."[210]

Political culture in the postwar South celebrated secession and secession heroes while treating Unionists as untouchables. Howe complained, "The uniform of the rebellion is still worn and its songs still sung."[211] "I challenge the Senate to show me," he stated, "what rebel community has ever rebuked such displays."[212] The American flag was detested. "[T]hrough large portions of those States," Hill told fellow representatives, "the most hated banner that floats above the breeze under the whole heavens is the starry emblem that hangs above your head."[213] Southern loyalists were ostracized. H. Wilson observed how "persons who were loyal have been regarded very much . . . as a sort of inferior portion of the southern people."[214]

Proponents of congressional Reconstruction detailed how rebels exercised the same control over Southern politics that they did before the war. H. Wilson asserted "the confederate States reconstructed since the surrender of the rebel armies are as completely in the hands of the rebels now as on the day Jeff Davis was incarcerated at Fortress Monroe."[215] Former Confederates controlled state constitutional conventions. Loan observed that "candidates were voted for and elected because of their services in the armies of the rebellion[] and of their assured fidelity to the cause of the traitors."[216] Those same traitors triumphed when former Confederate states held elections for state offices. Representative Samuel McKee of Kentucky asked: "Do we not know that that these late rebellious States have elected and put into the highest offices men who are the most odious traitors[?]"[217] "Shouts are given for Lee in the *loyal* Legislature of Virginia," Ward stated. "A former member of the rebel congress, once a Speaker of this House, whose lips are steeped in violated constitutional oaths, is elected Governor of South Carolina. *Loyal* Alabama has a rebel general for Governor."[218] Former Confederate heroes were as successful when seeking federal office. "These reconstructed rebels have," Loan complained, "elected as Representatives to this Congress, notorious, defiant rebels, whose infamous career in treachery and crime renders it impossible for them to take the oaths of office prescribed by law without committing perjury."[219] McKee queried: "Do we not know that they are knocking at the doors of this Hall and asking for the admittance of men upon these floors whose hands are reeking with the blood of slain loyalists[?]"[220]

Military defeat increased the popularity of those who were most dedicated to the Lost Cause while destroying any possibility that persons who were Unionists in 1861 could have any political influence in an unreconstructed South. Van Aernam, after detailing the successes of former Confederate leaders in Southern elections held immediately after Appomattox, pointed out that

[a]ll the State officers elected because of their participation in the rebellion; and of the fourteen Senators chosen from the reconstructed States, two only, Governor Marvin and Judge Sharkey, can take the oath of office. Of the Representatives elected from these seven States but two can take the oath prescribed by the laws of the country.[221]

Beaman stated that the "wounds and scars received in an attempt to overthrow the Government are alone sufficient passports to office."[222] Past Unionism was a disqualification for public office in the former slave states. Senator James W. Nye of Nevada observed that "unconditional loyalists, except in a few localities, cannot be elected to office; that men if elected at all, must be elected on the strength of their notoriety as rebels." He continued: "[A]menities [are] awarded to the disloyal only, that every arrangement is undertaken and carried out that can by possibility make Unionism unpopular and odious, and treason popular and respectable."[223]

These features of Southern politics enabled those who led the secession effort in 1860–1861 to maintain control over all local institutions. Howe pointed out that new state governments "follow in the footsteps of those organizations which existed there at the time the rebellion surrendered its arms. They represent the same people, precisely the same constituency; substantially the Legislatures and Governors were elected by the same people."[224] The Civil War had remarkably little impact on constitutional politics in the former Confederacy. Ward captured the respective statuses of former rebels and staunch Unionists in postwar Southern politics when he declared that

[t]he courts are rebel, jurors rebel, Legislatures rebel; the men who fought our flag boast of scars won in behalf of treason as honorable, and receive in reward office, honor, and profit. They do not disguise their hate for Union men; who are excluded from all those honors and privileges because of their loyalty. Freedom of speech, as of old, is a mockery.[225]

Clark asserted that "elections have been held by traitors, conventions and Legislatures have been held by traitors, offices filled, and a public sentiment created which to-day is more hostile in many places than it was months ago."[226]

Requiring these traitors to take oaths of allegiance was pointless. Former Confederates who had not been bound by oaths of allegiance in the past would not be bound by oaths of allegiance in the future. G. Williams predicted that "those who were most forward to abjure their sworn allegiance here[] will be the first to violate their new-made vows, by swearing themselves back again into legislative honors and governmental favors."[227] Howe pointed out that "the oath they will take is no more binding than they were in 1861, when they made flagrant war upon you."[228] Presidential Reconstruction, which depended in the sincerity of former Confederates, was doomed. Deming, after observing "[t]hey have taken all these oaths before," concluded the national government would need to "require more irreversible guarantees from the returning prodigals than those which end with 'so help me God!'"[229] "I am told," he reminded Congress, "that Italian brigands are never so devout in kneelings, crossings, and paternosters, as when they are about to plunge afresh into crime."[230]

Southern assurances of good faith to the contrary, Republicans in Congress regarded the land of cotton as a place where organized mayhem was directed at all persons not identified with the Lost Cause. "From every part of the rebel territory comes the same story of wrong, outrage, and oppression," Beaman reported. He detailed how "[t]he shooting of the negro, the depriving him of all civil rights, the murder of Union men, the banishment of northern emigrants, the utterance of disloyal sentiments, and the commission of every conceivable crime[] have become the order of the day."[231] Moulton observed: "The constant and barbarous outrages committed by rebels in the South against Union men and freedmen would fill volumes and outrage the feeling of savages."[232] Private militias were running amuck, indiscriminately targeting freed persons of color and white Republicans. H. Wilson asserted that "the greatest outrages are perpetrated by armed men who go up and down the county searching houses, disarming people, committing outrages of every kind and description."[233] Former slaves often took the brunt of the violence that engulfed the former Confederacy. Sumner stated how, "abandoned to themselves, with unchecked power, the old slavemasters naturally continue the barbarism in which they have so long excelled." "The blood curdles at the thought of such enormities," he continued, "and especially at the thought that the poor freedmen to whom we owe protection[] are left to the unrestrained will of such a people."[234] Former Confederates often did not discriminate by race when persecuting the perceived enemies of the South. "The poor freedman is sacrificed," Sumner declared, as is "[t]he northern settler, who believes in Human Rights."[235]

Continued military rule was necessary if Unionists and persons of color were to enjoy even a modicum of safety. "Standing armies and martial law," Loan stated, "are yet required to enforce national authority and to protect the loyal people against rebel violence and outrage.[236] "Loyal victims of postwar rebel violence in Tennessee were calling for an increased military presence," Ward declared, were "saying the rebels there are as cruel, malignant, and insolent as ever."[237] Union soldiers found themselves as much a target of unrepentant secessionists as did former slaves and white Republicans. "Rebel leaders," H. Wilson observed, "bear themselves toward northern men, officers of the Army, and the tried and true loyal men of the South more insolently than ever."[238]

Republicans detailed how rebels in control of Southern government were reinstituting slavery in the former Confederate states. The Black Codes played a far more significant role in many speeches on Reconstruction and proposed constitutional reform[239] than in the Joint Committee's report. II. Wilson was one of many proponents of congressional Reconstruction who pointed to the Black Codes when discussing an early version of what evolved into the Civil Rights Act of 1866 and the Second Freedmen's Bureau Bill. "It has been said that the slave codes and the laws of these States in regard to persons of color fell with slavery," he declared, "but in fact those laws are being executed, and in some of them in the most merciless manner. In several of these States new laws are being framed containing provisions wholly inconsistent with the freedom of the freedmen."[240] Representative Leonard Myers of Pennsylvania discussed the Black Codes in some detail when explaining why former Confederate states should not be immediately represented in Congress. He noted, for example, that Mississippi had "passed laws so violative of equal liberty under the Constitution and equal rights before the law that the President had instructed General Thomas to disregard them."[241]

The Thirteenth Amendment was a parchment barrier in the unreconstructed South. "Slavery is said to be abolished," Kelso stated. "In name it is, but not in reality."[242] Ward pointed out: "We are told, sir, that they have ratified the constitutional amendment abolishing slavery, Ay, so they have; but their courts have sold the freedmen the next day under some pretense of punishing him for vagrancy or something else equally absurd."[243] Former Confederates were devising new systems of forced labor. After quoting Schurz's observation that Southerners desired to "establish[] . . . a new form of servitude," Deming reminded his colleagues that "reconstructed North Carolina is now selling black men into slavery for petty larceny, and reconstructed South Carolina, Mississippi, and Louisiana are fettering the contract system with so many subtle formalities, forfeitures, and conditions[] that a modern labor contract is much like an old-fashioned slave-pen, a trap to hold the freedman to his work and cheat him of his wages."[244] Private arrangements stunted free labor. Sumner observed how planters in South

Carolina agreed not to hire any person of color without permission of his or her former owner or to rent land to a former slave.[245]

Former antislavery advocates in the North recognized that former slaves in the South still had no rights that a white person was bound to respect.[246] "In not a single southern State have they done justice by the freedmen," Ward stated. "In not one have they passed just and equitable laws that will protect him in his rights."[247] Representative Martin Welker of Ohio observed that

> [a] spirit of bitterness, a determination to oppress and harass them in every way possible, now pervades the legislation of most of these States. In many of them there is no protection afforded the colored men. Many of these States have now in force "black codes," in which all rights are denied to them. Several of them will not allow a colored man to own or rent a foot of land; deny him the benefit of schools [and] protection under the poor laws or rights in court by which he can obtain redress for grievances or secure protection.[248]

Legal proceedings were worthless as a means for vindicating Black rights. "You say that they have given the colored man a standing in court," Ward pointed out. "A standing in court, with, as I have said, hostile judges, jurors, witnesses, church and state all hostile. Such a standing in court is mockery; it is worse, it is insult."[249] Senator Lot Morrill of Maine anticipated the contemporary concern with "preservation through transformation"[250] when he observed that "the contest for chattel slavery is over, but the struggle for the possession of the negro as a forced laborer goes on."[251]

Persons of color in the South were the victims of an unprecedented terror campaign. H. Wilson reported that "great atrocities and cruelties are perpetrated upon the freedmen in various sections of the country."[252] Former members of the Confederate military were particularly prone to racist brutality. The junior senator from Massachusetts observed how "[r]eturned rebel soldiers and kindred spirits are avenging themselves for the humiliations of defeat by insults, outrages, barbarities, and murders of harmless freedmen."[253] The cruelties that freed persons of color experienced in 1865 reminded Republicans of how Southerners treated fugitive slaves before the Civil War. Kelso asked: "Does not every southern breeze still bring to our ears the sound of the lash, the baying of the bloodhound, the cries of the slave, and the screams of murder?"[254]

Proponents of congressional Reconstruction spoke as passionately about the sufferings of white Unionists in the postwar South as they did about the plight of former slaves. The Black Codes, Republicans believed, were only one of many means Southerners employed for persecuting the loyal. W. Lawrence described "loyal Union men" as "a persecuted and despised class in all the South."[255] Loyal whites continued to live in fear throughout most of the former Confederacy. Representative George R. Latham of West Virginia asserted that "the Union men are now as much proscribed, if not actively persecuted, throughout the great portion of the South as they were during the rebellion."[256] "Unionists are menaced in their safety," Sumner bluntly stated.[257] Southern opponents of secession who were not murdered or physically assaulted continued to suffer devastating property losses and deprivations. Howe pointed to "men whose whole estates had been confiscated by the rebel authorities for no other offense than having been true to the flag of the nation."[258] "The Union men," Moulton commented, "now are being compelled to leave the rebel States to save their property and lives."[259]

THE FUTURE

Premature restoration jeopardized the fruits of the Civil War. "If the eleven seceded States are immediately invested with their proportionate power in the administration of the Government," Beaman declared, "that glorious fabric of nationality created by the hands of our fathers, and so gallantly defended by the best blood of this generation, will be speedily demolished and utterly destroyed."[260] Representative Ephraim R. Eckley of Ohio declared: "To admit such members of Congress as they would elect from the States lately in rebellion would . . . permit them to gain everything, through congressional action, that they sought to accomplish by arms."[261] Congress would have wasted the several billions of dollars necessary to fight the Civil War. More than 350,000 Union soldiers would have died for no reason. Beaman stated: "Recognize their *status* as States, and admit them to representation in Congress with their present disloyal temper and disposition, and the outlays in life and treasure of the last five years will have been incurred in vain."[262] The Lost Cause might be found in the halls of Congress. Should former Confederate states "send their Senators and Representatives here," Hill predicted, "through their action they should obtain a reversal of the arbitrament of arms, and thus, not being able to commit murder upon the nation, should accomplish its suicide."[263]

Republicans offered apocalyptic visions of an unreconstructed South restored to the Union. Loyal state governments in the former Confederacy would collapse. "The presence of United States soldiers all over the South is conclusive evidence," Holmes declared, "that the President does not believe that civil governments could be maintained without them."[264] An immediate end to Reconstruction promised financial disaster and a restoration of discredited Southern labor systems. Howe foretold a dark future:

> Having at your dictation agreed to the act of emancipation, they will, after their own fashion, proceed to show you what it is worth. Having at your bidding waived the payment of the rebel debt, they will proceed to cancel the old bonds and issue new ones for the amount. And when, under their new code, the freedman is excluded from the jury box, the witness stand, the courts, and from the whole remedial law, and from the schools; when their labor is charged with an enormous debt contracted in the effort to perpetuate and intensify their servitude; when the regenerated State shouts to them "Work!" and yet denies them all chance to work except in the employ of their late owners, the great landholders; when the freedman sees that his utmost efforts only secure him a subsistence, which he always had, and the strictest fidelity secures him no friends, which he once had; when he finds that the tie which linked him to the family of his old master is severed, and that no new tie links him to the family of man, what then?[265]

THE FUTURE OF RIGHTS

Restoration without additional constitutional or legal securities threatened disaster for loyal persons of every race. Representative John F. Farnsworth of Illinois stated that "to restore the States lately in insurrection to the *status* which they enjoyed as States before the war would only be putting power into the hands of rebels and traitors, whose hatred of the Union and of Union men has become intensified rather than mollified since the termination of the war" and that "no Union man, whether white or black, would be able to live in those States one moment after the withdrawal of the troops that now protect them and preserve order."[266] Holmes questioned whether "as soon as the United States Army is withdrawn will not the State governments pass into the hands of disloyal men who are waiting only for this last and full recognition of their rights to wipe out, by unfriendly legislation or otherwise, every person, white as well as black, suspected of unconditional loyalty to the General Government?"[267] Rebel rule promised to invert the common call to "punish treason, reward loyalty." Ending Reconstruction prematurely, Stewart asserted, would give "unreconstructed rebels license . . . to reward[] traitors and persecute[e] Union men."[268] Former Confederates in power would engage in equal opportunity persecution with respect to anyone thought to be loyal to the national government. "[T]heir hate toward the Union men and the colored race is intense and diabolical in the extreme," Moulton observed, "[a]nd their power would be constantly exercised to oppress, harass, and extirpate the entire Union element of the South."[269] He continued:

> [S]uppose the Union people, we here in this Hall, yield up these great principles of justice and right, and the principles of the Opposition and the rebel leaders prevail; the rebel States would be admitted with all their disloyalty, treason, hatred of the Government, hatred of the freedmen and the Union men in the South, and with the unrepentant rebel smarting under the humiliation of defeat. What would be the consequences? The rebel States would have entire and exclusive control of their State governments. Their State laws would comport with their bitter feelings against the Government, Union men, and the freedmen; they would at once be persecuted, hunted down like dogs, their property confiscated, discriminated against in every law, deprived of suffrage and all rights, and could be exterminated or compelled to leave the States.[270]

Local authorities in an unreconstructed former Confederacy would not check private violence directed at any of the Union faithful. H. Wilson laid out "an unbroken chain of testimony going to show that the withdrawal of the troops of the United States is immediately followed by outrages upon the freedmen and upon men of known loyalty."[271] Representative Burton C. Cook of Illinois predicted that "the State laws . . . which were designed to protect Union men and freedmen[] would be swept away, and the judges appointed by . . . loyal Governors . . . would have to give place to men who would execute the will of the rebel majorities." "The recognition of these States now," he continued, "means the abandonment of the loyal men and the freedmen of the South to the mercy of men who hate and despite them for their loyalty."[272] The fates of former slaves and white Republicans in an unreconstructed south were entwined. "If . . . we disfranchise the loyal blacks," Kelso asked, "what hope will remain to the loyal whites after the Federal troops are withdrawn and the rebels restored to power?"[273] Windom maintained that under rebel rule "the freedmen of the South . . . shall have no protection for their persons and property" and that "loyal white men . . . shall have no political advantages over the rebels."[274]

The Thirteenth Amendment would be a dead letter in an unreconstructed south. Re-enslavement or worse, Republicans agreed, would likely follow if Southerners were left in control of Southern politics. "They acknowledge that slavery, as it once existed, is overthrown," Julian maintained, "but the continued inferiority and subordination of the colored race, under some form of vassalage or serfdom, is regarded by them as certain."[275] Stevens stated how, "if we leave them to the legislation of their late masters, we had better have left them in bondage. Their condition would be worse than that of our prisoners at Andersonville."[276] African Americans would barely eke out a subsistence, if that. Howe contended: "[T]hey mean, in spite of emancipation, to monopolize still the labor of the freedmen, to control its wages, and to appropriate all of its proceeds not demanded for their bare support."[277] This exploitation was the first step to re-enslavement. "[T]hey mean to do more than monopolize the labor of the freedmen," Howe continued. "[T]hey mean to convince the American people that emancipation was a blunder and a crime."[278] "Four million people," Wade agreed, would "be ostracized from this Government, to be made serfs forever."[279] Former Confederates in power might even declare unconstitutional the Thirteenth Amendment. Representative George S. Boutwell of Massachusetts reminded his peers that the former Confederate vice president, Alexander Stephens, "denies the constitutional efficacy of our amendment abolishing slavery,"[280]

No trace of civil rights legislation could survive a premature end to Reconstruction. Farnsworth declared that the white Southerners in power would "repeal . . . the civil rights bill, . . . grinding to the very depths of misery, compared with which slavery would be a boon, the four million freedmen."[281] Black Codes would be entrenched the day the last Union soldier left Dixie. G. Williams asked:

> How, then, is the condition of the negro improved by emancipation, under a policy that cuts him off from the enjoyment of all protection in person or property, and is intended obviously to keep him in the bonds of servitude, and to prove to the world that the real victory is theirs, and that the boon of freedom was only a cheat and a delusion? What is there to prevent the reenactment of the whole black code in any of these States as soon as they shall have been relieved from our control by readmission into the Union upon the terms of the Executive.[282]

The combination of nominal freedom and no legal protection made bondage seem attractive. Proponents of congressional Reconstruction worried that masters had more interest in the well-being of their slaves than employers had in the well-being of their at-will employees. "[I]f we leave all power in the hands of the dominant race," Representative John M. Broomall of Pennsylvania foresaw, "we will have done the negro little kindness in abolishing slavery. We will have abolished the duties of the slaveholder while we will have preserved his power and his spirit, only transferring them from the individual to the mass. We will have the negro a slave to the community, with no one man pecuniarily interested in his well-being."[283]

Former slaves would have no legal rights in a regime that repealed all civil rights laws and made a mockery of the constitutional ban on slavery. Howe thought that, in an unreconstructed South, "the freedmen shall not come to the polls; shall not enter the witness box or the jury box, or sue in the courts; shall not hold lands, nor inherit or transmit property."[284] Gaining formal legal rights would do little for persons of color stuck in the former Confederacy. The Radical Republican senator from Wisconsin asked: "[W]ill you tell me how, with all these disabilities heaped upon them, they are to be able to employ an attorney to appear for them? Or how, with all this prejudice arrayed against them, they are to find an attorney who dare appear for them? Or how, with all this indignity piled upon them, they are to find a jury that is not instructed to credit what they say?"[285]

Republican proponents of congressional Reconstruction were as concerned with what they believed were the ominous financial consequences of a politically empowered South as with what they predicted would be the dire consequences for race relations in the former Confederate states. Yates observed: "They are as defiant in their dangerous dogma of State sovereignty as when the war began. They are clamoring for the payment of the rebel debt. They are opposing the payment of the debt incurred by the United States. They are demanding compensation for their slaves."[286] Price warned Republicans to anticipate "an attempt to assume the rebel debt in some shape, and to repudiate the national debt in some manner, and also to pay for the slaves who have been made free."[287] The neediest of the Union faithful would suffer as much as the Union creditor and the Union taxpayer. Representative Ebenezer Dumont of Indiana feared that representatives from the rebel states would join Northern allies "in repudiating the national debt, or adding the confederate debt to it, in repealing the laws granting pensions to our living disabled soldiers, and to the widows and orphan children of those who are dead, and perchance to insert the names of their own traitors on our pension rolls, and tax our people to pay them."[288]

Proponents of congressional Reconstruction feared that Southern representatives in Congress would have no reason to pay the national debt, compensate disabled veterans, or provide for the families of deceased soldiers. Former Confederates had no political or economic incentives to fulfill national obligations incurred during the Civil War. Broomall pointed out that

[t]hese men are expected to represent their States in Congress. They are large holders of the rebel debt. Are they therefore especially qualified to vote for taxation to pay the cost of their own subjugation? Some of them have lost a limb in the rebel service; others have lost sons and brothers. Are they therefore especially qualified to vote pensions to our wounded soldiers and the widows of our dead ones?[289]

"Shall we intrust to their decision the question whether we shall preserve the public faith by repaying the money which loyal men among us have advanced to sustain the Government in the time of its need," Cook asked, "and whether we shall pay the pensions we have proposed to the soldiers who, in endeavoring to sustain the Government, have in the hands of these same men been mutilated and disabled?"[290] Southern promises made at gunpoint were not to be trusted. "You say that they have repudiated the rebel debt," Ward declared. "Indeed they have, in form; but how long do you suppose it will be after they get their members back into Congress before they will repeal all such legislation?"[291] Cook pointed out: "If this debt was repudiated with such intense reluctance, is it certain that when all political power is again given to their hands they will not rescind their action?"[292]

Southerners in power would prevent the national government from satisfying legitimate obligations incurred to Union creditors and Union soldiers by draining federal and state coffers to satisfy illegitimate demands made by Confederate creditors, former slaveholders, other Confederate property holders, and Confederate soldiers or their survivors. Republicans anticipated that former rebels in Congress would funnel money southward. H. Wilson warned that "the rebel slavemasters hope for compensation for slaves emancipated by national authority" and would "demand some compensation" for "the widows and orphan children of men fallen in battle," as well as for "the holders of thousands of millions of confederate bonds and obligations."[293] "Every man of them," Representative Ebon C. Ingersoll of Illinois stated, "will vote to assume the rebel debt and pension the disabled rebel soldiers, and the widows and children of those who lost their lives in the rebel cause, and pay for the property that has been destroyed by our armies that marched through the South."[294] These Southern financial demands would be enormous. "They will demand $2,000,000,000 for slaves, untold hundreds of millions of dollars for depredations committed by our armies," Boutwell predicted. He warned his partisan allies that "[a]n aggregate of thousands of millions of claims, or demands having the color of claims, will be marshaled against the Government."[295] Former Confederates might gain from the national judiciary what they did not gain from the national legislature. G. Williams thought "they will at least stagger your courts with the question, by what authority under the Constitution you have presumed to deprive the people of a State within the Union, by proclamation and without judgment of law, of any of their franchise or property."[296]

The resulting economic burdens would be devastating. A renewed Southern Democrat presence in the national government, Boutwell maintained, "portend[s] the destruction of the public credit, the repudiation of the public debt, and the disorganization of society."[297] Repudiation of federal obligations would destroy national finance. G. Williams asserted that "the next phase of the reunited Democracy of the North and South . . . will be opposition to the payment of this debt. . . . Readmit them here and every prudent man will endeavor to get rid of your securities."[298] The market for federal securities would collapse as soon as former Confederates entered national politics, no matter what assurances the federal government gave to potential moneylenders. "It will say you mock it," G. Williams told his peers, "when the makers of that debt, and the disloyal slaveholder himself, shall be exalted by your votes into legislators, to cooperate with the party here that has decried your obligations, and declared them to be worthless."[299]

The Northern faithful from all walks of life would suffer from the ruinous financial policies most likely to be adopted by a restored Southern elite. H. Wilson detailed how Southern financial demands threatened "[t]he holders of public securities, the possessors of the currency founded upon the public faith, the scarred soldiers of the Republic, the heirs of fallen heroes."[300] Such policies, Ingersoll agreed, promised "the bankruptcy of this Government," the "repudiation" of "your own loyal debt," and "annihilat[ion]" of "the credit of your Government." "You will no longer be able to pay the pensions to your own disabled soldiers, or the widows and orphans that have been caused by this war," he concluded.[301] Permitting Southern states to pay Confederate obligations would be as ruinous. "[T]he rebel States, if unconstrained by the Constitution of the Union," Baker asserted, "will, as soon as they get full control of themselves, set aside the little arrangements which have been made at the point of the bayonet, and burden their people with the great debts they have contracted for the overthrow of this Government—thus absorbing their revenues in their payment of these debts, and so crippling their ability to aid the exchequer of the nation."[302] Bodies as well as wallets would soon be decimated. Desperate for funds, the United States was likely to engage in military adventures abroad. A government faced with this "vast and overwhelming weight of indebtedness," Boutwell warned, would soon be engaged in "a foreign war."[303]

The Future of Politics

The North would suffer financial ruin, Southern Republicans would be decimated, and persons of color would be reduced to forced labor by a premature end to Reconstruction when a Congress open to Southern representatives was swarmed by former rebels who would immediately reestablish their alliance with those Northern Democrats who lacked any commitment to Union obligations incurred in the Civil War, were more committed to undermining a Southern Republican Party, and were even more committed to "a white man's government." Former Confederates lusted to establish the control over the national government necessary to settle scores with white Unionists and former slaves. J. L. Thomas observed that Southerners "have the determination to seize hold of the political power[] and to use it if possible to punish those who have made them submit to the laws."[304] Former Confederate heroes were poised to lead the fight for a revived slave power. Baker feared an "impending irruption of rebel celebrities into the chief seats of the Republic, which they have been unable to subvert by stealth, fraud, and perjury, or to overthrow by armed force in the field." He predicted "it will not be long before we shall see the floors of these legislative Halls speckled over with generals and colonels who won the popularity which elevated them to office by leading on the serried rebel column, under a strange and detested flag, to the slaughter of the patriot sons of the Republic."[305] Democrats were champing at the bit for Southern assistance in their quest to overthrow the Republican majority. Windom maintained that

> [r]ebels vanquished in the field are encouraged from unexpected quarters to renew the contest in other and more dangerous forms. . . . Rebellion having failed through the inability of those allies to keep their pledges, the rebels now propose to try the other mode, namely, to take their seats in Congress and carry on the contest "from the inside." In this they have renewed assurances of aid from the North.[306]

Yates thought these Northern doughfaces stood ready "to receive in the Senate and House of Representatives Senators and Representatives-elect fresh from secession State Legislatures and from battle-fields where their hands were imbrued in the blood of our loyal countrymen."[307] Rebel warriors-turned-politicians welcomed the opportunity to revitalize their antebellum coalition with Northern doughfaces. H. Wilson anticipated that "these baffled and ruined men, smarting under defeat, poverty, and wounded pride, will be ready ever to make combinations with those who in the dark and troubled night of the rebellion predicted the scaling down or the repudiation of the national debt, to secure payment for rebel debts and emancipated slaves."[308] R. Clarke spoke of a future "crime inspiring coalition of rebels and copperheads."[309] He observed: "Copperheads, attracted by natural affinitions and affections, have joined them in their conclaves, and are aiding them to heal up their wounds, revive their hopes, and prepare the material for another struggle for empire."[310]

Proponents of congressional Reconstruction, far more than free-state journalists, repeatedly emphasized how the Thirteenth Amendment would empower this unholy alliance between Northern Democrats and former Confederates. Republicans by December 1865 understood how the constitutional destruction of slavery threatened to facilitate the rebirth of the slave power. Instead of having an eighteen-vote advantage in the House of Representatives and the Electoral College, as was the case before the Civil War, members of the majority party in the Thirty-Ninth Congress estimated that the Thirteenth Amendment gave Southern whites a thirty-vote slaveocracy bonus in their quest to regain control of the national government.[311] G. Williams observed that "the conversion of the chattel into a freeman will greatly enlarge the representation of those States and bring into Congress some thirty votes on the basis of this peculiar population, while the loyal States must suffer from the increase."[312] This slaveocracy bonus dwarfed the representation of many Union states. Windom estimated that "[r]epresentatives taken from the loyal and transferred to the disloyal States" would result in "a gain in this House to the South against the North greater than the political power exercised by the States of Minnesota, Wisconsin, Iowa, Kansas, Nevada, Oregon, and California, or equal to all the New England States combined." This power was "handed over to the traitors to be wielded for the oppression of our defenders who live among them[] and against the welfare of the country."[313]

Armed with this representational boon, slaveholders might enjoy the same hegemony in national politics that they had before the Civil War. The reincarnated slave power would have the control over the presidency, the Congress, and the federal judiciary necessary to determine the official meaning of any enumerated constitutional right, including new constitutional rights to freedom and equality, to exercise any enumerated power, including new constitutional powers to implement the constitutional commitment to liberty and equality under law, and to manage the finances of the Union. Slaveholders in all three branches of the national government could initially determine the meaning of the constitutional ban on slaveholding, then repeal any constitutional provision that interfered with their pretensions. Stevens warned the Republican majority in the House of Representatives that,

[w]ith the basis [of representation] unchanged, the eighty-three southern members, with the Democrats that will in the best times be elected from the North, will always give them a majority in Congress and in the Electoral College. They will at the very first election take possession of the White House and the halls of Congress. I need not depict the ruin that would follow. Assumption of the rebel debt or repudiation of the Federal debt would follow. The oppression of the freedmen; the reamendment of their State constitutions, and the reestablishment of slavery would be the inevitable result.[314]

The fruits of Republican rule would be swept into the dustbin of history. Representative Rufus P. Spalding of Ohio predicted that a Democratic Party majority, amplified by the increased representation provided by the Thirteenth Amendment, would "repeal many, if not all, of the measures which we have adopted for the welfare and salvation of the country."[315]

Crime was paying and paying off dearly. Noting how the repeal of the Three-Fifths Clause augmented the slaveocracy bonus, Welker stated that "in this effort to overthrow the Government they have really increased their power and influence in the administration of the affairs of the Government."[316] Senator John Sherman of Ohio spoke of the "anomaly of allowing the rebel States an increased political power in Congress."[317] Again, treason was to be rewarded and loyalty punished. Baker pointed out that the basis of apportionment, if left unchanged, gave "to the recent traitors of the South, man for man, nearly double the political power in the popular branch of the Government, and over the future destinies of the Republic, which belongs to the loyal citizens of the country who have saved it from the destruction at the hands of these very traitors."[318] Windom complained that "[t]he vote of a South Carolina rebel is to be made equal to the votes of three of my own State, thus reaffirming by law the old insulting boast that 'one of the chivalry is equal to three northern mudsills.'"[319]

Windom detailed at some length the rebel redress for success, the strategy that would "in less than two years" enable "every disloyal district" to be "represented by a traitor, and traitors" to "control the legislation of the country."[320] The first step was subverting the test oath by finding persons who, while not technically guilty of treason, fully supported the Southern cause. "It will be an easy matter," Windom observed, "for the South to select men for the present Congress who have not borne arms against the Government or voluntarily given aid and comfort to the rebellion, yet who are at heart no more loyal than many who were in the rebel army."[321]

These Southern representatives in office would repeal the test oath, which required federal officers to swear that they had never committed treason. Repeal would increase rebel power in the national government by opening all offices to all former traitors. Windom noted: "At the next election every disloyal district will send men who thoroughly represent the feelings and sentiments of the people, those who have been most obnoxious for their treason having the preference."[322] The combination of constitutional rules and partisanship prevented such representatives from being removed from office no matter what their past or present disloyal behavior. "[I]t requires a two-thirds vote to expel a member," Windom pointed out, and "aided by their Democratic allies everybody knows that it would be an utter impossibility to expel Jeff. Davis himself should he be elected."[323] Rebel representatives and senators would exert far more influence than warranted by the number of their white electors. The former Confederate bloc in Congress, augmented by thirteen additional members from the repeal of the Three-Fifths Clause and supported by at least half the representatives from "the other five states which belonged to the slaveholding class"[324] (i.e., former slave states that did not secede), although elected by "less than one sixth of the people (a large majority of whom are disloyal)," would exercise "more than one third of the political power of the whole." Traitors needed only "one sixth more of the representation" to "have a majority in Congress and in the Electoral College" necessary to "elect their own President and make laws to suit themselves."[325] Northern Democrats would immediately make up that difference. Windom asked in conclusion:

> Does any one who has given the least attention to the working of political parties in this country believe for a moment that a compact, well-drilled organization at the South, which needs only one sixth of the representation from the North to give it control of the Government, will have any difficulty in obtaining that sixth? I think not? That party at the North which is now willing, for the sake of political alliance with rebels, to thus disfranchise its own section and inflict so wicked an injustice upon the loyal people, may well be trusted to go far enough to reap the fruits of such an unholy alliance.[326]

Presidential Reconstruction promised a national legislature pliant to the national executive. After pointing out that President Johnson's call for immediately seating representatives from former slave states would add fifty-eight new members of the House of Representatives and twenty-two new members of the Senate, Howe asked "what independence has that Legislature into which the Executive may at his pleasure pour so many votes[?]"[327]

These eighty extra elected members of Congress also translated into eighty extra electoral votes to be controlled by the president. Howe continued: "[W]ho is not so blind as not to see the terrible advantage which would be placed in his hands by conceding him the power to add to the vote of the Electoral College more than one third of its present number[?]"[328]

Secession would be back on the table in this reconstituted Jacksonian regime. Representatives from the former Confederate states would espouse the states' rights principles of the former Confederacy. R. Clarke declared: "If they had a right to secede, they insist that right shall still be available to them. If rebellion and waging war on the Union were lawful, ... then, they say, let us return with that privilege."[329] History, Republicans feared, was likely to repeat if reconstruction was done wrong. "[T]he apostles of secession," R. Clarke warned Republicans, "are boldly preaching treason in our Capitol, and preparing the disaffected for a second crusade against their country."[330]

Slaughter-House *Revisited*

The Republican and Unionist members of the Thirty-Ninth Congress who voted for the exclusion resolution and the Fourteenth Amendment told a different story of the constitutional history of the United States from 1860 to 1866 than did Justice Samuel Miller when he wrote the majority opinion in the *Slaughter-House Cases*. Miller claimed that the Civil War was about slavery.[331] The Fourteenth Amendment was directed at Black Codes.[332] Stevens and his political allies insisted that the Civil War about secession. The problem before the Thirty-Ninth Congress was preventing former rebels from regaining control over state and national politics.

The problem of rebel rule was a central theme in every Republican speech on Reconstruction and many speeches ostensibly devoted to proposed Fourteenth Amendments. Windom charged Democrats and President Johnson with adopting policies that empowered traitors. Presidential reconstruction was based on the notion that the

> grand panacea for all our political ills is based upon the theory that the people who attempted by violence and perjury to destroy the Government, ... that this people, without any evidences of repentance, but with every indication of sorrow for the "lost cause," of bitter hatred toward the Government and its defenders, have suddenly become sufficiently loyal to be trusted with all the rights and franchises they have renounced and forfeited.[333]

Representative Shelby M. Cullom of Illinois questioned whether former Confederate states that could be governed only by martial law were fit to send representatives to Congress. "If it is true that we are required to patrol those States with an army to protect the loyal white men and poor freedmen and to suppress treason," he pointed out, then "where is the propriety of admitting them to representation?"³³⁴ A Confederate army aside, Republicans looking southward in 1866 saw exactly what they saw when they looked southward in 1863. "[T]hey have barely ceased to be rebels, but hold to the faith of secessionists, which is rebellion in a chrysalis state," R. Clarke maintained. In his view, "[a] secessionist[] at heart is a traitor in principle"; "give him an opportunity and he will prove himself a rebel in practice."³³⁵

Republican backbenchers were as determined to prevent rebel rule as were the Republicans most responsible for framing the Fourteenth Amendment. H. Lane of Indiana stated that "it will not do to give power in the rebel States to the rebels."³³⁶ Howe described the South as a "boiling caldron of passion and excitement" into which "we are cordially invited to throw all the loyalty there is there, while treason is employed to tend the fires."³³⁷ No proponent of congressional Reconstruction wanted to be ruled by traitors. "The people of the North," Beaman asserted, "do not desire to see their political interests in the hands of disloyal men."³³⁸ Wade declared that he would "never consent to let unwashed traitors, dyed in the blood of our dearest friends, participate in the councils of the Government that they have endeavored to overthrow."³³⁹

Constitutional politics in the former Confederate states needed a complete overhaul before the United States could again be composed of all the united states. "[T]hey will never come as loyal States," Loan stated, "as long as unrepentant rebels are permitted to control their political destiny and rule the loyal people there."³⁴⁰ Representative Godlove S. Orth of Indiana summarized a common Republican view when he declared that Southern states would not be restored "until I am thoroughly satisfied that it can be done without jeopardizing in the least the peace, safety, and prosperity of our people."³⁴¹ An overhaul of Southern constitutional politics was necessary because Southern rebels were neither Republicans nor republicans. Nye captured the Republican disdain for the treasonous Southern elite:

A class that started the rebellion into growth and attempted a revolution upon the idea that "republican government was a failure"; that "the real civilization of a country is in its aristocracy, which should be made permanent by laws of entail and primogeniture"; that regards popular government as "the mistaken civilization of the age"; [and]

that would institute in the place of republican government, "an heredity Senate and Executive," is neither fit to represent or to be represented in any political body, State or national, within the bounds of this Union.[342]

This problem of rebel rule dwarfed the Black Codes as a motivating factor for constitutional reform. In contrast to the *Slaughter-House* majority, Republican members of the Thirty-Ninth Congress did not think the status of slavery settled after ratification of the Thirteenth Amendment. Rebels in control of former Confederate states had largely circumvented the constitutional ban on slavery and could be counted on to repeal in practice or in law that abolitionist edict as soon as they gained power nationally. Farnsworth spoke of the ways the constitutional ban on slavery "is avoided and got around by these cunning rebels."[343] In contrast to the *Slaughter-House* majority, Republicans did not think that granting persons of color more constitutional rights was the solution to the problems of Southern constitutional politics. Rebels who had never shown any inclination to respect constitutional limits on the expansion of slavery and were demonstrating no more respect for the constitutional ban on slavery could hardly be expected to respect constitutional provisions guaranteeing an even greater degree of racial equality. "[T]o commit their fortunes to the tender mercies of white rebels," Julian declared, "would be like committing the lamb to the jaws of the wolf."[344] In contrast to the *Slaughter-House* majority, Republican members thought that the status of former slaves was only one of many serious problems with ongoing rebel rule in the former Confederate states. If the South rose again, then white Unionists, white immigrants to the South, white Union soldiers, white widows of white Union soldiers, and white financial interests would all suffer. Windom complained that traitors had "entitled themselves to step at once, unquestioned, from the rebel congress and the rebel camps into the halls of legislation to make laws for the Republic which they have so recently tried in vain to destroy; to become the guardians of our widows, orphans, and disabled soldiers, and custodians of all the civil and political rights of the humble colored patriots whom they held in slavery as long as they could."[345] In even sharper contrast to the *Slaughter-House* majority, proponents of congressional Reconstruction recognized that constitutional reform needed to encompass all of Reconstruction, not merely race relations. "[R]ebel sentiments, rebel flags, rebel generals, rebel valor, rebel memories, and rebel debts" all had to be repudiated.[346]

This potential for government by disloyal rebels was the problem Republicans were trying to solve when they discussed, framed, and eventually passed the Fourteenth Amendment. Stevens's speech opening the debate on Reconstruction described "what we ought to do before these inveterate rebels are invited to participate in our legislation."[347] Representative John A. Bingham of Ohio, when introducing a stand-alone version of what became Section 1, pointed to "a conspiracy extending through every State lately in insurrection, and perchance beyond their limits, among these returning prodigal rebels, . . . to take possession of the legislative power of this country[] and accomplish by corrupt legislation what they failed to accomplish by arms."[348] Republican backbenchers echoed the leadership's fears of rebel rule. Representative Giles Hotchkiss of New York, in a speech commonly thought to explain the demise of the stand-alone version of what became Section 1, was blunt in stating his position: "I do not want rebel laws to govern and be uniform throughout this Union."[349]

The persons most responsible for the entire Fourteenth Amendment were dedicated to ensuring that the Lost Cause remained lost. The Fourteenth Amendment, as explained by the Joint Committee on Reconstruction, was designed to provide "adequate guarantees against future treason and rebellion."[350] The Joint Committee's report declared that the need for constitutional reform was "apparent from the bitter hostility to the government and people of the United States yet existing throughout the conquered territory."[351] Steven's last speech on the Fourteenth Amendment concluded: "The danger is that before any constitutional guards shall have been adopted Congress will be flooded by rebel and rebel sympathizers."[352]

Making Treason Odious

Republican members of the Thirty-Ninth Congress heartily endorsed Tennessean Andrew Johnson's claim, when he accepted the Republican/Unionist nomination for the vice presidency in 1864, that "treason must be made odious."[353] Forty-five Republicans repeated or paraphrased that quotation during the debates on the Fourteenth Amendment and Reconstruction. Representative Sidney Perham of Maine reported that Northern constituencies "demand that 'treason be made odious.'"[354] Stewart described the mission of the Republican Party as ensuring that "treason is blotted out, and . . . traitors are odious."[355] The House of Representatives on June 4 passed a resolution, proposed by Representative Thomas Williams of Pennsylvania, declaring President Johnson's assertion that "treason should be made odious" was "the undoubted sentiment of the people of the loyal states."[356] A related presidential quote was almost as popular. Thirteen Republicans repeated or paraphrased now-President Johnson's assertion that "traitors should take a back seat in the work of restoration."[357] Representative James M. Ashley of Ohio combined these quotations when pointing out that President Johnson was "talking about making treason odious, and declaring that traitors should take a back seat."[358] Democrats may have supported presidential Reconstruction, but none repeated those quotations on the floor of the House or Senate.

This Republican enthusiasm for quoting President Johnson hardly reflected a commitment to presidential Reconstruction or executive policies. Proponents of congressional Reconstruction agreed that "making treason odious" was the standard for judging presidential actions. Sherman declared that "we have a right to expect that the President of the United States shall fulfill his promise upon which he was elected, that he could do all he could to make treason odious."[359] Republican after Republican insisted that the president was failing his prescribed test. "Instead of making treason odious, as he promised to do," Ingersoll asserted, "he has done all that he well could to restore traitors to political power and to shield them from the legitimate results of their crimes."[360] Beaman, after quoting the seventeenth president at length and then documenting the woes of white Unionists in the South, asked "is this the way to make treason odious?"[361] Many Republicans flipped the president's claim when criticizing executive policies. Julian observed, "The legions of armed traitors . . . are all to be crowned with the honor and dignity of the ballot; and, as if to make treason respectable and loyalty odious, the colored people of the country . . . are to be handed over to the unbridled hate and fury of their old masters."[362] "Treason has been made popular in the South," Broomall complained, "and loyalty odious."[363]

Criminal trials were one means for making treason odious. Criminal punishment was President Johnson's preferred means for "making treason odious."[364] Some Republicans agreed. Nye "would hang enough to fulfill the assertion of the President that treason should be made odious."[365] Representative George F. Miller of Pennsylvania declared that "[t]reason ought to be made odious and there should be no procrastination in the trial of such offenders."[366]

Far more proponents of congressional Reconstruction quoted Johnson when discussing post–Civil War constitutional politics than when considering possible uses of the noose.[367] Rebel rule, Republicans agreed, was the consequence of not making treason odious.[368] "Is this the way 'treason is to be made odious[?]'" Windom asked when observing how the constitutional rules for apportionment would result in "vast political power to be taken from the loyal people of the North" and "handed over to the traitors to be wielded for the oppression of our defenders who live among them."[369]

H. Lane described as "a strange mode of punishing traitors and making treason odious" Democratic calls for "inviting these rebels into the Halls of Congress with an increase of fourteen members to their representation."[370] Treason trials distracted from the more vital concern: preventing traitors from governing former Confederate states and the national government. J. Ashley "was more anxious to secure justice to our friends and allies than to execute vengeance on our enemies."[371] Representative John D. Baldwin of Massachusetts worried that the failure to acknowledge that "treason is a crime to be punished and made odious" was inhibiting efforts to fashion "effective guarantees . . . against a return of the rebel spirit to political control of the country, or of any part of it."[372]

Making treason odious required policies that stripped rebel leaders and rebel constituencies of their power. Bans on officeholding and disenfranchisement were one means for making treason odious. Eckley would "contribute in rendering 'treason odious'" by "never vot[ing] to admit unconditionally a rebel Representative to a seat in this Hall or to place the ballot unrestricted in the hands of a traitor."[373] Apportionment reform was another. W. Lawrence quoted President Johnson's assertions that "treason must be made odious" and that "traitors should take a back seat in the work of restoration" when urging that "the basis of representation and direct taxes should be changed" so that "none can doubt but those who would reward traitors with a premium of political power for their treason."[374] Former Confederate states could be restored only when they were committed to President Johnson's catechisms. Benjamin would support admitting representatives from Tennessee only when "'[t]reason is made odious' there" and "bloody-handed traitors compelled to take a back seat."[375]

Making treason odious meant empowering the faithful. Black suffrage was a means for ensuring treason was made odious. Stewart feared government policy would not make "loyalty odious and treason honorable" unless persons of color were granted the ballot.[376] "Treason must be made odious," Sumner stated, "and to this end power must be secured to loyal fellow-citizens."[377] Proponents of congressional Reconstruction who opposed Black suffrage nevertheless agreed that making treason odious required making fundamental changes in constitutional politics that empowered those who had demonstrated steadfast allegiance to the Union. Latham, after observing "disloyalty to the United States is made honorable and loyalty made odious," insisted that "[i]f political power is in the hands of those who should not be its custodians, . . . let us wrest it from them."[378]

3

Protecting and Empowering the Loyal

If rebels were the problem, then loyalty was the solution. Senator Timothy O. Howe of Wisconsin maintained that a central goal of Reconstruction was "to conserve what loyalty there is in [former Confederate states], . . . hasten its development," and "demonstrate to the world that it is no longer dangerous to be loyal."[1] Representatives of former Confederate states could play no role in national policymaking until Congress was assured that the state they represented was loyal. The Indiana Union convention resolved: "Until the people of these States prove themselves loyal to the Government they should not be restored to the rights enjoyed before the rebellion."[2] "I would exact of them all," Representative Henry J. Raymond of New York declared, "needed and all just guarantees for their future loyalty to the Constitution and laws of the United States."[3] These guarantees included protections for those who had remained loyal during the Civil War. Representative John M. Broomall of Pennsylvania proposed that "Congress should [not] confer upon [the former Confederate states] the necessary power to form their own State governments and local institutions . . . until the rights of those among them, or whatever caste or color, who remain always true to their allegiance, are effectively protected and guarantied."[4] A petition from citizens of Massachusetts insisted that, "before recognition of the late rebellious districts as States and their admission to the national councils, a due regard must be had for the rights of the loyal people, and for security for the future."[5] Republicans and allied Unionists also wanted guarantees that those who remained loyal during the Civil War would be empowered. "[W]e should know," Representative Benjamin F. Loan of Missouri insisted, "that the political power in the State seeking recognition is confined exclusively to loyal hands and that equal privileges and exact justice have been secured by law alike to all loyal citizens."[6]

An overwhelming consensus existed in the Thirty-Ninth Congress that loyal people should be protected and empowered. Tables A.3 and A.4 document how Republicans, Democrats, and Unionists all celebrated the states that did not secede as "loyal states," just as all members of Congress condemned the states that seceded as "rebel states." Senator William M. Stewart of Nevada spoke of "the people of the loyal States who have succeeded in abolishing slavery."[7] Senator Edgar Cowan of Pennsylvania discussed "the almost unanimous, if not the unanimous expression of the opinion of the loyal States as to the object and purpose of the war."[8] Again, proponents of congressional Reconstruction were somewhat more likely than proponents of presidential Reconstruction to speak of "loyal states" and to use "loyal" as an adjective or noun. All members of Congress agreed that the rights of loyal persons had to be scrupulously honored. Senator James Dixon of Connecticut, a leading congressional supporter of presidential Reconstruction, obtained unanimous consent when he proposed that Congress pass "legislation . . . for the protection of loyal citizens of the United States whose property . . . has been confiscated by the so-called confederate government, and for the restoration of such property to the loyal owners."[9] The same bipartisan consensus supported government by the loyal.

Proponents and opponents of congressional Reconstruction differed on who constituted the loyal people of the United States. Democrats insisted that their party was as loyal to the Union as Republicans. Republicans, even those who opposed congressional Reconstruction, disagreed. The Republican Party and only the Republican Party, Republicans insisted, was the party of the people who remained loyal to the United States during the Civil War. Democrats maintained that most white Southerners had been loyal, were prepared to be loyal, or had good excuses for disloyal behavior. Republicans believed the only loyal white Southerners in 1866 were the relatively few who had actively supported the Union in 1861. Democrats never referred to persons of color as loyal. Republicans celebrated African American fidelity to the Union and military prowess during the Civil War. They maintained that Black Southerners were the only large constituency of loyal citizens in the former Confederate states.

The differences between the Reconstruction policies championed by proponents and opponents of congressional Reconstruction followed from these differences in who constituted the loyal people of the United States. President Andrew Johnson and his allies sought to empower most white Southerners who either had been loyal or were prepared to be loyal. Representative Thaddeus Stevens of Pennsylvania and his political allies sought to protect and empower loyal former slaves and the few loyal white Southerners in ways that would enable those who remained faithful during the Civil

War to live among most white Southerners who proponents of congressional Reconstruction recognized had been and remained disloyal. Democrats decried policies aimed at partisan advantage. Republicans, regarding their coalition as composed of the loyal people of the United States, insisted that the Union could enjoy the fruits of the Civil War only if the party of the Union continued to control the national government and gained control over the governments of former Confederate states.

Debates over Reconstruction and constitutional reform were fueled by significant differences in the numbers of persons the political actors of the time thought were loyal. Proponents of presidential Reconstruction saw loyalty as triumphant throughout the United States. Both major parties in the North were and had always been loyal. Union military victories freed most faithful white Southerners from the tyranny of the rebel minority, although some hangings and selective disenfranchisement might be useful for maintaining that allegiance. Confident that the numbers of faithful citizens guaranteed loyal control of the national government and former Confederate states once all loyal Southerners were represented in Congress, President Johnson and his political allies saw no need for substantial constitutional reform. Proponents of congressional Reconstruction believed the number of loyal persons in the United States too few under existing constitutional arrangements to maintain constitutional governments in the former Confederate states and in the nation. Only one major political party in the North was loyal. Most white Southerners were disloyal. Constitutional reform was necessary to protect loyal Southerners from rebels, to protect loyal Northerners from a rebel/Copperhead coalition, and to empower all loyal Americans in ways that would prevent rebels from governing the South and rebels/Copperheads from governing the nation.

Democrats

Democrats and other proponents of presidential Reconstruction who thought the Civil War ended at Appomattox believed as fervently that loyalty to the Union was restored when General Robert E. Lee surrendered to General Ulysses H. Grant. Mass disloyalty, in their view, did not exist in the North. Differences between Northern Democrats and Republicans were normal partisan disputes over the best means for combatting secession. Lee was sincere when he maintained that the only interest his remaining soldiers had was returning home to plant their fields in loyal submission to the Union. A politics of immediately restoration, Democrats maintained, was the best politics of loyalty.

IDENTIFYING THE LOYAL

Proponents of presidential Reconstruction identified the loyalty by race. Virtually all Northern whites were loyal during the Civil War. Loyalty was bipartisan. Northern white Democrats were as loyal to the Union as Northern white Republicans. Most white Southerners were as loyal, either because they had never been committed to the Confederacy or had sincerely foresworn secession. Former Black slaves, who had sided and would likely continue to side with the rebel elite, were the largest numerical class of disloyal persons in the United States during Reconstruction.

Bipartisanship. Democrats understood themselves as the loyal opposition.[10] They were not traitors because, opposing secession, Democrats were neither rebels nor rebel sympathizers. Party members disputed the means for fighting the Civil War and the goals of the war, but they agreed (at least the Democrats in Congress did) with Republicans that secession was illegal, that those who led the movement for secession were rebels, that rebels were traitors, and that traitors deserved to be punished.[11] After pointing out that Democrats had sent "its hundreds of thousands of volunteers into the ranks of the Federal armies," Representative Benjamin M. Boyer of Pennsylvania insisted "[n]o one party can rightfully boast of having saved the country."[12] Representative Charles A. Eldredge of Wisconsin described Democrats as composed of "men who will respect the Constitution, who will respect the Union and the sacrifices that have been made for it, and who are willing to restore, preserve, and perpetuate that Union."[13]

The real disunion faction in the North, prominent proponents of presidential Reconstruction charged, were Radical Republicans, many of whom had supported William Lloyd Garrison's public burning of the Constitution before the Civil War and who were opposing the policies that would unify the United States after the surrender at Appomattox. Boyer accused Republicans of "fight[ing] for disunion as zealously as ever armed traitors at the South fought for it during the rebellion."[14] Harkening back to Stephen Douglas's attack on the sectional Republican Party that began his first debate with Abraham Lincoln,[15] President Johnson's political allies in Congress maintained that national parties were the best means for achieving national unity. "Let a network of both parties ramify everywhere, spread over the whole country," Cowan pleaded, and "the cement of two parties interwoven like a network over the whole country will contribute a hundred times more to keep it together than any other device, or even the Constitution itself."[16] Republican calls for constitutional amendments were rooted in a partisanship inconsistent with true allegiance to the Constitution. "Show me a man who for a temporary advantage, either for himself or his party, would set foot upon one of his country's laws," Cowan stated, "and he is not loyal."[17]

White Southerners. When Democrats and their allies looked southward, they saw more white victims than unrepentant rebels.[18] Some were victims of rebel domination. Numerous Southern loyalists had supported the Union cause at great personal cost. Cowan insisted that "a great many of them did not engage in rebellion; a great many of them engaged to suppress it; some of them shed their blood in that attempt, and some of them struggled through all manner of difficulties to be true and faithful."[19] More were victims of Radical Republicans. Senator Garrett Davis of Kentucky insisted that Southerners "are more loyal than those who keep them out of their rights."[20] Most were victims of both the rebel and radical elite. "[T]he masses of the people in the South are not to blame for this war at all," Representative Andrew J. Rogers of New Jersey announced. "It was the leaders of the South . . . and the fanatical demagogues of the North . . . who are guilty of this war."[21]

President Johnson and his allies maintained that most Southerners during the Civil War were far more loyal to the Union than membership in and support for the Confederate army might indicate. Proponents of presidential Reconstruction asserted that numerous white Southerners had been coerced by secessionists or placed in situations in which loyalty was no longer a feasible option.[22] Many Southerners were compelled to assist the Confederate effort. G. Davis insisted: "The whole country was hunted over to find every man who was capable of bearing arms, and, without regard to his own judgment or his own disposition to enter into the rebellion or keep out it, he was forced by a resistless power to become a conscript in the rebel army."[23] Representative Green C. Smith spoke of "a large number of good and loyal men who never of their own free choice abandoned their love of the Republic."[24] Desertion rates proved that most Confederate soldiers were faithful to the Union in their hearts. "[A]n enormous desertion," G. Davis maintained, "could only have resulted from the fact that the greater proportion of them were forced into the service and were required to fight for a cause against which they were opposed in principle and sentiment and if left to their own free will would never have entered."[25] Democrats and allied Unionists insisted that the law of nations excused those Southerners who reluctantly supported the Confederacy. The withdrawal of practical Union protection in 1861 justified the withdrawal of obedience. If "allegiance and protection [were] reciprocal,"[26] then the Union had no right to expect loyalty from persons the national government could not defend in the immediate wake of secession. G. Davis maintained that "[t]he true and loyal men who constituted large majorities in many of the southern States were abandoned, they were left wholly without defense and protection by the Government that wants now to oppress them."[27]

This absence of Union protection in an environment of pervasive coercion counseled against limiting the loyal to those white Southerners who had supported the Union throughout the Civil War. Senator Thomas A. Hendricks of Indiana thought all persons who supported the Union in 1860 should be counted among the faithful. He considered loyal those "men who displayed heroic courage in standing out against the secession movement, but who afterward yielded obedience to and served the established government *de facto*."[28] G. Davis thought a patriotic heart sufficient. He considered loyal "every man who was willing to remain faithful to the Government of the United States, provided he had received such protection and support from the Government as would have enabled him to maintain that position."[29]

Proponents of presidential Reconstruction maintained that most white Southerners satisfied their loyalty standards. When protection returned, they recanted their disloyal sentiments and announced they were prepared to pledge undying allegiance to the Constitution of 1787. President Johnson and his political allies took their once and future citizens at their word. Senator James Guthrie of Kentucky maintained that "the great mass of the people accept the situation, and mean to be loyal to the United States."[30]

African Americans. When Democrats cast their southward gaze away from white Southerners, they saw former slaves who had been more loyal to the Confederacy than to the Union. Boyer complained how, "as a race, they did far more to sustain the rebellion than to suppress it. By their patient labor they sustained and fed the armies of the rebellion. They rose nowhere in insurrection."[31] Representative Charles Sitgreaves of New Jersey agreed that the "evidence is overwhelming that they were loyal to their masters."[32] Black military prowess and accomplishments were substantially overrated. "All the blacks in the South," Hogan insisted, "were not 'loyal'; were not our 'friends'[;] did not rush to 'our rescue'; did not 'fly to arms' for 'our defense.'"[33] White men and white men only were responsible for the Union military triumph. Rogers, after waxing eloquent on white soldiers, stated that the "records of the war show that while a few [former slaves] came into the ranks of the Federal Army, the great body of them remained true and loyal to the South."[34] "The white soldier did more," G. Davis stated.[35]

PROTECTING AND EMPOWERING THE DEMOCRATIC LOYAL

Democratic opposition to constitutional reform was rooted in Democratic understandings of who was and was not loyal. Loyal white Southerners, proponents of presidential Reconstruction repeatedly declared, were entitled to be represented and, if elected, represent their jurisdictions. Boyer insisted that, should "the people of the South . . . send loyal men to represent them in this Hall, they have a right to be here and a right to heard in the affairs of the Government."[36] Loyal whites were entitled to representation even if they were a small minority. Should "bloody-handed traitors, though numbering nine tenths of the people [be] disfranchised," Boyer maintained, Congress should "let the loyal people carry on the republican government of the State."[37] Many traitors responsible for secession by 1866 were dead or discredited. Others could be hung until dead after treason trials or discredited by disenfranchisement. "[L]et these men be tried; if guilty, let them be convicted," Smith proclaimed.[38] This combination of policies, which empowered white Southerners with loyal hearts and politically neutered secessionists with disloyal tongues, promised to return the United States to the constitutional politics of 1859, if not 1832, minus the fire-eaters who manipulated Southern people into leaving the Union and precipitated the Civil War.

No need existed for constitutional amendments that reformed national politics by adjusting apportionment or expanding suffrage. The loyal would govern no matter which party won national elections. A Southern alliance with Northern Democrats was normal republican politics, given that Northern Democrats were at least as loyal to the Union as were Northern Republicans. Black suffrage was the only threat to rule by the loyal, given the past tendency of slaves and former slaves to side with their treasonous masters. Black rights and protection in a "white persons' government" remained for superior whites to determine.

Further constitutional guarantees for loyal whites were unnecessary because loyal whites could protect themselves politically. Crippled Union soldiers and the widows of deceased Union soldiers could trust "the pledge of the honor and hearts of the people."[39] Hendricks thought that "pensions and bounties need no guarantee" given their widespread support in Northern states.[40] Loyal majorities would never assume any Confederate obligation. Representative William E. Finck asserted, "[N]o one can be found in this country silly enough to believe the rebel debt ever will be paid."[41] Democratic proposals in the Thirty-Ninth Congress for compensating former slaveholders were limited to "payment for the slaves which were enlisted in the United States Army in loyal slave States."[42] Many Republicans who supported compensation supported compensating only these loyal slaveholders.[43]

Republicans

Republican proponents of congressional Reconstruction who believed the Civil War did not end at Appomattox as fervently believed that disloyalty in the United States was as endemic in 1866 as in 1861. Disloyal white Southerners remained in power. Disloyal Northern Democrats remained beholden to the slaveholding elite for a share of national power. Former Black slaves were loyal but disempowered and distressed. A politics of massive reconstruction was necessary to fashion a politics of loyalty.

IDENTIFYING THE LOYAL

Republicans maintained that their coalition was the party of the loyal. Politics was a contest between the loyal and disloyal, not between two parties that competed for control of the government by offering somewhat different and often overlapping visions of the public good. Loyal Southern whites were few, far between, and in danger of extinction. Disloyal slaveholders had overwhelming influence on Southern constitutional politics, but most white Southerners could not be trusted as long as the slaveholding elite dominated politics in the former Confederate states. Freed slaves and Black citizens were the only Southerners who as a group in 1866 were loyal to the Union.

The Republican Party. Republicans identified the cause of the Republican Party (or Union Party) with the cause of freedom. Prominent Republicans regarded their coalition as a divine instrument for justice. Senator Henry Wilson of Massachusetts on March 2, 1866, asserted:

> Mr. President, the House, the Senate, the Cabinet, the President, each and all should not now forget to remember that they were clothed with authority by a party inspired by patriotism and liberty, a party that proclaims as its living faith the sublime creed of the equal rights of man and the brotherhood of all humanity, embodied in the New Testament and the Declaration of Independence. Let Representatives, Senators, Cabinet ministers, and the President amid the trials and temptations of the present, fully realize that the great Republican party, embracing in its ranks more of moral and intellectual worth than was ever embodied in any political organization in any age or in any land, was created by no man or set of men, that it was brought

into being by Almighty God to represent the higher and better sentiments of Christian America, to bear the flag of patriotism and liberty,
of justice and humanity. Brought into being in 1854 to resist the repeal of the prohibition of slavery in Kansas and Nebraska, the further
expansion of slavery into the depths of the continent, and the longer
domination of the slave power, it has for twelve years, in defeat and in
victory, ever been true to country, ever faithful to its flag, ever devoted
to the rights of struggling humanity. No political party in any country or in any age has fought on a plain so lofty, or achieved so much
for country, republican institutions, the cause of freedom, of justice,
and of Christian civilization. If it should perish now in the pride of
strength and of power, by the hands of suicide, or by the follies or
treacheries of men it has generously trusted, it will leave to after times
a brilliant record of honor and of glory.[44]

The Republican Party that H. Wilson celebrated had won the Civil War.
Representative Ephraim R. Eckley of Ohio thought that "the Union party"
had "sustained . . . our gallant Army in the field."[45] "[T]he Union party,
composed of the soldiers in the field and the loyal patriotic masses of the
loyal States," Representative Hezekiah S. Bundy of Ohio agreed, "contend-
ing successfully with the armed legions in the field and the more cowardly
allies in the North and West, saved our heritage."[46] If united, Republicans
would win the peace. Representative James Garfield of Ohio called "upon
the great Union party to stand together, and with all their manhood resist the revolutionary schemes not only of these rebels at the South, but of
their coadjudicators and abettors on this floor and everywhere who would
unite with them and trample not only upon the prostrate body of the Union
party, but, as I believe, of liberty herself."[47]

The identification of the Republican Party as the party of Americans who
remained loyal during the Civil War reflected how most partisans viewed
their coalition in the nineteenth century. Politically active citizens in Jacksonian America did not hold twentieth-century understandings of a two-
party system as structured by competition between coalitions representing
different groups of people who fought over the spoils of government.[48] A
political party was the best vehicle for maintaining the Constitution. Martin
Van Buren, the person most responsible for mass American political parties,
believed that "[a] democratic Constitution . . . required the institution of
the political party, by which the democracy could defend the Constitution against aristocratic sapping and mining."[49] The party of the people was
just as responsible for maintaining democracy in the United States. Gerald

Leonard and Saul Cornell point out how "such a party was not to be just one of two parties in roughly equal competition under the Constitution. Rather, it would be the party of the entire democracy in defense of majoritarianism itself."[50] Democrats, Whigs, and Republicans thought their coalition was the party of the people who were loyal to the Constitution and that their party was engaged in deadly battle against a minority dedicated to undermining the fundamental law of the land. Antebellum Democrats labeled that minority "the Money Power." Antebellum Republicans labeled that minority "the Slavepower." Both groups of partisans heartily endorsed the Van Burenite understanding that "only the permanent entrenchment of a party of the democracy would preserve the Constitution against an ever-ready aristocracy."[51]

Constitutional democracy was at stake in every election. Democracy was at stake because only one party truly represented the loyal majority of the United States. The Constitution was at stake because only one party was truly committed to playing by the constitutional rules, working within constitutional limits, and achieving constitutional aspirations. Leonard and Cornell observe that "political competition" in the United States was "between . . . those in the party who would 'secure the Constitution on a firm basis' and . . . those outside the party who would 'overturn the Constitution.'"[52]

Republicans were Van Burenites on partisan competition, even as they regarded Van Buren's beloved Jacksonian coalition as the mortal enemy of the constitutional republic. "Whenever party is necessary to sustain the Union," Stevens proclaimed, "I say rally to your party and save the Union." Stevens and his fellow partisans regarded themselves as constituting America's party because the Republican Party was the only coalition during that 1860s that was faithful to the Constitution. Representative Samuel McKee of Kentucky stated, "I do desire that party still to rule this land, because they alone having been loyal, they alone should rule."[53] Republicans, Representative William D. Kelley of Pennsylvania proclaimed, were charged with "maintain[ing] beyond all cavil or dispute" against Democrats the "proposition" that "the Constitution of the United States is the supreme law of the land."[54] Elections that determined "who ought to govern the county," in his view, were between "[t]he men who for more than four years sustained the bloody war for its overthrown or . . . the great Union party who maintained the Government against the most gigantic rebellion since that which Satan led."[55]

Democrats were the party of the disloyal. They were "copperheads."[56] Members were disloyal during the Civil War. Kelley declared that "the

Democratic party of the North fought for the rebellion where there was no personal danger as zealously as the Democratic party of the South did on the field of mortal danger."[57] Garfield accused the minority party of having "undertaken to reject and resist our scheme of restoring the Union for five years."[58] Democrats were no more loyal after Appomattox. Garfield accused party members of uniting "to reject the scheme of the great Union party and of the people to build up liberty in this country and put down traitors and treason everywhere."[59] Representative George S. Boutwell spoke of "insidious and dangerous doctrines, which are responded to by the whole Democratic party of the country," that "portent the destruction of the public credit, the repudiation of the public debt, and the disorganization of society."[60] "Every traitor of the South and every sympathizer with treason in the North," he declared, "sustains the policy of the Democratic Party and the President."[61]

Representative John A. Bingham of Ohio was the most important exception to this partisan consensus. Bingham insisted that he could not "approach the discussion of this great question, which concerns the safety of all, in the spirit of a partisan."[62] The Ohio Republican broke dramatically with the Jacksonian understandings of partisanship articulated by his fellow Republicans when he claimed,

> [t]he want of the Republic to-day is not a Democratic Party, is not a Republican party, is not any party save a party for the Union, for the Constitution, for the supremacy of the laws, for the restoration of all the States to their political rights and powers under such irrevocable guarantees as will forevermore secure the safety of the Republic, the equality of the States, and the equal rights of all the people under the sanctions of inviolable law.[63]

Crucial elements of this call to elevate fundamental rights to a place beyond political competition echo Justice Robert Jackson's famous assertion almost a hundred years later that "[o]ne's right to life, liberty, and property, to free speech, a free press, freedom of worship and assembly, and other fundamental rights may not be submitted to vote; they depend on the outcome of no elections."[64] Bingham was nevertheless not echoing the sentiments of other prominent Republicans in 1866 who thought the electoral triumph of the political party of the loyal people essential for protecting fundamental rights. Bingham may have anticipated the future regime, but the Thirty-Ninth Congress was controlled by Republicans who were Van Burenites on the vital role of partisanship for protecting constitutional rights.

White Unionists in the South. When Republicans looked southward, they saw far fewer loyal whites than did Democrats and President Johnson. All Northern factions agreed that white Southerners who supported the Union during the Civil War were loyal. Proponents of congressional Reconstruction, however, had little patience for the pleas of coercion that so moved President Johnson and his allies. The coercion excuse was cheap talk. Senator Waitman T. Willey of West Virginia observed that even Alexander Stephens, the vice president of the Confederacy, was now claiming "he never entered into the rebellion voluntarily."[65] Republicans found no more believable professions of loyalty from white Southerners who supported the Confederacy during the Civil War but claimed renewed devotion to the Union after the Confederate army surrendered. Proponents of congressional Reconstruction wanted a South ruled by the persons who had been loyal to the Union during the Civil War, not by those who pledged eternal fidelity to the Constitution of the United States only when staring down the barrel of a gun.

Republicans agreed with Democrats that elites dominated Southern politics, but Stevens and his allies insisted that domination took place through undue influence rather than, as many Democrats claimed, through duress. Antislavery advocates before, during, and immediately after the Civil War condemned a slave power that exercised hegemonic control over slave states by shaping public opinion.[66] Representative Thomas D. Eliot of Massachusetts spoke of "the masses of men who do not direct affairs, but are themselves guided and controlled by others."[67] These Confederates "engaged in the rebellion more by force of the will of others than of their own."[68] Representative Nathaniel P. Banks of Massachusetts captured this Republican understanding of the South as the land of elite manipulation when he declared,

> I do not believe that there is a State in this Union where at least a clear majority of the people were not from the beginning opposed to the war; and could you remove from the control of public opinion one or two thousand in each of these States, so as to let up from the foundations of political society the mass of common people, you would have a population in all these States as loyal and true to the Government as the people of any portion of the East or West.[69]

Hegemonic politics created a gulf between the Southern leadership and the Southern people. Representative John F. Farnsworth of Illinois spoke of "politicians in the South who, keeping themselves out of danger, set on the ignorant and brave to fight for what they were told by these rascals were 'their rights.'" As victims of elite propaganda, ordinary Southerners were far more likely to become loyal citizens than their supposed betters after events had discredited the slave power. "[T]he almost universal testimony from the rebel States," Farnsworth reported, "is that the soldiers who fought us in the field accept their situation of 'defeated and vanquished' with a much better grace than the politicians and non-combatants."[70]

"Misguided"[71] Confederates nevertheless had to be shown the light before they could be represented in Congress. Long-standing Southern elites, Republicans repeatedly pointed out, still controlled public opinion. Committed rebels had been elected to public office before the Civil War, were being elected to public office in 1866, and would be elected to public office for the foreseeable future until they were neutered politically as well as militarily. Former Confederate soldiers who "accept[ed] their situation," Farnsworth pointed out, were still supporting "unrepentant and unwashed murderers and traitors" when voting.[72] Time was needed to remove the baneful influence of the slave power and develop a Southern public opinion more favorable to the Union, free labor, and racial equality. The possibility that Reconstruction policies could break the dominance of the Southern elite gave Republicans hope for a more loyal future, but that loyal future had not yet been sufficiently realized to seat in Congress delegations from the former Confederate states.

The differences between proponents of congressional and presidential Reconstruction regarding which white Southerners were loyal was put on full display during a debate over staffing the post office. Identifying the loyal was the critical issue when the Senate considered what should be done when not enough otherwise qualified and interested residents of former Confederate states could take the test oath necessary for officeholding. Supporters of President Johnson called for abandoning the test oath or other proofs of loyalty during the Civil War. White Southerners who were not loyal in 1863 might be loyal in 1866. J. Dixon believed that "a man may be loyal and true to the Government at this time who cannot take the required oath."[73] Republicans disagreed. Persons who could not swear that they were loyal in 1863 were not sufficiently loyal in 1866 to participate in politics or hold public office. Offices that could not be filled by persons loyal in the Civil War should not be filled. "[I]f it is true that there are not loyal men enough in the States lately in rebellion to fill the post offices," Senator James W. Nye of Nevada declared, "this Government should not furnish them postal facilities."[74]

African Americans. Freedmen were "loyal."[75] Loan described "colored soldiers" and "colored citizens" as "the only considerable portion of the inhabitants" of the former Confederate states "that is or has recently been loyal to the Republic."[76] Stewart stated: "Two fifths of the people of the eleven States are colored, and are instinctively loyal and real friends of the Government."[77] Almost every Republican who spoke at some length in the Thirty-Ninth Congress on Reconstruction at some point emphasized that former slaves, freedmen, or persons of color were faithful to the United States during and immediately after the Civil War. Senator George H. Williams of Oregon maintained that Black Southerners "compris[e] a majority of the loyal people" in the former Confederate states.[78] Nye declared the Black man "is loyal and attached to the government."[79]

Republicans often used "black" and "loyal" as synonyms or otherwise treated all former slaves as putatively loyal. Garfield noted "those loyal millions who were made free."[80] Representative George W. Julian of Indiana spoke of "four million loyal colored people."[81] When proponents of congressional Reconstruction called for "extend[ing] the elective franchise to every loyal male citizen of the Republic," they were calling for Black suffrage.[82] Senator Samuel C. Pomeroy asked: "Have we made loyalty secure in the seceded States if only a portion of the men vote, and especially if that disfranchised portion be of the ranks of the truly loyal?"[83] Stewart, when insisting freedmen be granted the ballot, spoke of "exten[ding] the franchise to the loyal as well as the disloyal." "The question," he continued, "is shall this Government be in loyal or disloyal hands—in the hands of its friends or the hands of its enemies."[84]

Proponents of congressional Reconstruction repeatedly contrasted Black loyalists and white traitors. McKee "prefer[red] to trust the meanest black man with a loyal heart who ever wore the chains of slavery to the most intelligent traitor who has waged war against my country."[85] A petition from citizens of Wisconsin observed how "that portion of our people of African descent resident in the late insurgent States . . . were ever found faithful and loyal while treason seemed to be or was the normal condition of many of the whites in the insurgent States."[86] Senator Richard Yates of Illinois compared bondsmen favorable with their owners. "The poor loyal slave of the South," he asserted, "was more religious and more loyal than his slave-master."[87] Republicans who expressed concerns with "readmitting rebels to equal rights with loyal persons"[88] often made race the dividing line between loyal and disloyal Southerners. Kelley criticized Democrats for claiming "four sevenths of the people, every soul of them were loyal, should be disfranchised, and three sevenths, every soul of whom were disloyal, should govern the whole seven hundred thousand people of the state."[89] Representative Josiah B. Grinnell of Iowa stated, "I will never prefer a white traitor to a loyalist black."[90] Racist tropes on Black mental inferiority went hand in hand with assertions of Black patriotic superiority. Representative John R. Kelso of Missouri asserted: "The whites with all their intelligence were traitors, the blacks with all their ignorance were loyal."[91]

African American soldiers were particularly loyal. Representative John W. Longyear of Michigan declared "we should not ignore the services of the freedmen who heroically bled in defense of their country."[92] Nye noted "[t]he exhibition of his bravery . . . most recently in our own civil war."[93] Republicans gave Black soldiers substantial credit for the Union triumph in the Civil War. Julian stated, "They have done their full share in saving the nation's life. Many of them went into the Army as the substitutes of white ruffians . . . whose unprofitable lives were saved by the black column which stood between them and the bullets of the rebels."[94] Stewart maintained, "[w]hile his labor was added to the power of treason traitors were triumphant; when it was subtracted and added to the material resources of the Government the Union forces were victorious."[95]

Black military service extended beyond the battlefield. Senator Luke P. Poland of Vermont detailed the various services persons of color performed during the Civil War. He remembered "how loyal and faithful these people ever proved; how they fed, clothed, concealed, and guided our prisoners who had escaped from rebel prisons and starvation; how faithfully and truly they brought us information and guided our troops; and more than all, how gallantly they fought by the side of our men, and how nobly they yielded their lives to save the nation."[96] Other Republicans shared similar memories. "[W]herever they found a suffering solider of the Republic they ministered to his every need to the fullest extent of their humble ability," Representative James F. Wilson of Iowa observed. He continued: "Did he need food, they divided their scanty store with him; did he need shelter, they found for him that which was safe; did he need a guide, they gave up their hours of rest and led him through forest and swamp to the lines of the union."[97]

Protecting and Empowering the Republican Loyal

Congressional Reconstruction promised government of the loyal, by the loyal, and for the loyal. Reconstruction and constitutional reform were designed to protect the loyal from rebel rule and prevent rebel rule by empowering the loyal. Republicans would admit in Congress representatives from former Confederate states only when former rebels were replaced by or transformed into loyal citizens. Loyal persons who had remained faithful throughout the Civil War were responsible for reconstructing former Confederate states and were the beneficiaries of Reconstruction. Loyal people determined what guarantees were necessary to protect loyal persons.

Bingham maintained that the persons responsible for determining the commitments former rebels should make before restoration were "the loyal people of the loyal States, who saved the Union, and are represented on this floor," and that those loyal people were "the final judges upon that question, and from their decision there lies no appeal."[98] Representative Hiram Price of Iowa called on "the Representatives of a free and loyal constituency" to pass a constitutional amendment prohibiting payment of the rebel debt.[99] Many proponents insisted that only loyal states ratify those guarantees that took the form of constitutional amendments.[100] No need existed to include the rebel states in the deliberations over the Fourteenth Amendment and other guarantees. Banks stated, "The proposition is for the loyal States to determine upon what terms they will restore to the Union the insurgent States."[101] The constitutional guarantees Republicans sought were designed to protect and empower the loyal. McKee spoke for his partisan allies when he maintained that "in order to protect the loyal people of this land something must be done by a law ingrafted into the Constitution to protect them in their loyalty."[102] Proponents regarded punishing treason as another means of increasing security for the loyal. Treason trials, Jo. Henderson asserted, would "sustain the confidence of loyal people[] and warn the refractory for all time to come."[103]

Reconstruction protected and empowered people who Republicans thought were loyal. A central goal of Reconstruction and constitutional reform was entrenching the power of the Republican Party as the primary institutional vehicle for the people who were loyal during the Civil War. The white people who received rights guarantees were those Southern Unionists, Union soldiers, widows of Union soldiers, and Northern investors who had been loyal during the Civil War. African Americans played crucial roles in Republican efforts to protect and empower the loyal, but that role was primarily as the main loyal constituency in the former Confederate states rather than as the primary object of a "new birth of freedom."

Substantial constitutional reform was necessary because the Constitution of 1865 did not adequately empower or protect the persons or the political party that remained faithful to the Union during the Civil War. Loyal persons lacked the numbers necessary to ensure they could establish the control of the national and state governments necessary to protect loyal white Southerners, loyal white Northerners, and loyal persons of color. Most white Southerners were disloyal. The strong Democratic minority in the North was as disloyal. The loyal national majority could govern and protect the loyal throughout the United States only if constitutional politics was transformed by constitutional amendment.

THE CENTRALITY OF LOYALTY

Proponents of congressional action on Reconstruction were far more concerned with fashioning a loyal South than a South committed to free labor, racial equality, or some notion of fundamental human rights. A loyal South would be a safe place for loyal people. As such, former Confederate states could demonstrate their renewed allegiance to the Union by not violating the rights of former slaves and white Unionists. Nevertheless, the bottom line for most Republicans was allegiance as manifested by the treatment of the loyal, rather than the protection of fundamental rights as an end independent from loyalty. As Mark Wahlgren Summers explains, Republicans "would have *liked* to see justice done; but they *must* have security — a settlement that would stick, assuring that there would be no new war, no new wounds."[104] "The defense of equal rights," he continues, "depended not on a sense of justice alone but on a sense of urgency, the need for protection for the Union."[105]

Loyalty determined when Congress would restore the antebellum prerogatives of former Confederate states. The first condition for restoration, Senator Charles Sumner of Massachusetts demanded, was "[t]he complete reestablishment of loyalty."[106] "[T]he era of fraternity will be secured," Representative William Lawrence of Ohio stated, "with unqualified loyalty restored."[107] This loyalty required deeds, not the bland promises or mere oaths that President Johnson and his political allies thought were sufficient for restoration. Representative Hamilton Ward, Sr., of New York thought that when "former rebels" should "be admitted to a share in the Government . . . will depend much upon their loyalty and the ability they manifest to take loyal part on the Government."[108] W. Lawrence set out the conditions and consequences of loyalty when he asserted:

> When loyalty returns, when permanent civil government shall be practicable, in the sense that it shall bring obedience to national authority, and protect the Union population and the freedmen in the enjoyment of their rights, with security for the future assured, then can the work of restoration be made complete. When there shall be a loyal majority in any State able to control State government and prevent it from falling into the hands of traitors, then can State government be restored.[109]

Former Confederate states would enjoy representation in Congress — the most important prerogative of restored states — only when they were deemed loyal. The national legislature, Senator Lyman Trumbull of Illinois asserted, had to determine whether there "was a loyal government, representing the loyal people of the State, and in a condition that entitled them to representation in the two Houses of Congress."[110] Whether a particular representative had been faithful to the Union had no bearing on whether that representative could represent a state that had seceded from the Union. Republicans insisted that persons who had always supported the Union cause could not represent those whose allegiance remained with the Confederacy. "Do not tell me there are loyal representatives waiting for admission," Stevens stated; "until their States are loyal they can have no standing here. They would merely *mis*represent their constituents."[111] The loyal residents of former Confederate states were no more entitled to representation than the loyal neighbors they elected were entitled to represent. Boutwell insisted Congress require that, "in each of these States before they are allowed representation, the masses of the people shall be loyal, for the representative will reflect the views of the people."[112] Loyal members of Congress had to represent loyal voters. "I must know," Representative George R. Latham of West Virginia agreed, "that the constituency from which the applicants comes is of sufficient loyalty to preserve or maintain, as against home disaffection, a republican State government in harmony with that of the United States."[113] In his view, "until these prerequisites are met and satisfied, whether it be one year or ten years, or more, I would govern them by martial law and without representation[] . . . to preserve the territory in the interest of loyalty."[114]

Loyal people staffed the governing institutions responsible for reconstruction. McKee stated bluntly: "I desire that the loyal alone shall rule the country which they alone have saved."[115] Banks resorted to metaphor. "In a dark night, on a stormy sea," he averred, "the humblest man on ship-board would know enough to advise that the helm should be put in the hands of a man who wanted to save the ship, and not in his whose purpose was to destroy it."[116] Proponents of congressional Reconstruction insisted that loyalty was an absolute qualification for public office. Sumner's fifth condition for restoration was "[t]he choice of citizens for office, whether State or national, of constant and undoubted loyalty."[117] Nye maintained that "[t]he Government should see to it that every officer in it is loyal, or there should be no officers."[118] Professed loyalty in 1866 was not sufficient. The loyal persons entitled to represent had to demonstrate their allegiance to the Union from 1860 and before to 1866 and afterward. Latham declared: "[T]he applicant claiming a seat upon this floor must be loyal; and I would not accept *whitewashed* loyalty, or loyalty of a recent growth; he must have been loyal all the time—all the way through."[119] Some more conservative Unionists endorsed the test oath requirement. "[I]f they do not send the right kind of men, good men, loyal men, men who can do as we have done—stand before the altar of this House, and with uplifted hand swear before

God and man that they have never done anything to overthrow and destroy this Government," Smith declared, "send them back and let their people send another, and if he cannot take the oath, let them keep on sending men until they give us one who can be properly qualified to sit in the great Legislature of the nation."[120]

Only loyal need apply for reconstructing the South. Numerous petitioners called on Congress to "punish treason at least with ineligibility to office and loss of power."[121] Twelve hundred good citizens of Missouri insisted that admitting rebels to office was "a wanton insult to the whole loyal people."[122] Rebels need not apply for state and local offices or vote in state or local elections. Representative Rufus P. Spalding of Ohio stated that "it would have been right and proper in culling the first legislative bodies into action, in the rebel States, to have used the suffrages of all loyal freemen, without respect to color, and to have rejected the votes of all who had participated in the war against the Government."[123] Rebels need not apply for federal offices, either. Representative Martin Welker of Ohio put it succinctly: "No traitor should ever be allowed to contaminate these beautiful Halls."[124]

Loyal people made the rules for Reconstruction. Representative M. Russell Thayer of Pennsylvania called for "some scheme upon which the loyal people of the country might unite to effect a perfect restoration of peace and harmony throughout the United States."[125] Representative Jehu Baker of Illinois hoped "the loyal white men and the loyal black men, working side by side, will yet reconstruct the South."[126] Loyal persons in the national legislature oversaw Reconstruction. The House and Senate should be entrusted with the responsibility for determining Reconstruction policy, Nye stated, because "Congress represent[ed] the loyalty of the nation."[127] Broomall declared that "the loyal people of this nation, through their Representatives in Congress, should be the judge of what great and just guarantees will make them secure in the future."[128] Loyal people in the unreconstructed South were responsible for drafting and ratifying new state constitutions. Representative James M. Ashley of Ohio introduced a bill "to enable the loyal citizens of the United States whose constitutional governments were usurped or overthrown by the recent rebellion . . . to form a constitution and State government for each of said States preparatory to resuming as States their constitutional relations to the national government."[129] Kelso "call[ed] upon all the loyal people of those Territories, and none but the loyal, to form constitutions, republican in form, and apply for admission as States of the Union."[130]

Loyal persons were entitled to protection. Stewart stated: "To protect the southern loyal men, to protect the freedmen . . . is our first and paramount duty."[131] Representative Reader W. Clarke of Ohio declared that he was "bound in duty and affection to those who have stood firm in their integrity and preserved the nation from the wrath of its assailants."[132] Proponents of congressional Reconstruction emphasized Congress's responsibility to prevent traitors from oppressing loyalists. Stevens insisted that Congress "sufficiently protect the loyal men of the rebel States from the vindictive persecutions of their victorious rebel neighbors."[133] Longyear wanted "thorough and reliable protection for the loyal men in the rebel states."[134] Martial law and continued exclusion were necessary to achieve a bare modicum of security for persons of all races in the South who had always pledged allegiance to the Union. Restoring former Confederate states without further securities for the faithful, Representative Burton C. Cook of Illinois explained, would mean "the abandonment of the loyal men and the freedmen of the South to the mercy of men who hate and despise them for their loyalty."[135] Ward reported, "Tennessee loyalists are begging to have the military retained for the protection of loyal men."[136]

Loyal persons were entitled to be empowered. "Justice and a due regard to our national safety," Ward maintained, "would take the government of those States from the hands of our country's enemies and place it in the hands of its friends."[137] When defending his proposed constitutional amendment banning race discrimination in voting, Senator John B. Henderson of Missouri declared: "Let us permit the loyal minority to govern."[138] Proponents of congressional Reconstruction anticipated the contemporary sports adage that the best defense is a good offense when maintaining that empowering the loyal was the best bulwark against the disloyal. Kelso suggested how, "[t]he power being thus established in the hands of the loyal people, they would be able to keep the rebels in subjection, and we could recall our armies. Emigration, sure of protection, would pour into those States, and soon the element of treason would be swallowed up and lost."[139] A confident Longyear proclaimed that "[r]ebels must be taken care of here in the Halls of Congress; and so long as the loyal people of the country remain true to themselves and the Government, traitors will be taken care of here."[140]

GUARANTEES FOR THE PARTY OF THE LOYAL

Empowerment meant sustaining the strength and unity of the Republican Party. Stevens was particularly adamant that proponents of congressional Reconstruction obtain the guarantees necessary to entrench in government the Republican Party as the party of the people who remained loyal to the Union during the Civil War. His speech-opening debate on Reconstruction policy urged Republicans "to secure perpetual ascendancy to the party of the Union; and so as to render our republican Government firm and stable forever."[141] Stevens immediately before the House vote on the first version of the omnibus Fourteenth Amendment declared that the provision disenfranchising many former rebels "is there to save or destroy the Union by the salvation of destruction of the Union party."[142] Republican rule, if successfully maintained through various guarantees, would culminate in the South being remade in the image of the Republican Party. When Julian called for a constitutional amendment "whose darling purpose would be to Yankeeize and abolitionize the entire South, and put the old slave dynasty hopelessly under their feet,"[143] he was proposing constitutional reforms that would transform former Confederates into Republicans.

Prominent Republicans agreed that the success of Reconstruction depended on Republican rule. H. Wilson maintained: "The enduring interests of the regenerated nation, the rights of man, and the elevation of an emancipated race alike demand that the great Union Republican party, the outgrowth and development of advancing civilization in America, shall continue to administer the Government it preserved, and frame the laws for the nation it saved."[144] Senator John Sherman of Ohio insisted, "you must not sever the great Union party from this loyal element of the southern States."[145] Constitutional reform was necessary to ensure that the party responsible for the Northern victory in the Civil War remained the party responsible for ensuring that loyal citizens enjoyed the fruits of that noble achievement. McKee supported constitutional amendments that would "continue in power the great party which sustained our armies in the field."[146] G. Williams demanded that constitutional politics be restructured so that "control of this Government should remain in the hands of the men who stood up for the Union during the late war."[147] Republican journalists agreed. The *Springfield Republican* asserted that Republican Party had a "duty . . . to retain power as long as it can by honorable means, for the good of the country."[148]

GUARANTEES FOR THE LOYAL (WHITES)

Loyal Americans needed three kinds of insurance against future rebel rule. Loyal Southerners, Southern immigrants, soldiers, widows, and creditors needed financial guarantees. Loyalists of all races in the South needed civil rights guarantees. Most important, the people who had remained loyal during the Civil War needed the political guarantees necessary to ensure that rebels would never again rule. While proponents of congressional reform sometimes spoke of the loyal people without mentioning race or the loyal

people without regard to race, loyal white people were often the main beneficiaries of Republican reform proposals. Sometimes the racial beneficiaries
were explicit.

Financial guarantees. Loyal people needed financial guarantees. The Joint
Committee's report emphasized the need to "protect the loyal people
against future claims for the expenses incurred in support of rebellion and
for manumitted slaves."[149] Proponents of congressional Reconstruction emphasized how repudiating the rebel debt prevented white Unionists from
being overburdened by ruinous taxes. Welker justified a constitutional
amendment forbidding states "to levy any tax or imposts to pay the rebel
debt" by pointing out "[m]any loyal men are there who did not favor the
rebellion who should be protected from the payment of this debt."[150] "We
ought not to leave the question whether the loyal Union men of the South
shall be taxed to refund to rebels the money advanced by them to secure
the destruction of the lives and property of loyal men," Cook agreed, "to
the decision of the rebels who have advanced the money and seek its repayment."[151] Northerners who moved to the South needed the same protection
from levies aimed at compensating Confederate creditors or former slaveholders. Senator Daniel Clark of New Hampshire declared, "I do not want
that any citizen of my State or any citizen of any other loyal State who shall
go down into that country shall ever be taxed to pay one cent of the rebel
debt."[152] Financial guarantees protected the loyal people who remained in
the Union states from paying the taxes needed to raise revenue for compensating Confederate creditors and former slaveholders. "The loyal people
of the United States who risked their private interests in support of the
national authority have a right to demand," J. Wilson stated, "that the Government shall require, as a condition precedent to the admission of rebel
States, that the fundamental law shall be so amended as to make it forever
impossible that the public debt shall ever be endangered by the payment of
a single dollar for emancipated slaves or confederate obligation."[153]

Members of the military and their survivors—the vast majority of whom
were white—were in particular need of financial guarantees. "The late war,"
Representative Ralph P. Buckland of Ohio stated,

> has imposed great obligations upon the national Government, the
> most important and sacred of which is that of providing for the dis-
> abled soldiers, the soldiers' widows, and the soldiers' orphans. The
> Government is also bound to provide for the future protection of the
> lives, the liberty, and the rights of property of the loyal white people

and of the loyal colored people of the rebellious States. These obligations must be faithfully discharged, and I am not willing by any act of mine to transfer the control of the Government to the party or to the men who would be likely to disregard these obligations.[154]

Senator Benjamin F. Wade of Ohio called for doing "something to protect those wounded patriots who have been stricken down in the cause of their country and to put the security of their pensions and their means of support beyond the power of wavering majorities in Congress."[155]

Loyal creditors who had loaned money to the Union—almost all of whom were white—were in as much need of financial guarantees as were loyal soldiers. A petition from citizens of Massachusetts equated Union bondholders with former slaves when insisting that "the national faith of the United States also shall be guarded carefully, both with regard to our creditors and with regard to our freedmen."[156] Representative Thomas Williams of Oregon made the connection between honoring the national debt and paying pensions to Northern soldiers and their widows when he called for measures guaranteeing "obligations . . . to the families of those brave men who have gone down to death upon so many Southern battlefields."[157] The financiers who provided the national government with the funds for military pensions were entitled to reap the contracted-for benefits of their largess. T. Williams stated: "We must provide for the payment of its interest, as well as the redemption of all the pledges we have made to the disabled soldier, and to the widows and orphans of those who have perished in the field."[158]

Proponents of congressional Reconstruction played up numerous themes on loyalty when championing financial guarantees. They called for financial guarantees in the name of the loyal. Farnsworth maintained that "repudiating the rebel debt, and claims for slaves, will be most heartily adopted and approved by every loyal man in the nation."[159] They insisted on financial guarantees as a measure of loyalty. Former Confederates could demonstrate their allegiance to the Union by foreswearing payment of their debt and by committing themselves to maintaining the integrity of the Union debt. "As regards loyalty to the Union," Representative William A. Newell of New Jersey maintained, "we should be satisfied that they will repudiate all their debts incurred in the prosecution of the late war; and on the other hand respect the debts contracted by us in putting down the rebellion."[160] Repudiating the rebel debt simultaneously punished treason and rewarded loyalty. "I do not believe in paying traitors," Senator Jacob M. Howard of Michigan declared; "nor do I believe in indemnifying men abroad who, with their eyes open and a malignity in their heart beyond all parallel, gave them aid and comfort."[161]

Civil rights guarantees. Civil rights guarantees protected the fundamental rights of those who remained faithful to the Union during the Civil War. Loyal people had rights that needed securing. The rights of the disloyal were left to Democrats. Representative Joseph W. McClurg of Missouri sponsored a resolution calling for "giv[ing] the loyal citizens of those States protection in their natural and personal rights enumerated in the Constitution of the United States."[162] A petition from citizens of Massachusetts declared that "a due regard must be had for the rights of the loyal people."[163] J. Ashley would protect the rights of "all loyal men, . . . especially . . . the soldiers and sailors who served in the Union Army and Navy."[164] Many proposed rights guarantees supported protecting all loyal people, white and Black. A petition from Gloversville, New York, called on Congress to "provide security and equality before the law to loyal men of the South, without distinction of color."[165] J. Ashley spoke of the need for guaranteeing "the rights of all loyal men, without regard to race or color."[166] Proponents of congressional Reconstruction were explicit that loyal whites needed and were entitled to the same protections as loyal Blacks. Representative John H. Rice of Maine championed homestead laws that protected "the freedmen and the loyal whites of the South."[167]

Some Republicans proposed civil rights guarantees aimed squarely at loyal white persons. Bingham was explicit. He declared that an early version of Section 1 was designed "to protect the thousands of loyal white citizens of the United States whose property, by State legislation, has been wrested from them under confiscation, and protect them also against banishment."[168] Howe was speaking of Southern white unionists when he maintained that "[w]e must therefore furnish protection. . . . for that other class of their population . . . which is not black, but which is almost equally as unfortunate by reason of having been loyal."[169] Republicans, without mentioning race, often called for rights guarantees designed to prevent and remedy the rights violations that white persons had experienced during the Civil War and were experiencing in the early days of Reconstruction. "Gentleman who oppose this amendment," Bingham declared, "simply declare to these rebel States, go on with your confiscation statutes, your statutes of banishment, your statutes of unjust imprisonment, your statutes of murder and death against men because of their loyalty to the Constitution and Government of the United States."[170] This list speaks of the persecutions that loyal whites experienced during the Civil War, ignoring the discrimination loyal

Blacks experienced upon the formal cessation of hostilities. Representative Fernando C. Beaman of Michigan similarly emphasized the rights of white Unionists when he spoke of the need to protect the "loyal southern men for their sacrifices, services, and patriotism, who have braved prisons and loss of property, and the scorn and threats of bloody-handed traitors, and even death itself, rather than betray their country?"[171] Whites were asked to betray their country during the Civil War and were imprisoned if they did not. Rebels did not believe persons of color had a country to betray. Blacks who helped the Union were whipped and murdered, not imprisoned.

Political guarantees. Political guarantees empowered the loyal. Bans on officeholding guaranteed government by the people who remained faithful to the Union during the Civil War. Apportionment reform transferred power from Southern rebels to Northern loyalists. Political guarantees that empowered the loyal also protected the loyal by providing strong foundations for financial and civil rights guarantees. Proposals to disenfranchise former Confederates or bar them from public office punished treason and rewarded loyalty. McKee spoke of both traitors and loyalists when defending a constitutional ban on former Confederates holding public office. "Let us adopt this amendment," he declared, "and the men who made war upon us can never assume control of this Government again. Adopt this amendment, and you put the legal stamp of condemnation upon them and forever secure to the loyal the victory over armed treason."[172] Politically neutering traitors empowered the faithful. Trumbull declared "the object" of bans on officeholding was "to place these rebellious States in the hands of loyal men."[173] McKee thought officeholding bans would "encourage . . . the loyal men . . . because the nation will say to them 'You alone who have remained true, shall hold office.'"[174] Disenfranchisement was a more powerful means for punishing treason and rewarding loyalty. "We find that every southern State which is in the hands of loyal men," Trumbull observed, "has not only excluded from office, but from the right of suffrage also, the leading traitors."[175]

Apportionment reform empowered the loyal by ending the slavocracy bonus that enabled Southern whites to gain representation for slaves and freedmen who did not vote. R. Clarke proposed "equalizing representation in Congress so that a South Carolina rebel shall at most[] not possess more political power than a loyal Ohioan."[176] Farnsworth, when calling for apportionment reform, insisted that free Blacks "shall not be used to swell their rebel masters into giants and dwarf the loyal and patriotic men of the free states into Tom Thumbs."[177] Almost every Republican who called for apportionment reform contrasted the disloyal Southern rebel with the faithful Northern voter. G. Williams condemned the existing system that made "one unrepentant traitor the equal, in many instances, of two or three loyal northern men."[178] The question before Congress, H. Wilson insisted, was "whether one rebel in South Carolina shall count as much in the Electoral College and in the House of Representatives as two loyal men of New England, or of the great central States, or of the West."[179] Proponents of apportionment reform were particularly prone to compare members of the Confederate army to Northern soldiers. "I could not return to my own gallant State," Eckley maintained, "and say to her loyal people and to the three hundred thousand gallant sons she sent to the field that by my vote I had reduced their political power until it required five of these scarred veterans to equal two of the rebels against whom they fought."[180] H. Wilson spoke of "the men in the loyal States who believe the soldier who fought the battles of the Republic is the equal of the traitor who fought against the country."[181]

Proponents of congressional Reconstruction supported electoral reforms that empowered loyal whites and the loyal white majority in the loyal states. When tinkering with various apportionment schemes, Republicans and allied Unionists emphasized those features of their preferred alternative that punished treason and rewarded loyalty. Bingham thought unnaturalized immigrants should be included in the basis of representation because that population was largely "confined to the free loyal States."[182] Many Republicans favored apportionment on the basis of population rather than by voters because apportionment by population would enable border states to disenfranchise former Confederates without diminishing the political power of those citizens who had been faithful to the Union during the Civil War.[183] Representative John L. Thomas, Jr., of Maryland maintained that representatives to Congress and the Electoral College should not be based on the number of eligible voters in each state because that standard would disadvantage the "loyal States" that had banned disloyal rebels from voting.[184] Republicans scrutinized proposals for enfranchising persons of color to make sure they did not disenfranchise other loyal persons. J. Wilson rejected proposals combining Black suffrage and literacy tests because the latter "depriv[ed] . . . loyal white men of the right of voting."[185]

Republicans championed political guarantees that empowered the loyal as important means for sustaining the financial and civil rights guarantees that protected the loyal. Political guarantees provided strong foundations for financial guarantees. McKee pointed out that, "[i]n order to secure the payment of the national debt, in order to prevent the payment of compensation for slaves who have become freemen, and the assumption of the rebel debt, the control of this Government must be by the loyal men of the land."[186] Government by the party of the loyal was as necessary to "reward[] the heroes who survive with broken and maimed limbs and feeble bodies" and "deal[] out pensions and bounties to the orphans of the slain soldiers of the Republic."[187] Political guarantees for the loyal were more effective than civil rights guarantees for the loyal. As noted in chapter 2, Stevens warned Republicans that without apportionment reform "[a]ssumption of the rebel debt or repudiation of the Federal debt would follow" and "the reestablishment of slavery would be the inevitable result."[188] Suffrage reform was as important for protecting civil rights. "In less than six months," Stewart predicted, "every Union man will see that there is no protection, no freedom, for the blacks without the ballot, and the universal sentiment of the loyal masses will demand the enfranchisement of the oppressed race."[189]

GUARANTEES FOR LOYAL BLACKS

Proponents of congressional Reconstruction stressed loyalty when protecting and empowering persons of color. Republicans spoke of civil rights guarantees for loyal freedmen rather than civil rights guarantees for freedman, former slaves, or Black/Negro/colored citizens.[190] Advocates of Black suffrage maintained that persons of color should be given the ballot because Black citizens could be trusted to vote for loyal candidates. Sumner aside, few placed the same emphasis on voting as a fundamental right of male citizens. Black suffrage, proponents of congressional Reconstruction maintained, was a vital means for protecting and empowering loyal Blacks and, at least as important, protecting and empowering loyal whites.

Republicans insisted that Black Americans earned rights by being faithful to the Union during the Civil War. The Joint Committee's report, when discussing Section 2, declared: "It did not seem just or proper that all the political advantages derived from their becoming free should be confined to their former masters, who had fought against the Union, and withheld from themselves, who had always been loyal."[191] Much Republican rhetoric justified granting persons of color rights because they were loyal. Julian asked Republicans to "place the ballot in the hands of the loyal freedmen."[192] "If the States are to be organized immediately," Senator James H. Lane of Kansas agreed, then "the only question is whether the right of suffrage shall be given to rebel white men or loyal black men."[193] Boutwell feared that Black loyalty could not be taken for granted. "If you fail to secure the black man in his rights," the Massachusetts Republican warned party members, "he will be ready to accept the right of suffrage from the southern leaders, and transfer his allegiance, sympathy, and support from you to them."[194]

Many Republicans emphasized the military service performed by persons of color when justifying proposals for protecting and empowering newly minted Black citizens. The Joint Committee's report stated:

> [A] large proportion of the population had become, instead of mere chattels, free men and citizens. Through all the past struggle these had remained true and loyal and had in large numbers fought on the side of the Union. It was impossible to abandon them without securing them their rights as free men and citizens. The whole civilized world would have cried out against such base ingratitude, and the bare idea is offensive to all right-thinking men. Hence it became important to inquire what could be done to secure their rights, civil and political.[195]

"The soldier who aided in crushing out this wicked oppression upon the rights of honest labor, under whatever skin it may be found," Representative Burt Van Horn of New York stated, "thus established forever in this land by his suffering those sacred rights will stand ever before by the side of every citizen of the Republic, of whatever color, in defense of the rights for which he has fought."[196] Gratitude provided one basis for Black rights earned on the battlefield. Representative James R. Hubbell of Ohio maintained that "[a]mple and complete protection to the freedmen . . . is demanded . . . by the unmistakable voice of their grateful countrymen."[197] Republicans often spoke of an implicit contract with persons of color: service in exchange for rights. "In the extremity of our distress we called upon the black man to help us save the Republic," Garfield declared, "and amid the very thunder of battle, we made a covenant with him, sealed both with his blood and ours, and witnessed by Jehovah, that when the nation was redeemed, he should be free and share with us the glories and blessings of freedom."[198] Baker spoke of the "precious boon of civil freedom which has been pledged to the colored people of the South, in consideration of their great service to the Government in its hour of need."[199]

Proponents of voting rights were particularly prone to emphasize Black loyalty and military service as the primary foundation for extending the ballot to persons for color. "I am for suffrage to our friends in the South," Wade declared, "the men who have stood by us in this rebellion, the men who have hazarded their lives and all that they hold dear to defend our country."[200] "[D]id not the Congress of the United States pass a law for enrolling into the service of the United States the black man as well as the white man," Farnsworth asked when defending universal male suffrage.[201] Kelley pointed to Black heroism on the battlefield when defending his view that Congress should pass legislation granting all male persons of color the right to vote.

He asked: "Has the gentleman forgotten Port Hudson and Milliken's Bend? Do the papers he reads belong to that class which excluded from their columns everything about colored soldiers and American victories? If they do, let him study the story of Battery Wagner."[202] Clark declared similarly: "I would rather have the vote of the loyal black man, who periled his life to save the country, without probation, than of the rebel white man who periled his to destroy it."[203] Americans risked divine punishment should they not acknowledge and reward Black sacrifice. "If having called one hundred and eighty thousand men of the colored race, native-born American citizens, to fight our battles, after the aid they have given us, after they refused to take the musket for the defense of the confederacy when the confederacy appealed to them to do it," H. Wilson prophesized, "if we refuse to extend to them the suffrage, the weapon of protection, it will bring upon this nation, as slavery brought upon it, the curse of an offended God."[204]

Sumner, the Republican who most relied on claims rooted in human rights when calling for guarantees protecting and empowering persons of color,[205] made ample references to Black loyalty when championing bans on discrimination in civil, criminal, and voting laws. He spoke of "the supplemental promises only recently made to the freedman as the condition of allegiance and aid against the Rebellion."[206] The senior senator from Massachusetts waxed eloquent on Black military service when demanding Black suffrage. He declared that

> no government of a State recently in rebellion can be accepted as republican, where large masses of citizens who have been always loyal to the United States are excluded from the elective franchise, and especially where the wounded soldier of the Union, with all his kindred and race, and also the kindred of others whose bones whiten on the battle-fields where they died for their country are thrust away from the polls to give place to the very men by whose hands wound and death were inflicted; more particularly where, as in some of these States, the result would be to disenfranchise the majority of the citizens who were always loyal, and give to the oligarchical minority recently engaged in carrying on the rebellion the power to oppress the loyal majority.[207]

Black veterans had particular claims to participate in the writing of new state constitutions. Sumner maintained that the members of state constitutional conventions should be "the citizens of the State who have taken no part in the rebellion, especially those whose exclusion from the ballot enabled the rest to carry the State into the rebellion, and still more especially those who became soldiers in the armies of the Union, and by their valor on the battle-field turned the tide of war and made the Union triumphant."[208]

Black loyalty and military service played major roles in the debate over Black suffrage in the District of Columbia, a matter that was less contentious than Black suffrage in the states because a broad consensus existed that Congress could determine who voted in the nation's capital.[209] J. Wilson, when defending granting the ballot to persons of color, observed how, "mixed or black, they are citizens of this Republic, and they have been, and are today, true and loyal to their Government, and this is vastly more than many of their contemners can claim for themselves."[210] Every Republican who called for Black suffrage in the nation's capital spoke of Black military heroism. Grinnell described African Americans as "a race which has established its manhood by fighting our battles."[211] According to Price: "Does not every man in this country know that the negroes took up arms in defense of the old flag just as soon as this Government would allow them to do so[?]"[212] Many Republicans pointed to the total number of Blacks in Union military forces when justifying Black suffrage in the nation's capital. Bingham spoke of "one hundred and seventy-five thousand arraigned in arms under your banners doing firmly, unshrinkingly, and defiantly their full share in security the final victory of our arms."[213] Speaking with specific reference to the District of Columbia, Thayer pointed to "thirty-five hundred of those men wore the uniform of the union in the great war which has ended, and bore in that glorious struggle their share of the peril, the labor, and the suffering."[214] Several Republicans who opposed universal suffrage supported granting Black veterans the ballot. Representative Robert S. Hale of New York insisted "that men [who] have honorably served their country in arms does entitle them to the favorable consideration of Congress; and as a matter of gratitude we may fairly extend to the discharged soldiers of our loyal armies the right of suffrage."[215] Representative John A. Kasson of Iowa declared: "Let the blacks who gallantly fought go and vote."[216]

Republicans frequently compared African Americans, whose allegiance and military service had earned rights, to former Confederates, whose treason justified punishment. J. Rice pointed out that a proposed homestead law prohibiting rebels from taking advantage of various provisions enabled "more of the black race to avail themselves of its provisions than the white race of the South, for the reason that they are mostly loyal, and the whites are mostly disloyal."[217] "The colored population of this District, as a class, have shown as much devotion to our country during the severe struggle through which it has passed as their white neighbors," B. Van Horn declared. He noted: "While many with a whiter skin were plotting treason and conspiring to overthrow the Government which had made them all they were, and given them their daily bread, no treason or conspiracy was ever found in their ranks, or stained their hands with the innocent blood of the loyal and faithful defenders of the Republic."[218] The Black/white rebel contrast was particularly salient when Republicans considered qualifications for voting. "[W]ho is best entitled to vote," Farnsworth asked, "the loyal black man or the rebel white man[?]"[219] Julian pointed out: "If civil government is to be revived at all in the South, it is perfectly self-evident that the loyal men there must vote, but the loyal men are the negroes, and the disloyal are the whites."[220] Stewart made multiple contrasts between loyal Blacks and disloyal whites when defending Black suffrage:

> Dare you deny protection to the friends of the Union while you demand political rights for its enemies? Dare you say that a Union soldier shall not vote, but a rebel soldier shall? Dare you say that he who fed our starving prisoners shall not vote, but that he who starved them shall? Dare you say that this Government shall punish its friends and reward its enemies? Dare you contend that four million loyal citizens shall be outlawed and trampled under foot and allowed to perish because our enemies are exasperated against them on account of their friendship for us, and at the same time as enfranchisement for our enemies so that they may destroy our friends, menace our liberty, and embarrass our finances. Dare you deny liberty to the loyal and claim power for the disloyal?[221]

Suffrage rights, Stevens agreed, would "put the loyal freedman on an equal footing at the polls with the disloyal white man."[222]

Allegiance trumped perceptions of racial inferiority when many champions of Black suffrage defended their position. A few Republicans proponents of bans on race discrimination in voting laws rejected the common racist stereotypes of the 1860s. Representative Sidney Clarke of Kansas, during the debates over Black suffrage in Washington, DC, observed that "the colored people of this District show as good tests of intelligence, so far as that can be seen by the proportion of education among them, the amount of religious character, the quality of industry, freedom from poverty, payment of taxes, and loyalty as evinced by military service, as can be found in the constituencies of gentlemen speaking in opposition to this bill."[223] More commonly, proponents of Black suffrage made concessions to common claims of racial inferiority but then insisted that such racist considerations had no bearing on the right to vote or were outweighed by superior Black loyalty. Nye maintained that allegiance was the best measure of capacity to vote. "If loyalty and fidelity to the Government are a test of capacity to appreciate," he stated, "then most certainly has the colored man at least one of the highest and best of all qualifications."[224] Stewart rejected intelligence as a voting qualification. When championing Black suffrage, he declared, "if you allow, as you must, ignorant men who are disloyal to vote, why not let ignorant loyal men vote."[225] J. Wilson detailed why a less erudite loyal Black was more qualified to cast a ballot than a more sophisticated disloyal white. "[L]et us remember," he explained,

> that it is not always the ignorant man who makes the unsafe voter. The vicious man is the unsafe voter. The educated rebel voted against the best interests of the country long before he took up arms to destroy the Government which protected him. A man who loves his country and feels a personal interest in the success of free institutions will never make a dangerous voter, though he may not be able to read. The free white voters, however well they can read, who destroyed the orphan asylum in New York City, are far more dangerous to the permanency of free institutions than would be the liberty-loving colored men of this city if they should be instrusted with the ballot. And the case is quite as strong against the pardoned rebel whose hands are still red with the blood of murdered loyal soldiers, and whose heart is filled with bitterness toward the Government which has forced him to submit to its authority. While such men are allowed to vote, why should we close the doors against citizens who have always been true, and who have manifested, and still manifest, the most devoted attachment to the Government?[226]

Loyal government, proponents of Black suffrage insisted, was the priority of any system for allocating the ballot. When Cowan asked whether states in which persons of color voted would "send you more intelligent, more learned, more virtuous, and more independent Senators and Representatives," H. Wilson responded "[t]hey will send more loyal men."[227] Julian urged his fellow representatives not to "be particularly nice or fastidious in the choice of a man to vote down a rebel."[228]

African Americans emphasized their loyalty when petitioning Congress for voting and other rights. A petition from Black men in South Carolina asked Congress whether,

> in consideration of their unquestioned loyalty, exhibited by them alike as bond or free, as soldier or laborer, in the Union lines under the protection of the Government, or within the rebel lines under the

domination of the rebellion, that . . . they may have an equal voice with all loyal citizens, and that Congress will not sanction any State constitution which does not secure the exercise of the right of the elective franchise to all loyal citizens otherwise qualified in the common course of American law, without distinction of color.[229]

In a similar vein, Black citizens of Tennessee spoke of the "services we have rendered to the cause of the preservation of the Union."[230] Former slaves and other freedmen stressed past military service when petitioning Congress for the right to vote. Wade summarized a petition from "colored soldiers in the department of the Mississippi" as "setting forth that they have faithfully served their country in the Army, and assisted in defending the country against its enemies, and praying for the right of suffrage to be extended to them and to all other colored persons."[231] A petition from a committee of colored citizens residing in the state of Mississippi simply pointed out "we have fought in favor of liberty, justice, and humanity."[232]

Loyal freedmen were not the only or even the main beneficiary of Black suffrage. Loyal white Southerners needed Black votes for their protection and empowerment. Yates pointed out that "the time may arrive when the southern slaveholders and their northern sympathizers may come so near having the control of the Government, that the loyal black vote may be the balance of power and cast the scale in favor of Union and liberty."[233] Kelso insisted that, "though we may deny that the loyal blacks have any right to the elective franchise, we must nevertheless grant it to them in order thus to protect the loyal whites, whom all admit we are bound to protect." Channeling the interest-convergency thesis that Derrick Bell would advance more than a hundred years later,[234] Kelso highlighted the vital importance for white citizens of measures granting rights to Black citizens. In his view, "[i]f . . . we disfranchise the loyal blacks, what hope will remain to the loyal whites after the Federal troops are withdrawn and the rebels restored to power?"[235] G. Williams agreed that "[o]ur best security is to erect a breakwater against the encroachments of the dissatisfied white man by enlisting the counteracting influence, the cheap support in peace, of the loyal black man, to whom we have so successfully appealed in war."[236] Even Stevens, who was a vigorous champion of racial equality, celebrated Black suffrage as a means "which alone can give protection to the colored race and the loyal whites in the rebel States."[237]

Stewart, who became the leading moderate/conservative Republican champion of Black suffrage, insisted that granting male persons of color voting rights was the solution to the problem of rebel rule that threatened both loyal Blacks and loyal whites. He would "chain ['the leaders of the rebellion'] to the ballot of the loyal blacks[] and hold them in the strong grasp of a loyal people." Republican and republican government, Stewart claimed, depended on Southern Black voters. The more conservative of Nevada's two senators maintained that "[w]hile [black] political power is ignored or added to disloyalty free government in the South is impossible. When it is withdrawn from rebels and added to the loyal forces the Union and republican institutions will be safe."[238] Black voting guaranteed a loyal South. Former slaves could be trusted to cast their ballots for loyal candidates and would be part of majority coalitions in the new Republican/republican South when joined by loyal whites. Steward asked:

> Does any one suppose that the Senators and Representatives from South Carolina would not soon have a loyal constituency if the ballot were within reach of the black man? In that State over one half of the people would be a solid column (a black column, if you please). Does any one doubt that there would be whites enough to join them to obtain control of the State?[239]

Ambitious politicians campaigning in a political universe in which the ballot was distributed free from race discrimination would almost immediately see the loyal Black light. All candidates for public office would be "compelled to respect the loyal sentiments of their constituents in order to retain power."[240] The result would be a South committed to racial equality and opposed to secession. Representatives in this happy future, Stewart predicted, would "make equal laws and sustain the Union."[241]

Interest-Convergence in 1866

The Republican commitment to preventing rebel rule by empowering and protecting the persons, white and Black, who remained loyal during the Civil War de-centers racial equality and Section 1 from that commitment and provision's place at the heart of Reconstruction and constitutional reform.[242] Proponents of congressional Reconstruction were as concerned with protecting loyal white Southerners from persecution as they were with protecting loyal Black freedmen from an even more vicious discrimination. Safeguarding the loyal white soldier or his widow, the loyal white Southern taxpayer, and the loyal Northern creditor was as pivotal to Reconstruction as making secure the loyal Black victim of Southern persecution and discrimination. Stevens and his political allies thought that empowerment was at least as vital (if not far more important than) protection. Reconstruction and constitutional reform would be successful, congressional Republicans and their Unionist allies maintained, only when loyal persons controlled the national government and the governments of former Confederate states. Sections 2, 3, and 4 of the Fourteenth Amendment, from this perspective, form the core of the amendment, particularly if Section 1 is (mis)understood as concerned primarily with securing racial equality.

Chapter 4 confirms these Republican priorities. When proponents of congressional Reconstruction laid out the constitutional reforms they believed were vital for preventing rebel rule by empowering and protecting the loyal, they emphasized political guarantees. The heart of various Fourteenth Amendment proposals was some combination of provisions that altered the basis of apportionment, guaranteed Black suffrage, banned former Confederates from holding office, or disenfranchised persons who had supported the Confederacy. Constitutional guarantees for financial interests were as important as constitutional guarantees for fundamental rights. If Republicans were seeking a new birth of freedom, they were doing so by empowering the loyal rather than by constraining constitutional politics with a new set of limitations on state governments.

The Republican effort to protect and empower the loyal as the best means for combating the threat of rebel rule suggests the value of Bell's interest-convergence thesis for all the guarantees that proponents demanded before restoring former Confederate states. Bell observed: "The interest of blacks in achieving racial equality will be accommodated only when it converges with the interests of whites."[243] White interest was on full display during the debates over the exclusion resolution and constitutional reform. White citizens were the primary beneficiaries of financial guarantees. Few persons of color held Union war bonds. White Southern unionists who held property were far more likely than impecunious freedmen to bear the burden of taxes imposed to pay the Confederate debt or compensate former slaveholders. Republicans often presented white citizens as the primary beneficiary of political guarantees. Yates, Kelso, and Stewart detailed how Black suffrage would enable loyal Southern whites to control former Confederate states. Senator B. Gratz Brown of Missouri blamed Black disenfranchisement for the subordinate status of poor whites and the massive loss of life white Confederate soldiers suffered during the Civil War. "It was this disfranchising feature of the slave code that not only acted directly to degrade the laboring blacks," he said, "but also acted indirectly to paralyze the laboring whites, to destroy their political influence, to subject them to slaveholding opinion, and thus make any treason possible that was heralded as being in the interest of the dominant class."[244] Loyal Southern whites were the primary beneficiaries of bans on officeholding, especially in jurisdictions where persons of color were not permitted to hold office. Bundy pointed out how apportionment reform served the interests of loyal whites in the North. "[T]he loyal white men in this country demand [what became Section 2 of the Fourteenth Amendment] as a part of the fundamental law of the land," he asserted, "so that a white voter in the North shall hereafter be just as good and no better than a white voter in the South."[245] White citizens might even be the primary beneficiary of civil rights guarantees. Bingham, as noted above, when introducing what eventually became Section 1 of the Fourteenth Amendment, emphasized how protections for fundamental rights would prevent persecution of Southern whites.

Proponents of congressional reform demonstrated the relative priority they placed on rule by the loyal and on racial equality when laying out various proposals for constitutional reform and when considering Colorado statehood. Most Republicans and allied Unionists, when offering various Fourteenth Amendment proposals, gave equal if not far more weight to political and financial guarantees that protected and empowered the loyal than they gave to rights guarantees that promised racial equality. Apportionment reform was at the core of more calls for constitutional change than for equal protection. When, as in the issue of Colorado statehood and related matters, preventing rebel rule by protecting and empowering the loyal did not compel protecting or empowering persons of color, most proponents of congressional Reconstruction voted against protecting or empowering persons of color.

4

Guarantees

Representative Roscoe Conkling of New York, a member of the Joint Committee on Reconstruction, on January 16, 1866, offered the following resolution listing the five guarantees he proposed Congress require as conditions for restoring former Confederate states to their antebellum status in the Union:

Resolved, That in reestablishing Federal relationships with the communities lately in rebellion so as to permit them again to participate in administering the General Government, the following are necessary and proper requirements, and ought to be secured by such measures as will render them as far as possible immutable.

1. The absolute renunciation of all the pretensions and evasions of secession as a doctrine and as a practice.

2. The repudiation both by the State and by the national Governments of all public debts and obligations, including State and municipal liabilities contracted or assumed in aid of the late rebellion, and including also all claims by or on behalf of those who were in the military or naval service of the insurgents for bounty, pay, or pensions, and all claims by persons not loyal to the United States for damages or losses suffered by reason of the rebellion and for advances made in its aid.

3. The assurance of human rights to all persons within their borders, regardless of race, creed, or color, and the adoption of such provisions against barbarism, disorder, and oppression, as will relieve the General Government from the necessity of standing guard over any portion of our country to protect the people from domestic violence and outrage.

4. The impartial distribution of political power among all sections of the country so that four million people shall no longer be represented in Congress in the interest of sectional aggrandizement and at the same time be excluded from political privileges and rights.

5. The election of Senators and Representatives in truth loyal to the United States, and never ringleaders in the late revolt, nor guilty of dastardly betrayals which preceded the war or of atrocities which war cannot extenuate.[1]

The Conkling resolution called for anti-secession, financial, political, and civil rights guarantees. Conkling's list of the necessary statutory or constitutional reforms included bans on race discrimination, but that guarantee or other civil rights protections for former slaves was not given the place of pride by being the first condition to be enumerated,[2] declared the main priority of reconstruction or elaborated in a way that suggested the distinctive importance of securing practical freedom for persons of color in the South. Conkling's call for guarantees "secured by such measures as will render them as far as possible immutable" implied that the conditions for restoring former Confederate states should take the form of federal constitutional amendments, but the text did not rule out embodying at least some conditions in federal legislation, state law, or compacts between former Confederate states and the national government. The Conkling resolution did not clarify whether the conditions for restoring former Confederate states were limited to the eleven states that seceded from the Union or whether, after adoption, such states as Illinois would be barred from paying pensions to Confederate soldiers or denying the human rights of Black persons residing in those jurisdictions.

More than fifty Republicans and more than fifty petitioners provided similar lists of the "irreversible guarantees" or "securities" that they believed necessary for restoring former Confederate states to their antebellum status. Tables A.7 and A.8 summarize these reform packages. Members of Congress and petitioners, when setting out the guarantees necessary for reunion, covered the full spectrum of Reconstruction issues. Their proposals included bans on secession and nullification; financial concerns such as the rebel debt, the national debt, bans on compensation for emancipated slaves and other wartime damages to Confederates and their supporters, pensions for loyal soldiers, constitutional permission for national export taxes, and adjustments to the basis for allocating direct taxes; political matters such as the apportionment of representation in the House of Representatives and the Electoral College, bans on officeholding, Black suffrage, and Confederate disenfranchisement; and various civil rights, most notably (but not exclusively) the rights of persons of color to be free from racial discrimination.

Proponents of congressional reform did not agree on or always specify the legal forms that would embody their proposed guarantees. Some proposals made during the early sessions of the Thirty-Ninth Congress called for state constitutional and legal reforms. Senator Charles Sumner of Massachusetts on opening day proposed "five several conditions, which conditions precedent must be submitted to a popular vote, and be sanctioned by a majority of the people of each State."[3] Representative John A. Kasson of Iowa in late January offered four "propositions to each of the States lately in rebellion, for adoption by the Legislatures or conventions thereof, as a fundamental compact between each of the said States and the United States, irrepealable without mutual consent."[4] With rare exceptions, Republicans after January insisted that guarantees be embedded in federal law. Some reform proposals consisted exclusively of federal constitutional amendments. Others included a mixture of federal constitutional amendments and federal legislation. Many did not specify how the federal government should implement their proposed guarantees.

The information presented in tables A.7 and A.8 permits gross generalizations, but no person should attempt a quantitative analysis. Reconstruction proposals varied in their format and comprehensiveness. Many speeches and petitioners provided numbered lists of conditions. Others did a disservice to future historians by failing to clarify the precise guarantees they believed necessary for restoring former Confederate states. Some Republicans listed numerous anti-secession, financial, rights, and political guarantees. Their presentations give the impression that the speaker/proposer intended the lists to be complete and that the reason for leaving out an anti-secession or some other guarantee was that the speaker did not regard that condition for restoration desirable or necessary. Other proponents of congressional Reconstruction identified only one or two conditions for restoring former Confederate states. Their presentations usually left open whether the speaker believed other conditions were unnecessary or undesirable or, perhaps, not as important or omitted by accident. Further confusing questions of comprehensiveness, Republicans tended to engage in parallel play when setting out the guarantees they believed Congress should require of former Confederate states. Apart from Black suffrage, which Republicans debated at some length, few proponents explained why their list left out a guarantee that was included in the previous speech or included a guarantee left out of all lists proffered the week before.

Categorizing Republican proposals as anti-secession, financial, political, and civil rights guarantees fails to capture how many proposals crossed these boundary lines. Radicals commonly combined political and civil rights guarantees when insisting that state laws not make any racial distinctions, a demand that entailed granting persons of color the right to vote and various liberties under common law. Some lists treated no compensation for slaves as a financial guarantee. Others placed that demand alongside demands for racial equality. Republicans and their Unionist allies did not regard different categories of guarantees as independent. Most notably, proponents thought that establishing political guarantees would provide foundations for civil rights and financial guarantees.

The petitions, memorials, and remonstrances present other problems. Many appear identical, at least from their presentation. On February 23, for example, Sumner, Senator James W. Grimes of Iowa, and Senator Edgar Cowan of Pennsylvania presented, respectively, petitions from citizens of Philadelphia, citizens of Iowa, and citizens of Butler County, Pennsylvania. Each senator described the petition he was presenting as calling for a constitutional amendment prohibiting any state from making "any distinction in civil rights and privileges among the [naturalized[5]] citizens of the United States . . . on account of race, color or descent."[6] Several other members of Congress in the weeks immediately before or after described petitions they had presented in identical or nearly identical language.[7] In such circumstances, the best inference is that the petition was drawn up by the leadership of a national organization and did not reflect conclusions and language independently arrived at by, say, the citizens of Philadelphia, Iowa, and Butler County. Congressional presentations of petitions were often truncated. Sometimes a member of Congress making a presentation stated that the petition contained unspecified conditions for restoration. In other instances, the member stated that the petition called for "adequate security" or the like without indicating whether the petition was more specific.

Examining the reform packages that Republicans and a few Unionists offered, warts and all, during the first session of the Thirty-Ninth Congress provides a fuller picture of the menu for constitutional changes when the Fourteenth Amendment was being drafted than the conventional "John Bingham spoke for all Republicans." Such an examination makes clear that Republicans were going to order a multicourse meal. Most packages included a selection from at least three of four different categories including anti-secession guarantees, financial guarantees, political guarantees, and civil rights guarantees. No one looking at table A. 7 would think that rights guarantees, especially bans on racial discrimination, were the main course or centerpiece of the undertaking. Some proposals, most notably anti-secession guarantees and constitutional permission for export taxes, were largely abandoned before the final draft was finished.

Table A.7 and the content of Republican speeches setting out the guarantees necessary for restoring former Confederate states further de-center the place of racial equality in Reconstruction and in the Fourteenth Amendment. The cornerstone of many proposed conditions for restoration was a political guarantee: either apportionment reform or Black suffrage. Few proponents of congressional action on Reconstruction regarded civil rights guarantees or racial equality in the civil and criminal law as the primary condition necessary for allowing states that had seceded to resume their status within the Union. Many guarantees were as popular as bans on race discrimination. With the same frequency and intensity, Republicans demanded financial reforms—most notably measures forbidding the repayment of the Confederate debt—and political reforms—most notably measures adjusting the basis of representation—as they did protections for the civil rights or bans on race discrimination. A greater consensus existed among Republicans that financial and political reform had to take place constitutionally, at least more so than achieving new protections for individual rights through constitutional amendment. Republicans who specified the mode of reform almost always insisted that constitutional amendments were needed for financial and political reforms. Many claimed that Congress already had the power to pass laws prohibiting racial discrimination in the civil and criminal laws. When such federal statutes were passed by Congress in late March 1866, far fewer members included guarantees for racial equality in their conditions for restoring former Confederate states.

Table A.8 nevertheless provides evidence for more conventional accounts of Reconstruction and the Fourteenth Amendment as primarily concerned with civil rights and racial equality. In sharp contrast to the speeches made by members of Congress, a very high percentage of petitions to Congress emphasized protections for persons of color as the primary security against rebel rule. Almost all petitioners demanded as a condition for restoration Black suffrage, bans on racial discrimination in the civil and criminal laws, or both. Many petitioners would require of former Confederate states seeking representation in Congress only that they provide persons of color with some combination of political and civil rights.

Whether the petitions sent to the Thirty-Ninth Congress were a fair reflection of Northern thought on the necessary conditions for restoring former Confederate states is doubtful. In antebellum America, abolitionists had engaged in the frequent petition campaigns that inspired the decade-long fight over the "gag rule."[8] The more moderate Republicans that Abraham Lincoln represented tended to communicate to Congress by voting for representatives rather than by petitioning. Many petitions bluntly "pray[ed] for the imposition of such conditions upon the rebel States as shall punish treason . . . and reward loyalty with confidence and honor."[9] These petitions often do not appear to have offered any particular guarantees for restoration, but their sentiments are more consistent with the Reconstruction effort to prevent rebel rule by empowering and protecting the loyal than the somewhat more numerous petitions that emphasized the rights of former slaves.

Anti-secession Guarantees

Many Republicans listed anti-secession guarantees first when laying out the conditions for permitting former Confederate states to be represented in Congress. This security prevented rebel rule by outlawing rebellion. Representative Henry C. Deming of Connecticut insisted that "the Government shall be absolutely protected from a repetition of the secession experiment by a provision in our organic law."[10] Representative Martin Welker of Ohio called for an anti-nullification measure. He wanted "satisfactory evidence that loyal governments are organized that will not array themselves against the execution of the law that may be enacted by Congress, under the Constitution, for the common welfare."[11] Representative Reader W. Clarke of Ohio combined these proposals when he asked for "[a]n outspoken denial of the right of nullification and secession, putting an end to the dogma of supreme State sovereignty."[12] Representative Rufus P. Spalding of Ohio similarly advocated inserting a provision in the Constitution of the United States prohibiting "'nullification' and 'secession.'"[13]

Calls for anti-secession guarantees were often combined with attacks on state rights. R. Clarke wanted Congress to "put[] an end to the dogma of supreme State sovereignty."[14] An anti-secession amendment, Representative Jehu Baker of Illinois believed, would have an important influence on public attitudes toward the nature of the Union. "Are the opinions that a State has a sovereign right to secede, and that the Constitution is broken by coercing it back, quite given up in our land?" he asked the House of Representatives. "Now, sir, upon this great point of nationality, we want the victory of force to draw with it the logical consequence of passing on to a victory of permanent, quieting law, so literally certain that no future Calhoun, Davis, or Yancey will be able to mislead any portion of the people."[15] Other Republicans sought a broader statement of fundamental principles as a condition for restoration. "The so-called sovereignty of the States was the main cause of the rebellion," citizens of Missouri declared, "it is therefore eminently necessary to get rid of this evil."[16] "The terms of surrender," Senator James Nye of Nevada stated, "involve[] surrender of the doctrine of 'state sovereignty,' the right to secede, and all other political heresies that had involved the nation in civil war."[17]

Determining how many petitions called for anti-secession guarantees is difficult. Petitioners often asked Congress "not to restore any State that has rebelled, &c. to its place and power as a governing partner in the Union till adequate security has been obtained against its renewing the attempt to secede."[18] Whether citizens calling for adequate security against secession were asking for an explicit anti-secession guarantee, or regarded financial, political, and civil rights guarantees as vital means for preventing secession, is not always clear. Context helps. Some petitions combined calls for adequate security against secession with requests for financial, political, and civil rights guarantees. These petitioners appear to be requesting explicit anti-secession guarantees. On their list of conditions for readmission, the citizens of Huron and Erie Counties in Ohio included both "adequate security against secession" and a constitutional amendment declaring "[t]he Union of the United States of America shall be perpetual."[19] This suggests that "adequate security" was to be obtained through other guarantees. Some petitions, at least as presented by the members of Congress, called only for adequate security against secession.[20] No inference about whether this was a call for an anti-secession guarantee can be made in these circumstances.

Several Republicans maintained that criminal penalties for secessionists would help guarantee national union. Representative Samuel W. Moulton of Illinois declared "the Government shall be absolutely protected from the repetition of secession and rebellion by providing for the punishment of treason."[21] Representative James H. D. Henderson of Oregon, in a speech not directed specifically at conditions for readmission, declared "there should be a sufficient number of leading rebels from each of the States lately in rebellion against the United States Government arraigned for treason."[22] Representative Thaddeus Stevens of Pennsylvania called for providing homesteads for persons of color by confiscating Southern plantations.[23] The citizens of Hendrick County, Indiana, prayed that "the leading traitors may be tried and punished."[24] More often, when petitions demanded that treason be punished, they were demanding a political guarantee. Petitions commonly declared that Congress should "punish treason with at least ineligibility to office."

When Republicans and petitioners specified the form an anti-secession measure should take, they almost always demanded constitutional reform. Representative William Lawrence of Ohio, Spalding, Deming, Baker, R. Clarke, and Moulton favored federal constitutional amendment. Representatives Sidney T. Holmes of New York and Samuel J. Kuykendall of Illinois were the only proponents of congressional Reconstruction who thought that federal legislation was appropriate. Sumner was the rare Republican who focused on state action. He asserted that representatives from the former Confederacy should not be seated in Congress until "a majority of the people of each State" by "popular vote" demonstrated "[t]he complete reestablishment of loyalty, as shown by an honest recognition of the unity of the Republic, and the duty of allegiance to it at all times, without mental reservation or equivocation of any kind."[25]

Explicit anti-secession guarantees were controversial. Several proponents rejected such guarantees as pointless. The Constitution of 1860, in their view, plainly prohibited secession. No future behavior would likely be influenced by making that prohibition even more explicit. "I want no such change of the Constitution," Representative James A. Garfield of Ohio declared. He continued:

> They never had by the Constitution the right to secede. If we have not settled that question by war it can never be settled by a court. . . . I care not what provision might be in the Constitution; if any States of this Union desire to rebel and break up the Union, and are able to do it, they will do it in spite of the Constitution."[26]

Representative George R. Latham of West Virginia implicitly invoked Lucifer when criticizing attempts to forestall secession by constitutional amendment. "But I hear it said that we must reconstruct upon a basis which will forever preclude the possibility of another rebellion," he exclaimed. "Why, sir, the Almighty himself cannot organize a Government with provisions or guarantees which shall preclude the possibility of a rebellion against it."[27] Representative Henry J. Raymond of New York, who opposed the exclusion resolution but voted for the Fourteenth Amendment, pointed out "there have been a good many things put in the Constitution of the United States which South Carolina did not deem beyond her power."[28]

Republican enthusiasm for bans on secession waned over time. Most reform packages proposed in December, January, and early February include an anti-secession guarantee. Most reform packages proposed afterward do not. In sharp contrast to every other guarantee proposed by a member of Congress during the first session, no member publicly drafted an explicit anti-secession amendment or offered a resolution calling on Congress to adopt such an amendment. Little evidence exists that might explain this development. No extensive debate took place in the Thirty-Ninth Congress or even in the Joint Committee on Reconstruction on the merits of a constitutional amendment banning secession or some other means for repudiating state sovereignty as understood by Confederate secessionists. Perhaps Garfield and Latham were convincing when they insisted that a constitutional amendment prohibiting secession and nullification was pointless. Perhaps Republicans who called for such amendments were engaging in symbolic politics, hoping, as David Mayhew would note a century later, to "make pleasing judgmental statements" without "mak[ing] pleasing things happen."[29] Perhaps the absence of an anti-secession or an anti-nullification amendment is simply one of those mysteries that cannot be solved with the tools and information currently available to modern legal historians.

Financial Guarantees

Republicans and their Unionist allies insisted on various financial guarantees as conditions for restoring former Confederate states to their previous position in the Union. Sumner called on Republicans to take the steps necessary to prevent "the oligarchical enemies of the Republic . . . to break faith with national soldiers and national creditors to whose generosity it was indebted during a period of peril."[30] Although no proponent of congressional Reconstruction thought financial guarantees sufficient, almost every major reform package included at least one financial guarantee. More Republicans called for a constitutional ban on repaying the Confederate debt than demanded any other constitutional amendment, in particular a constitutional amendment banning race discrimination.

Proponents of congressional Reconstruction trotted out numerous financial guarantees when listing the conditions for restoration. Most reform packages included a constitutional amendment that forbade the national government from repudiating the national debt and state governments from repaying Confederate debts contracted during the Civil War.[31] Representative Leonard Myers of Pennsylvania declared: "The war debt of the Union must be sacred, that of the rebellion forever excluded."[32] Holmes stated: "We must do justice to the public creditor who furnished the Government the means to carry on this war" but that "[t]he debt created to aid the rebellion must be repudiated."[33] Others spoke only of prohibiting payment of the rebel debt.[34] Representatives John R. Kelso of Missouri, Thomas Williams of Pennsylvania, and Ralph P. Buckland of Ohio spoke only of securing the national debt. Some Republicans supplemented these debt provisions with a prohibition on compensating former slaveholders.[35] Representative Hiram Price of Iowa combined all three when he introduced a resolution declaring that "no State which has recently been in rebellion against the General Government ought to be entitled to a representation in Congress until such State" ratified a constitutional amendment forbidding any effort to "assume the rebel debt . . . , repudiate the national debt. . . . , and to pay for slaves who have been made free."[36] A few Republicans called for guarantees that promised pensions to Union soldiers would be paid.[37] W. Lawrence insisted that "obligations to Union soldiers" be "placed beyond repudiation."[38] Buckland spoke of the "great obligations [of] the national Government, the most important and sacred of which is that of providing for the disabled soldiers, the soldiers' widows, and the soldier's orphans."[39] Others wanted guarantees that former Confederate soldiers and their families would not receive pensions and that no Confederate would be compensated for any losses incurred during the Civil War. Conkling, as noted above, called for repudiating "all claims by on behalf of those who were in the military or naval service of the insurgents for bounty, pay, or pensions, and all claims by persons not loyal to the United States for damages or losses suffered by reason of the rebellion and for advances made in its aid."[40] The disloyal need not apply.

Congress, several proponents of congressional Reconstruction maintained, ought to require former Confederate states to pay for the Civil War before being restored to their antebellum prerogatives. On February 26, 1866, the House of Representatives approved a resolution proposed by Representative Joseph W. McClurg of Missouri calling on the Joint Committee on Reconstruction "to inquire into the expediency of levying contributions on the disloyal inhabitants of such seceding States, to defray the extraordinary expense that will otherwise be imposed on the General Government."[41] Nye thought the best way "to bring this rebellion to a close" was to "lay[] contributions upon the seceded States to pay every dollar of the expenses which contumacy adds to the Government."[42] Some members of Congress proposed specific measures for wiping out the public debt incurred in suppressing the Confederate rebellion. Kelso would confiscate rebel property to pay for the national war debt.[43] Stevens insisted on an "amendment to allow Congress to lay a duty on exports," which he believed necessary to ensure the South would contribute significantly to federal revenues for the foreseeable future.[44]

Republicans did not debate the differences in the financial guarantees they explicitly sought. Some financial guarantees were more popular than others. Repudiating the Confederate debt enjoyed broad support. Far fewer

Republicans, when making speeches on Reconstruction, endorsed the Stevens proposal for taxing exports or called for prohibiting compensation to former slaveholders. Republicans and their Unionist allies kept secret their reasons for championing a particular set of financial guarantees. No proponents of the exclusion resolution and the Fourteenth Amendment explained at any time why they included some financial guarantees in their reform packages but not others. Buckland was the only proponent of congressional Reconstruction who raised questions about any financial guarantee. When he explaining why his constitutional reform package did not include a ban on compensating slaveholders, Buckland declared: "I have no fear that the United States will ever pay for any emancipated slaves in any State; and as to Tennessee, I do not believe any precautionary conditions are necessary."[45] This absence of controversy over the what financial guarantees were necessary for the restoration of former Confederate states suggests the best inference that can be made as to why a member of Congress proposed, for example, repudiating the Confederate debt but not securing the federal debt is that said representative or senator thought that repudiating the Confederate debt was of particular importance and that securing the federal debt was of lesser significance (but not that he was opposed in principle to securing the federal debt). Sheer happenstance—what a representative had for breakfast, say, or the last person that representative spoke to before taking the floor—may also be the accurate explanation in many cases.

Financial guarantees required federal constitutional amendments.[46] When proponents of congressional Reconstruction specified how rebel debts would be repudiated, the national debt secured, compensation for emancipated slaves prohibited, pensions for Union soldiers guaranteed, pensions for Confederate soldiers banned, and taxes on exports permitted, they called for changes in the "organic law." Welker urged Congress to "[a]mend the organic law so as to put it out of the power of these States to levy any tax or imposes to pay the rebel debt."[47] Baker wanted "perfect security against the possibility of ever being burdened with the payment of the enormous rebel debt which was contracted in the satanic effort to lay the Republic in ruins."[48] Repealing the constitutional ban on export taxes obviously entailed a constitutional amendment.

Only a few Radicals disputed the consensus that constitutional amendments were necessary to secure financial guarantees. Senator Richard Yates of Illinois insisted the national government already had the power to enact the necessary economic reforms.[49] Sumner called for state constitutional reform in December 1865[50] but later submitted a federal constitutional amendment forbidding payment of the Confederate debt or repudiation of the national debt.[51]

Political Guarantees

Republicans united on the importance of political guarantees, even while disputing the precise electoral reforms necessary to restore the former Confederate states to their antebellum status in the Union. Representative John A. Bingham of Ohio and a few others aside, every proponent of congressional Reconstruction who offered a comprehensive reform package included one or more political guarantees. Some proposals were general. Representative Ebon C. Ingersoll of Illinois called for a constitutional amendment requiring former Confederate jurisdictions "to maintain a republican form of State government."[52] Proponents of congressional reform more often demanded specific political guarantees. Different members of Congress and petitioners proposed five measures that would alter the composition of Congress directly or indirectly by altering the congressional electorate in ways that they thought would empower the loyal. The most popular reform was an adjustment to the basis of representation. Some Republicans called for enfranchising persons of color. Proponents of congressional reform who would not punish most Confederates under criminal law insisted that leading rebels be barred from holding office, disenfranchised, or declared noncitizens. In sharp contrast to their behavior when proposing financial guarantees, Republicans often explained why they championed one set of political guarantees rather than another. Many proponents of apportionment reform declared they opposed Black suffrage. Senator William M. Stewart of Nevada combined support for Black suffrage with opposition to bans on officeholding and disenfranchisement.

Proponents of congressional Reconstruction were adamant that former Confederate states not be allocated representatives (and votes in the Electoral College) based on disenfranchised persons of color. Spalding called on Congress to "[a]mend the Constitution of the United States in respect to the apportionment of Representatives and direct taxes among the several States of the Union, in such manner, that people of color, shall not be counted with the population making up the ratio, except it be in States where they are permitted to exercise the elective franchise."[53] "Who can stand before the people of the North," Baker asked, "and tell them that the late rebel communities in Congress ought, as a matter of right, to have between thirty and forty Representatives in Congress upon no better basis than the unvoting and therefore unrepresented colored people of the South?"[54] Southern whites, Republicans emphasized, should no longer be allowed to speak politically for persons of color. Senator George H. Williams of Oregon described political arrangements in early 1866 as "a double outrage on the black man. It is not only to deny him a representative, but to give that office to his enemy."[55] Rather than apportion by population as mandated by the Constitution of 1787, many Republicans called for apportionment by voters. "Representation and the ballot," Holmes argued, "must go hand in hand."[56] Welker declared: "Let the Constitution be amended that representation in the House of Representation shall be based substantially on voting population and not general population."[57]

Apportionment reform often received the place of pride when Republicans spoke of the conditions for seating representatives from the Southern states. Senator John Sherman of Ohio, supported by Unionist members of the Ohio state legislature, maintained that an amendment changing the basis of apportionment was the only supplement necessary to President Johnson's proposed conditions for readmission. Sherman approved a resolution declaring "inexpedient and unnecessary . . . other conditions to a full restoration of their place and rights in the Union."[58] The one constitutional amendment Representative John M. Broomall of Pennsylvania demanded before former Confederate states were granted their antebellum prerogatives a reformed apportionment so that "a representative from South Carolina will not be elected by a fourth of the number of electors required by one from Pennsylvania."[59] Stevens was particularly adamant on the need for apportionment reform. "The first of those amendments" that he regarded as necessary before former Confederate states were "recognized as capable of acting in the Union" was "to change the basis of representation among the States from Federal numbers to actual voters."[60]

Proponents of congressional Reconstruction observed how changing the basis of representation from population to voters would place former Confederate states in a dilemma. Should South Carolina and friends attempt to preserve their numerical strength in Congress and the Electoral College by enfranchising persons of color, Black voters would provide Republicans with the electoral margins necessary to retain control of the national government. Stevens pointed out that "If they should grant the right of suffrage to persons of color, I think there would always be Union white men enough in the South, aided by the blacks, to divide the representation, and thus continue the Republican ascendency."[61] Former Confederate states that failed to enfranchise persons of color would lack the numbers in Congress and the Electoral College necessary to wrest control of the national government from Republicans. Stevens continued: "[If they should refuse to . . . alter their election laws it would reduce the representatives of the late slave States to about forty-five and render them powerless for evil."[62]

Many Republicans were hopeful that former Confederates, when placed in this dilemma, would choose Black suffrage. Stevens in December 1865 was particularly optimistic that apportionment reform would induce Black suffrage. His speech opening debate on Reconstruction proposed apportionment reform rather than Black suffrage, but the House Majority Leader made clear that obtaining the ballot for persons of color was the goal. Stevens informed fellow representatives that, "[i]n a country where political divisions will always exist," the "power" of Black voters, "joined with just white men, would greatly modify, if it did not entirely prevent, the injustice of majorities." Stevens continued: "Without the right of suffrage in the late slave States . . . I believe the slaves had far better been left in bondage."[63] G. Williams spoke similarly of apportionment reform as the road to Black suffrage in the South:

> If the white men of the South will insist that the negro shall have no political rights in the States, which he is to appear here to claim a recognition at our hands only to add to the power of the oligarchy in this Government, then I would insist that they shall appear here either in person, or by his attorney, or curator, or next friend, and not by a guardian or trustee under the appointment of his quondam master, which would be the sublimest of farces. If they are not content with this, then I would say to them, wait until by a constitutional amendment we can offer you the fairer basis of suffrage, which will enable you to swell your numbers as soon as you shall be prepared to do justice to the black man.[64]

Apportionment reform had the "virtue" of inducing Black suffrage in the South, although not in the North, where disenfranchised persons of color were not sufficiently numerous to reduce the number of representatives in Congress or the Electoral College. Proponents of congressional Reconstruction pointed out that loyal Black votes were needed to maintain loyal governments in the former Confederate states and in Washington, DC, but not elsewhere. Representative George W. Julian of Indiana, when championing Black suffrage in Washington, DC, asserted:

> Negro suffrage in the districts lately in revolt is thus a present political necessity, dictated by the selfishness of the white loyalist as well as his sense of justice. But in our western States, in which the negro population is relatively small, and the prevailing sentiment of the white people is loyal, no such emergency exists. Society will not be endangered by the temporary postponement of the right of negro suffrage till public opinion shall render it practicable, and our western

Representatives can thus vote for this bill without encountering any reasonable hostility from their conservative constituents, and leaving the question of suffrage in the loyal States to be decided by them on its merits.[65]

G. Williams insisted that constitutional commitments to republicanism (lowercase *r*) required giving Southern Blacks, but not Northern Blacks, the ballot:

Whether these States could be regarded as strictly republican with such a limitation of the elective franchise, if the necessities of the country or the protection of a numerous class of citizens required the presentation of the question to the consideration of Congress, is more than doubtful. The paucity of the blacks, however, in the Northern States, where there is no disposition to oppress them, and their uniform enjoyment, without molestation, of every social and civil right, without molestation, of every social and civil right, without the protection of the political privilege of the ballot, has made it a question of no practical importance to the country, and led to no formal complaint, although the overshadowing influence of the slave power has robbed them in many of the States of that privilege which the overthrow of slavery will sooner or later restore to them.[66]

Other Republicans believed immediately that enfranchising persons of color was the superior political guarantee. Radical Republicans were particularly likely to call for measures permitting former slaves to cast ballots. Sumner on the first day the Thirty-Ninth Congress was in session proposed a resolution declaring that "no government can be accepted as 'a republican form of government' where a large proportion of native-born citizens, charged with no crime and no failure of duty, is left wholly represented, although compelled to pay taxes, and especially where a particular race is singled out and denied all representation, although compelled to pay taxes; more especially where such race constitutes the majority of the citizens."[67] Deming conditioned Southern reinstatement in Congress on laws that "endowed" the freedmen "with every political right necessary to maintain . . . equality."[68] Proponents of Black suffrage insisted that political rights were as central to citizenship as civil rights. Representative William A. Newell of New Jersey maintained that, "[f]rom the very nature of republicanism, as understood by the fathers, freedom and suffrage are concomitant, twin sisters, inseparable, mutually dependent on each other for support and existence."[69] "[F]reedom and citizenship carry with them," he concluded, "the right of suffrage."[70] Representative Roswell Hart of New York regarded Black suffrage as both a political and anti-secession guarantee. He asked: "What more rational, proper, humane, and consistent course can be adopted than to enfranchise the freedmen to create an irreversible guarantee for the future peace and safety of the nation?"[71]

Enfranchisement proposals were most often phrased as antidiscrimination measures rather than as affirmative guarantees of voting rights. A few more radical members of Congress spoke out for voting as a fundamental right independent of discrimination. "The freedmen," Moulton stated, "shall be endowed with every political right necessary to maintain [their] equality."[72] More commonly, Republicans and their Unionist allies demanded that race not be a barrier to the ballot. Stewart called for "the extension of the elective franchise to all persons upon the same terms and conditions, making no discrimination on account of race, color, or previous condition of servitude."[73] The Friends Association of Philadelphia for the Aid and Elevation of Freedmen "pray[ed] that the right of suffrage be conferred irrespective of race or color."[74] Implementing Black suffrage through antidiscrimination measures permitted proponents of congressional Reconstruction to champion other restrictions on voting. Some petitions, for example, combined proposals to end race discrimination in voting with demands for literacy tests. Fifty citizens of Windsor, Vermont, called for "limiting the privileges of voting for those officers to citizens who can read; and requiring that no one shall be abridged or affected in his enjoyment of the elective franchise by reason of race, color, descent, or social condition."[75]

Many Republicans favored restricting political participation by former rebels. General agreement existed that some policy had to be put in place to ensure that former Confederates did not return to public office. Test oaths or their equivalent were popular. Raymond "would exercise a rigid scrutiny into the character and loyalty of the men whom [the former Confederate states] may send to Congress."[76] Sumner demanded, as a condition precedent for representation, "[t]he choice of citizens for office, whether State or national, of constant and undoubted loyalty, whose conduct and conversation shall give assurance of peace and reconciliation."[77] Constitutional bans on officeholding received substantial support. Representative Samuel McKee of Kentucky declared, "I would like so to amend the Constitution that no man who had raised his arm against the flag should ever be allowed to participate in any of the affairs of the Government."[78] Baker would ban from all federal offices any person who "has voluntarily participated in the civil, military, or naval services of the late so-called confederate States of America, or who has voluntarily adhered to the said so-called confederate

States of America by giving them aid and comfort."[79] "The loyal people of the country, North and South," he continued, want "permanent, reliable security that their eyes shall never behold that insufferable spectacle, some Robert E. Lee from Virginia, some Wade Hampton from South Carolina, some Jacob Thompson from Mississippi, some Gideon J. Pillow, or Fort Pillow Forrest from Tennessee, walking into the other end of the Capitol or into this Hall to make laws for the people of the United States!"[80] Most Republicans urged Congress to give bans on officeholding a broad scope. Spaulding asked Congress to "[p]rovide in the Constitution that no person, who has, at any time, taken up arms against the United States, shall ever be admitted to a seat in the Senate or House of Representatives in Congress."[81] Confederate creditors might suffer the same fate. The Union League Club of New York City called for "the exclusion from office of all who have borne arms as officers in the military or naval service or held office under or willingly contributed money to the so-called confederate government."[82]

Some proponents of congressional Reconstruction called for disenfranchising former Confederates, either as a distinctive political guarantee or in combination with bans on officeholding. "[W]e must see to it that the disloyal are permanently disfranchised," Representative Benjamin F. Loan of Missouri insisted.[83] Representative Godlove S. Orth would strip former Confederates of all political rights. "[A]ny person who has been, or shall hereafter be, engaged in rebellion against the Government of the United States," he proposed, "shall be disfranchised and rendered incapable of holding any office of honor or emolument under the Government against which he rebelled."[84] Representative Daniel Morris of New York championed as comprehensive a ban. He agreed that "no leader in this rebellion, no man who has been educated at the expense of the Government or who has ever held an office under it and then sought its overthrow, can ever hope to fill any position of trust, or exercise the elective franchise."[85] Some Republicans claimed that rebels were already disenfranchised because they were no longer citizens of the United States. Representative Ebenezer Dumont of Indiana claimed that Confederates had stripped themselves of all political rights. They had "renounce[d] . . . citizenship," which made them ineligible for federal office and probably ineligible to vote under most state laws.[86]

Proponents of limiting political participation proposed bans of different duration. While Loan and Morris called for permanent disenfranchisement, other Republicans favored more temporary political guarantees. They emphasized the need to bar former rebels from participating in Reconstruction, leaving their suffrage afterward to the sufferance of loyal citizens. Kelso would establish "the safety of the loyal people" and ensure "slavery [was] forever abolished" by ensuring "[t]he rebels should have no part nor lot in the formation of [state] constitutions, and their restoration to the elective franchise should devolve upon the loyal State governments after such have been established."[87] Banned today, rebels might regain their rights when the loyal had entrenched their political control of a former Confederate state.

A few called for Congress to reconstruct the former Confederate states and nation more thoroughly. Several urged Congress to guarantee states a republican form of government in ways indicating that this was a distinct condition of restoration and not merely the federal power justifying other conditions. Hart claimed that "it is the duty of the United States to guaranty that they have [a republican form of government] speedily ... as shall entitle them to admission into full and complete relation with the Federal Union."[88] Some suggestions went beyond concerns with preventing rebel rule by empowering and protecting the loyal. Women's suffrage made brief appearances in the debates over Reconstruction. Representative James A. Ashley of Ohio insisted that proponents of congressional Reconstruction refrain from using the word "male" in voting rights provisions because he was "unwilling to prohibit any State from enfranchising its women if they desire to do so."[89]

Far more debate occurred among Republicans over the proper political guarantees for restoration than over any other condition for readmitting Southern representations. With the clear exception of Moulton[90] and the possible exception of Broomall, Republicans supported either adjusting the basis of representation or enfranchising persons of color, but not both. Many speeches analyzed, at some length, the relative merits of enfranchising persons of color and limiting the representation of states that disfranchised persons of color. Proponents of apportionment reform emphasized expedience. Sherman asked those who favored enfranchising persons of color: "Will you, by your demand of universal suffrage, destroy the power of the Union party to protect them in their dearly purchased liberty?"[91] Proponents of Black suffrage emphasized principle. Frederick Douglass and others petitioned Congress "to favor no amendment to the Constitution of the United States which will grant or allow any one of the States of the Union to disfranchise any class of citizens on the ground of race or color."[92]

Republican proponents of apportionment reform often explained why they did not support Black suffrage. Some professed white supremacy. "If this is to continue to be exclusively a white man's Government," Buckland stated, "none but the white man should be represented in Congress or have any influence in the election of the President."[93] Other Republicans insisted that persons of color lacked the preparation necessary to vote. Representative Delos R. Ashley of Nevada maintained that "the time will come when negroes, becoming educated and acquiring property, will be allowed to vote, but they must be introduced to the full enjoyment of right and powers of citizenship gradually."[94]

Several proponents of apportionment reform pointed to Northern public opinion when rejecting proposals granting persons of color voting rights. Representative George V. Lawrence of Pennsylvania looked to his district when claiming "the constituency I represent will not expect me to make the extension of suffrage to the colored race a condition."[95] Senator Henry Wilson of Massachusetts favored "impartial suffrage" but did not believe that he had the political support necessary to "secure that great measure of justice and mercy."[96]

Republicans who favored congressional Reconstruction less vigorously disputed whether bans on political participation by former Confederates supplemented other political guarantees. Many proponents of apportionment reform or Black suffrage also supported bans on officeholding or disenfranchisement. Stewart and Representative George W. Anderson of Missouri were exceptions. Their call for "universal amnesty and universal suffrage" treated Black suffrage as a substitute for banning former Confederates from active participation in public life.[97] Stewart proposed on March 16 that, if states amended their constitutions to forbid race discrimination in voting, the federal government should "exonerate[e] all persons from all pains, penalties, or disabilities to which they may have become liable by reason of their connection with the rebellion."[98] Other Republicans who championed bans on political participation, but did not explicitly advocate for apportionment or Black suffrage, did so in speeches that left open the possibility that they supported or could be induced to support one of the latter two political guarantees.[99]

The mode of political reform sometimes depended on the political reform. When they specified the mode of reform, those Republicans who favored apportionment reform insisted on a constitutional amendment. Proponents of Black suffrage were more likely to call for statutory reform,[100] though many called for constitutional change. Stewart initially thought that Black suffrage was best implemented as a state constitutional amendment, at least if former Confederates were willing to grant persons of color the ballot as a condition of restoration. "I want the South to have an opportunity to vote upon it," he declared. "[I]f they refuse to adopt it," he continued, "it will be time enough to consider other propositions."[101] A month later, after seeing no evidence of Southern support for Black suffrage, Stewart endorsed constitutional reform.[102]

Similar differences arose when members of Congress proposed limiting political participation by former Confederates. Some proponents of bans on holding public office insisted on constitutional amendments. Spalding called on Congress to "[p]rovide in the Constitution that no person, who has, at any time, taken up arms against the United States, shall ever be admitted to a seat in the Senate or House of Representatives."[103] McKee proposed a constitutional amendment declaring that "[n]o person shall be qualified or shall hold [various federal offices] who has been or shall hereafter be engaged in any armed conspiracy or rebellion against the United States."[104] Others were satisfied with maintaining existing loyalty oaths. Representative Joseph H. Defrees of Indiana stated: "The iron-clad oath, that members are required to take before they get seats in this House is a bulwark against traitors, and no disloyal man can pollute these Halls with his impious feet as long as that remains on the statute-book."[105] Kuykendall celebrated "the test oath" as "a monument of loyalty."[106] Some proponents of disenfranchisement insisted on a constitutional amendment. Dumont disagreed. He suggested that all Congress had to do was recognize that seceding Confederates had disenfranchised themselves by abjuring citizenship in the United States. Dumont asked: "What could mortal man do to renounce his citizenship that these men have not done?"[107]

Civil Rights Guarantees

Most Republicans demanded civil rights guarantees. Most proposals for readmitting Southern representatives to Congress including measures protecting certain fundamental rights or securing racial equality. Many sought to enshrine equality under law more generally as a fundamental regime principle. As was the case with financial guarantees, but not with anti-secession and political guarantees, no Republican objected to any civil rights guarantee, though considerable differences emerged over details. The few Republicans who offered packages that did not include an antidiscrimination proposal or a protection for civil rights were no less inclined to support civil rights measures during the Thirty-Ninth Congress than the many proponents of congressional Reconstruction who offered reform packages that included civil rights conditions.

Baker articulated the Republican vision of the postwar free labor order when he attacked "class rule and aristocratic principles." Baker began with an assertion Democrats endorsed, that "class rule and aristocratic principles of government have burdened well nigh all Europe with enormous public debts and standing armies." He then declared distinctively Republican Party principles when insisting that slavery was rooted in class rule and aristocratic principles. The Republican from Illinois pointed out how "the class rule and aristocratic element of slaveholding which found a place in our republic has proven itself, in like manner, hurtful to our people." Baker's reconstruction was rooted in an antipathy to all status hierarchies, with particular emphasis on status hierarchies rooted in race. Congress, he asserted, "in restoring the normal relations of States lately in rebellion, . . . should have done [away] with class rule and aristocracy as a privileged power before the law in this nation." Baker concluded that the national legislature could prevent a new oligarchy from arising by passing legislation designed "to realize and secure the largest attainable liberty to the whole people of the Republic, irrespective of class or race."[108] Loyal Blacks were to be protected from unequal laws; loyal whites would enjoy the same protection.

Most Republican calls for civil rights guarantees included explicit bans on race discrimination. Proponents used such phrases as "irrespective of race or color"[109] or "without distinction of race or color."[110] "[T]he Constitution should be so amended that Congress shall be fully authorized to protect the freedmen in all their rights of 'life, liberty, and the pursuit of happiness' in the States," Welker declared, "and prohibit the passage of all laws, by any of the States, making any difference in the civil rights of their inhabitants, but that all, both white and black, shall stand equal before the civil and criminal law."[111] Petitioners regularly prayed for "the abolition of all distinctions . . . on account of color and race."[112] Citizens of New York asked Congress "to act on the principle that emancipation is not complete so long as any black code exists, whether affecting civil or political rights."[113] Some Republicans and petitioners phrased their civil rights guarantees as protections for former slaves. Kuykendall would "guaranty such protection to the freedmen as would insure them against harm or violence, and give them full and equal protection in all their rights."[114]

Others called for race-neutral individual rights provisions. The first version of Bingham's proposed rights guarantee would "empower Congress to pass all necessary and proper laws to secure to all persons in every State of the Union equal protection in their rights, life, liberty, and property."[115] Representative Columbus Delano of Ohio insisted on "proper assurance that in your capacity as a State for local and domestic purposes you will conform to those great principles of justice which lie at the basis of our Government, and which require that all men shall be secure in their lives, their liberties, and in their pursuit of happiness."[116] J. Ashley championed race-neutral privileges and immunities, due process, and equal protection clauses, although his conditions for restoration were largely an edited version of the Fourteenth Amendment originally proposed by the Joint Committee on Reconstruction.[117] Many race-neutral civil rights conditions were maddingly vague in ways that make determining precisely what the speaker meant practically impossible. Ingersoll sought guarantees for "justice to all men."[118] Morris insisted former Confederate states "protect loyal men."[119]

Some reform packages combined a general call for equality with a specific prohibition on race discrimination. Several speakers separated race-neutral guarantees and bans on race discrimination into two separate conditions. Moulton's campaign to entrench the passive voice insisted that "the freedmen shall be secured an absolute equality with the white man" and that "civil rights shall be guaranteed to all with the means to enforce them."[120] The Union League Club of New York City prayed for "equality before the law to all men without regard to race or color" and "the prohibition of all class legislation."[121] Other Republicans combined race-neutral rights and antidiscrimination proposals into what appears to be one guarantee. Sumner proposed a resolution declaring "there shall be no denial of rights, civil or political, on account of color or race; but that all persons shall be equal before the law."[122] Representative Samuel Shellabarger of Ohio more succinctly insisted on "irreversible guarantees for the rights of American citizens of every race and condition."[123] At times, Republicans used the conjunction to describe conditions that seem, at least to modern eyes, to be nearly identical. Ingersoll, after insisting that former rebels establish state governments that "recognize[] the rights of mankind irrespective of color," called for establishing "state constitutional obligations as shall require them to do justice to all men, of all conditions, the low as well as the high."[124] Welker similarly urged Congress to "secure equal and exact justice to all men" and "to pass laws here protecting the rights of these freedmen, making the same laws for them that are made for the white man."[125]

A few Republicans called for civil rights guarantees that were idiosyncratic. Myers insisted that "no law of any State lately in insurrection shall impose by indirection a servitude which the Constitution now forbids."[126] Kasson made one proposal for race equality in the civil law and criminal law and another proposal for race equality in property law.[127] Most propositions combined the two.

Whether most Republicans thought different phrases made a difference is unclear. Proponents of congressional Reconstruction continued engaging in parallel play when discussing civil rights guarantees. No Republican during the debates over the exclusion resolution or other Reconstruction matters explained why their preferred text was better than other draft proposals. Members attached little significance to differences between race-neutral language and explicit bans on race discrimination. Garfield proposed a race-neutral civil rights guarantee after he pleaded at length for Congress to protect former slaves.[128] Republicans did not even comment on differences in the proposals they made at different times during the first session of the Thirty-Ninth Congress. Stevens on December 6 proposed a constitutional amendment prohibiting race discrimination that declared "[a]ll national and State laws shall be equally applicable to every citizen, and no discrimination shall be made on account of race and color."[129] Less than two weeks later, he called for a constitutional amendment "to make all laws uniform" and for federal legislation protecting persons of color.[130] No reason exists for thinking that on December 18 Stevens was referred to anything other than the constitutional amendment he proposed on December 6, even though the earlier text explicitly banned race discrimination and the later constitutional proposal did not.[131]

Whether proponents of congressional Reconstruction distinguished between calls for "the abolition of all distinctions . . . on account of color and race" and claims that "civil rights should be secured by laws applicable alike to whites and blacks" is more difficult to assess. Many, but not all, Republicans in Congress believed that voting was not a civil right.[132] Context is often helpful. Most proponents of congressional Reconstruction offered both civil rights and political guarantees that clarified their position on whether former slaves had a right to vote or at least a right to voting laws that did not make racial discriminations. Many members of Congress when speaking on other matters took positions on the scope of civil rights that provide clues, often definitive, on whether they thought guarantees for civil rights included voting rights. Petitions from citizens are more difficult to assess. The best guess is that petitioners who called for bans on race discrimination in civil rights, without more, were not advocating Black suffrage, but this is just a best guess.

Proponents sometimes attached jurisdictional limitations to their civil rights guarantees. Loyal states could regulate persons of color as white persons saw fit. Rebel states could not. Buckland declared: "The Government is . . . bound to provide for the future protection of the lives, the liberty, and the rights of property of the loyal white people and of the loyal colored people of the rebellious States."[133] Sumner on February 2, 1866, proposed a resolution providing civil rights guarantees that was limited to "all States lately declared in rebellion."[134] Petitioners often restricted the scope of civil rights guarantees to former Confederate states or territories. A petition from citizens from Ohio would prohibit any "State which shall hereafter be admitted into this Union, or which may have attempted to withdraw from it," from making "any distinction in its constitution, laws, or municipal regulations on account of color or descent."[135] The citizens of Portland, Maine, called for the same constitutional amendment and for legislation prohibiting race discrimination in Washington, DC,[136] but not for laws mandating racial equality throughout the United States. Again, one privilege of loyalty was the right to discriminate against persons of color.

Several Republicans advocated rights guarantees that ranged beyond protection for garden-variety civil rights and race discrimination. Buckland wanted to make sure (white) residents of the Union states were free to travel south. After insisting "it is the duty of the Government to provide for its future safety, and insist upon such measures as will secure to every American citizen the natural rights of life, liberty, and property, in all the States," he stated: "If any citizen of Ohio chooses to go into South Carolina, or Mississippi, or any other State, for pleasure, for business, or for permanent settlement, his rights must be respected and protected."[137] This protection was due against both public and private rights violations. Buckland continued: "If the State authorities refuse or are unable to protect them against unlawful combinations or any kind, then the people of that State should be declared in insurrection against the national Government and treated accordingly."[138] Some Radical Republicans championed a positive right to education. Sumner insisted that states recognize that both Black and white residents were entitled to "an educational system for the equal benefit of all without distinction of color or race."[139] Among the "irresistible guarantees" that W. Lawrence insisted be a condition of readmission was that "every State pledged to provide common schools for all its youth."[140] Stevens thought legislation mandating homesteads for former slaves was vital to Reconstruction. Noting "[w]e have turned, or are about to turn, loose four million slaves without a hut to shelter them or a cent in their pockets," he declared that, "[i]f we do not furnish them with homesteads, if we leave them to the legislation of their late masters, we had better have left them in bondage."[141] A convention of "Colored" people in Florida asked for "education" and "homesteads," in addition to "protection of their civil rights, including the right of the elective franchise."[142] Latham proposed a confiscation program designed to benefit Northern whites: "[I]f necessary to preserve the territory in the interest of loyalty—if the present population should prove incorrigible—I would sweep their landed estates from them by confiscation, and recolonize the country with loyal citizens."[143]

Civil rights did not occupy a distinctive place of pride on the reform agenda of the Thirty-Ninth Congress. With few exceptions, no Republican conditioned the return of the South solely on securing guarantees for fundamental rights or formal racial equality. Hart was the rare Republican whose proposals centered on ending race discrimination: "We cannot ... restore these States to their full relations to the Union until the bondsmen we have set free shall stand erect in all the rights of citizenship, protected in person, property, and liberty, and burdened by no restriction imposed because of race or color."[144] Far more proponents considered a ban on race discrimination, or a demand for equality, to be only one among many securities that had to be established before Southern representatives could be seated in Congress. Few Republicans indicated that civil rights guarantees should be the priority of Reconstruction. When Republicans merely listed conditions for readmission, individual rights were typically placed in the middle or at the end of the enumeration. Conkling, for example, placed third the protection of human rights, and those of persons of color in particular, when submitting five resolutions on Reconstruction. Some Republicans who gave longer speeches explaining the securities necessary before seating Southern representatives did emphasize the importance of protecting civil rights and preventing race discrimination. More often, lengthy Republican speeches gave place of pride to financial or political reforms, most notably changing the basis of apportionment.

Republicans did not demand constitutional amendments for securing civil rights as often as they demanded constitutional amendments for securing economic and political reforms. Many Republicans called on the national government to secure racial equality through federal statutory law. Raymond declared as a condition of readmission that Congress "make such laws as may be requisite to carry [the Thirteenth Amendment] into effect, which includes such legislation as may be required to secure from them protection of their civil and personal rights."[145] Representative Burton C. Cook of Illinois called for passing the Second Freedmen's Bureau Bill and what became the Civil Rights Act of 1866. "[T]he nation did guaranty to them the civil rights of freedmen that pledge must be redeemed," he declared, "by the legislation of Congress."[146] Legislation was sufficient because Congress under the Constitution of 1865 was already authorized to adopt whatever measures were necessary to secure racial equality. J. Ashley maintained that "the Constitution of the United States confers on Congress ample power for the protection of the emancipated slaves and freedmen in the States recently in rebellion."[147]

The most radical members of the Thirty-Ninth Congress were particularly prone to call for legislation promoting Black civil rights. Stevens combined calls for a race-neutral constitutional amendment with legislative proposals protecting Black civil rights. The House Majority Leader noted that a constitutional amendment "to make all laws uniform" was "of vital importance," but he insisted that passing constitutional amendments "is not all that we ought to do before these inveterate rebels are invited to participate in our legislation." Stevens called for legislation that would "furnish [freedmen] with homesteads" and grant them "equal rights" and the "right of suffrage."[148] Sumner refrained from advocating for a federal constitutional amendment when he insisted that "a majority of the people of each [seceding] State by popular vote agree to . . . [t]he complete suppression of all oligarchical pretensions . . . so that there shall be no denial of rights on account of color or race; but justice shall be impartial; and all shall be equal before the law," as well as "an educational system for the equal benefit of all without distinction of color or race."[149] On February 2, the senior senator from Massachusetts maintained that Congress under the Guarantee Clause and Thirteenth Amendment had the power to prohibit racial discrimination in all political and civil rights.[150]

These calls to protect persons of color through legislation rather than through constitutional amendment were often self-conscious. At least nine Republicans who championed constitutional amendments to entrench various anti-secession, political, and financial guarantees either proposed legislation only for civil rights guarantees or did not specify the mode of reform for achieving civil rights guarantees. Broomall, who advocated a constitutional amendment changing the basis of apportionment, called for legislation that would grant persons of color the right to vote "in the District of Columbia, the Territories, and in the country reclaimed from the rebellion" and would "guard the rights of those who, in the midst of rebellion, periled their lives and fortunes for its honor, of whatever caste or lineage they be."[151] Defrees made a similar distinction between matters requiring constitutional reform and civil rights guarantees that could be embodied in federal statutes. He first insisted on a constitutional amendment changing the basis of apportionment and then declared that former Confederate states could be represented in Congress, provided "this amendment [was] adopted and the necessary laws passed by Congress to secure to 'the citizens of each State all the privileges and immunities of citizens of the several States.'"[152] Deming split the difference, calling for a constitutional amendment only if federal law proved insufficient. "[U]nless the equality of the freedman both before civil and criminal law can be fortified by legislation here, under the second clause of the amendment to the Constitution, giving universal freedom to the slave," he declared, "we shall require . . . an amendment."[153] When Republicans and petitioners proposed a mixture of constitutional and legislative reforms, rights guarantee were almost always on the legislative side of the ledger. Sherman endorsed a resolution of the Union members of the Ohio legislature that called for a constitutional amendment on the apportionment of representatives and then declared "we deem it the duty of Congress to provide by just and prudent but effective legislation for the protection of the freedmen."[154] G. Lawrence, in a speech made during the debates over the Fourteenth Amendment and after passage of the Civil Rights Act, omitted civil rights protections from his list of guarantees. He insisted only that former Confederate states "agree faithfully to administer the law passed by Congress to guaranty civil rights to all classes."[155]

G. Lawrence was typical in his omission of new civil rights guarantees articulated by Republicans and allied Unionists who spoke in the spring of 1866. Specific calls for protecting persons of color decreased sharply after Congress passed the Civil Rights Act of 1866. Before passage of that statute, most Republicans who specified multiple conditions for restoration included bans on race discrimination, differing only on whether these bans should take constitutional or statutory form. Fifteen Republicans gave speeches setting out conditions for restoration between the time the Civil Rights Act became law and the Joint Committee proposed the omnibus Fourteenth Amendment. None explicitly called for a constitutional amendment banning race discrimination or protecting civil rights. Morris and Ingersoll were the only Republicans who gave speeches in April or May 1866 on Reconstruction who called for any kind of civil rights guarantee.[156] The Joint Committee's proposed omnibus, which included such a constitutional guarantee, did not inspire more enthusiasm for civil rights guarantees. H. Wilson, as well as G. Lawrence, while Congress was debating the Fourteenth Amendment, each gave a speech on Reconstruction setting out conditions for restoring the former Confederate states that omitted civil rights guarantees or guarantees of racial equality.[157] The Black Codes, most Republicans seemed to have concluded, were dealt with adequately by legislation in the months before they debated and sent the Fourteenth Amendment to the states.

Civil rights and racial equality played a far greater role in petitions to the first session than in congressional speeches. As tables A.7 and A.8 indicate, compared to members of Congress, far more petitioners gave the rights of persons of color place of pride when listing the "adequate securities" necessary for restoring former Confederate states. Almost all petitions whose conditions were spelled out on the floor of Congress asked for civil rights guarantees. A high percentage called for explicit bans on race discrimina-tion. Many asked only for a civil rights guarantee, sometimes couched as a guarantee of republican government. Petitioners more closely resembled members of Congress in their ambivalence about the proper mode of secur-ing civil rights guarantees. Petitions that specified the form of reform when calling for anti-secession, financial, and political guarantees (other than bans on race discrimination in voting) almost always called for constitutional amendments. Many petitions that proposed to end race discrimination in civil rights or in both civil and political rights called only for legislation.

Powers Guarantees

Several petitions and a few members of Congress insisted on a constitutional amendment granting congressional powers as a condition for readmission. Some petitioners asked for a constitutional amendment authorizing Con-gress to enforce the other proposed constitutional amendments in the reform package. The citizens of Huron and Erie Counties, Ohio, after proposing four substantive amendments, added a fifth, declaring "Congress shall have power to enforce these articles by appropriate legislation."[158] Senator Henry S. Lane of Indiana called for Congress to be given power to enforce the Guarantee Clause in Article IV, Section 1. He "wish[ed] Congress, by a constitutional amendment, to furnish power to carry out every single guar-antee of the Constitution, most especially that provision of the Constitution guarantying a republican form of government to every State."[159] Garfield spoke more generally when he stated "we must see to it that hereafter per-sonal liberty and personal rights are placed in the keeping of the nation."[160]

Bingham was the most tenacious exponent of a powers guarantee. The Ohio Republican on December 6, 1865, proposed a constitutional amend-ment empowering Congress to pass "all necessary and proper laws to secure to all persons in every State of the Union equal protection in their rights, life, liberty, and property."[161] A month later, Bingham made clear that pas-sage of this amendment was his most vital condition for restoring former Confederate states. He justified combining a rights guarantee with a powers guarantee by claiming that the Constitution of 1787 and 1791 did not vest Congress with the power of enforcing either the Privileges and Immuni-ties Clause in Article IV or the Due Process Clause in the Fifth Amend-ment. Bingham asserted that "it has been the want of the Republic that there was not an express grant of power in the Constitution to enable the whole people of every State, by constitutional enactment, to enforce obedience to these requirements of the Constitution."[162]

Bingham's reading of the Constitution of 1865 went both unsupported and uncontested when other members of Congress and petitioners presented their reform packages. Representatives discussed congressional power to enforce Article IV during the debates over the Civil Rights Act of 1866,[163] but not when considering the conditions under which former Confederate states would be restored to their antebellum status. No other member of Congress, when proposing a powers guarantee, indicated that he agreed with Bingham on congressional power to enforce Article IV, provided an alternative justification for the powers guarantee, or explained the significance of a powers guarantee. No members of Congress or petitioner explained the absence of a powers guarantee from the list of the conditions they thought necessary for restoring former Confederate states to their antebellum status. Parallel play again thwarts the modern commentator who wishes to understand what anyone other than Bingham thought was the importance or insignificance of a powers guarantee.

Guarantees for What and for Whom?

Constitutional reform after the Civil War encompassed numerous subjects. The speeches that proponents of congressional Reconstruction made on the status of former Confederate states demonstrated a broad consensus among Republicans that political and financial guarantees were at least as necessary as civil rights guarantees before South Carolina and friends could resume their antebellum status. That the Fourteenth Amendment turned out to be an omnibus was a historical accident only in the sense that, had constitutional politics played out differently, then financial, political, and civil rights guarantees—and perhaps an explicit anti-secession guarantee—might have been embodied in separate constitutional amendments rather than as different provisions in the same constitutional amendment. The post–Civil War Constitution, however, was likely to encompass some financial and political guarantees. As great a consensus, if not a much greater consensus, existed on reforming apportionment and on the repudiating the Confederate debt than existed for legally obliterating the Black Codes.

The Republican suite of proposals for constitutional reform confirms that abolishing Black Codes played a secondary role in almost all Republican thinking about the constitutional guarantees necessary for restoring former Confederate status to their antebellum status in the Union. Political guarantees were front and center when proponents considered the conditions under which former Confederate states could be represented in Congress. Bingham aside, the vast majority of Republicans thought they had provided a sufficient guarantee for civil rights and racial equality when Congress passed the Civil Rights Act of 1866.[164] Had Bingham left Congress in a pique after his stand-alone rights amendment failed to gain much support in late February,[165] the national legislature almost certainly would have adopted some version of the financial and political guarantees proposed by various proponents of congressional Reconstruction. Judging by the lack of interest in additional constitutional guarantees for racial equality after the Civil Rights Act of 1866 became law, the Constitution of the United States would probably lack citizenship, privileges and immunities, equal protection, and due process clauses.[166] The proposals that became Sections 2, 3, and 4 were not nearly as dependent on aggressive advocacy by one or a few members of Congress.

The predominance of financial and political guarantees in Republican speeches highlights how proponents of congressional Reconstruction had broader concerns than ensuring that the former Confederate states respected the rights of former slaves. Republicans were as committed to protecting white Unionists, civil war veterans, and Northern creditors as they were Southern Blacks. They were disturbed by all the pathologies of Southern constitutional politics in the wake of the Civil War. Changing the balance of power in the national government and in the states was more fundamental to the project of Reconstruction than determining what loyal people did once loyal people were empowered.

The petitioners who called on Congress to adopt various financial, political, and civil rights guarantees as a means for obtaining "adequate security" against former Confederate states "renewing the attempt to secede" captured the ideas that united Republican conditions for restoring former Confederate states, their proposed constitutional amendments, and the different provisions of what became the Fourteenth Amendment. The various proposals detailed in this chapter that Republicans made for constitutional and legal reforms were connected by an overarching concern with preventing rebel rule rather than by a singular obsession with thwarting one manifestation of rebel rule, however egregious that manifestation may have been. Hart aside, no proponents of congressional Reconstruction placed the abolition of Black Codes at the heart of their preferred constitutional and legal reforms. Bingham, who more than any other Republican emphasized civil rights guarantees, expressed more concern for the rights of loyal whites in the South than for the rights of former slaves. Republicans and allied Unionists understood that rebels in power threatened far more than former slaves; that many threats could not be alleviated by changing the relevant constitutional constraints, even if former Confederates could be trusted to observe those constraints scrupulously; and that rebels in power were unlikely to be constrained by constitutional provisions inconsistent with their nefarious interests in white supremacy and national hegemony. Acknowledging the diversity of loyal persons, white and Black, who needed protection from rebel rule, most directed constitutional and legal reforms toward empowering at least some loyal persons rather than toward adding new rights provisions to the Constitution.

Constitutional politics in 1866 was in greater need of alteration than constitutional law. The lists of conditions that proponents of congressional Reconstruction championed expressed the broad consensus that only a Republican Party empowered by new political guarantees could win the peace and protect loyal people throughout the nation. Who exercised the powers vested in the national government by the Thirteenth Amendment and the Thirteenth Amendment's Constitution was more vital to constitutional reform than enumerating more specific or different powers and constraints. Republicans and allied Unionists demonstrated these priorities in circumstances when they could empower loyal whites without providing new protections for loyal Blacks. Colorado statehood and several other matters offered Congress the possibility of altering constitutional politics for the better without altering the legal rights of loyal Blacks. In each circumstance, most proponents of congressional Reconstruction were content to alter constitutional politics and maintain the racial status quo.

To Colorado and Beyond

The debate over Colorado statehood that took place in the Thirty-Ninth Congress just before representatives considered the omnibus Fourteenth Amendment offers an abridged version of many debates over Reconstruction for those who prefer reading two-hour-long Charles Sumner speeches to two-day-long Sumner speeches. The central issue was whether Republicans should empower the loyal even when that meant denying persons of color the ballot, at least in the short run. Most Republicans during the debate over Colorado statehood supported empowering loyal whites rather than protecting loyal Blacks. Most senators and representatives were willing to grant loyal Coloradans statehood, even though the territory was underpopulated, the proposed state constitution was not drafted consistently with federal law, and the state constitution as proposed limited voting to white persons. President Andrew Johnson and his political allies, who uniformly opposed Colorado statehood, emphasized the small population and procedural irregularities. Some Radical Republicans demanded Black suffrage. Combined, Radical Republicans and Democrats were not able to prevent Congress from passing legislation authorizing Colorado to become a state, but Republican defections prevented Congress from overriding President Johnson's veto of the Colorado statehood bill. Colorado would not become a state until 1876.

The debates over Colorado statehood were structured by the same Republican concerns and strategies that structured Reconstruction and the proposed constitutional reforms discussed in chapter 4. Colorado statehood, Reconstruction, and proposed constitutional reforms were attempts to empower the loyal. Given the choice between configuring constitutional politics by changing how government offices were staffed and constraining constitutional politics by placing limits on government action, Republicans consistently choose to emphasize reforms that constructed constitutional politics. In part on the assumption that persons of color would eventually be enfranchised, most Republicans preferred constitutional reforms and statehood policies that strengthened the party of persons who remained loyal during the Civil War over providing special protections for persons of color. Proponents of congressional Reconstruction, when considering the conditions under which former Confederate states would be restored to the Union, sought to foster government by the loyal by barring leading traitors from public office and diminishing the political power of states that did not allow the faithful to vote. Republicans, when considering admitting such new states to the Union as Colorado, sought to foster government by the loyal by providing the faithful with two more votes in the Senate, one more vote in the House of Representatives, and three more votes in the Electoral College.

The debate over Colorado statehood is intrinsically worth excavating. How members of the Thirty-Ninth Congress debated questions of population, territorial government, rule by law, republican equality, African American rights, and political expediency when considering Colorado statehood casts light on constitutional thinking at the time the Fourteenth Amendment was framed and ratified; the debate also sheds light on questions that remain vibrant in the third decade of the twenty-first century. The controversy over Colorado statehood provides valuable perspectives on state equality in the Senate. Senator Charles Buckalew of Pennsylvania during the debate over the apportionment resolution, and Senator Thomas A. Hendricks of Indiana during the debate over Colorado statehood, anticipated contemporary complaints that state inequality in the Senate violates constitutional and republican commitments to political equality.[1] Republicans who insisted on majority rule when allocating seats in the House of Representatives demurred when Democrats detailed how admitting underpopulated Western states would aggravate the majoritarian deficiencies of equal state representation in the Senate. Most Republicans believed that admitting Nevada, Colorado, Nebraska, and other Western territories represented a vital means for securing passage of the Thirteenth Amendment, ratifying the Thirteenth Amendment, reelecting President Abraham Lincoln, and ensuring the West would be a bulwark against repeated attempts at secession. A more *Republican* Senate outweighed the cost of a less *republican* Senate. The lesson may be that constitutional movements must pick and choose among possible reforms.

The Republican push for Colorado statehood highlights the ominous possibilities that were present from the very beginning of Reconstruction and the framing of the Fourteenth Amendment. In 1866, the interests of white loyalists and Black citizens largely coincided in almost all the former Confederate states. Congress could prevent rebel rule only by empowering and protecting loyal whites and loyal Blacks. The West presented more of a challenge. In Colorado, Nebraska, and other Western territories, and also in Tennessee, white and Black interests diverged. Protecting and empowering the loyal to prevent rebel rule did not require a new birth of freedom. The decisions Republicans made in these situations demonstrate the centrality of preventing rebel rule and rewarding loyalty to both Reconstruction and the Fourteenth Amendment.

Settling the West

Secession was a boon to Western development.[2] The backlash to the Kansas–Nebraska Act and the Lecompton Constitution paralyzed territorial policy during the late 1850s. A national government divided over slavery could neither admit new Western states nor organize new Western territories. Gridlock ended immediately after Southern representatives and senators resigned their seats. Kansas joined the Union on January 29, 1861.[3] Strong bipartisan Northern majorities voted to organize the Nevada, Colorado, and Dakota Territories. President James Buchanan signed the relevant legislation before leaving office.[4] Three years later, Republicans, to buttress support for the Thirteenth Amendment and President Lincoln's reelection, successfully pushed Nevada statehood.[5]

Nevadans' loyalty to the Union and Republican Party policy was front and center when that territory petitioned for statehood. State residents announced their opposition to secession and nullification when framing the state constitution. The crucial provision declared that

the Paramount Allegiance of every citizen is due to the Federal Government in the exercise of all its Constitutional powers as the same have been or may be defined by the Supreme Court of the United States; and no power exists in the people of this or any other State of the Federal Union to dissolve their connection therewith or perform any act tending to impair, subvert, or resist the Supreme Authority of the government of the United States. The Constitution of the United States confers full power on the Federal Government to maintain and Perpetuate its existence, and whensoever any portion of the States, or people thereof attempt to secede from the Federal Union, or forcibly resist the Execution of its laws, the Federal Government may, by warrant of the Constitution, employ armed force in compelling obedience to its Authority.[6]

Republicans in 1864 were eager to admit a state that promised two more Republican senators and one more Republican in the House of Representatives, all of whom would support the Thirteenth Amendment and federal war policies. Nevada would provide three more Republican votes in the Electoral College for President Lincoln and one more vote for ratifying the constitutional ban on slavery.[7] Previous population requirements took a back seat.[8] Senator Benjamin F. Wade of Ohio, defending Nevada statehood, imagined the past when asserting that, "[i]n enabling the Territories to come into the Union as States, I believe it will be found that the history of the Government is that very little attention has been paid to the number of inhabitants at the time the people have been authorized to form a State government."[9] No one commented that the proposed Nevada constitution limited voting to white males.[10]

Colorado proved more difficult.[11] One set of problems was the weak support for statehood within that territory and the irregular processes by which the proposed state constitution was approved. Congress had authorized the territory to apply for statehood,[12] but Coloradans overwhelming rejected the proposed constitution drafted by the territorial convention that followed the federal rules, in part because the territory's sizeable Hispanic population and mining interests in the western regions in that territory feared Denver control. The proposed state constitution that Coloradans sent to Congress was drafted by a convention organized without federal permission by territorial political leaders and approved by a bare majority of voters in an election in which far fewer persons voted than had done so in previous territorial elections. Population was a second problem. Colorado had far fewer than the 60,000 persons that territorial practice before 1860 typically required for statehood. The subsequent admission of Kansas and Nevada suggested that practice had been abandoned. Still, strong evidence existed that, unlike the population in previous underpopulated territories granted statehood, the population in Colorado was decreasing rather than increasing as unsuccessful miners and entrepreneurs left for greener pastures in the West or for ancestral homes in the East.

Colorado statehood presented Republicans with a choice between loyalty and Black suffrage. Colorado had been a loyal Republican bastion during the Civil War. Many Coloradans joined the Union army. The Colorado militia successfully turned back a Texas invasion of Union territories in the

Battle of Glorieta Pass. The most prominent Colorado politicians were staunch Republicans. Republicans were likely to retain control of Colorado for the foreseeable future. Colorado was as committed to white supremacy, and the proposed state constitution limited voting to white persons. Race discrimination in the civil law was rampant.[13]

The fate of Colorado statehood waxed and waned during the first months of 1866. The Senate initially rejected statehood in March by a vote of 21–14 (or 23–16, if senators who announced their positions but were paired off are counted).[14] Two months later, the upper chamber of Congress reversed course and approved Colorado statehood by vote of 19–13 (or 25–19 if senators who announced their positions but were paired off are counted).[15] The House of Representatives in May, after a very short debate, concurred by an 81–57 vote (four Representatives were paired off).[16] The Republican leadership in both the Senate and the House beat back proposals to require as a condition of statehood that Colorado permit persons of color to vote.[17] President Johnson vetoed the Colorado statehood bill on May 15.[18] Lacking the votes to overcome the veto in the Senate, the measure was temporarily shelved.[19]

Congressional divisions over Colorado statehood between March and May 1866 became more partisan and more consistent with congressional divisions over the Fourteenth Amendment. Tables A.1 and A.2 highlight how the change in Colorado's fortunes in the Senate was entirely the result of Republican proponents of the Fourteenth Amendment switching their votes in favor of statehood. Republicans who would vote for the omnibus Fourteenth Amendment in June divided evenly (14–13) in the March Senate vote on statehood, as did Republicans (1–1) who would vote against the omnibus Fourteenth Amendment. Significant swings occurred two months later. Republicans who would vote for the omnibus Fourteenth Amendment favored Colorado statehood in May by almost a three-to-one margin (23–8),[20] while three of the four Republicans who would vote against the Fourteenth Amendment opposed Colorado statehood. Wade had the honor of leading the fight against statehood in March but became one of the most vocal supporters of statehood in May. The only two Senate Democrats who supported Colorado statehood in March either switched their vote (James A. McDougall of California) or did not vote (James W. Nesmith of Oregon) in May. The House vote in May was as partisan as the May Senate vote. No Democrat voted for Colorado statehood. Republicans, all of whom would vote for the Fourteenth Amendment, divided by an almost three-to-one margin (77–31) in favor of statehood.[21]

Presidential Reconstruction and Colorado

Democrats, joined by the very conservative Republicans who supported presidential Reconstruction and opposed the Fourteenth Amendment, asserted that process and population concerns were sufficient to deny Colorado statehood. Coloradans, having rejected the congressional process for joining the Union, had no legal authority to take a second bite at the statehood apple. President Johnson and his political allies agreed that the initial invitation to join the Union should never have been issued. Colorado lacked the population necessary for statehood and was unlikely to achieve that population in the foreseeable future. Opponents of the exclusion resolution and Fourteenth Amendment agreed that statehood decisions, like decisions to amend the Constitution, should await the restoration of former Confederate states to full representation in Congress. That Coloradans limited voting to white persons had nothing to do with the case. Only a few proponents of the Fourteenth Amendment cared about the mandate for race discrimination in the constitution proposed by Colorado citizens.

President Johnson's veto message summarized each element of the Democratic opposition to Colorado statehood. The seventeenth president complained about the process by which Coloradans drafted their state constitution. The second convention was "without any legal authority," and the majority for statehood was tiny. Noting that more than 70 percent of Coloradans rejected the state constitution drafted according to the rules laid down by Congress, he concluded: "It does not seem to me entirely safe to receive this last-mentioned result, so irregularly obtained, as sufficient to outweigh the one which had been legally obtained in the first election."[22] Statehood was inconsistent with Democrats' understandings of republican government. Giving representation to a state as sparsely populated as Colorado would violate the constitutional commitment to "an approximation toward equality among the several States compromising the Union."[23] President Johnson insisted, as did Democrats throughout 1866, that Congress should take no decisive actions while the former Confederate states were not represented in Congress. His veto message stated: "It is a common interest of all the States, as well those represented as those unrepresented, that the integrity and harmony of the Union should be restored as completely as possible, so that all those who are expected to bear the burdens of the Federal Government shall be consulted concerning the admission of new States."[24]

Those representatives who opposed the exclusion resolution, the

Fourteenth Amendment, and Colorado statehood maintained that the process by which Coloradans approved a state constitution did not merit admission to the Union. That process was illegal. Congress authorized the election of delegates to a convention, Coloradans selected delegates according to the congressional rules, that convention drafted a state constitution, and an overwhelming number of Coloradan voters rejected that constitution. End of story. Hendricks noted that "[t]here was no provision in [federal] law for the holding of a second convention."[25] The second constitutional convention failed to follow the federal rules. Hendricks observed when leading the fight against statehood from the Democratic side that the selection process established by territorial party leaders resulted in "a most irregular election, in no sense, neither in law nor in equity, in accordance with the statute."[26] The vote on the second state constitution was hardly definitive. Hendricks pointed out that the second constitution passed by only a 155-vote majority in an election in which fewer than six thousand persons voted.[27]

Colorado did not have the population for statehood. The number of residents was miniscule. Many lacked what Democrats believed were the racial characteristics necessary for republican citizenship. Senator Reverdy Johnson of Maryland asserted that Colorado could at best claim a population of 35,000 but that 10,000 of those were "Mexicans by birth, wholly unacquainted with our institutions." He thought further investigation likely to reveal that "the population is much below that number."[28] Even that small number of Colorado residents was decreasing. Hendricks, in opposing Colorado statehood, noted that far fewer Coloradans voted in the 1865 territorial election than in the 1861 territorial election.[29] Senator James R. Doolittle of Wisconsin recanted his earlier support for statehood in light of territorial population losses during the Civil War. "[T]he population of Colorado is much less than I supposed it was when the enabling act was passed," he maintained, "and my conviction is that the population now is not to exceed twenty-five thousand in that Territory."[30]

This small, diminishing population was far below what past practice had required for statehood. Democrats claimed that the necessary population for membership was either the 60,000 persons mandated by the Northwest Ordinance[31] or the number of persons federal law established as composing a congressional district within an existing state, which in 1866 was about 120,000 people. The population of Colorado was not close to approximating either of these figures. Hendricks asserted that "it would require about one hundred and twenty thousand to secure a Representative in the House of Representatives; and here with a population, upon the best information we can get, of about fifteen thousand, it is asked to give two Senators and a

Representative to Colorado."[32] McDougall agreed that past precedents on population barred Colorado statehood. He declared:

> It has been regarded heretofore as a rule that no State shall come into the Federal Union until her population would come up to what was required by the enumeration for a member of the House of Representatives. I do not remember the precise number now required, but I know it is something over one hundred thousand. Two Senators in the Federal Senate for a population of fifteen thousand would be a great injustice; and to that injustice I cannot be a party.[33]

Granting statehood to underpopulated territories violated constitutional commitments to republican equality in all elected branches of the national government. Hendricks complained about inequitable representation in the House of Representatives. He maintained: "I shall not vote to admit a State to the same political power that Indiana possess, when it does not represent in point of population a fifth of the population of one of our congressional districts."[34] "[A] population of 12,000 or 14,000 ought not to have the voice in the legislation of this country," he insisted, "that the 1,300,000 of the people of Indiana have."[35] McDougall grumbled about inequitable representation in the Senate. He stated: "I do not think the Territory of Colorado is so populated and has such a number of permanent inhabitants as to justify her representation by two Senators in this Senate hall."[36] Senator James Guthrie of Kentucky protested inequitable representation in both Houses of Congress. He declared:

> Colorado ought not to be admitted as a State; that she had not the population nor the ability to sustain a State government; that she could not demand from the amount of her population, to be placed on an equal footing with the other States. She has not the population enough to entitle her to a Representative in the other House. If she should be admitted, she would be entitled to two Senators here, which would greatly in disproportion, and overbalancing with another small State the popular majority of large States in this body.[37]

Hendricks added the presidency to this list of complaints. He asked that, "when you come to select a President of the United States in 1868, is it right, it is just, is it consistent with the policy of our Government, that one man in Colorado shall have the voice of ninety men in Indiana[?]"[38]

Democrats acknowledged that constitutional commitments to federalism entailed some inequalities in representation, but the disparities that would result from Colorado statehood were unprecedented, unwarranted, and unjustified. That Americans had deviated from the one-person, one-vote ideal when framing the Constitution, Hendricks stated, "does not justify us in carrying that inequality beyond any point known in our history heretofore."[39] He concluded that "[r]epresentation must be equal and just, else representation of itself becomes tyranny."[40] R. Johnson regarded past population disparities to be the result of political compromises that the persons responsible for the Constitution of 1787 understood were "not republican" and "hostile to all the ideas of republican liberty entertained at that period."[41] This deviation should neither be repeated nor extended. Colorado statehood would have been a bridge too far for the founders, given that the disparity in population between Colorado and other states in 1866 was far greater than the disparity between the more populated and less populated states when the Constitution was framed. R. Johnson insisted that, "if the proposition had come from any member of the Convention that States thereafter to be admitted might be admitted if they had a population such as is the population of Colorado, the suggestion would not have received the sanction of any other member of the body."[42]

Republicans had no business rushing to admit an underpopulated state with a dubious commitment to statehood just to gain two Republican senators, one Republican representative, and three Republican votes in the Electoral College.[43] Delay was particularly appropriate for the same reason that Democrats maintained constitutional reform should be delayed. Congress should make momentous decisions, such as changing the fundamental law and admitting new Union members, only when all existing states were fully represented in the House and Senate. Senator Willard Saulsbury, Sr., of Delaware stated: "I prefer that when Colorado shall be admitted into the Union as we have heretofore understood and known it to be, as our fathers intended it should be, and not into a partial Union with a certain limited number of States."[44]

The representatives and senators who opposed the exclusion resolution, the Fourteenth Amendment, and Colorado statehood did not care that Colorado prohibited persons of color from voting. Doolittle insisted that suffrage rules in Colorado were none of Congress's business. He maintained that "each State had a right for itself to determine the question, and that the Federal Government had no right or constitutional power to impose on a State negro suffrage." "[T]he right of a State to determine that question for itself," in his view, "was one of the reserved rights of every State under the Constitution."[45] Enabling acts were no exception to the rule that states determined suffrage laws. Doolittle declared that "it did not belong to the Federal Government to impose [suffrage requirements] on the other States as a condition to their being in this Union."[46] Guthrie praised the proposed constitution for limiting suffrage to white males. "I should not object to [the proposed Colorado] Constitution because it had the word 'white' in it in relation to voters," he informed the Senate. Guthrie's Thirteenth Amendment had freed former slaves without making them full members of the political community in the United States. The Democrat from Kentucky did "not believe that black people are citizens of the United States even though they are born here."[47] Guthrie spoke for his party when concluding: "I think it is better for the African that he should be governed by the people where he lives, who know his habits, and understand all about him."[48]

Congressional Reconstruction and Colorado

Proponents of congressional Reconstruction splintered over Colorado statehood. Senator Charles Sumner of Massachusetts and a handful of other Republicans, mostly Radicals, insisted that Colorado not be admitted to the Union until white territorial citizens agreed to grant Black territorial citizens the right to vote. Colorado had to make the commitments to racial equality Sumner was demanding that former Confederate states make before being allowed representation, not the (weak) commitments to racial equality prevalent in those states already represented in the Thirty-Ninth Congress. Most Republicans were content to admit Colorado if the new state was as republican and as Republican as Ohio. Loyal states were free to enfranchise whomever they thought best. Besides, proponents of Colorado statehood assured others, and perhaps themselves, that Black suffrage was an idea whose time was clearly coming no matter what policies Congress adopted for admitting underpopulated states in the West.

REPUBLICANS AGAINST STATEHOOD

Sumner summarized the position of those Republicans who opposed Colorado statehood but supported the Fourteenth Amendment when he listed "three distinct objections . . . to the admission of Colorado as a State."[49] The first two objections animated those opponents of Colorado statehood who also opposed the Fourteenth Amendment. Sumner endorsed the Democratic Party's objections to process and population. He spoke of "the irregularity of the proceedings which have ended in the seeming adoption of the constitution presented to us" and "the small number of people constituting the population of that Territory, not being sufficient . . . to justify us in investing it with all the great prerogatives of a State."[50] The third objection was unique to those Republican proponents of the Fourteenth Amendment who opposed Colorado statehood. Coloradans, Sumner insisted, did "not come before us now according to the requirements of the enabling act with a constitution republican in form[] and consistent with the Declaration of Independence."[51] Unless Coloradans granted persons of color the right to vote, then Sumner and his allies would not support Colorado statehood. "[S]uch a community as now exists in Colorado," he insisted, "deficient in population, failing already in agriculture, failing already in mineral resources, and with a constitution which sets at defiance the first principle of human rights, should not at this moment be recognized as a State of the Union."[52]

Sumner was as steadfast and uncompromising in defense of Black suffrage during the debates over Colorado statehood as he was whenever Black suffrage was debated by the Thirty-Ninth Congress. Two months before the statehood debate began in earnest, the senior senator from Massachusetts presented a petition from African Americans in Colorado requesting that "the word 'white' be expunged from [the state] constitution wherever it may occur before [Colorado] be permitted to count herself and become one of the sisters of this great and most glorious Republic."[53] When Senator James H. Lane of Kansas suggested that "excluding one hundred negroes from the right of suffrage" did not require "a great deal of discussion,"[54] Sumner responded, "[a] great question that, sir, whether one hundred persons on account of their color shall be shut out from the exercise of the elective franchise."[55] Discuss he did. "I may be told, sir," Sumner said, "that there are but ninety colored persons in this distant Territory who are to be sacrificed. If there were but one, that would be enough to justify my opposition."[56] Sumner during the debate over Colorado statehood spoke often, repeatedly insisting that the phrase "every white male citizen" in the constitution proposed for Colorado "is not republican, and . . . is repugnant to the principles of the Declaration of Independence."[57] His first speech on Colorado statehood in the Thirty-Ninth Congress declared that restricting voting to white men "is not republican for the first principle of republican government is equality. Let that be denied, and you fail in your republican government."[58] This discrimination extended beyond the ballot box. Sumner when objecting to Colorado statehood pointed out that "these same colored men while despoiled of the elective franchise are nevertheless compelled to pay taxes to support the public schools from which their children are excluded."[59]

Colorado in 1866 was less egalitarian than Colorado in 1861. "There has been a regression in republican principle," Sumner announced.[60] Sumner pointed out that the word "white" did not appear in territorial electoral laws.[61] Colorado law when the territory was organized enfranchised "citizens of the United States."[62] Persons of color in 1861, Sumner claimed, were citizens of the United States and thus entitled to vote under territorial law. He pointed out that "[t]he language was broad and general; it was applicable to every male person of the age of twenty-one years or upward."[63]

This defense of Black suffrage was grounded in an opinion issued by Attorney General Edward Bates in 1862 declaring that persons of color were citizens of the United States.[64] Sumner insisted the Bates opinion, not the Supreme Court's contrary claim in *Dred Scott v. Sandford*,[65] was the official constitutional law of the land. The senior senator from Massachusetts maintained that "[b]y that opinion [Bates] fixed the law of this country forever; that all colored persons are citizens of the United States; and that opinion was emphatically the law of this distant Territory."[66] Whether Coloradans were aware of Bates's opinion and thought themselves bound by that opinion "did not alter the case by a hair's breadth."[67] Sumner insisted that senators when passing the enabling act understood that the Lincoln administration had overruled the Supreme Court on Black citizenship. They "supposed that all persons, without distinction of color in that Territory, were electors."[68] At least Sumner did. "[W]hen I voted for this enabling act," he stated, "I did not vote with the idea that there could be a discrimination founded on color."[69]

The serpent entered the Colorado garden only on March 11, 1864, after Congress had passed the enabling act authorizing Coloradans to form a state constitution.[70] On that day, race was introduced into Colorado law. A new territorial law declared: "Every male citizen of the age of twenty-one years or upward, not being negro or mulatto, shall be deemed a qualified voter."[71] Sumner excoriated what he believed to be a statutory novelty. He asserted: "[B]y express language, open and barefaced, negroes and mulattoes were put under the ban. A caste was established. A discrimination, odious, offensive, and unchristian was organized in the statutes of the Territory."[72] This introduction of race discrimination and the backsliding on commitments to equality under law were unprecedented. Jurisdictions had banned Black voting but none had ever taken existing suffrage rights away from citizens of color. Sumner insisted that "[n]o other Territory which has undertaken to recognize the rights of man has afterward undertaken to overthrow them."[73]

The proposed constitutional provision limiting voting to white persons violated the federal law that obliged Coloradans to adopt a state constitution that met the republican standards set out in the texts that gave birth to the United States.[74] The enabling act authorizing a constitutional convention in Colorado, Sumner pointed out, mandated that "the constitution when formed shall be republican and not repugnant to the Constitution of the United States and the principles of the Declaration of Independence."[75] This statute acknowledged that the Constitution of the United States, interpreted consistently with the Declaration of Independence, held territories seeking statehood to a higher republican standard than states. Existing state constitutions were not subject to federal inspection for republic infirmities, most notably the failure to grant Black suffrage. Proposed state constitutions were. The Territorial Clause and federal law imposed upon Congress a duty to appraise the proposed Colorado state constitution to determine whether all state residents, Black and white, were guaranteed a republican government. Sumner reminded the Senate that "⌊w⌋e have no occasion now to review the constitution of Connecticut or of New York, but we have occasion at this moment in the discharge of a solemn duty to review the constitution of this proposed state."[76]

Colorado failed this mandated constitutional and statutory test. A state constitution that disenfranchised African Americans was not republican. No Senator, Sumner insisted, could "say that a constitution which undertakes to exclude persons from their rights on account of color is consistent with the fundamental principles of the Declaration of Independence."[77] That the proposed Colorado constitution might have passed republican muster in the past had no bearing on the status of that constitution in light of updated Republican Party commitments in the wake of the Thirteenth Amendment. "In other times we have caught the cry, *No more slave States*," he observed. "There is another cry which must be ours, *No more States recognizing Inequality of Rights*."[78] Republicans could no more sacrifice this revised principle for partisan expedience than they could previously have admitted slavery in the West to prevent a civil war. Sumner:

> Better far than any number of votes will be loyalty to this great cause. Tell me not that it is expedient to create two more votes in this Chamber. Permit me to say nothing can be expedient that is not right. If I were now about to pronounce the last words that I could ever utter in this Chamber, I would say to you, Senators, do not forget that right is always the highest expediency. You can never sacrifice the right without suffering for it.[79]

Abandoning the principle that "[n]o more States recognizing Inequality of Rights" in the case of Colorado risked a precedent that might undo Reconstruction in the South. Sumner maintained that Congress was committed to admitting states in the West and readmitting states in the South with constitutions that "are republican in form and not repugnant to the principles of the Declaration of Independence."[80] If Colorado could fore-swear Black suffrage, so could Alabama. Opposing the motion to reconsider Colorado statehood, the senior Senator from Massachusetts stated

> at this moment the most important practical question before the coun-try is[] whether we shall allow the word "white" to be in the constitu-tions of the late rebel States. Sir, with what just weight can you insist that the word "white" shall be excluded from those constitutions when you yourself deliberately receive into the Union a new State which has that principle of exclusion?[81]

Never shy about repeating himself for those who did not get the point the seventh time, Sumner more bluntly asked: "[H]ow can you insist that it shall be excluded from constitutions and statutes there, when you receive into the Union this new community with a constitution which tolerates this principle of exclusion[?]"[82]

The word "white" in Colorado's proposed constitution was particularly obnoxious because the persons of color Coloradans proposed to disenfran-chise had been loyal during the Civil War. "[M]ore than seventy-five" of the ninety persons of color in Colorado, Sumner pointed out, "have borne arms for you in the late war; and yet these people are now positively disfranchised in the constitution which is it proposed to recognize."[83] As proponents of Black suffrage had argued at length when setting out conditions for restor-ing former Confederate states and distributing the ballot in Washington, DC, Sumner claimed that the African American citizens of Colorado who performed military service earned the right to vote in that jurisdiction. "We are told they are few in number, perhaps a hundred; but out of that hundred there are some seventy who promptly went forth as soldiers to do battle for your flag," he asserted. "[B]ut when they returned to their homes they found that the franchise that they had already enjoyed was taken from them; that they who had periled life for to save the Republic and to aid it in estab-lishing the rights of all, when they once more found themselves at their own firesides were despoiled of their own."[84]

Every Republican proponent of the Fourteenth Amendment who op-posed Colorado statehood condemned the exclusion of Black voters in the proposed state constitution. "This word 'white' in the constitution," Wade stated, "constitutes a very great reason why she should not be admitted."[85] Race discrimination violated those fundamental republican norms that ani-mated the Republican Party. Senator George Edmunds of Vermont called on the Senate to "discard[] the dogma of delusion and of wrong which de-clares that [voting] qualifications and distinctions are to rest upon unreal and accidental foundations."[86] Republicans committed to "the political equality of all men," he maintained, "cannot turn [their] backs[s] to those principles which are cardinal and essential for the sake of any temporary success."[87] Many Republican opponents of Colorado statehood connected their concerns with race discrimination in new states to race discrimination in the South. Senator B. Gratz Brown of Missouri, when opposing the motion to reopen debate on Colorado, declared:

> The chief objection which I wish to state—not that there are no others—is that the constitution under which it claims admission contains a clause denying the right of suffrage to persons on account of color and race. I will never indorse by any vote of mine in this Senate any such odious discrimination, and as I propose to exercise my constitutional right in that behalf in regard to other States of the Union which have lately been in rebellion, so I am willing that the political reform, the assertion of this fundamental principle, should begin in the house of my friends, and apply first to the admission of Colorado.[88]

Brown and his political allies believed that Colorado should not be allowed to set a precedent for the restoration of former Confederate states. Grimes asked of a Republican convert to Colorado statehood: "With what sort of a face can he get up here to-morrow and insist that the people of the State of Virginia or the people of the State of Tennessee shall allow certain classes of the population in those States to vote when he says that it is competent and proper for the people of the Territory of Colorado to forever exclude the colored population of that State from voting?"[89]

Past precedents granting statehood to or organizing territories in localities that did not permit persons of color to vote were justified by special circumstances immediately before and during the Civil War. Republican proponents of the Fourteenth Amendment who opposed Colorado statehood insisted that Kansas was a unique case. Congress accepted a proposed state constitution that discriminated against persons of color because granting statehood was necessary to curb violence and promote emancipation. Grimes declared that his vote to admit Kansas was not "a precedent for the government of [his] conduct respecting any other state." That support was motivated by his desire "to get the question out of the halls of Congress, to have the conflict that was then going on in Kansas and throughout the country and in Congress settled."[90] "I would have admitted [Kansas] as a State with any population that would make it a free State," Wade admitted, "and settle that threatening question."[91] Territorial policy during the Civil War was rooted in expedience rather than principle. Wade acknowledged that "we organized some four or five Territories in the winter . . . of 1861, and it was done by a kind of compromise to settle this terrible question that was agitated in the Territories with regard to slavery."[92] Loyalty during the Civil War trumped equal rights and population concerns. Senator John Conness of California claimed that in 1864 Nevada had been admitted to the Union and that an enabling act was passed for Colorado without regard to Black suffrage only because "there was a very strong disposition on the part of a very large portion of Congress . . . to create and admit loyal free States."[93]

These compromises of principle were no longer necessary during Reconstruction. Times changed. Conness asserted the "necessity does not exist today" that justified past permission for territories becoming states to maintain or adopt race discrimination, "and we are not to be governed or controlled by it."[94] Values changed. Grimes noted that Americans, since the enabling act for Colorado was passed, had become far more committed to racial equality. When H. Lane noted that Congress did not require Coloradans to permit persons of color to vote when authorizing territorial residents to draft a state constitution, Grimes responded with a series of hard questions: "[D]oes not the Senator know that we have all made vast progress since 1863? Has not the Senator himself made vast progress since then? Have we not declared emancipation throughout the whole land? Are we to be governed by the same principles that we acted upon at that time?"[95] The enabling act for Colorado statehood contained one example of the changing times. Edmunds pointed out that Congress had never before inserted into an enabling act the requirement that "the constitution when formed shall be republican and not repugnant to the Constitution of the United States and the principles of the Declaration of Independence."[96] This renewed commitment to republicanism and the Declaration of Independence, combined with greater understanding that race discrimination was inconsistent with republicanism and with the Declaration, required Congress to abjure the past practice of admitting states constitutionally committed to white supremacy. Edmunds observed:

I am not to be told, for one, that the rejection of a constitution because it imposes the qualification of color upon its electors is a thing that has never been done before. . . . In all preceding time the condition of the country, the rights of States, the situation of the people were different. We have reached the culminating point where the bitter fruits of errors of years ago have been reaped in a large degree, and where now, turning our faces once more toward the arts of peace and hopes of prosperity and of equality and fraternity too, I should hope, we are to begin a new era.[97]

This demand—that Colorado refrain from making a constitutional commitment to white supremacy—was not necessarily a demand for a constitutional commitment to racial equality. Edmunds conceded that states admitted to the Union could disenfranchise whom they pleased, including persons of color. He asked: "Is it not the subject of ordinary legislation to declare who shall vote and under what circumstances?"[98] What Congress could not sanction was constitutional commitments to disenfranchising African Americans or any other similarly situated group of persons. Constitutional commitments to white supremacy were a far greater abridgement of republican principles than potentially transient legal bans on Black suffrage in the state elections code. Edmunds insisted that "[i]t is not . . . the question whether it is right or fit that a State should decide for itself who or what portion of its citizens should vote, but it is the fundamental question whether we will allow a Territory over which we have control to impose upon itself an obligation which it cannot recede from, to exclude from any of the political rights of government any class of its citizens."[99] Constitutional restrictions on Black suffrage were unnecessary. White majorities, if they wished, could disenfranchise persons of color by statute. "What is there so sacred, what is there so fundamental," Edmunds asked, "in the right of the white men to rule the black, that the white men cannot be trusted with the power of wielding it by a majority[?]"[100] As important, the constitutional commitment to white supremacy inhibited popular efforts to obtain racial equality. States might disenfranchise persons of color today, but they could not make a constitutional commitment that made such disenfranchisement permanent or, as the Supreme Court would suggest more than one hundred years later, require persons of color seeking the ballot to run more difficult obstacles than other persons seeking rights.[101] Edmunds declared: "I fail to perceive how we can be appealed to to give to these people a constitution which ties up their own hands from doing what every one of my political brethren says is an act of justice."[102]

Republicans who supported the Fourteenth Amendment and opposed Colorado statehood agreed with their otherwise Democratic rivals that Colorado lacked the population necessary for admission to the Union. The number of people in Colorado, they maintained, was small and diminishing. Grimes, the member of this group who rested most of his argument on this premise, estimated that "there cannot be to exceed fifteen thousand people in the Territory."[103] Wade declared, when opposing Colorado statehood in March,[104] that "the population since 1860 has rather been decreasing."[105] This small, diminishing population did not meet the standard for statehood. Grimes would admit new states to the Union only when they "had the population required to send a Representative to Congress under the then existing rules."[106] Making an exception for Colorado would violate all existing precedents. Wade maintained: "I do not think in any instance it can be found that a Territory has been converted into a State with the meager population that seems to exist in Colorado at this time."[107]

Colorado statehood in 1866 would harm the nation. Wade spoke of the damage that admitting Colorado would inflict on the practice of republican government in the United States. Colorado statehood, he declared, would be "a departure from the great American principle that political power shall be distributed equally, or at all events as equally as convenience will admit."[108] Colorado statehood would make a mockery of state equality in the Senate and weaken commitment to representation by population in the House. Wade observed: "To say a population of twenty-five or thirty thousand, which is the utmost extent of the population of this Territory now, shall have two Senators on this floor and a Representative in the other House is an inequality amounting to almost the old rotten-borough system of England."[109] Sumner elaborated on this injury to republicanism. He complained that admitting Colorado would "impart to it a full equality in this Chamber with the largest States in the Union; with New York, with Pennsylvania, with Ohio, with Massachusetts; and that in the exercise of this equality the Senators from this small community on all questions of legislation, of diplomacy, and of appointments, might counterbalance the Senate of these large States."[110]

Coloradans themselves would be harmed by premature statehood. Residents could not afford the transition from territorial status in 1866. Grimes, when noting the increased taxation and other burdens entailed by statehood, predicted that "nothing . . . could possibly be more injurious to the people of Colorado themselves than to permit her to erect herself into a State with a population of only from 15,000 to 25,000."[111] Playing an interesting variation on a theme from *Federalist No. 10*,[112] Grimes maintained that republican government was unlikely to thrive in a jurisdiction with so few people. A small-population state could easily be dominated by a small oligarchy. The senior senator from Iowa worried "that it is proposed to create a little insignificant State in the mountains, with only about 12,000 to 15,000 people, that a powerful, rich, and influential man can carry in his pocket, or which he can control by that which he does carry in his pocket."[113]

Sumner was the only Republican opposed to seating representatives from former Confederate states and from Colorado who spent substantial energy making procedural objections to Colorado statehood.[114] He insisted that "the enabling act had expired" the instant Coloradans voted down the first constitution. At that point, "[a]ll the obligations of Congress under that enabling act then and there ceased."[115] The second constitutional convention was illegal. Sumner pointed out that "[b]y the enabling act the convention was to be called by the Governor. How was it called? By the executive committees of political parties, being so many caucuses."[116] Coloradans who failed to comply with the enabling act could not claim statehood under the enabling act. Strict rule of law was the operative principle. Sumner maintained that "the State, in order to claim any benefit under this act, must comply with all the conditions of the act; its representatives must be chosen at the time mentioned and the constitution must be accepted by the people at the time mentioned, and everything must be 'in pursuance of this act.' Those conditions failing, the act fails."[117]

REPUBLICANS FOR STATEHOOD

Loyalty conquered all in the Thirty-Ninth Congress. Colorado merited statehood because Coloradans were loyal. Senator James Nye of Nevada captured the spirit of Republican proponents of statehood. "When a body of men comes here with the power to uphold and maintain a State government clothed with the garments of loyalty," he stated, "let them come in."[118] Republicans favoring statehood insisted that Colorado had substantially complied with the enabling act. They claimed that Congress had waived whatever population requirements existed when passing an enabling act that did not make Black suffrage a condition of statehood. Senator Aaron Cragin of New Hampshire maintained that "not a single reason exists to-day for refusing this Territory admission that did not exist when the enabling act was passed."[119] Coloradans had valid reliance interests. Senator Alexander Ramsey of Minnesota declared that "at this time, to reject the admission of the State . . . would be a gross breach of faith to these people, who can very ill bear the expense of these two movements for admission into the Union."[120] Besides, Republican proponents of Colorado statehood predicted, Coloradans would soon adopt Black suffrage, even when not mandated by Congress.

Coloradans earned statehood on the battlefield and at the ballot box. "I presume no question will be raised here as to the loyalty of the people of Colorado," Senator Samuel Pomeroy of Kansas informed fellow senators, "because they volunteered largely, they helped us through the war, and they have sent here two of the most loyal and earnest Republicans (if that is any test of loyalty) that they have in the Territory."[121] Coloradans, he observed, "have never assumed any other position than that of the most radical, loyal, devoted, and earnest men for the country and the Government."[122]

Territories could earn promotion to statehood by displays of martial virtue. "Colorado never showed us as many evidences why she should be admitted as a State," Nye asserted, "as is presented by the very fact that regiment after regiment was sent from her territory to guard and protect the travel across the plains from the savage and to contend upon the field of strife with the rebels themselves."[123] This fidelity merited admission of the Union, Nye declared: "I am loath to turn by back upon any population that has shown such devotion to the Federal Government as Colorado has done. I assert that she comes here to-day in the attractive habiliments of loyalty, the proudest vestment with which man was ever clothed; out of her misfortunes and from the smoke and din of arms she comes here and presents herself with the spotless robes of undying loyalty."[124]

The consequences of admitting a faithful territory mattered as much to proponents of Colorado statehood as did the intrinsic merit of rewarding loyalty with statehood. Western votes were as important as Southern votes for maintaining control over the national government. Senator Henry Lane of Indiana stated:

The great controversy is transferred from the field of battle to this high Chamber, and we need votes and support here as much as we ever did during our military campaigns. I believe Colorado should be admitted. I shall vote to admit her for good and substantial reasons, and among those reasons is the very fact that I regard her people as essentially and intensely and thoroughly loyal. For no mere partisan purpose—my purpose arises higher than party—for the good of the country, the safety of the country, and to prolong the lifetime of the nation, I wish loyal votes to be multiplied here.[125]

Loyal states meant loyal votes. Nye asked, "[W]ould you have hesitated during the rebellion to have two [senators] from Colorado?"[126] Opponents of Colorado "heard it whispered . . . that we want two more votes," he commented. Darn right. Nye stated: "Sir, I want twenty and two more, but I want them loyal, and I care not how many votes we have if they are of the right kind; and I do not intend that we shall have any other here, by my vote."[127] "We may need their votes, we may need the votes of loyal men; we shall need their votes, doubtless, before this great controversy is over," H. Lane agreed.[128] Loyal Western states also served as a geographical barrier against past and any current Southern ambitions. Nye noted if "the process of making new States could be successfully carried out on the more distant portion of the continent it would strengthen us in that direction and make a counterbalancing power to the southern element that was flying off."[129]

Rushing loyal territories toward statehood prevented destructive conflicts over the future of the West. Senator John Creswell of Maryland observed that "the sooner we fill up that vast territory with States, remove from the arena of angry and perhaps dangerous controversy on the floor of Congress all that immense section of the country, the sooner shall we be in a position to bear our present heavy burdens of taxation[] and to advance more rapidly in the path of prosperity."[130]

Loyalty trumped race equality during the debate over Colorado statehood. H. Lane was blunt about his Republican priorities. He informed the Senate: "I will not vote to exclude Colorado simply because she does not permit negro suffrage. . . . If I believe that they are essentially right and loyal in every other respect, and if they disfranchise their rebel voters, I would not stand upon this qualification."[131] Senator George H. Williams of Oregon believed states with a substantial loyal white population could dispense with Black suffrage. Black suffrage was an antidote to rebel rule. G. Williams pointed out:

> If negro suffrage be required of the States lately in rebellion, it must be upon two grounds: first, because the black people of those States constitute a large proportion of the population; they are largely interested in all State matters and State questions, and there is such a deep-rooted prejudice against them that suffrage becomes necessary for them as a protection for their lives, liberty, and property; and again upon the ground that these black men have everywhere been unchangeably loyal to the Government during the late struggle, and by extending to them the right of suffrage we enable the loyal sentiment of that country to predominate over the rebel and disorganizing sentiment, and in that way secure the perpetuity, the peace, and the integrity of the nation.[132]

Those reasons "for requiring negro suffrage in the lately rebellious States," G. Williams announced, "do not exist so far as the Territory of Colorado is concerned."[133] There was no threat of rebel rule in Colorado. The white population of Colorado was loyal. Black votes were not needed to keep the disloyal white minority out of power. Coloradans of color, living in a jurisdiction where slavery had never been legal, had little to fear from the white majority. Black citizens if statehood came to pass would be protected even when not empowered. G. Williams insisted that "there is no feeling or prejudice, I imagine, in that Territory that would greatly endanger the substantial rights and privileges of the colored people."[134]

Precedent supported admitting Colorado and accepting the proposed state constitution rejecting Black suffrage. Congress had never demanded any commitment to racial equality when previously considering proposed state constitutions. H. Lane declared: "I should prefer that that word ['white'] had been left out, but it has not been left out in any single State organization of any Territory that we have ever admitted. I believe that there is no instance in the whole history of the admission of new States where that word 'white' has not been the prefix to the qualification for holding office and voting."[135] Congress, he concluded, should not make Black suffrage "a test in the case of Colorado when it has never been made a test in the case of any other State or Territory."[136] Recent precedents supported the congressional decision that republican governments might forbid Black suffrage. Representative James A. Ashley of Ohio observed: "The State of Nevada, having accepted the conditions prescribed by Congress[,] was admitted into the Union, with a provision precisely like the one now objected to in the constitution of Colorado."[137] G. Williams asserted as binding precedent for Colorado statehood the congressional decision when organizing Montana Territory that voters be limited to white persons. He pointed out:

> In 1864 the Congress of the United States decided that the organic act of a Territory should exclude black men from the right of suffrage; and can Congress now, with any consistency, turn around and condemn the people of Colorado because they, about the same time, decided in the same way? Had they not good reason to suppose that this decision, under the precedents and under the circumstances, would be entirely acceptable to Congress?[138]

Republican proponents of Colorado statehood observed that Republican opponents of Colorado statehood had endorsed without objection these past congressional decisions to organize territories based on white suffrage. G. Williams suggested that Sumner "ought not to be too harsh upon the people of Colorado because they thought in 1865 just as he thought in 1863."[139] State practice was as compelling as territorial precedent. Republicans representing states that forbade persons of color from voting were hardly able to insist that Colorado adopt more egalitarian suffrage laws. Colorado should not be left out of the Union, Senator Jacob Howard of Michigan stated, just "because her people happen to have exercised the same right, the same power, be it right or wrong, which is exercised in the constitution of almost every other State in the Union."[140]

Congress was estopped from insisting on Black suffrage because no such demand was made in the enabling act.[141] Senator Henry Wilson of Massachusetts, when moving for reconsideration of Colorado statehood, emphasized that Colorado had followed the rules set down in 1864. He declared:

> I do not think it is fair play, after we passed the bill, which we did pass
> in 1864, and after the most enterprising and vigorous men in that Territory, who agree with a majority of us in this Chamber, have framed
> a constitution, and come here for admission, for us to refuse their application on the ground of a distinction which they have made in their
> constitution, when we did not ask them to refrain from making such
> a distinction; when we imposed no conditions on them; when we did
> not suggest any.[142]

Senator William Stewart of Nevada agreed that Coloradans in 1864 had no notice that denying Black suffrage would prompt the Senate to reject the proposed state constitution in 1866. He observed: "Congress, in March 1864, were willing, at the time they extended this invitation to Colorado, that a government should be formed by the whites alone and that the negroes should be excluded."[143] Reliance interests rooted in both the enabling act and past practice supported statehood. Stewart thought "[t]he people of Colorado had no reason to believe that Congress would object" to using the word "white" in the state constitution. The race discrimination mandated by the proposed state constitution, he concluded, was consistent with "the theory and practice of our Government" and "corresponds with the invitation by Congress."[144]

Senator Lyman Trumbull of Illinois maintained that Coloradans by mandating or permitting Black suffrage in the proposed state constitution would have violated the enabling act. The enabling act declared: "All persons qualified by law to vote for representatives to the General Assembly . . . are hereby authorized to vote for and choose representatives to form a convention." On the possibly contestable assumption that "all" meant "all and only all," and the even more contestable assumption that the enabling act barred representatives to the state constitutional convention from expanding suffrage rights, Congress had compelled territorial politicians to limit the suffrage to existing voters. Trumbull, based on this dubious interpretation, insisted that federal law required Coloradans to disenfranchise persons of color because "the law of the Territory at that time did not allow any but white persons to vote."[145] Trumbull's interpretation of Colorado law was no more set in stone than his interpretation of federal law. The relevant territorial statute granted suffrage rights to "Citizens of the United States" and some "persons of foreign birth."[146] As Sumner pointed out, whether the proposed constitutional ban on Black suffrage complied with the enabling act depended on whether Coloradans of color were citizens of the United States when white Coloradans framed the state constitution. The senior senator from Massachusetts, as noted above, relied on an opinion issued by United States Attorney General Edward Bates declaring persons of color to be citizens of the United States.[147] Trumbull rejected Bates's authority in favor of local practice. The senior senator from Illinois asserted that "such was not the understanding in Colorado, and no colored person ever did vote there."[148]

Neither Sumner nor Trumbull were judicial supremacists, at least when Colorado citizenship was on the table. The Supreme Court was missing in action when senators considered the meaning of "citizen" in Colorado law. Both Sumner and Trumbull looked to extrajudicial authority when determining constitutional rights: Sumner to the executive branch, Trumbull to popular understandings. No Republican suggested Congress should acknowledge that the Supreme Court's decision in *Dred Scott* settled that former slaves were not citizens of the United States in 1861.

Howard, when agreeing with Trumbull that Coloradans had adhered to the requirement in the enabling act that the state constitution be consistent with republican principles, offered another defense of the provisions in the proposed Colorado constitution limiting voting to white citizens. Suffrage, in his view, was not an element of republican government. Howard "was never able to discover in the Declaration of Independence that it was the right of every person, white or black, to vote at the polls."[149] The people in republican governments determined who voted, just as the people in republican governments determined who had the capacity to exercise other rights. Howard stated that "it is the right of every organized political community to regulate the right of suffrage according to the opinions and desires of a majority of that community."[150] Colorado exercised this power of a republican regime when excluding persons of color from the ballot box. "If . . . it be the will of the majority to exclude certain classes from the right of suffrage, where that will is exercised freely," Howard concluded, "I do not know any higher law pertaining to a republican government than that will."[151]

G. Williams insisted that republican principles properly understood supported the right of the white Colorado majority to disenfranchise the Black Colorado minority. A republican government was one in which popular majorities governed. In the case of Colorado, the republican stakes were the right of the white majority to govern. The question before Congress, G. Williams maintained, was "whether the thirty thousand white people of the State of Colorado shall have the right of suffrage, or whether seven-five or one hundred black men shall have that right."[152] The Republican answer to this question was to adopt the policy that maximized enfranchisement. G. Williams asked that Congress "extend to these thousands of white men the right of suffrage and their privileges as American citizens rather than to deny them those rights and privileges for the supposed necessity of providing similar rights and privileges for a handful of black people."[153] The spirit of 1776 compelled Congress to admit Colorado. The Republican senator from Oregon accused Sumner of abandoning the proscription on taxation without representation, one of the senior senator from Massachusetts's most cherished principles:

> The twenty-five or thirty thousand white people of the Territory of Colorado are taxed like the citizens of Massachusetts, and they have paid more revenue tax than some of the States of this Union, and yet those people have no representation whatever in the Government which imposes these taxes. I take up what the honorable Senator then said; I apply it to this case; I answer his argument with it, and I say that taxation without representation is tyranny.[154]

No proponent of Colorado statehood considered the obvious point that under the proposed state constitution Black Coloradans would be taxed without representation. Apparently, white Coloradans had sufficient unity of interest to virtually represent Coloradans of color, but the people of Kansas and other Western states lacked the unity of interest to represent Colorado.

Republican principles were violated every moment territorial status was maintained. G. Williams believed that "territorial organizations only result from necessity[] and are incompatible with the spirit and genius of our Government; for under them American citizens are ruled by a Government in the making of which they have no voice."[155] This "state of colonial dependence and subjection"[156] should end. G. Williams wanted new states formed and admitted as quickly as could be done. "[W]henever the people in such a Territory are competent to maintain a State government, and desire so to do," he maintained, "it seems to me justice and good policy dictate the consent of Congress, for by the multiplications of new States, we add to the greatness and power of the nation."[157]

Republican supporters of Colorado statehood claimed that they supported Black suffrage as fervently as those Republicans who opposed statehood but that Congress had to think pragmatically when admitting new states to the Union. Howard stated: "I believe that it is as much the right of the colored man to vote at an election as the white man; but still we must look to these matters in a practical sense; we must contemplate them as practical questions of legislation, and not as mere theoretical questions."[158] Pragmatism was warranted because the number of otherwise qualified persons excluded by the word "white" in the proposed constitution was minute. H. Lane complained: "We are to stop and have our hands tied because these seventy or eighty negroes are not permitted to vote."[159] "[T]he number there is only some forty or fifty," Howard declared when explaining why he did not "regard this restriction of the right of suffrage in the Colorado constitution as of importance enough to withhold my vote."[160] Pragmatism was also warranted because Coloradans would undoubtedly abandon race discrimination in the very near future. Nye predicted "the sun will not make his annual course before you will see white men and black men voting in Colorado."[161] Loyal states were particularly prone to make racially egalitarian reforms over time. Howard happily stated: "I shall vote under the expectation that that generous and enterprising people who have done so much according to their numbers to uphold the Government of the United States during the late war will see to it hereafter that this error shall be corrected in their constitution, and that all persons, black or white, shall be permitted to vote in that State."[162] J. Ashley, a leader in the fight for Black suffrage, assured fellow Republicans that Coloradans who had demonstrated extraordinary loyalty and military prowess would soon exhibit as strong commitments to racial equality. "We leave the question of suffrage to the people of Colorado," he told the House, "and I would rather intrust that question or any other to the loyal people of Colorado, who furnished three regiments of as good soldiers as ever entered the Union Army, than to commit the question of enfranchising the black man to the white electors of the late rebel States."[163]

Pragmatism was especially warranted because Black suffrage was inevitable throughout the United States. H. Lane looked forward to "the future, and no distant future, when the force of public opinion, mightier in this land than an army with banners, will strike the word 'white' out of every State constitution."[164] "[T]the day is not far distant," G. Williams prophesized, that "the Constitution of the United States will be so changed as to entitle men of all classes, without distinction of race or color, to enjoy the elective franchise."[165] Republican proponents of Colorado statehood promised to support this egalitarian trend by requiring Black suffrage in future territorial measures. "Under no circumstances whatever," H. Wilson vowed, "will I ever authorize any of the other Territories which have not yet had enabling acts[] to frame a constitution which shall make such a distinction."[166] Stewart took the same pledge. Colorado should not be excluded if "they have acted in good faith thus far," he asserted, but Congress should "go forward and announce hereafter the principles that enter into a republican form of government."[167]

Republican proponents of Colorado statehood rejected claims that long-standing and immediate precedents demonstrated that Colorado lacked the population necessary to join the Union. Congress in the more distant and recent past, they pointed out, had admitted low-population states. G. Williams insisted "there is no provision of the Constitution, and no precedents in our history[,] that require a Territory to contain any particular number of inhabitants to be qualified for admission into the Union." He maintained that "from the formation of the Government up to this time Territories have been admitted without respect to numbers, and the question of population has been subordinated." J. Lane denied any "rule as to population has governed the reception of new States." Colorado compared favorably to many territories that had achieved statehood before the Civil War. J. Lane declared: "Colorado has to-day more white inhabitants within her borders than Florida had when she was admitted." "To-day," he added, "Colorado has almost as many souls within her border as Kansas had when every Republican in both branches of Congress voted for her reception."[168] J. Ashley pointed to territories in all regions of the United States that had become states with fewer residents than Colorado. "The population of Colorado," he informed the House, "is to-day twice as great as that of the State of Florida at the time of its admission" and "greater than that of the State of Arkansas when it was admitted [and] the State of Oregon at the time of its admission."[169] The most recent precedents again favored Colorado statehood. Howard pointed out that Nevada had been admitted to the Union with a population in 1860 that was no greater than that of Colorado.[170] Wade insisted that population requirements demanded by opponents of statehood existed in theory but not in practice. "It has been said," he observed, "that there should be population enough for a Representative in Congress, but that rule has not been adhered to."[171] Ramsey suggested that Western states should not have to meet traditional population requirements. He insisted "this is a far outlying population that we ought not to require the same population that we ought of a community conterminous to ourselves."[172]

Americans had never been constitutionally committed to the principle of equal representation or one-person, one-vote underlying Democratic objections to Colorado statehood. Senator Samuel Kirkwood of Iowa bluntly stated that "[i]t is not the policy of our Government . . . to have equality in these things, and we do not have it."[173] Republican proponents of Colorado statehood noted that the framers in 1787 recognized the problem of unequal population and resolved that problem by providing for state equality in the

Senate and proportional representation in the House. G. Williams pointed out: "When the Union was formed, the State of New York contained eight to ten times the population contained in the State of Rhode Island; Pennsylvania contained eight to ten times the population of the State of Delaware; but those small States were allowed equal suffrage in the Senate with the large States, and their proportionate power was preserved in the House of Representatives."[174] Colorado was no different. Besides, the existing partisan alliances made the probability low that population inequalities would make a practical difference. As a good loyal state, Colorado would vote with other good and more populous loyal states on the issues of the day. "[I]n ninety-nine cases out of a hundred of general legislation, tending to the prosperity, greatness, and glory of this nation," G. Williams insisted, "Colorado would have the same interest as the State of New York; and there is therefore no necessary conflict or antagonism between the two States."[175]

Congress waived whatever population requirements past precedents arguably required when passing the enabling act authorizing Coloradans to apply for statehood. Trumbull asked: "[A]re we not bound by our acts . . . [w]hen the Congress of the United States says . . . to the people of Colorado, although you have less than thirty or forty thousand people, whatever the number may be, you are authorized to go on and form a State government, call your convention, without any further action of Congress you shall be a State?"[176] This congressional decision to authorize a state constitutional convention was binding. Trumbull thought it "wholly out of place" for Congress "to go into this question of population now." In his view, "The Senate is committed, Congress is committed, by its previous action."[177] G. Williams made the same plea for estoppel based on the enabling act:

> Congress then decided that the population of the Territory was sufficient to authorize the people to form a State constitution; and I say that the people of the Territory had a right to expect that that question was settled by the action of Congress. And now when this application is made for admission, they ought not to be met and defeated upon the ground that the population of the Territory is not sufficient to authorize the formation of a State government.[178]

Republican supporters of statehood argued that Colorado had more population in actuality than the opponents of statehood maintained. H. Lane and J. Ashley estimated that 50,000 lived in Colorado.[179] Stewart thought the proper number was 35,000.[180] Lower population estimates failed to consider the consequences of Coloradans' loyalty during the Civil War. S. Pomeroy suggested that fewer Coloradans voted in the referendum on the second proposed state constitution than in the referendum on the first proposed state constitution because many supporters of the second state constitution and Colorado statehood were out of the state fighting rebels. He claimed: "If they had been called to the polls at any other period, they would not only have polled a larger vote, but they would have undoubtedly polled a larger majority in favor of the constitution; but at the time their young men were almost all in the military service."[181]

Population estimates were likely to be inaccurate. Ramsey thought that "[n]o man can say what the population of Colorado is. . . . The probability is just as great that it is 50,000 or 60,000 as it is that it is 20,000 or 30,000."[182] Several Republican proponents of statehood pointed to the difficulties estimating the population of Western regions. Statehood opponents who relied on voting data when claiming Colorado was underpopulated had engaged in bad social science. G. Williams insisted that the vagaries of Western life made the number of voters in a particular election a poor proxy for population. He asserted how "that vote is a very poor criterion as to the actual population of the Territory, for in these Territories votes are controlled by accidental circumstances, and a vote on year may be double what it may be another year, and all controlled by accidental circumstances."[183] The number of voters in an election, Cragin maintained, was a dubious means for estimating the population of any jurisdiction and "is no evidence whatever of population, especially in a mining Territory."[184]

Proponents of Colorado statehood tossed aside procedural irregularities in favor of what they claimed was material compliance. How the state constitutional convention was called and conducted had little bearing on Colorado's qualifications for statehood. "[T]he practice of the Government heretofore," Creswell maintained, "has never been to require . . . any special form of proceedings."[185] The end justified the means—in this case a republican constitution drafted somewhat informally. The crucial factor justifying statehood was that the proposed state constitution adhered strictly to congressional mandates. Trumbull declared: "Everything in regard to slavery, everything in regard to public lands, everything in regard to the toleration of religion, everything that was required as a condition by Congress on the part of the people of Colorado in the formation of their State constitution, the people of Colorado have literally complied with."[186] Substantial compliance was the triumphant congressional rule. H. Lane agreed that, "even though [Colorado] did not comply technically with the enabling act, they did comply substantially."[187] This strict compliance with congressional conditions for the content of the state constitutional convention outweighed any legalistic defect that may have marred the convention. Howard stated that "it is the substance, it is the promise, the encouragement, the pledge which we in our sincerity held out to the people of Colorado, that ought to govern us."[188]

Any irregularity in the process by which Colorado's proposed constitution was framed was cured by the popular process for ratifying that text. Popular consent was a higher value than procedural form, as demonstrated by the decision of the Constitution's framers in 1787 to ignore the rules for constitutional change mandated by the Articles of Confederation. Echoing the central theme of *Federalist No. 40*,[189] Trumbull asked: "Is it at all material how they were elected to the convention, if there was an acquiescence of the people—and does he doubt that—in the mode that was adopted?"[190] The appropriate governing principle and cliché was "if first you do not succeed," not "you get only one bite at the apple." Trumbull stated: "I think that when the Congress of the United States has submitted to the people of a Territory whether they shall form a State constitution, and has authorized them to form it, if on one trial they do not do so they may go on to do so afterward."[191] Reliance interests trumped legalistic form. H. Lane maintained that the people of Colorado had a right to expect that Congress welcomed statehood. The enabling act, even if "null and void and expired by its own terms," he insisted, "was an invitation for them to come, an intimation that their coming would be welcome."[192]

Loyalty Versus Racial Equality in the West (and in Tennessee)

Members of the Thirty-Ninth Congress faced a series of Colorado-type decisions in the last days before the first session adjourned, and they reached similar conclusions. Wade proposed a bill outlawing race discrimination in both political and civil rights in the territories. Tennessee applied for restoration while denying Black suffrage. Nebraska applied for admission with a constitution that did not permit persons of color to vote. The Senate debated whether to seat David Patterson, the senator-elect from Tennessee, who nominally held a judicial office under the Confederacy, had nevertheless been unquestionably loyal to the Union, but shared Andrew Johnson's racial beliefs. In each case, the new birth of freedom failed to trump loyalty. The territorial bill was tabled. Tennessee was restored to "practical relations with the Union." The Senate voted to admit Nebraska. Patterson took his seat in the Senate.

THE TERRITORIES

On July 2, 1866, Wade, without argument, proposed that Congress avoid another Colorado-type debate by banning all forms of race discrimination in the territories. His proposed bill contained a provision declaring "[t]hat within the Territories aforesaid there shall be no denial of the elective franchise to citizens of the United States because of race or color, and all persons shall be equal before the law."[193] Some senators had excused their vote for Colorado statehood by claiming that Congress, when authorizing the territory to propose a state constitution, had not insisted on Black suffrage. Wade's territorial bill foreclosed that alibi for the future.

A brief debate followed. Stewart defended Black suffrage in part by referencing the Declaration of Independence. He pointed out that "we do say that all men are equally entitled to the pursuit of happiness and to the protection of the law."[194] Voting was a means of protection, although Stewart did not add, as he had in previous debates, that voting was a means of protecting the loyal. Continued violence was the alternative to Black suffrage. Stewart observed: "[N]ow that the negro in the South is manumitted . . . he must be protected, and if you do not allow him to protect himself with the ballot you must protect them with the sword."[195] The other Republicans remained silent as Saulsbury and Hendricks made conventional Democratic arguments against Black suffrage. The former, who spoke at some length, insisted that "the founders of this Government meant to establish a white man's Government"[196] and that no one supposed "essential to the welfare of the white race that the negroes there be admitted to participate in the government of those Territories."[197] Both Democrats insisted on the principle "physician heal thyself." "If you recognize the principle here as contemplated by this bill, to be consistent with yourselves and to be logical in your own reasoning," Saulsbury insisted, "you must say that they ought to be clothed with this franchise wherever the race exists."[198] No Republican took the challenge. The territorial bill was laid over until the next session of the Thirty-Ninth Congress.

TENNESSEE

Loyalty and republicanism were on full display when the Thirty-Ninth Congress, ten days before adjourning, began the debate over restoring Tennessee to the Union.[199] A broad consensus existed that Tennessee was loyal. Prominent Republicans, however, denied that Tennessee was republican because that state disenfranchised persons of color. Those dissenters successfully challenged the language by which Tennessee gained the right to be represented in Congress and exercise other prerogatives of a state. Once the language was sanitized, proponents of Black suffrage could not prevent restoration of a state with a populace that most proponents of congressional Reconstruction believed was no longer a threat to make renewed attempts at secession.

Tennessee was loyal. Representative George F. Miller of Pennsylvania observed that "Tennessee has sixty thousand loyal voters."[200] The more radical Senator Timothy O. Howe of Wisconsin stated that the "only reason I have for voting" for restoring Tennessee "springs from the consideration that local government in Tennessee is in the hands of loyal men" and "that there is a probability that it will continue in such hands."[201] Grimes spoke of "a growing spirit of loyalty."[202] White Unionists in Tennessee had earned the right to restoration for the same services to the Union that many Republicans believed entitled persons of color to be granted political rights. The staunch white patriots of Tennessee, Miller proclaimed, "during the late rebellion stood firm and undaunted for the Constitution and flag of this Republic," "suffered from persecution and hunger beyond description," "raised a large force," and "entered the conflict for the preservation of the Union."[203] Loyal Tennessee had politically neutered the disloyal by denying them the ballot. Wade identified the "thing that moves me stronger to the admission of the State than anything else"; "they have disfranchised their rebels and denied them the privilege of participating in the State government."[204] Tennessee statehood would embolden loyal white citizens throughout the former Confederacy. Miller thought restoration would "give encouragement to the loyal element and teach the other southern States that the only way for them to be represented in the councils of the nation will be to follow the example of Tennessee."[205]

Most proponents of Tennessee restoration vigorously insisted that Tennessee was republican. Miller declared the state had "so changed her constitution and laws as to protect her citizens and make it truly a republican form of government."[206] Representative John A. Bingham of Ohio performed remarkable feats of mathematics when purporting to demonstrate the republican pedigree of bans on Black suffrage. A lesser mortal might consider the small number of eligible voters in Tennessee to be an insurmountable bar to meeting standards for republican government. Bingham thought otherwise. He began by insisting that the relatively small number of enfranchised loyal whites had a much larger constituency. The "sixty-three thousand white loyal voters in Tennessee," Bingham maintained, "represent four hundred and forty thousand of the white population of the State."[207] These 440,000 white persons were a political majority in Tennessee. That white population was almost double the size of the Black population. Bingham then pointed out that majority rule was the central principle of republican government. He declared that "the right of the law-abiding majority of the people to govern" was "the very principle out of which the Constitution and the Union have been maintained through these five years of war."[208] From these premises, Bingham deduced that the white "majority" should be permitted disenfranchise the Black "minority," even though the number of loyal males in each racial group was approximately equal. Demanding that Blacks vote, Bingham concluded, would be "to deny the right of the loyal majority . . . to rule."[209] Other majorities disenfranchised minorities. Tennessee was no different. Bingham pointed out that "Tennessee today is as republican as Massachusetts," which placed significant literacy conditions on voting "on the principle that the majority of the law-abiding citizens of a State who have not forfeited their privileges by treason have the right to control its political power."[210]

A few supporters of restoration had doubts about the state's republicanism. Senator John B. Henderson of Missouri observed that "a majority of the people of Tennessee today—that is, the original white voters—are not loyal and have not been since 1861." "I do not pretend she is loyal," he informed the House of Representatives minutes before the first session of the Thirty-Ninth Congress ended.[211] These doubts did not justify scuttling Tennessee's restoration. Jo. Henderson supported minority white rule. He differed from Bingham only in acknowledging that minorities would soon govern Tennessee. Still, Jo. Henderson did not doubt the right of that minority to govern. In his view, "a minority of the people have a right to representation when they show that they are able to control the politics of the State."[212] No persons of color were included in this minority. If empowering loyal whites was a sufficient condition for a loyal state, then restoration did not require empowering loyal Blacks.

Republicans could not insist that Tennessee mandate Black suffrage without "slaughtering the whole company," to quote the Fairy Queen from William Gilbert and Arthur Sullivan's comic opera *Iolanthe*. If Tennessee was not republican, then no state was republican. Trumbull pointed out: "Most of us are here under republican forms of government just like this in Tennessee."[213] "[W]hile the States we represent exclude negro suffrage," Miller concluded, "we cannot with much grace insist upon these States doing that which our own refused to do."[214] Bingham pointed out that the same principles that would exclude Tennessee would also exclude such border states as Missouri, which "has a like population disfranchised [and] a like white rebel population disfranchised" and for that reason is "in the hands of a white minority, and a very small white minority if you count the disfranchised rebel population together with the disfranchised colored population."[215] That Missouri was "never a rebel State"[216] did not affect the calculus, Bingham stated, "unless . . . rebels in a State that did not secede are entitled to more consideration than rebels in a State that did secede."[217]

The Fourteenth Amendment clinched the deal for restoration. Ratification gave Tennesseans the opportunity to demonstrate they and their state were loyal. Miller suggested that the congressional decision to allow Tennessee to be represented in the House and Senate, and to enjoy all other state prerogatives, be contingent on ratification of the Fourteenth Amendment, something he regarded as "indispensable to the injunction of 'guarantying to every State in the Union a republican form of government.'"[218] Bingham maintained that national ratification would guarantee that African Americans would be protected in Tennessee, even if they were not empowered.[219]

Bingham was particularly and uniquely insistent that persons of color did not need the ballot if they had the Fourteenth Amendment. On the assumption that the Fourteenth Amendment would be ratified, former slaves could trust that Congress would step in should the loyal white citizens of Tennessee violate whatever fundamental rights persons of color enjoyed as free citizens. In an argument echoed by no other member of the Thirty-Ninth Congress, Bingham asserted that "any abuse by any State of its reserved powers by a denial of the inherent rights of any portion of the people or of the privileges of any citizen[] may be corrected at once by the law of the whole people of the United States."[220] With Bingham and friends protecting persons of color, Black suffrage could be dispensed with. The Fourteenth Amendment gave "the power . . . to the American people to throw the shield of the law of the land over these unfortunate human beings, lately slaves, now emancipated citizens."[221]

Remarkably, considering his claim that the Fourteenth Amendment might guarantee republican government in states that wished to deviate from the republican path, Bingham did not consider national ratification of the Fourteenth Amendment necessary for Tennessee to be restored or for the restoration of any other former Confederate states. When Stevens proposed that restoration of any state be contingent on both the state and nation ratifying the Fourteenth Amendment,[222] Bingham proposed that state ratification would be sufficient.[223] J. Wilson immediately proposed that state ratification and state commitment to universal male suffrage be sufficient for restoration.[224] Representative William D. Kelley of Pennsylvania, sensing an intractable division among Republicans, made a motion to table, which succeeded by a 101–35 vote.[225] The restoration of Tennessee would depend on factors unique to Tennessee. The broader contest between loyalty and the new birth of freedom would have to wait for another day.

Several Radical Republicans objected to claims that Tennessee was, in fact, republican.[226] Sumner, unsurprisingly, led the fight in the Senate, although, more surprisingly, he did so succinctly. The senior Senator from Massachusetts invoked Jefferson when insisting that republican governments did not distribute access to the ballot based on race. He proclaimed

> that constitution of Tennessee is not founded on the consent of the governed. It cannot invoke for it that principle of the Declaration of Independence; it is not a government republican in form; and when you undertake to allege that it is republican in form, permit me to say you make an allegation which is false in fact. I do not intend to raise any question of theory, but I submit to the Senate that a constitution which on its face disfranchises more than one fourth of the citizens cannot be republican in form.[227]

Representative George S. Boutwell of Massachusetts led the fight in the House. He maintained that "the government which they submit here, and which by your preamble and by your vote you declare under the Constitution to be a republican form of government, is not, as it appears to me, such in fact."[228] Boutwell did not believe in universal suffrage but insisted that republicanism required near-universal suffrage. "[T]he terms and conditions" placed on access to the ballot "must be reasonable; they must be such as to render it not only possible but probable that the great majority will be able to meet the requirements of the law."[229] Bans on Black suffrage did not meet this condition. "Whenever a man and his posterity are forever disfranchised from all participation in the government," Boutwell declared, "that government is not republican in form."[230] Boutwell brushed aside claims that Blacks had not been and were not entitled to vote in almost all states by pointing to the Thirteenth Amendment. Anticipating a version of "living originalism"[231] (and ignoring women entirely), he noted:

> The abolition of slavery by the Constitution has given a new meaning to the phrase "republican government"; for it is now settled that a State in which slavery exists is not republican in form according to our Constitution, though previous to the ratification of the amendment the fact may have been otherwise. While slavery existed it was generally true, however, that all free citizens were voters. To this rule there were some exceptions, but they were few and relatively unimportant.[232]

Republican opponents of restoration maintained that Black citizens in Tennessee, if not empowered, would not be protected. Brown accused his fellow partisans of adopting policies that would "not . . . exact justice at the hands of rebellion toward those late in slavery, not such as guaranty safely to the loyal people against the numerical superiority of treasonable elements."[233] Sumner pointed out that persons of color were faring no better in Tennessee than elsewhere in the former Confederacy. The Memphis riots that winter were "an outrage of unparalleled atrocity grown out of this very rebel spirit." Tennessee was no different than any of the other former Confederate states that no good Republican thought should be represented in Congress. Loyal people were no safer in Tennessee than in Mississippi. Sumner observed a "deep-seated hatred, amounting in many cases to a spirit of revenge toward the white Unionists of the State, and a haughty contempt for the negro whom they cannot treat as a freeman."[234] Public opinion and the persons who controlled public opinion in Tennessee remained largely unchanged from secession to proposed restoration. A party existed in the state, Sumner observed, that "sympathizes with the men and principles of the rebellion" and controlled the press. Religion was on the side of the rebels: "Hundreds of rebel ministers[] who glory in having led off in the rebellion . . . are still in the confidence of their people." Restoring a Tennessee still under the thumb of rebels promised the restoration of rebel rule. Sumner predicted that in "the first general action the entire civil and judicial power of the State must pass into the hands of those who have so long oppressed . . . and made actual war upon" persons of color.[235]

The tensions between loyalty and republicanism played out during the debate over the appropriate preamble to the resolution restoring Tennessee to "her proper, practical relations to the Union."[236] The original joint resolution declared that Tennessee had ratified "a constitution of government, republican in form."[237] The Joint Committee on July 19 omitted that language but pointed to "a proper spirit of obedience in the body of her people."[238] The new resolution also substituted ratification of the Fourteenth Amendment for the requirement that the state not repeal laws disenfranchising former Confederates, barring former Confederates from holding public office, repudiating the Confederate debt, and forbidding compensation for emancipated slaves.[239] The Senate Judiciary Committee further muddied the waters by proposing a resolution that included both "republican in form" and "a proper spirit of obedience."[240] Some Republicans suggested deleting the preamble entirely,[241] while Democrats wanted a preamble that indicated that Tennessee had always been a state in the Union entitled to representation in the House and Senate.[242]

The reference to "republican in form" proved particularly controversial, even among supporters of Tennessee's restoration. Jo. Henderson acknowledged that Radicals had a point when they objected to the language of the original resolution. "There are perhaps four or five hundred thousand negroes in the State of Tennessee entirely excluded by this constitution," he asserted, "and Congress is called upon to declare that the constitution is republican in form."[243] Yates, speaking for Sumner and probably for himself, pointed out: "Some gentlemen on this floor believe no constitution is republican in form which excludes from suffrage all of a particular class of individuals."[244] Brown, speaking for himself, declared: "Republicanism means nothing if it means not impartial, universal suffrage."[245]

Loyalty trumped the new birth of freedom. The House restored Tennessee by a 125–12 vote, with forty-six Representatives not voting.[246] The Senate agreed to delete any reference to Tennessee's constitution being "republican,"[247] but Sumner's motion to require Black suffrage as a condition of restoration was defeated by a 34–4 vote, with ten senators not voting.[248] The House immediately agreed to the Senate modifications to the bill restoring Tennessee.[249] The final preamble declared that Tennessee

> did ... by a large popular vote[] adopt and ratify a constitution or government whereby slavery was abolished and ordinances and laws of secession and debts contracted under the same were declared void; and ... a State government has been organized under said constitution, which has ratified the amendment to the Constitution of the United States abolishing slavery; also the amendment proposed by the Thirty-Ninth Congress, and has done other acts proclaiming and denoting loyalty.[250]

Tennessee had pledged allegiance to the United States, but the nature of any commitment to "liberty and justice for all" remained ambiguous at best.

Nebraska

On July 24, 1866, the day Tennessee representatives were seated in the House,[251] Wade successfully moved to begin Senate consideration of Nebraska statehood.[252] That territory met the requirements for statehood that Republicans laid out during the Colorado debate. Nebraska was what former Confederate states were not, a place that Nye thought promised to send "men here with loyal principles, backed by a loyal constituency."[253] Nebraska was unsullied with secession. Nye observed that Nebraska came to the Senate "with virgin robes, ... whose skirts hang none of the fragrance of the fumes or fragrance of rebellion."[254] Nebraska was loyal. Wade pointed out that "this State has never in her progress from a Territory to a State been hostile to the glorious flag of the country, she never raised an impious arm against the General Government."[255] Nebraska was loyal to the party of the loyal. Nye believed "the real objection . . . to the admission of this State is that she has been guilty of sending here loyal men."[256] "They do not want two Republican Senators here," he said of the opposition to statehood.[257] Nebraska promised more votes for congressional Reconstruction. "[T]here should be a row of States across the continent," Nye asserted, "in order to protect the great works that are now being constructed."[258]

Nebraska also presented the same issues that almost derailed Colorado statehood in Congress. Questions existed as to whether Nebraskans had followed the rules laid out in the enabling act for Nebraska statehood. The enabling act called for a constitutional convention, but the actual constitution approved by the people was drafted by the territorial legislature.[259] The population of Nebraska was less that the number used to allocate seats in the House of Representatives. Buckalew, after stating "a State shall not be admitted into the Union until it has an adequate number of inhabitants to authorize it to have one member in the House of Representatives under the ratio which may exist at the time," pointed out that, under the most liberal estimates advanced by advocates of statehood, Nebraska "has only one half the number requisite to elect a member in the House of Representatives, but according to the statistics which we have before us the population must be much less than that."[260] The number of voters was even less, threatening to further aggravate the antimajoritarian consequences of state equality in the Senate. Sumner asked: "[W]ill you invest those eight thousand voters with the same powers and prerogatives in this Chamber which are now enjoyed by New York and Pennsylvania[?]"[261] Nebraskans' commitment to statehood was weak. The margin of support for the state constitution was small, approximately a hundred votes.[262] Rumors of fraud existed, alleging that soldiers from Iowa had crossed the Nebraska frontier to cast ballots in favor of statehood.[263] These matters needed at least some congressional investigation before the statehood vote.[264] Buckalew pointed out that "we should not incur the peril of admitting a State into the Union when a majority of the qualified electors of that State have actually voted against it."[265] Most important, from the perspective of Radical Republicans: Nebraska did not allow the tiny population of African American citizens to vote. Sumner "challenged" proponents of Nebraska statehood "to show that a constitution which on its face disqualifies citizens on account of color and disfranchises them can be republican in form."[266]

Most Republicans cast all these objections aside. Wade and Representative

John H. Rice of Maine, who shepherded Nebraska statehood through the Senate and House, respectively, urged their colleagues not to be deterred by legal technicalities. Wade declared that the "people of Nebraska . . . proceeded . . . in the spirit of the [enabling] act."[267] J. Rice insisted that the territory "has substantially complied with all the requirements we have imposed upon her."[268] Previous federal permission for a territory to draft a state constitution was another unnecessary formality. Wade claimed that "an enabling act was not essential," that is to say, Congress could approve any constitution approved by territorial majorities.[269] Rumors of fraud were mere gossip. Wade asked: "Does the Senator suppose that he is to impeach the integrity of the people of a Territory upon the bare breath of scandal he has heard from the mouths of men or from party newspapers[?]"[270] A close vote on statehood was as authoritative as a landslide. Wade pointed out that "many of the most important questions that ever came before this nation, . . . questions which have fixed the character of our institutions for ages, have been decided by a single vote."[271] Nebraska met all the demographic requirements for a state. The territory was "wealthy"[272] and had "a reasonable amount of population,"[273] which Wade thought could not "be less than sixty thousand."[274] J. Rice pointed out that Nebraska "has a very desirable climate and a rich soil, capable of supporting a very large population; that the Pacific railroad is being built through this Territory; and that the tide of emigration is flowing there with great rapidity."[275] Besides, maintaining territories was a financial burden for the national government. Congress could protect federal coffers by granting Nebraska statehood. Wade stated that a "Territory is always an incumbrance to the General Government; it is attended with a good deal of expense."[276]

Granting statehood when the people of a territory wanted statehood was consistent with constitutional commitments to popular sovereignty.[277] "[W]hen the intelligent people of the United States residing in a Territory anywhere have deliberately made up their minds that they are wealthy enough and numerous enough to set up for themselves," Wade told the Senate, "their decision out to be respected."[278] S. Pomeroy added: "If there is anything the American people like, it is their own government."[279] Territorial rule, Howard thought, was a form of serfdom. Territorial government was a "constitution of vassalage," the "most corrupting and embarrassing of all governments upon the face of the earth."[280] Republicans promoted republican government and avoided political enslavement by granting statehood to territories as rapidly as possible. J. Rice championed "the policy of admitting new States as fast as they can be properly formed[] and as soon as the people are in a condition to govern themselves."[281]

Nebraska was republican—or as republican as Congress required Nebraska to be when passing the enabling act. With respect to Black suffrage, J. Rice conceded that "the constitution [Nebraska] presents is not in form such as I would desire it to be; and but for the fact that we have invited her to come in with such a constitution as she has formed, I would vote against her admission to-day."[282] Nebraska was as republican as any other state. Wade insisted: "The State constitution is republican in form, it is not as perfectly so, as far as suffrage is concerned, as I wish it was; but it is just as good as its neighbors are now."[283] The ban on Black suffrage in the constitution Nebraskans submitted to Congress was no different than the ban on Black suffrage in constitutions citizens of other territories had submitted to Congress in their successful applications statehood. "It is in vain now at this time of day to make a discrimination against this State because she has done like every other State that has come into the Union," Wade stated, "with a constitution precisely the same as every other had[] and not at all different in this respect."[284] Nebraska statehood had the implicit support of the sainted Republican martyr. Nye pointed out that the word "white" was in the proposed state constitution of Nevada, "and yet the lamented Lincoln hesitated not a moment to admit her."[285]

Put simply, Nebraska was "republican enough." The Nebraska constitution was "republican in form" because very few if any states met the Radicals' interpretation of "republican in form" when the Constitution was ratified.[286] Nye concluded: "[It] may not be in the fullest sense[] republican; but it is republican in the sense in which every State since the original thirteen has been admitted into this Union."[287] Nebraska's constitution was also republican in form because the ban on Black suffrage excluded only a handful of persons. Wade noted: "I do not suppose . . . there are fifty colored persons in the whole Territory."[288] Besides, Nye claimed, Nebraska's deviation from republican perfection was temporary. Persons of color would soon get the right to vote under the Civil Rights Act of 1866. "That bill," he asserted, "clothed every man with citizenship," and "the judge was yet living who would declare under it that every born citizen of this country had a right to vote."[289]

Nebraska statehood survived the Senate debate and a rushed vote in the House of Representatives. Doolittle's motion to refer statehood back to a committee was defeated by a close 22–18 vote, with ten senators not voting.[290] The Senate more decisively defeated Sumner's motion conditioning Nebraska statement on there being "no denial of the elective franchise or of any other right on account of color or race; but all persons shall be equal before the law."[291] Sumner gained the support of only five other senators:

Edmunds, William P. Fessenden of Maine, Edwin D. Morgan of New York, and Luke P. Poland of Vermont, though Brown, Lot M. Morrill of Maine, and Daniel Clark of New Hampshire, who might have been yes votes, appear to have been absent from the Senate that day. The Senate on July 27, the day before the scheduled adjournment, approved Nebraska statehood by a 24–18 vote.[292] The House moved swiftly. Debate lasted no more than fifteen minutes. Representatives first defeated Kelley's motion to make Nebraska statehood conditional on the state constitution mandating universal male suffrage[293] and then by the same 62–52 passed the Nebraska statehood bill.[294]

Haste was temporarily wasted when President Johnson pocket-vetoed the Nebraska statehood bill. Unlike Colorado, however, Republicans in the Thirty-Ninth Congress were able to get their Republican state. Republicans in the second session of the Thirty-Ninth Congress (December 3, 1866– March 4, 1867), after agreeing that Black suffrage would be a condition of statehood, had the votes to overcome a presidential veto. Nebraska joined the Union in 1867.

DAVID PATTERSON

Loyalty again trumped racial equality when Congress, just before adjourning, debated whether to seat Senator David Patterson of Tennessee.[295] Patterson, who was President Johnson's son-in-law, had a past very similar to the Tennessee Unionist, with an important twist. No one disputed Patterson's commitment to the Union.[296] Patterson, however, had been a judge in Tennessee while the Confederacy reigned. Unlike his spouse's father, he could not take the statutorily mandated test oath, which obligated him to swear that he had never held office in the Confederacy. A few Radical Republicans aside, everyone agreed that Patterson ought to be seated. The debate was over how to get around the test oath. After a bit of a congressional roundabout, a solution was reached. The Senate administered a special version of the test oath, deleting the reference to holding office.

Democrats and a few Republicans insisted that Patterson be allowed to take the oath immediately, with the proviso that he would be expelled if the Senate concluded that the Tennessean had committed perjury. Some Democrats insisted that the test oath was unconstitutional.[297] Others claimed that Patterson had done nothing in the past inconsistent with the test oath. Hendricks claimed that Patterson could take the test oath in good conscience because he had not actually held a Confederate office or assisted the Confederacy. If secession was "null and void," Hendricks maintained, "the acts of the State governments during the entire period of the revolution, which were not political in their character, and which were not to contribute aid to the rebellion, were legal and valid."[298]

More common, proponents of seating Patterson immediately maintained that a refusal to seat could be based only on constitutional qualifications for office, as would be the case if Patterson was constitutionally too young to be a senator. Violation of the test oath merited expulsion, which presumed a seated senator. R. Johnson stated: "He has a right to take [the test oath] . . . subject . . . to the responsibility of sinning against the law or the Constitution by taking a false oath. If he takes a false oath he can be proceeded against, or the Senate can proceed against him afterwards."[299] "Heretofore," Grimes agreed, "the case has always been that, *prima facie*, the man presenting credentials was entitled to the occupation of the seat."[300] Expulsion differed from exclusion in requiring a supermajority vote. Senator Edgar Cowan of Pennsylvania insisted that "we cannot superadd any additional qualifications."[301] If a senator committed an "offense," he maintained, "then two thirds may expel him, but it requires two thirds, and that is the security of the body."[302]

More Republicans thought that the Senate could not proceed with business as usual when swearing in a senator who had held office in the Confederacy. Trumbull disagreed with Grimes's call to swear in first and ask questions later. The chair of the Judiciary Committee reminded his colleagues that the presumption of regularity was rebuttable. "If," Trumbull claimed, "facts are presented which overcome the *prima facie* case . . . , making it proper to inquire, I shall not hesitate to vote to refer such credentials and make the inquiry before the person is sworn in."[303] Howard pointed out that Patterson might not be an innocent. A judge in a Confederate state was responsible for implementing "cruel and proscriptive laws of confiscation" that put the property of "Union citizens residing in the insurrectionary States . . . into the confederate fisc for public use."[304] Howard would exclude on this basis. The junior senator from Michigan pointed out that Patterson was squarely within the letter of the law mandating the test oath. Patterson "was confessedly an officer of the State of Tennessee," "the evidence . . . does not show that he was in the slightest peril at the that moment," and the senator-elect "took that oath as willingly, as intelligently, and as understandingly as he ever took any oath to support the Constitution of the United States as members of this body."[305]

The resulting debate demonstrated all the problems that occur when legislatures are faced with more than two choices that cannot be easily rank-ordered.[306] The Senate Judiciary Committee recommended that Patterson be allowed to take the oath.[307] Clark, when supporting that recommendation, declared that "the object of the oath is to prevent rebels and secessionists from coming into the Senate, not to exclude Union men like the Senator elect from Tennessee."[308] That proved unacceptable to the Senate majority. Trumbull worried that looking the other way when Patterson swore falsely would set a precedent that would enable actual rebels to take the test oath. "If you say today that a person who has admittedly accepted an office and exercised the duties of it under a government in hostility to the United States may[,] notwithstanding, swear that he has not done that," he asked, "how would you keep Alexander Stephens or anybody else from being admitted" if they asserted "'I was really opposed to this thing, and I really did this for the purpose of protecting the Union'[?]"[309] Trumbull suggested a joint resolution modifying the test oath in Patterson's case so that Patterson would not have to swear that he "had neither sought, nor accepted, nor attempted[] to exercise the functions of any office whatever under any authority or pretended authority hostile to the United States."[310] "[I]f there is a case where the loyal man ought to be admitted," he stated, "it is our duty to remove the statute, so that he may take his seat."[311] The Senate concurred,[312] but the House of Representatives was not as accommodating. Members feared setting a precedent that might enable a future Democratic majority in Congress to waive the test oath for former rebels. "If we do this act, it will be a precedent which will carry fatality in its train," Representative Roscoe Conkling of New York declared. "From Jefferson Davis to the meanest tool of despotism and treason[] every rebel may come here, and we shall have no reason to assign against his admission except the arbitrary reason of numbers."[313] The seating of David Patterson was a matter for the upper chamber of Congress only. When moving to table the joint resolution, Conkling stated: "The Senate has passed it; upon the Senate be the responsibility. The Senate has absolute power over the admission or rejection of Mr. Patterson, and there is no reason for our dividing with the Senate the responsibility of its exercise."[314] Conkling's motion passed.[315] The House returned the issue to the Senate with the clock ticking toward adjournment.

Faced with the risk of an infinite regress, Trumbull and most of his political allies relented and agreed to have Patterson take the test oath. Poland observed: "The vote of the Senate today on the joint resolution that was passed was a declaration on the part of the Senate that Mr. Patterson, who presents himself as a Senator here, is a fit and proper man to be a Senator."[316] If Jefferson Davis took the oath, Howe consoled the Senators, "your remedy for it . . . is simply to go to a magistrate here and enter a complaint against Mr. Davis for perjury."[317]

This legal subterfuge enabled a loyal white man and the loyal white men he represented to be empowered. No member of Congress during the debate over Patterson's credentials explored whether the senator-elect was committed to protecting and empowering former slaves and other Black citizens. As with the statehood debates for Colorado, Tennessee, and Nebraska—when most Republicans were confident that they had successfully empowered loyal whites—concerns with empowering and protecting loyal Blacks were tabled.

Patterson served in the Senate without distinction for three years. His name cannot be found in the index to any major history on Reconstruction. While in office, Patterson consistently voted with those Democrats and border-state Unionists who in the first session of the Thirty-Ninth Congress had opposed both the exclusion resolution and the Fourteenth Amendment.[318] His most notable vote was for acquitting his father-in-law when President Johnson was impeached. A. Johnson was acquitted by one vote. Had Senate Republicans demanded a senator from Tennessee committed to racial equality, Johnson might have been impeached, and Wade, as president pro tempore of the Senate and next in the line of succession, might have become president of the United States in 1868 when that office became vacant.

The debate over seating Patterson highlights how most Republicans, while not wanting white Southern Unionists such as Andrew Johnson running the country, were quite willing to permit white Southern Unionists such as Johnson's son-in-law and political ally to represent Tennessee in the Senate and control local Tennessee politics. White supremacy was and would be the informal law of the land in Andrew Johnson's Tennessee and David Patterson's new South. Jim Crow would replace Black Codes with very little improvement in the condition of African Americans. Government officials would find ways to evade constitutional provisions and statutes enfranchising persons of color. Private violence performed free from legal sanction would in practice nullify any remaining pretense of racial equality under law. Nevertheless, no Republican would ever worry that a former Confederate state might take another stab at secession when men such as Johnson and Patterson were in charge or, after redemption, at least partners in the ruling coalition.

The Triumph of Loyal Whites

History is a motion picture, not a snapshot. A still taken during the last week of the first session of the Thirty-Ninth Congress reveals Stevens getting little support for several bills proposing that Southern states be restored only on the condition that they adopt universal male suffrage.[319] Snapshots taken during the second session of the Thirty-Ninth Congress reveal how Republican electoral gains during the 1866 midterms enabled party majorities to pass Wade's territorial bill, attach Black suffrage conditions to Nebraska and Colorado statehood, and adopt Stevens's proposed bill mandating universal male suffrage in new states. Everyone reading this book who has gotten this far knows what happens in the next part of the movie.[320]

Republicans regarded territorial policy and congressional Reconstruction as two sides of the same coin. Admitting Colorado and Nebraska to statehood was part of a general Republican strategy to maintain control of the national government by looking westward as well as in a southerly direction.[321] As support ebbed for reconstructing former Confederate states, many Republicans found that admitting underpopulated Western states was an effective alternative to African American suffrage for fashioning a constitutional politics that privileged the values and interests of the white persons who remained loyal during the Civil War.[322] Before the Civil War, a general consensus existed that territories could be granted statehood only when their populations entitled them to one representative in the House of Representatives. Republicans during and after the Civil War abandoned this practice when successfully admitting many Republican-leaning territories with populations substantially below this "ratio of representation" while simultaneously delaying the admission of several Democratic-leaning territories that met antebellum statehood requirements. Nevada, which consistently supported Republicans for the White House and consistently sent two Republicans to the Senate, was admitted in 1864, despite having less than one-fifth the population of the least populous state. Democratic-leaning Utah, which in 1864 had seven times the population of Nevada, joined the Union only in 1896. The lame-duck Republican majority in Congress on March 3, 1875, passed a Colorado statehood bill that, by expediting the territorial referendum on statehood, ensured that Colorado would be in the Union in time for state residents to vote in the 1876 national elections.[323] That state's three electoral votes provided Republican Rutherford Hayes with his margin of victory.

This turn to the West belied the majoritarian pretensions underlying the original Republican attack on the slave power. Republicans before, during, and immediately after the Civil War complained that the Three-Fifths Clause and the imminent disenfranchisement of persons of color enabled one voter in states such as South Carolina to exercise the same influence on the partisan composition of the national government as several voters in states such as New York. During the debates over admitting Western territories, the script was flipped. Democrats complained that one voter in such underpopulated states as Nevada exercised the same influence over national policy as several voters in South Carolina. President Johnson, when vetoing a bill authorizing statehood for Colorado, stated:

> The population, it will be observed, is but slightly in excess of one-fifth of the number required as the basis of representation for a single congressional district in any of the States—the number being 127,000.
>
> I am unable to perceive any good reason for such great disparity in the right of representation, giving, as it would, to the people of Colorado not only this vast advantage in the House of Representatives, but an equality in the Senate, where the other States are represented by millions. With perhaps a single exception, no such inequality as this has ever before been attempted. I know that it is claimed that the population of the different States at the time of their admission has varied at different periods, but it has not varied much more than the population of each decade and the corresponding basis of representation for the different periods.[324]

Republicans were, unsurprisingly, indifferent to previously expressed majoritarian concerns or the one-person, one-vote principle when Western statehood was on the table.

The way in which Republicans manipulated Western statehood had substantial electoral and political consequences throughout the last third of the nineteenth century and the first decades of the twentieth. Had states been admitted according to pre–Civil War population norms, Democrats would have either controlled the national government from 1877 to 1889 or had control over one of the elected institutions of the national government necessary to prevent Republican majorities in the other branches from repealing laws passed during the years when Democrats controlled the presidency, Senate, and House of Representatives. In fact, aided by Republican senators and Electoral College votes from underpopulated Western states, Republicans controlled the Senate for all but two years during this period and the presidency for all but four years. Republicans maintained this control during the lifetime of almost everyone who was politically active during the Civil War and Reconstruction. Democrats, during the period from the Civil War to the inauguration of President Woodrow Wilson, had control over the national institutions necessary to repeal Republican measures and enact Democratic substitutes only from 1893 to 1895. Republican policies first enacted during the Civil War and Reconstruction such as high tariffs,

Civil War pensions, aid to railroads, and federal internal improvements survived the nineteenth century because the votes cast by Republican senators
from underpopulated states prevented Democrats from realizing their constitutional visions and preferred policies.

This effort to construct a constitutional politics that privileged the values
and interests of the white voters who remained loyal to the Union during
the Civil War resurrected Republican Party commitments announced before
the Civil War. Antislavery advocates during the 1840s and 1850s bitterly
complained that slaveholders exercised disproportionate power in the national government in general and over territorial policies in particular.[325] Van
Buren Democrats and Northern Whigs/Republicans sharply criticized the
James K. Polk administration (1845–1949) for settling the Oregon boundary dispute with Great Britain and failing to support internal improvement
projects in what were then considered western states (formed out of the old
Northwest Territory).[326] The Wilmot Proviso, which prohibited slavery in
all territories acquired from Mexico after hostilities, was advertised as an
attempt to populate the West with free white settlers. Representative David
Wilmot of Pennsylvania maintained that slaves should be kept out of the
Southwest to "preserve to free white labor a fair country."[327] These white
settlers, antislavery advocates agreed, would return control over national
policy to free states. "We will engage in competition for the virgin soil of
freedom," Senator William Seward of New York declared after the passage
of the Kansas–Nebraska Act, "and God give the victory to the side which
is stronger in numbers as it is in right."[328] The vast majority of Republicans
immediately before the Civil War, in sharp contrast to Stevens and other
Radical Republicans immediately after that war, declaimed any immediate
interest in reforming race relations within the Southern states. President
Lincoln spoke for almost the entire Republican Party when, in his First
Inaugural Address, he declared that he had neither the power nor the interest in emancipating slaves in existing states.[329] When Lincoln claimed that
confining human bondage to existing states would eventually lead to the
ultimate extinction of slavery in the future, his emphasis was as much on
the "future" as on "extinction." He admitted that, if Republicans governed
consistently with their 1856 and 1860 platforms, a Supreme Court staffed
by the Republican Party for much of the twentieth century would still recognize the existence and legality of human bondage. "I do not suppose that
in the most peaceful way ultimate extinction would occur in less than a
hundred years," Lincoln asserted in the debates with Stephen Douglas.[330]
Slaves would till southern fields as late as 1954, the year the Supreme Court
decided *Brown v. Board of Education*.[331] Lincoln's immediate program was

designed to secure the interests of the "free white people" interested in Western settlement, not the enslaved persons of color dreaming of liberty.[332]

By 1896, the Republican Party had achieved every one of that coalition's pre–Civil War goals (and more). Antislavery advocates during the 1850s maintained they were in a race with the South to settle and control the West.[333] Republicans won. Republican congressional majorities during and after the Civil War determined the boundaries of Western states, the conditions under which Western states would be admitted, and the timing of Western states' admission to the union. The resulting territorial and statehood policies ensured that, at the turn of the twentieth century, most Western states had more in common politically, economically, and culturally with Republican states in the Midwest than with Democratic former Confederate states.[334] Antislavery advocates before the Civil War maintained that control over the West was an essential means for ensuring that voters in the free states determined national policy.[335] National policy after the Civil War on such matters as the tariff and internal improvements promoted Northern interests in large part because Republicans representatives from underpopulated Western states cast crucial votes in favor of tariffs and aid for economic development.[336] As Lincoln promised when running for president, Southern racial policies did not spread through the country. Racism was prevalent in the North and West in 1860 and at the turn of the twentieth century.[337] Nevertheless, no state or territory in which slavery was banned before the Civil War in 1900 disfranchised most male citizens of color or adopted comprehensive racial segregation policies. Race relations in Colorado resembled those in Indiana more so than in Alabama.

Each Western state admitted to the Union pushed the Republican Party further toward that coalition's original pre–Civil War commitments to white voters and away from the egalitarian commitments that animated many party members (Thaddeus Stevens in particular) immediately after the Civil War. While some Western Republicans during Reconstruction initially supported the radical wing of the Republican Party,[338] most in the following decades exhibited diminished interest in protecting persons of color in the South.[339] Republican members of Congress from new Western states preferred championing policies (such as silver coinage) that promoted Western economic development. Mining interests trumped concerns for racial equality.[340] Former Republican proponents of Black suffrage such as Stewart proved quite willing to make deals with Southerners that served the interests of white constituencies in the South and West. The final nail in Reconstruction's coffin was hammered in 1890, when Stewart and other Silver Republicans in the West, after securing increased Southern opposition to the gold standard, abandoned the effort of Senator Henry Cabot Lodge of Massachusetts to push through Congress a bill protecting Black voting rights.[341] "We have fallen upon bad times for the party," Senator John C. Spooner of Wisconsin, a more traditional Republican supporter of racial equality, complained. Spooner regretted the Republican willingness in 1866 to aggravate the democratic problems with state equality in the Senate by admitting underpopulated states with loyal white majorities. He observed that the "Confederacy and the Western mining camps are in legislative supremacy. Think of it—Nevada, in 1870 about 45,000 people, in 1880 about 65,000, and in 1890 about 47,000—barely a respectable county, furnished two senators to betray the Republican party and the rights of citizenship for silver."[342]

Conclusion
Rebels, Loyalists, and Racial Equality

President Abraham Lincoln famously maintained that his primary commitment was saving the Union and not emancipating slaves. On August 22, 1862, he wrote a public letter to Horace Greeley, a prominent Republican and editor of the influential *New York Daily Tribune*, declaring:

> My paramount object in this struggle *is* to save the Union, and is *not* either to save or to destroy slavery. If I could save the Union without freeing *any* slave I would do it, and if I could save it by freeing *all* the slaves I would do it; and if I could save it by freeing some and leaving others alone I would also do that. What I do about slavery, and the colored race, I do because I believe it helps to save the Union; and what I forbear, I forbear because I do *not* believe it would help to save the Union.[1]

When writing this letter, Lincoln was contemplating issuing the Emancipation Proclamation.[2] Conventional wisdom maintains that this executive decree transformed the Civil War from a struggle to save the Union into a crusade for human freedom. John Hope Franklin, in his acclaimed study of the Emancipation Proclamation, wrote that "the war became more than a war to save the integrity and independence of the Union. It also became a war to promote the freedom of mankind."[3] Lincoln's priorities nevertheless remained unchanged throughout the Civil War. According to Franklin: "Lincoln saw no contradiction between the contents of his reply to Greeley and the contents of the Emancipation Proclamation."[4] The sixteenth president concluded simply that emancipating slaves, first in regions controlled by Confederate states and then throughout the nation, was the best means of saving the Union. Lincoln informed Thomas T. Eckert, who witnessed the drafting of the Emancipation Proclamation, that he was "giving freedom to the slaves in the South for the purpose of hastening the end of the war."[5] Franklin observes: "First and foremost, the Proclamation was a military measure."[6] The edict freeing all slaves under the control of Confederate states weakened the laboring capacity of the South, inhibited efforts to enlist slaves in the Confederate army, paved the way for the Union to recruit Black soldiers, and foreclosed foreign recognition of the Confederate states.[7] Lincoln issued the Emancipation Proclamation in his capacity as commander in chief, not in his role as keeper of the national conscience.

The best view may be that Lincoln and his political allies regarded saving the Union and ending slavery as entangled in ways that cannot be fully disaggregated rather than as either in harmony or in opposition. Lincoln before the Civil War maintained that the existence of slavery was a grave threat to national union. His famous "House Divided" speech insisted that "this government cannot endure, permanently half slave and half free."[8] Democrats claimed such rhetoric was the greater menace to the ongoing coexistence of the free and slave states.[9] Ideals concerning race and bondage remained entwined with interests in national security and union during the Civil War.[10] What Lincoln and his contemporaries thought about the morality of slavery influenced the importance they attached to winning (as opposed to ending) the Civil War, what constituted victory in the conflict, and how victory was best achieved. Almost all Republicans who shared Lincoln's moral antipathy to slavery concluded, sooner or later, that abolition was both a vital end and a vital means for restoring and maintaining national union. Senator Charles Sumner of Massachusetts wrote: "Let the doctrine of Emancipation be proclaimed as an essential and happy agency in subduing a wicked rebellion."[11] Freeing slaves was part of the strategy for military victory. Frederick Douglass asserted that the "union cause would never prosper till the war assumed an Anti-Slavery attitude."[12] Greeley "hail[ed]" the Emancipation Proclamation as "a great stride toward the restoration of the Union."[13] Almost all Democrats, who did not think abolition to be a vital end, did not think of abolition as a means for restoring and maintaining national union. The Hartford *Times* declared that the Emancipation Proclamation "will work an injury rather than any good to the Union cause."[14] The New York *Herald* accused Lincoln of "possibly destroying the Union instead of saving it."[15]

The proponents of congressional Reconstruction responsible for framing the Fourteenth Amendment updated Lincoln's priorities. They regarded preventing rebel rule as a more immediate fundamental regime commitment than racial equality. Had Senator Lyman Trumbull of Illinois, Representative Jehu Baker of Illinois, or many other moderate Republicans written to Frederick Douglass during the first session of the Thirty-Ninth Congress,

that hypothetical letter might have echoed Lincoln's language in his letter
to Greeley as follows:

> Our paramount object *is* to prevent rebel rule by empowering and
> protecting the loyal, and is *not* either to achieve or frustrate racial
> equality. If we can prevent rebel rule without mandating *any* form
> of racial equality we would do it, and if we could achieve that end by
> mandating absolute racial equality we would do it; and if we could
> save that end by mandating some forms of racial equality but not oth-
> ers, we would also do that. What we do about the colored race, we do
> because we believe it helps prevent rebel rule; and what we forbear,
> we forbear because we do *not* believe it would help prevent rebel rule.

Chapter 2 documented that the primary goal of congressional Reconstruction was to prevent rebel rule, not to abolish the Black Codes. Chapter 3
detailed the Republican commitment to preventing rebel rule by protecting
and empowering all loyal people, Black and white, as individuals, and the
Republican Party as the institutional vehicle for the people who remained
faithful to the United States during the Civil War. Chapter 4 pointed out
that proponents of congressional Reconstruction were more likely to call
for constitutional reforms that empowered loyal white citizens, most notably changing the basis of apportionment, and that protected loyal white
people, most notably repudiating the Confederate debt and securing the
Union debt, than they were to call for constitutional reforms that protected
and empowered loyal Black citizens. Chapter 5 observed that, when Republicans could prevent rebel rule by empowering and protecting loyal white
citizens, they did not insist that loyal citizens of color be empowered and
protected.

   If understood as attempts to prevent rebel rule by empowering and
protecting loyal whites, Reconstruction, the Fourteenth Amendment, and
Colorado statehood seem wildly successful rather than dismal failures. The
proto-Confederates who redeemed Southern governments were committed
white supremacists, but they were no longer secessionists. Former Confederates returned to Congress, the federal judiciary, and local politics, although
as junior partners in national coalitions dominated by politicians from the
free states. The South became the most patriotic region in the country, even
as Confederate flags and monuments to Confederate heroes proliferated.
Secessionist sentiments by the end of the nineteenth century existed only at
the margins of American constitutional politics, where they have remained
to this day. Republicans—with considerable aid from newly admitted, underpopulated Western states—controlled the national government until the

New Deal. The party of the persons who remained loyal during the Civil War, augmented by Westerners whose lives were often untouched by either secession or persons of color, retained the power to determine how the Thirteenth and Fourteenth Amendments would be implemented and the course of national policy more generally. Continued Republican control of the national government was nevertheless purchased by diminished Republican commitment to former slaves. Republicans, most notably Republicans from the underpopulated Western states, by the late nineteenth century determined that emancipation and thin formal legal equality were more than sufficient to redeem whatever commitments were made to persons of color during the Civil War. More radical visions would have to await new political coalitions and new forms of constitutional politics.

Mark Wahlgren Summers details how Republicans accomplished fundamental regime change, even if that regime change was not what was anticipated by the more radical members of the party. He points out that if "the chief end of reconstruction was to bring the nation back together and this time for good, to banish the prospect of future war, to break the power of the former slave states to menace or overawe the majority, [and] to end slavery and give that freedom more than a nominal meaning," then Reconstruction "ranked as an unqualified success."[16] The people who remained loyal to the Union were empowered.[17] With the exception of Woodrow Wilson, every president of the United States until Lyndon Johnson hailed from a state that fought on the side of Abraham Lincoln during the Civil War. Most Supreme Court justices who ascended to that bench during the last third of the nineteenth century resided in the North. Republicans almost always controlled at least one branch of the national legislature. Representative Frederick Crisp of Georgia (1891–1895) was the only resident of a former Confederate state who from Appomattox until 1931 served as Speaker of the House. The people who remained loyal to the Union were protected. National policy skewed northward even as Southerners were allowed to police race relations as they thought best in former Confederate states. Summers observes: "Well into the twentieth century, half or more of the money the government spent went to service or redeem the Union war debt or to pay pensions to Union veterans."[18] The wish of Representative Thaddeus Stevens of Pennsylvania to make rebels pay for the Civil War was granted. "That revenue," Summers continues, "came largely from the protectionist Morrill 'War Tariff' and its offspring, the duties of which fell with much more crushing weight on the South with comparatively few items to protect."[19] Northern soldiers and their widows received their promised pensions. Northern creditors and their descendants saw their bonds paid with full interest.

Republicans also achieved their antebellum goal of ending slavery and providing persons of color with a modicum of civil rights. However horrible the condition of free Blacks in the late nineteenth century, that condition was far better than slavery. Many African Americans by 1900 enjoyed some degree of economic success that was impossible under slavery and next to impossible in antebellum Northern states. All were free to marry, raise families, and exercise a far greater degree over their lives than had been the case before the Civil War.

The substantially improved state of African Americans after the post–Civil War Amendments became law highlights how the better view remains that the issues of preventing rebel rule and achieving racial equality immediately after the Civil War were as entangled as were the issues of achieving military victory and abolishing slavery during the Civil War. Preventing rebel rule and racial equality were not, to use the modern social science vernacular, "independent variables." The relationship between the two depended on who different partisans thought remained a rebel in 1866 and who had been loyal in 1863, in addition to the merits of Black citizenship. Proponents of congressional Reconstruction regarded rebel rule as a threat to racial equality. Chapter 2 detailed how members of Congress who supported the exclusion resolution feared that the practical abandonment of the Thirteenth Amendment in former Confederate states was the nearly certain evil consequence of a renewed alliance between the antebellum Southern elite and Northern Democrats. Racial equality was one solution to the problem of rebel rule. Chapter 3 pointed out that Republicans and allied Unionists agreed that loyal Blacks, particularly those who served in the military, were a crucial component of the loyal citizens who were to be empowered and protected by constitutional and statutory reforms. Chapter 4 documented how all proponents of congressional action on Reconstruction agreed that Congress ought to mandate racial equality, even while disputing whether that mandate ought to take the form of a constitutional amendment barring race discrimination.

The problem Republicans faced was that support for racial equality did not extend beyond their core constituency. Committed Republicans hoped for an American republic united by commitments to racial equality and free labor. Republicans in many Northern states during and after the Civil War repealed legal restrictions on persons of color and desegregated public schools. Less committed Republicans or "swing voters" separated issues of loyalty from racial equality. They accepted and sometimes celebrated home rule by former Confederates committed to paying the national debt and not paying the rebel debt. A West controlled by the Republican Party was worth the price of a West more interested in internal improvements than racial equality. The electoral imperatives that before the Civil War led many Republicans to emphasize the harm the slave power did to white interests led crucial Republicans after the Civil War to emphasize the interests of the white persons who had remained loyal when those interests clashed with loyal African Americans.

The next volumes of The Forgotten Fourteenth Amendment series will further explore the complex relationship, during the period the Fourteenth Amendment was being framed, between racial equality and preventing rebel rule. The next anticipated volume—tentatively titled *Making the Anti-Slavery Constitution Work*—will elaborate the state of the constitutional law and politics of racial equality when the Thirty-Ninth Congress met, with particular emphasis on what Republicans thought were the primary legal and political obstacles to preventing rebel rule and achieving their cherished free labor regime. *Reconfiguring Constitutional Politics*, the third volume, will detail how various Republicans attempted to construct and constitute a constitutional politics that would simultaneously prevent rebel rule and achieve racial equality.

This and the future volumes detail why the Fourteenth Amendment cannot be understood solely by reading the congressional speeches of Representative John A. Bingham of Ohio or even all congressional speeches in the first session of the Thirty-Ninth Congress under the header "Constitutional Amendment." Constitutional reform was integral to the series of debates in the Thirty-Ninth Congress over how best to prevent rebel rule by empowering and protecting the loyal. Modern obsessions with Republican commitments to legal guarantees for racial equality and fundamental rights obscure the far more robust and far more crucial debates that members of the Thirty-Ninth Congress engaged in over the exclusion resolution, territorial policy, and the proposed constitutional reforms that eventually became Sections 2, 3, and 4 of the Fourteenth Amendment. The exclusion resolution played a vital role in Republican efforts to secure control of the national government by retaining control of the South. Colorado statehood complemented the exclusion resolution by enabling Republicans to maintain control of the national government through control of the West. Both measures, as well as many proposed constitutional reforms, empowered the faithful to protect the loyal. All were central to the Republican strategy to construct and constitute a constitutional politics that would punish treason and reward loyalty.

The exclusion resolution, proposed constitutional reforms, and Colorado

statehood were unified by this Republican commitment to punishing treason and rewarding loyalty. The exclusion resolution did so by denying
seceding states representation in Congress until former Confederates demonstrated firm allegiance to the Union. Proposed constitutional reforms
punished treason by reducing the representation in the House of Representatives and the Electoral College of states that disenfranchised a significant
number of former slaves and by barring certain former Confederates from
holding public office. Proposed constitutional reforms rewarded loyalty by
stating more clearly that Congress had the power to protect former slaves
and those whites who had remained faithful during the Civil War, guaranteeing payment of Union obligations, and temporarily turning control over
former Confederate states to those who had always supported the Union
cause. Colorado statehood rewarded loyalty by granting statehood to persons who had fought for the Union during the Civil War, even though their
jurisdiction was underpopulated, they did not follow the rules that Congress mandated for drafting a state constitution, and they ratified a constitution that limited voting to white persons. What Senator James W. Nye of
Nevada said about Colorado statehood was true across the board for most
members of the Thirty-Ninth Congress: "When a body of men comes here
with the power to uphold and maintain a State government clothed with
the garments of loyalty, let them come in."[20] Allegiance, as the debates over
Colorado and Tennessee statehood highlight, had privileges. One was membership. Another, apparently, was the right to discriminate against persons
of color.

Republicans, when debating the exclusion resolution, constitutional reforms, and Colorado statehood, were attempting to construct rather than
create constitutional politics. Members of the majority party in the Thirty-
Ninth Congress acknowledged that loyal people needed protection from
former Confederates, but they also believed that those protections were
best secured by empowering the faithful rather than by constraining the
unsympathetic. Republicans during the debates over the exclusion resolution and Colorado statehood maintained that the fate of persons of color
and other loyal citizens was far better secured by political arrangements that
entrenched the Republican Party—the party of the loyal—in power than
by erecting legal barriers against racial injustice. The Black Codes served
as a reminder (as if any reminder was needed) that former Confederates in
power were unlikely to be constrained by parchment declarations, particularly declarations as vague as Section 1 of the Fourteenth Amendment. The
North would enjoy the fruits of the Civil War, persons of color would not

be re-enslaved, Southern Republicans would not be persecuted, and secession attempts would not be repeated, Stevens and his political allies thought,
only by a constitutional politics that temporarily prevented former Confederate states from being represented in Congress, vested control over those
states in persons who remained loyal to the United States, further weakened
former Confederate states politically if they did not allow persons of color
to vote, and augmented the political power of Union states by admitting
to the Union new states from the West who shared the free labor commitments of the North and Midwest (then considered the Northwest). Senator
George H. Williams of Oregon assured Republicans that "Colorado would
have the same interest as the State of New York."[21] He did not claim that
Colorado would vote with Mississippi or even Missouri. More loyal voters
and more loyal representatives were a more secure guarantee against rebel
rule than more nice phrases in constitutional texts.

The sincerity of these commitments to racial equality may be questioned.
Derrick Bell, as discussed in chapter 3, famously maintained that racial majorities obtain favorable policies only when those policies advance white
interests.[22] History provides much evidence for this "interest-convergence
dilemma." Eric Foner notes that the antebellum Republican Party succeeded where abolitionist parties failed by highlighting how the slave power
threatened the liberties of Northern whites.[23] Mary Dudziak details how
Americans concerned with the impact of race segregation on American foreign policy played crucial roles in the decisions that eventually dismantled
Jim Crow.[24] Mainstream Republican commitments to granting former slaves
access to the ballot during the Thirty-Ninth Congress provide another instance of politicians supporting African American interests when and only
when white people were the main beneficiaries of expanded black rights.
G. Williams unwittingly anticipated Bell's interest-convergence thesis when
he noted that Black suffrage in former Confederate states was more vital
than Black suffrage in Colorado because "by extending to [Southern blacks]
the right of suffrage we enable the loyal sentiment of that country to pre-
dominate over the rebel and disorganizing sentiment, and in that way [Con-
gress can] secure the perpetuity, the peace, and the integrity of the nation."[25]
Black suffrage was important when Black votes were needed to maintain
loyal whites in power. When loyal whites were sufficiently numerous to win
elections without Black help, Republicans dispensed with Black suffrage, at
least during the time the Fourteenth Amendment was being framed.

Republican commitments to persons of color should nevertheless not
be dismissed as purely instrumental or hypocritical. Many proponents of
congressional Reconstruction who opposed on pragmatic grounds Black

suffrage as a condition for restoring former Confederate states or admitting new Western states were and remained ardent proponents of racial equality.[26] Senator Henry Wilson of Massachusetts helped organize the Free Soil Party, drafted the bill that permitted persons of color to join the Union army, and fought to seat Black senators when they were elected during Reconstruction.[27] Representative James M. Ashley of Ohio was the main sponsor of the Thirteenth Amendment in the House and a tireless advocate for granting former slaves substantial political and economic rights.[28] Senator Jacob M. Howard of Michigan was one of the more influential Radical Republicans in the Reconstruction Congress.[29] Nye as territorial governor of Nevada risked his political career when fighting to give persons of color the right to testify and when battling to give all persons the right to marry a partner of a different race.[30]

These members of Congress who supported constitutional reforms and territorial policies that directly empowered and protected loyal white persons looked forward to a bright future marked by a steady if not accelerated march toward a regime that realized commitments to free labor and human equality. When defending his vote for Colorado statehood, Howard predicted that the "generous and enterprising people who have done so much according to their numbers to uphold the Government of the United States during the late war will see to it hereafter that this error shall be corrected in their constitution[] and that all persons, black or white, shall be permitted to vote in that State."[31] Howard and his political allies had witnessing a remarkable transformation in Northern attitudes toward slavery and racial equality, as persons on the home front became aware of Black heroism on Civil War battlefields.[32] Time plainly seemed to be on the side of those who believed Black and white Americans could share the same civic space as legal equals. Experience was demonstrating that the arc of the moral universe did indeed bend toward justice.[33] The members of the Thirty-Ninth Congress responsible for congressional Reconstruction and the constitutional reforms that became the Fourteenth Amendment would not be the only Americans committed to racial equality ever to hold that faith.

TABLE A.I: HOUSE VOTES ON THE FOURTEENTH AMENDMENT, THE EXCLUSION RESOLUTION, AND STATEHOOD FOR COLORADO AND NEBRASKA

Name	State	Party	Exclusion resolution[1]	Fourteenth Amendment[2]	Colorado voting rights for blacks[3]	Colorado statehood[4]	Nebraska statehood[5]
Donald C. McRuer	California	Republican	Yes	Yes	Yes	No	Absent
William Higby	California	Republican	Yes	Yes	Absent	No	No
John Bidwell	California	Republican	Yes	Yes	No	Yes	Yes
Henry C. Deming	Connecticut	Republican	Yes	Absent	No	Yes	Absent
Samuel L. Warner	Connecticut	Republican	Yes	Yes	No	Yes	Absent
Augustus Brandegee	Connecticut	Republican	Yes	Absent	Yes	Absent	Absent
John H. Hubbard	Connecticut	Republican	Yes	Yes	Absent	Absent	Yes
John Wentworth	Illinois	Republican	Yes	Yes	Absent	Absent	Yes
John F. Farnsworth	Illinois	Republican	Yes	Yes	Absent	No	Yes
Elihu B. Washburne	Illinois	Republican	Yes	Absent (Yes)	Yes	Yes	Absent
Abner C. Harding	Illinois	Republican	Yes	Yes	No	Yes	No
Ebon C. Ingersoll	Illinois	Republican	Yes	Absent	No	Yes	Yes
Burton C. Cook	Illinois	Republican	Yes	Yes	Absent	Absent	Absent
Henry P. H. Bromwell	Illinois	Republican	Yes	Yes	No	Yes	Yes
Shelby M. Cullom	Illinois	Republican	Yes	Yes	No	Yes	Yes
Jehu Baker	Illinois	Republican	Yes	Yes	No	Yes	Yes
Andrew J. Kuykendall	Illinois	Republican	Absent	Yes	No	No	Yes
Samuel W. Moulton	Illinois	Republican	Yes	Yes	No	Yes	Absent
Ralph Hill	Indiana	Republican	Absent	Absent (Yes)	Absent	Absent	Absent
John H. Farquhar	Indiana	Republican	Yes	Yes	No	Yes	Yes
George W. Julian	Indiana	Republican	Yes	Yes	Yes	No	No
Ebenezer Dumont	Indiana	Republican	Absent	Yes	No	Yes	Yes
Henry D. Washburn[6]	Indiana	Republican	N/A	Yes	No	No	Absent
Godlove S. Orth	Indiana	Republican	Yes	Yes	No	Yes	Yes
Schuyler Colfax	Indiana	Republican		Yes	No		
Joseph H. Defrees	Indiana	Republican	Yes	Yes	No	Yes	Yes
Thomas N. Stilwell	Indiana	Republican	Absent	Yes	Yes	No	Absent
James F. Wilson	Iowa	Republican	Yes	Yes	Yes	No	Absent
Hiram Price	Iowa	Republican	Yes	Yes	Absent	Absent	No
William B. Allison	Iowa	Republican	Yes	Yes	Yes	No	No

First Name	Last Name	State	Party					
Josiah B.	Grinnell	Iowa	Republican	Yes	Yes	Yes	Yes	Absent
John A.	Kasson	Iowa	Republican	Absent	Absent	Yes	Yes	Absent
Asahel W.	Hubbard	Iowa	Republican	Yes	Yes	Yes	Yes	Absent
Sidney	Clarke	Kansas	Republican	Yes	Absent	Absent	No	Absent
John	Lynch	Maine	Republican	Yes	Yes	Yes	No	No
Sidney	Perham	Maine	Republican	Yes	Yes	Yes	No	No
James G.	Blaine	Maine	Republican	Yes	Yes	Yes	No	Absent
John H.	Rice	Maine	Republican	Yes	Yes	Yes	No	Yes
Frederick A.	Pike	Maine	Republican	Yes	Yes	Yes	No	Absent
Thomas D.	Eliot	Massachusetts	Republican	Absent (Yes)	Yes	Yes	Yes	No
Oakes	Ames	Massachusetts	Republican	Absent	Yes	Yes	Yes	Absent
Alexander H.	Rice	Massachusetts	Republican	Yes	Yes	Yes	Absent	Yes
Samuel	Hooper	Massachusetts	Republican	Absent (Yes)	Yes	Absent	No	Yes
John B.	Alley	Massachusetts	Republican	Yes	Yes	Yes	No	No
Nathaniel P.	Banks	Massachusetts	Republican	Yes	Yes	No	No	Yes
George S.	Boutwell	Massachusetts	Republican	Yes	Yes	Yes	Absent	No
John D.	Baldwin	Massachusetts	Republican	Yes	Yes	Yes	Absent	Absent
William B.	Washburn	Massachusetts	Republican	Yes	Yes	Absent	Absent	Absent
Henry L.	Dawes	Massachusetts	Republican	Yes	Yes	Absent	Yes	Absent
Fernando C.	Beaman	Michigan	Republican	Yes	Yes	No	No	Absent
Charles	Upson	Michigan	Republican	Yes	Yes	No	No	Absent
John W.	Longyear	Michigan	Republican	Yes	Yes	No	No	Absent
Thomas W.	Ferry	Michigan	Republican	Yes	Yes	No	Yes	Absent
Rowland E.	Trowbridge	Michigan	Republican	Yes	Yes	No	No	Absent
John F.	Driggs	Michigan	Republican	Yes	Yes	No	Yes	Yes
William	Windom	Minnesota	Republican	Yes	Yes	Yes	No	Absent
Ignatius L.	Donnelly	Minnesota	Republican	Yes	Yes	No	Yes	No
Henry T.	Blow	Missouri	Republican	Absent	No	No	Yes	Absent
Thomas E.	Noell	Missouri	Republican	Absent	Absent	Absent	No	Absent
Joseph W.	McClurg	Missouri	Republican	Yes	Yes	Yes	Yes	Absent
Robert T.	Van Horn	Missouri	Republican	Absent	Absent	Yes	No	Absent
Benjamin F.	Loan	Missouri	Republican	Yes	Yes	Yes	Yes	No
John F.	Benjamin	Missouri	Republican	Yes	Yes	No	Yes	Yes
George W.	Anderson	Missouri	Republican	Yes	Absent	No	Absent	Yes
Delos R.	Ashley	Nevada	Republican	Absent	Yes	No	No	Yes

(continued)

Table A.1 (*continued*)

Name	State	Party	Exclusion resolution[1]	Fourteenth Amendment[2]	Colorado voting rights for blacks[3]	Colorado statehood[4]	Nebraska statehood[5]
Gilman Marston	New Hampshire	Republican	Yes	Absent (Yes)	No	Yes	Absent
Edward H. Rollins	New Hampshire	Republican	Absent (Yes)	Absent (Yes)	No	Yes	Yes
James W. Patterson	New Hampshire	Republican	Yes	Absent	No	Yes	Yes
John F. Starr	New Jersey	Republican	Yes	Absent	Absent	Absent	Absent
William A. Newell	New Jersey	Republican	No	Yes	No	No	Yes
James Humphrey[7]	New York	Republican	Absent	Absent (Yes)	N/A	N/A	N/A
Henry J. Raymond	New York	Republican	No	Yes	No	No	Absent
William E. Dodge[8]	New York	Republican	N/A	Yes	No	Yes	Yes
William A. Darling	New York	Republican	Absent	Yes	No	No	Absent
John H. Ketcham	New York	Republican	Yes	Yes	No	Yes	Yes
John A. Griswold	New York	Republican	Yes	Yes	Absent	No	Absent
Robert S. Hale	New York	Republican	No	Absent	Absent	Absent	Absent
Calvin T. Hulburd	New York	Republican	Yes	Yes	Absent	Absent	Absent
James M. Marvin	New York	Republican	Absent	Absent (Yes)	Absent	Absent	Absent
Demas Hubbard Jr.	New York	Republican	Yes	Yes	Absent	Absent	Absent
Addison H. Laflin	New York	Republican	Yes	Yes	No	Yes	Yes
Roscoe Conkling	New York	Republican	Yes	Yes	No	Yes	Yes
Sidney T. Holmes	New York	Republican	Yes	Yes	No	Yes	Yes
Thomas T. Davis	New York	Republican	Absent	Yes	Absent	Absent	Absent
Theodore M. Pomeroy	New York	Republican	Yes	Yes	Absent	Absent (Yes)	Absent
Daniel Morris	New York	Republican	Yes	Yes	Yes	No	Yes
Giles W. Hotchkiss	New York	Republican	Yes	Yes	Absent	Yes	Yes
Hamilton Ward Sr.	New York	Republican	Yes	Yes	Absent	Absent	Absent
Roswell Hart	New York	Republican	Yes	Absent (Yes)	Absent	Yes	Yes
Burt Van Horn	New York	Republican	Yes	Yes	No	Yes	Yes
Henry H. Van Aernam	New York	Republican	Yes	Yes	Absent	Yes	No
Benjamin Eggleston	Ohio	Republican	Yes	Yes	Absent	Absent	Yes
Rutherford B. Hayes	Ohio	Republican	Yes	Yes	Absent	Absent	Yes
Robert C. Schenck	Ohio	Republican	Yes	Yes	No	Yes	Yes
William Lawrence	Ohio	Republican	Yes	Absent (Yes)	No	Yes	Yes

[226]

	State	Party					
Reader W. Clarke	Ohio	Republican	Absent	Absent	No	Yes	Absent
Samuel Shellabarger	Ohio	Republican	Yes	Yes	No	Yes	Yes
James R. Hubbell	Ohio	Republican	Yes	Yes	No	Yes	Yes
Ralph P. Buckland	Ohio	Republican	Yes	Yes	No	Yes	Absent
James M. Ashley	Ohio	Republican	Absent	Absent	No	Yes	Absent
Hezekiah S. Bundy	Ohio	Republican	Absent	Absent	No	Absent	Absent
Columbus Delano	Ohio	Republican	Yes	Yes	No	Yes	Yes
Martin Welker	Ohio	Republican	Yes	Yes	No	Yes	Yes
Tobias A. Plants	Ohio	Republican	Yes	Yes	No	Yes	Yes
John A. Bingham	Ohio	Republican	Yes	Yes	No	Yes	Yes
Ephraim R. Eckley	Ohio	Republican	Yes	Yes	No	Yes	Yes
Rufus P. Spalding	Ohio	Republican	Yes	Yes	No	Yes	No
James A. Garfield	Ohio	Republican	Yes	Yes	Yes	Yes	Absent
James H. D. Henderson	Oregon	Republican	Yes	Yes	No	Yes	Yes
Charles O'Neill	Pennsylvania	Republican	Yes	Yes	No	Yes	Yes
Leonard Myers	Pennsylvania	Republican	Yes	Yes	No	Yes	No
William D. Kelley	Pennsylvania	Republican	Yes	Yes	Yes	No	Absent
M. Russell Thayer	Pennsylvania	Republican	Yes	Absent (Yes)	Absent	Absent	No
John M. Broomall	Pennsylvania	Republican	Yes	Yes	Yes	No	No
Thaddeus Stevens	Pennsylvania	Republican	Yes	Yes	No	No	Yes
Ulysses Mercur	Pennsylvania	Republican	Yes	Yes	No	Yes	Yes
George F. Miller	Pennsylvania	Republican	Absent (Yes)	Yes	No	N/A	Yes
William H. Koontz[9]	Pennsylvania	Republican	N/A	N/A	N/A	N/A	Yes
Abraham A. Barker	Pennsylvania	Republican	Absent	Absent	No	Yes	Yes
Stephen F. Wilson	Pennsylvania	Republican	Yes	Yes	Absent	Absent	Yes
Glenni W. Scofield	Pennsylvania	Republican	Yes	Yes	Absent	Absent	Yes
Charles V. Culver	Pennsylvania	Republican	Absent	Absent	Absent	Absent	Absent
James K. Moorhead	Pennsylvania	Republican	Yes	Yes	No	Yes	Yes
Thomas Williams	Pennsylvania	Republican	Yes	Yes	Yes	Yes	No
George V. Lawrence	Pennsylvania	Republican	Yes	Yes	No	Yes	Yes
Thomas A. Jenckes	Rhode Island	Republican	Yes	Absent	Yes	Yes	No
Nathan F. Dixon, Jr.	Rhode Island	Republican	Absent	Absent	Yes	No	Absent
Frederick E. Woodbridge	Vermont	Republican	Absent	Absent	Yes	No	Absent
Justin S. Morrill	Vermont	Republican	Yes	Yes	Yes	No	No
Portus Baxter	Vermont	Republican	Yes	Yes	Yes	No	No

(continued)

Table A.1 (*continued*)

Name		State	Party	Exclusion resolution[1]	Fourteenth Amendment[2]	Colorado voting rights for blacks[3]	Colorado statehood[4]	Nebraska statehood[5]
Halbert E.	Paine	Wisconsin	Republican	Yes	Yes	Yes	No	No
Ithamar C.	Sloan	Wisconsin	Republican	Yes	Yes	Absent	Absent	Absent
Amasa	Cobb	Wisconsin	Republican	Yes	Yes	Absent	Yes	Yes
Philetus	Sawyer	Wisconsin	Republican	Yes	Yes	No	Yes	Yes
Walter D.	McIndoe	Wisconsin	Republican	Yes	Absent (Yes)	Absent	Absent	Absent
John R.	Kelso	Missouri	Independent Republican	Yes	Yes	Yes	Yes	Absent
Nathaniel G.	Taylor[10]	Tennessee	Unionist	N/A	N/A	N/A	N/A	No
Edmund	Cooper[11]	Tennessee	Unionist	N/A	N/A	N/A	N/A	No
Lovell H.	Rousseau[12]	Kentucky	Unconditional Unionist	No	Absent	No	No	N/A
Green C.	Smith	Kentucky	Unconditional Unionist	No	Yes	No	Yes	Absent
William H.	Randall	Kentucky	Unconditional Unionist	Yes	Yes	Absent	Absent	Absent
Samuel	McKee	Kentucky	Unconditional Unionist	Yes	Yes	Absent	Yes	Absent
John L.	Thomas Jr.	Maryland	Unconditional Unionist	Yes	Yes	No	Absent	Yes
Charles E.	Phelps	Maryland	Unconditional Unionist	No	Yes	Absent	Absent (No)	No
Francis	Thomas	Maryland	Unconditional Unionist	Absent	Yes	No	Absent (Yes)	Absent
Horace	Maynard[13]	Tennessee	Unconditional Unionist	N/A	N/A	N/A	N/A	No
William B.	Stokes[14]	Tennessee	Unconditional Unionist	N/A	N/A	N/A	N/A	Yes
John W.	Leftwich[15]	Tennessee	Unconditional Unionist	N/A	N/A	N/A	N/A	No

Chester D.	Hubbard	West Virginia	Unconditional Unionist	Yes	Yes	No	Yes	Yes	Yes
George R.	Latham	West Virginia	Unconditional Unionist	No	Yes	No	Yes	Yes	Yes
Kellian V.	Whaley	West Virginia	Unconditional Unionist	No	Yes	No	Yes	Yes	Yes
John A.	Nicholson	Delaware	Democrat	No	No	Absent	Absent	No	No
Lewis W.	Ross	Illinois	Democrat	No	No	No	No	No	No
Anthony	Thornton	Illinois	Democrat	No	No	No	No	No	No
Samuel S.	Marshall	Illinois	Democrat	No	No	No	No	No	No
William E.	Niblack	Indiana	Democrat	No	No	No	Absent	Absent	Absent
Michael C.	Kerr	Indiana	Democrat	No	No	Absent	Absent	No	Absent
Daniel W.	Voorhees[16]	Indiana	Democrat	N/A	N/A	N/A	N/A	N/A	N/A
Lawrence S.	Trimble	Kentucky	Democrat	No	No	Absent	Absent	No	No
Burwell C.	Ritter	Kentucky	Democrat	No	No	No	No	No	No
Henry	Grider	Kentucky	Democrat	No	No	No	No	No	Absent
Aaron	Harding	Kentucky	Democrat	No	No	No	No	No	Absent
George S.	Shanklin	Kentucky	Democrat	No	No	No	No	No	No
Hiram	McCullough	Maryland	Democrat	No	No	No	Absent (No)	No	No
Benjamin G.	Harris	Maryland	Democrat	No	No	No	Absent	No	No
John	Hogan	Missouri	Democrat	No	No	No	Absent	No	No
Charles	Sitgreaves	New Jersey	Democrat	No	No	No	No	Absent	Absent
Andrew J.	Rogers	New Jersey	Democrat	No	No	No	No	Absent	Absent
Edwin R. V.	Wright	New Jersey	Democrat	No	No	No	No	No	No
Stephen	Taber	New York	Democrat	No	No	No	Absent	Absent	No
Teunis G.	Bergen	New York	Democrat	No	No	No	No	No	No
Morgan	Jones	New York	Democrat	Absent	Absent	Absent	Absent	Absent	Absent
Nelson	Taylor	New York	Democrat	No	No	No	No	No	No
John W.	Chanler	New York	Democrat	No	No	Absent	No	No	No
James	Brooks[17]	New York	Democrat	No	N/A	No	N/A	N/A	N/A
William	Radford	New York	Democrat	No	Absent (No)	Absent (No)	Absent (No)	Absent	No
Charles H.	Winfield	New York	Democrat	Absent	No	No	No	No	No
Edwin N.	Hubbell	New York	Democrat	Absent	Absent (No)	Absent	Absent (No)	Absent	Absent
Charles	Goodyear	New York	Democrat	No	No	Absent	Absent	Absent	Absent
James M.	Humphrey	New York	Democrat	No	No	Absent	Absent	Absent (No)	Absent

(continued)

Table A.1 (*continued*)

Name		State	Party	Exclusion resolution[1]	Fourteenth Amendment[2]	Colorado voting rights for blacks[3]	Colorado statehood[4]	Nebraska statehood[5]
Francis C.	Le Blond	Ohio	Democrat	Absent (No)	No	No	No	No
William E.	Finck	Ohio	Democrat	No	No	No	No	No
Samuel J.	Randall	Pennsylvania	Democrat	No	No	Absent	Absent	Absent
Benjamin M.	Boyer	Pennsylvania	Democrat	Absent (No)	No	No	No	No
Sydenham E.	Ancona	Pennsylvania	Democrat	No	No	No	No	No
Myer	Strouse	Pennsylvania	Democrat	No	No	No	No	No
Philip	Johnson	Pennsylvania	Democrat	Absent (No)	Absent (No)	Absent	Absent	Absent
Charles	Denison	Pennsylvania	Democrat	Absent	No	No	No	No
Adam J.	Glossbrenner	Pennsylvania	Democrat	No	No	No	No	No
Alexander H.	Coffroth[18]	Pennsylvania	Democrat	No	No	No	No	N/A
John L.	Dawson	Pennsylvania	Democrat	No	No	No	No	Absent
Charles A.	Eldredge	Wisconsin	Democrat	No	No	No	No	No

1. *Congressional Globe*, 39th Cong., 1st Sess., 950.
2. *Congressional Globe*, 39th Cong., 1st Sess., 3149.
3. *Congressional Globe*, 39th Cong., 1st Sess., 2272.
4. *Congressional Globe*, 39th Cong., 1st Sess., 2374.
5. *Congressional Globe*, 39th Cong., 1st Sess., 4476.
6. Washburn replaced Daniel Vorhees on February 23, 1866, after the House determined Daniel Vorhees had won the election in their district.
7. James Humphrey died on June 16, 1866.
8. Dodge replaced James Brooks on April 7 after Congress determined he had won the election in their district.
9. Koontz replaced Alexander Coffroth after Congress determined he had won the election in his district.
10. Taylor became a member of Congress on July 24, 1866.
11. Cooper became a member of Congress on July 24, 1866.
12. Rousseau resigned from Congress on July 21, 1866. He was not replaced during the 39th Congress, 1st Session.
13. Maynard became a member of Congress on July 24, 1866.
14. Stokes became a member of Congress on July 24, 1866.
15. Leftwich became a member of Congress on July 24, 1866.
16. Vorhees was replaced on February 23 by Henry Washburn after the House determined Washburn won the election in their district.
17. Brooks was replaced on April 7, 1866, after Congress determined William E. Dodge won the election in his district.
18. Coffroth was replaced on July 18 by William Dodge when Congress determined that Dodge had won the election in their district.

TABLE A.2: SENATE VOTES ON THE FOURTEENTH AMENDMENT, THE EXCLUSION RESOLUTION, AND STATEHOOD FOR COLORADO AND NEBRASKA

Name		State	Party	Exclusion resolution[1]	Fourteenth Amendment[2]	First Colorado vote[3]	Second Colorado vote[4]	Nebraska statehood[5]
John	Conness	California	Republican	Yes	Yes	No	Yes	Yes
Lafayette S.	Foster	Connecticut	Republican	Yes	Yes	No	Yes	No
James	Dixon	Connecticut	Republican	No	Absent	Absent	Absent (No)	Absent
Lyman	Trumbull	Illinois	Republican	Yes	Yes	Yes	Yes	Yes
Richard	Yates	Illinois	Republican	Yes	Yes	Absent	Absent (Yes)	Yes
Henry S.	Lane	Indiana	Republican	Yes	Yes	Yes	Yes	Yes
Samuel J.	Kirkwood	Iowa	Republican	Yes	Yes	Yes	Yes	Yes
James W.	Grimes	Iowa	Republican	Yes	Yes	No	No	Absent
Samuel C.	Pomeroy	Kansas	Republican	Yes	Yes	Yes	Yes	Yes
James H.	Lane[6]	Kansas	Republican	No	Yes	Yes	Yes	N/A
Edmund	Ross[7]	Kansas	Republican	N/A	N/A	N/A	N/A	No
Lot M.	Morrill	Maine	Republican	Yes	Yes	No	Absent	Absent
William Pitt	Fessenden	Maine	Republican	Yes	Yes	No	Absent (No)	No
Charles	Sumner	Massachusetts	Republican	Yes	Yes	No	No	No
Henry	Wilson	Massachusetts	Republican	Yes	Yes	No	Yes	Yes
Zachariah	Chandler	Michigan	Republican	Yes	Yes	Yes	Yes	Yes
Jacob M.	Howard	Michigan	Republican	Absent (Yes)	Yes	Absent	Yes	Yes
Alexander	Ramsey	Minnesota	Republican	Yes	Yes	Yes	Yes	Yes
Daniel S.	Norton	Minnesota	Republican	No	No	Yes	Yes	No
John B.	Henderson	Missouri	Republican	Yes	Yes	Absent (Yes)	Absent (Yes)	Yes
B. Gratz	Brown	Missouri	Republican	Yes	Absent	Absent	Absent	Absent
William M.	Stewart	Nevada	Republican	No	Yes	Yes	Yes	Yes
James W.	Nye	Nevada	Republican	Yes	Yes	Absent	Yes	Yes
Daniel	Clark	New Hampshire	Republican	Yes	Yes	Absent	Yes	Absent
Aaron H.	Cragin	New Hampshire	Republican	Yes	Yes	Yes	Yes	Absent
Ira	Harris	New York	Republican	Yes	Yes	No	Absent (No)	No
Edwin D.	Morgan	New York	Republican	No	Yes	Absent	Absent (No)	No
Benjamin F.	Wade	Ohio	Republican	Yes	Yes	No	Absent (Yes)	Yes
John	Sherman	Ohio	Republican	Yes	Yes	Yes	Yes	Yes
George H.	Williams	Oregon	Republican	Yes	Yes	Yes	Absent (Yes)	Yes
Edgar	Cowan	Pennsylvania	Republican	No	No	Absent	Absent (No)	No

First Name	Last Name	State	Party	Vote 1[1]	Vote 2[2]	Vote 3[3]	Vote 4[4]	Vote 5[5]
Henry B.	Anthony	Rhode Island	Republican	Yes	Yes	Absent	Absent	Yes
William	Sprague	Rhode Island	Republican	Yes	Yes	No	Yes	Yes
Solomon	Foot[8]	Vermont	Republican	Absent (Yes)	N/A	Absent	N/A	N/A
George F.	Edmunds[9]	Vermont	Republican	N/A	Yes	N/A	No	No
Luke P.	Poland	Vermont	Republican	Yes	Yes	No	No	No
Waitman T.	Willey	West Virginia	Republican	Yes	Yes	Absent (Yes)	Absent	Yes
James R.	Doolittle	Wisconsin	Republican	No	No	No	No	No
Timothy O.	Howe	Wisconsin	Republican	Yes	Yes	Absent	Yes	Yes
Garrett	Davis	Kentucky	Unionist	No	No	No	No	No
Joseph S.	Fowler[10]	Tennessee	Unionist	N/A	N/A	N/A	N/A	No
John A. J.	Creswell	Maryland	Unconditional Unionist	Yes	Yes	No	Yes	Yes
Peter G.	Van Winkle	West Virginia	Unconditional Unionist	No	No	No	Yes	Yes
James A.	McDougall	California	Democrat	No	No	Yes	No	No
Willard	Saulsbury, Sr.	Delaware	Democrat	No	No	Absent (No)	Absent (No)	Absent
George Read	Riddle	Delaware	Democrat	No	No	No	No	No
Thomas A.	Hendricks	Indiana	Democrat	No	No	No	No	No
James	Guthrie	Kentucky	Democrat	No	No	No	No	No
Reverdy	Johnson	Maryland	Democrat	No	No	Absent (no)	Absent (No)	No
William	Wright	New Jersey	Democrat	Absent	Absent	Absent	Absent	Absent
John P.	Stockton[11]	New Jersey	Democrat	No	N/A	No	N/A	N/A
James W.	Nesmith	Oregon	Democrat	No	Absent	Yes	Absent	No
Charles R.	Buckalew	Pennsylvania	Democrat	No	Absent	No	No	No

1. *Congressional Globe*, 39th Cong, 1st Sess., 1147.
2. *Congressional Globe*, 39th Cong, 1st Sess., 3042.
3. *Congressional Globe*, 39th Cong, 1st Sess., 1365.
4. *Congressional Globe*, 39th Cong, 1st Sess., 2180.
5. *Congressional Globe*, 39th Cong, 1st Sess., 4222.
6. James Lane died on July 11, 1866. He was replaced by Edmund Ross.
7. Ross replaced James Lane on July 19, 1866.
8. Solomon Foot died on March 28, 1866. He was replaced by George Edmunds.
9. George Edmunds replaced Solomon Foot on April 3, 1866.
10. Fowler became a member of the Senate on June 24, 1866.
11. Stockton was removed from the Senate on March 27, 1866, when the Senate determined he had not been constitutionally elected by the state legislature.

TABLE A.3: REFERENCES TO "REBEL" AND "LOYAL" IN THE HOUSE OF REPRESENTATIVES

Name	Party	ExV[1]	14V[2]	Pages[3]	RP[4]	Rebel[5]	RebelP[6]	Loyal[7]	BLoyal[8]
McRuer	Republican	Yes	Yes	21	0	1	1	0	
Higby	Republican	Yes	Yes	36	12	8	6	18	Yes
Bidwell	Republican	Yes	Yes	32	0	0	0	3	
Deming	Republican	Yes	Absent	13	4	10	4	5	
Warner	Republican	Yes	Yes	3	0	0	0	0	
Brandegee	Republican	Yes	Absent	16	1	0	0	0	
J. Hubbard	Republican	Yes	Yes	21	2	0	0	1	
Wentworth	Republican	Yes	Yes	40	0	5	2	2	
Farnsworth	Republican	Yes	Yes	56	9	35	18	21	Yes
Washburne	Republican	Yes	Absent (Yes)	106	1	14	1	6	
Aa. Harding	Republican	Yes	Yes	39	2				
Ingersoll	Republican	Yes	Absent	53	10	27	18	38	Yes
Cook	Republican	Yes	Yes	28	8	19	12	50	
Bromwell	Republican	Yes	Yes	21	13	3	2	8	
Cullom	Republican	Yes	Yes	14	6	26	8	15	
Baker	Republican	Yes	Yes	17	11	34	23	33	
Kuykendall	Republican	Absent	Yes	7	5	9	7	12	
Moulton	Republican	Yes	Yes	17	6	73	64	19	
Hill	Republican	Absent	Absent (Yes)	16	5	6	4	12	
Farquhar	Republican	Yes	Yes	19	0	7	4	2	
Julian	Republican	Yes	Yes	41	12	74	47	40	Yes
Dumont	Republican	Absent	Yes	16	5	13	13	6	
Washburn	Republican	N/A	Yes	12	0	2	1		
Orth	Republican	Yes	Yes	21	8	35	22	15	
Colfax	Republican	N/A	Yes	5	0	2	0	9	
Defrees	Republican	Yes	Yes	7	7	6	2	12	
Stilwell	Republican	Absent	Yes	6	3	4	3		
J. Wilson	Republican	Yes	Yes	109	20	21	13	15	Yes
Price	Republican	Yes	Yes	44	8	2	2	12	
Allison	Republican	Yes	Yes	36	0	0	0	0	
Grinnell	Republican	Yes	Yes	46	6	17	5	5	Yes
Kasson	Republican	Absent	Absent	104	4	7	3	9	
A. Hubbard	Republican	Yes	Yes	18	0	0	0	1	
S. Clarke	Republican	Yes	Yes	17	7	35	32	23	
Lynch	Republican	Yes	Yes	25	0	2	1	0	
Perham	Republican	Yes	Yes	28	5	23	13	34	Yes
Blaine	Republican	Yes	Yes	60	5	4	1	26	
Rice	Republican	Yes	Yes	20	1	3	2	7	

1. Vote on the exclusion resolution.
2. Vote on the Fourteenth Amendment.
3. Approximate number of pages for speeches and resolutions in the *Congressional Globe*.
4. Approximate number of pages for speeches and resolutions on Reconstruction, suffrage in Washington, DC, and admission of Western states.
5. References to "rebel."
6. References to "rebel" in the present tense.
7. References to "loyal."
8. References to whether Blacks were loyal.

Name	Party	ExV[1]	14V[2]	Pages[3]	RP[4]	Rebel[5]	RebelP[6]	Loyal[7]	BLoyal[8]
Pike	Republican	Yes	Yes	43	2	1	1	2	
Eliot	Republican	Yes	Yes	44	26	14	9	22	
Ames	Republican	Absent (Yes)	Yes	0	0	1	1	1	
A. Rice	Republican	Absent	Yes	33	0	5	1	1	
Hooper	Republican	Yes	Yes	34	0	2	0	5	
Alley	Republican	Absent (Yes)	Yes	44	0	2	2	4	
Banks	Republican	Yes	Yes	52	4	11	2	9	
Boutwell	Republican	Yes	Yes	39	13	20	16	53	Yes
Baldwin	Republican	Yes	Yes	15	4	8	6	7	
Washburn	Republican	Yes	Yes	16	0	3	0	3	
Dawes	Republican	Yes	Yes	78	6	5	5	6	
Beaman	Republican	Yes	Yes	16	6	35	26	32	
Upson	Republican	Yes	Yes	14	0	1	0	0	
Longyear	Republican	Yes	Yes	5	1	5	5	5	
Ferry	Republican	Yes	Yes	9	0	2	2	0	
Trowbridge	Republican	Yes	Yes	17	0	1	0	3	
Driggs	Republican	Yes	Yes	24	0	0	0	1	
Windom	Republican	Yes	Yes	26	11	49	38	34	Yes
Donnelly	Republican	Yes	Yes	25	8	9	2	2	Yes
Blow	Republican	Absent	Absent	5	0	0	0	0	
Noell	Republican	Absent	Absent	3	0	0	0	3	
McClurg	Republican	Yes	Yes	5	0	0	0	3	
R. Van Horn	Republican	Absent	Yes	4	0	0	0	1	
Loan	Republican	Yes	Yes	15	4	73	38	23	
Benjamin	Republican	Yes	Absent	20	6	12	10	16	
Anderson	Republican	Yes	Absent	9	4	6	3	16	
D. Ashley	Republican	Absent	Yes	8	3	5	4	4	
Marston	Republican	Yes	Absent (Yes)	4	0	2	2	0	
Rollins	Republican	Absent (Yes)	Absent (Yes)	14	0	0	0	0	
Patterson	Republican	Yes	Absent	15	10	6	4	14	
Starr	Republican	Yes	Absent	0	0	0	0	0	
Newell	Republican	No	Yes	18	6	2	0	7	
J. Humphrey	Republican	Absent	Absent (Yes)	1	0	0	0	0	
Raymond	Republican	No	Yes	82	36	39	17	40	
Dodge	Republican	N/A	Yes	15	1	0	0	1	
Darling	Republican	Absent	Yes	26	2			1	
Ketcham	Republican	Yes	Yes	4	0	1			
Griswold	Republican	Yes	Yes	17	0				
Hale	Republican	No	Yes	70	11	7	1	3	
Hulburd	Republican	Yes	Absent	13	0	1		1	
Marvin	Republican	Absent	Yes	0	0			1	
D. Hubbard	Republican	Yes	Absent (Yes)	1	0				
Laflin	Republican	Yes	Yes	22	1	2	1	1	
Conkling	Republican	Yes	Yes	92	9	7	4	5	
Holmes	Republican	Yes	Yes	18	4	9	8	40	Yes
T. Davis	Republican	Absent	Yes	81	11	20	3	25	
T. Pomeroy	Republican	Yes	Yes	3	0				
Morris	Republican	Yes	Yes	6	4	2	1	15	
Hotchkiss	Republican	Yes	Yes	19	1	4	4	1	
Ward	Republican	Yes	Yes	22	5	26	11	30	

(continued)

Table A.3 (*continued*)

Name	Party	ExV[1]	14V[2]	Pages[3]	RP[4]	Rebel[5]	RebelP[6]	Loyal[7]	BLoyal[8]
Hart	Republican	Yes	Yes	10	4	10	8	15	Yes
B. Van Horn	Republican	Yes	Absent (Yes)	12	3	1	0	7	
Van Aernam	Republican	Yes	Yes	8	4	24	13	9	Yes
Eggleston	Republican	Yes	Yes	7	0				
Hayes	Republican	Yes	Yes	1	0				
Schenck	Republican	Yes	Yes	177	11	18	2	23	Yes
W. Lawrence	Republican	Yes	Absent (Yes)	64	23	58	36	52	Yes
R. Clarke	Republican	Absent	Yes	16	9	59	40	30	
Shellabarger	Republican	Yes	Yes	75	32	43	25	32	
J. Hubbell	Republican	Yes	Yes	4	4	12	8	9	
Buckland	Republican	Yes	Yes	5	5	11	7	23	Yes
J. Ashley	Republican	Yes	Yes	22	8	23	8	50	Yes
Bundy	Republican	Absent	Yes	10	5	31	22	29	
Delano	Republican	Absent	Yes	52	10	11	8	40	
Welker	Republican	Yes	Yes	10	3	10	8	4	
Plants	Republican	Yes	Yes	9	6	14	5	3	
Bingham	Republican	Yes	Yes	55	32	54	39	88	Yes
Colfax	Republican			5	0	1	1		
Eckley	Republican	Yes	Yes	9	3	4	4	7	
Spalding	Republican	Yes	Yes	58	8	17	10	20	Yes
Garfield	Republican	Yes	Yes	108	8	24	11	21	
Jo. Henderson	Republican	Yes	Yes	28	5	9	2	10	
O'Neill	Republican	Yes	Yes	34	0	1		1	
Myers	Republican	Yes	Yes	32	5	19	11	10	
Kelley	Republican	Yes	Yes	110	32	23	16	23	Yes
Thayer	Republican	Yes	Yes	74	13	7	4	12	
Broomall	Republican	Yes	Absent (Yes)	30	13	40	27	22	Yes
Stevens	Republican	Yes	Yes	201	27	87	61	42	Yes
Mercur	Republican	Yes	Yes	6	0	0	0	1	
Miller	Republican	Absent (Yes)	Yes	33	12	47	20	41	
Koontz	Republican	N/A	N/A	5	0	0	0	1	
Barker	Republican	Absent	Yes	0	0	0	0	0	
S. Wilson	Republican	Yes	Yes	2	0	0	0	0	
Scofield	Republican	Yes	Yes	38	7	30	22	11	Yes
Culver	Republican	Absent	Absent	0	0	0	0	0	
Moorhead	Republican	Yes	Yes	20	5	2	1	0	
T. Williams	Republican	Yes	Yes	25	15	16	15	42	
G. Lawrence	Republican	Yes	Yes	15	8	7	4	14	
Jenckes	Republican	Yes	Yes	51	5	7	3	4	
N. Dixon	Republican	Absent	Absent	0	0	0	0	0	
Woodbridge	Republican	Yes	Absent	36	2	3	0	1	
J. Morrill	Republican	Yes	Yes	150	0	4	2	0	
Baxter	Republican	Yes	Yes	0	0	0	0	0	
Paine	Republican	Yes	Yes	67	5	19	4	5	Yes
Sloan	Republican	Yes	Yes	23	2	1	1	3	
Cobb	Republican	Yes	Yes	18	0	1	0	0	
Sawyer	Republican	Yes	Yes	1	0	0	0	0	
McIndoe	Republican	Yes	Absent (Yes)	3	0	0	0	0	
Burleigh	Republican	N/A	N/A	23	0	2	2	3	

Name	Party	ExV[1]	14V[2]	Pages[3]	RP[4]	Rebel[5]	RebelP[6]	Loyal[7]	BLoyal[8]
Anonymous	Republican	N/A	N/A	0	0	1	1	0	
Kelso	Independent Republican	Yes	Yes	8	4	40	33	33	Yes
Taylor	Unionist	N/A	N/A	1	1	9	0	5	
Cooper	Unionist	N/A	N/A	0	0	0	0	0	
Rousseau	Unconditional Unionist	No	Absent	23	12	22	9	40	
Smith	Unconditional Unionist	No	Yes	46	19	94	42	49	
W. Randall	Unconditional Unionist	Yes	Yes	1	0	2	1	0	
McKee	Unconditional Unionist	Yes	Yes	24	12	23	12	49	
J. L. Thomas	Unconditional Unionist	Yes	Yes	24	13	35	24	8	
Phelps	Unconditional Unionist	No	Yes	15	8	10	4	14	
F. Thomas	Unconditional Unionist	Absent	Yes	27	0	0	0	0	
Maynard	Unconditional Unionist	N/A	N/A	3	3	13	0	10	
Stokes	Unconditional Unionist	N/A	N/A	3	3	7	3	13	
Leftwich	Unconditional Unionist	N/A	N/A	0	0	0	0	0	
C. Hubbard	Unconditional Unionist	Yes	Yes	5	1	0	0	0	
Latham	Unconditional Unionist	No	Yes	22	11	11	4	22	
Whaley	Unconditional Unionist	No	Yes	14	2	2	0	1	
Nicholson	Democrat	No	No	10	8	0	0	0	
Ross	Democrat	No	No	24	0	1	1	1	
Thornton	Democrat	No	No	14	9	0	0	10	
Marshall	Democrat	No	No	44	10	5	3	6	
Niblack	Democrat	No	No	23	9	3	2	3	No
Kerr	Democrat	No	No	34	25	11	4	5	
Voorhees	Democrat	No	N/A	0	0	1	1	1	
Trimble	Democrat	No	No	14	11	2	2	10	
Ritter	Democrat	No	No	10	7	0	0	5	
Grider	Democrat	No	No	7	3	1	1	11	
Ab. Harding	Democrat	No	No	39	2	6	3	34	No
Shanklin	Democrat	No	Absent (No)	7	5	3	1	6	
McCullough	Democrat	No	Absent	1	0	0	0	0	
Harris	Democrat	Absent (No)	Absent	7	3	2	2	0	
Hogan	Democrat	No	No	25	10	4	0	9	No
Sitgreaves	Democrat	No	No	8	7	2	0	9	No
Rogers	Democrat	No	No	76	35	21	17	5	No
Wright	Democrat	No	No	25	4	0	0	10	No
Taber	Democrat	No	No	3	2	1	0	0	
Bergen	Democrat	No	No	11	0	1	0	0	
Jones	Democrat	Absent	Absent	0	0	0	0	0	

(continued)

Table A.3 (*continued*)

Name	Party	ExV[1]	14V[2]	Pages[3]	RP[4]	Rebel[5]	RebelP[6]	Loyal[7]	BLoyal[8]
Taylor	Democrat	No	No	17	3	1	0	1	
Chandler	Democrat	No	No	50	26	3	0	12	
Brooks	Democrat	No	N/A	32	4	1	1	1	
Radford	Democrat	No	Absent (No)	5	0	1	0	0	
Winfield	Democrat	Absent	No	4	0	1	1	0	
E. Hubbell	Democrat	Absent	No	2	0	00	0	0	
Goodyear	Democrat	No	Absent (No)	4	4	2	2	0	
J. M. Humphrey	Democrat	No	No	14	0	0	0	1	
Le Blond	Democrat	Absent (No)	No	41	19	4	1	5	
Finck	Democrat	No	No	30	19	2	2	6	
S. Randall	Democrat	No	No	51	15	27	11	22	
Boyer	Democrat	No	No	20	9	8	4	4	
Ancona	Democrat	Absent (No)	No	10	0	0	0	0	
Strouse	Democrat	No	No	10	2	4	1	4	
P. Johnson	Democrat	Absent (No)	Absent (No)	31	11	1	1	0	
Denison	Democrat	Absent	No	4	4	3	3	0	
Glossbrenner	Democrat	No	No	1	0	0	0	0	
Coffroth	Democrat	No	No	9	0	9	0	1	
Dawson	Democrat	No	No	9	6	2	0	4	
Eldredge	Democrat	No	No	24	14	20	14	10	
McLean[9]	Democrat	N/A	N/A	2	0	1	0	0	

Note: Tables A.1, A.2, A.3, and A.4 were compiled by hand using standards that were not perfectly consistent. While the tables support gross conclusions, minor differences are at least as likely to be caused by tabulation issues than reflect anything about the 39th Congress, 1st Session.

9. Samuel McLean was a nonvoting delegate from Montana Territory.

TABLE A.4: REFERENCES TO "REBEL" AND "LOYAL" IN THE SENATE

Name	Party	ExV	14V	Pages	RP	Rebel	RebelP	Loyal	BLoyal
Conness	Republican	Yes	Yes	166	14	10	9	22	
Foster	Republican	Yes	Yes	8	0	1	0	8	
J. Dixon	Republican	No	Absent	30	21	15	13	31	
Trumbull	Republican	Yes	Yes	263	103	116	54	133	Yes
Yates	Republican	Yes	Yes	31	14	36	29	13	Yes
H. Lane	Republican	Yes	Yes	35	13	86	71	18	Yes
Kirkwood	Republican	Yes	Yes	33	2	0	0	1	
Grimes	Republican	Yes	Yes	196	15	13	2	14	
S. Pomeroy	Republican	Yes	Yes	95	14	6	2	16	Yes
J. Lane	Republican	No	Yes	24	8	3	2	19	
Ross	Republican	N/A	N/A	0	0	0	0	0	
L. Morrill	Republican	Yes	Yes	99	18	9	5	2	
Fessenden	Republican	Yes	Yes	257	56	19	15	24	
Sumner	Republican	Yes	Yes	200	72	88	58	43	Yes
H. Wilson	Republican	Yes	Yes	160	35	154	108	105	
Chandler	Republican	Yes	Yes	57	1	8	0	0	
Howard	Republican	Absent (Yes)	Yes	137	31	116	60	57	
Ramsey	Republican	Yes	Yes	31	3	2	0	0	
Norton	Republican	No	No	8	1	1	0	0	
Jo. Henderson	Republican	Yes	Yes	161	42	66	46	75	
Brown	Republican	Yes	Absent	26	3	9	7	4	Yes
Stewart	Republican	No	Yes	92	39	27	18	107	Yes
Nye	Republican	Yes	Yes	79	18	33	20	48	Yes
Clark	Republican	Yes	Yes	118	17	79	57	58	Yes
Cragin	Republican	Yes	Yes	8	1	0	0	0	
Harris	Republican	Yes	Yes	47	0	5	1	1	
Morgan	Republican	No	Yes	13	0	3	1	2	
Wade	Republican	Yes	Yes	118	43	16	11	21	
Sherman	Republican	Yes	Yes	197	28	45	29	29	
G. Williams	Republican	Yes	Yes	89	23	68	44	32	Yes
Cowan	Republican	No	No	103	52	43	25	38	
Anthony	Republican	Yes	Yes	51	5	6	3	4	
Sprague	Republican	Yes	Yes	51	1	12	2	7	
Foot	Republican	Absent (Yes)	N/A	14	0	0	0	0	
Edmunds	Republican	N/A	Yes	75	9	4	3	12	
Poland	Republican	Yes	Yes	44	5	24[1]	10	35	
Willey	Republican	Yes	Yes	28	10	12	7	50	
Doolittle	Republican	No	No	165	54	50	4	26	
Howe	Republican	Yes	Yes	133	36	44	25	61	Yes
G. Davis	Unionist	No	No	164	78	45	15	23	No
Fowler	Unionist	N/A	N/A	1	1	0	0	0	
Creswell	Unconditional Unionist	Yes	Yes	39	13	9	5	9	
Van Winkle	Unconditional Unionist	No	No	40	8	2	2	3	
McDougall	Democrat	No	No	93	36	0	0	3	
Saulsbury	Democrat		No	95	43	5	3	6	

(continued)

Table A.4 (*continued*)

Name	Party	ExV	14V	Pages	RP	Rebel	RebelP	Loyal	BLoyal
Riddle	Democrat	No	No	10	0	1	0	0	
Hendricks	Democrat	No	No	221	64	9	7	12	
Guthrie	Democrat	No	No	74	17	12	11	6	
R. Johnson	Democrat	No	No	192	71	6	6	27	
Wright	Democrat	Absent	Absent	0	0	0	0	0	
Stockton	Democrat	No	N/A	0	0	0	0	0	
Nesmith	Democrat	No	Absent	48	6	15	8	8	
Buckalew	Democrat	No	Absent	39	19	0	0	3	

1. Poland's numbers are inflated by counting a committee report he read on Senator-elect Patterson that used "rebel" nine times, all referring to past activity.

TABLE A.5: REFERENCES PAIRED WITH "REBEL" IN THE THIRTY-NINTH CONGRESS, FIRST SESSION: ALL

	TYY-NY[1]	PYY-NY[2]	TYY[3]	PYY[4]	TNY[5]	PNY[6]	TNN[7]	PNN[8]
No. of Representatives	212		145		10		57	
(noun)	1123	663	876	539	57	25	190	99
states[9]	857	588[10]	757	530	19	8	81	50
army	177	14	120	13	17	0	39	1
debt[11]	165	154	115	109	25	22	25	23
government	50	4	41	3	2	0	7	1
soldiers	37	19	28	17	1	1	8	1
service	28	1	21	1	2	0	5	0
leaders	27	10	27	10	0	0	0	0
sympathizers	27	20	20	14	2	2	5	4
districts	25	15	22	13	1	0	2	2
confederacy[12]	21	0	18	0	0	0	3	0
prison[13]	20	1	19	1	0	0	1	0
forces[14]	20	1	14	1	3	0	3	0
authorities	18	6	14	6	1	0	3	0
communities	17	10	16	9	0	0	1	1
unrepentant rebel	16	16	16	16	0	0	0	0
legislature	16	8	13	8	3	0	0	0
element	15	13	13	12	2	1	0	0
congress	15	1	13	1	0	0	2	0
general	14	6	13	6	0	0	1	0
white rebel[15]	13	13	13	13	0	0	0	0
side	13	2	7	2	0	0	6	0
reconstructed rebel	12	12	12	12	0	0	0	0
pardoned rebel[16]	11	10	9	8	0	0	2	2
armed rebel	11	2	6	2	3	0	2	0

1. Total uses of "rebel" by persons who voted for the Fourteenth Amendment. This table presumes that persons who were absent for one vote voted as they did in the other vote unless strong evidence exists to the contrary. Seven members of Congress were absent for both votes. Four members—N. Dixon, Culver, Jones, and Wright—did not speak during the First Session of the Thirty-Ninth Congress. I have classified Kasson, Blow, and Noell as Republicans who voted for the exclusion resolution and the Fourteenth amendment based on their speeches and, in Blow's case, his membership on the Joint Committee on Reconstruction.

2. Present uses of "rebel" by persons who voted for the Fourteenth Amendment.

3. Total uses of "rebel" by persons who voted for the Fourteenth Amendment and the exclusion resolution.

4. Present uses of "rebel" by persons who voted for the Fourteenth Amendment and the exclusion resolution.

5. Total uses of "rebel" by persons who did not vote for the exclusion resolution but did vote for the Fourteenth Amendment.

6. Present uses of "rebel" by persons who did not vote for the exclusion resolution but did vote for the Fourteenth Amendment.

7. Total uses of "rebel" for all who voted against the exclusion resolution and the Fourteenth Amendment.

8. Present uses of "rebel" for all who voted against the exclusion resolution and the Fourteenth Amendment.

(continued)

Table A.5 (*continued*)

	TYY-NY[1]	PYY-NY[2]	TYY[3]	PYY[4]	TNY[5]	PNY[6]	TNN[7]	PNN[8]
power	10	5	10	5	0	0	0	0
cause	10	3	6	3	0	0	4	0
population	9	9	9	9	0	0	0	0
defeated rebel[17]	9	9	8	8	1	1	0	0
master[18]	9	7	9	7	0	0	0	0
governor[19]	9	1	1	1	3	0	5	0
hordes	8	1	7	1	0	0	1	0
spirit	8	8	7	7	0	0	1	1
recent rebel	7	7	7	7	0	0	0	0
representatives	7	4	4	4	3	0	0	0
blood stained rebel	7	4	4	2	0	0	3	2
invasion	7	1	7	1	0	0	0	0
constituency	6	6	6	6	0	0	0	0
ex-vice president[20]	6	6	6	6	0	0	0	0
majority	6	6	6	6	0	0	0	0
returning rebel[21]	6	6	4	4	2	2	0	0
southern rebel	6	3	6	3	0	0	0	0
state governments	6	1	3	0	1	1	2	0
pirates	6	0	6	0	0	0	0	0
victories	6	0	6	0	0	0	0	0
conquered rebel	5	5	5	5	0	0	0	0
influence	5	5	5	5	0	0	0	0
Senators	5	5	5	5	0	0	0	0
territory	5	5	4	4	1	1	0	0
red-handed rebel	5	5	3	3	0	0	2	2
hands	5	4	5	4	0	0	0	0
neighbors	5	4	5	4	0	0	0	0
chiefs[22]	5	1	5	1	0	0	0	0
flag	5	1	5	1	0	0	0	0
lines	5	0	5	0	0	0	0	0
Morgan's men[23]	5	0	5	0	0	0	0	0
bayonets	5	0	2	0	0	0	3	0
class	4	4	4	4	0	0	0	0
Democratic rebel scheme	4	4	4	4	0	0	0	0
unpardoned	4	4	4	4	0	0	0	0
voluntary rebel	4	4	4	4	0	0	0	0
newspapers	4	3	3	2	0	0	1	1
vote	4	2	4	2	0	0	0	0
citizens	4	2	3	1	0	0	1	1
people	4	2	2	2	2	0	0	0
South Carolina rebel	4	2	2	2	2	0	0	0
laws	4	1	4	1	0	0	0	0
organization	4	1	4	1	0	0	0	0
portions	4	1	4	1	0	0	0	0
oaths	4	1	3	1	0	0	1	0
raiders	4	0	4	0	0	0	0	0
ranks	4	0	4	0				
war steamers[24]	4	0	4	0	0	0	0	0
Democratic rebel theory	3	3	3	3	0	0	0	0
end	3	3	3	3	0	0	0	0
leading rebel	3	3	3	3	0	0	0	0
militia	3	3	3	3	0	0	0	0

	TYY-NY[1]	PYY-NY[2]	TYY[3]	PYY[4]	TNY[5]	PNY[6]	TNN[7]	PNN[8]
owners	3	3	3	3	0	0	0	0
section	3	3	3	3	0	0	0	0
friends	3	2	3	2	0	0	0	0
masses	3	2	3	2	0	0	0	0
traitor	3	2	2	1	0	0	1	1
capital	3	1	3	1	0	0	0	0
conquered rebel	3	1	3	1	0	0	0	0
officer	3	1	3	1	0	0	0	0
party	3	1	3	1	0	0	0	0
slaveholders	3	1	3	1	0	0	0	0
dead	3	1	2	1	1	0	0	0
arms	3	1	2	1	0	0	1	0
official	3	1	1	1	0	0	2	0
hosts	3	0	3	0	0	0	0	0
piratical vessel	3	0	3	0	0	0	0	0
portion	3	0	3	0	0	0	0	0
ship (named)	3	0	3	0	0	0	0	0
emissaries	3	0	2	0	0	0	1	0
defiant rebel	2	2	2	2	0	0	0	0
disenfranchised rebel	2	2	2	2	0	0	0	0
guilty rebel	2	2	2	2	0	0	0	0
journals	2	2	2	2	0	0	0	0
mob	2	2	2	2	0	0	0	0
music/song	2	2	2	2	0	0	0	0
presses	2	2	2	2	0	0	0	0
repentant rebel[25]	2	2	2	2	0	0	0	0
rule	2	2	2	2	0	0	0	0
speculators	2	2	2	2	0	0	0	0
white-washed rebel	2	2	2	2	0	0	0	0
whites[26]	2	2	1	1	0	0	1	1
allies/alliances	2	1	2	1	0	0	0	0
camps	2	1	2	1	0	0	0	0
country	2	1	2	1	0	0	0	0
enemy	2	1	2	1	0	0	0	0
port	2	1	2	1	0	0	0	0
man[27]	2	1	1	1	0	0	1	0
archives	2	0	2	0	0	0	0	0
belligerent	2	0	2	0	0	0	0	0
cannon	2	0	2	0	0	0	0	0
conscription	2	0	2	0	0	0	0	0
conspirators	2	0	2	0	0	0	0	0
constitution	2	0	2	0	0	0	0	0
control	2	0	2	0	0	0	0	0
General Pickett and Hoke	2	0	2	0	0	0	0	0
judiciary	2	0	2	0	0	0	0	0
pirate Shenandoah	2	0	2	0	0	0	0	0
property	2	0	2	0	0	0	0	0
slavery	2	0	2	0	0	0	0	0
senate	2	0	2	0	0	0	0	0
spy	2	0	2	0	0	0	0	0
raid	2	0	1	0	0	0	1	0
troops	2	0	1	0	0	0	1	0
martial law	2	0	0	0	0	0	2	0

(continued)

Table A.5 (*continued*)

	TYY-NY[1]	PYY-NY[2]	TYY[3]	PYY[4]	TNY[5]	PNY[6]	TNN[7]	PNN[8]
aristocracy	1	1	1	1	0	0	0	0
armed and hostile rebel	1	1	1	1	0	0	0	0
barbarism	1	1	1	1	0	0	0	0
bayonets and fortifications	1	1	1	1	0	0	0	0
bitter rebel	1	1	1	1	0	0	0	0
brethren	1	1	1	1	0	0	0	0
celebrities	1	1	1	1	0	0	0	0
column	1	1	1	1	0	0	0	0
conquered rebel	1	1	1	1	0	0	0	0
cotton	1	1	1	1	0	0	0	0
cruel rebel	1	1	1	1	0	0	0	0
delegation	1	1	1	1	0	0	0	0
domestic rebel	1	1	1	1	0	0	0	0
encouraged rebel	1	1	1	1	0	0	0	0
estates	1	1	1	1	0	0	0	0
fallen rebel	1	1	1	1	0	0	0	0
flagitious rebel	1	1	1	1	0	0	0	0
flame	1	1	1	1	0	0	0	0
General Hampton	1	1	1	1	0	0	0	0
hearts	1	1	1	1	0	0	0	0
heresy	1	1	1	1	0	0	0	0
impatient rebel	1	1	1	1	0	0	0	0
impenitent rebel	1	1	1	1	0	0	0	0
inhabitants	1	1	1	1	0	0	0	0
incensed rebel	1	1	1	1	0	0	0	0
infuriate rebel	1	1	1	1	0	0	0	0
in-heart	1	1	1	1	0	0	0	0
interest	1	1	1	1	0	0	0	0
inveterate rebel	1	1	1	1	0	0	0	0
Jefferson Davis	1	1	1	1	0	0	0	0
memories	1	1	1	1	0	0	0	0
oppressors	1	1	1	1	0	0	0	0
outbreaks	1	1	1	1	0	0	0	0
persecuting rebel	1	1	1	1	0	0	0	0
plowman	1	1	1	1	0	0	0	0
policy	1	1	1	1	0	0	0	0
prodigal rebel	1	1	1	1	0	0	0	0
rapacity	1	1	1	1	0	0	0	0
rebel constitutions or states	1	1	1	1	0	0	0	0
South Carolina	1	1	1	1	0	0	0	0
rebellious person	1	1	1	1	0	0	0	0
Rebellious power of slavery	1	1	1	1	0	0	0	0
reeking rebel	1	1	1	1	0	0	0	0
rights	1	1	1	1	0	0	0	0
rubbish	1	1	1	1	0	0	0	0
Secretary of the Treasury	1	1	1	1	0	0	0	0
Secretary of War	1	1	1	1	0	0	0	0
Semmes	1	1	1	1	0	0	0	0
sentiments	1	1	1	1	0	0	0	0

	TYY-NY[1]	PYY-NY[2]	TYY[3]	PYY[4]	TNY[5]	PNY[6]	TNN[7]	PNN[8]
sequestration	1	1	1	1	0	0	0	0
sheriff	1	1	1	1	0	0	0	0
South	1	1	1	1	0	0	0	0
spectre	1	1	1	1	0	0	0	0
Spratt	1	1	1	1	0	0	0	0
sources	1	1	1	1	0	0	0	0
state forces	1	1	1	1	0	0	0	0
state legislature	1	1	1	1	0	0	0	0
supremacy	1	1	1	1	0	0	0	0
surrender	1	1	1	1	0	0	0	0
sympathizing England	1	1	1	1	0	0	0	0
Texas	1	1	1	1	0	0	0	0
torpedo[28]	1	1	1	1	0	0	0	0
trophies	1	1	1	1	0	0	0	0
tyranny	1	1	1	1	0	0	0	0
unamnestied rebel	1	1	1	1	0	0	0	0
uniform	1	1	1	1	0	0	0	0
United States judge	1	1	1	1	0	0	0	0
unrelenting rebel	1	1	1	1	0	0	0	0
valor	1	1	1	1	0	0	0	0
vanquished rebel	1	1	1	1	0	0	0	0
vilest rebel	1	1	1	1	0	0	0	0
Virginia	1	1	1	1	0	0	0	0
violent	1	1	1	1	0	0	0	0
violence	1	1	1	1	0	0	0	0
white voters	1	1	1	1	0	0	0	0
wounded rebel	1	1	1	1	0	0	0	0
yoke	1	1	1	1	0	0	0	0
black (race) rebel	1	1	0	0	0	0	1	1
letters	1	1	0	0	0	0	1	1
utterances	1	1	0	0	0	0	1	1
act	1	0	1	0	0	0	0	0
agent	1	0	1	0	0	0	0	0
allegiance	1	0	1	0	0	0	0	0
apologist	1	0	1	0	0	0	0	0
aristocratic rebel	1	0	1	0	0	0	0	0
arrant rebel	1	0	1	0	0	0	0	0
bands	1	0	1	0	0	0	0	0
barbarous rebel	1	0	1	0	0	0	0	0
brawl	1	0	1	0	0	0	0	0
bullets	1	0	1	0	0	0	0	0
center	1	0	1	0	0	0	0	0
commission	1	0	1	0	0	0	0	0
competitor	1	0	1	0	0	0	0	0
city	1	0	1	0	0	0	0	0
coast	1	0	1	0	0	0	0	0
collector	1	0	1	0	0	0	0	0
craft	1	0	1	0	0	0	0	0
cruisers	1	0	1	0	0	0	0	0
currency	1	0	1	0	0	0	0	0
defeated rebel	1	0	1	0	0	0	0	0
defeats	1	0	1	0	0	0	0	0
domination	1	0	1	0	0	0	0	0
fighting rebel	1	0	1	0	0	0	0	0

(continued)

Table A.5 (*continued*)

	TYY-NY[1]	PYY-NY[2]	TYY[3]	PYY[4]	TNY[5]	PNY[6]	TNN[7]	PNN[8]
General Sterling Price	1	0	1	0	0	0	0	0
General Thomas	1	0	1	0	0	0	0	0
Gibraltar-Vicksburg	1	0	1	0	0	0	0	0
graves	1	0	1	0	0	0	0	0
guiltiest rebel	1	0	1	0	0	0	0	0
gun	1	0	1	0	0	0	0	0
heroes	1	0	1	0	0	0	0	0
hope	1	0	1	0	0	0	0	0
ladies	1	0	1	0	0	0	0	0
legions	1	0	1	0	0	0	0	0
magazines (military)	1	0	1	0	0	0	0	0
major	1	0	1	0	0	0	0	0
military movement	1	0	1	0	0	0	0	0
military organization	1	0	1	0	0	0	0	0
military role	1	0	1	0	0	0	0	0
oppression	1	0	1	0	0	0	0	0
orders	1	0	1	0	0	0	0	0
ordinance of secession	1	0	1	0	0	0	0	0
pay	1	0	1	0	0	0	0	0
persecution	1	0	1	0	0	0	0	0
pillage	1	0	1	0	0	0	0	0
programme	1	0	1	0	0	0	0	0
prisoner	1	0	1	0	0	0	0	0
rag (military)	1	0	1	0	0	0	0	0
revolutionary rebel	1	0	1	0	0	0	0	0
shout	1	0	1	0	0	0	0	0
sovereignty	1	0	1	0	0	0	0	0
spirits	1	0	1	0	0	0	0	0
straps	1	0	1	0	0	0	0	0
supplies	1	0	1	0	0	0	0	0
triggers	1	0	1	0	0	0	0	0
volunteers	1	0	1	0	0	0	0	0
war	1	0	1	0	0	0	0	0
wife	1	0	1	0	0	0	0	0
willful rebel	1	0	1	0	0	0	0	0
educated rebel	1	0	0	0	1	0	0	0
powers	1	0	0	0	1	0	0	0
privateer Florida	1	0	0	0	1	0	0	0
surgeon	1	0	0	0	1	0	0	0
armed and organized rebel	1	0	0	0	0	0	1	0
candidate	1	0	0	0	0	0	1	0
fierce rebel	1	0	0	0	0	0	1	0
fort	1	0	0	0	0	0	1	0
invading rebel	1	0	0	0	0	0	1	0
military despotism	1	0	0	0	0	0	1	0
military power	1	0	0	0	0	0	1	0
Secretary Benjamin	1	0	0	0	0	0	1	0
scrapes	1	0	0	0	0	0	1	0
sharpshooters	1	0	0	0	0	0	1	0
shot	1	0	0	0	0	0	1	0
troops	1	0	0	0	0	0	1	0

9. Includes "rebellious states."
10. "late rebel states" counted as reference to the past.
11. Includes "war debt" and "debtor."
12. Includes "rebel confederation."
13. Includes "prison-pen."
14. Includes "rebel armed forces" and "rebel military forces."
15. Includes "rebel white man" and "rebel white people."
16. Includes "amnestied rebel" and "restored rebel."
17. Includes "subdued rebel."
18. Includes "rebel slave-masters."
19. Includes "rebel Governor of Tennessee."
20. Includes "vice president."
21. Includes "returned rebel."
22. Includes chieftains.
23. Includes "John Morgan" and "Morgan."
24. Includes "rebel steamer Florida."
25. Includes "repenting."
26. Includes "white citizens."
27. Includes "men."
28. Used as a metaphor.

	Total	PTotal	TRNN[1]	PRNN[2]	TUNN[3]	PUNN[4]	TDNN[5]	TDNN[6]
No. of Representatives	57		4		2		51	
(noun)	190	99	94	40	86	57	10	2
states	81	50	35	23	46	27	0	0
army	39	1	18	1	20	0	1	0
debt	25	23	6	4	19	19	0	0
soldiers	8	1	2	0	4	1	2	0
government	6	1	2	0	4	1	0	0
sympathizers	5	4	0	0	4	4	1	0
side	6	0	6	0	0	0	0	0
governor	5	0	5	0	0	0	0	0
service	5	0	5	0	0	0	0	0
cause	4	0	2	0	1	0	1	0
blood-stained rebel	3	2	0	0	2	2	1	0
authorities	3	0	1	0	1	0	1	0
bayonets	3	0	0	0	0	0	3	0
confederacy	3	0	3	0	0	0	0	0
forces	3	0	0	0	3	0	0	0
districts	2	2	1	1	1	1	0	0
pardoned rebel	2	2	0	0	2	2	0	0
red-handed rebel	2	2	0	0	2	2	0	0
armed rebel	2	0	1	0	1	0	0	0
congress	2	0	2	0	0	0	0	0
martial law	2	0	2	0	0	0	0	0
official	2	0	2	0	0	0	0	0
state government	2	0	0	0	2	0	0	0
communities	1	1	1	1				
citizens	1	1			1	1		
letters	1	1	0	0	1	1	0	0
spirit	1	1	0	0	1	1	0	0
traitors	1	1	0	0	1	1	0	0
utterances	1	1	0	0	1	1	0	0
whites	1	1	0	0	1	1	0	0
newspapers	1	1	0	0	0	0	1	1
emissaries	1	0	1	0	0	0	0	0
general	1	0	1	0	0	0	0	0
man	1	0	1	0	0	0	0	0
military despotism	1	0	1	0	0	0	0	0
arms	1	0	0	0	1	0	0	0
fierce rebel	1	0	0	0	1	0	0	0
fort	1	0	0	0	1	0	0	0
hordes	1	0	0	0	1	0	0	0
invading rebel	1	0	0	0	1	0	0	0
prison	1	0	0	0	1	0	0	0
raid	1	0	0	0	1	0	0	0
sharpshooters	1	0	0	0	1	0	0	0
shot	1	0	0	0	1	0	0	0
armed and organized rebel	1	0	0	0	0	0	1	0

	Total	PTotal	TRNN[1]	PRNN[2]	TUNN[3]	PUNN[4]	TDNN[5]	TDNN[6]
candidate	1	0	0	0	0	0	1	0
military power	1	0	0	0	0	0	1	0
oaths	1	0	0	0	0	0	1	0
Secretary Benjamin	1	0	0	0	0	0	1	0
sway	1	0	0	0	0	0	1	0
troops	1	0	0	0	0	0	1	0

1. Total uses of "rebel" for Republicans who voted against the exclusion resolution and the Fourteenth Amendment.

2. Present uses of "rebel" for Republicans who voted against the exclusion resolution and the Fourteenth Amendment.

3. Total uses of "rebel" for Unionists and unconditional Unionists who voted against the exclusion resolution and Fourteenth Amendment.

4. Present uses of "rebel" for Unionists and unconditional Unionists who voted against the exclusion resolution and the Fourteenth Amendment.

5. Total uses of "rebel" for Democrats who voted against the exclusion resolution and the Fourteenth Amendment.

6. Present uses of "rebel" for Democrats who voted against the exclusion resolution and the Fourteenth Amendment.

TABLE A.7: CONDITIONS FOR READMISSION OF FORMER CONFEDERATE STATES: MEMBERS OF CONGRESS

(continued)

	AS[1]	RD[2]	ND[3]	CP[4]	EP[5]	AP[6]	BV[7]	BO[8]	DE[9]	RD[10]	XD[11]	Other
Sumner[12]	i	iii	iii									iv: Education
J. Ashley[13]	i, iv, v						ii	v		ii		iii: pensions for soldiers
Stevens[14]	iii	3–4	3–4							5	3–4	iv: freedom of religion
Bingham[15]		1	2		2	1					2	
Price[16]		1	2	3	?							
Stillwell[17]	I	ii								iv		iii: Ratify 13
Spalding[18]	3	4	4			2	1[19]	5				
Shellabarger[20]												1
Howe[21]	1,3	5	6							7	2	6: peace / 8: loyalty / 9: rights of Union men
Conkling[22]	1	2				4		5		3		
Deming[23]	1	4	3				2			2		
Stewart (1/26)[24]								2		1		
Baker[25]	1	2				3		4		5		
Broomall[26]	1	2				5	4[27]	2				iii: ratify 13
Garfield[28]						3				1		
J. Hubbell[29]						1				2		
W. Lawrence[30]	1	3	5	4		2		2			6	5: duty to union soldiers / 7: education
Welker[31]	2	2	4			1	6[32]	5		3		

1. Proposals to ban secession.
2. Proposals to ban payment of the Confederate/rebel debt.
3. Proposals to mandate payment of the national debt.
4. Proposals to ban compensation for emancipated slaves.
5. Proposals to repeal the constitutional ban on export taxes.
6. Proposals to change the constitutional rules for apportioning representatives between the states.
7. Proponents to ban race discrimination in voting.
8. Proponents to ban some former Confederates from holding office.
9. Proposals to disenfranchise some former Confederates.
10. Proposals to ban race discrimination.
11. Proposals to ban discrimination.

Table A.7 (*continued*)

	AS[1]	RD[2]	ND[3]	CP[4]	EP[5]	AP[6]	BV[7]	BO[8]	DE[9]	RD[10]	XD[11]	Other
H. Lane[34]		2	2				1			4		**3: empower Congress** 5: suffrage in DC
Delano[35]								ii		i		
Ward[36]				3			2			1		
T. Williams[37]			2							1		
G. Williams[38]		iii	iv			1		ii		iii		
Newell[39]							*1*	5		2		
Defrees[40]						1		3		2		
Cook[41]		1				2				3		
W. Lawrence[42]	2	3				4				6		1: ratify 13 5: change rule for direct taxes
Cullom[43]						2				*1*		
H. Wilson[44]	ii	4								5		**I: ban slavery** iii: ratify 13
R. Clarke[45]	1	4	3		5	2						
Beaman[46]												1: unspecified "guarantee for future good conduct" **iii: prohibit slavery** i: ratify 13 and **prohibit slavery**
J. Lane[47]	I	iii								iv		
Sherman[48]		iii				5		iii		iv		
Stewart (3/1)[49]		1?				2?		3+				
McKee[50]		X						1				
Loan[51]							2	1				
Kuykendall[52]	*1*							3		2		
J. Ashley[53]		3		3				*1*; i		2		
Orth[54]		1				2		3				
D. Ashley[55]		2		4		1	X	3	3			
Holmes[56]	4	3	2			5		1		6		**3: no pensions to rebels**

		ii	iii		iv		X	i	iv	5
Stewart 3/16[57]	I	ii								
Dumont[58]		ii	?		1		X	5	2	5?
Anderson[59]	1	4			2		X?	X?	2	X?
Moulton[60]		3		3	4	X				5
Myers[61]					4		X			
Buckland[62]		3	X	4	X					
Hart[63]		4?		2	2				1	
Stewart (4/4)[64]	I	2 iii	2		1	1		1	1	
J. Lane[65]		iii		iv	v		v	1		
Baldwin[66]					1					
W. Lawrence[67]										
R. Clarke[68]	4	1	2	3	v	2	1	v	1	
Perham[69]	4	3	3	3	2		2	1	2	
Miller[70]		2		3	1					
J. L. Thomas[71]		3		1	1		2	2		
Smith[72]		1					2	1		
Shellabarger[73]							1			
Scofield[74]	3	2		1						
Moorhead[75]		2	4		1			1	1	1
G. Lawrence[76]		3		1	1		2	4		
Ingersoll[77]		1	2		3		2			1
H. Wilson[78]		1						1		1
Morris[79]										
Patterson[80]		2		3	3	2?	2			
J. Ashley[81]		4	4	3	2	6	1			

iii: no slavery

1: No slavery in form

1: protect former soldiers and their families
2: protect loyal people in rebel states
3/3: Protect rights in all states
3: republican government

ii: prohibit slavery

V: republican government

4: no pensions to rebels

2: republican government

5: Empower Congress

(continued)

Note: Numbers are in the order the proposal was made. Arabic numerals: proposal for federal reform. Roman numerals: proposal for state reform. Bold numerals: proposal for constitutional reform. Italic numerals: proposal for legislation. Neither bold nor italic: unclear whether constitutional reform or legislation. X: proposal explicitly rejected.

12. *Congressional Globe*, 39th Cong., 1st Sess., 1251. See also *Congressional Globe*, 1224 (listing bans on officeholding and voting rights as conditions of readmission).

13. H.R. No. 54, 39th Cong., 1st Sess., 7–8.

14. *Congressional Globe*, 39th Cong., 1st Sess., 10, 72–75. Stevens on March 10 added a constitutional amendment forbidding repudiation of the national debt to his original proposal and changed the order of amendments slightly. Stevens repeated this list on March 10, more clearly placing financial guarantees third and rights guarantees fourth.

15. *Congressional Globe*, 39th Cong., 1st Sess., 157–158. Bingham proposed an amendment permitting Congress to tax exports on December 6 (*Congressional* Globe, 39th Cong., 1st Sess., 14) but did not mention that proposal when on January 9 he elaborated conditions for restoration.

16. *Congressional Globe*, 39th Cong., 1st Sess., 69.

17. *Congressional Globe*, 39th Cong., 1st Sess., 71, 669.

18. *Congressional Globe*, 39th Cong., 1st Sess., 133.

19. District of Columbia only.

20. *Congressional Globe*, 39th Cong., 1st Sess., 145 (demanding without specification "irreversible guarantees for the rights" of American citizens of every race and condition").

21. *Congressional Globe*, 39th Cong., 1st Sess., 170 (stated as reasons for exclusion rather than conditions for admission).

22. *Congressional Globe*, 39th Cong., 1st Sess., 252.

23. *Congressional Globe*, 39th Cong., 1st Sess., 331 (Deming indicated that a constitutional amendment would be necessary if Congress could not pass legislation mandating "the equality of the freedman, before both civil and criminal law").

24. *Congressional Globe*, 39th Cong., 1st Sess., 445.

25. *Congressional Globe*, 39th Cong., 1st Sess., 462–464.

26. *Congressional Globe*, 39th Cong., 1st Sess., 468–470.

27. In the South only.

28. *Congressional Globe*, 39th Cong., 1st Sess., App., 67–68.

29. *Congressional Globe*, 39th Cong., 1st Sess., 662.

30. *Congressional Globe*, 39th Cong., 1st Sess., 667.

31. *Congressional Globe*, 39th Cong., 1st Sess., 727–728.

32. Soldiers only.

33. *Congressional Globe*, 39th Cong., 1st Sess., 732–733 (Kelso called for confiscation of rebel property to cover the national war debt and would limit black suffrage to former Confederate states)

34. *Congressional Globe*, 39th Cong., 1st Sess., 740–742.

35. *Congressional Globe*, 39th Cong., 1st Sess., 90–91.

36. *Congressional Globe*, 39th Cong., 1st Sess., 783.

37. *Congressional Globe*, 39th Cong., 1st Sess., 911.

38. *Congressional Globe*, 39th Cong., 1st Sess., App., 96–97 (G. Williams did not indicate whether state reform would be sufficient for states other than Tennessee and Arkansas, which had substantial populations that remained loyal during the Civil War).

39. *Congressional Globe*, 39th Cong., 1st Sess., 867–868.

40. *Congressional Globe*, 39th Cong., 1st Sess., 872.

41. *Congressional Globe*, 39th Cong., 1st Sess., 903.

42. *Congressional Globe*, 39th Cong., 1st Sess., 909.

43. *Congressional Globe*, 39th Cong., 1st Sess., 910–912.

44. *Congressional Globe*, 39th Cong., 1st Sess., 931.

45. *Congressional Globe*, 39th Cong., 1st Sess., 1010 (R. Clarke also favored civil rights legislation and maintaining the test oath but did not specifically include those proposals when listing conditions for readmission).

46. *Congressional Globe*, 39th Cong., 1st Sess., 1016.

47. *Congressional Globe*, 39th Cong., 1st Sess., 1026 (J. Lane set out these conditions when discussing whether senators from Arkansas should be seated)

48. *Congressional Globe*, 39th Cong., 1st Sess., App. pp, 127, 131–132.

49. *Congressional Globe*, 39th Cong., 1st Sess., 1103–1105 (Stewart recommended but did not demand constitutional amendments on the Confederate debt and apportionment).

50. *Congressional Globe*, 39th Cong., 1st Sess., 1162–1165.

51. *Congressional Globe*, 39th Cong., 1st Sess., App., 143–145 (Loan insisted that Confederate debts be repudiated before explicitly listing conditions for readmission).

52. *Congressional Globe*, 39th Cong., 1st Sess., 1171–1172.

53. *Congressional Globe*, 39th Cong., 1st Sess., 1189 (J. Ashley called for federal legislation and state constitutional provisions prohibiting race discrimination).

54. *Congressional Globe*, 39th Cong., 1st Sess., 1307.

55. *Congressional Globe*, 39th Cong., 1st Sess., 1314, 1316.

56. *Congressional Globe*, 39th Cong., 1st Sess., 1318–1319.

57. *Congressional Globe*, 39th Cong., 1st Sess., 1437.

58. *Congressional Globe*, 39th Cong., 1st Sess., 1476.

59. *Congressional Globe*, 39th Cong., 1st Sess., 1479. Anderson claimed to support Stewart's call for "universal amnesty and universal suffrage," but his speech explicitly indicated support only for "restricted negro suffrage." *Congressional Globe*, 39th Cong., 1st Sess., 1479.

60. *Congressional Globe*, 39th Cong., 1st Sess., 1618. The antisecession amendment focused on the punishment for treason.

61. *Congressional Globe*, 39th Cong., 1st Sess., 1619, 1622–1623.

62. *Congressional Globe*, 39th Cong., 1st Sess., 1627. Buckland thought unnecessary constitutional or statutory provisions prohibiting payment for emancipated slaves.

63. *Congressional Globe*, 39th Cong., 1st Sess., 1628–1630. Hart rejected constitutional amendments to protect "the rights of the freedmen" and "to repudiate the rebel debt" as impossible to obtain. He called for congressional action on the rights of freedmen but did not discuss legislature on financial guarantees.

64. *Congressional Globe*, 39th Cong., 1st Sess., 1754.

65. *Congressional Globe*, 39th Cong., 1st Sess., 1799 (but property limits on persons of color not applied to white persons).

66. *Congressional Globe*, 39th Cong., 1st Sess., 1828.

67. *Congressional Globe*, 39th Cong., 1st Sess., 1835–1836.

68. *Congressional Globe*, 39th Cong., 1st Sess., 1840.

69. *Congressional Globe*, 39th Cong., 1st Sess., 2084–2085.

70. *Congressional Globe*, 39th Cong., 1st Sess., 2089. Miller repeated his claim that the apportionment, rebel debt, and export tax amendments were the only guarantees necessary during the debate over the omnibus Fourteenth Amendment. *Congressional Globe*, 39th Cong., 1st Sess., 2511.

71. *Congressional Globe*, 39th Cong., 1st Sess., 2094.

72. *Congressional Globe*, 39th Cong., 1st Sess., 2097.

73. *Congressional Globe*, 39th Cong., 1st Sess., 2102.

74. *Congressional Globe*, 39th Cong., 1st Sess., 2248.

75. *Congressional Globe*, 39th Cong., 1st Sess., 2256.

76. *Congressional Globe*, 39th Cong., 1st Sess., App., 203–204.

77. *Congressional Globe*, 39th Cong., 1st Sess., 2406.

78. *Congressional Globe*, 39th Cong., 1st Sess., 2488.

79. *Congressional Globe*, 39th Cong., 1st Sess., 2691.

80. *Congressional Globe*, 39th Cong., 1st Sess., 2692. Patterson would either grant persons of color voting rights or disenfranchise "the disloyal."

81. *Congressional Globe*, 39th Cong., 1st Sess., 2879. Ashley proposed a modified version of the Joint Committee's recommended omnibus that included the Privileges and Immunities, Due Process, and Equal Protection Clauses.

TABLE A.8: CONDITIONS FOR READMISSION OF FORMER CONFEDERATE STATES: PETITIONS

(continued)

	AS[1]	RD[2]	ND[3]	CP[4]	EP[5]	AP[6]	BV[7]	BO[8]	DE[9]	RD[10]	XD[11]	Other
Vermont Legislature[12]	1						1			1		
Citizens of Massachusetts[13]		4	3				2			1	2	5: Education
Puritan Church, NY[14]							1			1		
Citizens of Washington, DC[15]		3		3								
Citizens of Michigan[16]	1	3		4		2				4		5: Congress enforces
African Episcopal, Methodist, MO[17]							1			1		"adequate security"
Citizens of Will County, IL[18]							1					1: citizenship
Citizens of Wisconsin[19]							3			2		4: Freedmen's Bureau; 5: education
Citizens of Connecticut[20]	1	3				2				4		"adequate security"
Citizens of Massachusetts[21]		1								2		3: unspecified constitutional amendments
Citizens of Harris County, IN[22]	1	2										"sufficient security"
Citizens of Muscatine County, IA[23]	1	3				2				4		
Citizens of Buffalo, NY[24]	1	3		3		2				4		
Citizens of Indiana and Ohio[25]		3		3		2				4		
Citizens of Michigan[26]	1	3		3		2				4		
500 "Colored" Soldiers[27]							2			1		
Citizens of New York[28]							1			1		1: secure republican government; 2: unspecified
Citizens of Portland, ME[29]		2		6		4			2: in DC	3		1,3,5 . . . : unspecified
Union League Club, NYC[30]						5		1		3	4	2: unspecified

1. Proposals to ban secession.
2. Proposals to ban payment of the Confederate/rebel debt.
3. Proposals to mandate payment of the national debt.
4. Proposals to ban compensation for emancipated slaves.
5. Proposals to repeal the constitutional ban on export taxes.
6. Proposals to change the constitutional rules for apportioning representatives between the states.
7. Proponents to ban race discrimination in voting.
8. Proponents to ban some former Confederates from holding office.
9. Proposals to disenfranchise some former Confederates.
10. Proposals to ban race discrimination.
11. Proposals to ban discrimination.

Table A.8 (continued)

	AS[1]	RD[2]	ND[3]	CP[4]	EP[5]	AP[6]	BV[7]	BO[8]	DE[9]	RD[10]	XD[11]	Other
Citizens of Defiance County, OH[32]	1											2: unspecified
Citizens of Hendricks County, IN[33]												2: traitors be punished
Citizens of Mahoning County, OH[34]	1	2					3			1		
Citizens of Windsor, VT[35]	1							1		2		
Citizens of Burke, VT[36]	1											Adequate security against secession
Citizens of 3rd Cong. Dist., IL[37]	1											
Citizens of Huron and Erie Counties, OH[38]	3: adequate security	5	6				4			2: DC	**6: Rebel states**	7: Congress enforces
Citizens of Illinois[39]	1: adequate security											
Citizens of Wisconsin[40]			1							1		"permanent guarantees for future security"
Union Party, IN[41]	i	ii						2				1: proof of loyalty; iii: ratify 13
Union Members, OH Legislature[42]										5		
Citizens of Ohio[43]	1	3	4			2	4			4		5: Congress enforces
Citizens of the US[44]												
Citizens of Chester County, PA[45]										2		**1: Adequate security**; **1: Punish treason, reward loyalty**
Citizens of Byberry Township, PA[46]								1		2		**Punish treason, reward loyalty**
Citizens of Michigan[47]	1	3	4			2				4		**5: Congress enforces**
Citizens of St. Lawrence County, NY[48]						2	1					**"Proper guarantees"**
Citizens of Kenosha, WI[49]							1	2				"Punish treason,... reward loyalty"
Citizens of Essex County[50]							1					"Punish treason,... reward loyalty"
Citizens of Ohio, Indiana, Illinois, and Michigan[51]							1					
Citizens of Louisiana[52]							_1_					

12. *Congressional Globe*, 39th Cong., 1st Sess., 7.

13. *Congressional Globe*, 39th Cong., 1st Sess., 88.

14. *Congressional Globe*, 39th Cong., 1st Sess., 88.

15. *Congressional Globe*, 39th Cong., 1st Sess., 107.

16. *Congressional Globe*, 39th Cong., 1st Sess., 2.

17. *Congressional Globe*, 39th Cong., 1st Sess., 224.

18. *Congressional Globe*, 39th Cong., 1st Sess., 806.

19. *Congressional Globe*, 39th Cong., 1st Sess., 591.

20. *Congressional Globe*, 39th Cong., 1st Sess., 699.

21. *Congressional Globe*, 39th Cong., 1st Sess., 913.

22. *Congressional Globe*, 39th Cong., 1st Sess., 951.

23. *Congressional Globe*, 39th Cong., 1st Sess., 951.

24. *Congressional Globe*, 39th Cong., 1st Sess., 806.

25. *Congressional Globe*, 39th Cong., 1st Sess., 829.

26. *Congressional Globe*, 39th Cong., 1st Sess., 829.

27. *Congressional Globe*, 39th Cong., 1st Sess., 848.

28. *Congressional Globe*, 39th Cong., 913 (unclear whether call for "irreversible guarantees" refers to requested reforms or other specified constitutional amendments).

29. *Congressional Globe*, 39th Cong., 1st Sess., 913.

30. *Congressional Globe*, 39th Cong., 1st Sess., 930.

31. *Congressional Globe*, 39th Cong., 1st Sess., 931.

32. *Congressional Globe*, 39th Cong., 1st Sess., 978.

33. *Congressional Globe*, 39th Cong., 1st Sess., 1006.

34. *Congressional Globe*, 39th Cong., 1st Sess., 1006.

35. *Congressional Globe*, 39th Cong., 1st Sess., 1006.

36. *Congressional Globe*, 39th Cong., 1st Sess., 1006.

37. *Congressional Globe*, 39th Cong., 1st Sess., 1006.

38. *Congressional Globe*, 39th Cong., 1st Sess., 1024.

39. *Congressional Globe*, 39th Cong., 1st Sess., 1025.

40. *Congressional Globe*, 39th Cong., 1st Sess., 1025.

41. *Congressional Globe*, 39th Cong., 1st Sess., App. 132.

42. *Congressional Globe*, 39th Cong., 1st Sess., App. 132.

43. *Congressional Globe*, 39th Cong., 1st Sess., 1176–1177 (the petition also called for a legislative ban on race discrimination in Washington, D.C.).

44. *Congressional Globe*, 39th Cong., 1st Sess., 1177.

45. *Congressional Globe*, 39th Cong., 1st Sess., 1200.

46. *Congressional Globe*, 39th Cong., 1st Sess., 1200.

47. *Congressional Globe*, 39th Cong., 1st Sess., 1251.

48. *Congressional Globe*, 39th Cong., 1st Sess., 1251.

49. *Congressional Globe*, 39th Cong., 1st Sess., 1272.

50. *Congressional Globe*, 39th Cong., 1st Sess., 1272.

51. *Congressional Globe*, 39th Cong., 1st Sess., 1406.

52. *Congressional Globe*, 39th Cong., 1st Sess., 1706.

	Senate	House of Representatives
December 4	Protection of Freedmen	Southern representatives excluded Joint Committee approved
December 5	other business	other business
December 6	other business	other business
December 7	adjourned	adjourned
December 8	adjourned	adjourned
December 9	adjourned	adjourned
December 10	adjourned	adjourned
December 11	other business	Farnsworth constitutional amendment proposed Jenckes constitutional amendment proposed Delano constitutional amendment proposed Benjamin Export Tax amendment proposed Julian black suffrage in DC introduced
December 12	Joint Committee approved with revisions	other business
December 13	Protection of Freedmen	revised Joint Committee approved
December 14	other business	members of Joint Committee appointed
December 15	adjourned	adjourned
December 16	adjourned	adjourned
December 17	adjourned	adjourned
December 18	other business	Reconstruction
December 19	Johnson letter on Reconstruction	Debt constitutional amendment passed
December 20	Protection of Freedmen	other business
December 21	Protection of Freedmen Civil Rights Act introduced 2nd Freedmen's Bureau introduced	Reconstruction
December 22	adjourned	adjourned
December 23	adjourned	adjourned
December 24	adjourned	adjourned
December 25	adjourned	adjourned
December 26	adjourned	adjourned
December 27	adjourned	adjourned
December 28	adjourned	adjourned
December 29	adjourned	adjourned
December 30	adjourned	adjourned
December 31	adjourned	adjourned
January 1	adjourned	adjourned
January 2	adjourned	adjourned
January 3	adjourned	adjourned
January 4	adjourned	adjourned

	Senate	House of Representatives
January 5	2nd Freedmen's Bureau referred	Reconstruction Apportionment Amendment
January 6	adjourned	adjourned
January 7	adjourned	adjourned
January 8	other business	Reconstruction Apportionment Amendment
January 9	other business	Reconstruction
January 10	Provisional Governments introduced	other business
January 11	Provisional Governments Civil Rights Act reported 2nd Freedmen's Bureau reported	other business
January 12	Provisional Governments Colorado Civil Rights Act 2nd Freedmen's Bureau Bill	Colorado statehood
January 13	adjourned	adjourned
January 14	adjourned	adjourned
January 15	other business	other business
January 16	other business	Conkling resolutions on Reconstruction
January 17	Provisional Governments	other business
January 18	Provisional Governments 2nd Freedmen's Bureau	2nd Freedmen's Bureau
January 19	2nd Freedmen's Bureau	Reconstruction
January 20	Colorado statehood 2nd Freedmen's Bureau	adjourned
January 21	adjourned	adjourned
January 22	Apportionment Amendment 2nd Freedmen's Bureau	Apportionment Amendment J. Ashley Constitutional Amendment proposed
January 23	2nd Freedmen's Bureau	Apportionment Amendment
January 24	2nd Freedmen's Bureau	Apportionment Amendment
January 25	2nd Freedmen's Bureau passed	Apportionment Amendment
January 26	Reconstruction	Apportionment Amendment
January 27	adjourned	Reconstruction
January 28	adjourned	adjourned
January 29	Civil Rights Act	Apportionment Amendment
January 30	Civil Rights Act	Apportionment Amendment 2nd Freedmen's Bureau
January 31	Civil Rights Act	Apportionment Amendment passed
February 1	Civil Rights Act	2nd Freedmen's Bureau
February 2	Civil Rights Act passed	2nd Freedmen's Bureau
February 3	adjourned	2nd Freedmen's Bureau
February 4	adjourned	adjourned
February 5	Apportionment Amendment	2nd Freedman's Bureau Civil Rights Act Reconstruction
February 6	Apportionment Amendment	2nd Freedman's Bureau passed with revisions
February 7	Debt Amendment referred Apportionment Amendment	Reconstruction
February 8	Apportionment Amendment 2nd Freedman's Bureau passed with more revisions	other business

(continued)

Calendar (*continued*)

	Senate	House of Representatives
February 9	Apportionment Amendment	Revised Second Freedman's Bureau passed
February 10	adjourned	Reconstruction
February 11	adjourned	adjourned
February 12	other business	other business
February 13	Bingham Rights Amendment Apportionment Amendment	other business
February 14	Apportionment Amendment	other business
February 15	Apportionment Amendment	Reconstruction
February 16	Apportionment Amendment	other business
February 17	adjourned	Reconstruction
February 18	adjourned	adjourned
February 19	Apportionment Amendment 2nd Freedmen's Bureau veto	Reconstruction Resolutions
February 20	Exclusion Resolution 2nd Freedmen's Bureau veto not over-ridden	Exclusion Resolution passed
February 21	Exclusion Resolution Apportionment Amendment	other business
February 22	adjourned	adjourned
February 23	Exclusion Resolution	other business
February 24	adjourned	Reconstruction
February 25	adjourned	adjourned
February 26	Exclusion Resolution	Bingham Rights Amendment
February 27	Exclusion Resolution	Bingham Rights Amendment
February 28	Exclusion Resolution	Bingham Rights Amendment postponed
March 1	Exclusion Resolution	Civil Rights Act
March 2	Exclusion Resolution passed	Civil Rights Act
March 3	adjourned	Reconstruction
March 4	adjourned	adjourned
March 5	Apportionment Resolution	Tennessee Resolution
March 6	Apportionment Resolution	other business
March 7	Apportionment Resolution	other business
March 8	Apportionment Resolution	Civil Rights Act
March 9	Apportionment Resolution rejected	Civil Rights Act
March 10	adjourned	Reconstruction
March 11	adjourned	adjourned
March 12	Apportionment Amendments proposed Colorado statehood	other business
March 13	Colorado statehood rejected	Civil Rights Act passed with revisions
March 14	other business	other business
March 15	Revised Civil Rights Act passed	other business
March 16	Stewart Resolution on voting rights	other business
March 17	adjourned	Reconstruction
March 18	adjourned	adjourned
March 19	other business	other business
March 20	other business	other business
March 21	other business	other business
March 22	other business	other business
March 23	other business	other business
March 24	adjourned	Reconstruction
March 25	adjourned	adjourned
March 26	other business	other business

	Senate	House of Representatives
March 27	Civil Rights Act veto	other business
March 28	adjourned	other business
March 29	adjourned	other business
March 30	adjourned	adjourned
March 31	adjourned	adjourned
April 1	adjourned	adjourned
April 2	other business	other business
April 3	other business	other business
April 4	Civil Rights Act veto override	other business
April 5	Civil Rights Act veto override	other business
April 6	Civil Rights Act veto override passed	other business
April 7	adjourned	Reconstruction
		Civil Rights Act veto override
April 8	adjourned	adjourned
April 9	other business	Civil Rights Act veto override passed
April 10	other business	other business
April 11	other business	other business
April 12	other business	other business
April 13	other business	other business
April 14	adjourned	adjourned after speech celebrating
		Lincoln
April 15	adjourned	adjourned
April 16	other business	other business
April 17	Colorado statehood	other business
April 18	other business	other business
April 19	Colorado statehood	other business
April 20	other business	other business
April 21	adjourned	Reconstruction
April 22	adjourned	adjourned
April 23	other business	Tennessee Restoration
April 24	Colorado statehood	Tennessee Restoration other business
April 25	Colorado statehood passed	other business
April 26	other business	other business
April 27	other business	other business
April 28	adjourned	Reconstruction
April 29	adjourned	adjourned
April 30	Omnibus 14th introduced	Omnibus 14th introduced
		Tennessee Restoration
May 1	other business	other business
May 2	Tennessee Restoration	other business
May 3	other business	Colorado statehood passed
May 4	other business	other business
May 5	adjourned	Reconstruction
May 6	adjourned	adjourned
May 7	other business	other business
May 8	other business	Omnibus 14th
May 9	other business	Omnibus 14th
May 10	other business	Omnibus 14th passes
May 11	other business	adjourned
May 12	adjourned	adjourned
May 13	adjourned	adjourned
May 14	other business	other business
May 15	Colorado statehood veto	Tennessee Restoration postponed
May 16	Colorado statehood veto override	other business

(continued)

Calendar (*continued*)

	Senate	House of Representatives
May 17	other business	other business
May 18	other business	other business
May 19	adjourned	Reconstruction
May 20	adjourned	adjourned
May 21	Colorado statehood veto override	other business
May 22	other business	other business
May 23	Omnibus 14th	New 2nd Freedmen's Bureau
May 24	Omnibus 14th	New 2nd Freedmen's Bureau
May 25	other business	other business
May 26	Adjourned	other business
May 27	Adjourned	Adjourned
May 28	other business	other business
May 29	Omnibus 14th	New 2nd Freedmen's Bureau passed Tennessee Restoration
May 30	Omnibus 14th	Tennessee Restoration
May 31	Omnibus 14th	other business
June 1	adjourned	adjourned
June 2	adjourned	adjourned
June 3	adjourned	adjourned
June 4	Omnibus 14th	Tennessee Restoration
June 5	Omnibus 14th	other business
June 6	Omnibus 14th	other business
June 7	Omnibus 14th	other business
June 8	Omnibus 14th with revisions passed	other business
June 9	adjourned	Reconstruction
June 10	adjourned	adjourned
June 11	adjourned	Tennessee restoration bill
June 12	other business	other business
June 13	other business	Omnibus 14th with Senate revisions passed
June 14	other business	Tennessee restoration
June 15	New 2nd Freedmen's Bureau introduced	Tennessee restoration
June 16	adjourned	Reconstruction
June 17	adjourned	adjourned
June 18	other business	Export Tax Amendment defeated Tennessee Restoration
June 19	other business	other business
June 20	other business	Tennessee Restoration tabled
June 21	other business	other business
June 22	other business	other business
June 23	other business	other business
June 24	adjourned	adjourned
June 25	other business	other business
June 26	New 2nd Freedmen's Bureau passed with revisions	other business
June 27	other business	other business
June 28	other business	New 2nd Freedmen's Bureau conference request
June 29	Black Suffrage in Territories	other business
June 30	New 2nd Freedmen's Bureau Conference agreed	other business
July 1	adjourned	adjourned
July 2	New 2nd Freedmen's Bureau passed	other business

	Senate	House of Representatives
July 3	other business	New 2nd Freedmen's Bureau passed
July 4	adjourned	adjourned
July 5	other business	other business
July 6	other business	other business
July 7	other business	other business
July 8	adjourned	adjourned
July 9	other business	other business
July 10	other business	other business
July 11	other business	other business
July 12	other business	other business
July 13	other business	other business
July 14	other business	other business
July 15	adjourned	adjourned
July 16	New 2nd Freedmen Bureau veto override passed	New 2nd Freedmen Bureau veto override passed
July 17	other business	other business
July 18	other business	other business
July 19	other business	Tennessee Restoration
July 20	Tennessee Restoration	Tennessee Restoration passed
July 21	Tennessee Restoration passed with revisions	other business
July 22	adjourned	adjourned
July 23	Nebraska statehood introduced	Revised Tennessee Restoration passed
July 24	other business	other business
July 25	Nebraska statehood	Stevens Reconstruction bill read
July 26	Patterson introduced	other business
July 27	Nebraska statehood passed Patterson reported and revised oath passed Patterson regular oath passed	Nebraska statehood passed Patterson revised oath tabled
July 28	Final adjournment	Stevens Reconstruction bill presented Final adjournment

NOTES

SERIES FOREWORD

1. Walter F. Murphy, "Who Shall Interpret? The Quest for the Ultimate Constitutional Interpreter," *Review of Politics* 48, no. 3 (Summer 1986): 401–423.

A PREFACE TO THE FORGOTTEN FOURTEENTH AMENDMENT SERIES

1. Julia Bess Frank taught me this joke.
2. Many prominent texts with "Fourteenth Amendment" in the title discuss only Section 1. See., e.g., Randy E. Barnett and Evan D. Bernick, *The Original Meaning of the 14th Amendment: Its Letter and Spirit* (Cambridge, MA: Harvard University Press, 2021); Ilan Wurman, *The Second Founding: An Introduction to the Fourteenth Amendment* (New York: Cambridge University Press, 2020); William E. Nelson, *The Fourteenth Amendment: From Political Principle to Judicial Doctrine* (Cambridge, MA: Harvard University Press, 1998); Judith A. Baer, *Equality under the Constitution: Reclaiming the Fourteenth Amendment* (Ithaca, NY: Cornell University Press, 1983); Raoul Berger, *Government by Judiciary: The Transformation of the Fourteenth Amendment* (Cambridge, MA: Harvard University Press, 1977). Scholars have produced as extensive a literature on the Citizenship Clause, the Due Process Clause, the Equal Protection Clause, and the Privileges and Immunities Clause of the Fourteenth Amendment.
3. At least until Donald Trump, who seemed to exist for the purpose of renewing interest in what had previously been ignored provisions of the constitutional text. See also Michael Abramowicz, "Beyond Balanced Budgets, Fourteenth Amendment Style," 33 *Tulsa Law Journal* 561, 562 (1997) (Section 4 "has become obscure, less likely to be cited in policy discussion than in a Washington joke").
4. This Congress convened from March 4, 1865, to March 4, 1867, including special, first, and second sessions; the debates that are the subject of this volume occurred mainly during the first session, December 1865 to July 1866.
5. Slaughter-House Cases, 83 U.S. 36, 70 (1872) ("Among the first acts of legislation adopted by several of the States in the legislative bodies which claimed to be in their normal relations with the Federal government, were laws which imposed upon the colored race onerous disabilities and burdens, and curtailed their rights in the pursuit of life, liberty, and property to such an extent that their freedom was of little value, while they had lost the protection which they had received from their former owners from motives both of interest and humanity.").
6. Slaughter-House Cases, at 70.
7. See Thomas M. Cooley, *A Treatise on the Constitutional Limitations Which Rest Upon the Legislative Power of the States of the American Union*, 5th ed. (Little, Brown, 1883), 492; Jack M. Balkin, *Living Originalism* (Cambridge, MA: Harvard University Press, 2011), 184; Laura F. Edwards, *A Legal History*

of the Civil War and Reconstruction (New York: Cambridge University Press, 2015), 103; Kate Masur, *Until Justice Be Done: America's First Civil Rights Movement, From the Revolution to Reconstruction* (New York: W. W. Norton & Company, 2021), 331; Michael Les Benedict, *Preserving the Constitution: Essays on Politics and the Constitution in the Reconstruction Era* (New York: Fordham University Press, 2006), 6–7.

8. National Labor Relations Board v. Houston Distribution Services, Inc., 573 F. 2d 260 (5th Cir. 1978).

9. See, e.g., Tennessee v. Lane, 541 U.S. 509, 561–562 (2004) (Scalia, J., dissenting).

10. Nikolas Bowie and Daphna Renan, "The Separation-of-Powers Counterrevolution," 131 *Yale Law Journal* 2020, 2050 (2022). See McDonald v. City of Chicago, 561 U.S. 742, 775 (2010) (opinion of Alito, J.) ("Today, it is generally accepted that the Fourteenth Amendment was understood to provide a constitutional basis for protecting the rights set out in the Civil Rights Act of 1866.").

11. Eric Foner, *The Second Founding: How Civil War and Reconstruction Remade the Constitution* (New York: W. W. Norton & Company, 2019). 68. See Balkin, *Living Originalism*, 185 ("The central purpose of the Fourteenth Amendment was to recognize and protect the twin principles of equal citizenship and equality before the law."); Paul Gowder, *The Rule of Law in the United States*, 4 (unpublished manuscript) ("the Fourteenth Amendment" is "our most direct textual representation of the ideal of the rule of law"); Edwards, *Legal History*, 6 ("secured the people's civil and political rights through federal authority").

12. Steven G. Calabresi and Lena Barsky, "An Originalist Defense of *Plyler v. Doe*," 2017 *Brigham Young University Law Review* 225, 270 (2017). See Edwards, *Legal History*, 105.

13. Sanford Levinson, *Framed: America's 51 Constitutions and the Crisis of Government* (New York: Oxford University Press, 2012), 19.

14. Alexis De Tocqueville, *Democracy in America*, vol. 1, edited by Phillips Bradley (New York: Vintage Books, 1990), 280.

15. See Grutter v. Bollinger, 539 U.S. 306 (2003); Gratz v. Bollinger, 539 U.S. 244 (2003).

16. See McDonald v. City of Chicago, 561 U.S. 742 (2010).

17. See *McDonald*, at 806 (Thomas, J., concurring).

18. See Obergefell v. Hodges, 576 U.S. 644, 672–673 (2015).

19. See *McDonald*; Duncan v. Louisiana, 391 U.S. 145 (1968).

20. Texas v. Johnson, 491 U.S. 397 (1989).

21. See *Texas*, at 403, 404, 406, 407, 410–411, 415, 418 (citing Spence v. Washington, 418 U.S. 405 (1974).

22. Dobbs v. Jackson Women's Health Organization, 597 U.S. ___ (2022).

23. Kennedy v. Bremerton School District, 597 U.S. ___ (2022); Carson v. Makim, 596 U.S. ___ (2022); New York State Rifle & Pistol Association, Inc. v. Bruen, 597 U.S. ___ (2022).

24. See Mark A. Graber, "Teaching the Forgotten Fourteenth Amendment and the Constitution of Memory," 62 *St. Louis University Law Journal* 639, 653 (2018).

25. See Franita Tolson, "What Is Abridgment? A Critique of Two Section Twos," 67 *Alabama Law Review* 433, 434 (2015) ("Section 2 of the Fourteenth Amendment has the unfortunate privilege of being dead as long as it has been alive.");

Gabriel J. Chin, "Reconstruction, Felon Disenfranchisement, and the Right to Vote: Did the Fifteenth Amendment Repeal Section 2 of the Fourteenth Amendment," 92 *Georgetown Law Journal* 259, 260 (2004) ("no discriminating state lost even a single seat in the House of Representatives when Congress reapportioned itself").

26. See Mark A. Graber, "Their Fourteenth Amendment, Section 3 and Ours," *Just Security*, February 16, 2021, justsecurity.org.

27. See Abramowicz, "Beyond Balanced Budgets."

28. Charles Howard McIlwain, *Constitutionalism: Ancient and Modern* (Ithaca, NY: Cornell University Press, 1947), 21. See Giovanni Sartori, "Constitutionalism: A Preliminary Discussion," 56 *American Political Science Review* 853, 855 (1962) (a constitution as "a fundamental law, or a fundamental set of principles, and a correlative institutional arrangement, which would restrict arbitrary power and ensure a 'limited government'"); Gabor Halmai, "Populism, Authoritarianism and Constitutionalism," 20 *German Law Journal* 296, 312 (2019) ("the main characteristic of constitutionalism is the legally limited power of the government"); Steven G. Calabresi, "Originalism and James Bradley Thayer," 113 *Northwestern University Law Review* 1419, 1440 (2019); Stephen Gardbaum, *The New Commonwealth Model of Constitutionalism: Theory and Practice* (New York: Cambridge University Press, 2013), 21–22.

29. See, e.g., Jamal Greene, *How Rights Went Wrong: How Our Obsession with Rights is Tearing America Apart* (Boston: Houghton Mifflin Harcourt, 2021).

30. Sartori, "Constitutionalism," 855. For a general discussion of the centrality of rights to liberal constitutionalism, see Mark A. Graber, *A New Introduction to American Constitutionalism* (New York: Oxford University Press, 2013), 35–37.

31. Lorraine E. Weinrib, "The Postwar Paradigm and American Exceptionalism," *The Migration of Constitutional Ideas*, edited by Sujit Choudhry (New York: Cambridge University Press, 2006), 90.

32. Ronald Dworkin, "The Forum of Principle," 56 *New York University Law Review* 469 (1981).

33. Weinrib, "The Postwar Paradigm," 92.

34. See, e.g., John Harrison, "Reconstructing the Privileges or Immunities Clause," 101 *Yale Law Journal* 1385, 1408 (1992) ("(The Amendment was an omnibus proposal that dealt simultaneously with four of the leading problems of Reconstruction: the status of the Civil Rights Bill, apportionment of representatives, suffrage, and eligibility of former rebels for state and federal office."); Calabresi and Barsky, "An Originalist Defense of *Plyler v. Doe*," 270.

35. See, e.g., Harrison, "Reconstruction" 1408 n. 81 ("The Amendment also deals with national and rebel debt, but those issues were not of much practical consequence.").

36. I should live so long.

37. *Congressional Globe*, 39th Cong., 1st Sess., 688 (House); 747 (Senate), 775 (House concurring in Senate amendments).

38. *Congressional Globe*, 39th Cong., 1st Sess., 916–917 (A. Johnson veto); 943 (Senate fails to override veto).

39. *Congressional Globe*, 39th Cong., 1st Sess., 606–607 (Senate), 1367 (House), 1413–1416 (Senate concurring in House amendments).

40. *Congressional Globe*, 39th Cong., 1st Sess., 1679–1681 (A. Johnson veto), 1809 (Senate override), 1861 (House override).

41. *Congressional Globe*, 39th Cong., 1st Sess., 2878 (House), 3413 (Senate), 3524 (Senate concurs in amendments), 3562 (House concurs in amendments).

42. *Congressional Globe*, 39th Cong., 1st Sess., 3838–3839 (A. Johnson veto), 3842 (Senate override), 3850 (House override).

43. *Congressional Globe*, 39th Cong., 1st Sess., 311.

44. Republicans in Congress became more committed to African American suffrage during the Thirty-Ninth Congress, Second Session.

45. See Graber, *A New Introduction to American Constitutionalism*, 212–249.

46. Max M. Edling, *A Revolution in Favor of Government: Origins of the U.S. Constitution and the Making of the American State* (New York: Oxford University Press, 2003).

47. Marbury v. Madison, 5 U.S. 137, 177 (1803).

48. For a discussion of partisan supremacy, see Mark A. Graber, "Separation of Powers," *The Cambridge Companion to the United States Constitution*, edited by Karen Orren and John W. Compton (New York: Cambridge University Press, 2018), 235–242.

49. 60 U.S. 393 (1856).

50. Abraham Lincoln, "First Inaugural Address—Final Text," *Collected Works of Abraham Lincoln*, vol. 4, edited by Roy P. Basler (New Brunswick, NJ: Rutgers University Press, 1951), 268.

51. For a discussion of legislative primacy, see Mark A. Graber, "Korematsu's Ancestors," 74 *Arkansas Law Review* 425, 446–455 (2021).

52. Michael McConnell's survey of that debate highlights the numerous Republicans who sought to prohibit school segregation. What he misses is that all Republicans supporting bans on segregation were speaking of congressional power under Section 5 of the Fourteenth Amendment. None claimed that courts could independently use Section 1 to outlaw school segregation. Michael W. McConnell, "Originalism and the Desegregation Decisions," 81 *Virginia Law Review* 947 (1995).

53. See Lawrence B. Solum, "The Fixation Thesis: The Role of Historical Fact in Original Meaning," 91 *Notre Dame Law Review* 1 (2015).

54. See Leo Strauss, *Persecution and the Art of Writing* (Chicago: University of Chicago Press, 1988).

55. The classic study of constitutional reform as a means of altering constitutional politics is Ran Hirschl, *Towards Juristocracy: The Origins and Consequences of the New Constitutionalism* (Cambridge, MA: Harvard University Press, 2004).

56. See Alexander Hamilton, James Madison, and John Jay, *The Federalist Papers*, edited by Clinton Rossiter (New York: New American Library, 1961), 308.

57. See Larry D. Kramer, "Madison's Audience," 112 *Harvard Law Review* 611, 612–613 (1999) (detailing the extensive scholarship on *Federalist No. 10*).

58. See Gordon S. Wood, *The Creation of the American Republic* (Chapel Hill: University of North Carolina Press, 1969), 471.

59. See George S. Boutwell, *Reminiscences of Sixty Years in Public Affairs*, vol. 2 (New York: McClure, Phillips, 1902), 42. See also Charles Fairman, *Reconstruction and Reunion, 1864–1888* (Part One A) (New York: Cambridge University Press, 2010), 121 (quoting a letter from Salmon Chase describing Bingham as "inclined to impractical views").

60. Slaughter-House Cases, see 76–82.

61. 17 *Stat.* 13 (1871). See Christopher R. Green, "The Original Sense of the (Equal) Protection Clause: Subsequent Interpretation and Application," 19 *George Mason Civil Rights Law Journal* 219, 224–252 (2009).

62. 18 *Stat.* 335 (1875). See Alfred Avins, "The Civil Rights Act of 1875: Some Reflected Light on the Fourteenth Amendment and Public Accommodations," 66 *Columbia Law Review* 873 (1966).

63. 17 *Stat.* (142) (1872). See Gerard N. Magliocca, "Amnesty and Section Three of the Fourteenth Amendment," 36 *Constitutional Commentary* 87 (2021).

64. This will be the subject of the final volume in The Forgotten Fourteenth Amendment series or a series of articles.

65. See Jack M. Balkin, "Lawyers and Historians Argue About the Constitution," 35 *Constitutional Commentary* 345 (2020); Benedict, *Preserving the Constitution*, ix–x.

66. Cass R. Sunstein, "The Idea of a Useable Past," 95 *Columbia Law Review* 601, 603 (1995).

67. See Kurt T. Lash, *The Fourteenth Amendment and the Privileges and Immunities of American Citizenship* (New York: Cambridge University Press, 2014), xiv–xv, 277–279.

68. Randall Kennedy, "Reconstruction and the Politics of Scholarship," 98 *Yale Law Journal* 521, 521 (1989).

69. See, e.g., Lawrence B. Solum, "Originalism and Constitutional Construction," 82 *Fordham Law Review* 453 (2013).

70. See, e.g., Richard H. Fallon, Jr., "A Constructivist Coherence Theory of Constitutional Interpretation," 100 *Harvard Law Review* 1189 (1987).

71. For a sampling of the legal literature, see Barnett and Bernick, *The Original Meaning of the 14th Amendment*; Wurman, *The Second Founding*; Berger, *Government by Judiciary*; Lash, *The Fourteenth Amendment*.

72. See Peter Westin, "The Empty Idea of Equality," 95 *Harvard Law Review* 937 (1982).

73. See Douglas Rae et al., *Equalities* (Cambridge, MA: Harvard University Press, 1983).

74. See Fallon, Jr., "A Constructivist Coherence Theory of Constitutional Interpretation," 1189.

75. See Levinson, *Framed*.

76. See *McDonald*, at 805–858 (Thomas, J., concurring).

77. See Matthew Ing, "Birthright Citizenship, Illegal Aliens, and the Original Meaning of the Citizenship Clause," 45 *Akron Law Review* 719 (2012); Gerald Walpin, David B. Rivkin Jr., and John C. Yoo, "Birthright Citizenship: Two Perspectives," 17 *Federalist Society Review* 9 (2016).

78. See Michael Kent Curtis, *No State Shall Abridge: The Fourteenth Amendment*

and the Bill of Rights (Durham, NC: Duke University Press, 1986); Charles Fairman, "Does the Fourteenth Amendment Incorporate the Bill of Rights," 2 *Stanford Law Review* 5 (1949).

79. See McConnell, "Originalism and the Desegregation Decisions," 947; Alexander M. Bickel, "The Original Understanding and the Segregation Decision," 69 *Harvard Law Review* 1 (1955).

80. See Darrell A. H. Miller, "Text, History, and Tradition: What the Seventh Amendment Can Teach Us About the Second," 122 *Yale Law Journal* 852 (2013); Don B. Kates, Jr., "Handgun Prohibition and the Original Meaning of the Second Amendment," 82 *Michigan Law Review* (1983).

81. See Jack Balkin, "Abortion and Original Meaning," 24 *Constitutional Commentary* 291 (2007); Joshua J. Craddock, "Protecting Prenatal Persons: Does the Fourteenth Amendment Prohibit Abortion?" 40 *Harvard Journal of Law & Public Policy* 539 (2017).

82. See Michael B. Rappaport, "Originalism and the Colorblind Constitution," 89 *Notre Dame Law Review* 71 (2013); Eric Schnapper, "Affirmative Action and the Legislative History of the Fourteenth Amendment," 71 *Virginia Law Review* 753 (1985).

83. See Levinson, *Framed*.

84. See Graber, "Teaching the Forgotten Fourteenth Amendment and the Constitution of Memory," 639.

85. See Sanford Levinson, *Our Undemocratic Constitution: Where the Constitution Goes Wrong (And How We the People Can Fix It)* (New York: Oxford University Press, 2006).

86. For a scholarly effort to revive the Marque and Reprisal Clause, see Kenneth B. Moss, *Marque and Reprisal: The Spheres of Public and Private Warfare* (Lawrence: University Press of Kansas, 2019).

87. See Tolson, "What Is Abridgment?," 433; Jack M. Balkin, *"The Not-So-Happy Anniversary of the Debt-Ceiling Crisis,"* The Atlantic (July 31, 2012), www.theatlantic.com/politics/archive/2012/07/the-not-so-happy-anniversary-of-the-debt-ceiling-crisis/260458/ [https://perma.cc/LR74-SEHK]; Magliocca, "Amnesty and Section 3 of the Fourteenth Amendment," 87.

88. See Jack M. Balkin, "The Reconstruction Power," 85 *New York University Law Review* 1801, 1805 (2010).

89. 521 U.S. 507 (1997).

90. 529 U.S. 598 (2000).

91. See., e.g., Balkin, "The Reconstruction Power," 1805; Erwin Chemerinsky, "The Religious Freedom Restoration Act Is a Constitutional Expansion of Rights," 39 *William and Mary Law Review* 601, 604–629 (1998); Michael W. McConnell, "Institutions and Interpretation: A Critique of *Boerne v. Flores*," 111 *Harvard Law Review* 153 (1997).

92. See Robert C. Post and Reva B. Siegel, "Legislative Constitutionalism and Section Five Power: Policentric Interpretation of The Family and Medical Leave Act," 112 *Yale Law Journal* 1943 (2003); Robert C. Post and Reva B. Siegel, "Protecting the Constitution from the People: Juricentric Restrictions on Section Five Power," 78 *Indiana Law Journal* 1 (2003).

93. See David E. Pozen and Adam M. Samaha, "Anti-Modalities," 119 *Michigan Law Review* 729 (2021).

94. See Balkin, "The Reconstruction Power," 1806, n.17.

95. For a sampling of the literature, see Charles Beard, *An Economic Interpretation of the Constitution of the United States* (New York: The Free Press, 1986); Forrest McDonald, "A New Introduction," in Charles Beard, *An Economic Interpretation of the Constitution of the United States* (New York: The Free Press, 1986); David Brian Robertson, *The Constitution and America's Destiny* (New York: Cambridge University Press, 2005); Gordon S. Wood, *The Radicalism of the American Revolution* (New York: Alfred A. Knopf, 1992); Michael J. Klarman, *The Framers' Coup: The Making of the United States Constitution* (New York: Oxford University Press, 2016).

96. Jack N. Rakove, *Original Meanings: Politics and Ideas in the Making of the Constitution* (New York: Alfred A. Knopf, 1996).

97. Klarman, *The Framers' Coup*, 606.

98. For some examples, see Tom Ginsburg, *Judicial Review in New Democracies: Constitutional Courts in Asian Cases* (New York: Cambridge University Press, 2003); Yvonne Tew, *Constitutional Statecraft in Asian Courts* (New York: Oxford University Press, 2020); Tamir Moustafa, *The Struggle for Constitutional Power: Law, Politics, and Economic Development in Egypt* (New York: Cambridge University Press, 2009); Margit Cohn, *A Theory of the Executive Branch: Tension & Legality* (New York: Oxford University Press, 2021); Madhav Khosla, *India's Founding Moment: The Constitution of a Most Surprising Democracy* (Cambridge, MA: Harvard University Press, 2020); Zachary Elkins, Tom Ginsburg, and James Melton, *The Endurance of National Constitutions* (New York: Cambridge University Press, 2009); Mark Tushnet, *The New Fourth Branch: Institutions for Protecting Constitutional Democracy* (New York: Cambridge University Press, 2021). See generally Ran Hirschl, *Comparative Matters: The Renaissance of Comparative Constitutional Law* (New York: Oxford University Press, 2014).

99. Hirschl, *Towards Juristocracy*, 12.

100. Adam Chilton and Mila Versteeg, *How Constitutional Rights Matter* (New York: Oxford University Press, 2020).

101. Gregory P. Downs, *After Appomattox: Military Occupation and the Ends of War* (Cambridge, MA: Harvard University Press, 2019); Lisset Marie Pino and John Fabian Witt, "The Fourteenth Amendment as an Ending: From Bayonet Justice to Paper Rights," 10 *The Journal of the Civil War Era* 5 (2020).

102. Michael Les Benedict, *A Compromise of Principle: Congressional Republicans and Reconstruction, 1863–1869* (New York: W. W. Norton & Company, 1974); Earl M. Maltz, "The Forgotten Provision of the Fourteenth Amendment: Section 2 and the Evolution of American Democracy," 76 *Louisiana Law Review* 149 (2015). See also Benedict, *Preserving the Constitution*, x (noting that Americans in the mid-nineteenth century "relied for the day-to-day freedom on the actions and self-restraint of their legislative representatives").

103. Richard M. Vallely, *The Two Reconstructions: The Struggle for Black*

Enfranchisement (Chicago: University of Chicago Press, 2004), 29–30. See Fairman, *Reunion and Reaction*, 128 (the "first concern" of the Joint Committee on Reconstruction "was representation").

104. Forrest A. Nabors, *From Oligarchy to Republicanism* (Columbia: University of Missouri Press, 2017).

105. Mark Wahlgren Summers, *The Ordeal of the Reunion: A New History of Reconstruction* (Chapel Hill: University of North Carolina Press, 2014).

106. Harold Melvin Hyman, *Era of the Oath: Northern Loyalty Tests During the Civil War and Reconstruction* (Philadelphia: University of Pennsylvania Press, 1954); William A. Blair, *With Malice Toward Some: Treason and Loyalty in the Civil War Era* (Chapel Hill: University of North Carolina Press, 2014).

107. Garrett Epps, *Democracy Reborn: The Fourteenth Amendment and the Fight for Equal Rights in Post-Civil War America* (New York: Henry Holt and Company, 2013).

108. Edwards, *Legal History*, 6.

109. Foner, *The Second Founding*, xix.

110. Fairman, *Reunion and Reaction*, 131. See Maltz, "Section 2," 150 ("Sections 2 and 3 were generally viewed as equally important and controversial.").

111. Kate Masur, *Until Justice Be Done*, 331. See Benedict, *Preserving the Constitution*, 6–7.

112. Benedict, *Preserving the Constitution*, xi, 12–13.

113. See Masur, *Until Justice Be Done*, 294–297. See Edwards, *Legal History*, 108.

114. The classic article is Paul L. Murphy, "Time to Reclaim: The Current Challenge of American Constitutional History," 69 *American Historical Review* 64 (1963). See Anthony Brundage and Richard A. Cosgrove, *The Great Tradition: Constitutional History and National Identity in Britain and the United States, 1870–1960* (Stanford, CA: Stanford University Press, 2007). See also Hirschl, *Comparative Matters*, 163–168 (noting that law professors dominate scholarship on comparative constitutionalism).

115. Benedict, *Preserving the Constitution*, x.

116. See Summers, *The Ordeal of the Reunion*, 90–95; Fairman, *Reunion and Reaction*, 128–132; Edwards, *Legal History*, 104–108.

117. Vallely, *The Two Reconstructions*, 29.

118. See David K. Thomson, *Bonds of War: How Civil War Financial Agents Sold the World on the Union* (Chapel Hill: University of North Carolina Press, 2022).

119. See Blair, *With Malice Toward Some*.

120. See Benedict, *Preserving the Constitution*, 6–7.

121. This point is developed in the conclusion of this volume.

122. The seminal article complaining about the use of history in legal argument is Alfred H. Kelly, "Clio and the Court: An Illicit Love Affair," 1965 *Supreme Court Review* 119 (1965). More recent important interventions include Jonathan Gienapp, "Written Constitutionalism, Past and Present," 39 *Law and History Review* 321 (2021); Saul Cornell, "Meaning and Understanding in the History of Constitutional Ideas: The Intellectual History Alternative to Originalism," 82 *Fordham Law Review* 721, 724 (2013); Jack N. Rakove, "Joe the Ploughman Reads the Constitution, or, the Poverty of Public Meaning

Originalism," 48 *San Diego Law Review* 575 (2011). See also Jonathan Gienapp, *The Second Creation: Fixing the American Constitution in the Founding Era* (Cambridge, MA: Harvard University Press, 2018); Balkin, "Lawyers and Historians"; Rakove, *Original Meanings*.

123. Mazur, *Until Justice be Done*; Martha S. Jones, *Birthright Citizens: A History of Race and Rights in Antebellum America* (New York: Cambridge University Press, 2018); Simon J. Gilhooley, *The Antebellum Origins of the Modern Constitution: Slavery and the Spirit of the Modern Constitution* (New York: Cambridge University Press, 2020).

124. Marbury v. Madison, 5 U.S. 137 (1803).

125. See especially Sylvia Snowiss, *Judicial Review and the Law of the Constitution* (New Haven, CT: Yale University Press, 1990).

126. Hamilton, Madison, and Jay, *The Federalist Papers*, 196.

127. Hamilton, Madison, and Jay, *The Federalist Papers*, 466.

128. Cooper v. Aaron, 358 U.S. 1, 18 (1958).

129. Sylvia Snowiss, *Judicial Review and the Law of the Constitution* (New Haven, CT: Yale University Press, 1990).

130. Gerald Leonard and Saul Cornell, *The Partisan Republic: Democracy, Exclusion, and the Fall of the Founders' Constitution, 1780s–1830s* (New York: Cambridge University Press, 2019).

131. Larry D. Kramer, *The People Themselves: Popular Constitutionalism and Judicial Review* (New York: Oxford University Press, 2004), 73–213.

132. Kramer, *The People Themselves*, 213.

133. Kramer, *The People Themselves*, 213–215.

134. See Stanley Kutler, *Judicial Power and Reconstruction Politics* (Chicago: University of Chicago Press, 1968).

135. Kutler, *Judicial Power*, 162.

136. See Williams Lasser, *The Limits of Judicial Power: The Supreme Court in American Politics* (Chapel Hill: University of North Carolina Press, 1988), 110.

137. See, e.g., William A. Dunning, *Essays on the Civil War and Reconstruction* (New York: Harper & Row, 1965), 87–99, 118–119. See generally Kennedy, "Reconstruction," 523–525; Edwards, *Legal History*, 7.

138. See, e.g., Kenneth Stampp, *The Era of Reconstruction, 1865–1877* (New York: Vintage Books, 1965), 11–12, 135–145. See generally Kennedy, "Reconstruction," 525–526.

139. See, e.g., Benedict, *Preserving the Constitution*, 6–7; Alfred H. Kelly, "Comment on Harold M. Hyman's Paper," *New Frontiers of the American Reconstruction*, edited by Harold M. Hyman (Urbana: University of Illinois Press, 1966). See generally Kennedy, "Reconstruction," 527–528.

140. For histories of the history of Reconstruction, see Kennedy, "Reconstruction," 523–528.

141. See Edwards, *Legal History*, 108.

142. See Edwards, *Legal History*, 110.

143. Dunning, *The Civil War and Reconstruction*, 93.

144. Benedict, *Preserving the Constitution*, xiii. See Benedict, *Preserving the Constitution*, 6–7.

145. Nabors, *From Oligarchy to Republicanism*, 16 (emphasis in original).

146. Benedict, *Preserving the Constitution*, 6–7.
147. See Karen Orren and Stephen Skowronek, *The Search for American Political Development* (New York: Cambridge University Press, 2004).
148. Martin Shapiro, "Political Jurisprudence, Public Law, and Post-Consequentialist Ethics: Comment on Professors Barber and Smith," 2 *Studies in American Political Development* 88 (1989).
149. See William Michael Treanor, "The Case of the Dishonest Scrivener: Gouverneur Morris and the Creation of the Federalist Constitution," 120 *University of Michigan Law Review* 1 (2021); David S. Schwartz, "Gouverneur Morris, the Committee of Style, and the Federalist Constitution: A Comment on Treanor's Gouverneur Morris," 120 *Michigan Law Review Online* (forthcoming 2022).
150. See Boutwell, *Reminiscences*, vol. 2, 42; Fairman, *Reconstruction and Reunion*, 121; Christopher R. Green, "Incorporation, Total Incorporation, and Nothing But Incorporation?" 24 *William & Mary Bill of Rights Journal* 93, 124–125 (2015).
151. McCulloch v. Maryland, 17 U.S. 316, 407 (1819).
152. See Mark A. Graber, "Conflicting Representations: Lani Guinier and James Madison on Electoral Systems," 13 *Constitutional Commentary* 291 (1996).
153. See Mila Versteeg and Emily Zackin, "American Constitutional Exceptionalism Revisited," 81 *University of Chicago Law Review* 1641, 1652–1668 (2014).
154. See Emily Zackin, *Looking for Rights in All the Wrong Places: Why State Constitutions Contain America's Positive Rights* (Princeton, NJ: Princeton University Press, 2013).
155. See Graber, *A New Introduction to American Constitutionalism*, 243–248.

INTRODUCTION: THREE REPUBLICAN SOLOISTS AND THE REPUBLICAN CHORUS

1. *Congressional Globe*, 39th Cong., 1st Sess., 72, 461.
2. *Congressional Globe*, 39th Cong., 1st Sess., 3974.
3. Kurt Lash's otherwise magnificent collection of materials on the Reconstruction Amendments, for example, includes materials from the debates over the Civil Rights Act of 1866 and the Second Freemen's Bureau but none of the speeches on Johnson's December Message to Congress or the exclusion resolution that discuss at length constitutional reform in general and proposed Fourteenth Amendments in particular. See Kurt T. Lash, ed., *The Reconstruction Amendments: The Essential Documents*, vol. 2 (Chicago: University of Chicago Press, 2021).
4. Excellent discussions exist, but none treat the constitutional arguments on federalism and the separation of powers with the same loving detail given to Bingham's speeches on what became Section 1 of the Fourteenth Amendment. See, e.g., Downs, *After Appomattox*, 113–135.
5. *Congressional Globe*, 39th Cong., 1st Sess., 1162 (citizens of Bridgewater, Massachusetts), 1200 (citizens of Chester County, Pennsylvania), 1662 (citizens of Massachusetts). See *Congressional Globe*, 39th Cong., 1st Sess., 1006 (citizens of Windsor, Vermont) ("punish treason with loss of power and ineligibility to office and reward loyalty with confidence and honor"), 1099 (citizens of Maine) ("punish treason, reward loyalty"), 1200 (citizens of Byberry Township, Pennsylvania) ("punish treason with ineligibility to office, and reward loyalty

with confidence and honor"), 1349 (citizens of Bucksport, Maine) (same), 1436 (citizens of Peru, New York) (same), 1752 (citizens of Massachusetts) (same), 1272 (citizens of Danvers, Massachusetts) ("punish treason with ineligibility to office and loss of power, and reward loyalty with confidence and honor"), 1272 (citizens of Kenosha, Wisconsin), 1772 (citizens of New Hampshire).

6. *Congressional Globe*, 39th Cong., 1st Sess., 74.

7. *Congressional Globe*, 39th Cong., 1st Sess., 74.

8. *Congressional Globe*, 39th Cong., 1st Sess., 74.

9. *Congressional Globe*, 39th Cong., 1st Sess., 74.

10. See Hyman, *Era of the Oath*, 83.

11. The classic Jacksonian expression of partisan supremacy is Martin Van Buren, *Inquiry into the Origin and Course of Political Parties in the United States* (New York: Augustus M. Kelley, 1967 [1867]).

12. Forty-seven if one includes "ex-rebel."

13. *Congressional Globe*, 39th Cong., 1st Sess., 461–466. Stevens used the word "rebel" or "rebels" twelve times and the word "loyal" once in his speech, which spans two and a half pages in the *Congressional Globe*.

14. *Congressional Globe*, 39th Cong., 1st Sess., 463.

15. *Congressional Globe*, 39th Cong., 1st Sess., 461.

16. *Congressional Globe*, 39th Cong., 1st Sess., 463.

17. *Congressional Globe*, 39th Cong., 1st Sess., 461.

18. *Congressional Globe*, 39th Cong., 1st Sess., 464. A month earlier, Baker had proposed a resolution condemning "class rule and aristocratic principle" that concluded, "in restoring the normal relations of States lately in rebellion, it is the high and sacred duty of the Representatives of the people to proceed upon the true, as distinguished from the false, democratic principle, and to realize and secure the largest attainable liberty to the whole people of the Republic, irrespective of class or race." *Congressional Globe*, 39th Cong., 1st Sess., 69.

19. *Congressional Globe*, 39th Cong., 1st Sess., 3978.

20. *Congressional Globe*, 39th Cong., 1st Sess., 3978.

21. *Congressional Globe*, 39th Cong., 1st Sess., 3979.

22. *Congressional Globe*, 39th Cong., 1st Sess., 3979.

23. *Congressional Globe*, 39th Cong., 1st Sess., 3980.

24. *Congressional Globe*, 39th Cong., 1st Sess., 3980.

25. *Congressional Globe*, 39th Cong., 1st Sess., 3979.

26. *Congressional Globe*, 39th Cong., 1st Sess., 3979.

27. *Congressional Globe*, 39th Cong., 1st Sess., 3978.

28. But not during the second session of the Thirty-Ninth Congress.

29. Friends have described what follows as an annotated version of the relevant pages in the *Congressional Globe*.

30. The expression "fake news" is obviously an anachronism. Chapter 2 will nevertheless show affinities between Democratic descriptions of the postwar South and the descriptions of political reality Donald Trump offered during and immediately after his presidency.

31. See Philip A. Klinkner and Rogers M. Smith, *The Unsteady March: The Rise and Decline of Racial Equality in America* (Chicago: University of Chicago Press, 1999), 58–71.

1. THE EXCLUSION DEBATE

1. See *Congressional Globe*, 39th Cong., 1st Sess., 2. Sumner's conditions are discussed in Chapter 4.

2. Andrew Johnson, "First Annual Message," in *A Compilation of the Messages and Papers of the Presidents, 1789–1897*, vol. 6, edited by James D. Richardson (Washington, DC: Government Printing Office, 1897), 357–358.

3. *Congressional Globe*, 39th Cong., 1st Sess., 943, 1147.

4. *Report of the Joint Committee on Reconstruction, at the first session, Thirty-Ninth Congress* (Washington, DC: Government Printing Office, 1866) (hereafter *Report of the Joint Committee*).

5. The debate over the post office bill concerned presidential appointment and removal powers. Discussion soon concerned President Johnson's effort to use the appointment power to buttress presidential Reconstruction, which in turn caused a discussion of Reconstruction more generally. See *Congressional Globe*, 39th Cong., 1st Sess., 2308–2309 (Jo. Henderson), 2418–2419 (Poland), 2451–2453 (H. Wilson), 2454–2455 (Doolittle), 2456–2458 (Cowan), 2585–2588 (H. Wilson), 2588–2592 (Cowan), 2493–2494 (Doolittle), 2495–2497 (Nye), 2523–2526 (Nye), 2526–2528 (Doolittle), 2550–2555 (Howard), 2557–2559 (Cowan).

6. *Congressional Globe*, 39th Cong., 1st Sess., 3–5. See Eric Foner, *Reconstruction: America's Unfinished Revolution, 1863–1877* (New York: Harper & Row, 1988), 239; Hyman, *Era of the Oath*, 88–90.

7. See Johnson, "First Annual Message," in *Messages and Papers*, vol. 6, 357–358; Andrew Johnson, "To the Senate of the United States," in *Messages and Papers*, vol. 6, 373; Andrew Johnson, "To the Senate and House of Representatives," in *Messages and Papers*, vol. 6, 391–392 (urging Congress not to send the Fourteenth Amendment to the states); Andrew Johnson, "To the House of Representatives," 397 (comments on bill restoring Tennessee); Andrew Johnson, "To the Senate of the United States," 403–404 (veto of Second Freedmen's Bureau Bill); Andrew Johnson, "To the House of Representatives," 416 (veto of Colorado Statehood Bill); Andrew Johnson, "To the House of Representatives," 423 (veto of Revised Second Freedmen's Bureau Bill).

8. See *Congressional Globe*, 39th Cong., 1st Sess., 917.

9. *Congressional Globe*, 39th Cong., 1st Sess., 943, 950.

10. *Congressional Globe*, 39th Cong., 1st Sess., 1147.

11. *Congressional Globe*, 39th Cong., 1st Sess., 4303.

12. *Congressional Globe*, 39th Cong., 1st Sess., 982.

13. *Congressional Globe*, 39th Cong., 1st Sess., 991.

14. See, e.g., *Congressional Globe*, 39th Cong., 1st Sess., 1105 (Stewart) (discussing the apportionment resolution), 1196 (Second Freedmen's Bureau Bill), 1136 (Cowan) (apportionment resolution), 2079 (Nicholson) (discussing the Bingham amendment), 2398 (Phelps) (Fourteenth Amendment), 2883–2884 (Latham) (same), 2905 (Bromwell) (same), 3069 (Van Aernam) (same), 3169–3170 (Windom) (same), 3201 (Orth) (same); *Congressional Globe*, 39th Cong., 1st Sess., App., 124 (Sherman) (apportionment resolution), 210 (Bundy) (Fourteenth Amendment), 253–254 (Cullom) (same). The debates over the exclusion resolution, Johnson's Message, the restoration bill, and other matters also bled

into the debates over the civil rights bills. See *Congressional Globe*, 39th Cong., 1st Sess., 1832–1837 (W. Lawrence) (discussing the Civil Rights Act of 1866), 2261–2264 (Finck), 3217 (Niblack) (same).

15. See Thurman W. Arnold, "Criminal Attempts-The Rise and Fall of an Abstraction," 40 *Yale Law Journal* 53, 58 (1930) (quoting Thomas Reed Powell).

16. As noted, Kurt Lash's collection of "essential documents" on the "Reconstruction Amendments" does not contain one reading on the debate on the exclusion or restoration of former Confederate states, even readings on those frequent occasions when members of Congress proposed or discussed various constitutional reforms. Lash, *The Reconstruction Amendments*, vol. 2.

17. *Congressional Globe*, 39th Cong., 1st Sess., 6.

18. *Congressional Globe*, 39th Cong., 1st Sess., 24–30.

19. *Congressional Globe*, 39th Cong., 1st Sess., 46–47.

20. *Congressional Globe*, 39th Cong., 1st Sess., 57.

21. *Congressional Globe*, 39th Cong., 1st Sess., 106.

22. *Report of the Joint Committee*, iv–vi.

23. *Report of the Joint Committee*, vii.

24. *Report of the Joint Committee*, xxi. See Downs, *After Appomattox*, 113, 127.

25. "Views of the Minority," *The Reports of the Committees of the House of Representatives made during the First Session Thirty-Ninth Congress, 1865–66* (Washington, DC: Government Printing Office, 1866).

26. See *Congressional Globe*, 39th Cong., 1st Sess., 2332 (Williams) (proposing that Tennessee and Arkansas be admitted upon ratification, that other ratifying states be admitted on March 4, 1867, if the Fourteenth Amendment was ratified, and that Congress admit representatives from all former Confederates states should the Fourteenth Amendment not be ratified), 2947 (H. Wilson) (proposing a restoration bill conditioning representation on ratification of the Fourteenth Amendment and bans on race discrimination in voting and other laws), 3090 (Kelley (same), 3201 (Orth) (conditioning representation on ratifying the Fourteenth Amendment).

27. See, e.g., *Congressional Globe*, 39th Cong., 1st Sess., 3979–3980 (Bingham), *Congressional Globe*, 39th Cong., 1st Sess., App., 255–258 (Baker), 305 (Miller).

28. Pino and Fabian Witt, "The Fourteenth Amendment as an Ending."

29. Four unconditional Unionists from border states in the House—George Lathan of West Virginia, Charles Phelps of Maryland, Green Smith of Kentucky, and Kellian Whaley of West Virginia—voted against the exclusion resolution but for the Fourteenth Amendment.

30. "Views of the Minority," *Reports of the Committees*, 2.

31. "Views of the Minority," 1.

32. "Views of the Minority," 2.

33. "Views of the Minority," 4.

34. "Views of the Minority," 4.

35. "Views of the Minority," 6.

36. See "Views of the Minority," 11.

37. "Views of the Minority," 11.

38. See *Congressional Globe*, 39th Cong., 1st Sess., 150 (Voorhees) ("no States or number of States confederated together can in any manner sunder their

connection with the Federal Union"), 193 (R. Johnson ("notwithstanding their acts of secession and hostility, they were still States"), 1044–455 (J. Dixon), 1170 (Kuykendall), 2696–2697 (Ross), ("every department of the Government . . . has uniformly recognized them as States in the Union"), 2884 (Latham) ("Who, until the present time, ever heard of a sovereign Power governing in time of peace any portion of its subjects as belligerents under the law of nations?"), 3248 (Raymond) ("You tell me these eight millions have forfeited their rights; that they have ceased to be States; that they are conquered provinces, subject only to the laws of war. . . . The theory has no warrant in our Constitution or in the theory of our government.").

39. Harris endorsed the "right of secession." He insisted that the Confederate states "by their ordinances of secession . . . did go out, and thereby became to this Union foreign States." One consequence of secession was that "the south ern seceded States have no right to Representation on this floor or in the Senate" until "admitted into this Union . . . by an act of Congress." *Congressional Globe*, 39th Cong., 1st Sess., 3172–3173.

40. See *Congressional Globe*, 39th Cong., 1st Sess., 85.

41. *Congressional Globe*, 39th Cong., 1st Sess., 2253. See *Congressional Globe*, 39th Cong., 1st Sess., 139 (Latham) ("The so-called ordinances of secession adopted by the people of some of the southern States are of no more legal effect by way of dissolving their allegiance to the General or national Government than the blank paper upon which they are written."), 189 (R. Johnson) ("Will any member of the Senate seriously maintain . . . that the ordinance of secession had any validity whatever?"), 288 (Grider); 869 (Strouse) ("I have from the beginning opposed secession and disunion in every from. . . . [T]he acts of secession of Virginia, South Carolina, or any of the southern States, were utterly void and invalid."); *Congressional Globe*, 39th Cong., 1st Sess., App., 48 ("We denounced secession as a heresy, as unwarranted by the Constitution."), 73 (Rousseau) ("The right of secession was denied by all the Union men in the United States.").

42. *Congressional Globe*, 39th Cong., 1st Sess., 117. See *Congressional Globe*, 39th Cong., 1st Sess., 140 (Latham).

43. *Congressional Globe*, 39th Cong., 1st Sess., 26.

44. *Congressional Globe*, 39th Cong., 1st Sess., 40. See *Congressional Globe*, 39th Cong., 1st Sess., 662 (S. Randall) (states may leave the Union "only . . . by the consent of the States in the Union").

45. *Congressional Globe*, 39th Cong., 1st Sess., 1830. See *Congressional Globe*, 39th Cong., 1st Sess., 1830 (Le Blond) ("nowhere is it provided that thereby the State whose people are in rebellion shall lose its identity as a State in the Union and become a Territory"), 3175 (Le Blond).

46. *Congressional Globe*, 39th Cong., 1st Sess., 115.

47. *Congressional Globe*, 39th Cong., 1st Sess., App., 243.

48. *Congressional Globe*, 39th Cong., 1st Sess., 26.

49. *Congressional Globe*, 39th Cong., 1st Sess., 2095. See *Congressional Globe*, 39th Cong., 1st Sess., App., 49 (Smith).

50. *Congressional Globe*, 39th Cong., 1st Sess., 28.

51. See *Congressional Globe*, 39th Cong., 1st Sess., 193 (R. Johnson).

52. Johnson, "First Annual Message," 353, 356.
53. Johnson, "To the Senate," 372.
54. *Congressional Globe*, 39th Cong., 1st Sess., 251. See *Congressional Globe*, 39th Cong., 1st Sess., 218 (Chanler) ("Rebellion has been put down, and secession made impossible hereafter.").
55. *Congressional Globe*, 39th Cong., 1st Sess., 29. See *Congressional Globe*, 39th Cong., 1st Sess., 42 (Saulsbury) ("[T]here is not a particle of resistance from the Potomac to the Rio Grande, or from Ohio to the Gulf of Mexico. . . . Everybody knows that war has ceased, and the rebellion as it is called has ceased."). More conservative Republicans agreed. Stillwell proposed a resolution that began, "Whereas the war for the preservation of the Union and the Constitution is now over." *Congressional Globe*, 39th Cong., 1st Sess., 71. See *Congressional Globe*, 39th Cong., 1st Sess., 109 (Stewart) (quoting President Johnson).
56. *Congressional Globe*, 39th Cong., 1st Sess., 289. See *Congressional Globe*, 39th Cong., 1st Sess., 51 (Smith) ("There is no rebel Legislature in any of these States.").
57. *Congressional Globe*, 39th Cong., 1st Sess., 23.
58. Johnson, "To the Senate," 372.
59. *Congressional Globe*, 39th Cong., 1st Sess., App., 51.
60. *Congressional Globe*, 39th Cong., 1st Sess., 1167.
61. *Congressional Globe*, 39th Cong., 1st Sess., 1168.
62. *Congressional Globe*, 39th Cong., 1st Sess., 22. See *Congressional Globe*, 39th Cong., 1st Sess., 113 (Saulsbury).
63. *Congressional Globe*, 39th Cong., 1st Sess., 1863. See *Congressional Globe*, 39th Cong., 1st Sess., 118 (Finck), 1049 (Stewart), 2264 (Finck) ("The States, then, being in the Union, and peace having been completely restored, there is no constitutional right whatever for depriving them of just and constitutional representation.").
64. *Congressional Globe*, 39th Cong., 1st Sess., 40. See *Congressional Globe*, 39th Cong., 1st Sess., 40 (R. Johnson) ("the moment the insurrection was terminated there was no power whatsoever left in the Congress of the United States over those States"), 153 (Voorhees), 190 (R. Johnson), 193 (R. Johnson) ("the cure becomes absolute and effectual by removal the cause of that temporary paralysis, and that ended, the States stand as they stood before the disease assailed them; they stand perfect, with all the health of living and vital and powerful States, and entitled to the benefits of the Constitution and the laws").
65. *Congressional Globe*, 39th Cong., 1st Sess., 2254. See *Congressional Globe*, 39th Cong., 1st Sess., 29 (Guthrie) ("We have suppressed that insurrection. They are now States of the Union."), 139 (Latham) ("who questioned the right of the loyal people of these States to reestablish their governments . . . when they recovered the power to do so?"), 151 ("those States are in full, formal, and real submission and obedience as the other States"), 312–313 (Doolittle) (noting loyalty had returned to Florida), 1107 (R. Johnson) ("[T]he insurrection . . . has terminated. There is no hostile force now to be found in any one of the States in which the rebellion or the insurrection or the civil war existed. There is no opposition found anywhere in any of other States, by act, to the authority of the Government of the United States."), 2097 (Smith); *Congressional Globe*,

39th Con., 1st Sess., App., 302 (G. Davis) ("Whenever the insurrection is suppressed, the work of both Congress and the President is fully and completely performed, and all government power over the subject is exhausted.").

66. *Congressional Globe*, 39th Congress. 1st Sess., 118.

67. *Congressional Globe*, 39th Cong., 1st Sess., 2407. See *Congressional Globe*, 39th Cong., 1st Sess., 1043 (J. Dixon) ("We have no right to say that the State of Illinois shall not be represented in time of peace."), 1049 (Saulsbury), 1052 (J. Dixon), 1080 (Stewart), 1168 (Thornton) ("The right . . . to be represented in the Senate and House of Representatives, is as fully secured as the right to local government."), 2455 (Doolittle) ("the people of this country . . . demand . . . the loyal representatives of the southern States in the Congress of the United States"), 2696 (Ross) (claiming that excluding states violated the constitutional requirements that "each State shall have at least one Representative" in the House and that "the Senate of the United States shall be composed of two Senators from each State"), 3246 (Raymond) ("the absolute right of representation").

68. *Congressional Globe*, 39th Cong., 1st Sess., 118.

69. *Congressional Globe*, 39th Cong., 1st Sess., App., 2. See *Congressional Globe*, 39th Cong., 1st Sess., 43 (Saulsbury).

70. *Congressional Globe*, 39th Cong., 1st Sess., 350.

71. *Congressional Globe*, 39th Cong., 1st Sess., 2095. See *Congressional Globe*, 39th Cong., 1st Sess., 152 (Voorhees), 2096 (S. Randall) ("if the loyal one tenth have to pay taxes have they not certainly the right of representation?"), 2098 (Ritter) ("the idea of being taxed without the right of representation is one that has always been abhorred and detested by the American people"), 3172 (Harris) ("Let taxation be suspended where representation is denied."); *Congressional Globe*, 39th Cong., 1st Sess., App., 260 (Trimble) ("They are taxed, and should be entitled to vote, with representatives here.").

72. *Congressional Globe*, 39th Cong., 1st Sess., 28. See *Congressional Globe*, 39th Cong., 1st Sess., 152 (Voorhees); *Congressional Globe*, 39th Cong., 1st Sess., App., 262 (Trimble).

73. *Congressional Globe*, 39th Cong., 1st Sess., 2096.

74. *Congressional Globe*, 39th Cong., 1st Sess., 3. See *Congressional Globe*, 39th Cong., 1st Sess., 118 (Finck). Exclusion may also have been futile. "It is not to be supposed that by holding these people off at arm's length after they have adopted constitutions that are republican in form," Defrees claimed, "will have a tendency to make them more loyal." *Congressional Globe*, 39th Cong., 1st Sess., 872.

75. *Congressional Globe*, 39th Cong., 1st Sess., App. 302. See *Congressional Globe*, 39th Cong., 1st Sess., 271 (Doolittle) ("The President alone is made the judge of the time when the insurrection is suppressed and when the Army shall be withdrawn.").

76. *Congressional Globe*, 39th Cong., 1st Sess., 29.

77. *Congressional Globe*, 39th Cong., 1st Sess., 124.

78. *Congressional Globe*, 39th Cong., 1st Sess., App. 2.

79. See Foner, *Reconstruction*, 193–194.

80. See Paul E. Herron, *Framing the Solid South: The State Constitutional*

Conventions of Secession, Reconstruction, and Redemption (Lawrence: University Press of Kansas, 2017), 123–126, 136–144.

81. *Congressional Globe*, 39th Cong., 1st Sess., 32. See *Congressional Globe*, 39th Cong., 1st Sess., 42 (Saulsbury) ("He has asked them to ratify the constitutional amendment. They have done it. He has asked them to abolish slavery. They have done it."), 118 (Finck) (noting that the former Confederate states had renounced slavery and secession), 189 (Nesmith) (endorsing Johnson's plan), 273 (Doolittle) (asserting that allegiance, repudiation of the rebel debt, emancipation, and ratification of the Thirteenth Amendment were the conditions for representation), 1311 (Goodyear) (endorsing President Johnson's Reconstruction policies), 2098 (Ritter), 2395 (Phelps) (same), 2494 (Cowan) (noting that former Confederate states had ratified the Thirteenth Amendment, ratified state constitutional bans on slavery, and ratified state constitutional bans on paying the rebel debt), 2697 (Ross) (endorsing Johnson's plan); *Congressional Globe*, 39th Cong., 1st Sess., App. 51 (Smith) (endorsing Johnson's plan), 304 (G. Davis) (same).
  The Joint Committee on Reconstruction was willing to admit Tennessee on these conditions. See *Congressional Globe*, 39th Cong., 1st Sess., 1189.
82. *Congressional Globe*, 39th Cong., 1st Sess., 71.
83. *Congressional Globe*, 39th Cong., 1st Sess., 96.
84. *Congressional Globe*, 39th Cong., 1st Sess., 78. *Congressional Globe*, 39th Cong., 1st Sess., 1175–1176 (Finck) (readmission is justified because Southern states claim to accept emancipation and promise to treat persons of color fairly).
85. *Congressional Globe*, 39th Cong., 1st Sess., 110.
86. *Congressional Globe*, 39th Cong., 1st Sess., 193.
87. *Congressional Globe*, 39th Cong., 1st Sess., 153.
88. See Johnson, "To the Senate of the United States," 373–374.
89. *Congressional Globe*, 39th Cong., 1st Sess., 153. See *Congressional Globe*, 39th Cong., 1st Sess., 157 (Voorhees).
90. *Congressional Globe*, 39th Cong., 1st Sess., 290. See *Congressional Globe*, 39th Cong., 1st Sess., 3095 (Rousseau) ("All has been done but one thing, namely, the admission of representatives from the States lately in rebellion.").
91. *Congressional Globe*, 39th Cong., 1st Sess., 3094. See *Congressional Globe*, 39th Cong., 1st Sess., 3242 (Raymond) ("we have no right, no power, under the Constitution of the United States to impose such conditions of representation at all"); *Congressional Globe*, 39th Cong., 1st Sess., App. 262 ("we demand no conditions for the restoration of the Union").
92. *Congressional Globe*, 39th Cong., 1st Sess., 140.
93. *Congressional Globe*, 39th Cong., 1st Sess., 290.
94. Johnson, "First Annual Message," 358.
95. *Congressional Globe*, 39th Cong., 1st Sess., 25. See *Congressional Globe*, 39th Cong., 1st Sess., 28 (Hendricks), 29 (J. Dixon), 1139–1140 (Doolittle), 1166 (Thornton).
96. *Congressional Globe*, 39th Cong., 1st Sess., 1042.
97. *Congressional Globe*, 39th Cong., 1st Sess., 1311.
98. For the history of the test oath, see Hyman, *Era of the Oath*.
99. *Congressional Globe*, 39th Cong., 1st Sess., 1046. See *Congressional Globe*, 39th

Cong., 1st Sess., 140 (Latham), 445 (Stewart) ("have we not a test oath that will keep them out?"), 1172 (Kuykendall, who did not vote on the exclusion resolution) ("I am not in favor of repealing the test oath, but am in favor of its remaining there as a monument of loyalty."), 2095 (Smith), 2332 (J. Dixon), 3245 (Raymond) ("[I]f he can take the oath we have prescribed, if he can abide by any test of loyalty we may impose, then it is our duty to admit him if duly elected and returned to his seat in Congress."); *Congressional Globe*, 39th Cong., 1st Sess., App., 244 (Sitgreaves) ("He is willing to accept our understanding of the allegiance due from the citizen; that the allegiance to the General Government is paramount, and is willing to seal it with an oath."). See also *Congressional Globe*, 39th Cong., 1st Sess., 3092 (Rousseau) ("Lincoln . . . never dreamed of rejecting loyal men legally elected from the insurrectionary States.").
Several Republicans who supported (Defrees) or did not vote (Kuykendall) on the exclusion resolution indicated that the test oath was an adequate substitute for exclusion. See *Congressional Globe*, 39th Cong., 1st Sess., 872 (Defrees) ("The iron-clad oath that members are required to take before they get seats in this House is a bulwark against traitors, and no disloyal man can pollute these Halls with his impious feet as long as that remains on the statute-book."); 1172 (Kuykendall) ("I am not in favor of repealing the test oath, but am in favor of its remaining there as a monument of loyalty.").

100. *Congressional Globe*, 39th Cong., 1st Sess., 2397.
101. *Congressional Globe*, 39th Cong., 1st Sess., 665. See *Congressional Globe*, 39th Cong., 1st Sess., 71 (Stillwell), 1413 (Hendricks) ("[A] Senator must take an oath that he has had no voluntary connection with the rebellion; he must show by his oath that he has been loyal throughout the whole unfortunately controversy."), 3176 (S. Randall), 3176 (Eldridge), 3245 (Marshall) ("We have had it to be an outrage to exclude men who were loyal to the Government, have risked their lives and all that is dear to them in the cause of the Union, and can take the oath prescribed by law.").
102. *Congressional Globe*, 39th Cong., 1st Sess., 1169. See *Congressional Globe*, 39th Cong., 1st Sess., App., 262 (Trimble) ("What is the test a great nation should make of loyalty other than submission to the Constitution as it is and the laws passed in pursuance thereof.").
103. *Congressional Globe*, 39th Cong., 1st Sess., 29. See *Congressional Globe*, 39th Cong., 1st Sess., 1172 (Marshall) ("the better mode is to repeal the test oath and determine the question as to each member when he presents himself here").
104. *Congressional Globe*, 39th Cong., 1st Sess., 1173. See *Congressional Globe*, 39th Cong., 1st Sess., 1172 (Rogers) ("the oath is unconstitutional"), 1863 (Saulsbury), 2261 (Finck).
105. See *Congressional Globe*, 39th Cong., 1st Sess., 1049. President Johnson in the early days on Reconstruction suggested that Mississippi might consider enfranchising persons of color "who can read the Constitution of the United States in English and write their names, and to all persons of color who own real estate valued at not less than $250, and pay taxes." See *Congressional Globe*, 39th Cong., 1st Sess., 1437 (quoting Johnson to Sharkey, August 8, 1865). The suggestion was ignored and abandoned.
106. *Congressional Globe*, 39th Cong., 1st Sess., 2098–2099.

107. *Congressional Globe*, 39th Cong., 1st Sess., App., 2–3.
108. *Congressional Globe*, 39th Cong., 1st Sess., 70. See *Congressional Globe*, 39th Cong., 1st Sess., 119 (Finck) ("I deny the right of this Congress, or of the Federal Government, either directly or indirectly to regulate the right of the elective franchise within the several States.")
109. *Congressional Globe*, 39th Cong., 1st Sess., 118.
110. See *Congressional Globe*, 39th Cong., 1st Sess., 118–119.
111. *Congressional Globe*, 39th Cong., 1st Sess., App., 3.
112. *Congressional Globe*, 39th Cong., 1st Sess., 1827.
113. *Congressional Globe*, 39th Cong., 1st Sess., 3169.
114. *Report of the Joint Committee*, xiii.
115. *Report of the Joint Committee*, xviii.
116. *Report of the Joint Committee*, xii.
117. *Report of the Joint Committee*, xix. See *Report of the Joint Committee*, xi.
118. *Report of the Joint Committee*, xii.
119. *Report of the Joint Committee*, ix. See *Report of the Joint Committee*, xviii, xx ("The authority to restore rebels to political power in the federal government can be exercised only with the concurrence of all the departments in which political power is vested.").
120. *Report of the Joint Committee*, xxi. See *Report of the Joint Committee*, x ("It was an equally important inquiry whether their restoration to their former relations with the United States should be granted upon certain conditions and guarantees which would effectually secure the nation against a recurrence of evils so disastrous as those from which it had escaped at so enormous a sacrifice."), xi ("security against the recurrence of such outrages in the future"), xx ("adequate guarantees against future treason and rebellion").
121. *Report of the Joint Committee*, xviii–xix, xxi.
122. See *Congressional Globe*, 39th Cong., 1st Sess., 899 (Cook) ("it is impossible that the action of any State can take such State out of the Union"), 665 (W. Lawrence) ("the constitutional right of secession . . . is denied by all loyal men"), 1007–1008 (R. Clarke) (secession acts were "without constitutional sanction, mere nullities, and needed no repeal to render them void").
123. *Congressional Globe*, 39th Cong., 1st Sess., 920.
124. *Congressional Globe*, 39th Cong., 1st Sess., 142. See *Congressional Globe*, 39th Cong., 1st Sess., 164 (Howe) (a state "is charged with duties also, and if it persistently disregard those, or willfully persist in the exercise of powers not intrusted to it, it may thereby forfeit its right to being"), 2879 (J. Ashley) ("constitutional State government ceased in each of the States so confederated together"); *Congressional Globe*, 39th Cong., 1st Sess., App., 66 (Garfield) ("there was not in one of the States a single government we did or could recognize").
125. See *Congressional Globe*, 39th Cong., 1st Sess., 132 (Spalding) ("forfeited its privileges as a part of the governing Power"), 166 (Howe) ("by rebellion they forfeited the right"), 900 (Cook) ("a State may go out of the Union in such sense as to lose all right to exercise any authority in the Government, and all right to be represented in the national councils"), 911 (Cullom), 1020 (Bromwell), 2691 (Morris) ("these States are still in the Union, but by reason of their criminal acts, they have forfeited their right of being represented in our national

councils"), 2693 (Patterson) ("the rebel States have . . . forfeited all their political rights"), 3068 (Van Aernam) ("the rebellious States have forfeited, abdicated, and lost their position, and all the rights and privileges which they held as governing members in the Union"); *Congressional Globe*, 39th Cong., 1st Sess., App., 65 (Garfield) ("by their own act of treason and rebellion they had forfeited their rights in the Union"), 93 (G. Williams) ("the rights which these rebel States had under the Constitution prior to the rebellion by that rebellion became forfeited and passed into the hands of the Federal Government").

126. *Congressional Globe*, 39th Cong., 1st Sess., 72. See *Congressional Globe*, 39th Cong., 1st Sess., 469 (Broomall of Pennsylvania), 2096 (Boutwell) (former Confederate states' right of representation "ceased to exist").

127. *Congressional Globe*, 39th Cong., 1st Sess., App., 86. See *Congressional Globe*, 39th Cong., 1st Sess., 868 (Newell).

128. *Congressional Globe*, 39th Cong., 1st Sess., 3172.

129. *Congressional Globe*, 39th Cong., 1st Sess., 2. See *Congressional Globe*, 39th Cong., 1st Sess., 98 (Broomall), 919 (Bromwich) (proposing a joint resolution declaring "the States of this Union which did not renounce their allegiance to the Federal Government during the late rebellion . . . are the only States clothed with the legal power to consider and decide upon amendments to that Constitution").

130. *Congressional Globe*, 39th Cong., 1st Sess., 74. See *Congressional Globe*, 39th Cong., 1st Sess., 1310 (Stevens) ("in adopting those amendments their aid will neither be desired nor permitted").

131. *Congressional Globe*, 39th Cong., 1st Sess., 1310.

132. *Congressional Globe*, 39th Cong., 1st Sess., 1474.

133. See *Congressional Globe*, 39th Cong., 1st Sess., 188 (Howe) ("they assumed the legal character of Territories"), 564 (Paine), 731–733, 736–739 (H. Lane), 783 (Ward), 784 (T. Williams) ("these States had ceased to be members of the Union, and passed into the condition of Territories"), 3067 (Van Aernam), 3793 (Wade), 4302 (Howe). See also *Congressional Globe*, 39th Cong., 1st Sess., 3177 (Boutwell) (denying that former Confederate states were states in the Union).

134. *Congressional Globe*, 39th Cong., 1st Sess., 142 (Shellabarger). See *Congressional Globe*, 39th Cong., 1st Sess., 1021 ("it is evident that the Constitution of the United States is a part of the constitution of Alabama, and such a part that without it the constitution of Alabama cannot exist even for a moment").

135. *Congressional Globe*, 39th Cong., 1st Sess., 2555. See *Congressional Globe*, 39th Cong., 1st Sess., 24 (Howard) ("conquered communities"), 73 (Stevens) ("conquered provinces"), 98 (Broomall) ("a conquered people"), 873 (citizens of Alexandria, Virginia), 988 (Fessenden) ("Is there anything more certain than that the conqueror has a right, if he chooses, to change the form of government, . . . that he has a right to take entire control of the nation and the people, that he has a right to exact security for the future, and such secure for his own safety as he may demand."), 1309 (Stevens) ("conquered people" and "conquered provinces"), 2318 (Stevens), 2535 (Howard), 2879 (J. Ashley), 3627 (Stevens). But see, *Congressional Globe*, 39th Cong., 1st Sess., 109 (Stewart) (rejecting claims that former Confederate states were "conquered provinces"), 122 (Raymond) (same).

136. *Congressional Globe*, 39th Cong., 1st Sess., 158 (Bingham), 465 (Baker), 1021 (Bromwell), 1827 (Baldwin), 1840 (R. Clarke), 3177 (Dawes) ("They have always been States, but States disorganized, and therefore unable to elect Representatives.").
137. *Congressional Globe*, 39th Cong., 1st Sess., 989 (Fessenden).
138. *Congressional Globe*, 39th Cong., 1st Sess., 73 (Stevens) ("a dead corpse"), 125 (Jenckes) ("they simply died out"), 900 (Cook) ("such State government is destroyed and dead").
139. *Congressional Globe*, 39th Cong., 1st Sess., 163 (Howe), 4302 (Howe).
140. *Congressional Globe*, 39th Cong., 1st Sess., 88 (petition from citizens of Massachusetts).
141. *Congressional Globe*, 39th Cong., 1st Sess., 1470.
142. *Congressional Globe*, 39th Cong., 1st Sess., 2, 92, 592 (Sumner).
143. *Congressional Globe*, 39th Cong., 1st Sess., 73 (Stevens), 140 (Latham) ("the suspension of the proper practical relations between the people of these States and the national Government"), 157 (Bingham) ("if the functions of a State are suspended the powers of the State cannot be exercised"), 162 (Howe) ("the political functions formerly granted to those people have been suspended"), 1827 (Baldwin), 2091 (J. L. Thomas), 2250 (Scofield), 2690 (Morris), 2693 (Patterson) ("It was not a case of death but suspended animation."), 3995 (G. Williams).
144. *Congressional Globe*, 39th Cong., 1st Sess., 2087 (Miller).
145. *Congressional Globe*, 39th Cong., 1st Sess., App., 66 (Garfield) ("every vestige of municipal authority in those States was, by secession, rebellion, and the conquest of the rebellion, utterly destroyed"); *Congressional Globe*, 39th Cong., 1st Sess., 73 (Stevens), 900–901 (Cook), 904 (W. Lawrence) ("[w]ith all lawful civil government abandoned and destroyed in the rebellious States"), 2091 (J. L. Thomas), 3201 (Orth) ("The local governments in the several rebel States were undoubtedly destroyed by the act of rebellion."), 3995 (G. Williams).
146. *Congressional Globe*, 39th Cong., 1st Sess., 2 (Sumner) ("We all know that the State organizations in certain States of the Union have been usurped and overthrown."), 75 (J. Ashley) ("[s]tates whose constitutional governments were usurped or overthrown by the recent rebellion"), 2162 (Howe), 465 (Baker), 2091 (J. L. Thomas); *Congressional Globe*, 39th Cong., 1st Sess., App., 142 (Shellabarger) ("during such usurpation, such States and their people ceased to have any of the rights or powers of government as States of this Union").
147. See *Congressional Globe*, 39th Cong., 1st Sess., App., 65–66 (Garfield); *Congressional Globe*, 39th Cong., 1st Sess., 2 (Sumner) ("sundry states which, by reason of rebellion, were without Legislatures"), 904 (Lawrence) ("the people were thus left without any State government; that it is the duty of the United States to guarantee it, and until this is done there can be no valid *de jure* permanent civil State government and no right to representation in Congress or the Electoral College").
148. *Congressional Globe*, 39th Cong., 1st Sess., 988 (Fessenden) ("In order to constitute a State of the Union there should be a republican government; that government must be acknowledged by Congress."), 1826–1827 (Baldwin) (requirement that that state be republican), 2091 (J. L. Thomas) (requiring Congress consider "the republican character of their State governments"), 3177

(Dawes) ("until" former Confederate states "erect and maintain a State government republican in form, they are not capable of electing Representatives").

149. *Congressional Globe*, 39th Cong., 1st Sess., 1072. See *Congressional Globe*, 39th Cong., 1st Sess., App., 126 (Sherman) ("Having taken up arms against the United States, they by that act lose their constitutional powers within the United States to govern and control our councils.").

150. Abraham Lincoln, "Last Public Address," in Basler, *Collected Works*, 8:404. See *Congressional Globe*, 39th Cong., 1st Sess., 121 (Raymond) ("Their practical relations to the Constitution of the United States have been disturbed."), 782 (Ward) ("They are out of their practical relation with the Union."), 911 (Cullom) (same), 930 (Union League Club of NY), 1121 (Kelley) ("destroyed or suspended . . . the practical relations which made them parts of the Union?"), 1304 (Orth), 1318 (Holmes), 1473 (Dumont), 1477 (Anderson) ("the ordinances of secession . . . dissolve[d] the practical relations of the States adopting them with the Union"), 1619 (Myers), 1827 (Baldwin), 2083 (Perham), 2091 (J. L. Thomas), 2488 (H. Wilson), 3090 (Kelley), 3997 (Trumbull); *Congressional Globe*, 39th Cong., App., 86 (Shellabarger). See *Congressional Globe*, 39th Cong., 1st Sess., 1048 (Trumbull) ("Before the State of Tennessee can be again in constitutional relations with this Government, there must be set up an organization loyal to the Government."), 3209 (Orth) ("outside of the constitutional relations to the Union"); *Congressional Globe*, 39th Cong., 1st Sess., App., 143 (Loan) ("they have had no political relations to the Federal Government than those of rebellious subjects").
The joint resolution declaring Tennessee reconstructed asserted "the State of Tennessee is hereby restored to her former proper, practical relations to the Union." *Congressional Globe*, 39th Cong., 1st Sess., 4056.

151. *Congressional Globe*, 39th Cong., 1st Sess., 3246.

152. *Congressional Globe*, 39th Cong., 1st Sess., 1837. See *Congressional Globe*, 39th Cong., 1st Sess., 1007 (R. Clarke) ("They were once States in the Union.").

153. *Congressional Globe*, 39th Cong., 1st Sess., 2488.

154. *Congressional Globe*, 39th Cong., 1st Sess., 3177.

155. *Congressional Globe*, 39th Cong., 1st Sess., 158.

156. *Congressional Globe*, 39th Cong., 1st Sess., 165. See *Congressional Globe*, 39th Cong., 1st Sess., 2082 (Perham) ("[I]t is of but little importance whether we regard these States as dead, according to the theory of some members of Congress, or their functions suspended, as the President declares.").

157. *Congressional Globe*, 39th Cong., 1st Sess., 726.

158. *Congressional Globe*, 39th Cong., 1st Sess., 734.

159. *Congressional Globe*, 39th Cong., 1st Sess., 3999. See *Congressional Globe*, 39th Cong., 1st Sess., 24 (Howard).

160. *Congressional Globe*, 39th Cong., 1st Sess., 56.

161. Downs, *After Appomattox*, 114.

162. *Congressional Globe*, 39th Cong., 1st Sess., 3177. See *Congressional Globe*, 39th Cong., 1st Sess., 42 (Trumbull), 140 (Latham) ("They have been declared by proclamation of the Executive in rebellion . . . and I am yet notified of no proclamation of peace."), 1319 (Holmes) ("the rebellion" must be "suppressed in fact as well as name").

163. See *Congressional Globe*, 39th Cong., 1st Sess., 132.
164. *Congressional Globe*, 39th Cong., 1st Sess., App., 144.
165. *Congressional Globe*, 39th Cong., 1st Sess., 1049.
166. No Republican who supported exclusion maintained that the status of states was for judges to decide. H. Wilson's claim—"Once admit that the right of a State to secede is a debatable question to be determined by the courts, and you will have done more toward the destruction of this Government than was ever done by armed treason on the field of battle"—seems to have expressed the Republican attitude toward judicial review of exclusion as well as secession. *Congressional Globe*, 39th Cong., 1st Sess., 2948. See *Congressional Globe*, 39th Cong., 1st Sess., 165 ("No one pretends that the judicial department has this power."). Chapter 3 discusses Republican understandings of constitutional authority. Dawes maintained that "the three branches representing the Government of the United States—the two Houses and the President" had to "pass judgment upon" state constitutions before former Confederate states could be represented in Congress. *Congressional Globe*, 39th Cong., 1st Sess., 3176–3177.
167. *Congressional Globe*, 39th Cong., 1st Sess., App., 125. See *Congressional Globe*, 39th Cong., 1st Sess., 24 (Howard), 72 (Stevens) ("it is very plan that it requires the action of Congress to enable them to form a State Government and sent representatives to Congress"), 88 (petition from citizens of Massachusetts), 98 (Broomall) ("the future political condition of these people must be fixed by the supreme power of the conqueror"), 112 (H. Wilson) ("It is committed . . . to an Administration and a Congress placed in power by the American people."), 124 (Spalding), 125 (Jenckes), 786 (G. Williams), 900 (Cook), 909 (W. Lawrence) ("The power to determine when State government is restored . . . is the power of the people speaking through Congress, and can never be surrendered."), 912 (Cullom) ("Congress has the full power of reconstructing the rebellious States."), 920 (Longyear), 1007–1008 (R. Clarke), 1019 (Broomall), 1072 (Nye) ("Congress can prescribe the conditions."), 1143 (Fessenden), 1304–1305 (Orth), 1310 (Stevens), 1470–1471 (Hill), 1474 (Dumont) ("Congress alone has the power to speak their sins forgiven and set their captive souls at liberty."), 1477 (Anderson) ("I deny their right to admission until Congress shall settle the terms upon which their members shall be admitted."), 1617–1618 (Moulton), 1621 (Myers) ("Congress is to judge of the condition of these people."), 1625 (Buckland) ("It is a question for Congress to decide when the people of a State who have been in rebellion are in a condition to resume the right of representation."), 1800 (Wade), 1825 (Baldwin) ("It belongs to Congress, primarily, and to no other branch of the Government, to guarantee to each State a republican organization; and it belongs exclusively to Congress to decide whether the reorganization of a State that has been disorganized by any cause whatever is republican in form and in all respects satisfactory."), 2418–2419 (Poland), 2451 (H. Wilson), 2550–2552, 2554–2544 (Howard) ("the business of reconstructing the States belongs exclusively to Congress, and not to the Executive; that that is a thing to be done by the exercise of the law-making power only"), 1837 (W. Lawrence), 2083 (Perham) ("the law-making power of the Government alone is competent to perform this important duty"), 2091 (Miller) ("It is for Congress

to decide not only whether these State governments having been once subverted, have been again reconstructed, but to examine and see how they have been reconstructed, and whether they have been so reconstructed as to entitle them to representation here."), 2689–2690 (Morris) ("The relations thus changed and the rights thus affected can be restored to these States only by the legislative branch of the Government."), 2693 (Patterson) ("Congress . . . should decide when these States have been properly reorganized and fitted to renew their legitimate functions in the Union."), 3067 (R. Clarke) (Congress "decide[s] upon what terms and guarantees the rebel States shall be restored to their practical relations in the Union"), 3068 ("Congress not only has the right, but that it is its bounded duty, to legislate upon and determine this question."), 3095 (Price), 3201 (Orth), 3210 3211 (Julian) ("The restoration of civil government in the South is undeniably necessary. That Congress alone, in cooperation with the people can do this, is equally certain."). *Congressional Globe*, 1st Sess., App., 132 (resolution of the Indiana Union Convention), 208 (Bundy) ("Congress has the absolute right, and it is its duty to . . . determine who shall and who shall not be admitted to seats therein from the rebel States.").

168. *Congressional Globe*, 39th Cong., 1st Sess., 294. See *Congressional Globe*, 39th Cong., 1st Sess., 159 (Bingham), 1008 (R. Clarke) ("we, the Representatives of the loyal people of the Union, propose to become the sole judges ourselves of the terms and time of that restoration"); *Congressional Globe*, 39th Cong., 1st Sess., App., 66 ("belongs exclusively to the legislative authority of the Government to determine the political status of the insurgent States").

169. *Congressional Globe*, 39th Cong., 1st Sess., 1050.

170. *Congressional Globe*, 39th Cong., 1st Sess., 56.

171. *Congressional Globe*, 39th Cong., 1st Sess., 5. See *Congressional Globe*, 39th Cong., 1st Sess., 73 (Stevens), 142 (Shellabarger), 465 (Baker) (describing "the duty of Congress . . . to secure to the people of such usurped or disorganized State a republican form of government"), 868 (Newell), 900 (Cook), 904 (W. Lawrence), *Congressional Globe*, 39th Cong., 1st Sess., App., 88 (Delano).

172. *Congressional Globe*, 39th Cong., 1st Sess., 920.

173. *Congressional Globe*, 39th Cong., 1st Sess., 2. See *Congressional Globe*, 39th Cong., 1st Sess., 91 (Sumner) ("It must be performed by the national government."), 461 (Baker) ("another precedent condition is that the revolted States should each present a government republican in form, and of this Congress is the exclusive judge").

174. *Congressional Globe*, 39th Cong., 1st Sess., 92. See *Congressional Globe*, 39th Cong., 1st Sess., 2 (Sumner),

175. *Congressional Globe*, 39th Cong., 1st Sess., 2082. See *Congressional Globe*, 39th Cong., 1st Sess., 988 (Fessenden) ("In order to constitute a State of the Union there should be a republican government; that government must be acknowledged by Congress."), 2091 (J. L. Thomas) (requiring Congress consider "the republican character of their State governments").

176. *Congressional Globe*, 39th Cong., 1st Sess., 56.

177. *Congressional Globe*, 39th Cong., 1st Sess., 73. See *Congressional Globe*, 39th Cong., 1st Sess., 166 (Howe), 564 (Paine) ("when in the judgment of Congress

it shall be proper to admit these Territories as States of the Union, it will be for Congress to provide the necessary legislation").

178. *Congressional Globe*, 39th Cong., 1st Sess., 2318. See *Congressional Globe*, 39th Cong., 1st Sess., 2334 (Sumner) (claiming resolutions calling for former Confederate states to be represented in Congress "failed to make any provision for that security which common sense and common prudence, the Law of Nations and every instinct of the human heart require").

179. *Congressional Globe*, 39th Cong., 1st Sess., 564.

180. See *Congressional Globe*, 39th Cong., 1st Sess., 188 (Howe), 564.

181. *Congressional Globe*, 39th Cong., 1st Sess., 132–133. Baker tossed in the General Welfare Clause and the power to suppress insurrections. *Congressional Globe*, 39th Cong., 1st Sess., 464.

182. *Congressional Globe*, 39th Cong., 1st Sess., 1043.

183. *Congressional Globe*, 39th Cong., 1st Sess., 1043.

184. *Congressional Globe*, 39th Cong., 1st Sess., 165.

185. *Congressional Globe*, 39th Cong., 1st Sess., 166.

186. *Congressional Globe*, 39th Cong., 1st Sess., 1075.

187. *Congressional Globe*, 39th Cong., 1st Sess., 2400.

188. *Congressional Globe*, 39th Cong., 1st Sess., 2400.

189. *Congressional Globe*, 39th Cong., 1st Sess., 2400. See *Congressional Globe*, 39th Cong., 1st Sess., 2405.

190. *Congressional Globe*, 39th Cong., 1st Sess., 2400.

191. *Congressional Globe*, 39th Cong., 1st Sess., 1177 (Citizens of the United States).

192. *Congressional Globe*, 39th Cong., 1st Sess., 2 (Sumner) ("proper guarantees for security in the future"), 95 ("insist on guarantees"), 727 (Welker) ("guarantees for the future"), 902 (Cook) ("guarantees), 909 (W. Lawrence) ("guarantees"), 912 (Cullom) ("a sure guarantee against any more rebellions"), 1007 (R. Clarke) ("unmistakable guarantee against all possible contingency whereby the peace, the prosperity, the life of the nation may again be put in peril"), 1016 (Beaman) ("We should also obtain . . . some guarantee for future good conduct before consenting to place such mean in power.").

193. *Congressional Globe*, 39th Cong., 1st Sess., 112. See *Congressional Globe*, 39th Cong., 1st Sess., 122 (Raymond) ("guarantees for the future"), 124 (Bingham) ("a perpetual guarantee for the future"), 782 (Ward) ("future security of the nation"), 785 (Williams) ("All the safeguards which the circumstances of the case required."), 1019 (Bromwell) ("some security should be demanded of the States lately in rebellion").

194. See *Congressional Globe*, 39th Cong., 1st Sess., 1251. See *Congressional Globe*, 39th Cong., 1st Sess., 1025 (petition from citizens of Wisconsin) ("permanent guarantees for future security"), 1099 (petition from Brasher Galls, New York) ("against the admission of southern States until proper guarantees are established"). In many cases the congressmen presenting those petitions did not mention any particular guarantees that those petitions may have requested.

195. See *Congressional Globe*, 39th Cong., 1st Sess., 699 (citizens of Connecticut), 806 (citizens of Will County, Illinois) (same), 806 (petition of citizens of Buffalo), 829 (petition of citizens of Indiana and Ohio) (same), 828 (petition of

citizens of Michigan) (same), 931 (citizens of Massachusetts), 951 (petition of citizens of Henry County, Indiana) (same), 978 (petition or citizens of Defiance County, Ohio) (same), 1006 (citizens of Mahoning County, Ohio) (same), 1006 (petition from the third congressional district, Illinois (same), 1024 (petition from citizens of Huron and Erie Counties, Ohio) (same), 1099 (petition from citizens of Iowa). See *Congressional Globe*, 39th Cong., 1st Sess., 1099 (citizens of Maine) (same), 1099 (citizens of Indiana) (same). The good people of Burke, Vermont, used the phrase "ample security." *Congressional Globe*, 39th Cong., 1st Sess., 1006. See *Congressional Globe*, 39th Cong., 1st Sess., 951 (petition from citizens of Muscatine County, Iowa) ("sufficient security is given for the future").

196. *Congressional Globe*, 39th Cong., 1st Sess., 88. See *Congressional Globe*, 39th Cong., 1st Sess., 107 (same).

197. *Congressional Globe*, 39th Cong., 1st Sess., 1015.

198. *Congressional Globe*, 39th Cong., 1st Sess., 1007. See *Congressional Globe*, 39th Cong., 1st Sess., 1008 (R. Clarke) ("who does not know that an uncondi-tional restoration of those States would result in fresh revolts, and that all our bloody battles will have to be fought over again").

199. *Congressional Globe*, 39th Cong., 1st Sess., 469. See *Congressional Globe*, 39th Cong., 1st Sess., 465–466 (Baker), 1015 (Beaman) (admitting "without delay these traitors direct from the battlefield" would enable them to "attempt to accomplish by political skill and dark intrigue what they failed to do by the sword").

200. *Congressional Globe*, 39th Cong., 1st Sess., 2.

201. *Congressional Globe*, 39th Cong., 1st Sess., 508.

202. *Congressional Globe*, 39th Cong., 1st Sess., 72–75.

203. *Congressional Globe*, 39th Cong., 1st Sess., 1016. See *Congressional Globe*, 39th Cong., 1st Sess., 157 (Bingham).

204. See Mark A. Graber and Howard Gillman, *The Complete American Constitu-tionalism*, vol. 5, pt. 1: The Constitution of the Confederate States (New York: Oxford University Press: 2018), xvii–xxi.

205. See Arthur Bestor, "State Sovereignty and Slavery: A Reinterpretation of Pro-slavery Constitutional Doctrine, 1846–1860," 54 *Illinois State Historical Soci-ety Journal* 117 (1961).

206. See H. Robert Baker, *The Rescue of Joshua Glover: A Fugitive Slave, the Con-stitution, and the Coming of the Civil War* (Athens: Ohio University Press, 2006), 135–161.

207. See Joel H. Silbey, *A Respectful Minority: The Democratic Party in the Civil War Era, 1860–1868* (New York: W. W. Norton & Co., 1977).

208. For excellent surveys of partisan divisions over executive power during the Civil War, see Timothy S. Huebner, *Liberty & Union: The Civil War Era and American Constitutionalism* (Lawrence: University Press of Kansas, 2016), 211–248; Mark E. Neely, Jr., *The Fate of Liberty: Abraham Lincoln and Civil Liberties* (New York: Oxford University Press: 1991).

209. See Huebner, *Liberty & Union*; Neely, *The Fate of Liberty*.

210. See Eric Foner, *Free Soil, Free Labor, Free Men: The Ideology of the Republican*

Party before the Civil War (Oxford, UK: Oxford University Press, 1970), 73–102.

211. Abraham Lincoln, "Speech at Peoria, Illinois, October 16, 1854," in Basler, *Collected Works*, 2:268.

212. See Klinkner and Smith, *The Unsteady March*, 58–71.

2. THE PROBLEM OF REBEL RULE

1. *Congressional Globe*, 39th Cong., 1st Sess., App., 142–143. See *Congressional Globe*, 39th Cong., 1st Sess., App., 144 (Loan):

> [T]he rebel chieftains, shrewd, wily, and irrepressible, on the dispersion of their armies realized the utter and irretrievable failure of their attempt to divide and destroy this Republic by force, and at once comprehended the necessity for changing their plans. Fraud is the inevitable alternative of those who find themselves too weak to succeed by force, and the rebel leaders have transferred the contest which they waged for the division of the Republican from the battle-field to the political arena. There, in the guise of friends, in the name of loyalty, in the avowed cause of peace, harmony, and union, they have assumed to organize in the late rebellious districts civil State governments, and demand for them the recognition of political relations with the Federal Government as States in the Union, their real object and purpose being to secure a position which will enable them to form political combinations by which they can, as formerly, control the policy of the Government, that they may direct it to national destruction, for they have found it to possess a power that they cannot resist, and one that will control them unless they can destroy it.

2. *Congressional Globe*, 39th Cong., 1st Sess., 1616.

3. *Congressional Globe*, 39th Cong., 1st Sess., 732. See *Congressional Globe*, 39th Cong., 1st Sess., 011 (Cullom) ("they mean to come here and by political management attempt to do what they have not been able to do by the use of the sword"), 1470 (Hill) ("they should, through their State machinery, send their Senators and Representatives here, and through their action they should obtain a reversal of the arbitrament of arms, and thus, not being able to commit murder upon the nation, should accomplish its suicide"), 1616 (Moulton).

4. *Congressional Globe*, 39th Cong., 1st Sess., 783.

5. 60 U.S. 393 (1856).

6. 10 *Stat.* 277 (1854).

7. See, e.g., William M. Wiecek, *The Sources of Antislavery Constitutionalism in America, 1760–1848* (Ithaca, NY: Cornell University Press, 1984); Rebecca E. Zietlow, *The Forgotten Emancipator: James Mitchell Ashley and the Ideological Origins of Reconstruction* (New York: Cambridge University Press, 2018), 24–43.

8. Paul Finkelman, "John Bingham and the Background to the Fourteenth Amendment," 36 *Akron Law Review* 671, 681 (2003). The seminal statement of this position is Berger, *Government by Judiciary.* Supreme Court opinions routinely repeat this claim. The recent examples include United States v. Vaello

Madero, 596 U.S. ___. 142 S. Ct. 1539, 1548–1549 (2022) (Thomas, J., concurring), and Timbs v. Indiana, 586 U.S. ___, 139 S. Ct. 682, 689 (2019).

9. See Foner, *Free Soil, Free Labor, Free Men.*

10. *Congressional Globe,* 39th Cong., 1st Sess., 1412.

11. *Congressional Globe,* 39th Cong., 1st Sess., 1642.

12. See, e.g., *Congressional Globe,* 39th Cong., 1st Sess., 1389.

13. *Congressional Globe,* 39th Cong., 1st Sess., 1525,

14. *Congressional Globe,* 39th Cong., 1st Sess., 1391.

15. *Congressional Globe,* 39th Cong., 1st Sess., 1648.

16. *Congressional Globe,* 39th Cong., 1st Sess., 1528.

17. *Congressional Globe,* 39th Cong., 1st Sess., 4167.

18. *Congressional Globe,* 39th Cong., 1st Sess., 743.

19. *Congressional Globe,* 39th Cong., 1st Sess., 1057. See *Congressional Globe,* 39th Cong., 1st Sess., 1413 (Hendricks) ("question is not whether rebels, guilty parties, shall be admitted to the deliberations of the Senate, but whether loyal men, men who can take the oath, shall be admitted").

20. See, e.g., *Congressional Globe,* 39th Cong., 1st Sess., 354 (Kelley), 387 (Hill), 535 (Benjamin), 675 (Sumner), 685 (Sumner), 705 (Fessenden), 737 (H. Lane), 835 (Clark), 1090 (Bingham), 1095 (Hotchkiss), 1183 (S. Pomeroy), 1254 (Wilson), 1281 (Fessenden), 1284 (Anthony), 1285 (Trumbull), 2405 (Ingersoll), 2460 (Stevens), 2464 (Garfield), 2508 (Boutwell), 2509 (Spalding), 2535 (Eckley), 2536 (Longyear), 2540 (Farnsworth), 2768 (Howard), 2800 (Stewart), 2964 (Stewart), 3148 (Stevens); *Congressional Globe,* 39th Cong., 1st Sess., App., 109–110 (Jo. Henderson), 297 (Schenck).

21. See, e.g., *Congressional Globe,* 39th Cong., 1st Sess., 141 (Blaine) ("rebellious States"), 354 (Thayer) ("States lately in rebellion"), 379 (Sloan) (same), 404 (Lawrence), 432 (Bingham) ("States lately in rebellion"), 453 (McKee) ("rebellious States"), 674 (Sumner) ("States lately in rebellion"), 675 (Sumner), 739 (H. Lane), 982 (Sherman), 1065 (Hale) ("States lately in rebellion"), 1067 (Price) (same), 1094 (Bingham), 1094 (Hotchkiss), 1183 (S. Pomeroy), 1230 (Sumner), 1254 (Wilson), 2460 (Stevens), 2464 (Thayer), 2468 (Kelley), 2510 (Miller) ("States lately in rebellion"), 2768 (Howard); *Congressional Globe,* 39th Cong., 1st Sess., App., 58 (J. L. Thomas) ("States lately in rebellion"), 92 (G. Williams), 131 (Sherman), 155 (Morrill).

22. See, e.g., *Congressional Globe,* 39th Cong., 1st Sess., 74 (Stevens), 491 (Raymond), 675 (Sumner), 740 (H. Lane), 991 (Sherman), 2405 (Ingersoll), 2499 (Broomall), 2505 (McKee), 2509 (Spaulding), 2511 (Miller), 2540 (Farnsworth), 2768 (Howard), 2801 (Stewart), 2964 (Stewart); *Congressional Globe,* 39th Cong., 1st Sess., App., 99 (Yates), 127 (Sherman),

23. See, e.g., *Congressional Globe,* 39th Cong., 1st Sess., 404, 739 (H. Lane) ("rebel white voters"), 1284 (Anthony).

24. *Congressional Globe,* 39th Cong., 1st Sess., App., 58. See *Congressional Globe,* 39th Cong., 1st Sess., 1228 (Sumner) (rebel class).

25. See *Congressional Globe,* 39th Cong., 1st Sess., 535. See *Congressional Globe,* 39th Cong., 1st Sess., 2901 (Stewart) ("rebel elements"); *Congressional Globe,* 39th Cong., 1st Sess., App., 96.

26. *Congressional Globe,* 39th Cong., 1st Sess., 116.

27. *Congressional Globe*, 39th Cong., 1st Sess., App., 99.

28. *Congressional Globe*, 39th Cong., 1st Sess., App., 140.

29. *Congressional Globe*, 39th Cong., 1st Sess., 740. See also *Congressional Globe*, 39th Cong., 1st Sess., 1233 (Anthony) (condemning those who "engage in war on the rebel side").

30. See, e.g., *Congressional Globe*, 39th Cong., 1st Sess., 1616–1619 (Moulton); *Congressional Globe*, 39th Cong., 1st Sess., App., 142–145 (Loan).

31. See, *Congressional Globe*, 39th Cong., 1st Sess., 1616–1619 (Moulton); *Congressional Globe*, 39th Cong., 1st Sess., App., 142–145 (Loan).

32. *Congressional Globe*, 39th Cong., 1st Sess., 1008.

33. *Congressional Globe*, 39th Cong., 1st Sess., 143.

34. Garrett Epps, "The Undiscovered Country: Northern Views of the Defeated South and the Political Background of the Fourteenth Amendment," 13 *Temple Political & Civil Rights Law Review* 411, 413 (2004). This section owes much to Professor Epps's study.

35. *Congressional Globe*, 39th Cong., 1st Sess., 465 (Baker), 1017 (Beaman).

36. *Congressional Globe*, 39th Cong., 1st Sess., 92. See *Congressional Globe*, 39th Cong., 1st Sess., 92 (quoting A. Warren Kelsey) ("they deem it better to rule in the Union than to serve in the confederate army").

37. *Congressional Globe*, 39th Cong., 1st Sess., 443 (Howe), 909 (W. Lawrence), 1016 (Beaman).

38. "Declaration of Rights and Wrongs," *Proceedings of the Colored People's Convention of State of South Carolina* (Charleston: South Carolina Leader Office, 1865), 27.

39. Carl Schurz, "Report on the Condition of the South," Senate Document No 2, 39th Cong., 1st Sess. (1865), 39. See Schurz, "Report," 48, 50; Whitelaw Reid, *After the War: A Tour of the Southern States, 1865–1866* (New York: Harper & Row Publishers, 1965), 321, 578; John T. Trowbridge, *The Desolate South, 1865–1866: A Picture of the Battlefields and of the Devastated Confederacy* (Boston: Little, Brown, 1956), 152; John Richard Denning, *The South As It Is: 1865–1866* (New York: Viking Press, 1965), 41.

40. *Congressional Globe*, 39th Cong., 1st Sess., 93.

41. *Congressional Globe*, 39th Cong., 1st Sess., 93.

42. Trowbridge, *The Desolate South*, 152.

43. *Congressional Globe*, 39th Cong., 1st Sess., 92.

44. Sidney Andrews, *The South since the War: As Shown by Fourteen Weeks of Travel and Observation in Georgia and the Carolinas* (Boston: Ticknor and Fields, 1866), 283. See Andrews, *The South since the War*, 287 ("They admit the supremacy of the Federal Constitution, but they reaffirm the legality of secession.").

45. Andrews, *The South since the War*, 333. See Andrews, *The South since the War*, 363 ("It seems to be the common average sentiment that only a secondary allegiance is due the general government.").

46. *Congressional Globe*, 39th Cong., 1st Sess., 92.

47. Reid, *After the War*, 238.

48. *Congressional Globe*, 39th Cong., 1st Sess., 92.

49. Schurz, "Report," 47, 52 (quoting Major General Steedman).

50. Schurz, "Report," 13.
51. *Congressional Globe*, 39th Cong., 1st Sess., 873 (Howard) (presenting a memorial from citizens of Alexandria, Virginia).
52. See *Congressional Globe*, 39th Cong., 1st Sess., 92–93.
53. Denning, *The South*, 358.
54. *Congressional Globe*, 39th Cong., 1st Sess., 1017 (Beaman), 1076 (Nye) (same). See *Congressional Globe*, 39th Cong., 1st Sess., 313 (Sumner) (quoting a correspondent from Florida) ("The people of Florida are more hostile than they ever have been."), 465 (Baker) (quoting A.J. Fletcher to Baker, December 20, 1865) ("there are as many disloyal persons in Tennessee to-day as at any time since the beginning of 1861"), 1305 (Orth) (quoting a correspondent from Georgia) ("they are as intolerant and rebellious as any time during the war").
55. Schurz, "Report," 24.
56. Schurz, "Report," 7.
57. Denning, *The South*, 369.
58. *Congressional Globe*, 39th Cong., 1st Sess., 95. See *Congressional Globe*, 39th Cong., 1st Sess., 93 (Sumner) (quoting a correspondent from North Carolina) ("If anything otherwise, more hatred exists towards the Government. I know there is more toward Union men, both black and white."), 1629 (Hart) (quoting a correspondent) ("There is not one spark of love for the Union in all that I have seen or can judge, but bitter unrelenting hate, full of the spirit of hell and death to the black man and his white benefactor.").
59. Schurz, "Report," 57.
60. *Congressional Globe*, 39th Cong., 1st Sess., 2775.
61. *Congressional Globe*, 39th Cong., 1st Sess., 914.
62. *Congressional Globe*, 39th Cong., 1st Sess., 95.
63. *Congressional Globe*, 39th Cong., 1st Sess., 1147. See *Congressional Globe*, 39th Cong., 1st Sess., 94 (Sumner) (quoting a letter from Alabama) ("The existing feeling is, that no man who did not support the confederacy is worthy of trust; and that all offices are given to those who did their best to break up the country.").
64. Schurz, "Report," 13. See also Hyman, *Era of the Oath*, 84–86.
65. *Congressional Globe*, 39th Cong., 1st Sess., 873 (Howard) (presenting a memorial from citizens of Alexandria, Virginia).
66. *Congressional Globe*, 39th Cong., 1st Sess., 92. See *Congressional Globe*, 39th Cong., 1st Sess., 294 ("our old enemies on this floor, whom we banished for treason, may come back here to-day if their people see fit to send them").
67. Andrews, *The South since the War*, 158.
68. Reid, *After the War*, 405.
69. Reid, *After the War*, 408–409.
70. *Congressional Globe*, 39th Cong., 1st Sess., 93.
71. *Congressional Globe*, 39th Cong., 1st Sess., 873 (Howard) (presenting a memorial from citizens of Alexandria, Virginia).
72. For suppression of political dissent in the antebellum South, see Michael Kent Curtis, *Free Speech, "The People's Darling Privilege:" Struggles for Freedom of Expression in American History* (Durham, NC: Duke University Press, 2000),

117–299; Clement Eaton, *The Freedom of Thought Struggle in the Old South*, revised and enlarged ed. (New York: Harper & Row, 1964).

73. *Congressional Globe*, 39th Cong., 1st Sess., 93.

74. *Congressional Globe*, 39th Cong., 1st Sess., 95.

75. Andrews, *The South since the War*, 385. See Andrews, *The South since the War*, 372–373 (quoting a former Southern Unionist) ("There isn't any freedom of speech here, or anywhere in the State, unless you speak just as the Secessionists please to let you. I should be shot before to-morrow morning if I were to publicly say what I've said to you. Take the troops away, and off the great lines of travel there would be a reign of terror in a month.").

76. Denning, *The South*, 313. See Reid, *After the War*, 86 ("Nobody could stand up in the State who should advocate promiscuous negro suffrage.").

77. *Congressional Globe*, 39th Cong., 1st Sess., 95. See *Congressional Globe*, 39th Cong., 1st Sess., 1616 (Moulton) ("There is neither freedom of speech, or of the press, or protection to life, liberty, or property.").

78. *Congressional Globe*, 39th Cong., 1st Sess., 914. See *Congressional Globe*, 39th Cong., 1st Sess., 264 (petition from "colored men of the city of Montgomery, Alabama") (expressing concern about a state policy requiring "the arming of two militia companies in every county of the State").

79. *Congressional Globe*, 39th Cong., 1st Sess., 94.

80. *Congressional Globe*, 39th Cong., 1st Sess., 914.

81. *Congressional Globe*, 39th Cong., 1st Sess., 95.

82. *Congressional Globe*, 39th Cong., 1st Sess., 127. See *Congressional Globe*, 39th Cong., 1st Sess., 128 (petitioner from "colored citizens of the State of Mississippi") (complaining that "owing to the prejudice existing there, they have not been able to assemble in convention"), 914 (General Tillson) ("the withdrawal of troops has been followed by outrages on the freed people; their schoolhouses have been burned, their teachers driven off or threatened with death, and the freed people by fraud, and even by violence, made to enter into unjust and fraudulent contracts").

83. See *Congressional Globe*, 39th Cong., 1st Sess., 92–95.

84. *Congressional Globe*, 39th Cong., 1st Sess., 873 (Howard) (presenting a memorial from citizens of Alexandria, Virginia).

85. *Congressional Globe*, 39th Cong., 1st Sess., 466. See *Congressional Globe*, 39th Cong., 1st Sess., 93–95.

86. *Congressional Globe*, 39th Cong., 1st Sess., 94.

87. *Congressional Globe*, 39th Cong., 1st Sess., 95.

88. *Congressional Globe*, 39th Cong., 1st Sess., 94.

89. *Congressional Globe*, 39th Cong., 1st Sess., 94. African Americans residing in the territories had lesser, if serious, complaints. See *Congressional Globe*, 39th Cong., 1st Sess., 128 (petition by African American citizens in Colorado complaining "that they are taxed in that constitution without representation; they are even taxed to support public schools to educate the children of white people, while they are excluded from those schools themselves").

90. Schurz, "Report," 22.

91. Schurz, "Report," 4.

92. *Congressional Globe*, 39th Cong., 1st Sess., 93. Sumner heard from other correspondents that "northern men . . . do not consider themselves safe," that "northern lessees do not dare remain in their places," and that "respectable men . . . are refugees from their homes . . . , being recently expelled on account of their Union sentiments." *Congressional Globe*, 39th Cong., 1st Sess., 95.

93. *Congressional Globe*, 39th Cong., 1st Sess., 3095.

94. *Congressional Globe*, 39th Cong., 1st Sess., 95.

95. *Congressional Globe*, 39th Cong., 1st Sess., 1305.

96. *Congressional Globe*, 39th Cong., 1st Sess., 902 (Cook) (quoting a memorial from the Union State Central Committee of Tennessee). See *Congressional Globe*, 39th Cong., 1st Sess., 1305 (Orth) (quoting a correspondent from Georgia) ("I have seen the smoldering ruins of the property of northern settlers.").

97. *Congressional Globe*, 39th Cong., 1st Sess., 1147.

98. *Congressional Globe*, 39th Cong., 1st Sess., 1305.

99. *Congressional Globe*, 39th Cong., 1st Sess., 912.

100. *Congressional Globe*, 39th Cong., 1st Sess., 465 (Baker), 1917 (Beaman).

101. *Congressional Globe*, 39th Cong., 1st Sess., 94 (emphasis in original). See *Congressional Globe*, 39th Cong., 1st Sess., 92–95 (Sumner quoting various correspondents) ("many of them hope as long as the black race exists here to be able to hold it in a condition of practical serfdom. All expect the negro to be killed in one way or another by emancipation"; "a good many men are unwilling yet to believe that the 'peculiar institution' of the South has been actually abolished, and still have the lingering hope that slavery, though not in name, will yet in some form practically exist"; "[i]f legal chicanery can avail, these rights will be but nominal, and they will remain as they have ever been, isolated and part; free in name, but slave in fact"; "if . . . the unfortunate negro is to be left in the hands of his infuriated and disappointed former owners to legislature and fix his status, God help him, for his cup of bitterness will overflow indeed").

102. *Congressional Globe*, 39th Cong., 1st Sess., 93.

103. *Congressional Globe*, 39th Cong., 1st Sess., 902 (Cook) (quoting Union State Central Committee of Tennessee).

104. Trowbridge, *The Desolate South*, 316.

105. Schurz, "Report," 17–19.

106. Schurz, "Report," 50.

107. Schurz, "Report," 17.

108. Schurz, "Report," 51.

109. Schurz, "Report," 75.

110. Andrews, *The South since the War*, 178.

111. See Mark Tushnet, "Constitutional Workarounds," 87 *Texas Law Review* 1499 (2009).

112. John Trowbridge, *The Desolate South*, 222–223. See Schurz, "Report," 32, 35–36, 45, 50–51, 53, 91, 105; Reid, *After the War*, 44, 51, 146, 151, 343; *Congressional Globe*, 39th Cong., 1st Sess., 465 (Baker) (quoting Brownlow) (former slaves "would have hard times if the military were withdrawn").

113. *Congressional Globe*, 39th Cong., 1st Sess., 1017 (Beaman) (quoting the Union Party of Tennessee).

114. Andrews, *The South Since the War*, 378. See Denning, *The South*, 5, 42 ("persecution of Unionists").

115. Schurz, "Report," 105 (quoting A.P. Ketchum). See Schurz, "Report," 8 (noting that "if the troops were . . . withdrawn," Unionists "would not be permitted to live" in Charleston, and "the lives of northern men in Mississippi would not be safe").

116. *Congressional Globe*, 39th Cong., 1st Sess., 873 (Howard) (presenting a memorial from citizens of Alexandria, Virginia).

117. *Congressional Globe*, 39th Cong., 1st Sess., 465 (Baker), 1017 (Beaman). The same conditions existed in Georgia. See *Congressional Globe*, 39th Cong., 1st Sess., 1305 (Orth) (quoting a correspondent) ("The moment the troops are removed the citizens say openly that they intended to send every Yankee where they belong, and will attend to the negroes as they deserve.").

118. *Congressional Globe*, 39th Cong., 1st Sess., 902 (Cook) (quoting Governor Brownlow of Tennessee), 1017 (Beaman) (same), 1076 (Nye) (same).

119. *Congressional Globe*, 39th Cong., 1st Sess., 465; *Congressional Globe*, 39th Cong., 1st Sess., 1017. See *Congressional Globe*, 39th Cong., 1st Sess., 465 (Baker) (quoting A.J. Fletcher to Baker, December 20, 1865) ("Teachers from the North engaged in teach negroes would not be admitted into society, and in many places be driven away.").

120. *Congressional Globe*, 39th Cong., 1st Sess., 465 (Baker) (quoting A. J. Fletcher to Baker, December 20, 1865).

121. Trowbridge, *The Desolate South*, 316. See Schurz, "Report," 14; Denning, *The South*, 91; Andrews, *The South since the War*, 36, 284; Andrews, *The South since the War*, 97, 324, 371.

122. *Congressional Globe*, 39th Cong., 1st Sess., 313. The Union State Central Committee of Tennessee predicted restoration would ensure "patronage" to "the late rebels," "medals to southern heroes," payment of the "confederate debt," and Black Codes. *Congressional Globe*, 39th Cong., 1st Sess., 902.

123. *Congressional Globe*, 39th Cong., 1st Sess., 92. Sumner quoted another correspondent, who declared: "They will do all in their power to resist negro suffrage, and to reduce taxation and expenditures, and would attack the national debt if they saw any reason to believe repudiation possible. They will continue to assert the inferiority of the African." *Congressional Globe*, 39th Cong., 1st Sess., 92. Sumner quoted Southern politicians who explicitly denied Southern responsibility for the national debt. *Congressional Globe*, 39th Cong., 1st Sess., 92 (quoting a candidate from Congress in Virginia) ("I am opposed to the southern States being taxed at all for the redemption of this debt, either directly or indirectly."), 92 ("The idea that the national will pay the South for her slaves extensively prevails.").

124. Andrews, *The South since the War*, 267. Sumner quoted that speech as declaring: "Let us repudiate only under the lash and the application of military power, and then, as soon as we are an independent sovereignty, restored to our equal rights and privileges in the Union, let us immediately call another convention and resume the debt." *Congressional Globe*, 39th Cong., 1st Sess., 93. See Andrews, *The South since the War*, 260–268.

125. *Congressional Globe*, 39th Cong., 1st Sess., 92 (Sumner) (quoting A. Warren Kelsey).
126. *Congressional Globe*, 39th Cong., 1st Sess., 93.
127. *Congressional Globe*, 39th Cong., 1st Sess., 92.
128. *Congressional Globe*, 39th Cong., 1st Sess., 94.
129. Reid, *After the War*, 439.
130. *Congressional Globe*, 39th Cong., 1st Sess., 95. See *Congressional Globe*, 39th Cong., 1st Sess., 93–95 ("If we act wisely we shall be joined by what is called the Copperhead party, and even by many of the Black Republicans.").
131. Reid, *After the War*, 403–444. See Epps, "The Undiscovered Country," 418–419.
132. Andrews, *The South since the War*, 355. See Andrews, *The South since the War*, 216, 233; Reid, *After the War*, 77, 305, 393–394; Denning, *The South*, 351, 355.
133. Andrews, *The South since the War*, 44.
134. *Congressional Globe*, 39th Cong., App., 1st Sess., 155.
135. Salmon Portland Chase and Charles Dexter Cleveland, *Anti-Slavery Addresses of 1844 and 1845* (Philadelphia: J. A. Bancroft and Co., 1867), 97. See Foner, *Free Soil, Free Labor, Free Men*, 89. Republicans in the Thirty-Ninth Congress continued to condemn the Three-Fifths Clause. See *Congressional Globe*, 39th Cong., 1st Sess., 404 (Lawrence), 410 (Broomall). *Congressional Globe*, 39th Cong., 1st Sess., App., 296.
136. See Paul Finkelman, "How the Proslavery Constitution Led to the Civil War," 43 *Rutgers Law Journal* 405, 424–429 (2013).
137. See "Report and Resolutions of the Hartford Convention," *Documents of American History*, vol. 1, edited by Henry Steele Commager (New York: Appleton-Century Crofts, 1963), 1263; *Annals of Congress*, 16th Cong., 1st Sess., 153–154, 217, 965, 1192; *Annals of Congress*, 15th Cong., 2nd Sess., 1213; Masur, *Until Justice be Done*, 169–173.
138. "Letter from Robert Dale Owen: Negro Suffrage and Representative Population," *New York Tribune*, June 24, 1865, 8.
139. "News from Washington," *Richmond Examiner*, January 9, 1866, 1.
140. *Congressional Globe*, 39th Cong., 1st Sess., 92.
141. Denning, *The South*, 362.
142. *Congressional Globe*, 39th Cong., 1st Sess., App., 2.
143. *Congressional Globe*, 39th Cong., 1st Sess., 78.
144. *Congressional Globe*, 39th Cong., 1st Sess., 78.
145. *Congressional Globe*, 39th Cong., 1st Sess., 78.
146. *Congressional Globe*, 39th Cong., 1st Sess., 78.
147. *Congressional Globe*, 39th Cong., 1st Sess., 78.
148. *Congressional Globe*, 39th Cong., 1st Sess., 78.
149. *Congressional Globe*, 39th Cong., 1st Sess., 78.
150. *Congressional Globe*, 39th Cong., 1st Sess., 78.
151. *Congressional Globe*, 39th Cong., 1st Sess., 78.
152. *Congressional Globe*, 39th Cong., 1st Sess., 78.
153. *Congressional Globe*, 39th Cong., 1st Sess., 78.
154. "Views of the Minority," *Reports of the Committees*, 8.
155. "Views of the Minority," 8.

156. "Views of the Minority," 7.
157. "Views of the Minority," 8–9.
158. *Congressional Globe*, 39th Cong., 1st Sess., 40.
159. *Congressional Globe*, 39th Cong., 1st Sess., 117. See *Congressional Globe*, 39th Cong., 1st Sess., 1026 (J. Lane) ("I feel authorized to declare that the situation of the State of Arkansas today is as peaceable and quiet as any other State in the Union."), 1311 (Goodyear) ("the southern people profess entire submission and fealty to the Constitution and laws of the United States and their acts correspond with their words"), 2468 (Boyer) ("the people of the South, once rebels, are rebels no longer"); *Congressional Globe*, 39th Cong., 1st Sess., App., 172 (Grider) ("Tennessee is certainly more loyal now than she was then."), 185 (G. Davis) (its "citizens are now loyal"). For a rare proponent of congressional Reconstruction who agreed with this claim, see *Congressional Globe*, 39th Cong., 1st Sess., 1626 (Buckland) ("the great mass of the southern people are submitting to the Government in good faith").
160. *Congressional Globe*, 39th Cong., 1st Sess., 96.
161. *Congressional Globe*, 39th Cong., 1st Sess., 96.
162. *Congressional Globe*, 39th Cong., 1st Sess., 96.
163. *Congressional Globe*, 39th Cong., 1st Sess., 1407. See *Congressional Globe*, 39th Cong., 1st Sess., 1411 (G. Davis) ("I do not believe one word" of "the general charges made by the Senator from Massachusetts of cruel and inhumane treatment of the negro soldiers in Kentucky," other claims of "outrage(s) are "as basely false as it is possible for something to be.").
164. *Congressional Globe*, 39th Cong., 1st Sess., 96.
165. See *Congressional Globe*, 39th Cong., 1st Sess., 97. See *Congressional Globe*, 39th Cong., 1st Sess., 111 (Stewart) (quoting Grant), 870 (Strouse) (citing Grant). The minority report for the Joint Committee on Reconstruction also relied heavily on Grant when claiming that rebels no longer ruled the South. See "Views of the Minority," 23. The Democrats on the committee in February urged that Tennessee be represented in Congress because, although "at some localities there have been some irregularities and temporary disaffection, . . . the great body of the people in said State are not only loyal and willing, but anxious to have and maintain amicable, sincere, and patriotic relations with the General Government." *Congressional Globe*, 39th Cong., 1st Sess., 944.
166. *Congressional Globe*, 39th Cong., 1st Sess., 96. See *Congressional Globe*, 39th Cong., 1st Sess., 95 (Saulsbury) ("Private letters and correspondence are not to be supposed to have much weight with the Senate of the United States.").
167. *Congressional Globe*, 39th Cong., 1st Sess., 96.
168. *Congressional Globe*, 39th Cong., 1st Sess., 1411.
169. *Congressional Globe*, 39th Cong., 1st Sess., 109.
170. Governor Brownlow and Carl Schurz were particular sources of reference. See *Congressional Globe*, 39th Cong., 1st Sess., 909 (W. Lawrence) (quoting Schurz on Southern loyalty and commitment to maintaining revised forms of slavery), 1305 (Orth).
171. *Report of the Joint Committee*, xvii.
172. *Report of the Joint Committee*, xvii.
173. *Report of the Joint Committee*, xvii.

174. *Report of the Joint Committee*, xvii. See *Report of the Joint Committee*, xvi ("The national banner is openly insulted, and the national airs scoffed at"), xviii ("the proof of a condition of feeling hostile to the Union and dangerous to the government throughout the insurrectionary States would seem to be overwhelming.").

175. *Report of the Joint Committee*, xvii.

176. *Report of the Joint Committee*, x. See *Report of the Joint Committee*, ix ("There was no evidence of loyalty of those who had participated in these conventions."), xvii.

177. *Report of the Joint Committee*, xvi.

178. *Report of the Joint Committee*, xi. See *Report of the Joint Committee*, vii ("They . . . laid down their arms only because there was no longer any power to use them.").

179. *Report of the Joint Committee*, xv.

180. *Report of the Joint Committee*, xi.

181. *Report of the Joint Committee*, xvii.

182. *Report of the Joint Committee*, xvii.

183. *Report of the Joint Committee*, xvii.

184. *Report of the Joint Committee*, xviii.

185. *Report of the Joint Committee*, xviii.

186. *Report of the Joint Committee*, xvii.

187. *Report of the Joint Committee*, xvii.

188. *Report of the Joint Committee*, xx.

189. *Congressional Globe*, 39th Cong., 1st Sess., 444. See *Congressional Globe*, 39th Cong., 1st Sess., 903 (Cook) ("in all the southern States the spirit of the majority of the people is hostile to the Government of the United States"), 2947 (H. Wilson) ("[a] majority of the people of those States who engaged in the rebellion are as hostile to the Government as they were at any period of the war").

190. *Congressional Globe*, 39th Cong., 1st Sess., 295.

191. *Congressional Globe*, 39th Cong., 1st Sess., 909. See *Congressional Globe*, 39th Cong., 1st Sess., 2947 (H. Wilson) ("The destructive doctrine of secession is not dead, nor is it even sleeping. It is as firmly rooted in the minds of those who waged war to enforce it as it was before the first gun was fired in the late great civil war. They have not yielded one iota of the claim they made of the right of a State to secede."), 3064 (R. Clarke) ("the heresies that led to the late rebellion . . . are still retained by the rebels").

192. *Congressional Globe*, 39th Cong., 1st Sess., 3069.

193. *Congressional Globe*, 39th Cong., 1st Sess., 466. See *Congressional Globe*, 39th Cong., 1st Sess., 469 (Broomall) ("can we safely intrust to these governments the rights and interests of the Union men of the South?").

194. *Congressional Globe*, 39th Cong., 1st Sess., 1008. See *Congressional Globe*, 39th Cong., 1st Sess., 1617 ("To stop fighting does not make them cease to be public enemies, because they may have ceased fighting for want of means, not will."), 1629 (Hart) ("the rebels, who, a few months ago, believed themselves forever beaten in their attempts to destroy the Government, now stand erect with unconquerable hate to renew the struggle").

195. *Congressional Globe*, 39th Cong., 1st Sess., 3066.

196. *Congressional Globe*, 39th Cong., 1st Sess., 739. See *Congressional Globe*, 39th Cong., 1st Sess., 168 ("having found they cannot successfully fight against the United States, they would doubtless, like the privilege of sending here some hundred or more representatives to vote against it"), 332 (Deming).

197. *Congressional Globe*, 39th Cong., 1st Sess., 787. See *Congressional Globe*, 39th Cong., 1st Sess., 1183 (S. Pomeroy) ("If suffrage in the rebel States is now placed in the hands of only those who voted before, what reason can any one give why they will not vote again to make war on the United States when the times and occasion shall promise success more certainly. Does an inability to prosecute longer the war and a surrender on that account change the character or purpose of the people engaged in it? When did exhaustion or defeat ever eradicate the conscientious convictions of a great people, struggling, as they supposed, for their rights and their liberties, deluded though they were?").

198. *Congressional Globe*, 39th Cong., 1st Sess., App., 61.

199. *Congressional Globe*, 39th Cong., 1st Sess., 3166.

200. *Congressional Globe*, 39th Cong., 1st Sess., 796. See *Congressional Globe*, 39th Cong., 1st Sess., 1007 (R. Clarke) ("No penitence, no acknowledgement of error, no manifestation of the turn of filial or fraternal regard, but a sullen, reluctant submission to the force of circumstances they cannot control."), 1395 (Orth).

201. *Congressional Globe*, 39th Cong., 1st Sess., 834. See *Congressional Globe*, 39th Cong., 1st Sess., 3064 (R. Clarke) ("the rebels are importunate to get back, and they are very careful to insist upon their rehabilitation under circumstances as nearly like those under which they left").

202. *Congressional Globe*, 39th Cong., 1st Sess., 1016.

203. *Congressional Globe*, 39th Cong., 1st Sess., 331. See *Congressional Globe*, 39th Cong., 1st Sess., 1305 (Orth) ("I could give instances almost without number of the spirit of disloyalty constantly manifesting itself in very large portions of the rebellious districts."), 1319 (Holmes) (citing "an entire want of loyalty in these States. . . . [H]ow widespread and universal is the felling of hostility to the General Government in most if not all of these States[?]").

204. *Congressional Globe*, 39th Cong., 1st Sess., 169.

205. *Congressional Globe*, 39th Cong., 1st Sess., 332. See *Congressional Globe*, 39th Cong., 1st Sess., 168 (Howe) (describing Southerners as advising to "[k]eep still till we get in a position where they cannot put any more restraints upon us").

206. *Congressional Globe*, 39th Cong., 1st Sess., 1319.

207. *Congressional Globe*, 39th Cong., 1st Sess., 444.

208. *Congressional Globe*, 39th Cong., 1st Sess., 168. See *Congressional Globe*, 39th Cong., 1st Sess., 1319 (Holmes) ("Is not hostility to the Government as widespread and unyielding as during the balmy days of the revolution?").

209. *Congressional Globe*, 39th Cong., 1st Sess., 782.

210. *Congressional Globe*, 39th Cong., 1st Sess., 1472.

211. *Congressional Globe*, 39th Cong., 1st Sess., 168.

212. *Congressional Globe*, 39th Cong., 1st Sess., 168. See *Congressional Globe*, 39th Cong., 1st Sess., 168–169 (Howe) (noting the frequency with which former Confederates hissed at national airs and cheered Southern songs).

213. *Congressional Globe*, 39th Cong., 1st Sess., 1471.

214. *Congressional Globe*, 39th Cong., 1st Sess., 4046.
215. *Congressional Globe*, 39th Cong., 1st Sess., App., 140.
216. *Congressional Globe*, 39th Cong., 1st Sess., App., 144. See *Congressional Globe*, 39th Cong., 1st Sess., 463 (Baker) ("Look, sir, at the men who have already been elected . . . by most of these communities."); *Congressional Globe*, 39th Cong., 1st Sess., App., 99 (Yates) ("We know that the only passport to southern office, to the Legislature and to Congress, is fidelity in the rebel army and in the rebel cause.").
217. *Congressional Globe*, 39th Cong., 1st Sess., 453.
218. *Congressional Globe*, 39th Cong., 1st Sess., 782 (emphasis in original). See *Congressional Globe*, 39th Cong., 1st Sess., 1164 (McKee) (detailing the influence of former Confederates on reconstructed States and proposed congressional delegations after asking, "Have traitors a back seat in the restoration of the States recently in rebellion?").
219. *Congressional Globe*, 39th Cong., 1st Sess., App., 144.
220. *Congressional Globe*, 39th Cong., 1st Sess., 453.
221. *Congressional Globe*, 39th Cong., 1st Sess., 3070. See *Congressional Globe*, 39th Cong., 1st Sess., 3069–3070 (Van Aernam) (detailing former Confederate electoral successes in the former Confederate states).
222. *Congressional Globe*, 39th Cong., 1st Sess., 1016.
223. *Congressional Globe*, 39th Cong., 1st Sess., 1076.
224. *Congressional Globe*, 39th Cong., 1st Sess., 444.
225. *Congressional Globe*, 39th Cong., 1st Sess., 783. See *Congressional Globe*, 39th Cong., 1st Sess., 141 (Latham) ("from the tone of their press, and the general character and antecedents of those recently elected to offices of honor and trust, they are far, very far indeed, from . . . filling what I should consider prerequisites for the admission of their representatives").
226. *Congressional Globe*, 39th Cong., 1st Sess., 834.
227. *Congressional Globe*, 39th Cong., 1st Sess., 791. See *Congressional Globe*, 39th Cong., 1st Sess., 902 (Cook), 1007 (R. Clarke).
228. *Congressional Globe*, 39th Cong., 1st Sess., 168. See *Congressional Globe*, 39th Cong., 1st Sess., 167 (Howe) ("How has the consent of either of those communities to the decree of emancipation been obtained? How is it that some of them agreed to annul their ordinances of secession while others have only repealed them? How have some of these communities been induced *not* to forego, but to postpone, the charge of the debt contracted in aid of the rebellion upon the industry of those communities?"), 1470 (Hill), 1628 (Hart).
229. *Congressional Globe*, 39th Cong., 1st Sess., 332.
230. *Congressional Globe*, 39th Cong., 1st Sess., 332.
231. *Congressional Globe*, 39th Cong., 1st Sess., 1017. See *Congressional Globe*, 39th Cong., 1st Sess., 168 (Howe) ("men whom your law condemns to death wantonly assaulted me for no other reason than that your law proclaimed them free"), 1016 (Beaman) (pointing to "the daily murders of Union men in the districts lately in rebellion, . . . the disposition to extinguish the very existence of every man who during the war was found faithful among the faithless . . . , and their fiendish treatment of that unfortunate race who kissed the rod that smote them").

232. *Congressional Globe*, 39th Cong., 1st Sess., 1616. See *Congressional Globe*, 39th Cong., 1st Sess., 1629 (Hart) ("They persecute loyal men, they butcher the negroes; they enact laws which practically reenslave the negro."); *Congressional Globe*, 39th Cong., 1st Sess., App., 144 (Loan) ("standing armies and martial law are yet required to enforce national authority and to protect the loyal people against rebel violence and outrage").

233. *Congressional Globe*, 39th Cong., 1st Sess., 915.

234. *Congressional Globe*, 39th Cong., 1st Sess., 95.

235. *Congressional Globe*, 39th Cong., 1st Sess., 94.

236. *Congressional Globe*, 39th Cong., 1st Sess., App., 144.

237. *Congressional Globe*, 39th Cong., 1st Sess., 783. See *Congressional Globe*, 39th Cong., 1st Sess., 168 (Howe) ("There is another class of people there who, in my judgment, deserve the attention of Congress. I refer to that class who have the luck to be white but have had the singular taste during the past four years to be loyal."). See also *Congressional Globe*, 39th Cong., 1st Sess., 142 (Shellabarger) (pointing to the "indiscriminate and remorseless assassination or murder of every loyal man whom their treason could reach" during the Civil War).

238. *Congressional Globe*, 39th Cong., 1st Sess., App., 140.

239. As will be detailed in a forthcoming volume, the Black Codes were front and center when Republicans discussed such statutory reforms as the Civil Rights Act of 1866 and the Second Freedmen's Bureau Bill.

240. *Congressional Globe*, 39th Cong., 1st Sess., 39. See *Congressional Globe*, 39th Cong., 1st Sess., 442–444 (Howe) (condemning Black Codes); 733 (Kelso) (same), 793 (Williams) (same), 902 (Cook) (same), 908 (W. Lawrence), 1305 (Orth). For similar claims made in debates over legislation protecting free persons of color, see *Congressional Globe*, 39th Cong., 1st Sess., 41 (H. Wilson) ("the laws of Mississippi makes every one of these men whom we have made free practically a slave"), 93 (Sumner "a body of men calling themselves the Legislature . . . have undertaken to pass a Black Code, separating the two races, in defiance of every principle of Equality"), 111 (H. Wilson).

241. *Congressional Globe*, 39th Cong., 1st Sess., 1621.

242. *Congressional Globe*, 39th Cong., 1st Sess., 733. See *Congressional Globe*, 39th Cong., 1st Sess., 1319 (Holmes) ("These people are nominally free but really slaves.").

243. *Congressional Globe*, 39th Cong., 1st Sess., 783.

244. *Congressional Globe*, 39th Cong., 1st Sess., 331–332. See *Congressional Globe*, 39th Cong., 1st Sess., 470 (Broomall) (endorsing the Schurz Report), 1305 (Orth) (same).

245. *Congressional Globe*, 39th Cong., 1st Sess., 93.

246. See *Congressional Globe*, 39th Cong., 1st Sess., App., 154 (L. Morrill) ("they are not free men; they have no right whatever which that community is bound to respect; they are more than ever beyond the pale and protection of the Constitution; they have not even a master to serve with an interest in his service to care for his physical condition").

247. *Congressional Globe*, 39th Cong., 1st Sess., 783. See *Congressional Globe*, 39th Cong., 1st Sess., 740 (H. Lane) ("The slave codes in substance still in force . . . Not a single one of these rebel State Legislatures has protected the

rights of the freedmen."), 792–793 (G. Williams) ("[H]ow is it in regard to the marital relation, with all its incidents? How as to education and preparation for the ballot? Have the schools been thrown open to him? Is he free to work on his own terms, to acquire property, to go about wherever his interests or inclination may lead him, and to seek employment at such wages as he can fairly earn—or is he still subject to condemnation as a vagrant, and sale or apprenticeship for fines and jail fees?").

248. *Congressional Globe*, 39th Cong., 1st Sess., 727. See *Congressional Globe*, 39th Cong., 1st Sess., App., 99 (Yates) ("We know there is a bitter and unrelenting hostility toward the freedmen who have been emancipated by the constitutional amendment.").

249. *Congressional Globe*, 39th Cong., 1st Sess., 783.

250. Reva Siegel, "'The Rule of Love': Wife Beating as Prerogative and Privacy," 105 *Yale Law Journal* 2117, 2178 (1996).

251. *Congressional Globe*, 39th Cong., 1st Sess., App., 155.

252. *Congressional Globe*, 39th Cong., 1st Sess., 111. See *Congressional Globe*, 39th Cong., 1st Sess., App., 140 (H. Wilson) ("The poor freedmen are . . . everywhere subject to indignity, insult, outrage, and murder.").

253. *Congressional Globe*, 39th Cong., 1st Sess., App., 140.

254. *Congressional Globe*, 39th Cong., 1st Sess., 733.

255. *Congressional Globe*, 39th Cong., 1st Sess., 203.

256. *Congressional Globe*, 39th Cong., 1st Sess., 141.

257. *Congressional Globe*, 39th Cong., 1st Sess., 95.

258. *Congressional Globe*, 39th Cong., 1st Sess., 168.

259. *Congressional Globe*, 39th Cong., 1st Sess., 1618. See *Congressional Globe*, 39th Cong., 1st Sess., 2 (Sumner) (Southern loyalists are being "driv[en] . . . from their homes" and "depriv[ed] . . . of all opportunity of livelihood"), 1471 (Hill) ("men are fleeing the South for their lives, for no other crime than that they have been true to your government").

260. *Congressional Globe*, 39th Cong., 1st Sess., 1018. See *Congressional Globe*, 39th Cong., 1st Sess., 1018 (Beaman) (warning that "we should have on this floor fifty-eight Representatives, representing rebel constituencies").

261. *Congressional Globe*, 39th Cong., 1st Sess., 2535. See *Congressional Globe*, 39th Cong., 1st Sess., 357 (Conkling) ("Twenty-eight votes, to be more or less controlled by those who once betrayed the Government."), 404 (W. Lawrence) ("They will reward traitors with a liberal premium for treason."), 410 (Cook) ("The reward of treason will be an increased representation in this House, an increased influence in the Government."), 2962 (Poland) ("With no amendment on this subject the late slave States come into the lower House of Congress with a much larger representation than ever before. Is it safe to do this, is it just to the loyal portion of the nation who have borne such immense burdens to maintain its existence").

262. *Congressional Globe*, 39th Cong., 1st Sess., 1016 (emphasis in original).

263. *Congressional Globe*, 39th Cong., 1st Sess., 1470.

264. *Congressional Globe*, 39th Cong., 1st Sess., 1319. See *Congressional Globe*, 39th Cong., 1st Sess., 1319 (Holmes) ("Have the loyal people of either of these States the power to sustain a State government without the aid of Federal bayonets?").

265. *Congressional Globe*, 39th Cong., 1st Sess., 168. See *Congressional Globe*, 39th Cong., 1st Sess., 169 (Howe) (abandoning Reconstruction would "surrender the protection of its freedmen, its heroic soldiers, and its faithful friends to its direst enemies"). L. Morrill made similar observations.

> The rebel debts are still unrepudiated by those States and menace the public credit, while the national debt is unassumed by them. Secession is not annulled but repealed, and in condition for fresh opportunity to repeat its attack upon the national sovereignty. The freedmen have no protection in those States outside of that scanty and temporary protection, inadequate and precarious, which is afforded through the Freedmen's Bureau. Their rights of manhood are denied. Everybody knows that since these States have themselves become "reconstructed" they have enacted black codes and vagrant laws to take possession and control of these "freedmen." The great struggle to-day is for the possession of the negro now as in the past. That is the great struggle in the South. Slave-masters have lost their personal control over them. They demand now that they shall be remanded into their custody, they having the political power of the State. (*Congressional Globe*, 39th Cong., 1st Sess., App., 155.)

266. *Congressional Globe*, 39th Cong., 1st Sess., 207 (emphasis in original).
267. *Congressional Globe*, 39th Cong., 1st Sess., 1319. See *Congressional Globe*, 39th Cong., 1st Sess., 444 ("if we recommit the powers of the States to those people to-day, the rights and dearest interests of these two classes of men, one of which we have made free and the other of which we have found loyal, will be utterly disregarded and trampled upon").
268. *Congressional Globe*, 39th Cong., 1st Sess., 2800.
269. *Congressional Globe*, 39th Cong., 1st Sess., 1616.
270. *Congressional Globe*, 39th Cong., 1st Sess., 1618.
271. *Congressional Globe*, 39th Cong., 1st Sess., 914.
272. *Congressional Globe*, 39th Cong., 1st Sess., 903, 902. See *Congressional Globe*, 39th Cong., 1st Sess., 902 (Cook) (noting that without the military, "the Union men and freedmen can have no protection").
273. *Congressional Globe*, 39th Cong., 1st Sess., 732.
274. *Congressional Globe*, 39th Cong., 1st Sess., 3167.
275. *Congressional Globe*, 39th Cong., 1st Sess., 258. See *Congressional Globe*, 39th Cong., 1st Sess., 294 (Wade) ("will you desert them and leave them in the hands of their vindictive enemies to be destroyed").
276. *Congressional Globe*, 39th Cong., 1st Sess., 74. See *Congressional Globe*, 39th Cong., 1st Sess., 111 (describing the evidence of Southern abuse of former slaves as "enough to make the heart and soul sick").
277. *Congressional Globe*, 39th Cong., 1st Sess., 167. See *Congressional Globe*, 39th Cong., 1st Sess., App., 155 (L. Morrill) (condemning that who would "remand" freed persons of color "to their old masters who we know propose to press and deny them every civil right").
278. *Congressional Globe*, 39th Cong., 1st Sess., 167.
279. *Congressional Globe*, 39th Cong., 1st Sess., 294.

280. *Congressional Globe*, 39th Cong., 1st Sess., 2509.
281. *Congressional Globe*, 39th Cong., 1st Sess., 2540. See *Congressional Globe*, 39th Cong., 1st Sess., 792 (G. Williams) ("you have only made his condition worse"). See *Congressional Globe*, 39th Cong., 1st Sess., App., 132 (Sherman) ("What would be their miserable fate if now surrendered to the custody of the rebels of the South?").
282. *Congressional Globe*, 39th Cong., 1st Sess., 793. See *Congressional Globe*, 39th Cong., 1st Sess., 792–793 (G. Williams) ("You will only have mocked him with the mirage of liberty to make his condition tenfold worse than it was before.").
283. *Congressional Globe*, 39th Cong., 1st Sess., 470.
284. *Congressional Globe*, 39th Cong., 1st Sess., 167.
285. *Congressional Globe*, 39th Cong., 1st Sess., 167.
286. *Congressional Globe*, 39th Cong., 1st Sess., App., 99.
287. *Congressional Globe*, 39th Cong., 1st Sess., 69.
288. *Congressional Globe*, 39th Cong., 1st Sess., 1474. See *Congressional Globe*, 39th Cong., 1st Sess., App., 112 (Jo. Henderson) ("If admitted, . . . they are strong enough to repudiate the public debt, withdraw the pensions from the wounded veterans, or deny the claim of loyal States for expenses and the loyal men for damages.").
289. *Congressional Globe*, 39th Cong., 1st Sess., 470. See *Congressional Globe*, 39th Cong., 1st Sess., 1183 (S. Pomeroy) ("[I]f their wounded soldiers and widows go unpensioned will they vote and be taxed to pension ours? If their currency is worthless, will they maintain faith in ours? If their bonds are repudiated, will they make secure ours?").
290. *Congressional Globe*, 39th Cong., 1st Sess., 902. See *Congressional Globe*, 39th Cong., 1st Sess., 1471 (Hill), 1474 (Dumont) ("Do we not know that the national debt incurred to put down the rebellion is a stench in the nostrils of a reconstructed rebel and his northern allies[?]").
291. *Congressional Globe*, 39th Cong., 1st Sess., 783.
292. *Congressional Globe*, 39th Cong., 1st Sess., 902.
293. *Congressional Globe*, 39th Cong., 1st Sess., 701.
294. *Congressional Globe*, 39th Cong., 1st Sess., 2405. See *Congressional Globe*, 39th Cong., 1st Sess., 1471 (Hill) (Southern in Congress would seek "to pay their own debt incurred in their treasonable but vain attempt at the destruction of your Government"), 1621 (Myers), 2800 (Stewart).
295. *Congressional Globe*, 39th Cong., 1st Sess., 309. See *Congressional Globe*, 39th Cong., 1st Sess., 332 (Deming) ("the next Legislatures may reenact secession and reaffirm the debt").
296. *Congressional Globe*, 39th Cong., 1st Sess., 784.
297. *Congressional Globe*, 39th Cong., 1st Sess., 2509. See *Congressional Globe*, 39th Cong., 1st Sess., 92 (Sumner) ("of course such people already talk of repudiating the national debt"), 783 (Ward) ("have they given us any assurance that they in conjunction with their obsequious northern allies will not repudiate the national debt, which they say was incurred in their subjugation?"), 1075 (Nye) ("your admission just now and your alliance with northern sympathizers would not be propitious in raising the value of our public securities"), 1078 (Nye) ("a vast national debt which these forces would repudiate; by a basis

for illegitimate claims against the Government, that, if allowed, would destroy our national securities and prostrate the nation in finance"), 2800 (Stewart) ("I was forced to the conclusion that the fifteen original slave States must shortly be handed over to the enemies of the Government to aid the Democracy in repudiating the national debt."), 3066 (R. Clarke) ("[H]ow stand these great [financial] interests, if this Democratic-traitor logic is to be received as the gospel of the new party organization[?]").

298. *Congressional Globe*, 39th Cong., 1st Sess., 797.
299. See *Congressional Globe*, 39th Cong., 1st Sess., 797 (G. Williams) ("No sharp-sighted money-leader will trust a Government so administered.").
300. *Congressional Globe*, 39th Cong., 1st Sess., 701.
301. *Congressional Globe*, 39th Cong., 1st Sess., 2405. See *Congressional Globe*, 39th Cong., 1st Sess., 797 (G. Williams).
302. *Congressional Globe*, 39th Cong., 1st Sess., 463.
303. *Congressional Globe*, 39th Cong., 1st Sess., 309.
304. *Congressional Globe*, 39th Cong., 1st Sess., App., 61.
305. *Congressional Globe*, 39th Cong., 1st Sess., 463.
306. *Congressional Globe*, 39th Cong., 1st Sess., 3166–3167.
307. *Congressional Globe*, 39th Cong., 1st Sess., App., 98 (Yates).
308. *Congressional Globe*, 39th Cong., 1st Sess., 701.
309. *Congressional Globe*, 39th Cong., 1st Sess., 3066. See *Congressional Globe*, 39th Cong., 1st Sess., 1304 (Orth) ("The reconstruction, but I fear, unrepentant rebels, anxious doubtless to be able soon to strike hands with their northern sympathizers, who now, as during the war, are their willing champions."), 1618 (Moulton).
310. *Congressional Globe*, 39th Cong., 1st Sess., 3064. See *Congressional Globe*, 39th Cong., 1st Sess., 3065 (R. Clarke) ("[T]he copperheads are pressing for an early restoration of their southern brethren, and they, too, prefer no change in the order of restoration."), 3066 (R. Clarke) (predicting "cooperation" between "rebels and Democrats . . . in attempts to subvert the Government by fraud or force").
311. See generally Nelson, *The Fourteenth Amendment*, 46.
312. *Congressional Globe*, 39th Cong., 1st Sess., 794.
313. *Congressional Globe*, 39th Cong., 1st Sess., 3168.
314. *Congressional Globe*, 39th Cong., 1st Sess., 74.
315. *Congressional Globe*, 39th Cong., 1st Sess., 2509.
316. *Congressional Globe*, 30th Cong., 1st Sess., 726.
317. *Congressional Globe*, 39th Cong., 1st Sess., 982.
318. *Congressional Globe*, 39th Cong., 1st Sess., 462. See *Congressional Globe*, 39th Cong., 1st Sess., 404 (W. Lawrence) ("I would not allow this additional number of ten Representatives to the late slave States as the reward of treason"), 739 (H. Lane) ("I thought you were to punish traitors and to make treason odious; and how to you propose to punish traitors? By an amnesty wise and sweeping in its operation, and by inviting these rebels into the Halls of Congress with an increase of fourteen members to their representation? Is this not a strange mode of punishing traitors and making treason odious?"), 794 (G. Williams) ("The benefit of your act of emancipation then is to inure the master who has

endeavored to break up your Government, while the black man still holds substantially the relation of a slave, and is only used to count for the benefit of his oppressors!").

319. *Congressional Globe*, 39th Cong., 1st Sess., 3169.

320. *Congressional Globe*, 39th Cong., 1st Sess., 3168.

321. *Congressional Globe*, 39th Cong., 1st Sess., 3168.

322. *Congressional Globe*, 39th Cong., 1st Sess., 3168.

323. *Congressional Globe*, 39th Cong., 1st Sess., 3168.

324. *Congressional Globe*, 39th Cong., 1st Sess., 3169. Windom included West Virginia in this list.

325. *Congressional Globe*, 39th Cong., 1st Sess., 3169.

326. *Congressional Globe*, 39th Cong., 1st Sess., 3169.

327. *Congressional Globe*, 39th Cong., 1st Sess., 166.

328. *Congressional Globe*, 39th Cong., 1st Sess., 166.

329. *Congressional Globe*, 39th Cong., 1st Sess., 3065.

330. *Congressional Globe*, 39th Cong., 1st Sess., 3065.

331. Slaughter-House Cases, at 68 ("whatever auxiliary causes may have contributed to bring about this war, undoubtedly the overshadowing and efficient cause was African slavery").

332. Slaughter-House Cases, at 70–71.

333. *Congressional Globe*, 39th Cong., 1st Sess., 3167,

334. *Congressional Globe*, 39th Cong., 1st Sess., 912.

335. *Congressional Globe*, 39th Cong., 1st Sess., 3064.

336. *Congressional Globe*, 39th Cong., 1st Sess., 740.

337. *Congressional Globe*, 39th Cong., 1st Sess., 167.

338. *Congressional Globe*, 39th Cong., 1st Sess., 1016. See *Congressional Globe*, 39th Cong., 1st Sess., 727 (Welker) ("The rebels . . . cannot at once and without conditions take their original place in the Government against which they warred."), 796 (G. Williams) ("inviting the traitors themselves to reconstruct their States has had the worst possible effect upon them"), 1305 (Orth) ("Is the old slaveholder to be intrusted with the power of providing for the security and safety of the manumitted slave? Is the traitor, whether 'reconstructed' or not, to be transformed into the national legislator, with power to act upon such laws as the country demands for the punishment of treason, if not as an indemnity for the past at least as a security for the future?"), 1319 (D. Ashley) ("Who . . . can consistently with his duty to a loyal constituency vote to recognize as reconstructed, with the right of representation in the national Legislature, States that . . . select men to represent them who have distinguished themselves in the service of the rebellion, and who have held some of the highest offices in the government organized to secure its success[?]"), 1474 (Dumont) ("If their object in getting into Congress is not to preserve and perpetuate the Union, but to disrupt and destroy it, to play into the hands of some hostile power, is it not the duty of Congress to keep them out?").

339. *Congressional Globe*, 39th Cong., 1st Sess., 297.

340. *Congressional Globe*, 39th Cong., 1st Sess., App., 144.

341. *Congressional Globe*, 39th Cong., 1st Sess., 1307.

342. *Congressional Globe*, 39th Cong., 1st Sess., 1076.

343. *Congressional Globe*, 39th Cong., 1st Sess., 383.
344. *Congressional Globe*, 39th Cong., 1st Sess., App., 57. See *Congressional Globe*, 39th Cong., 1st Sess., 832 (Clark) (discussion why persons of color were demanding "the necessary right of suffrage to protect themselves against the rebels"); *Congressional Globe*, 39th Cong., 1st Sess., App., 132 (Sherman) ("What would be their miserable fate if now surrendered to the custody of the rebels of the South?").
345. *Congressional Globe*, 39th Cong., 1st Sess., 3167–3168.
346. *Congressional Globe*, 39th Cong., 1st Sess., App., 144. See *Congressional Globe*, 39th Cong., 1st Sess., 782 (Ward) ("when . . . former rebels [will] be admitted to a share in the Government . . . depends much upon their loyalty and the ability they manifest to take loyal part in the Government"); *Congressional Globe*, 39th Cong., 1st Sess., App., 67 (Garfield) (wanting "sufficient assurance" that "their actions in the future shall be such as loyal men can approve").
347. *Congressional Globe*, 39th Cong., 1st Sess., 74.
348. *Congressional Globe*, 39th Cong., 1st Sess., 1092.
349. *Congressional Globe*, 39th Cong., 1st Sess., 1095.
350. *Report of the Joint Committee*, xix.
351. *Report of the Joint Committee*, xxi.
352. *Congressional Globe*, 39th Cong., 1st Sess., 3148.
353. John Savage, *Life and Public Services of Andrew Johnson. Seventeenth President of the United States* (New York: Derby & Miller, Publishers, 1866), 296.
354. *Congressional Globe*, 39th Cong., 1st Sess., 2082. See *Congressional Globe*, 39th Cong., 1st Sess., 1035 (Orth) ("The people . . . are determined that 'traitors shall be punished and treason made odious.'"), 1616 (Moulton) ("If there is any question in which the people have more interest or feel more intensely than another, it is that . . . treason shall be made odious.").
355. *Congressional Globe*, 39th Cong., 1st Sess., 3528. See also *Congressional Globe*, 39th Cong., 1st Sess., 668 (W. Lawrence) (discussing "treason, infamous and odious").
356. *Congressional Globe*, 39th Cong., 1st Sess., 2945.
357. Savage, *Andrew Johnson*, 295. For direct quotes, see *Congressional Globe*, 39th Cong., 1st Sess., 1164 (McKee), 1633 (W. Lawrence), 1842 (Benjamin), 2102 (Shellabarger), 2402 (Ingersoll), 2487 (H. Wilson), 2499 (Broomall), 2523 (Nye), 2694 (Patterson), 2882 (J. Ashley), 3170 (Windom); *Congressional Globe*, 39th Cong., 1st Sess., App., 207 (Bundy), 227 (Defrees).
358. *Congressional Globe*, 39th Cong., 1st Sess., 2882.
359. *Congressional Globe*, 39th Cong., 1st Sess., App., 130. See *Congressional Globe*, 39th Cong., 1st Sess., 569 (Howard) (the administration's failure to try Jefferson Davis and others meant "[t]reason will not thus be made odious"), 731 (Kelso) (criticizing Johnson and Democrats for "not making treason odious"), 932 (Wade) ("so far from rendering treason odious by punishment, he has foisted into the highest and most delicate trusts many of the worst traitors"), 1164 (McKee), 1629 (Hart), 2093 (J. L. Thomas) ("I have yet to see wherein treason has been looked upon as a crime, or to find where any traitor has been made odious."), 2250 (Scofield), 2284 (Julian), 2401 (Ingersoll), 2499 (Broomall) ("the manner in which the present Administration has punished treason has made

it not odious"), 2880 (J. Ashley), *Congressional Globe*, 39th Cong., 1st Sess., App., 257 (Baker). But see *Congressional Globe*, 39th Cong., 1st Sess., 1047 (J. Dixon) (excluding rebels while seating in Congress loyal Southerners "'makes treason odious'"), 3622 (Willey) (criticizing Republicans who claimed "we will make treason odious and . . . make Unionism honorable, and yet make no distinctions between the traitor and the Union man").

360. *Congressional Globe*, 39th Cong., 1st Sess., 2402. See *Congressional Globe*, 39th Cong., 1st Sess., 2403 (Ingersoll) ("Failing to make it odious by punishing southern men, he himself has make it odious by his treachery to the party and the principles of the party which placed him in power."). See also *Congressional Globe*, 39th Cong., 1st Sess., 2402 (Ingersoll) ("he proclaimed to the world 'that traitors should take a back seat.' Now he proclaims that traitors should have a front seat").

361. *Congressional Globe*, 39th Cong., 1st Sess., 1016–1017.

362. *Congressional Globe*, 39th Cong., 1st Sess., 3210. See *Congressional Globe*, 39th Cong., 1st Sess., 1076 (Nye) (president Reconstruction had made "Unionism unpopular and odious, and treason popular and respectable").

363. *Congressional Globe*, 39th Cong., 1st Sess., 2499.

364. See Johnson, "First Annual Message," in *Messages and Papers*, vol. 6, 359.

365. *Congressional Globe*, 39th Cong., 1st Sess., 2526. See *Congressional Globe*, 39th Cong., 1st Sess., 569 (Howard), 1617 (Moulton), 1840 (S. Clarke), 2283–2284 (Julian), 2496–2497 (Nye). See also *Congressional Globe*, 39th Cong., 1st Sess., 2900 (Doolittle). But see *Congressional Globe*, 39th Cong., 1st Sess., 2882 (J. Ashley) ("I was more anxious to secure justice to our friends and allies than to execute vengeance on our enemies.").

366. *Congressional Globe*, 39th Cong., 1st Sess., 2089.

367. Sherman thought making treason odious meant acting with the Republican Party. *Congressional Globe*, 39th Cong., 1st Sess., App., 130.

368. See *Congressional Globe*, 39th Cong., 1st Sess., App., 208 (Bundy).

369. *Congressional Globe*, 39th Cong., 1st Sess., 3168. See *Congressional Globe*, 39th Cong., 1st Sess., 932 (Wade), 1076 (Nye). 1092 (Bingham) (proponents of "welcom[ing] back the returning prodigals . . . forget . . . that treason is a crime that must be made odious"), 1164 (McKee), 1629 (Hart); *Congressional Globe*, 39th Cong., 1st Sess., App., 208 (Bundy).

370. *Congressional Globe*, 39th Cong., 1st Sess., 739.

371. *Congressional Globe*, 39th Cong., 1st Sess., 2882.

372. *Congressional Globe*, 39th Cong., 1st Sess., 1827.

373. *Congressional Globe*, 39th Cong., 1st Sess., 2536. See *Congressional Globe*, 39th Cong., 1st Sess., 463 (Baker) (Congress could so something "about making treason odious" by passing a constitutional "amendment excluding rebels forever from all the high offices of honor or profit under the Government of the United States"), 739 (H. Lane) (changing the basis of apportionment will make treason odious), 758 (Price) (bans on officeholding), 834 (Clark) (bans on officeholding), 1164 (McKee) (quoting Johnson and then asserting "let us make all who have engaged in treason infamous in the eye of the law to all time by saying to them, you can neither make laws nor can you administer them for the loyal people of the country"), 1305 (Orth) ("there is no better way to make

treason odious than to place upon the traitor the brand that he shall forever be disqualified from holding any office under the Government which he attempted to destroy"), 1842 (Benjamin), 2084 (Perham) ("The leading intelligent traitors . . . should be deprived of all political rights." This "would demonstrate that 'treason is a crime to be punished and made odious.'"), 2102 (Shellabarger) (disenfranchisement), 2469 (Kelley) ("disenfranchisement" demonstrated "that treason is a crime which must be made odious"), 2509 (Spalding) (disenfranchisement will demonstrate that "treason against the Government is odious"), 2540 (Farnsworth) (bans on officeholding would make "treason odious"); *Congressional Globe*, 39th Cong., 1st Sess., App., 207–208 (Bundy), 227 (Defrees) ("traitors of this class mentioned in this proposition must never be permitted to hold any place of trust or power"), 257 (Baker) (bans on officeholding). See also *Congressional Globe*, 39th Cong., 1st Sess., 2524 (Nye) (confiscation); *Congressional Globe*, 39th Cong., 1st Sess., App., 228 (Defrees) (urging confiscation and disqualification from office as the means for making "treason odious"). See also *Congressional Globe*, 39th Cong., 1st Sess., 931 (petition of citizens of Missouri) (invoking President Johnson's claim that "treason must be made odious . . . against the restoration of any of the leaders, civil or military, to citizenship in the United States").

374. *Congressional Globe*, 39th Cong., 1st Sess., 1633.
375. *Congressional Globe*, 39th Cong., 1st Sess., 1842.
376. *Congressional Globe*, 39th Cong., 1st Sess., 2800.
377. *Congressional Globe*, 39th Cong., 1st Sess., 1224.
378. *Congressional Globe*, 39th Cong., 1st Sess., 2886.

3. PROTECTING AND EMPOWERING THE LOYAL

1. *Congressional Globe*, 39th Cong., 1st Sess., 170.
2. *Congressional Globe*, 39th Cong., 1st Sess., App., 132.
3. *Congressional Globe*, 39th Cong., 1st Sess., 125. See *Congressional Globe*, 39th Cong., 1st Sess., 1025 (petition of citizens of Wisconsin) ("permanent guarantees for future security").
4. *Congressional Globe*, 39th Cong., 1st Sess., 98. See *Congressional Globe*, 39th Cong., 1st Sess., 739 (H. Lane) ("upon what safe basis can the States be restored to their constitutional relations to the United States"), 1019 (Broomall) ("some security should be demanded of the States lately in rebellion"); *Congressional Globe*, 39th Cong., 1st Sess., App., 99 (Yates) ("these States are not to be permitted to resume their practical relation with the Union until they by their conduct show that they are willing to come into the Union upon terms which shall forever settle this question, and upon such a basis as will prevent the recurrence of another war, and secure, if not indemnity for the past, at least security for the future").
5. *Congressional Globe*, 39th Cong., 1st Sess., 88 (petition of citizens of Massachusetts).
6. *Congressional Globe*, 39th Cong., 1st Sess., App., 144.
7. *Congressional Globe*, 39th Cong., 1st Sess., 3528.
8. *Congressional Globe*, 39th Cong., 1st Sess., 2556.
9. *Congressional Globe*, 39th Cong., 1st Sess., 391.
10. See Silbey, *A Respectful Minority*.

11. See, i.e., *Congressional Globe*, 39th Cong., 1st Sess., 85 (Rogers), 2255 (Aa. Harding).

12. *Congressional Globe*, 39th Cong., 1st Sess., 2467.

13. *Congressional Globe*, 39th Cong., 1st Sess., 2507. See *Congressional Globe*, 39th Cong., 1st Sess., 2531 (Strouse) ("The history of the United States is the history of the Democratic party; its creed is the Constitution, and its principles have been for seventy-five years the operative cause of our country's rise, progress, strength, and greatness.").

14. *Congressional Globe*, 39th Cong., 1st Sess., 2468. See *Congressional Globe*, 39th Cong., 1st Sess., 2472 (Smith) ("There are two parties in this country who are against this Government, and are attempting to overthrow and destroy it—the one is an extreme party on the one side, and the other is an extreme party of the other side.").

15. See Stephen A. Douglas, "Mr. Douglas' Speech: First Debate with Stephen A. Douglas at Ottawa, Illinois," in Basler, *Collected Works*, 3:1–2.

16. *Congressional Globe*, 39th Cong., 1st Sess., 2988.

17. *Congressional Globe*, 39th Cong., 1st Sess., 2898.

18. See generally *Congressional Globe*, 39th Cong., 1st Sess., 2467 (Boyer) ("a majority of the whole people will stand by the country").

19. *Congressional Globe*, 39th Cong., 1st Sess., 2988.

20. *Congressional Globe*, 39th Cong., 1st Sess., App., 304.

21. *Congressional Globe*, 39th Cong., 1st Sess., 2539.

22. *Congressional Globe*, 39th Cong., 1st Sess., 2915 (Doolittle) (complaining that proposed bans on officeholding did not exempt "those who were forced into the rebel service"). Similar claims were made by Democrats when insisting that Confederate conscripts should be able to hold public office after the Civil War. See Hyman, *Era of the Oath*, 66–67, 72.

23. *Congressional Globe*, 39th Cong., 1st Sess., 2918.

24. *Congressional Globe*, 39th Cong., 1st Sess., App., 48.

25. *Congressional Globe*, 39th Cong., 1st Sess., 2918.

26. *Congressional Globe*, 39th Cong., 1st Sess., 2884 (Latham); *Congressional Globe*, 39th Cong., 1st Sess., App., 149 (Saulsbury). See *Congressional Globe*, 39th Cong., 1st Sess., 2918 (Willey) ("The duty of Government and the citizen is reciprocal. . . . The Government owes to its citizens protection; the citizens owes to the Government obedience and support.").

27. *Congressional Globe*, 39th Cong., 1st Sess., 2919.

28. *Congressional Globe*, 39th Cong., 1st Sess., 2940.

29. *Congressional Globe*, 39th Cong., 1st Sess., 2919.

30. *Congressional Globe*, 39th Cong., 1st Sess., 336.

31. *Congressional Globe*, 39th Cong., 1st Sess., 178.

32. *Congressional Globe*, 39th Cong., 1st Sess., App., 244. See *Congressional Globe*, 39th Cong., 1st Sess., App., 83 (Chanler) (contrasting "black freedmen" with "loyal white immigrants"), 243 (G. Davis) (questioning Black loyalty).

33. *Congressional Globe*, 39th Cong., 1st Sess., App., 62.

34. *Congressional Globe*, 39th Cong., 1st Sess., 203.

35. *Congressional Globe*, 39th Cong., 1st Sess., 217–218.

36. *Congressional Globe*, 39th Cong., 1st Sess., 2467. See *Congressional Globe*, 39th Cong., 1st Sess., App., 74 (Rousseau).

37. *Congressional Globe*, 39th Cong., 1st Sess., 2469.

38. *Congressional Globe*, 39th Cong., 1st Sess., 2471. See *Congressional Globe*, 39th Cong., 1st Sess., 2467 (Boyer) ("They who have committed treason are amenable to the laws, even after they have returned to allegiance.").

39. *Congressional Globe*, 39th Cong., 1st Sess., 2940.

40. *Congressional Globe*, 39th Cong., 1st Sess., 2940.

41. *Congressional Globe*, 39th Cong., 1st Sess., 2461 (Finck), 3845 (Aa. Harding), 3963–3964 (G. Davis). See *Congressional Globe*, 39th Cong., 1st Sess., 2467 (Boyer) ("there is no hot haste required to prohibit by a constitutional enactment the payment of this debt by the bankrupt States of the South; and I do not suppose that any man outside of a lunatic asylum ever dreamed it would be paid by any one else"), 2940 (Hendricks) ("who is so stupid as to have supposed these debts legal, or that they had any valid existence for one hour after the *de facto* government of the confederate states ceased to exist").

42. *Congressional Globe*, 39th Cong., 1st Sess., 2501 (Shanklin). See *Congressional Globe*, 39th Cong., 1st Sess., 3845 (Aa. Harding).

43. See *Congressional Globe*, 39th Cong., 1st Sess., 3574–3575.

44. *Congressional Globe*, 39th Cong., 1st Sess., App., 142.

45. *Congressional Globe*, 39th Cong., 1st Sess., 2534. See *Congressional Globe*, 39th Cong., 1st Sess., App., 226 (Howe) ("This Union party . . . have whipped the rebellion.").

46. *Congressional Globe*, 39th Cong., 1st Sess., App., 204.

47. *Congressional Globe*, 39th Cong., 1st Sess., 2464. See *Congressional Globe*, 39th Cong., 1st Sess., App., 132 (Sherman) ("But the division of the Whig party was an event utterly insignificant in comparison with the evil results of a division in the Union party."), 133 (Sherman) ("you must not sever the great Union party from this loyal element of the southern States").

48. The seminal expression of this position is Anthony Downs, *An Economic Theory of Democracy* (New York: Harper & Row, 1957).

49. Leonard and Cornell, *The Partisan Republic*, 215. For a discussion of Republican commitments to the Van Buren understanding of political parties, see Mark A. Graber, "Separation of Powers," in Orren and Compton, *Cambridge Companion to the Constitution*, 235–242.

50. Leonard and Cornell, *The Partisan Republic*, 215.

51. Leonard and Cornell, *The Partisan Republic*, 218.

52. Leonard and Cornell, *The Partisan Republic*, 219.

53. *Congressional Globe*, 39th Cong., 1st Sess., 2505. See *Congressional Globe*, 39th Cong., 1st Sess., 2505 (McKee) ("I desire that the loyal heart of the nation shall continue in power the great party which sustained our armies in the field.").

54. *Congressional Globe*, 39th Cong., 1st Sess., 2468.

55. *Congressional Globe*, 39th Cong., 1st Sess., 2468.

56. *Congressional Globe*, 39th Cong., 1st Sess., 2534 (Eckley), 2540 (Farnsworth), 2544 (Stevens); *Congressional Globe*, 39th Cong., 1st Sess., App., 203 (W.

Lawrence). See *Congressional Globe*, 39th Cong., 1st Sess., App., 209 (Bundy) (referring to "the Democratic rebel scheme" and "the Democratic rebel theory").

57. *Congressional Globe*, 39th Cong., 1st Sess., 2468.

58. *Congressional Globe*, 39th Cong., 1st Sess., 2464. See *Congressional Globe*, 39th Cong., 1st Sess., 2464 (Garfield) (accusing Democrats during the Civil War of having "helped to unite and rally the South against the Union"), 2534 (Eckley) ("With what pleasure would I recur to the Journals of the Thirty-Eighth Congress if I could find the name of my colleague recorded in favor of any of the measures necessary to levy men, raise money, provide means, or even to punish a guerilla for shooting down a soldier or a citizen[?]"), 2540 (Farnsworth) (speaking of "members of Congress who encouraged [rebels] and discouraged our soldiers"), 2963 (Poland) ("[D]id we not have many men in the North who sympathized with the rebels: who counseled resistance to the draft, and threw every obstacle in the way of the successful prosecution of the war; who rejoiced at our defeats and rebel victories? Did not a large party in a national convention resolve that the war for the suppression of the rebellion was a failure and ought to be stopped?"). See *Congressional Globe*, 39th Cong., 1st Sess., App., 226 (Howe).

59. *Congressional Globe*, 39th Cong., 1st Sess., 2464. See *Congressional Globe*, 39th Cong., 1st Sess., 2464 (Garfield) (accusing Democrats of calling on the South "to have the manliness to resist the operations of Congress and of the great Union party"), 2498 (Broomall) ("The gentlemen who have voted on all occasions upon the rebel side of all questions that have been before the country for six years could hardly be expected to change their positions at this time.").

60. *Congressional Globe*, 39th Cong., 1st Sess., 2509.

61. *Congressional Globe*, 39th Cong., 1st Sess., 2508.

62. *Congressional Globe*, 39th Cong., 1st Sess., 2542.

63. *Congressional Globe*, 39th Cong., 1st Sess., 2542.

64. West Virginia State Board of Education v. Barnette, 319 U.S. 624, 638 (1943).

65. *Congressional Globe*, 39th Cong., 1st Sess., 2918.

66. See Foner, *Free Soil, Free Labor, Free Men*.

67. *Congressional Globe*, 39th Cong., 1st Sess., 2511.

68. *Congressional Globe*, 39th Cong., 1st Sess., 2511.

69. *Congressional Globe*, 39th Cong., 1st Sess., 2533.

70. *Congressional Globe*, 39th Cong., 1st Sess., 2540.

71. *Congressional Globe*, 39th Cong., 1st Sess., 2540.

72. See *Congressional Globe*, 39th Cong., 2540 (Farnsworth).

73. *Congressional Globe*, 39th Cong., 1st Sess., 496.

74. *Congressional Globe*, 39th Cong., 1st Sess., 496.

75. See *Congressional Globe*, 39th Cong., 1st Sess., 737 (H. Lane). See *Congressional Globe*, 39th Cong., 1st Sess., 2963 (Poland) (the "only class of loyal people living" in the former Confederate states), 3977 (Boutwell), 3978 (Bingham) (referring to "loyal blacks" and "loyal freedmen"), 4007 (Brown) (pointing out that African Americans were "the largest section of [Tennessee's] loyal population"), 4304 (Stevens) ("loyal colored men"); *Congressional Globe*, 39th Cong., 1st Sess., App., 57 (Julian) ("loyal freedmen"), 297 (Schenck). See also

Congressional Globe, 39th Cong., 1st Sess., App., 127 (Sherman) (noting "the loyal men of the southern States include[ed] the colored as well as the white people"); 145 (Loan) (insisting "[a]ll loyal men must be enfranchised without regard to color").

76. *Congressional Globe*, 39th Cong., 1st Sess., App., 144. See *Congressional Globe*, 39th Cong., 1st Sess., 591. (petition of citizens of Wisconsin).

77. *Congressional Globe*, 39th Cong., 1st Sess., 2802.

78. *Congressional Globe*, 39th Cong., 1st Sess., 792.

79. *Congressional Globe*, 39th Cong., 1st Sess., 1075.

80. *Congressional Globe*, 39th Cong., 1st Sess., App., 66. See *Congressional Globe*, 39th Cong., 1st Sess., App., 96 (Jo. Henderson) ("the negroes who cultivate the soil in the southern States, and who are loyal men and have been loyal men"), 305 (Miller) ("they are loyal to the Government of the United States").

81. *Congressional Globe*, 39th Cong., 1st Sess., App., 57.

82. *Congressional Globe*, 39th Cong., 1st Sess., 2509 (Boutwell).

83. *Congressional Globe*, 39th Cong., 1st Sess., 1183.

84. *Congressional Globe*, 39th Cong., 1st Sess., 2800.

85. *Congressional Globe*, 39th Cong., 1st Sess., 2505.

86. See *Congressional Globe*, 39th Cong., 1st Sess., 591.

87. *Congressional Globe*, 39th Cong., 1st Sess., App., 104.

88. *Congressional Globe*, 39th Cong., 1st Sess., 88 (petition from citizens of Massachusetts).

89. *Congressional Globe*, 39th Cong., 1st Sess., 2469. See *Congressional Globe*, 39th Cong., 1st Sess., 3977 (Boutwell) ("You have four million discontented loyal persons made discontented by your actions.").

90. *Congressional Globe*, 39th Cong., 1st Sess., 223. See *Congressional Globe*, 39th Cong., 1st Sess., 224 (Grinnell) (condemning those who prefer "white treason to sable loyalty"); 259 (Julian) ("as between [blacks] and white rebels, who deserve to be hung, they are eminently fit").

91. *Congressional Globe*, 39th Cong., 1st Sess., 733.

92. *Congressional Globe*, 39th Cong., 1st Sess., 2537.

93. *Congressional Globe*, 39th Cong., 1st Sess., 1074. See *Congressional Globe*, 39th Cong., 1st Sess., 867 (Newell) ("the race was called upon to aid in the struggle, and they nobly responded to the appeal").

94. *Congressional Globe*, 39th Cong., 1st Sess., 259.

95. *Congressional Globe*, 39th Cong., 1st Sess., 2964.

96. *Congressional Globe*, 39th Cong., 1st Sess., 2963.

97. *Congressional Globe*, 39th Cong., 1st Sess., 175.

98. *Congressional Globe*, 39th Cong., 1st Sess., 159. See *Congressional Globe*, 39th Cong., 1st Sess., 1008 (R. Clarke) ("we, the Representatives of the loyal people of the Union, propose to become the sole judges ourselves of the terms and time of that restoration"), 2542 (Bingham) ("the final settlement of this grave question which touches the nation's life is at least with the people of the loyal States—the loyal people of the Union").

99. *Congressional Globe*, 39th Cong., 1st Sess., 69.

100. *Congressional Globe*, 39th Cong., 1st Sess., 2459.

101. *Congressional Globe*, 39th Cong., 1st Sess., 2533.

102. *Congressional Globe*, 39th Cong., 1st Sess., 2504.
103. *Congressional Globe*, 39th Cong., 1st Sess., 920.
104. Summers, *The Ordeal of the Reunion*, 3–4 (emphasis in original).
105. Summers, *The Ordeal of the Reunion*, 4.
106. *Congressional Globe*, 39th Cong., 1st Sess., 2.
107. *Congressional Globe*, 39th Cong., 1st Sess., 667. See *Congressional Globe*, 39th Cong., 1st Sess., 2962 (Poland) ("[C]an it be possible that we are at once bound to admit these people to actively participate with us in administering the General Government; that we have no more power or right to test their loyalty or require security for it than we have of the people of a State which has always been loyal and true?").
108. *Congressional Globe*, 39th Cong., 1st Sess., 782.
109. *Congressional Globe*, 39th Cong., 1st Sess., 909. See *Congressional Globe*, 39th Cong., 1st Sess., 42 (Trumbull) (federal oversight necessary until former Confederate states establish institutions that "should be recognized by the Federal Government as loyal and true to the Constitution"), 56 (Sumner) (discussing the need for "some evidence that the condition of loyalty and obedience is their true condition again"), 912 (W. Lawrence) ("If the people of the rebellious States are still disloyal, there is no provision of the Constitution entitling them to representation in the Congress of the United States. If it is true that we are required to patrol those States with an army to protect the loyal white men and poor freedmen and to suppress treason, where is the propriety of admitting them to representation?"), 1048 (Trumbull) ("Before the State of Tennessee can be again in constitutional relations with this Government, there must be set up an organization loyal to the Government."), 2464 (Thayer) (calling for "the reconstruction of those old relations of loyalty and fidelity to the Constitution which once characterized these States"), 4221 (Nye) ("just as fast as they will bring back men here with loyal principles, backed by a loyal constituency, I will vote to take back the rebellious States"); *Congressional Globe*, 39th Cong., 1st Sess., App., 67 (Garfield) ("Our duty is to demand that before we admit them, . . . their actions in the future shall be such as loyal men can approve."), 91 (Delano) ("Elect and return loyal men as Representations.").
110. *Congressional Globe*, 39th Cong., 1st Sess., 1050. See *Congressional Globe*, 39th Cong., 1st Sess., 24 (Howard) (Senate cannot admit Southern representatives until "loyalty is restored in the rebel States"), 726 (Welker) ("as States they are not entitled to representation here until loyal governments are organized within their territories").
111. *Congressional Globe*, 39th Cong., 1st Sess., 2459. See *Congressional Globe*, 39th Cong., 1st Sess., 2544 (Stevens) ("I regret that the true men of these States cannot brought in [to Congress], but they cannot be brought in with rebel constituencies behind them. They would misrepresent their States."), 3990 (Wade) ("You may admit a loyal man upon this floor who happens to be sent here by a disloyal constituency; but it is impossible upon the great principles of representative government that he can represent them.").
112. *Congressional Globe*, 39th Cong., 1st Sess., 2508. See *Congressional Globe*, 39th Cong., 1st Sess., 2509 (Boutwell) (declaring all Republicans agreed "that there shall be a loyal people in each applicant State before any representative

from that State is admitted in Congress"); *Congressional Globe*, 39th Cong., 1st Sess., App., 68 (Garfield) ("Satisfy me that there is a loyal State, loyal by the will of its people, that there are districts of loyal constituents, and that they send loyal Representatives, and those Representatives shall at once have my vote in favor of their admission.").

113. *Congressional Globe*, 39th Cong., 1st Sess., 140.

114. *Congressional Globe*, 39th Cong., 1st Sess., 141.

115. *Congressional Globe*, 39th Cong., 1st Sess., 2505. See *Congressional Globe*, 39th Cong., 1st Sess., 2532 (Banks), 2537 (Beaman) ("the Government should be administered by loyal hands"), 4270 (Shellabarger) (speaking of "the endeavor to hold and retain the Government in the hands and control of loyal men"); *Congressional Globe*, 39th Cong., 1st Sess., App., 207 (Bundy) ("the loyal people of the country must govern the country").

116. *Congressional Globe*, 39th Cong., 1st Sess., 2534.

117. *Congressional Globe*, 39th Cong., 1st Sess., 2.

118. *Congressional Globe*, 39th Cong., 1st Sess., 496.

119. *Congressional Globe*, 39th Cong., 1st Sess., 140.

120. *Congressional Globe*, 39th Cong., 1st Sess., App., 52.

121. *Congressional Globe*, 39th Cong., 1st Sess., 1006 (citizens of Windsor, Vermont), 1272 (citizens of Kenosha, Wisconsin), 1272 (Citizens of Essex County, Massachusetts).

122. *Congressional Globe*, 39th Cong., 1st Sess., 931 (petition of citizens of Missouri).

123. *Congressional Globe*, 39th Cong., 1st Sess., 132.

124. *Congressional Globe*, 39th Cong., 1st Sess., 728.

125. *Congressional Globe*, 39th Cong., 1st Sess., 2464.

126. *Congressional Globe*, 39th Cong., 1st Sess., 470. See *Congressional Globe*, 39th Cong., 1st Sess., 157 (Bingham) ("The Republic is in the hands of its friends, and its only safety is in the hands of its friends.").

127. *Congressional Globe*, 39th Cong., 1st Sess., 1075.

128. *Congressional Globe*, 39th Cong., 1st Sess., 461. See *Congressional Globe*, 39th Cong., 1st Sess., 462 (Baker) (describing proposed constitutional amendments as "guarantees of safety and justice to the loyal people who have saved this country at so great a cost of blood and treasure").

129. *Congressional Globe*, 39th Cong., 1st Sess., 75. See *Congressional Globe*, 39th Cong., 1st Sess., 732 (Kelso) ("Congress . . . is bound to see that all the loyal citizens are allowed a voice in the conventions that meet to frame the new State constitutions.").

130. *Congressional Globe*, 39th Cong., 1st Sess., 733. See *Congressional Globe*, 39th Cong., 1st Sess., 2 (Sumner), 732 (Kelso) ("all the loyal citizens should have a voice in the formation of the new State constitution").

131. *Congressional Globe*, 39th Cong., 1st Sess., 445. See *Congressional Globe*, 39th Cong., 1st Sess., 462 (describing proposed constitutional amendments as "protecting the loyal people of the nation from the crying injustice and palpable danger of restoring the late rebel communities"); *Congressional Globe*, 39th Cong., 1st Sess., App., 99 (Yates) ("we may regard the rebellious population as out of the Union for all purposes of representation until they comply with such just requirements as we may impose for securing protection to loyal men").

132. *Congressional Globe*, 39th Cong., 1st Sess., 1007.

133. *Congressional Globe*, 39th Cong., 1st Sess., 2460. See *Congressional Globe*, 39th Cong., 1st Sess., 734 (petition of David Burdick) (calling on the national government to "immediately use our power to protect the loyal from oppression").

134. *Congressional Globe*, 39th Cong., 1st Sess., 2537.

135. *Congressional Globe*, 39th Cong., 1st Sess., 902. See *Congressional Globe*, 39th Cong., 1st Sess., 2504 (McKee) (asking whether Congress was "willing to turn over the loyal men in these States . . . to the tender mercies of [rebels]").

136. *Congressional Globe*, 39th Cong., 1st Sess., 783.

137. *Congressional Globe*, 39th Cong., 1st Sess., 783. See *Congressional Globe*, 39th Cong., 1st Sess., App., 144 (Loan) ("we should know that the political power in the State seeking recognition is confided exclusively to loyal hands"), 204 (W. Lawrence) ("the future safely of the country can only be secured by the continuance of the true loyal Union men of the country in power").

138. *Congressional Globe*, 39th Cong., 1st Sess., App., 110.

139. *Congressional Globe*, 39th Cong., 1st Sess., 733.

140. *Congressional Globe*, 39th Cong., 1st Sess., 2537.

141. *Congressional Globe*, 39th Cong., 1st Sess., 74.

142. *Congressional Globe*, 39th Cong., 1st Sess., 2544.

143. *Congressional Globe*, 39th Cong., 1st Sess., App., 58.

144. *Congressional Globe*, 39th Cong., 1st Sess. App., 142. See *Congressional Globe*, 39th Cong., 1st Sess., 3038 (Yates) ("I always feel perfectly safe when I am in the hands of a good Republican Union party.").

145. *Congressional Globe*, 39th Cong., 1st Sess., App., 133.

146. *Congressional Globe*, 39th Cong., 1st Sess., 2505.

147. *Congressional Globe*, 39th Cong., 1st Sess., App., 96.

148. Nelson, *The Fourteenth Amendment*, 46.

149. *Report of the Joint Committee*, xxi.

150. *Congressional Globe*, 39th Cong., 1st Sess., 728.

151. *Congressional Globe*, 39th Cong., 1st Sess., 903.

152. *Congressional Globe*, 39th Cong., 1st Sess., 2770.

153. *Congressional Globe*, 39th Cong., 1st Sess., 701. See *Congressional Globe*, 39th Cong., 1st Sess., 2340 (Farnsworth) ("repudiating the rebel debt, and claims for slaves, will be most heartily adopted and approved by every loyal man in the nation.").

154. *Congressional Globe*, 39th Cong., 1st Sess., 1625.

155. *Congressional Globe*, 39th Cong., 1st Sess., 2769.

156. *Congressional Globe*, 39th Cong., 1st Sess., 931.

157. *Congressional Globe*, 39th Cong., 1st Sess., 792.

158. *Congressional Globe*, 39th Cong., 1st Sess., 797.

159. *Congressional Globe*, 39th Congress., 1st Sess., 2340. See *Congressional Globe*, 39th Cong., 1st Sess., 903 (Cook) ("The question whether Union men of the South shall be required to pay for the destruction of their own property and their own bitter persecution, when they were imprisoned in dungeons and were driven from their homes and hunted like a partridge upon the mountains, is a question to be decided by the loyal men of the nation, and not by the traitors who want the money.").

160. *Congressional Globe*, 39th Cong., 1st Sess., 868.

161. *Congressional Globe*, 39th Cong., 1st Sess., 2768.
162. *Congressional Globe*, 39th Cong., 1st Sess., 155.
163. *Congressional Globe*, 39th Cong., 1st Sess., 88.
164. *Congressional Globe*, 39th Cong., 1st Sess., 1187.
165. *Congressional Globe*, 39th Cong., 1st Sess., 1006.
166. *Congressional Globe*, 39th Cong., 1st Sess., 1189.
167. *Congressional Globe*, 39th Cong., 1st Sess., 717.
168. *Congressional Globe*, 39th Cong., 1st Sess., 1065.
169. *Congressional Globe*, 39th Cong., 1st Sess., 444.
170. *Congressional Globe*, 39th Cong., 1st Sess., 1092.
171. *Congressional Globe*, 39th Cong., 1st Sess., 1017.
172. *Congressional Globe*, 39th Cong., 1st Sess., 1164.
173. *Congressional Globe*, 39th Cong., 1st Sess., 2901. See *Congressional Globe*, 39th Cong., 1st Sess., 2902 (Trumbull) (noted than a proposed officeholding ban "will be a popular provision with loyal men, and how the disloyal regard it is not a matter of so much consequence").
174. *Congressional Globe*, 39th Cong., 1st Sess., 2505.
175. *Congressional Globe*, 39th Cong., 1st Sess., 2902.
176. *Congressional Globe*, 39th Cong., 1st Sess., 1008. See *Congressional Globe*, 39th Cong., 1st Sess., 2465 (Thayer) (declaring that apportionment reform is "the point to which they loyal millions of the country turn their eyes for future peace and security").
177. *Congressional Globe*, 39th Cong., 1st Sess., 2539–2540.
178. *Congressional Globe*, 39th Cong., 1st Sess., 794.
179. *Congressional Globe*, 39th Cong., 1st Sess., 1254. See *Congressional Globe*, 39th Cong., 1st Sess., 903 (speaking of the need to change apportionment in ways that "would secure to loyal men the same influence in the Government which is accorded to rebels").
180. *Congressional Globe*, 39th Cong., 1st Sess., 2535. See *Congressional Globe*, 39th Cong., 1st Sess., 728 (Welker) ("It gives a rebel white man two and a half votes to one for the Union soldier in the North.").
181. *Congressional Globe*, 39th Cong., 1st Sess., 1254.
182. *Congressional Globe*, 39th Cong., 1st Sess., 434.
183. *Congressional Globe*, 39th Cong., 1st Sess., 1257 (H. Wilson).
184. *Congressional Globe*, 39th Cong., 1st Sess., App., 59. See *Congressional Globe*, 39th Cong., 1st Sess., 535 (Benjamin).
185. *Congressional Globe*, 39th Cong., 1st Sess., 311.
186. *Congressional Globe*, 39th Cong., 1st Sess., 2595.
187. *Congressional Globe*, 39th Cong., 1st Sess., 2505.
188. *Congressional Globe*, 39th Cong., 1st Sess., 74.
189. *Congressional Globe*, 39th Cong., 1st Sess., 2802.
190. See, e.g., *Congressional Globe*, 39th Cong., 1st Sess., 3979 (Bingham) (claimed dedication to "the rights of loyal colored men").
191. *Report of the Joint Committee*, xiii.
192. *Congressional Globe*, 39th Cong., 1st Sess., App., 57. See *Congressional Globe*, 39th Cong., 1st Sess., 360 (memorial of the association of loyal Pennsylvanians) ("asking Congress . . . to confer upon all loyal citizens in this District

the elective franchise, without distinction of color"); *Congressional Globe*, 39th Cong., 1st Sess., 145 (Loan) ("All loyal men in those States must be enfranchised without regard to color. Those races who bear arms to defend a Republican must be allowed to participate in its Government.").

193. *Congressional Globe*, 39th Cong., 1st Sess., 740.

194. *Congressional Globe*, 39th Cong., 1st Sess., 309.

195. *Report of the Joint Committee*, xiii.

196. *Congressional Globe*, 39th Cong., 1st Sess., 284.

197. *Congressional Globe*, 39th Cong., 1st Sess., 662.

198. *Congressional Globe*, 39th Cong., 1st Sess., App., 66.

199. *Congressional Globe*, 39th Cong., 1st Sess., 462.

200. *Congressional Globe*, 39th Cong., 1st Sess., 2769. See *Congressional Globe*, 39th Cong., 1st Sess., 2537 (Longyear) ("we should have the manhood and magnanimity to declare that all men who have wielded the sword in defense of their country are fit to be intrusted with the ballot"), 2799 (Stewart) ("[C]an we not now claim that the loyal men of this nation by their valor and by their sacrifices have won not only for themselves but for every man in all this broad land the glorious right of self-government[?]"); *Congressional Globe*, 39th Cong., 1st Sess., App., 99 (Yates) (demanding voting rights for "the loyal men who have bared their breasts to the storm of battle"), 145 (Loan) ("Those races who bear arms to defend a Republic must be allowed to participate in its Government.").

201. *Congressional Globe*, 39th Cong., 1st Sess., 204. See *Congressional Globe*, 39th Cong., 1st Sess., 206 (Farnsworth) ("Tell me who will, that a man . . . who has shed his blood and given his right arm for the support of that same Government . . . has no right to a voice in the choice of his rulers[?]"), 732 (Kelso) ("They knew enough to cast bullets with judgment, and I have no doubt that they would soon learn to cast ballots with equal judgment.").

202. *Congressional Globe*, 39th Cong., 1st Sess., 182.

203. *Congressional Globe*, 39th Cong., 1st Sess., 834. See *Congressional Globe*, 39th Cong., 1st Sess., 727 (Welker) ("This Government by their emancipation is as solemnly bound to secure their freedom and protect their rights, as it is to pay off the debts incurred in saving the life of the nation."), 733 (Kelso) ("when the war hung in even balance, we called upon these poor slaves to help us, and promised in return to make the free"), 792 (T. Williams).

204. *Congressional Globe*, 39th Cong., 1st Sess., 1256.

205. See *Congressional Globe*, 39th Cong., 1st Sess., 667–683.

206. *Congressional Globe*, 39th Cong., 1st Sess., 674.

207. *Congressional Globe*, 39th Cong., 1st Sess., 3.

208. *Congressional Globe*, 39th Cong., 1st Sess., 2.

209. *Congressional Globe*, 39th Cong., 1st Sess., 173 (J. Wilson), 201 (Rogers), 215 (T. Davis), 255 (Julian), 261 (J. L. Thomas), 279 (Hale), and 281 (Thayer).

210. *Congressional Globe*, 39th Cong., 1st Sess., 174. See *Congressional Globe*, 39th Cong., 1st Sess., 285 (B. Van Horn) ("They have exhibited, to say the least, as high order of loyalty, and as much of it, as the white population. They were always true, always the friends of the Government, in sunshine or in storm, in victory or defeat.").

211. *Congressional Globe*, 39th Cong., 1st Sess., 223.

212. *Congressional Globe*, 39th Cong., 1st Sess., 241. See *Congressional Globe*, 39th Cong., 1st Sess., 241 (Price) (Blacks were "present at every time and under all circumstances to defend the flag and to suppress treason and put down traitors when they have had the opportunity and been allowed to do so").

213. *Congressional Globe*, 39th Cong., 1st Sess., 222. See *Congressional Globe*, 39th Cong., 1st Sess., 222 ("[T]hese people have borne themselves as bravely, as well, and . . . as wisely during the great contest just closed, as any people to whom he can point, situated in like circumstances, at any period of the world's history[.]").

214. *Congressional Globe*, 39th Cong., 1st Sess., 282. See *Congressional Globe*, 39th Cong., 1st Sess., 175 (J. Wilson) ("Three thousand five hundred and forty nine marched out from this District to defend the nation. . . . Many of them are buried with the white comrades on scores of battlefields.").

215. *Congressional Globe*, 39th Cong., 1st Sess., p.280.

216. *Congressional Globe*, 39th Cong., 1st Sess., 239. See *Congressional Globe*, 39th Cong., 1st Sess., 310 (C. Hubbard), 728 (Welker) (persons of color "[h]aving served in the Union Army . . . should at least be admitted to this right").

217. *Congressional Globe*, 39th Cong., 1st Sess., 717.

218. *Congressional Globe*, 39th Cong., 1st Sess., 285. Boutwell, who championed universal male suffrage, was the rare Republican who rejected the connection between military service and voting. See *Congressional Globe*, 39th Cong., 1st Sess., 308 (noting "we are bound to treat the colored people in this District in regard to the matter of voting precisely as we treat white people," but insisting, "[t]here is not the least possible connection between service in the Army and Navy and the exercise of the elective franchise"). See also *Congressional Globe*, 39th Cong., 1st Sess., 238 (Kasson) (suggesting that "a man old enough to fight for his country ought to be old enough to vote for his country" but noting that under present law "service in the Army of the country does not give this right" to any soldier under the age of twenty-one).

219. *Congressional Globe*, 39th Cong., 1st Sess., 206. See *Congressional Globe*, 39th Cong., 1st Sess., 717 (J. Rice) ("more of the black race will be able to avail themselves of [the proposed homestead law] than the white race of the South, for the reason that they are mostly loyal, and the whites are mostly disloyal").

220. *Congressional Globe*, 39th Cong., 1st Sess., 258.

221. *Congressional Globe*, 39th Cong., 1st Sess., 2802–2803. Farnsworth offered a resolution declaring that

> we agree with the President of the United States that "mercy without justice is a crime"; and the admitting of rebels and traitors, upon whose hands the blood of slain patriots has scarcely dried, and upon whose hearts is the damning crime of starving to death loyal men taken as prisoners in battle, to the rights of citizenship and suffrage, while we deny those rights to the loyal black man, who fought for the Union, and who fed and protected our staring soldiers, is a fit illustration of that truism. (*Congressional Globe*, 39th Cong., 1st Sess., 15.)

222. *Congressional Globe*, 39th Cong., 1st Sess., 4304.

223. *Congressional Globe*, 39th Cong., 1st Sess., 303.

224. *Congressional Globe*, 39th Cong., 1st Sess., 1074.

225. *Congressional Globe,* 39th Cong., 1st Sess., 2802.
226. *Congressional Globe,* 39th Cong., 1st Sess., 175.
227. *Congressional Globe,* 39th Cong., 1st Sess., 2989.
228. *Congressional Globe,* 39th Cong., 1st Sess., 259.
229. *Congressional Globe,* 39th Cong., 1st Sess., 107.
230. *Congressional Globe,* 39th Cong., 1st Sess., 107.
231. *Congressional Globe,* 39th Cong., 1st Sess., 806.
232. *Congressional Globe,* 39th Cong., 1st Sess., 128.
233. *Congressional Globe,* 39th Cong., 1st Sess., App., 105.
234. Derrick A. Bell, Jr., *"Brown v. Board of Education* and the Interest-Convergence Dilemma," 93 *Harvard Law Review* 518, 523 (1980) ("The interest of blacks in achieving racial equality will be accommodated only when it converges with the interests of whites.").
235. *Congressional Globe,* 39th Cong., 1st Sess., 732.
236. *Congressional Globe,* 39th Cong., 1st Sess., 793.
237. *Congressional Globe,* 39th Cong., 1st Sess., 4304.
238. *Congressional Globe,* 39th Cong., 1st Sess., 2964.
239. *Congressional Globe,* 39th Cong., 1st Sess., 2802.
240. *Congressional Globe,* 39th Cong., 1st Sess., 2802.
241. *Congressional Globe,* 39th Cong., 1st Sess., 2802.
242. For a notable exception, see Summers, *The Ordeal of the Reunion.*
243. Bell, *"Brown v. Board of Education* and the Interest-Convergence Dilemma," 518, 523.
244. *Congressional Globe,* 39th Cong., 1st Sess., 4007.
245. *Congressional Globe,* 39th Cong., 1st Sess., App., 210.

4. GUARANTEES

1. *Congressional Globe,* 39th Cong., 1st Sess., 252.
2. Commentators often emphasize the firstness of the First Amendment. See, e.g., Akhil Reed Amar, "The First Amendment's Firstness," 47 *University of California, Davis Law Review* 1015 (2014); Edmond Cahn, "The Firstness of the First Amendment," 65 *Yale Law Journal* 464 (1956).
3. *Congressional Globe,* 39th Cong., 1st Sess., 2.
4. *Congressional Globe,* 39th Cong., 1st Sess., 508.
5. The petition Grimes presented did not include the word "naturalized."
6. *Congressional Globe,* 39th Cong., 1st Sess., 979.
7. See *Congressional Globe,* 39th Cong., 1st Sess., 413 (Cowan presenting a petition from citizens of Indiana County, Pennsylvania), 494 (S. Pomeroy presenting a petition from citizens of Pennsylvania), 640 (Cowan presenting a petition from citizens of Fayette County, Pennsylvania), 829 (Cragin presenting a petition from citizens of Buffalo, New York), 951 (G. Lawrence presenting a petition from citizens of Washington County, Pennsylvania), 1036 (Kelley presenting a petition from citizens of Philadelphia), 1480 (Sumner presenting a petition from citizens of Jefferson County, Pennsylvania), 1728 (Brown presenting a petition from citizens of Beverly, New Jersey).
8. See William Lee Miller, *Arguing About Slavery: The Great Battle in the United States Congress* (New York: Alfred A. Knopf, 1996).

9. *Congressional Globe*, 39th Cong., 1st Sess., 1200 (petition of citizens of Byberry Township, Pennsylvania). See *Congressional Globe*, 39th Cong., 1st Sess., 1099 (petition of S. A. Boothby and others) ("punish treason, reward loyalty"), 1162 (petition from Bridgewater, Massachusetts) (asking "for an amendment to the Constitution to impose such conditions upon the rebel States as shall punish treason and reward loyalty"), 1200 (petition of citizens of Chester County, Pennsylvania) (praying for Congress to condition readmission on measures that would "punish treason, reward loyalty"); 1272 (petition of citizens of Kenosha, Wisconsin) (same), 1272 (petition of citizens of Essex County, Massachusetts) (same). See also *Congressional Globe*, 39th Cong., 1st Sess., 1131 (petition of citizen from Barre, Massachusetts) ("asking for an amendment to the Constitution so as to protect all loyal citizens"),

10. *Congressional Globe*, 39th Cong., 1st Sess., 331. See *Congressional Globe*, 39th Cong., 1st Sess., 252 (Conkling), 462 (Baker) 508 (Kasson); *Congressional Globe*, 39th Cong., 1st Sess., 91 (Delano) ("show your obedience to the Constitution and laws").

11. *Congressional Globe*, 39th Cong., 1st Sess., 728.

12. *Congressional Globe*, 39th Cong., 1st Sess., 1010.

13. *Congressional Globe*, 39th Cong., 1st Sess., 133.

14. *Congressional Globe*, 39th Cong., 1st Sess., 1010. See *Congressional Globe*, 39th Cong., 1st Sess., 123 (Raymond).

15. *Congressional Globe*, 39th Cong., 1st Sess., 462–463. See *Congressional Globe*, 39th Cong., 1st Sess., 1010 (R. Clarke) (claiming an antisecession/antinullification constitutional amendment was necessary because "[m]any of the leaders of the rebellion adhere to this favorite assumption with as much tenacity as ever, and proclaim without reserve that they only await the favorable occasion to try their cherished principles in another forum where success will more likely attend the effort").

16. *Congressional Globe*, 39th Cong., 1st Sess., 931.

17. *Congressional Globe*, 39th Cong., 1st Sess., 1077. See *Congressional Globe*, 39th Cong., 1st Sess., 1319 (Holmes) ("the political heresies that engendered the war . . . must be repudiated").

18. *Congressional Globe*, 39th Cong., 1st Sess., 978 (petition of citizens of Defiance County, Ohio). See *Congressional Globe*, 39th Cong., 1st Sess., 1006 (petitions of citizens of Mahoning County, Ohio, and citizens of the Third Congressional District, Illinois). Standing alone, such calls might be asking for political guarantees, such as a ban on former Confederates holding office. Given, however, that such petitions often also separately called for bans on former Confederates holding office, this phrase seems best interpreted as a request for an explicit antisecession guarantee.

19. *Congressional Globe*, 39th Cong., 1st Sess., 1024.

20. See, e.g., *Congressional Globe*, 39th Cong., 1st Sess., 1025 (petition of citizens of Illinois).

21. *Congressional Globe*, 39th Cong., 1st Sess., 1618.

22. *Congressional Globe*, 39th Cong., 1st Sess., 729. See *Congressional Globe*, 39th Cong., 1st Sess., 783 (Kelso) ("We should convict and hang for treason the leaders of the rebellion."), 920 (Ja. Henderson).

23. *Congressional* Globe, 39th Cong., 1st Sess., 74. See *Congressional Globe*, 39th Cong., 1st Sess., 732 (Kelso).

24. *Congressional Globe*, 39th Cong., 1st Sess., 1006.

25. *Congressional Globe*, 39th Cong., 1st Sess., 2. See *Congressional Globe*, 39th Cong., 1st Sess., 132–333 (Spaulding) (calling on Congress to by legislation to "use[] the suffrages of all loyal freedmen" in "the rebel States" and "[e]xtend a qualified right of suffrage to the freedmen in the District of Columbia").

26. *Congressional Globe*, 39th Cong., 1st Sess., 68.

27. *Congressional Globe*, 39th Cong., 1st Sess., 141.

28. *Congressional Globe*, 39th Cong., 1st Sess., 123.

29. David R. Mayhew, *Congress: The Electoral Connection* (New Haven, CT: Yale University Press, 1974), 62; David Bateman, Stephan Stohler, and Robinson Woodward-Burns, "Judicial Power and the Shifting Purpose of Article V" (unpublished manuscript under review and on file with author).

30. *Congressional Globe*, 39th Cong., 1st Sess., 2.

31. See *Congressional Globe*, 39th Cong., 1st Sess., 74 (Stevens), 133 (Spalding) (calling on Congress to "insert a provision in the Constitution prohibiting the repudiation of the national debt, and also prohibiting the assumption by Congress of the rebel debt"); 252 (Conkling), 331 (Representative Henry C. Deming of Connecticut), 462 (Baker), 508 (Kasson) 728 (Welker) ("our public creditors shall be protection from any repudiation of the public debt of the nation; that our credit may at all times be sustained"); 1075 (Nye) ("the majority in Congress is very tenacious on the subject of the Union war debt; that it is determined to keep faith with the national creditors; that it is bent on adopting and throwing round it all the safeguards and precautions possible"); 1177 (petition of citizens of Ohio). See also *Congressional Globe*, 39th Cong., 1st Sess., 2 (Sumner) (calling for "a majority of the people of each (seceding) State" by "popular vote" to agree to "[t]he rejection of the rebel debt, and at the same time the adoption, in just proportion, of the national debt and the national obligations to Union soldiers, with solemn pledges never to join in any measure, direct or indirect, for their repudiation, or in any way tending to impair the national credit").

32. *Congressional Globe*, 39th Cong., 1st Sess., 1622.

33. *Congressional Globe*, 39th Cong., 1st Sess., 1319.

34. See *Congressional Globe*, 39th Cong., 1st Sess., 902 (Cook), 1307 (Orth), 1618 (Moulton),

35. See *Congressional Globe*, 39th Cong., 1st Sess., 1316 (D. Ashley) (rebel debt and no compensation), 1437 (Stewart) (same). Many petitioners linked bans on compensation with bans on race discrimination. See, e.g., *Congressional Globe*, 39th Cong., 1st Sess., 1251 (memorial of citizens of Michigan).

36. *Congressional Globe*, 39th Cong., 1st Sess., 69.

37. *Congressional Globe*, 39th Cong., 1st Sess., 2.

38. *Congressional Globe*, 39th Cong., 1st Sess., 667.

39. *Congressional Globe*, 39th Cong., 1st Sess., 1625.

40. *Congressional Globe*, 39th Cong., 1st Sess., 252. See *Congressional Globe*, 39th Cong., 1st Sess., 1316 (D. Ashley) (calling for a constitutional amendment

"prohibiting the States from levying taxes to pay pensions to the men engaged in the rebellion against the Government of the United States").

41. *Congressional Globe*, 39th Cong., 1st Sess., 1032.

42. *Congressional Globe*, 39th Cong., 1st Sess., 1077.

43. *Congressional Globe*, 39th Cong., 1st Sess., 732.

44. *Congressional Globe*, 39th Cong., 1st Sess., 74. See *Congressional Globe*, 39th Cong., 1st Sess., 1010 (R. Clarke) calling for "The power to be given to Congress to levy export duties, whereby the great stable of the South, cotton, may be subjected to the burden of paying a liberal share of our great public debt, incurred in a struggle in which cotton was indirectly and remotely, but surely, the inciting cause").

45. *Congressional Globe*, 39th Cong., 1st Sess., 1624.

46. But see *Congressional Globe*, 39th Cong., 1st Sess., 1622 (Myers) (favoring a constitutional, but noting "if every other guarantee were obtained, we might trust to the acts of the several Legislatures in reference to this question").

47. *Congressional Globe*, 39th Cong., 1st Sess., 728. Curiously, Welker did not specific whether a constitutional amendment was necessary to ensure "our public creditors shall be protected from any repudiation of the public debt of the nation." *Congressional Globe*, 39th Cong., 1st Sess., 728.

48. *Congressional Globe*, 39th Cong., 1st Sess., 462.

49. *Congressional Globe*, 39th Cong., 1st Sess., 472.

50. *Congressional Globe*, 39th Cong., 1st Sess., 2.

51. *Congressional Globe*, 39th Cong., 1st Sess., 129.

52. *Congressional Globe*, 39th Cong., 1st Sess., 2406.

53. *Congressional Globe*, 39th Cong., 1st Sess., 133. See *Congressional Globe*, 39th Cong., 1st Sess., 1307 (Orth) ("Representation should be based on actual voters in each State, and so long as the right of suffrage is withheld from the freedmen, so long should the States in which they reside be deprived of the exercises of political power based upon that population."), 1622 (Myers) ("when any class is excluded from the elective franchise we are not entitled to representation for such excluded class").

54. *Congressional Globe*, 39th Cong., 1st Sess., 463.

55. *Congressional Globe*, 39th Cong., 1st Sess., 794.

56. *Congressional Globe*, 39th Cong., 1st Sess., 1319. See *Congressional Globe*, 39th Cong., 1st Sess., 1618 ("representation in Congress shall be founded on and in proportion to numbers entitled to suffrage"), 1627 (Buckland) ("representation should be founded solely upon voters").

57. *Congressional Globe*, 39th Cong., 1st Sess., 727.

58. *Congressional Globe*, 39th Cong., 1st Sess., App., 132.

59. *Congressional Globe*, 39th Cong., 1st Sess., 470.

60. *Congressional Globe*, 39th Cong., 1st Sess., 74.

61. *Congressional Globe*, 39th Cong., 1st Sess., 74.

62. *Congressional Globe*, 39th Cong., 1st Sess., 74.

63. *Congressional Globe*, 39th Cong., 1st Sess., 74–75.

64. *Congressional Globe*, 39th Cong., 1st Sess., 794. See *Congressional Globe*, 39th Cong., 1st Sess., 728.

65. *Congressional Globe*, 39th Cong., 1st Sess., 258.
66. *Congressional Globe*, 39th Cong., 1st Sess., 795.
67. *Congressional Globe*, 39th Cong., 1st Sess., 2.
68. See *Congressional Globe*, 39th Cong., 1st Sess., 2 (Sumner) (asserting representatives from the former Confederacy would not be seated in Congress until "a majority of the people of each State" by "popular vote" agreed to the "complete enfranchisement of all citizens").
69. *Congressional Globe*, 39th Cong., 1st Sess., 867.
70. *Congressional Globe*, 39th Cong., 1st Sess., 867.
71. *Congressional Globe*, 39th Cong., 1st Sess., 1630.
72. *Congressional Globe*, 39th Cong., 1st Sess., 1618.
73. *Congressional Globe*, 39th Cong., 1st Sess., 1439.
74. *Congressional Globe*, 39th Cong., 1st Sess., 848.
75. *Congressional Globe*, 39th Cong., 1st Sess., 1006.
76. *Congressional Globe*, 39th Cong., 1st Sess., 125.
77. *Congressional Globe*, 39th Cong., 1st Sess., 2. See *Congressional Globe*, 39th Cong., 1st Sess., 1224 (Sumner) ("all who have been untrue to the Republic must for a certain time, constituting the *transition period*, [must] be excluded from the partnership of government").
78. *Congressional Globe*, 39th Cong., 1st Sess., 451.
79. *Congressional Globe*, 39th Cong., 1st Sess., 1148. See *Congressional Globe*, 39th Cong., 1st Sess., 1162 (McKee) (same). See also *Congressional Globe*, 39th Cong., 1st Sess., 732 (Welker) ("no man whose heart was filled with sentiments of treason, whose hand is red with the blood of our martyred heroes, should ever be allowed to take a seat as a Representation in the American Congress"), 1105 (Stewart) ("we intend to exclude from both Halls of Congress all but loyal men"), 1319 (Holmes) ("no person, with my consent, shall ever hold office under the Government of the United States who has in any way voluntarily aided the rebellion"); *Congressional Globe*, 39th Cong., 1st Sess., App., 132 (resolutions of the Indiana Union convention) ("no man who voluntarily participated in the rebellion ought to be admitted to a seat in Congress").
80. *Congressional Globe*, 39th Cong., 1st Sess., 463.
81. *Congressional Globe*, 39th Cong., 1st Sess., 133. See *Congressional Globe*, 39th Cong., 1st Sess., 1306 (Orth) ("there is no better way to make treason odious than to place upon the traitor the brand that he shall forever be disqualified from holding office under the Government which he attempted to destroy").
82. *Congressional Globe*, 39th Cong., 1st Sess., 930.
83. *Congressional Globe*, 39th Cong., 1st Sess., App., 145.
84. *Congressional Globe*, 39th Cong., 1st Sess., 1307.
85. *Congressional Globe*, 39th Cong., 1st Sess., 2691.
86. *Congressional Globe*, 39th Cong., 1st Sess., 1476.
87. *Congressional Globe*, 39th Cong., 1st Sess., 732.
88. *Congressional Globe*, 39th Cong., 1st Sess., 1629.
89. *Congressional Globe*, 39th Cong., 1st Sess., 2879.
90. *Congressional Globe*, 39th Cong., 1st Sess., 1618.
91. *Congressional Globe*, 39th Cong., 1st Sess., App., 132.

92. *Congressional Globe*, 39th Cong., 1st Sess., 848 (memorial and protest of Frederick Douglass and others).
93. *Congressional Globe*, 39th Cong., 1st Sess., 1627.
94. *Congressional Globe*, 39th Cong., 1st Sess., 1315. See *Congressional Globe*, 39th Cong., 1st Sess., 1623 (Myers) (and as education is needed to give it fitness, I am satisfied not to demand of the South a policy my own State has not adopted").
95. *Congressional Globe*, 39th Cong., 1st Sess., App., 203.
96. *Congressional Globe*, 39th Cong., 1st Sess., 2488.
97. *Congressional Globe*, 39th Cong., 1st Sess., 1479. Whether Anderson endorsed all of Stewart's program is not clear. Shortly after supporting Stewart, Anderson stated, "I am today in favor of restricted negro suffrage in the States." *Congressional Globe*, 39th Cong., 1st Sess., 1479.
98. *Congressional Globe*, 39th Cong., 1st Sess., 1437.
99. See *Congressional Globe*, 39th Cong., 1st Sess., 1476 (Dumont).
100. See *Congressional Globe*, 39th Cong., 1st Sess., 1630 (Hart) ("the power exists in the Constitution").
101. *Congressional Globe*, 39th Cong., 1st Sess., 1437.
102. *Congressional Globe*, 39th Cong., 1st Sess., 1754.
103. *Congressional Globe*, 39th Cong., 1st Sess., 133.
104. *Congressional Globe*, 39th Cong., 1st Sess., 1162. See *Congressional Globe*, 39th Cong., 1st Sess., 462–464 (Baker), 1318–1319 (Orth), 2094 (J. T. Thomas), 2097 (Smith); *Congressional Globe*, 39th Cong., 1st Sess., App., 67–68 (Garfield).
105. *Congressional Globe*, 39th Cong., 1st Sess., 872. See *Congressional Globe*, 39th Cong., 1st Sess., 1007 (Clarke) ("in no event can any of the delinquent States be permitted to participate in the national councils until they will present such men as their Representatives who will take the oath all loyal Representatives are required to take, and who represent a loyal constituency").
106. *Congressional Globe*, 39th Cong., 1st Sess., 1172. See *Congressional Globe*, 39th Cong., 1st Sess., 140 (Latham); *Congressional Globe*, 39th Cong., 1st Sess., App., 131 (Sherman) ("I, for one, will never yield that test oath to enable any man whose hand is stained with the blood of my fellow-countrymen to take a seat on the floor of the Senate.").
107. *Congressional Globe*, 39th Cong., 1st Sess., 1476.
108. *Congressional Globe*, 39th Cong., 1st Sess., 69.
109. *Congressional Globe*, 39th Cong., 1st Sess., 508.
110. See *Congressional Globe*, 39th Cong., 1st Sess., 508 (Kasson), 1319 (Holmes) (former Confederate states must "guarantee to all their people, without distinction of race or color, the blessings and privileges of government"); 1437 (Stewart) ("do away with all existing distinctions as to civil rights and disabilities . . . by reason either of race or color, or previous condition of servitude").
111. *Congressional Globe*, 39th Cong., 1st Sess., 728.
112. *Congressional Globe*, 39th Cong., 1st Sess., 1006 (Windsor, Vermont); 1272 (citizens of Essex County, Massachusetts); 806 (citizens of Buffalo, New York). See *Congressional Globe*, 39th Cong., 1st Sess., 848 (petition of Lewis Tappan) ("praying that in all enactments the colored people may be treated

as white citizens"), 848 (petition of 500 "colored" soldiers) ("the same rights and privileges accorded to white men"), 913 (petition of citizens of Portland, Maine),

113. *Congressional Globe*, 39th Cong., 1st Sess., 913. See *Congressional Globe*, 39th Cong., 1st Sess., 931 (same).

114. *Congressional Globe*, 39th Cong., 1st Sess., 1171. See *Congressional Globe*, 39th Cong., 1st Sess., 591 (petition of citizens of Wisconsin), 662 (Hubbell) ("[a]mple and complete protection to the freedmen in all their rights of persons and of property to the full extent enjoyed by all non-voting classes"), 728 (Welker), 1319 (Holmes) ("the fulfillment of the pledges to the freedmen made in the emancipation proclamation must be placed beyond any contingency").

115. *Congressional Globe*, 39th Cong., 1st Sess., 14. See *Congressional Globe*, 39th Cong., 1st Sess., 868 (Newell) ("loyalty to human rights, the rights and privileges of every citizen").

116. *Congressional Globe*, 39th Cong., 1st Sess., App., 91. Delano added that this security was motivated by "the results of the war hav[ing] cast upon this nation a great duty toward the emancipated race." *Congressional Globe*, 39th Cong., 1st Sess., App., 91.

117. *Congressional Globe*, 39th Cong., 1st Sess., 2879.

118. *Congressional Globe*, 39th Cong., 1st Sess., 2604.

119. *Congressional Globe*, 39th Cong., 1st Sess., 2691.

120. *Congressional Globe*, 39th Cong., 1st Sess., 1618.

121. *Congressional Globe*, 39th Cong., 1st Sess., 930. See *Congressional Globe*, 39th Cong., 1st Sess., 88 (petition from "citizens of the United States") (praying that "no State may be admitted into the Union with the proscription of color in its constitution or laws," and Congress require of states seeking to join or rejoin the Union a commitment to "equality of all classes before the law, . . . secured and protected for all classes as for the whites").

122. *Congressional Globe*, 39th Cong., 1st Sess., 592. See *Congressional Globe*, 39th Cong., 1st Sess., 2 (Sumner), 931 (H. Wilson) ("civil rights should be secured by laws applicable alike to whites and blacks"), 1006 (petition of citizens of Hendrick County, Indiana) ("praying the rebel States may not be admitted back until they secure equal rights to all men, so that all men, white and black, may stand equal before the law"), 1006 (petition of citizens of Gloverstown, New York) ("security and equality before the law to loyal men of the South, without distinction of color"), 1162 (petition of citizens from Bridgewater, Massachusetts) (calling on Congress to "abolish all laws making distinctions on account of race or color"),

123. *Congressional Globe*, 39th Cong., 1st Sess., 145.

124. *Congressional Globe*, 39th Cong., 1st Sess., 2399, 2406.

125. *Congressional Globe*, 39th Cong., 1st Sess., 727.

126. *Congressional Globe*, 39th Cong., 1st Sess., 1622.

127. *Congressional Globe*, 39th Cong., 1st Sess., 508.

128. *Congressional Globe*, 39th Cong., 1st Sess., App., 67–68. For a similar proposal of a race neutral rights guarantee designed to prevent race discrimination, see *Congressional Globe*, 39th Cong., 1st Sess., 1622 (Myers) ("That each State shall provide for equality before the law, equal protection to life, liberty, and

property, equal right to be sued, to inherit, make contracts and give testimony. Not one of the rebel States allows a negro to give testimony against a white man; several impose punishments which different according to the color of the offender.").

129. *Congressional Globe*, 39th Cong., 1st Sess., 10.

130. *Congressional Globe*, 39th Cong., 1st Sess., 74.

131. A petition from citizens of Massachusetts after declaring "emancipation is not complete as long as the black codes exist" called for a constitutional amendment (or "irreversible guarantees") that included "enfranchisement and equality before the laws," but did not refer specially to race discrimination. *Congressional Globe*, 39th Cong., 1st Sess., 88.

132. See *Congressional Globe*, 39th Cong., 1st Sess., 173 (J. Wilson), 179 (Scofield), 215 (T. Davis).

133. *Congressional Globe*, 39th Cong., 1st Sess., 1625.

134. *Congressional Globe*, 39th Cong., 1st Sess., 592.

135. *Congressional Globe*, 39th Cong., 1st Sess., 1177. See *Congressional Globe*, 39th Cong., 1st Sess., 979 (petitions of citizens of Philadelphia, Pennsylvania, Iowa, and Butler County, Pennsylvania), 1024 (petition of citizens of Huron and Erie Counties, Pennsylvania) (limiting discrimination prohibitions to "rebel states"), 1189.

136. *Congressional Globe*, 39th Cong., 1st Sess., 913.

137. *Congressional Globe*, 39th Cong., 1st Sess., 1627.

138. *Congressional Globe*, 39th Cong., 1st Sess., 1627.

139. *Congressional Globe*, 39th Cong., 1st Sess., 2.

140. *Congressional Globe*, 39th Cong., 1st Sess., 667.

141. *Congressional Globe*, 39th Cong., 1st Sess., 74. See *Congressional Globe*, 39th Cong., 1st Sess., 716 (J. Rice), "it is impossible for us to give liberty, protection, and justice to the people of those States, unless we secure them in their homes and their homesteads").

142. *Congressional Globe*, 39th Cong., 1st Sess., 913. See *Congressional Globe*, 39th Cong., 1st Sess., 256 (Julian).

143. *Congressional Globe*, 39th Cong., 1st Sess., 141.

144. *Congressional Globe*, 39th Cong., 1st Sess., 1628.

145. *Congressional Globe*, 39th Cong., 1st Sess., 124.

146. *Congressional Globe*, 39th Con., 1st Sess., 903. See *Congressional Globe*, 39th Cong., 1st Sess., 124 (Raymond), 911 (Cullom) (same).

147. *Congressional Globe*, 39th Cong., 1st Sess., 1189.

148. *Congressional Globe*, 39th Cong., 1st Sess., 74. See *Congressional Globe*, 39th Cong., 1st Sess., 1171 (Kuykendall).

149. *Congressional Globe*, 39th Cong., 1st Sess., 2. See *Congressional Globe*, 39th Cong., 1st Sess., 508 (Kasson).

150. *Congressional Globe*, 39th Cong., 1st Sess., 592.

151. *Congressional Globe*, 39th Cong., 1st Sess., 470.

152. *Congressional Globe*, 39th Cong., 1st Sess., 872.

153. *Congressional Globe*, 39th Cong., 1st Sess., 331. See *Congressional Globe*, 39th Cong., 1st Sess., 728 (Welker), 1627 (Buckland) ("If the Constitution of the United States does not now confer upon the national Government the power

to provide against such outrages upon the rights of American citizens, which I think it does, then I say it is the duty of Congress and the President to insist upon such an amendment as will confer that power."); *Congressional Globe*, 39th Cong., 1st Sess., App., 67 (Garfield) ("If our Constitution does not now afford all the powers necessary to that end, we must ask the people to add them.").

154. *Congressional Globe*, 39th Cong., 1st Sess., 132.

155. *Congressional Globe*, 39th Cong., 1st Sess., App., 203.

156. *Congressional Globe*, 39th Cong., 1st Sess., 2406 (Ingersoll), 2691 (Morris).

157. *Congressional Globe*, 39th Cong., 1st Sess., 2488 (H. Wilson); *Congressional Globe*, 39th Cong., 1st Sess., App., 203 (G. Lawrence).

158. *Congressional Globe*, 39th Cong., 1st Sess., 1024. See *Congressional Globe*, 39th Cong., 1st Sess., 1177 (citizens of Ohio) (likely the same petition), 1251 (citizens of Michigan), 2879 (J. Ashley).

159. *Congressional Globe*, 39th Cong., 1st Sess., 741.

160. *Congressional Globe*, 39th Cong., 1st Sess., App., 67. See *Congressional Globe*, 39th Cong., 1st Sess., 667 (W. Lawrence) ("the personal rights of every citizen secured").

161. *Congressional Globe*, 39th Cong., 1st Sess., 14.

162. *Congressional Globe*, 39th Cong., 1st Sess., 1034.

163. The members of Congress who spoke on this subject almost always thought Congress had the power to enforce Article IV. That debate will be discussed in a forthcoming volume.

164. This point will be developed at length in *The Thirteenth Amendment's Constitution*. For a flavor of some of the arguments, see Mark A. Graber, "The Second Freemen's Bureau Bill's Constitution," 94 *Texas Law Review* 1361 (2016).

165. See *Congressional Globe*, 39th Cong., 1st Sess., 1095.

166. This point will be developed at length in a subsequent volume.

5. TO COLORADO AND BEYOND

1. For Buckelew, see *Congressional Globe*, 39th Cong., 1st Sess., 959–965.

2. This paragraph largely summarized Michael Green, "Abraham Lincoln, Nevada, and the Law of Unintended Consequences," 52 *Nevada Historical Society Quarterly* 85, 87 (Summer 2009).

3. 12 *Stat.* 126 (1861).

4. 12 *Stat.* 172 (1861) (Colorado); 12 *Stat.* 126 (1861) (Nevada) 209; 12 *Stat.* 229 (1861) (Dakota).

5. 12 *Stat.* 30 (1864).

6. Francis Newton Thorpe, "Constitution of the State of Nevada—1864," *The Federal and State Constitutions* (Washington, DC: Government Printing Office, 1909), 2402. Green, "Abraham Lincoln," 89.

7. Some debate exists over which Republicans pushed hardest for the admission of Nevada. See F. Lauriston Bullard, "Abraham Lincoln and the Statehood of Nevada," 26 *American Bar Association Journal* 210 (1940), 26 *American Bar Association Journal* 313 (1940) (maintaining Lincoln pushed Nevada statehood); Earl S. Pomeroy, "Lincoln, the Thirteenth Amendment, and the Admission of Nevada," 12 *Pacific Historical Review* 362 (1943) (claiming Republicans in

Congress were more aggressive pushing Nevada statehood). For an excellent summary of this debate, see Green, "Abraham Lincoln," 91–98.

8. See Green, "Abraham Lincoln," 90.

9. *Congressional Globe*, 37 Cong., 3rd Sess., 1510.

10. Thorpe, "Constitution of the State of Nevada—1864," 2404.

11. This paragraph and the next borrow heavily from Eugene H. Berwanger, *The Rise of the Centennial State: Colorado Territory, 1861–76* (Urbana: University of Illinois Press, 2007); Carl Abbott, Stephan J. Leonard, and Thomas J. Noel, *Colorado: A History of the Centennial State*, 5th ed. (Boulder: University Press of Colorado, 2013).

12. 10 *Stat.* 32 (1864).

13. See Eugene H. Berwanger, "Hardin and Langston: Western Black Spokesmen of The Reconstruction Era," 64 *Journal of Negro History* (1979), 103–105; *Congressional Globe*, 39th Cong., 1st Sess., 2138 (Sumner).

14. *Congressional Globe*, 39th Cong., 1st Sess., 1365.

15. *Congressional Globe*, 39th Cong., 1st Sess., 2179.

16. *Congressional Globe*, 39th Cong., 1st Sess., 2373–2374.

17. The vote was 37–7 in the Senate with fifteen Senators not voting. *Congressional Globe*, 39th Cong., 1st Sess., 2180. The vote was 95–37 in the House with fifty-one representatives not voting. *Congressional Globe*, 39th Cong., 1st Sess., 2373.

18. *Congressional Globe*, 39th Cong., 1st Sess., 2589.

19. The Senate did bother taking a vote to override. See *Congressional Globe*, 39th Cong., 1st Sess., 2714.

20. Conness, Sprague, Wade, and H. Wilson switched. Clark, Howard, Howe, Nye and Yates, who did not state a preference in the March vote, voted for statehood in May.

21. The two Unconditional Unionists in the Senate (Creswell and Van Winkle) switched their votes from against in March to for in May. Unconditional Unionists in the House divided 6–2 in favor of statehood.

22. *Congressional Globe*, 39th Cong., 1st Sess., 2609.

23. *Congressional Globe*, 39th Cong., 1st Sess., 2609.

24. *Congressional Globe*, 39th Cong., 1st Sess., 2609.

25. *Congressional Globe*, 39th Cong., 1st Sess., 1355. See *Congressional Globe*, 39th Cong., 1st Sess., 2172 (Hendricks) ("Congress provided that the people at a time specified might elect delegates, "that those delegates should convene and organize into a convention, and being thus organized, should frame a constitution for the people of that Territory, and that that constitution thus made should be submitted to the people for their approval or rejection. Such an election was held; the convention met; a constitution was framed; it was submitted to the people, and by a large vote, three to one, they rejected it. Now I ask, was it competent for the people of Colorado to proceed further under the act of Congress?"), 2179 (R. Johnson).

26. *Congressional Globe*, 39th Cong., 1st Sess., 1360. See *Congressional Globe*, 39th Cong., 1st Sess., 2172 (Hendricks) ("a constitution irregular in every respect").

27. *Congressional Globe*, 39th Cong., 1st Sess., 1356.

28. *Congressional Globe*, 39th Cong., 1st Sess., 2178.

29. *Congressional Globe*, 39th Cong., 1st Sess., 1360.

30. *Congressional Globe*, 39th Cong., 1st Sess., 1361.

31. See *Congressional Globe*, 39th Cong., 1st Sess., 2173 (Hendricks).

32. *Congressional Globe*, 39th Cong., 1st Sess., 2173. *Congressional Globe*, 39th Cong., 1st Sess., 2174.

33. *Congressional Globe*, 39th Cong., 1st Sess., 2174. See *Congressional Globe*, 39th Cong., 1st Sess., 2373 (Finck) (noting comparisons between Colorado and such states as Delaware and Florida were inapt because that the "ratio of representation" when states were admitted before the Civil War "was much less than at present").

34. *Congressional Globe*, 39th Cong., 1st Sess., 1356.

35. *Congressional Globe*, 39th Cong., 1st Sess., 1355. See *Congressional Globe*, 39th Cong., 1st Sess., 2173 (Hendricks), 2179 (R. Johnson) ("in the true sense of a republican government, it is not right in principle to give to fifteen or twenty thousand people an equal voice in this body with one or two or three millions").

36. *Congressional Globe*, 39th Cong., 1st Sess., 2145. This assertion was made in the April debate over Colorado statehood. McDougall in the March debates had claimed that Colorado met past population standards. *Congressional Globe*, 39th Cong., 1st Sess., 1359. See *Congressional Globe*, 39th Cong., 1st Sess., 2173 (Hendricks) ("In the Senate of the United States one man in Colorado will have the voice of ninety men in the State of Indiana. Is that equality? Is that democracy? Is that justice? Or is it tyranny?").

37. *Congressional Globe*, 39th Cong., 1st Sess., 2141. See *Congressional Globe*, 39th Cong., 1st Sess., 2178 (R. Johnson) (complaining about letting "these twenty or thirty thousand persons be represented by one member certainly in the House of Representatives, although the number now required as the basis of representation in that House is 127,000, and to give them two Senators on this floor").

38. *Congressional Globe*, 39th Cong., 1st Sess., 2173.

39. *Congressional Globe*, 39th Cong., 1st Sess., 2173.

40. *Congressional Globe*, 39th Cong., 1st Sess., 2173.

41. *Congressional Globe*, 39th Cong., 1st Sess., 2178.

42. *Congressional Globe*, 39th Cong., 1st Sess., 2178.

43. See *Congressional Globe*, 39th Cong., 1st Sess., 2408 (S. Randall).

44. *Congressional Globe*, 39th Cong., 1st Sess., 1353.

45. *Congressional Globe*, 39th Cong., 1st Sess., 2143. See generally, *Congressional Globe*, 39th Cong., 1st Sess., App., p. 185 (G. Davis) (complaining with respect to Colorado, Nebraska and Nevada "the great consideration was that each one of these infant Territories that assumed the name of State would bring to its patronizing party two Senators and one Representative, and add that much to the material of a two-thirds majority in both Houses").

46. *Congressional Globe*, 39th Cong., 1st Sess., 2143.

47. *Congressional Globe*, 39th Cong., 1st Sess., 2142.

48. *Congressional Globe*, 39th Cong., 1st Sess., 2142.

49. *Congressional Globe*, 39th Cong., 1st Sess., 1327. See also *Congressional Globe*, 39th Cong., 1st Sess., 1983 (Sumner) ("The question was amply discussed on a former occasion; it was considered in every possible aspect. The condition

of the Territory of Colorado was exposed; its want of population was exhibited, and its constitution having in it the word 'white' was also exhibited to the Senate.").

50. *Congressional Globe*, 39th Cong., 1st Sess., 1327–1328.

51. *Congressional Globe*, 39th Cong., 1st Sess., 1328.

52. *Congressional Globe*, 39th Cong., 1st Sess., 2135.

53. *Congressional Globe*, 39th Cong., 1st Sess., 390.

54. *Congressional Globe*, 39th Cong., 1st Sess., 850.

55. *Congressional Globe*, 39th Cong., 1st Sess., 850.

56. *Congressional Globe*, 39th Cong., 1st Sess., 2033.

57. *Congressional Globe*, 39th Cong., 1st Sess., 1329.

58. *Congressional Globe*, 39th Cong., 1st Sess., 1329. Sumner pointed out that the word "white" or equivalent did not appear in territorial electoral laws. *Congressional Globe*, 39th Cong., 1st Sess., 1360. In his view, Senators when passing the enabling act "supposed that all persons, without distinction of color in that Territory, were electors." *Congressional Globe*, 39th Cong., 1st Sess., 2037. At least Sumner did. "[W]hen I voted for this enabling act," he stated, I did not vote with the idea that there could be a discrimination founded on color." *Congressional Globe*, 39th Cong., 1st Sess., 2036.

59. *Congressional Globe*, 39th Cong., 1st Sess., 2138.

60. *Congressional Globe*, 39th Cong., 1st Sess., 2138.

61. *Congressional Globe*, 39th Cong., 1st Sess., 1360.

62. *Congressional Globe*, 39th Cong., 1st Sess., 2138.

63. *Congressional Globe*, 39th Cong., 1st Sess., 2138.

64. Edward Bates, "Citizenship," 10 *Opinions of the Attorney General* 382 (1862).

65. 60 U.S. 393 (1856).

66. *Congressional Globe*, 39th Cong., 1st Sess., 2140.

67. *Congressional Globe*, 39th Cong., 1st Sess., 2140. See *Congressional Globe*, 39th Cong., 1st Sess., 2140 ("[I]t is in vain from the Senator from Illinois to remind us that in Colorado they did not consider colored persons citizens of the United States. Constitutionally and legally they are citizens, and there was no power in Colorado to deny them that citizenship.").

68. *Congressional Globe*, 39th Cong., 1st Sess., 2037.

69. *Congressional Globe*, 39th Cong., 1st Sess., 2036.

70. See *Congressional Globe*, 39th Cong., 1st Sess., 2140 (noting the enabling act was passed on February 24, 1864).

71. *Congressional Globe*, 39th Cong., 1st Sess., 2138.

72. *Congressional Globe*, 39th Cong., 1st Sess., 2139.

73. *Congressional Globe*, 39th Cong., 1st Sess., 2138.

74. See *Congressional Globe*, 39th Cong., 1st Sess., 1984 (Sumner) ("Let Colorado wait at least until she recognizes the Declaration of Independence."), 2033 (Congress should not "receive into this Union a community which choose to insult the age by appearing here with a constitution setting at defiance the fundamental principles of the Declaration of Independence"), 2713 ("the principle that no State shall be received into this Union from this time forward with a constitution which disavows the first principle of the Declaration of Independence").

75. 13 Stat. 32, 33 (1864). See *Congressional Globe*, 39th Cong., 1st Sess., 2036 (Sumner).

76. *Congressional Globe*, 39th Cong., 1st Sess., 1329. See *Congressional Globe*, 39th Cong., 1st Sess., 2139 ("Do not tell me that there are States in this Union which have such constitutions. That is no answer. We are not called to sit in judgment on those constitutions; we have no power to revise them; we are not to vote upon them; but here in this case we are called to sit in judgment upon this constitution, to revise, it and to vote upon it. You are to declare by your votes whether a constitution which tramples upon the principle of human equality is republican in form.").

77. *Congressional Globe*, 39th Cong., 1st Sess., 2036. See *Congressional Globe*, 39th Cong., 1st Sess., 2139 ("[W]hat is the first principle of the Declaration of Independence? Is it not in solemn words that all men are created equal, and that all just government stands on the consent of the governed?").

78. *Congressional Globe*, 39th Cong., 1st Sess., 2140 (emphasis in original).

79. *Congressional Globe*, 39th Cong., 1st Sess., 2140.

80. *Congressional Globe*, 39th Cong., 1st Sess., 1329. See *Congressional Globe*, 39th Cong., 1st Sess., 2036 (Sumner) (same).

81. *Congressional Globe*, 39th Cong., 1st Sess., 1983.

82. *Congressional Globe*, 39th Cong., 1st Sess., 2138. See *Congressional Globe*, 39th Cong., 1st Sess., 1329 ("it will hardly be decent for us in reviewing the constitution of a new State not to apply to it the highest possible test").

83. *Congressional Globe*, 39th Cong., 1st Sess., 2033. See *Congressional Globe*, 39th Cong., 1st Sess., 2135 ("at the close of the war, when by every obligation we are solemnly bound to maintain the rights of the colored race, you will err if you give your hand to such a community as I have described, which, so inferior in population and resources, comes forward with a constitution denying those rights").

84. *Congressional Globe*, 39th Cong., 1st Sess., 2138.

85. *Congressional Globe*, 39th Cong., 1st Sess., 1358.

86. *Congressional Globe*, 39th Cong., 1st Sess., 2176.

87. *Congressional Globe*, 39th Cong., 1st Sess., 2176.

88. *Congressional Globe*, 39th Cong., 1st Sess., 1982.

89. *Congressional Globe*, 39th Cong., 1st Sess., 2035.

90. *Congressional Globe*, 39th Cong., 1st Sess., 1357.

91. *Congressional Globe*, 39th Cong., 1st Sess., 1357.

92. *Congressional Globe*, 39th Cong., 1st Sess., 1357.

93. *Congressional Globe*, 39th Cong., 1st Sess., 1363.

94. *Congressional Globe*, 39th Cong., 1st Sess., 1363.

95. *Congressional Globe*, 39th Cong., 1st Sess., 2035. See also *Congressional Globe*, 39th Cong., 1st Sess., 2140 (Sumner) ("I have no recollection of the Nevada case. I do not know whether I voted on it or not, and I consider the question as absolutely irrelevant.").

96. *Congressional Globe*, 39th Cong., 1st Sess., 2176.

97. *Congressional Globe*, 39th Cong., 1st Sess., 2176.

98. *Congressional Globe*, 39th Cong., 1st Sess., 2176.

99. *Congressional Globe*, 39th Cong., 1st Sess., 2176.

100. *Congressional Globe*, 39th Cong., 1st Sess., 2176.

101. See Romer v. Evans, 517 U.S. 620 (1996).

102. *Congressional Globe*, 39th Cong., 1st Sess., 2176.

103. *Congressional Globe*, 39th Cong., 1st Sess., 2035. See *Congressional Globe*, 39th Cong., 1st Sess., 2035 (Grimes) ("I am irresistibly driven to the conclusion that there cannot be to exceed fifteen thousand people in the Territory.").

104. *Congressional Globe*, 39th Cong., 1st Sess., 1365. Wade did not vote when the Senate approved Colorado statehood in May. See *Congressional Globe*, 39th Cong., 1st Sess., 2179.

105. *Congressional Globe*, 39th Cong., 1st Sess., 1357. See *Congressional Globe*, 39th Cong., 1st Sess., 1363 (Grimes) ("the population of Colorado at this moment is probably not near as large . . . as it was last year").

106. *Congressional Globe*, 39th Cong., 1st Sess., 1353. See *Congressional Globe*, 39th Cong., 1st Sess., 1363 (Conness) (proposing a law "providing that no Territory should be received into the Union as a State until it had population enough to elect a member to Congress under the then existing apportionment law of the United States").

107. *Congressional Globe*, 39th Cong., 1st Sess., 1357.

108. *Congressional Globe*, 39th Cong., 1st Sess., 1357.

109. *Congressional Globe*, 39th Cong., 1st Sess., 1357. See *Congressional Globe*, 39th Cong., 1st Sess., 1363 (Grimes) ("the sum and substance of it all, is whether or not the Senate is prepared by its solemn vote to create a kind of rotten-borough State in the Rocky mountains, and give to that State the same representation and the same power on this floor as is given to the State of New York, Pennsylvania, and Ohio"), 2035 (Grimes) ("I am not willing to say that a population of that size and of that description shall be entitled to come into the Senate and be represented, and have the same power in our deliberations as the State of New York or Ohio or Pennsylvania.").

110. *Congressional Globe*, 39th Cong., 1st Sess., 2135–2136. See *Congressional Globe*, 39th Cong., 1st Sess., 2140 (Sumner) ("other States of the Union . . . ought not to find themselves voted down in this Chamber by two Senators from this small state").

111. *Congressional Globe*, 39th Cong., 1st Sess., 1353.

112. See Hamilton, Madison, and Jay, *The Federalist Papers*, 83 (noting the advantages to republican government of a "greater number of citizens").

113. *Congressional Globe*, 39th Cong., 1st Sess., 1363.

114. Fessenden briefly asked, "I want to know whether I understood rightly that the people of Colorado acted under that enabling act and refused to avail themselves of it." *Congressional Globe*, 39th Cong., 1st Sess., 1359. Wade made a similar point. *Congressional Globe*, 39th Cong., 1st Sess., 1357.

115. *Congressional Globe*, 39th Cong., 1st Sess., 2035.

116. *Congressional Globe*, 39th Cong., 1st Sess., 2139.

117. *Congressional Globe*, 39th Cong., 1st Sess., 2139.

118. *Congressional Globe*, 39th Cong., 1st Sess., 2145.

119. *Congressional Globe*, 39th Cong., 1st Sess., 1362.

120. *Congressional Globe*, 39th Cong., 1st Sess., 1362.

121. *Congressional Globe*, 39th Cong., 1st Sess., 1351.

122. *Congressional Globe*, 39th Cong., 1st Sess., 1351.

123. *Congressional Globe*, 39th Cong., 1st Sess., 2144.

124. *Congressional Globe*, 39th Cong., 1st Sess., 2144–2145.

125. *Congressional Globe*, 39th Cong., 1st Sess., 2170.

126. *Congressional Globe*, 39th Cong., 1st Sess., 2145.

127. *Congressional Globe*, 39th Cong., 1st Sess., 2144.

128. *Congressional Globe*, 39th Cong., 1st Sess., 2170.

129. *Congressional Globe*, 39th Cong., 1st Sess., 2142. See also *Congressional Globe*, 39th Cong., 1st Sess., 2171 (Williams) (the importance of representing the West).

130. *Congressional Globe*, 39th Cong., 1st Sess., 2177.

131. *Congressional Globe*, 39th Cong., 1st Sess., 2170.

132. *Congressional Globe*, 39th Cong., 1st Sess., 2172.

133. *Congressional Globe*, 39th Cong., 1st Sess., 2172.

134. *Congressional Globe*, 39th Cong., 1st Sess., 2171–2172.

135. *Congressional Globe*, 39th Cong., 1st Sess., 2034. See *Congressional Globe*, 39th Cong., 1st Sess., 2170 (H. Lane) ("Every single new State has been admitted with the word 'white' in its constitution. We have recognized them as republican in form for three quarters of a century. The grand triumphs of this country in three wars, and its grand improvement in material interests have all been brough out under this interpretation of the fathers that a State might be republican in form and still have the word 'white' in it.").

136. *Congressional Globe*, 39th Cong., 1st Sess., 2170.

137. *Congressional Globe*, 39th Cong., 1st Sess., 2373.

138. *Congressional Globe*, 39th Cong., 1st Sess., 2171.

139. *Congressional Globe*, 39th Cong., 1st Sess., 2171.

140. *Congressional Globe*, 39th Cong., 1st Sess., 2175.

141. See *Congressional Globe*, 39th Cong., 1st Sess., 1362 (Cragin).

142. *Congressional Globe*, 39th Cong., 1st Sess., 2034. See *Congressional Globe*, 39th Cong., 1st Sess., 2033 (H. Wilson) (noting Sumner "voted for the bill to allow Colorado to make a constitution and come here, and that bill authorized her to make this distinction or not to make it, just as she pleased. That bill did not even make a suggestion that she should secure equality before the law to all her citizens."), 2034 (H. Wilson) ("We, however, gave this people an enabling act, in which we did not tell them that they should not make this discrimination, and did not even suggest it; and that enabling act came, too, from the men of this body who profess to be the strongest in their devotion to the equal rights of man.").

143. *Congressional Globe*, 39th Cong., 1st Sess., 2141.

144. *Congressional Globe*, 39th Cong., 1st Sess., 2141.

145. *Congressional Globe*, 39th Cong., 1st Sess., 1360. See *Congressional Globe*, 39th Cong., 1st Sess., 2037 ("the law of Colorado, when [Sumner] voted for the enabling act, did not allow colored persons to vote").

146. *Congressional Globe*, 39th Cong., 1st Sess., 2139.

147. Edward Bates, "Citizenship," 10 *Opinions of the Attorney General* 382 (1862).

148. *Congressional Globe*, 39th Cong., 1st Sess., 2139.

149. *Congressional Globe*, 39th Cong., 1st Sess., 2175.

150. *Congressional Globe*, 39th Cong., 1st Sess., 2175.

151. *Congressional Globe*, 39th Cong., 1st Sess., 2175.
152. *Congressional Globe*, 39th Cong., 1st Sess., 2171.
153. *Congressional Globe*, 39th Cong., 1st Sess., 2171.
154. *Congressional Globe*, 39th Cong., 1st Sess., 2171.
155. *Congressional Globe*, 39th Cong., 1st Sess., 2172.
156. *Congressional Globe*, 39th Cong., 1st Sess., 2172.
157. *Congressional Globe*, 39th Cong., 1st Sess., 2172.
158. *Congressional Globe*, 39th Cong., 1st Sess., 2175.
159. *Congressional Globe*, 39th Cong., 1st Sess., 2170.
160. *Congressional Globe*, 39th Cong., 1st Sess., 2175.
161. *Congressional Globe*, 39th Cong., 1st Sess., 2143. See *Congressional Globe*, 39th Cong., 1st Sess., 2171 (Williams) (endorsing Nye and claiming "the day is not far distant with the Constitution of the United States will be so changed as to entitle men of all classes, without distinction of race or color, to enjoy the elective franchise"), 2175 (Howard) ("I think the time is not far distant when every citizen of the United States, black or white, ought to be and will be admitted to the right of suffrage."), 2373 (J. Ashley) ("I have no doubt that they loyal people of Colorado will enfranchise her blacks long before the blacks are enfranchised by the spirits who will control the late rebel States.").
162. *Congressional Globe*, 39th Cong., 1st Sess., 2175.
163. *Congressional Globe*, 39th Cong., 1st Sess., 2373.
164. *Congressional Globe*, 39th Cong., 1st Sess., 2170.
165. *Congressional Globe*, 39th Cong., 1st Sess., 2171.
166. *Congressional Globe*, 39th Cong., 1st Sess., 2034.
167. *Congressional Globe*, 39th Cong., 1st Sess., 2141.
168. *Congressional Globe*, 39th Cong., 1st Sess., 1357. See *Congressional Globe*, 39th Cong., 1st Sess., 1351 (S. Pomeroy) (noting the Kansas precedent), 2033 (H. Wilson) (noting the Nevada precedent); 2141 (Stewart) (citing the Nevada precedent), 2373 (J. Ashley) (noting the total vote in the most recent election in Colorado "is a larger number of votes than is cast in several Representative districts in a number of southern States. It is a larger vote than that cast in the State of Delaware or the State of Florida").
169. *Congressional Globe*, 39th Cong., 1st Sess., 2373.
170. *Congressional Globe*, 39th Cong., 1st Sess., 2174.
171. *Congressional Globe*, 39th Cong., 1st Sess., 2712.
172. *Congressional Globe*, 39th Cong., 1st Sess., 1362.
173. *Congressional Globe*, 39th Cong., 1st Sess., 2173. See *Congressional Globe*, 39th Cong., 1st Sess., 2177 (Creswell) ("the practice of our Government theretofore has never been to require any state population as a condition-precedent to the admission of a State").
174. *Congressional Globe*, 39th Cong., 1st Sess., 2170.
175. *Congressional Globe*, 39th Cong., 1st Sess., 2170–2171.
176. *Congressional Globe*, 39th Cong., 1st Sess., 1359.
177. *Congressional Globe*, 39th Cong., 1st Sess., 1359–1360.
178. *Congressional Globe*, 39th Cong., 1st Sess., 1364. See *Congressional Globe*, 39th Cong., 1st Sess., 2172 (Williams) ("Congress is estopped at this time from controverting that question. Whatever legal or technical questions may

be made upon the enabling act, I say that Congress then deliberately decided that the population of that Territory was sufficient to justify it in becoming a State."), 2174 (Stewart) ("Congress has passed upon the question of population. The Senate twice passed upon it by passing an enabling act in 1863, and again in 1864."), 2174 (Howard) (same), 2175 (Howard) ("I look upon the statute of 1864 as containing, . . . a pledge to the people of Colorado that they should come into the Union, as a pledge to them of the privilege of forming a State constitution, Congress having adjudged that their numbers were sufficient and that their situation at that remote point was such as to make it necessary and proper that they should form a State constitution and be admitted into the Union.").

179. *Congressional Globe*, 39th Cong., 1st Sess., 2034.

180. *Congressional Globe*, 39th Cong., 1st Sess., 2174 (H. Lane), 2373 (Ashley).

181. *Congressional Globe*, 39th Cong., 1st Sess., 1351. S. Pomeroy also claimed the possibility of being subject to the Civil War draft suppressed the vote for the state constitution. *Congressional Globe*, 39th Cong., 1st Sess., 1351.

182. *Congressional Globe*, 39th Cong., 1st Sess., 1363. See *Congressional Globe*, 39th Cong., 1st Sess., 2170 (H. Lane) ("no one knows what the population amounts to").

183. *Congressional Globe*, 39th Cong., 1st Sess., 1364.

184. *Congressional Globe*, 39th Cong., 1st Sess., 1362.

185. *Congressional Globe*, 39th Cong., 1st Sess., 2177.

186. *Congressional Globe*, 39th Cong., 1st Sess., 1360.

187. *Congressional Globe*, 39th Cong., 1st Sess., 2170.

188. *Congressional Globe*, 39th Cong., 1st Sess., 2175.

189. Hamilton, Madison, and Jay, *The Federalist Papers*, 253 ("They must have borne in mind that as the plan to be framed and proposed was to be submitted to *the people themselves*, the disapprobation of this supreme authority would destroy it forever; its approbation blot out antecedent errors and irregularities.") (emphasis in original).

190. *Congressional Globe*, 39th Cong., 1st Sess., 1360.

191. *Congressional Globe*, 39th Cong., 1st Sess., 1359.

192. *Congressional Globe*, 39th Cong., 1st Sess., 2170.

193. *Congressional Globe*, 39th Cong., 1st Sess., 3535.

194. *Congressional Globe*, 39th Cong., 1st Sess., 3528.

195. *Congressional Globe*, 39th Cong., 1st Sess., 3528.

196. *Congressional Globe*, 39th Cong., 1st Sess., 3525.

197. *Congressional Globe*, 39th Cong., 1st Sess., 3526.

198. *Congressional Globe*, 39th Cong., 1st Sess., 3526. See *Congressional Globe*, 39th Cong., 1st Sess., 3529 (Hendricks) ("If a Senator is in favor of extending the right of suffrage in every State, everywhere where a colored man is found, extending the right to him, he will vote for this bill.").

199. Chapter 1 details the controversies that broke out over issues related to the status of former Confederate states immediately after the Civil War.

200. *Congressional Globe*, 39th Cong., 1st Sess., App., 282.

201. *Congressional Globe*, 39th Cong., 1st Sess., 3992. See *Congressional Globe*, 39th Cong., 1st Sess., 3994 (H. Lane) ("I shall vote to admit Tennessee because she had . . . a full and complete loyal State government.").

202. *Congressional Globe*, 39th Cong., 1st Sess., 3998.

203. *Congressional Globe*, 39th Cong., 1st Sess., App., 282.

204. *Congressional Globe*, 39th Cong., 1st Sess., 3990.

205. *Congressional Globe*, 39th Cong., 1st Sess., App., 282.

206. *Congressional Globe*, 39th Cong., 1st Sess., App., 282.

207. *Congressional Globe*, 39th Cong., 1st Sess., App., 3978.

208. *Congressional Globe*, 39th Cong., 1st Sess., 3978.

209. *Congressional Globe*, 39th Cong., 1st Sess., 3978. Bingham repeated this mantra frequently. See *Congressional Globe*, 39th Cong., 1st Sess., 3979 ("the right of the majority of loyal freemen to rule"), 3780 ("a majority of the local freemen, citizens of the United States, within her limits shall be permitted to control the destiny and political power of that State").

210. *Congressional Globe*, 39th Cong., 1st Sess., 3978.

211. *Congressional Globe*, 39th Cong., 1st Sess., 4305.

212. *Congressional Globe*, 39th Cong., 1st Sess., App., 3992.

213. *Congressional Globe*, 39th Cong., 1st Sess., 3988.

214. *Congressional Globe*, 39th Cong., 1st Sess., App., 283. See *Congressional Globe*, 39th Cong., 1st Sess., 3980 (Bingham) ("if Tennessee is not entitled to representation in the House neither is New York or Ohio").

215. *Congressional Globe*, 39th Cong., 1st Sess., 3978. See *Congressional Globe*, 39th Cong., 1st Sess., 2988 (Trumbull) (making the Missouri analogy).

216. *Congressional Globe*, 39th Cong., 1st Sess., 3979 (Stevens).

217. *Congressional Globe*, 39th Cong., 1st Sess., 3979.

218. *Congressional Globe*, 39th Cong., 1st Sess., App., 282.

219. *Congressional Globe*, 39th Cong., 1st Sess., 3979–3980.

220. *Congressional Globe*, 39th Cong., 1st Sess., 3980.

221. *Congressional Globe*, 39th Cong., 1st Sess., 3979.

222. *Congressional Globe*, 39th Cong., 1st Sess., 3981. See *Congressional Globe*, 39th Cong., 1st Sess., 3993 (Fessenden) (supporting the same policy), 3999–4000 (Morrill) (same).

223. *Congressional Globe*, 39th Cong., 1st Sess., 3981.

224. *Congressional Globe*, 39th Cong., 1st Sess., 3981.

225. *Congressional Globe*, 39th Cong., 1st Sess., 3981.

226. See also *Congressional Globe*, 39th Cong., 1st Sess., 3978 (Higby) (objecting that "the voting power is confined exclusively to the white population").

227. *Congressional Globe*, 39th Cong., 1st Sess., 3998.

228. *Congressional Globe*, 39th Cong., 1st Sess., 3976. See *Congressional Globe*, 39th Cong., 1st Sess., 3988 (Brown) (questioning whether the proposed constitution of Tennessee was "republican in form . . . notwithstanding the fact that it disfranchises the whole colored population").

229. *Congressional Globe*, 39th Cong., 1st Sess., 3976.

230. *Congressional Globe*, 39th Cong., 1st Sess., 3976.

231. See Jack M. Balkin, *Living Originalism* (Cambridge, MA: Harvard University Press, 2011).

232. *Congressional Globe*, 39th Cong., 1st Sess., 3977.

233. *Congressional Globe*, 39th Cong., 1st Sess., 4007.

234. *Congressional Globe*, 39th Cong., 1st Sess., 3998.

235. *Congressional Globe*, 39th Cong., 1st Sess., 3998.

236. *Congressional Globe*, 39th Cong., 1st Sess., 3950.

237. *Congressional Globe*, 39th Cong., 1st Sess., 3948.

238. *Congressional Globe*, 39th Cong., 1st Sess., 3950. Bingham proposed adding "her return to her due allegiance to the Government, laws, and authority of the United States." *Congressional Globe*, 39th Cong., 1st Sess., 3975.

239. *Congressional Globe*, 39th Cong., 1st Sess., 3948, 3950.

240. *Congressional Globe*, 39th Cong., 1st Sess., 3987.

241. *Congressional Globe*, 39th Cong., 1st Sess., 4000, 4003 (Yates).

242. *Congressional Globe*, 39th Cong., 1st Sess., 4005 (Cowan), 4006 (McDougall).

243. *Congressional Globe*, 39th Cong., 1st Sess., 3991.

244. *Congressional Globe*, 39th Cong., 1st Sess., 3998.

245. *Congressional Globe*, 39th Cong., 1st Sess., 4007.

246. *Congressional Globe*, 39th Cong., 1st Sess., 3980.

247. *Congressional Globe*, 39th Cong., 1st Sess., 3998.

248. *Congressional Globe*, 39th Cong., 1st Sess., 4000.

249. *Congressional Globe*, 39th Cong., 1st Sess., 4056.

250. *Congressional Globe*, 39th Cong., 1st Sess., 4056.

251. *Congressional Globe*, 39th Cong., 1st Sess., 4106.

252. *Congressional Globe*, 39th Cong., 1st Sess., 4072.

253. *Congressional Globe*, 39th Cong., 1st Sess., 4221 (Nye).

254. *Congressional Globe*, 39th Cong., 1st Sess., 4220 (Nye).

255. *Congressional Globe*, 39th Cong., 1st Sess., 4208.

256. *Congressional Globe*, 39th Cong., 1st Sess., 4220.

257. *Congressional Globe*, 39th Cong., 1st Sess., 4220.

258. *Congressional Globe*, 39th Cong., 1st Sess., 4220.

259. See *Congressional Globe*, 39th Cong., 1st Sess., 4208 (Hendricks) ("the constitution never was adopted by a convention under the enabling act at all, but it is a constitution presented to the people by the Legislature of the Territory"), 4209 (Doolittle), 4211–4212 (Doolittle).

260. *Congressional Globe*, 39th Cong., 1st Sess., 4213. See *Congressional Globe*, 39th Cong., 1st Sess., 4207 (Sumner), 4213 (Buckalew) ("the number of inhabitants in the Territory of Nebraska cannot exceed forty thousand").

261. *Congressional Globe*, 39th Cong., 1st Sess., 4207. See also *Congressional Globe*, 39th Cong., 1st Sess., 4213 (Buckalew) (noting that Congress was making no attempt to admit New Mexico, even though that territory had a greater population than Nebraska).

262. See *Congressional Globe*, 39th Cong., 1st Sess., 4207 (Sumner), 4208 (Hendricks), 4209 (Doolittle).

263. See *Congressional Globe*, 39th Cong., 1st Sess., 4208 (Hendricks), 4209 (Doolittle), 4210–4211 (Doolittle).

264. *Congressional Globe*, 39th Cong., 1st Sess., 4212 (G. Davis) ("the facts revealed at this time show not only the importance but the necessity of an investigation of this whole subject by the Committee on Territories, or some other committee"), 4212 (Buckalew), 4221 (Sumner).

265. *Congressional Globe*, 39th Cong., 1st Sess., 4213.

266. *Congressional Globe*, 39th Cong., 1st Sess., 4208.

267. *Congressional Globe*, 39th Cong., 1st Sess., 4210 (S. Pomeroy). See *Congressional Globe*, 39th Cong., 1st Sess., 4209 (Wade) ("by passing an enabling act authorizing the people of a Territory to form a State government we commit ourselves to receive them whenever they do accept the invitation and form a State government"), 4211 (Howard) ("This pledge we voluntarily gave them two years ago.").

268. *Congressional Globe*, 39th Cong., 1st Sess., 4275.

269. *Congressional Globe*, 39th Cong., 1st Sess., 4209. See *Congressional Globe*, 39th Cong., 1st Sess., 4210 (Howard) (noting Michigan had formed a state constitution on the initiative of territorial citizens), 4211 (Howard).

270. *Congressional Globe*, 39th Cong., 1st Sess., 4208. See *Congressional Globe*, 39th Cong., 1st Sess., 4211 (Howard) ("too late in the day for Congress to enter into a question of that kind which ought to have been decided, and was decided if it was of sufficient importance to come before the board of election, by that board"), 4221 ("there is no proof of fraud, not even a reasonable suspicion of fraud"). See also *Congressional Globe*, 39th Cong., 1st Sess., 4212 (Kirkwood) (denying that any fraud occurred).

271. *Congressional Globe*, 39th Cong., 1st Sess., 4208.

272. *Congressional Globe*, 39th Cong., 1st Sess., 4210 (S. Pomeroy). See *Congressional Globe*, 39th Cong., 1st Sess., 4220 (Nye) ("the great interest surrounding that great work, the Pacific railroad, requires at the hands of every one of us that protection which can only be given by State laws").

273. *Congressional Globe*, 39th Cong., 1st Sess., 4210 (S. Pomeroy).

274. *Congressional Globe*, 39th Cong., 1st Sess., 4207.

275. *Congressional Globe*, 39th Cong., 1st Sess., 4275.

276. *Congressional Globe*, 39th Cong., 1st Sess., 4207 (Wade) ("A Territory is always an incumbrance to the General Government; it is attended with a good deal of expense.").

277. *Congressional Globe*, 39th Cong., 1st Sess., 4207.

278. *Congressional Globe*, 39th Cong., 1st Sess., 4207. See *Congressional Globe*, 39th Cong., 1st Sess., 4210 (Wade) ("Shall we defeat the will of those people who have sent their Senators here to represent them by the assent and approval of the whole community that voted for their constitution[?]").

279. *Congressional Globe*, 39th Cong., 1st Sess., 4210.

280. *Congressional Globe*, 39th Cong., 1st Sess., 4211.

281. *Congressional Globe*, 39th Cong., 1st Sess., 4275.

282. *Congressional Globe*, 39th Cong., 1st Sess., 4275.

283. *Congressional Globe*, 39th Cong., 1st Sess., 4208.

284. *Congressional Globe*, 39th Cong., 1st Sess., 4208. See *Congressional Globe*, 39th Cong., 1st Sess., 4308 ("no new State has yet knocked on our doors with a constitution admitting colored people to the franchise—not one").

285. *Congressional Globe*, 39th Cong., 1st Sess., 4220.

286. *Congressional Globe*, 39th Cong., 1st Sess., 4207–4208.

287. *Congressional Globe*, 39th Cong., 1st Sess., 4220.

288. *Congressional Globe*, 39th Cong., 1st Sess., 4208.

289. *Congressional Globe*, 39th Cong., 1st Sess., 4220.

290. *Congressional Globe*, 39th Cong., 1st Sess., 4222.

291. *Congressional Globe*, 39th Cong., 1st Sess., 4222.

292. *Congressional Globe*, 39th Cong., 1st Sess., 4222. Given a number of staunch Democrats, most notably Saulsbury, also missed that vote, the evidence is clear that the full Senate would have approved Nebraska statehood by approximately the same six year margin.

293. *Congressional Globe*, 39th Cong., 1st Sess., 4275–4276.

294. *Congressional Globe*, 39th Cong., 1st Sess., 4276.

295. For more details on the seating of David Patterson, see Hyman, *Era of the Oath*, 91–94.

296. *Congressional Globe*, 39th Cong., 1st Sess., 4214 (Trumbull) ("He was a loyal man himself."), 4243 (Trumbull), 4245 (Howe) ("an innocent, guiltless, loyal man"), 4267 (Maynard) ("a well-known and universally recognized loyal man"). See also *Congressional Globe*, 39th Cong., 1st Sess., 4269 (Shellabarger) (noting that the senators who vouched for Patterson were all "loyal"), 4271 (Eldridge) But see, *Congressional Globe*, 39th Cong., 1st Sess., 4243 (Wade) ("he was a judge on the bench sworn to maintain that government, sworn to defend its laws, sworn to enforce them against all loyal men"), 4215 (Trumbull), 4215 (Clark).

297. See *Congressional Globe*, 39th Cong., 1st Sess., 4168 (Guthrie), 4169 (G. Davis).

298. *Congressional Globe*, 39th Cong., 1st Sess., 4166. See *Congressional Globe*, 39th Cong., 1st Sess., 4166 (Patterson had "no duties to discharge in connection with the administration of . . . objectionable laws").

299. *Congressional Globe*, 39th Cong., 1st Sess., 4163. See *Congressional Globe*, 39th Cong., 1st Sess., 4165 (Cowan), 4167 (Hendricks) ("the proposed Senator is to take the oath . . . and if that oath be not true, then the question comes up before the Senate whether the Senate has been offended by that act, and upon that question two thirds alone can render an effective vote"), 4168 (Guthrie) (same), 4169 (G. Davis) ("if he is willing to take these oaths he is entitled *prima facie* to his seat in this body; and if he takes either oath falsely it becomes a subject of after inquiry by the Senate; and for the crime of perjury").

300. *Congressional Globe*, 39th Cong., 1st Sess., 4163.

301. *Congressional Globe*, 39th Cong., 1st Sess., 4165.

302. *Congressional Globe*, 39th Cong., 1st Sess., 4167,

303. *Congressional Globe*, 39th Cong., 1st Sess., 4164. See *Congressional Globe*, 39th Cong., 1st Sess., 4164 (Howard), 4164 (Sumner).

304. *Congressional Globe*, 39th Cong., 1st Sess., 4166.

305. *Congressional Globe*, 39th Cong., 1st Sess., 4215.

306. The classic study is Kenneth J. Arrow, *Social Choice and Individual Values* (third edition) (New Haven, CT: Yale University Press, 2012).

307. *Congressional Globe*, 39th Cong., 1st Sess., 4213–4214.

308. *Congressional Globe*, 39th Cong., 1st Sess., 4215.

309. *Congressional Globe*, 39th Cong., 1st Sess., 4214–4215.

310. *Congressional Globe*, 39th Cong., 1st Sess., 4216.

311. *Congressional Globe*, 39th Cong., 1st Sess., 4243.

312. *Congressional Globe*, 39th Cong., 1st Sess., 4245.

313. *Congressional Globe*, 39th Cong., 1st Sess., 4273.

314. *Congressional Globe*, 39th Cong., 1st Sess., 4273.

315. *Congressional Globe*, 39th Cong., 1st Sess., 4273.
316. *Congressional Globe*, 39th Cong., 1st Sess., 4245.
317. *Congressional Globe*, 39th Cong., 1st Sess., 4245.
318. See Benedict, *A Compromise of Principle*, 356, 360, 365, 367, 368, 373, 374, 376.
319. *Congressional Globe*, 39th Cong., 1st Sess., 4157.
320. As my Uncle Jack Englander would say at some point during the Passover service, "we all know the rest of the story. Let's eat."
321. See Paul Frymer, *Building an American Empire: The Era of Territorial and Political Expansion* (Princeton, NJ: Princeton University Press, 2017), 153.
322. This paragraph and the next summarize Charles Stewart III and Barry R. Weingast, "Stacking the Senate, Changing the Nation: Republican Rotten Boroughs, Statehood Politics, and American Political Development," 6 *Studies in American Political Development* 223 (1992). See also Frymer, *Building an American Empire*, 153.
323. See Berwanger, *The Rise of the Centennial State*, 141–153.
324. Andrew Johnson, "Veto Message," in *Messages and Papers*, vol. 6, 485–486.
325. See, e.g., Leonard L. Richards, *The Slave Power: The Free North and Southern Domination* (Baton Rouge: Louisiana State University Press, 2000), 134–215.
326. See Eric Foner, "The Wilmot Proviso Revisited," 56 *Journal of American History* 262 (1969).
327. *Congressional Globe*, 29th Cong., 2nd Sess., App., 317.
328. *Congressional Globe*, 33rd Cong., 1st Sess., App., 769. See David M. Potter, *The Impending Crisis, 1848–1861* (completed and edited by Don E. Fehrenbacher) (New York: Harper & Row, 1976), 199.
329. Abraham Lincoln, "First Inaugural Address—Final Text," in Basler, *Collected Works*, 4:263.
330. Abraham Lincoln, "Mr. Lincoln's Rejoinder: Fourth Debate with Stephen A. Douglas at Charleston, Illinois," in Basler, *Collected Works*, 3:181.
331. 347 U.S. 483 (1954).
332. See Abraham Lincoln, "Speech at Peoria, Illinois," in Basler, *Collected Works*, 2:268.
333. See Mark A. Graber, *Dred Scott and the Problem of Constitutional Evil* (New York: Cambridge University Press, 2006), 134.
334. Stewart and Weingast, "Stacking the Senate," 230–242.
335. See Graber, *Dred Scott*, 134–135.
336. See Stewart and Weingast, "Stacking the Senate," 260–264.
337. See Klinkner and Smith, *The Unsteady March*, 72–105.
338. Stewart and Weingast, "Stacking the Senate," 235–236.
339. Charles W. Calhoun, *Conceiving a New Republic: The Republican Party and the Southern Question, 1869–1900* (Lawrence: University Press of Kansas, 2006), 256–257.
340. See Green, Abraham Lincoln," 99–100.
341. See Paul Finkelman, "Civil Rights in Historical Context: In Defense of *Brown*," 118 *Harvard Law Review* 973, 887–888 (2005); Alexander Keyssar, *The Right to Vote: The Contested History of Democracy in the United States* (New York: Basic Books, 2000), 110.
342. Charles W. Calhoun, *Conceiving a New Republic*, 258.

CONCLUSION: REBELS, LOYALISTS, AND RACIAL EQUALITY

1. Abraham Lincoln, "To Horace Greeley, August 22, 1862," in Basler, *Collected Works,* 5:388–389.
2. John Hope Franklin, *The Emancipation Proclamation* (Garden City, NY: Doubleday & Company, 1963), 26–27, 135.
3. Franklin, *The Emancipation Proclamation,* 138.
4. Franklin, *The Emancipation Proclamation,* 136.
5. Franklin, *The Emancipation Proclamation,* 36. See Franklin, *The Emancipation Proclamation,* 38
6. Franklin, *The Emancipation Proclamation,* 126. See Klinkner and Smith, *The Unsteady March,* 57.
7. Franklin, *The Emancipation Proclamation,* 44, 80–81, 125–127, 130–135, 136–137, 148–151.
8. Abraham Lincoln, "'A House Divided': Speech at Springfield, Illinois," in Basler, *Collected Works,* 2:461.
9. See Stephen Douglas, "Mr. Douglas's Reply: First Debate with Stephen A. Douglas at Ottawa, Illinois," in Basler, *Collected Works,* 3:461. ("If it cannot endure thus divided, then he must strive to make them all free or all slave, which will inevitably bring about a dissolution of the Union.").
10. Kristin Luker made the same point when discussed the entangled relationships between ideals and interests in the abortion controversy. She observed: "The values that lead pro-life and pro-choice women into different attitudes toward abortion are the same values that led them at an earlier time to adopt different lifestyles that supported a given view of abortion." Kristin Luker, *Abortion & the Politics of Motherhood* (Berkeley: University of California Press, 1984), 199.
11. Franklin, *The Emancipation Proclamation,* 24. See Franklin, *The Emancipation Proclamation,* 61 (quoting Sumner) (the Emancipation Proclamation "strikes at the origin and mainspring of this Rebellion").
12. Franklin, *The Emancipation Proclamation,* 25. See Franklin, *The Emancipation Proclamation,* 61 (quoting Douglass) (the Emancipation Proclamation "invested" the Civil War with sanctity and England was morally bound to hold aloof from the Confederacy").
13. Franklin, *The Emancipation Proclamation,* 119–120 See Franklin, *The Emancipation Proclamation,* 62 (quoting Greeley) (the Emancipation Proclamation is "the beginning of the end of the rebellion"). See also Franklin, *The Emancipation Proclamation,* 16 (quoting Simon Cameron), 18 (noting sentiment among congressional Republicans that "[s]laves were . . . weapons of war that must not be in the hands of the enemy"), 63 (quoting a newspaper declaring that the Emancipation Proclamation was "a legitimate means of aiding military action"), 119 (quoting the *Washington Morning Chronicle*) ("President Lincoln now destroys the right arm of rebellion—African slavery."), 121 (quoting the Cincinnati *Daily Gazette*) ("In the struggle for the national existence, these blacks are unavoidably a power on one side of the other.").
14. Franklin, *The Emancipation Proclamation,* 66. See Franklin, *The Emancipation Proclamation,* 66 (quoting the *Boston Post*) the Proclamation would "introduce contention where harmony is necessary to our national salvation").

15. Franklin, *The Emancipation Proclamation*, 122.
16. Summers, *The Ordeal of the Reunion*, 395–396.
17. The next sentences summarize Summers, *The Ordeal of the Reunion*, 396.
18. Summers, *The Ordeal of the Reunion*, 396.
19. Summers, *The Ordeal of the Reunion*, 396–397.
20. *Congressional Globe*, 39th Cong., 1st Sess., 2145.
21. *Congressional Globe*, 39th Cong., 1st Sess., 2170–2171.
22. See Bell, *"Brown v. Board of Education* and the Interest-Convergence Dilemma,"* 518.
23. Mary L. Dudziak, *Cold War Civil Rights: Race and the Image of American Democracy* (Princeton, NJ: Princeton University Press, 2000).
24. Foner, *Free Soil, Free Labor, Free Men.*
25. *Congressional Globe*, 39th Cong., 1st Sess., 2172.
26. See Hans L. Trefousse, *The Radical Republicans: Lincoln's Vanguard for Racial Justice*, xiii (including H. Wilson, Howard and J. Ashley as among the radical leaders in Congress).
27. See also Richard H. Abbott, *Cobbler in Congress: The Life of Henry Wilson, 1812–1875* (Lexington: University Press of Kentucky, 1972); Benedict, *A Compromise of Principle*, 38 (noting H. Wilson was one of the most influential of the radical Republicans in the Reconstruction Congress).
28. See Zietlow, *The Forgotten Emancipator.*
29. See Benedict, *A Compromise of Principle*, 38; Foner, *Reconstruction*, 60.
30. Green, "Abraham Lincoln," 88–89.
31. *Congressional Globe*, 39th Cong., 1st Sess., 2175.
32. See Klinkner and Smith, *The Unsteady March*, 78–79.
33. Dr. Martin Luther King, Jr., "Where Do We Go From Here?" *A Testament of Hope: The Essential Writings and Speeches of Martin Luther King, Jr.*, edited by James M. Washington (New York: HarperCollins, 1991), 252. The persons responsible for the Constitution of 1787 had a similar experience with a dramatic rise in support for emancipated slaves that crested shortly after ratification. See Klinkner and Smith, *The Unsteady March*, 12–23; Graber, *Dred Scott*, 107–108.